Beiträge zum
ausländischen öffentlichen Recht und Völkerrecht

Edited by

the Max Planck Society
for the Advancement of Science
represented by Prof. Dr. Armin von Bogdandy
and Prof. Dr. Anne Peters

Volume 341

Catharina Ziebritzki

The EU's Liability for its Refugee Camps

Responsibility for Fundamental Rights Violations in the Integrated EU Hotspot Administration

Nomos

Open Access funding by the Max Planck Society.

The Deutsche Nationalbibliothek lists this publication in the Deutsche Nationalbibliografie; detailed bibliographic data are available on the Internet at http://dnb.d-nb.de

a.t.: Frankfurt am Main, Univ., Diss., 2024

Original title: The EU's Responsibility in the Asylum Administration. Administrative Integration, Judicial Protection and the Case of the EU Hotspots.

1st Edition 2025

Published by
Nomos Verlagsgesellschaft mbH & Co. KG
Waldseestraße 3–5 | 76530 Baden-Baden
www.nomos.de

Production of the printed version:
Nomos Verlagsgesellschaft mbH & Co. KG
Waldseestraße 3–5 | 76530 Baden-Baden

ISBN (Print): 978-3-7560-2323-3
ISBN (ePDF): 978-3-7489-4972-5

DOI: https://doi.org/10.5771/9783748949725

D30

Online Version
Nomos eLibrary

Acknowledgements

This book came out of a long journey. I would like to express my deep gratitude to all those who have made this journey possible, be it through their inspiration or their support, and to all those who have accompanied me, be it for a shorter or for a longer part of the way.

The journey began in summer 2015 in the refugee camp *Moria*, on the island of Lesvos, Greece. I had just completed my law degree in Heidelberg, and was drawn towards the shores of Europe, where I would see with my own eyes what European externalisation policies really do to our fellow humans. I realised two things. Firstly, I began to sense the extent of suffering caused by European policies. It became obvious to me that this suffering affects racialised people in particular and that it hits children and vulnerable people especially hard. Secondly, I realised that, contrary to what media reports at the time often suggested, the inhumane camps were projects not of Greece but of the EU. It seemed strange to me that officials from EU agencies and the European Commission had their office containers inside the camps and walked through the mud alongside their Greek colleagues while the EU fiercely denied any legal responsibility for human rights violations.

The journey continued in January 2016 when I started my work as a research fellow at the Max Planck Institute for Comparative Public Law and International Law in Heidelberg. This was a different world. Unlike in *Moria*, there was not always an urgent next thing to do. There was space and time for thought and reflection. The Institute offered me a truly wonderful space to discuss, learn, read, write, think, and discuss again. We had time for concentrated research, and we were given the possibility to follow our inclinations and interests.

I thank all those who have accompanied me during my time at the Institute, both intellectually and personally. I am truly grateful to Professor Armin von Bogdandy for his generous trust. From the very first moment, he gave me the greatest possible freedom to do things the way it seemed right to me – even when this meant things would take me longer. He managed to both inspire and challenge me. Without his support, the journey would have stopped before it really began.

I am deeply grateful to Kanad Bagchi, Leander Beinlich, Milan Tahraoui, Raffaela Kunz, Giacomo Rugge, Teddy Shulman, Silvia Steininger, Franz Ebert, Christoph Krenn, and all the others who travelled with me as PhD fellows and friends. You made those parts of the journey that we travelled together a wonderful time. I am equally grateful to Michalis Ioannidis, Laura Hering, and Erin Pobjie for their constant support and friendship. And I am grateful to Anuscheh Farahat, Christian Marxsen, Nora Markard, Jürgen Bast, Anna Lübbe, and Melanie Fink for their continuous advice and encouragement. Without you all, I would most likely not have completed this project.

I am equally grateful to Robert Nestler, Vinzent Vogt and Clara-Anne Bünger. We met in 2016 in Chios, a neighbour island to Lesvos, and what brought us together was the ambition to offer qualified legal advice to those trapped in the dangerous and chaotic sites that were labelled 'EU hotspots'. I am grateful to the three of you for our collaboration and friendship and for giving me the freedom to pursue both NGO work and academic work. I am indebted to Katharina Voß, Ansgar Gilster and Kristine Rembach for trusting in our ambitions.

The journey continued throughout the following years, with my mind and body oscillating between Heidelberg, Berlin, Athens and the Greek Aegean islands. I met wonderful people along the way. I am grateful to Cathryn Costello and Violeta Moreno-Lax. I am grateful to Yasar, Kate, Anne Pertsch, Niki Georgiou, Elli Kriona, Giorgos Maniatis, Corinna Ujkašević, Mustafa Noah, and Aora Helmzadeh. Thank you for your inspiration and your support, in different ways and times.

My journey was generously funded by the Max Planck Institute for Comparative Public Law and International Law, the Friedrich Ebert Foundation, and Equal Rights Beyond Borders. I thank my interview partners at the EU asylum agency and the European Commission for their time and openness. I am truly grateful to all those who have invested time and intellect to read and improve my sketches and drafts. I am indebted to Jamie Kessler, Carolyn Moser and Florian Kriener for final proofreading. I thank Johannes Rux, Andrea Schneider, Carola Spengler and their team at Nomos for the great collaboration and smooth publication process.

The journey has been long and rich, and it seems impossible to mention everyone I have met along the way. I thank all those who, knowingly or unknowingly, have accompanied, supported and inspired me.

And finally, thank you to those who have accompanied my soul over the last years, for I could not have made this journey with my mind alone.

Thank you, dear sisters and dear brother, Jojo, Valja, and Toni. Thank you, dear parents, Doris and Henning. Thank you, dear grandfathers and dear grandmothers, especially Werner and Heide, for passing on our own family's stories of flight. Thank you, dear friends. Thank you, Felix. Thank you, Antonia. Thank you, Sophia, Aljoscha, and Sigrid, for those parts of the journey that we shared. Thank you, Lin, thank you, Heidi and Emna. Thank you, dear Maxim; and thank you, little Jascha, for bursting into our lives.

Berlin, 5 September 2024

Overview of Content

Table of Contents

List of Abbreviations

AFSJ	Area of Freedom, Security and Justice
AMIF	Asylum, Migration and Integration Fund
AST	Asylum Support Team
CAT	Convention against Torture
CEAS	Common European Asylum System
ChFR	Charter of Fundamental Rights
CJEU	Court of Justice of the European Union; the same abbreviation is used to refer to the CJEU's predecessors, i.e. the Court of Justice of the European Coal and Steel Communities and the Court of Justice of the European Communities
COM	European Commission
CPT	European Committee for the Prevention of Torture and Inhuman or Degrading Treatment or Punishment
CRC	Convention on the Rights of the Child
DARIO	Draft Articles on the Responsibility of International Organizations
DARS	Draft Articles on Responsibility of States for Internationally Wrongful Acts
ECA	European Court of Auditors
EASO	European Asylum Support Office
EC	European Community
ECCHO	European Commission, Directorate General European Civil Protection and Humanitarian Aid Operations
ECGAB	European Code of Good Administrative Behaviour
ECHR	European Convention on Human Rights
ECtHR	European Court of Human Rights
EFCA	European Fisheries Control Agency

EMA	European Agency for the Evaluation of Medicinal Products
EMSA	European Maritime Safety Agency
ESM	European Stability Mechanism
EU	European Union
EUAA	European Union Agency for Asylum
eu-LISA	Agency for the Operational Management of Large-Scale IT Systems in the Area of Freedom, Security and Justice
Europol	European Union Agency for Law Enforcement Cooperation
EURTF	European Regional Task Force
FRA	European Union Agency for Fundamental Rights
Frontex	European Border and Coast Guard Agency, and formerly: European Agency for the Management of Operational Cooperation at the External Borders of the Member States of the European Union
GAS	Greek Asylum Service
HOME	European Commission, Directorate General Home Affairs
ICCPR	International Covenant on Civil and Political Rights
IMF	International Monetary Fund
IOM	International Organization for Migration
JMD	Joint Ministerial Decision
MMST	Migration Management Support Team
MoU	Memorandum of Understanding
MoU-JP	Memorandum of Understanding on a Joint Pilot
MP-RIC	Multi-Purpose Reception and Identification Centre (also referred to as 'EU Hotspot 2.0')
NGO	Non-Governmental Organisation
OHCHR	Office of the United Nations High Commissioner for Human Rights
OP	Operational Plan
RABIT	Frontex, Rapid Border Intervention Team
RIC	Greek Reception and Identification Centre

RIS	Greek First Reception and Identification Service
SoP	Standard Operation Procedures
TEU	Treaty on European Union
TFEU	Treaty on the Functioning of the European Union
ToC	Terms of Cooperation
UDHR	Universal Declaration of Human Rights
UN	United Nations
UNGA	United Nations General Assembly
UNHCR	United Nations High Commissioner for Refugees

Introduction

1 EU Hotspots as a Critical Challenge to Human Rights

In November 2019, the EU Fundamental Rights Agency (FRA) concluded that the EU hotspot approach, i.e., the approach to conduct asylum procedures in refugee camps at external borders, 'brings along built-in deficiencies' and 'creates fundamental rights challenges that appear almost unsurmountable.'[1] The agency's head was even more straightforward when they told the European Parliament that 'the EU hotspot approach as implemented in Greece is the single most worrying fundamental rights issue that we are confronting anywhere in the European Union'.[2]

The list of reports substantiating fundamental rights violations in EU hotspots is long. Consistent and extensive documentation by UN bodies, the Council of Europe, EU bodies, Greek national bodies, and NGOs clearly shows that deficiencies in EU hotspots are widespread and structurally inherent to their administration.[3] Fundamental rights violations, including violations of the prohibition of inhuman treatment as enshrined in Art. 3

1 Fundamental Rights Agency, Feb 2019, Update of the 2016 Opinion on fundamental rights in the 'hotspots' set up in Greece and Italy, p. 7. This study understands 'human rights' as encompassing 'fundamental rights'.

2 EU observer, 7 November 2019, Greek migrant hotspot now EU's 'worst rights issue', https://euobserver.com/migration/146541 (all links last accessed 1 May 2024, unless indicated otherwise).

3 For a few relevant reports, see, OHCHR, 3 November 2017, UN Special Rapporteur on the human rights of migrants concludes his follow up country visit to Greece, https://www.ohchr.org/EN/NewsEvents/Pages/DisplayNews.aspx?NewsID=19976&LangID=E; Council of Europe, 19 February 2019, Report to the Greek Government on the visit to Greece carried out by the European Committee for the Prevention of Torture and Inhuman or Degrading Treatment or Punishment (CPT) from 10 to 19 April 2018, CPT/Inf (2019) 4; Médecins Sans Frontières, 5 September 2019, A disastrous policy: vulnerable people trapped on the Greek islands pay the price of inhumane policies of the EU-Türkiye deal, https://www.doctorswithoutborders.ca/article/disastrous-policy-vulnerable-people-trapped-greek-islands-pay-price-inhumane-policies-eu; Danish Refugee Council, October 2017, Fundamental Rights and the EU Hotspot Approach, https://drc.ngo/media/4051855/fundamental-rights_web.pdf; Greek Ombudsman, Andreas Pottakis, April 2017, Special Report. Migration flows and refugee protection. Administrative challenges and human rights issues, https://www.synigoros.gr/?i=human-rights.en.recentinterventions.434107.

of the Convention of on Human Rights (ECHR) and Art. 4 of the EU Charter of Fundamental Rights (ChFR), occur regularly and result from the construction of the procedure as such. In this sense, the EU hotspot administration can be described as systemically deficient.[4]

Two kinds of systemic deficiencies can be distinguished: those related to reception conditions and those related to asylum procedures. Reception-related deficiencies include instances of inhuman or degrading treatment in violation of Art. 4 ChFR due to disastrous living conditions, in particular for vulnerable persons,[5] and violations of Art. 6 ChFR resulting from systemic detention practices.[6] Procedure-related deficiencies include violations of the right to be heard under Art. 41 ChFR, of the specific procedural guarantees for children under Art. 24 ChFR, and of the procedural dimension of the prohibition of refoulement as enshrined in Art. 4, 18, 19 ChFR.[7]

Systemic violations of fundamental rights in EU hotspots should not be seen in isolation. As numerous studies by scholars and NGOs have shown, the European asylum system as a whole has come to rest on practices that either per se constitute fundamental rights violations[8] or de facto result

4 On the concept of systemic deficiencies see Armin von Bogdandy, Michael Ioannidis, „Systemic Deficiency in the Rule of Law: What it is, what has to be done, what can be done", *Common Market Law Review* 51 (2014), p. 59-96, p. 60, 91; similarly, Iris Canor, „My brother's keeper? Horizontal solange: 'An ever closer distrust among the peoples of Europe'", *Common Market Law Review* 50 (2013), p. 383-422, p. 385: 'a systemic violation of core European fundamental rights'. For the concept in the specific context of the asylum system see Evangelia (Lilian) Tsourdi, Cathryn Costello, „'Systemic Violations' in EU Asylum Law: Cover or Catalyst?", *German Law Journal* 24 (2023), p. 982-994. On the qualification of the deficiencies in the EU hotspots as systemic see chapter 2, 3.

5 See the ECtHR's jurisprudence cited in fn. 33. Further chapter 2, 3.

6 This is more contentious, because the ECtHR has so far not found a violation of Art. 5 ECHR in the cases that were submitted to it. In detail on the argument for a violation of Art. 6 ChFR see chapter 2, 3.

7 See chapter 2, 3.

8 Consider, for instance, the practice of systemic pushbacks at the EU's external borders with Belarus during the 2020 (see further Catharina Ziebritzki, „Warum die ‚Instrumentalisierung'" Asylsuchender kein Argument für die Aussetzung ihrer Grundrechte ist", *Kritische Justiz* 55 (2022), p. 152-166) or the practice of systemic pushbacks at the EU's external border with Türkiye (see ECRE, 30 Sept 2022, Greece: Systematic Pushbacks Continue by Sea and Land as MEPs Demand EU Action, Deaths Up Proportionate to Arrivals, Number of People in Reception System Reduced by Half – Mitarachi Still Not Satisfied, https://ecre.org/greece-systematic-pushbacks-continue-by-sea-and-land-as-meps-demand-eu-action-deaths-up-proportionate-to-arrivals-number-of-people-in-reception-system-reduced-by-half-mitarachi-still-not/).

in fundamental rights violations and even the death of persons seeking refuge.[9] Considering this, it is truly unsettling that the second package of reforming the Common European Asylum System (CEAS), adopted in spring 2024, does not remedy existing shortcomings[10] but, on the contrary, further consolidates and partially even exacerbates practices that have already proven dysfunctional over the past decade.[11]

At a societal level, the current state of the European asylum system appears to reflect a gradual shift in attitudes towards forced displacement. After the Second World War, when the political focus was on refugees from Europe, European societies largely agreed that persons on flight must be offered refuge.[12] Seventy years later, this political and moral consensus seems to have eroded significantly. As the prevailing narrative increasingly conceptualises migration as a danger or threat – to security and social prosperity, to labour markets and education systems, or more generally to identity in terms of culture, religion, or race[13] – a deeply ingrained fear of 'others' prevails.[14] As a result, fundamental rights violations and even the death of persons on flight are increasingly considered empirically 'normal' and normatively acceptable. This shift in political evaluation is clearly reflected in current media coverage as a barometer of social attention: deaths

9 For the rising number of deaths see only UNHCR, Operational Data Portal as of 15 February 2022, Europe: Dead and Missing At Sea, https://data2.unhcr.org/en/dataviz/95; The Guardian, 20 June 2018, The list: It's 34,361 and rising: how the List tallies Europe's migrant bodycount, https://www.theguardian.com/world/2018/jun/20/the-list-europe-migrant-bodycount.

10 For a similar account, see, Evangelia (Lilian) Tsourdi, Cathryn Costello, „'Systemic Violations' in EU Asylum Law: Cover or Catalyst?" (fn. 4), p. 993: 'It is important to understand the role of EU law in creating the conditions for systemic breaches, (…). Where the CEAS leads to systemic human rights violations, then its reform is the appropriate response.'.

11 For the reform package see EU Official Journal L series daily view, 22 May 2024, https://eur-lex.europa.eu/oj/daily-view/L-series/default.html?&ojDate=22052024.

12 As reflected in the adoption of the Convention relating to the Status of Refugees (adopted 28 July 1951, entered into force 22 April 1954) 189 UNTS 137 (hereinafter: Refugee Convention), which was – prior to the adoption of Protocol Relating to the Status of Refugees (adopted 31 January 1967, entered into force 4 October 1967) 606 UNTS 267 (hereinafter: 1967 Protocol) – applicable only to refugees originating from Europe.

13 On the construction of identity based on these and further parameters see Kwame Anthony Appiah, *The Lies That Bind: Rethinking Identity. Creed, Country, Colour, Class, Culture*, Liveright Publishing 2018.

14 Zygmunt Baumann, *Strangers at Our Door*, Polity Press 2016.

during crossings to European shores, for instance, have long ceased to make the headlines.

From a legal perspective – with the standard being the law of the European society, including the ECHR as the minimal consensus on human rights as well as the ChFR as the corresponding document in EU constitutional law[15] – the EU's asylum policy has, in substantial parts, become unlawful. Practices that are commonly implemented by national authorities and EU bodies, and are partially even normatively sanctioned by EU secondary law, violate basic fundamental rights standards as enshrined in the ChFR. Examples range from regular pushbacks to inhumane reception conditions, the denial of children's and women's rights, or the deprivation of basic procedural rights.[16] In sum, the European asylum system in its current form is normatively misguided and empirically dysfunctional to an extent that structurally calls into question human rights and the rule of law. Put differently, the EU's asylum policy as of 2024 constitutes a threat to the EU's own foundational values as enshrined in Art. 2 of the Treaty on European Union (TEU).[17] This problem does not only concern refugees and asylum seekers. It concerns all EU citizens.[18]

---

15 On European law in a broad sense as the law of the European society, see Armin von Bogdandy, *The Emergence of European Society through Public Law. A Hegelian and Anti-Schmittian Approach*, Oxford University Press 2024 p. 15 et seq.

16 For a comprehensive assessment of the EU's asylum policy from the perspective of fundamental rights, see Jürgen Bast, Frederik von Harbou, Janna Wessels, *Human Rights Challenges to European Migration Policy. The REMAP Study*, Nomos 2022.

17 Art. 2 TEU reads: 'The Union is founded on the values of respect for human dignity, freedom, democracy, equality, the rule of law and respect for human rights, including the rights of persons belonging to minorities. These values are common to the Member States in a society in which pluralism, non-discrimination, tolerance, justice, solidarity and equality between women and men prevail.'.

18 Similarly, Barbara Grabowska-Moroz, Dimitry Vladimirovich Kochenov, „The Loss of Face for Everyone Concerned. EU Rule of Law in the Context of the 'Migration Crisis'", in V Stoyanova, S Smet (ed.), *Migrants' Rights, Populism and Legal Resilience in Europe*, Cambridge University Press 2022, p. 187-208; Evangelia (Lilian) Tsourdi, Cathryn Costello, „'Systemic Violations' in EU Asylum Law: Cover or Catalyst?" (fn. 4), p. 994, concluding that 'the CEAS (Common European Asylum System) itself brings about systemic human rights violations' (parenthesis added by the author).

2 Europe's Largest Refugee Camps

When the *New York Times* wrote about the most prominent EU hotspot – *Moria*, located on the Greek island of Lesbos – they referred to it as 'Europe's largest refugee camp'.[19] This is an insightful description. First, it makes explicit that EU hotspots, despite the somewhat euphemistic legal term, are, in fact, refugee camps.[20] Second, it correctly reflects the figures. The EU hotspots at the EU's external borders with Türkiye, located on five islands in the Greek Aegean, are indeed the largest refugee camps in Europe. *Moria* had hosted approximately 12,000 refugees and asylum seekers before it was destroyed in September 2020. In total, about 355,000 asylum seekers have stayed in EU hotspots between 2016 and 2023.[21] Third, and perhaps most importantly, the description aptly reflects the European dimension.

The original EU hotspot approach was put forward by the European Commission (Commission) in May 2015.[22] The main novelty in this

19 New York Times, 20 Sept 2020, Fire Destroys Most of Europe's Largest Refugee Camp, on Greek Island of Lesbos, https://www.nytimes.com/2020/09/09/world/europe/fire-refugee-camp-lesbos-moria.html.

20 In its broadest meaning, the term 'refugees' means forced migrants, i.e. all persons entitled to international protection and internally displaced persons, see e.g. UNHCR, Global Trends in Forced Displacement 2020, available online: https://www.unhcr.org/60b638e37/unhcr-global-trends-2020, p. 2. In the colloquial meaning, and the one that is referred to in this study where no other indication is given, refugees are persons entitled to international protection, i.e. refugees in the sense of the Refugee Convention (see fn. 12) and persons entitled to complementary protection under human rights law. The notion 'asylum seekers' is broader insofar as it encompasses all those who have lodged an application for international protection.

21 Per month, between 2,500 and 42,000 persons have stayed in EU hotspots. In 2023, the official capacity in total was between 13,000 or 17,000 places, depending on the source. The number of people staying in the EU hotspots changes on a weekly basis. For an overview and current figures see Boat Refugee Foundation, EU-Türkiye Deal. Visualising data from the Greek hotspots, 2016–2023, https://reliefweb.int/report/greece/eu-Türkiye-deal-visualising-data-greek-hotspots-2016-2023; UNHCR, Operational Data Portal, https://data.unhcr.org/en/search?type=news&sv_id=11&geo_id=640; Hellenic republic Ministry of Migration and Asylum Statistics, https://migration.gov.gr/en/statistika/; Scribr, Uploads by Hellenic Ministry of Migration and Asylum, https://de.scribd.com/user/507807805/Hellenic-Ministry-of-Migration-and-Asylum.

22 European Commission, 13 May 2015, Communication from the Commission to the European Parliament, the Council, the European Economic and Social Committee and the Committee of the Regions, A European Agenda on Migration, COM(2015) 240 final (hereinafter: European Agenda on Migration), p. 6; European Commission,

approach was that EU agencies – including the European Asylum Agency (EUAA, formerly European Asylum Support Office, EASO), Frontex (European Border and Coast Guard), FRA, Europol (European Union Agency for Law Enforcement Cooperation), Eurojust (European Union Agency for Criminal Justice Cooperation) and eu-LISA (European Union Agency for the Operational Management of Large-Scale IT Systems in the Area of Freedom, Security and Justice) – as well as the Commission itself were closely involved in the administrative procedures on the ground. Specifically, the agencies were tasked with providing administrative support and the Commission was entrusted with overall coordination and supervision.[23] In terms of geographical scope, the EU hotspot approach was conceived for implementation in several member states and EU hotspot camps were established in Italy and Greece.[24] Yet, this study focuses on the EU hotspots in Greece, which have functioned, since 2015 and until today, as a 'law and governance blueprint' or 'testing ground' for the EU's increased administrative involvement.[25]

In fact, the main difference between EU hotspots and other refugee camps located at the EU's external borders is that the former are co-managed by the European Union itself. EU hotspots are conceptualised and administered jointly by EU bodies and by national authorities. This specificity becomes clear when comparing the refugee camps located at the Hungarian-Serbian border to those at the Greek-Turkish border.[26] Both were established in the aftermath of the 2015 crisis of the CEAS when the EU was confronted with an increased number of asylum claims; both were situated at the EU's external borders; both operated on the basis of physical

July 2015, Explanatory Note on the 'Hotspot' Approach, available at: http://www.statewatch.org/news/2015/jul/eu-com-hotsposts.pdf (hereinafter: EU Hotspot Explanatory Note). See further chapter 1, 2.

23 See further chapter 1, 3.

24 For an overview see European Parliament, 2023, Briefing: The hotspot approach in Greece and Italy, https://www.europarl.europa.eu/thinktank/en/document/EPRS_BRI(2023)754569.

25 See further chapter 1, 2. The EU hotspots in Greece are located on the Aegean islands of Lesvos, Chios, Kos, Samos and Leros. This study takes into account developments from 2015 to 2022.

26 The Hungarian 'transit zones' were closed in May 2022, as a consequence of CJEU, Court (Grand Chamber), judgement of 17 December 2002, European Commission v Hungary, C-808/18. See ECRE, Country Report Hungary, 2022 Update, https://ecre.org/2022-update-aida-country-report-hungary/, p. 54.

confinement;[27] and both applied a border procedure that was based on a safe third country clause.[28] The difference, however, lies in the responsible public actors. Whereas the Hungarian camps were conceptualised and run by national authorities, the camps in Greece are conceptualised and co-managed by national authorities in close cooperation with EU bodies.[29]

Since 2015, the EU hotspot approach has been adjusted to changing practical needs and political preferences numerous times, with two milestones being of particular importance. The first was the adoption of the EU-Türkiye Statement in March 2016.[30] From the day of the entry into force of that Statement, the purpose of the EU hotspot administration was overhauled. Whereas EU hotspots had initially been conceived as relocation centres from where asylum seekers would be transferred to other member states, they were now reconceptualised as deportation centres from where asylum seekers would be forcibly returned to Türkiye. The criticism of this idea as a rather blunt externalisation strategy notwithstanding, the return policy also proved to be completely dysfunctional in practice. Between March 2016 and March 2020, only approximately 2,000 deportations to Türkiye were carried out,[31] and since March 2020, the return policy has even come to a complete standstill.[32] As a result, the number of asylum seekers that were 'trapped' in EU hotspots – not being allowed to travel to the Greek mainland or to other member states, but also not being returned

27 With differences in detail and over time. In more detail on the practice in the EU hotspots see chapter 2, 3.1.b. Only some practices qualify as 'detention', while others qualify simply a restriction of movement.

28 Again, with differences in detail and over time. In more detail on the practice in the EU hotspots see chapter 2, 3.2.c. The 'safe third country clause' is a specific 'protection elsewhere clause' which allow to reject asylum claims as inadmissible without examining the substance of the claim. The 'safe third country concept' presupposes that a person has already found protection in another country; it is similar to the 'country of first asylum concept' which presupposes that a person could find protection in another country.

29 On the EU's inconsistent approach towards Hungary and Greece see chapter 3, 2.1.

30 European Council, Press Release, EU-Türkiye statement, 18 March 2016, https://www.consilium.europa.eu/en/press/press-releases/2016/03/18/eu-Türkiye-statement/. See further chapter 1, 2.

31 UNHCR, Returns from Greece to Türkiye (in the framework of the EU-TUR Statement) as of 31 March 2020, https://data.unhcr.org/en/documents/details/75075. The main reason for these low numbers was that Türkiye did not qualify as a 'safe third country' for most asylum seekers, see further chapter 2, 3.2.c.

32 EU Observer, 19 Jan 2021, Türkiye snubs Greece on migrant returnees; European Commission, 24 May 2022, Sixth Annual Report on the Facility for Refugees in Türkiye, COM/2022/243 final, p. 3.

to Türkiye – grew exponentially. At the same time, the conditions in the camps deteriorated gravely, to the point that the European Court of Human Rights (ECtHR), in several cases, found a violation of the prohibition of inhumane treatment under Art. 3 ECHR.[33]

Eventually, these fatal developments resulted in an event that has become the second milestone in the history of EU hotspots. In September 2020, an uncontrolled fire broke out in the largest EU hotspot, *Moria,* and almost entirely destroyed the camp.[34] As it was clear that the EU hotspot had to be rebuilt in any case and considering the severe deficiencies in terms of administrative dysfunction and ongoing fundamental rights violations, the Commission took the opportunity to present an EU hotspot reform. The reform, enshrined in a Memorandum of Understanding between Greece and the EU,[35] has changed the operation of the EU hotspot administration so profoundly that it is referred to here as 'EU hotspot approach 2.0'. The most important novelty, apart from an expansion of detention practices, was a further increase of the EU's own involvement. The tasks of the EUAA and Frontex were further expanded, and the Commission's role was strengthened to the extent that EU hotspots are now truly 'co-managed' by Greece and the EU.[36]

---

33 ECtHR, Decision on interim measure of 14 May 2020, A.B. v Greece, Application no. 19614/20; ECtHR, Decision on interim measures of 7 April 2020, M.A. v. Greece, Application no. 15782/20; ECtHR, Decision on interim measures of 26 March 2020, M.A. v. Greece, Application no. 15192/20; ECtHR, Decision on interim measure of 16 April 2020, E.I. and Others v Greece, Application No 16080/20 (available at: https://www.proasyl.de/news/egmr-urteil-fluechtlinge-aus-moria-muessen-menschenwuerdig-untergebracht-werden/). See for further similar decisions: Refugee Support Aegean (RSA), European Court of Human Rights orders Greece to safeguard asylum seekers' life and limb on Lesvos, 24 September 2020, https://rsaegean.org/en/european-court-of-human-rights-orders-greece-to-safeguard-asylum-seekers-life-and-limb-on-lesvos/.

34 See fn. 19.

35 European Commission, Annex to the Commission Decision approving the Memorandum of Understanding between the European Commission, European Asylum Support Office, the European Border and Coast Guard Agency, Europol and the Fundamental Rights Agency, of the one part, and the Government of Hellenic Republic, of the other part, on a Joint Pilot for the establishment of a new Multi-Purpose Reception and Identification Centre in Lesvos, 2 December 2020, C(2020) 8657 final, Annex (hereinafter: MoU Joint Pilot). For now, the Joint Pilot is framed by the Commission as a Greece-specific project, thereby reinforcing the differences between the EU hotspots located in Greece and those in Italy.

36 See further chapter 1, 2; chapter 2.

As both milestones show, the development of EU hotspots is marked by informality. Neither the 2016 EU-Türkiye Statement nor the 2020 Memorandum of Understanding have a clear legal basis in primary law or even formal legal character.[37] As a consequence, the involved EU bodies initially carried out their administrative tasks on the basis of policy papers alone, and their activities were often vested with a legal basis in secondary legislation only years later.[38] Today, the main legal basis is enshrined in the EUAA Regulation and the Frontex Regulation.[39] First, they define a 'hotspot area' as 'an area in which the host Member State, the Commission, relevant Union agencies and participating Member States cooperate, with the aim of managing an existing or potential disproportionate migratory challenge characterised by a significant increase in the number of migrants arriving at the external borders.'[40] Second, they provide for specific agency teams that shall be deployed to EU hotspots for the provision of administrative support, the so-called migration management support teams (MMST).[41] Third, they define the Commission's responsibility to supervise the EU hotspot administration, providing that it 'shall establish the terms of cooperation at the hotspot area and shall be responsible for the coordination of the activities of the migration management support teams'.[42]

37 On the informal character of the EU's crisis response see chapter 1, 2.2.

38 Insofar as the activities of Frontex and the EUAA are concerned, the most important belated legalisation was adopted in the context of the first CEAS reform package between 2016 and 2021, see further chapter 1, 2.2; chapter 2, 1 and 2.

39 Regulation (EU) 2019/1896 of the European Parliament and of the Council of 13 November 2019 on the European Border and Coast Guard and repealing Regulations (EU) No 1052/2013 and (EU) 2016/1624 (hereinafter: Frontex Regulation); Regulation (EU) 2021/2303 of the European Parliament and of the Council of 15 December 2021 on the European Union Agency for Asylum and repealing Regulation (EU) No 439/2010 (hereinafter: EUAA Regulation).

40 Art 2 para 23 Frontex Regulation, Art. 16 para 2 lit. l EUAA Regulation.

41 Art. 2 para 19, Art. 36 para 1 lit d, Art. 40 Frontex Regulation; Art. 16 para 2 lit l, 21 EUAA Regulation.

42 Art. 40 para 3, recital 55 Frontex Regulation; Art. 21 para 2, recital 34 EUAA Regulation. Similarly already Art. 18 para 3 Regulation (EU) 2016/1624 of the European Parliament and of the Council of 14 September 2016 on the European Border and Coast Guard and amending Regulation (EU) 2016/399 of the European Parliament and of the Council and repealing Regulation (EC) No 863/2007 of the European Parliament and of the Council, Council Regulation (EC) No 2007/2004 and Council Decision 2005/267/EC (hereinafter: Frontex 2016 Regulation).

3 The EU's Judicial Responsibility (Research Question)

To address fundamental rights violations, both in individual cases and at a systemic level, it is essential to determine which actor is responsible. While responsibility can be assigned through different social practices, an especially important tool in this context is law.[43] Most legal structures allow to determine who is responsible for what. However, this is not the case in the specific context of asylum policies. To date, the question of who bears responsibility for fundamental rights violations that result from asylum policies largely remains open. This is partly due to sophisticated outsourcing strategies and consistent externalisation of the 'dirtiest' tasks to third countries or private actors, which makes chains of causation extremely difficult to establish. Another reason lies in the fact that the international law framework on allocating responsibility in multi-actor situations remains structurally weak.[44] As a result, legal scholarship on the matter has emerged only recently,[45] and practical possibilities for concerned asylum seekers to claim their rights are still largely lacking.

While legal responsibilities in the context of asylum and externalisation policies remain indeterminate for most countries in the Global North, legal

43 Responsibility in the legal context is often understood as accountability. For the prevalent notion of accountability see Mark Bovens, „Analysing and Assessing Accountability: A Conceptual Framework“, *European Law Journal* 13 (2007), p. 447-468, who defines accountability as 'a relationship between an actor and a forum, in which the actor has an obligation to explain and to justify his or her conduct, the forum can pose questions and pass judgement, and the actor may face consequences'. This study, however, focuses on legal accountability, i.e. on judicial review.

44 International Law Commission, Draft Articles on Responsibility of States for Internationally Wrongful Acts, November 2001, Supplement No. 10, A/56/10 (DARS); ibid., Draft Articles on the Responsibility of International Organizations, A/66/10 (DARIO). On the applicability of the DARIO to the European Union see Andrés Delgado Casteleiro, *The International Responsibility of the European Union. From Competence to Normative Control*, Cambridge University Press 2016, p. 54–109. For an innovative proposal see André Nollkaemper, Jean d'Aspremont, Christiane Ahlborn, Berenice Boutin, Nataša Nedeski, Ilias Plakokefalos, Dov (collaboration) Jacobs, „Guiding Principles on Shared Responsibility in International Law“, *European Journal of International Law* 31 (2020), p. 15-72.

45 Notably, Cathryn Costello, Itamar Mann, „Border Justice: Migration and Accountability for Human Rights Violations“, *German Law Journal* 21 (2020), p. 311-334; and the other articles in the cited special issue; Violeta Moreno-Lax, Mariagiulia Giuffré, „The Rise of Consensual Containment: From 'Contactless Control' to 'Contactless Reponsibility' for Forced Migration Flows“, in Satvinder Singh Juss (ed.), *Research Handbook on International Refugee Law*, Edward Elgar 2019, p. 82-108.

responsibility of the EU is particularly understudied. Research on whether, and if so, under which circumstances and in which manner, the EU bears responsibility for fundamental rights violations that occur as a result of its asylum policies remains scarce.[46] Although scholarly discourse has recently become increasingly aware of the necessity to examine the EU's role and its responsibilities in the asylum system, its findings to date remain rather limited. Most contributions focus on the EU's responsibility under international law[47] – an approach that comes with built-in practical obstacles and conceptual shortcomings.[48] Contributions that focus on the EU's responsibility under EU law often remain limited to non-judicial review fora such as the European Ombudsman or agency-internal complaints mechanisms.[49]

The lack of research on the EU's legal responsibility is striking when taking into account that the EU has become a very powerful, perhaps the most powerful, public actor in the European asylum system. The EU sets the central legal standards, concludes international agreements, negotiates influential 'deals', and increasingly implements its policies at the administrative level.[50] In terms of content, the EU pursues harsh externalisation policies. In short, the EU has become an 'ordinary' public actor of the Global North. Earlier conceptualisations of the EU as a human rights orga-

46 With research on the responsibility of Frontex in the context of border control being a notable exception.

47 See, for instance, Roberta Mungianu, *Frontex and Non-Refoulement. The International Responsibility of the EU*, Cambridge University Press 2016; Federico Casolari, „The EU's Hotspot Approach to Managing the Migration Crisis: A Blind Spot for International Responsibility?", *Italian Yearbook of International Law* 25 (2015), p. 109-134.

48 For an analysis of the conceptual shortcomings, see Itamar Mann, „Maritime Legal Black Holes: Migration and Rightlessness in International Law", *The European Journal of International Law* 29 (2018), p. 347-372.

49 A notable exception in this regard is the work of Melanie Fink, *Frontex and Human Rights. Responsibility in 'Multi-Actor Situations' under the ECHR and EU Public Liability Law*, Oxford University Press 2018; Melanie Fink, „The Action for Damages as a Fundamental Rights Remedy: Holding Frontex Liable", *German Law Journal* 21 (2020), p. 532-548.

50 For a comprehensive analysis of the EU's role in the administrative context, see Catharina Ziebritzki, *The EU's Responsibility in the Asylum Administration. Administrative Integration, Judicial Protection and the Case of the EU Hotspots*, Dissertation at Frankfurt University, Law Department January 2024.

nisation seem quite out of place.[51] Today, there can hardly be any doubt that the EU poses a severe threat to the fundamental rights of asylum seekers.

From an EU constitutional perspective, however, the EU's role continues to be conceived almost as if it still was a human rights organisation: its responsibilities lack legal contours.[52] There is no tailor-made remedy that would allow individuals to hold the EU responsible before the Court of Justice of the European Union (CJEU). Non-judicial review fora are designed in a deficient manner and, in any case, cannot replace judicial protection.[53] As the CJEU has consistently held since *Les Verts*, the rule of law – more precisely, the fundamental right to effective judicial protection enshrined in Art. 47 ChFR and the principle of effectiveness – require that all public acts, including those issued by the EU itself, are subject to judicial review.[54] This guarantee of judicial protection is comprehensive and applies regardless of whether the conduct in question is formally-binding or factual in nature.[55] Hence, the fact that the EU, in the context of the asylum administration, mainly acts through non-formally binding measures is no argument against judicial review.[56]

The question of the EU's responsibility becomes particularly acute in the case of EU hotspots where administrative integration is particularly ad-

51 Armin von Bogdandy, „The European Union as a Human Rights Organization? Human Rights and the Core of the European Union", *Common Market Law Review* 37 (2000), p. 1307-1338, p. 1317, 1336.

52 Jürgen Bast, Frederik von Harbou, Janna Wessels, *The REMAP Study* (fn. 16), p. 15: 'Today, the European Union (EU) has established itself as a powerful actor in migration policy (...) The EU has yet to adjust to its new role as potential threat to the Human Rights of migrants.'.

53 See further chapter 3, 1.

54 CJEU, Court, judgement of 23 April 1986, Parti écologiste 'Les Verts' v European Parliament, 294/83, para 23; CJEU, Court, judgement of 25 July 2002, Unión de Pequeños Agricultores v Council of the European Union, C-50/00 P, para 38–39: '[T]he European Community is, however, a community based on the rule of law in which its institutions are subject to judicial review of the computability of their acts with the Treaty and with the general principles of law which include fundamental rights. Individuals are therefore entitled to effective judicial protection (...)'.

55 For a comprehensive assessment of judicial review against the EU's factual conduct see Timo Rademacher, *Realakte im Rechtsschutzsystem der Europäischen Union*, Mohr Siebeck 2014; Timo Rademacher, „Factual Administrative Conduct and Judicial Review in EU Law", *European Review of Public Law* 30 (2017), p. 399-435.

56 In more detail on the EU's mode of operation, which can be described as 'determining without deciding', chapter 1, 4.3; chapter 2, 1 and 2.

vanced.[57] Close cooperation between EUAA, Frontex and the Commission, on the one hand, and national authorities, on the other, makes it especially difficult to establish who is responsible for what. Certainly, the host member state bears one share of the responsibility. This is apparent already from the numerous interim measures and judgements of the ECtHR condemning Greece for violations of Art. 3 ECHR and obliging it to provide humane reception conditions.[58] But blaming the host member state alone is too easy.[59] The EU's involvement – ranging from the conceptualisation of the EU hotspot approach to the provision of funding and the implementation at the operational level – strongly suggests that the EU bears its share of the responsibility, too. Power comes with responsibility, after all.

Yet, the question of the EU's legal responsibility for systemic fundamental rights violations in EU hotspots remains unanswered. The EU's role and its failures in the EU hotspots have not yet been subject to review before the CJEU. As this study will show, the main reason for this is that relevant stakeholders have no political interest in initiating judicial proceedings on these issues, and affected individuals have not yet been able to fully explore the potential of the EU legal protection system for that matter.[60] So far, there is also no pragmatic scholarly proposal on how to ensure judicial review. Research is mostly limited to evaluating non-judicial review mechanisms – but these fall short of the constitutional requirements, especially the fundamental right to an effective judicial remedy under Art. 47 ChFR, and have, moreover, brought little clarity. Although some proceedings have been initiated before the European Ombudsman, for instance, against the EUAA for its mistakes in connection with asylum interviews in the EU

57 Further on EU hotspots as a paradigm example and 'testing ground' for the EU's new role as central actor in the asylum administration see chapter 1, 2.

58 See fn. 33.

59 Relying on judicial remedies against Greece alone is neither conceptually convincing nor practically effective. Greece systemically fails to implement ECtHR judgements, especially in the areas of migration, borders and asylum, see European Parliament, Resolution of 7 February 2024 on the rule of law and media freedom in Greece, 2024/2502(RSP), para 15. The gravity of the implementation failures is such that the European Parliament in para 27 called 'for a Commission assessment under the Rule of Law Conditionality Regulation (i.e. Regulation (EU, Euratom) 2020/2092 of the European Parliament and of the Council of 16 December 2020 on a general regime of conditionality for the protection of the Union budget) of the consequences of the failure to implement relevant judgments by the European courts' (parentheses added by author).

60 See further chapter 3, 2 and 3.

hotspots[61] and against the Commission for its failures in planning and supervising the EU hotspot administration,[62] the Ombudsman's decisions appear to be characterised not only by a lack of enforceability but also by a lack of courage. Her inquiries regularly end with a mere reminder to the administration to do better in the future. Procedures before the agency's internal complaints mechanisms have remained futile, too. The EUAA's complaints mechanism is not even set up yet, and Frontex's mechanism is difficult to access and structurally weak.[63] Based on these or similar findings, existing studies tend to conclude that the EUAA appears 'out of control', that it is almost a 'mission impossible' to hold the EU accountable for its failures in the asylum system or even diagnose an outright 'failure of law' in the EU hotspot context.[64]

61 European Ombudsman, Decision of 5 July 2018, on the European Asylum Support Office's (EASO) Involvement in the Decision-Making Process Concerning Admissibility of Applications for International Protection Submitted in the Greek Hotspots, in particular Shortcomings in Admissibility Interviews, Case 735/2017/MDC; Decision of 30 September 2019, on the Conduct of Experts in Interviews with Asylum Seekers Organised by the European Asylum Support Office, Case 1139/2018/MDC.

62 European Ombudsman, Decision of 11 June 2023, How the European Commission ensures respect for fundamental rights in EU-funded migration management facilities in Greece, Case OI/3/2022/MHZ.

63 As a result, Frontex's complaints mechanism is also of limited practical relevance: between 2016 and 2021, only 69 complaints have been lodged, out of which only 22 were deemed admissible, see European Ombudsman, Decision of 15 June 2021, on the functioning of the European Border and Coast Guard Agency's (Frontex) complaints mechanism for alleged breaches of fundamental rights and the role of the Fundamental Rights Officer, Case OI/5/2020/MHZ. See further chapter 3, 1.

64 Salvatore F. Nicolosi, David Fernandez-Rojo, „Out of control? The case of the European Asylum Support Office", in Miroslava Scholten, Alex Brenninkmeijer (ed.), *Controlling EU Agencies. The Rule of Law in a Multi-jurisdictional Legal Order*, Edward Elgar 2020, p. 177-195; Evangelia (Lilian) Tsourdi, „Holding the European Asylum Support Office Accountable for its role in Asylum Decision-Making: Mission Impossible?", *German Law Journal* 21 (2020), p. 506-531; Max Pichl, *The "Moria Complex". Irresponsibility, Incompetence and Disenfranchisement Five Years After the EU-Turkey Accord and Launch of the Hotspot System. A Study for medico international*, 2021, p. 14–17. Similarly also Gaia Lisi, Mariolina Eliantonio, „The Gaps in Judicial Accountability of EASO in the Processing of Asylum Requests in Hotspots", *European Papers* 4 (2019), p. 589-602, concluding at p. 600 that 'effectively exerting control over the hotspot activities and in particular EASO's contribution (...) is frowned with considerable difficulties'.

4 The EU's Liability for EU Hotspots (Thesis)

This is where the present study seeks to contribute. Based on a comprehensive analysis of the EU hotspot administration, it makes two central claims.[65] The first is that the EU is the central actor in the EU hotspot administration. More precisely, it will be shown that EU bodies, although they refrain from issuing legally binding decisions towards individuals, de facto steer and guide the course of the EU hotspot administration. The second thesis is that the EU, in certain cases, bears legal responsibility for the fundamental rights violations occurring in EU hotspots. Specifically, it will be argued that the relevant EU bodies, i.e. the EUAA, Frontex and the European Commission, can be held responsible via the action for damages under Art. 41 para 3 ChFR, Art. 340 para 2 of the Treaty on the Functioning of the European Union (TFEU).[66]

With regard to the first thesis, it must be noted that analysing the EU's role in the EU hotspots is important not only for the sake of understanding the case as such but also for understanding the EU's new role in the asylum administration more generally. Since 2015, the EU has gradually evolved into a critical administrative actor, and its new role is particularly evident in the context of the EU hotspots where administrative integration is most advanced. What is more, the EU hotspots in Greece function as an 'administrative experiment' where advanced administrative integration is 'tested' – albeit often at the cost of fundamental rights.[67] As a result of this 'testing', the relevant practices are then perpetuated insofar as they are deemed 'useful' by the political actors in charge through subsequent consolidation in secondary law. The process is well illustrated with the

65 Building on earlier research, in particular: Catharina Ziebritzki, „Refugee Camps at the EU External Border – Is the Union responsible? The Integrated EU Hotspot Administration and the Potential of EU Public Liability Law", in Markus Kotzur, David Moya, Ülkü Sezgi Sözen, Andrea Romano (ed.), *The External Dimension of EU Migration and Asylum Policies. Human Rights, Development and Neighbourhood Policies in the Mediterranean Area*, Nomos 2020; Catharina Ziebritzki, *The EU's Responsibility in the Asylum Administration* (fn. 50).

66 On the details of the legal basis see chapter 3, 4.3. As will be shown in chapter 5 and in the conclusion, this argument is partly confirmed and partly challenged by the recent judgement in CJEU, General Court (Sixth Chamber), judgement of 6 September 2023, WS et al v Frontex, T-600/21.

67 Note that the fundamental rights of third country nationals are at stake here. If it were about the rights of EU citizens, the outcry would undoubtedly be huge – and rightly so.

CEAS reform of April 2024. The new standard procedure, consisting of a pre-entry screening, an extended border procedure, and a crisis mode,[68] largely appears as a consolidation of practices that have been implemented in the EU hotspots since 2015.[69]

The second thesis is useful beyond the specific case of the EU hotspots, too, because it shows that the most promising procedural option to hold the EU responsible for its non-formally binding conduct is via the action for damages. The argument hence implies that the action for damages has evolved into a 'makeshift' fundamental rights remedy.[70] While the most common counterarguments against this understanding refer to doctrinal difficulties in the context of causation and attribution, a comprehensive analysis in light of the CJEU's relevant case law will show that these arguments cannot persist. Based on the doctrine of EU liability law as it currently stands, the action for damages indeed allows concerned individuals to hold the EUAA, Frontex and the European Commission responsible for their misconduct. The present study's analysis thus points to a practically feasible way to hold the EU responsible for its failures not only in the specific context of the EU hotspots but also for other aspects of the asylum administration – e.g. for the provision of EU funding – and beyond that in all areas of the administration where the EU acts in non-formally binding ways.

Given the scarcity of legal research on the EU's legal responsibility in the context of the asylum system, two limitations concerning the second thesis require clarification. First, the focus here lies on the responsibility *of the EU*, leaving aside questions concerning the legal responsibility of the host member state or of the participating member states.[71] Second, the focus is

68 Regulation (EU) 2024/1349 of the European Parliament and of the Council of 14 May 2024 establishing a return border procedure, and amending Regulation (EU) 2021/1148 (hereinafter: Return Border Procedure Regulation 2024); Regulation (Eu) 2024/1356 of the European Parliament and of the Council of 14 May 2024 introducing the screening of third-country nationals at the external borders and amending Regulations (EC) No 767/2008, (EU) 2017/2226, (EU) 2018/1240 and (EU) 2019/817 (hereinafter: Screening Regulation II 2024); Regulation (EU) 2024/1359 of the European Parliament and of the Council of 14 May 2024 addressing situations of crisis and force majeure in the field of migration and asylum and amending Regulation (EU) 2021/1147 (hereinafter: Crisis Regulation).

69 On the EU hotspot procedure see chapter 2, 1.3.

70 In more detail on this understanding chapter 3, 3.

71 Thus, when this study concludes that the EU is liable, that finding must not to be misunderstood as implying that only the EU is liable; questions of joint liability simply

on the responsibility of the EU and its bodies *under EU law*. Questions concerning the EU's responsibility under international law will hence not be addressed.[72]

5 State of Research and Contribution of this Study

This study makes several contributions to European legal scholarship. Its findings contribute, first, to established studies on the integrated European administration, second, to rapidly evolving and increasingly relevant research on European asylum law, and third, to emerging scholarship on fundamental rights remedies against the EU. Fourth, and at a more general level, the study also contributes to recent research on strengthening the rule of law in the EU.

As regards the first relevant field, the integrated European administration, it should be recalled that increasing administrative cooperation of member state authorities and EU bodies is a much-debated and widely analysed phenomenon. The terms and concepts offered to describe and understand that phenomenon are accordingly numerous and diverse.[73] This study adopts the understanding of an integrated European administration, comprising national authorities and EU bodies, united by their function to implement EU law.[74] On this basis, it provides a reconstruction of the development and structure of the integrated EU hotspot administration.

---

fall outside the scope of this study. For an analysis of the host member state's and the participating member states' responsibility under the ECHR and under EU liability law in the case of Frontex operations see Melanie Fink, *Frontex and Human Rights* (fn. 49), p. 80–316. On joint liability more generally see Peter Oliver, „Joint Liability of the Community and the Member States", in Ton Heukels, Alison McDonnell (ed.), *The Action for Damages in Community Law*, Wolters Kluwer 1997, p. 285-309; John E. Noyes, Brian D. Smith, „State Responsibility and the Principle of Joint and Several Liability", *Yale Journal of International Law* 132 (1988), p. 225-267.

72 For an analysis of Frontex's responsibility under international law see Roberta Mungianu, *Frontex and Non-Refoulement* (fn. 47). For an analysis of responsibility of all involved actors in the EU hotspot approach under international law see Federico Casolari, „The EU's Hotspot Approach to Managing the Migration Crisis: A Blind Spot for International Responsibility?", *Italian Yearbook of International Law* 25 (2015), p. 109–134.

73 For an overview see Paul Craig, *EU Administrative Law*, Oxford University Press 2018, p. 3–4.

74 See, in particular, Herwig C. H. Hofmann, Alexander Türk, „The Development of Integrated Administration in the EU and its Consequences", *European Law Journal* 13 (2007), p. 253-271; Eberhard Schmidt-Aßmann, „Einleitung: Der Europäische

As will be explained in more detail below, this case study is particularly well-suited to further the study of the integrated asylum administration more broadly and integrated administration in other policy fields. The case study of the EU hotspots exemplifies with particular clarity and persistence the constitutional challenges and structural tensions underlying administrative integration. On the one hand, the challenges related to the EU's competences are aggravated by traditional sovereignty-related concerns, and on the other hand, challenges related to individual judicial protection come with pressing urgency due to fundamental rights violations occurring at a large scale.

This leads to the second field to which this study seeks to contribute, European asylum law. It provides an in-depth understanding of the European asylum administration and the EU's responsibility within it, thereby contributing to addressing the challenge of holding the EU responsible for outsourced or externalised human rights violations. Although legal research on the CEAS has increased exponentially since 2015, most contributions focus on substantial asylum law, thereby leaving the administration and administrative law relatively under-investigated. Where research on the European asylum administration is undertaken, it usually remains limited to specific parts thereof and has long focused on horizontal cooperation.[75] More recent studies take into account vertical forms of cooperation but still remain limited to individual aspects, and they usually adopt a rather policy-oriented perspective.[76] In particular, knowledge of the EU hotspot

---

Verwaltungsverbund und die Rolle des Europäischen Verwaltungsrechts", in Eberhard Schmidt-Aßmann, Bettina Schöndorf-Haubold (ed.), *Der Europäische Verwaltungsverbund. Formen und Verfahren der Verwaltungszusammenarbeit in der EU*, Mohr Siebeck 2005, p. 1-23.

75 For instance Cathryn Costello, „Administrative governance and the Europeanisation of asylum and immigration policy", in Herwig C.H. Hofmann, Alexander H. Türk (ed.), *EU Administrative Governance*, Edward Elgar 2006, p. 287-340, dedicating only p. 306–309 to Frontex; Jürgen Bast, „Transnationale Verwaltung des europäischen Migrationsraums: Zur horizontalen Öffnung der EU-Mitgliedstaaten", *Der Staat* 46 (2007), p. 1-32; Matthias Wendel, „The Refugee Crisis and the Executive: On the Limits of Administrative Discretion in the Common European Asylum System", *German Law Journal* 17 (2016), p. 1005-1032.

76 In particular the work of Evangelia (Lilian) Tsourdi, „Bottom-Up Salvation? From Practical Cooperation Towards Joint Implementation Through the European Asylum Support Office", *European Papers* 1 (2017), p. 997-1031; Evangelia (Lilian) Tsourdi, „Beyond the 'Migration Crisis': The Evolving Role of EU Agencies in the Administrative Governance of the Asylum and External Border Control Policies", in Johannes Pollak, Peter Slominski (ed.), *The Role of EU Agencies in the Eurozone and Migration*

administration – which is important to understand the functioning of the European asylum administration more generally – so far largely remains in the world of practitioners. As scholars have noted repeatedly, there is a 'knowledge gap' or 'simply a lack of information' on how the EU hotspots operate.[77]

Third, this study contributes to emerging research on individual remedies, and more specifically, fundamental rights remedies, against the EU. As EU agencies work hand in hand with member states, scholars devote increasing attention to agencification, including the question of legal protection.[78] At the same time, research on legal protection against the European Commission is increasing, too, both in the traditional context of competition law and, more recently, in the context of the Eurozone crisis.[79] Remarkably, however, the results of this research have not yet been sufficiently explored in the context of the asylum system, with research on Frontex's responsibility in the context of the border administration remaining a notable exception.[80] Research on the responsibilities of the Commission

---

Crisis. Impact and Future Challenges, Palgrave Macmillan 2021, p. 175-203. See also David Fernández-Rojo, *EU Migration Agencies. The Operation and Cooperation of FRONTEX, EASO and EUROPOL*, Edward Elgar 2021.

77 Sergio Carrera, Leonhard Den Hertog, Joanna Parkin, „The Peculiar Nature of EU Home Affairs Agencies in Migration Control: Beyond Accountability versus Autonomy?", *European Journal of Migration and Law* 15 (2013), p. 337-358, noting at p. 353 that 'there is often a simple lack of information'; David Fernández-Rojo, *EU Migration Agencies* (fn. 76), stating at p. 17 that 'a knowledge gap exists between the operational functions de jure conferred on Frontex, EASO and Europol and the activities that these agencies increasingly conduct de facto on the ground.'.

78 See only Madalina Busuioc, *European Agencies: Law and Practices of Accountability*, Oxford University Press 2013, p. 191–220; Merijn Chamon, *EU Agencies. Legal and Political Limits to the Transformation of the EU Administration*, Oxford University Press 2016, p. 327–368; Mariavittoria Catanzariti, Alexander H. Türk, „EU agencies and the rise of a mixed administration in the EU multi-jurisdictional setting: facing the challenges of the rule of law", in Miroslava Scholten, Alex Brenninkmeijer (ed.), *Controlling EU Agencies. The Rule of Law in a Multi-jurisdictional Legal Order*, Edward Elgar 2020, p. 18-38.

79 For an overview see Alexander Türk, „Judicial review of integrated administration in the EU", in Herwig Hofmann, Alexander Türk (ed.), *Legal Challenges in EU Administrative Law: Towards an Integrated Administration*, Edward Elgar 2009, p. 218-256; Mariolina Eliantonio, Nikos Vogiatzis, „Judicial and Extra-Judicial Challenges in the EU Multi- and Cross-Level Administrative Framework", *German Law Journal* 22 (2021), p. 315–324.

80 See in particular the work of Melanie Fink (fn. 49). See further, albeit from the perspective of international law, Roberta Mungianu, *Frontex and Non-Refoulement* (fn. 47); Matthias Lehnert, *Frontex und operative Maßnahmen an den europäischen*

and the EUAA, as well as on the EU's responsibility in the EU hotspot administration, is still largely lacking.

As scholars largely agree that judicial protection against the EU is constitutionally required but deficient in practice, the main discussion today concerns the question of which procedure is best suited to hold the EU responsible for its misconduct. One strand seeks to make use of the action for annulment,[81] and another argues in favour of the action for damages.[82] Contributing to the latter strand, this study explores the potential of the action for damages in the specific case of the EU hotspots.[83] It thereby tests and confirms the scholarly argument that the action for damages functions as a fundamental rights remedy and contributes to intricate doctrinal discussions on attribution and causation in the context of the integrated administration.[84] As set out above, these discussions are relevant beyond the asylum administration. EU institutions more generally tend to rely on non-formally binding measures such as EU soft law[85] and factual

---

Außengrenzen. Verwaltungskooperation – materielle Rechtsgrundlagen – institutionelle Kontrolle, Nomos 2014, p. 273–436.

81 See, in particular, Giulia Gentile, „Ensuring Effective Judicial Review of EU Soft Law via the Action for Annulment before the EU Courts: a Plea for a Liberal-Constitutional Approach", *European Constitutional Law Review* (2020), p. 466-492; for an overview see Herwig Hofmann, Morgane Tidghi, „Rights and Remedies in Implementation of EU Policies by Multi-Jurisdictional Networks", *European Public Law* (2014), p. 147-164, p. 155.

82 See, in particular, the work of Melanie Fink (fn. 49); Timo Rademacher (fn. 55); Nina Półtorak, „Action for Damages in the Case of Infringement of Fundamental Rights by the European Union", in Ewa Bagińska (ed.), *Damages for violations of human rights. A comparative study of domestic legal systems*, Springer 2016, p. 427-441; Angela Ward, „Damages under the EU Charter of Fundamental Rights", *ERA Forum* 12 (2012), p. 589-611.

83 The possibility of making use of the action for damages to hold the EU liable for misconduct in EU hotspots was already noted by Sergio Carrera, Leonhard Den Hertog, Joanna Parkin, „The Peculiar Nature of EU Home Affairs Agencies in Migration Control" (fn. 77), p. 344–345, however without further analysis. Similarly, Gaia Lisi, Mariolina Eliantonio, „The Gaps in Judicial Accountability of EASO in the Processing of Asylum Requests in Hotspots" (fn. 64), p. 601 conclude that 'further research is certainly needed to explore the potential for the liability action to ensure some degree of protection to individuals.'.

84 See, for instance, Melanie Fink, „EU Liability for Contributions to Member States' Breaches of EU Law", *Common Market Law Review* 56 (2019), p. 1227-1264; Martin Weitenberg, *Der Begriff der Kausalität in der haftungsrechtlichen Rechtsprechung der Unionsgerichte*, Nomos 2014.

85 On the notion of EU soft law see Francis Snyder, „Soft Law and Institutional Practice in the European Community", in Stephen Martin (ed.), *The Construction of Europe.*

administrative conduct. Examples include the Covid-19 pandemic and the Common Security and Defence Policy,[86] but also more traditional fields such as competition law.[87]

This leads to the last point. Seen from a broader constitutional perspective, this study also contributes to recent research on strengthening the rule of law in the European Union, which is urgently required in the context of the asylum system.[88] Unlike most existing studies,[89] however, it does not focus on enforcing EU law against member states; instead, it focuses on enforcing EU law against the EU itself. As set out above, the rule of law implies that all public entities, including the EU itself, are subject to judicial scrutiny. In the context of the asylum system, however, this guarantee largely runs empty. Overly complex and insufficiently regulated administrative structures lead to responsibility blurring and shifting. Consequently, the most powerful actors - including the EU - are mostly not held responsible, and fundamental rights violations persist. In order to address systemic deficiencies in the asylum system, it is thus fundamental to disentangle its administrative structures and hold EU bodies responsible for their misconduct. In this sense, the analysis of the EU's responsibility contributes to building an asylum system that is, not only on paper but also in administrative reality, based on the rule of law and human rights. Developing and advancing constitutional arguments, the core of which is anchored in Art. 2 TEU, contributes to building an EU that is closer to its

Essays in honour of Emile Noël, Springer 1994, p. 197-227; Fabien Terpan, „Soft Law in the European Union. The Changing Nature of EU Law", *European Law Journal* 21 (2015), p. 68-96.

86 Carolyn Moser, *Accountability in EU Security and Defence. The Law and Practice of Peacebuilding*, Oxford University Press 2020, in particular p. 6–7 where she notes that the 'discrepancy between law and practice in EU civilian crisis management is intriguing, not least because the de facto shift in power is likely to hamper or even harm accountability'.

87 Oana Andreea Stefan, „European Competition Soft Law in European Courts: A Matter of Hard Principles?", *European Law Journal* 14 (2008), p. 753–772.

88 Barbara Grabowska-Moroz, Dimitry Vladimirovich Kochenov, „The Loss of Face for Everyone Concerned" (fn. 18).

89 Armin von Bogdandy, Michael Ioannidis, „Systemic Deficiency in the Rule of Law" (fn. 4); Armin von Bogdandy, Pál Sonnevend (ed.), *Constitutional Crisis in the European Constitutional Area. Theory, Law and Politics in Hungary and Romania*, Nomos 2015, p. 204–267; András Jakab, Dimitry Kochenov (ed.), *The Enforcement of EU Law and Values. Ensuring Member States' Compliance*, Oxford University Press 2017.

own normative aspirations.[90] Ultimately, this study is hence motivated by the hope that change can be achieved through law.[91]

6 Typical Case Constellations

To illustrate and substantiate its findings, this study refers to six case constellations which describe typical situations in EU hotspot camps in Greece between 2015 and 2022.[92] These cases will be used as reference points and serve to support, substantiate and exemplify the argument of this study.

The cases were construed on the basis of on publicly available reports and practical experience of the author.[93] All cases reflect standard situations that affect a large number of persons. For the sake of argumentative clarity, however, the construed cases focus on one or two specific legal problems, whereas in practice, several of these issues would usually occur and overlap in a single case.

The legal assessments involved – including the findings of fundamental rights violations – are based on a comprehensive review of available reports by different actors, including EU institutions, UN bodies and NGOs, of the ECtHR's relevant case law on Art. 3 ECHR, especially in the context of EU

90 In the same direction Evangelia (Lilian) Tsourdi, Cathryn Costello, „'Systemic Violations' in EU Asylum Law: Cover or Catalyst?" (fn. 4) who at p. 993–994 conclude 'asylum-related failings should (...) be identified as rule of law issues and be incorporated in processes seeking to probe risks to EU values.'.

91 Karl E Klare, „Legal Culture and Transformative Constitutionalism", *South African Journal on Human Rights* 14 (1998), p. 146-188, at p. 150 speaks of 'transformative hopes'. For an application of this idea to the EU see Armin von Bogdandy, *The Emergence of European Society through Public Law* (fn. 15), p. 3 et seq., p. 78 et seq., p. 157 et seq., p. 242 et seq.

92 What is not typical, of course, is that the persons concerned claim compensation from the EU. Also, case 4 is not typical insofar as the number of deportations to Türkiye has been very low ever since March 2016, and that no deportations have been carried out since March 2020, see chapter 2, 2.1.c and 3.2.c. For the sake of the consequentiality of the case study, the cases are based on CEAS as it stood between 2015 and 2022. For the sake of actuality, however, reference is made – in addition – to the the legal basis under the reformed CEAS of 2024.

93 For an overview of the systemic deficiencies in the EU hotspot administration see chapter 2, 3. For the author's practical experience see fn. 103.

hotspots, and of the CJEU's relevant case law, including on Art. 4 and 41 ChFR in the context of the asylum system and external borders.[94]

Case 1 – Sara Esmaili – Inhumane reception conditions – Art. 4 and 41 ChFR
Sara Esmaili and her 9-year-old daughter Ayla, both of Afghan nationality, suffered from the living conditions in camp Moria during winter 2018. Ms Esmaili is a 35-year-old woman, single mother and pregnant. She is also a victim of severe sexual and gender-based violence and thus qualifies as vulnerable. According to the then applicable law, she should, therefore, have been exempted from the border procedure and referred to the Greek mainland.[95] The EUAA, however, failed to conduct a correct vulnerability assessment. The procedural mistakes were so grave that they amounted to a violation of Art. 41 ChFR. As a result of the deficient interview, Ms Esmaili was registered as non-vulnerable and obliged to stay in the EU hotspot camp. As the conditions in the camp amounted to inhumane and degrading treatment in the sense of Art. 4 ChFR, prolonged exposure to the dire conditions resulted in severe long-term consequences on the physical and psychological health of Ms Esmaili and her daughter. Ms Esmaili now claims compensation for violation of Art. 41 and of Art. 4 ChFR from the EUAA, the Commission, or the Union.

Case 2 – Magan Daud – Deficient asylum interview – Art. 41 ChFR
Magan Daud, a 40-year-old man of Syrian nationality, arrived on the island of Kos on 1 June 2019. Mr Daud qualified as vulnerable because he is a survivor of torture and suffers from a severe chronic heart disease. The EUAA, however, conducted the asylum interview in a deficient manner and failed to conduct a vulnerability assessment. On this basis, the EUAA concluded that Mr Daud was not vulnerable and that Türkiye could be considered a safe third country for him. It also recommended rejecting the asylum claim. The procedural errors committed by the EUAA were sufficiently grave to amount to a violation of Art. 41 ChFR. Yet, and in line with usual practice, the Greek Asylum Service rubber-stamped the EUAA's recommendation without any further examination, with the result that Mr Daud's claim for asylum was rejected. Mr Daud claims

94 See fn. 3 for relevant reports, and fn. 33 for the ECtHR's case law; further throughout this study.
95 See Art. 60 para 4 lit f Law 4375/2016 as reformed in April 2016.

compensation for the violation of Art. 41 ChFR from the EUAA, the Commission, or the Union.

Case 3 – Daniat Kidane – Age assessment through visual inspection – Art. 24, 41 and 4 ChFR
Daniat Kidane, a 16-year-old unaccompanied girl of Eritrean nationality, arrived to the island of Lesbos on 1 June 2018. The responsible Frontex expert estimated her age purely based on her physical appearance and informed the Greek authorities that she was born on 1 January 2002. Although this mistake amounts to a violation of the procedural rights of the child under Art. 24, 41 ChFR, the Greek authority accepted Frontex's assessment without further inquiry. Consequently, Daniat was neither exempted from the border procedure nor given access to the camp section dedicated to unaccompanied minors. Instead, she stayed in a camping tent like all other adults and families and was deprived of access to medical services; this situation severely affected her physical and mental health. The seriousness of her injuries was such that the threshold of a violation of Art. 4 ChFR was reached. The complete absence of state support also violated her rights as a child under Art. 24 para 1 and 2 ChFR. Daniat Kidane claims compensation for the violation of Art. 24, 41 and Art. 4 ChFR from Frontex, the Commission, or the Union.

Case 4 – Nabeeh Al Badawi – Return to Türkiye – Art. 4, 18, 19 ChFR
Nabeeh Al Badawi, a 22-year-old man of Syrian nationality, was deported from Lesbos to Türkiye on 1 December 2019. Given the specific circumstances of the case, and taking into account that Turkish authorities had forcibly returned Mr Al Badawi to Syria already in 2018, Türkiye could not be considered a safe third country for him. The deportation hence constituted a breach of the non-refoulement principle as enshrined in Art. 4, 18, 19 para 2 ChFR. Yet, Frontex supported the Hellenic Police by providing a vessel and escort officers, and failed to react to Mr Al Badawi's concerns raised during the process of deportation. After his arrival in Türkiye, Mr Al Badawi was subject to prolonged administrative detention and then again forcibly returned to Syria. Back in Aleppo, Mr Al Badawi claims compensation for the violation of the non-refoulement principle as enshrined in Art. 4, 18, 19 ChFR through his return to Türkiye from Frontex, the Commission or the Union.

Case 5 – Kareem Rashid – Limbo situation – Art. 41 and 4 ChFR
In March 2021, the asylum claim of Kareem Rashid, a 35-year-old man of Syrian nationality, was rejected as inadmissible in the EU hotspot in Chios. Due to the halt of readmissions since March 2020, it was clear that he would not be able to enter Türkiye. Yet, the EUAA applied its standard reasoning, concluded that Türkiye was safe, and recommended that he should seek protection there. Although this procedural mistake was so grave that it amounted to a violation of Art. 41 ChFR, neither the agency nor the Commission had adjusted the general operating procedures to the changed circumstances since March 2020. As a result, Mr Rashid was obliged to stay on the island of Chios, where, due to his status as a rejected asylum seeker, he did neither have access to any support services nor to the labour market. The prolonged stay of Mr Rashid in this limbo situation seriously harmed his physical and mental health, which amounted to a violation of his rights under Art. 4 ChFR. Mr Rashid thus claims compensation for the violation of Art. 4 ChFR from the EUAA, the Commission or the Union.

Case 6 – Reem Saeed – Prolonged detention – Art. 6 ChFR
Reem Saeed, a 30-year-old woman of Syrian nationality, arrived on the island of Kos in June 2020. Upon her arrival, she was immediately arrested and placed in detention. When her asylum claim was rejected in June 2021, a new detention order was issued, now referring to her imminent deportation as justification, notably despite the fact that readmissions to Türkiye had been effectively halted since March 2020. In October 2021, Ms Saeed found a lawyer representing her interests and, upon her intervention, was eventually released. As explained above, this generic detention scheme was a usual practice on Kos, yet the Commission failed to address the matter at the supervisory level.[96] Therefore, Ms Saeed claims compensation for the violation of her rights under Art. 6 ChFR from the Union or the Commission.

7 Method

This study relies on a combination of three methods: contextual doctrinal reconstruction, classical legal analysis, and empirical findings. The first

96 See chapter 2, 2 and 4.3.

method is to reconstruct the relevant legal field in order to provide a clear understanding of the object of investigation.[97] For instance, the EU hotspot administration is conceptualised as an integrated entity, encompassing member states' administrations and the relevant EU bodies including their horizontal and vertical interactions. This kind of defining and structuring a field of law on the basis of general principles, thereby giving legal and administrative phenomena a form and a name, can be referred to as doctrinal reconstruction. The reconstruction is contextual insofar as, in addition to the law, it also takes into account non-formally binding texts such as communications, policy notes, operational plans and internal administrative guidelines.[98] This is necessary because the European asylum administration evolves quicker than the formal law and, to a significant extent, operates on the basis of informal documents.[99]

Second, the study relies on classical legal analysis to develop a proposal on how to hold the EU responsible for its involvement in fundamental rights violations. Unlike other contributions, which often focus on developing proposals for doctrinal or legislative reform, this study's focus lies on proposing an interpretation of the law as it currently stands. This interpretational exercise is based on a comprehensive analysis of the CJEU's case law and is thus closely linked to legal practice. In this sense, the approach of this study can be seen as pragmatic: rather than proposing politically

97 See on that method, albeit with reference to the example of international law, Matthias Goldmann, „Dogmatik als rationale Rekonstruktion: Versuch einer Metatheorie am Beispiel völkerrechtlicher Prinzipien", *Der Staat* 53 (2014), p. 373-399.

98 In order to provide such contextual doctrinal reconstruction, several access to documents requests were made, not all of which were successful: Unlike in other fields of the AFSJ, the relevant documents are often not publicly available. The author has made numerous requests under Regulation (EC) No 1049/2011 of May 2011 regarding public access to European Parliament, Council and Commission documents (hereinafter: Transparency Regulation). Frontex has denied access to several documents with reference to the security exemption under Art 4 para 1 lit c Transparency Regulation. All documents obtained by EASO/EUAA, Frontex and the European Commission are on file with the author.

99 On the necessity of such approach for the analysis of the Area of Freedom, Security and Justice (hereinafter: AFSJ) more broadly see Jörg Monar, „Der Raum der Freiheit, der Sicherheit und des Rechts", in Armin von Bogdandy, Jürgen Bast (ed.), *Europäisches Verfassungsrecht. Theoretische und Dogmatische Grundzüge*, Springer 2009, p. 749-797, 753.

unrealistic reform,[100] it aims at developing practicable solutions to ensure fundamental rights under the law as it currently stands.

Third, these traditional legal methods are embedded within empirical findings. Empirical evidence is essential to understanding the operation of EU hotspots. The EU hotspot administration – and the European asylum administration more generally – develops at such a pace and often works on the basis of ad hoc agreements, or simply practical needs, that reading the law alone is not sufficient to understand what is actually going on. This is particularly true where implementation deficits are significant, widespread, and persisting. Accordingly, the reconstructive parts of this study draw on publicly available authoritative reports[101] and semi-structured qualitative interviews with representatives of the Commission and the EUAA.[102] These findings are supplemented by anecdotal insights gained by the author through her work as a practising lawyer.[103] Finally, the six typical cases described above are presented here. As explained, these cases were construed on the basis of authoritative reports and case law and, thus, reflect empirical reality. As will become clear in the course of this study, working with these case examples makes the argument more vivid and easier to understand, especially when it comes to intricate operational, administrative or doctrinal details. In sum, the added value of case examples is

100 In this direction, for instance, David Fernández-Rojo, *EU Migration Agencies* (fn. 76), who concludes at p. 157 that 'a legislative instrument that would regulate and detail the operational powers of Frontex, EASO and Europol should be adopted. Such a legislative instrument would (inter alia) clarify the allocation of responsibilities among the several actors that closely cooperate in the hotspots (...)'.

101 Including by EU bodies, UN bodies, and NGOs, see fn. 3.

102 Interviews with the EASO Union Contact Point conducted on 13 December 2019 and on 19 February 2021; interviews with Commission representative 1 (Unit C4) and Commission representative 2 (Unit C4) conducted on 12 February 2021; interview with Commission representative 3 (Unit C4) conducted on 16 February 2021; interview with Commission representative 4 (Unit E2) conducted on 26 February 2021; interview with Commission representative 5 (Dedicated Taskforce) conducted on 7 April 2021. Frontex has not replied to the author's requests for an interview. All interview transcripts are are on file with the author; the interviews will be referred to in the relevant footnotes.

103 The author is co-founder and board member the Greek-German NGO Equal Rights Beyond Borders which provides free legal services in the EU hotspots of Chios and Kos and engages in strategic litigation in European asylum law, see www.equal-rights.org. Between 2016 and 2018, she has worked as legal advisor for refugees and asylum seekers in Chios.

twofold: it makes the work easier to access and addresses the gap between law on paper and administrative reality on the ground.

Chapter 1: The EU's New Role in the Asylum Administration

This chapter presents the EU hotspot administration as a paradigm example of the EU's new role in the asylum administration. The first section briefly outlines how the role of the EU has changed in the aftermath of the 2015 crisis. The key observation is that EU bodies have become crucial to the functioning of the European asylum administration. As a consequence, the EU has become an 'ordinary' public actor in the sense that it not only protects refugee rights but also poses a potential threat thereto (1).[1] On this basis, the second section reconstructs the EU hotspot administration, including its history and regulatory framework. This shows that EU hotspots were conceived as an 'administrative experiment' and, until today, function as a 'testing ground' for the EU's new administrative role (2). The following sections then zoom in on the EU's new role and outline its main administrative actors and forms of operation. The third section portrays the EU asylum agency (EUAA, formerly EASO), the EU border agency (Frontex), and the European Commission (3). The fourth section presents support and supervision as the main forms of administrative conduct at the EU level and, on this basis, argues that the EU, in the context of the asylum administration, mainly 'determines without deciding'. This means that the EU steers and guides the course of the administration without, however, issuing formally-binding decisions to individuals – this task is always left to member states. The lack of formal bindingness in the EU's conduct is precisely what makes it so difficult, but at the same time utterly necessary, to establish possibilities for judicial protection (4).

---

1 An observation that might seem obvious considering the EU's colonial legacies – a perspective that is well-established in historical scholarship, see e.g. Peo Hansen, Stefan Jonsson, *Eurafrica: The Untold History of European Integration and Colonialism*, Bloomsbury Academic 2014, but only recently emerging in legal scholarship, see e.g. Hanna Eklund, „Peoples, Inhabitants and Workers: Colonialism in the Treaty of Rome", *The European Journal of International Law* 34 (2023), p. 831-854. Based on the still prevailing narrative in legal scholarship, however, the EU's role in the European asylum system is often reconstructed as a protector of refugee rights against member states, see in more detail 1.1.

1 Granting and Threatening Rights

From the perspective of the European Commission, the overarching aim of the 2015 crisis response was to reduce the number of asylum seekers that arrived in the EU and to 'restore order', as it was often framed, at external borders.[2] To this end, the EU considerably stepped up its own involvement at all levels of the European asylum system, ranging from external relations to administrative support in individual asylum procedures.[3]

As a result of this process, the traditional narrative of the EU as a defender of refugee rights against member states can no longer persist. Today, it is clear that the EU itself poses a potential threat to the rights of asylum seekers and refugees. The EU has become an 'ordinary' public actor in the sense that it does what most public actors in the Global North do: it pursues harsh externalisation policies by taking measures at all regulatory levels, including legislation and soft law, international agreements and 'deals', as well as, more recently, administrative regulation and administration.

1.1 The EU as an 'Ordinary' and Ambivalent Public Actor

In the founding phase and first decade of the Common European Asylum System, the EU was largely perceived as a guarantor of refugee rights. Indeed, several major achievements were made at EU level during this period. Among other things, the EU accomplished the creation of an internal allocation mechanism, harmonisation of legislative standards across member states, the introduction of the status of international protection and, arguably most importantly, the conception of refugee rights as fundamental rights. Critical voices focused on human rights violations 'occurring within the Union' rather than those committed by the Union itself and argued that these should be addressed through an even more proactive human

2 See only European Commission, Communication from the Commission to the European Parliament and the Council on the State of Play of Implementation of the Priority Actions under the European Agenda on Migration, 10.02.2016, COM(2016) 85 final, p. 3: 'Restoring orderly management of borders on the Eastern Mediterranean/Western Balkans route is the most pressing priority for the European Union today.', p. 8: 'Restoring order in these circumstances requires swift coordinated European action to address the immediate failings as well as to reduce the scale of the migratory inflows themselves.'.

3 In detail on the post-crisis reforms of Frontex and EASO see below 3.

rights policy by the EU.[4] From a constitutional perspective, there were good reasons to see the EU as a defender of refugee rights against member states.[5]

Today – and justified earlier critique from postcolonial studies notwithstanding[6] – such ideas must appear out of place, even from a conventional constitutionalist perspective. At the latest since the crisis, it has become obvious that the EU poses an increasingly serious threat to refugee rights.[7] In fact, the EU has since 2015 adopted a whole series of measures aimed at restricting access to the asylum system and lowering protection standards in Europe.[8] Rather than striving to realise the aspiration to provide international protection to those in need, as its mandate in Art. 78 para 1 TFEU provides, the EU's political focus today clearly lies on shifting responsibility for international protection to third countries and outsourcing responsibilities for the ensuing large-scale human rights violations, too. In brief, the EU has become a classic representative of externalisation policies.[9]

---

4 Philip Alston, J. H. H. Weiler, „An 'Ever Closer Union' in Need of a Human Rights Policy", *European Journal of International Law* 9 (1998), p. 658–723, p. 670, p. 718–719.

5 Armin von Bogdandy, „The European Union as a Human Rights Organization? Human Rights and the Core of the European Union", *Common Market Law Review* 37 (2000), p. 1307–1338, p. 1317, 1336.

6 See fn. 1.

7 Barbara Grabowska-Moroz, Dimitry Vladimirovich Kochenov, „The Loss of Face for Everyone Concerned. EU Rule of Law in the Context of the 'Migration Crisis'", in V Stoyanova, S Smet (ed.), *Migrants' Rights, Populism and Legal Resilience in Europe*, Cambridge University Press 2022, p. 187–208, p. 190: 'the rule of law is not secured sufficiently, either in the EU or by the EU, causing all concerned to lose face: EU values deserve better.', p. 208: 'both the national (...) and the EU regulatory levels have demonstrated eagerness to annihilate fundamental rights, undermining the basics of the rule of law (...).'.

8 Cathryn Costello, Minos Mouzourakis, „The Common European Asylum System. Where did it all go wrong?", in Maria Fletcher, Ester Herlin-Karnell, Matera Claudio (ed.), *The European Union as an Area of Freedom, Security and Justice*, Routledge 2017, p. 263-299, p. 298–294.

9 'Externalisation' refers to the externalisation of the responsibility to provide protection to refugees to third states. Externalisation policies mainly appear in the form of non-arrival policies; they are often referred to as 'policies of non-entrée', a term coined by James C. Hathaway, „The Emerging Politics of Non-Entrée", *Refugees* 91 (1992), p. 40. See further B. S. Chimni, „The Geopolitics of Refugee Studies: a View from the South", *Journal of Refugee Studies* 11 (1998), p. 350-374, p. 351; Thomas Gammeltoft-Hansen, James C. Hathaway, „Non-refoulement in a World of Cooperative Deterrence", *Columbia Journal of Transnational Law* 53 (2015), p. 235–284, p. 241: 'Whereas refugee law is predicated on the duty of *non-refoulement*, the politics of *non-entrée* is based on a commitment to ensuring that refugees shall not be allowed to arrive.'.

Consequently, the EU's role in the asylum system must be conceptualised as ambivalent: it is both a guarantor and a potential threat to refugee rights. While the EU's major achievements remain central safeguards for refugee protection in Europe, its externalisation policies and related measures clearly pose a threat thereto. Interestingly, this shift in the EU's role is rarely made explicitly in legal scholarship,[10] but most recent contributions seem to agree in substance.[11] Opinions differ, however, when it comes to judging or qualifying the EU's new role. Some argue that the main problem is the EU as such,[12] thereby implying that re-shifting power to regulate asylum to member states would improve refugee protection. But this assumption seems implausible. There is simply no reason why member states should be more open towards receiving refugees than the EU. Based on the understanding of the EU as the polity representing European society,[13] one cannot reasonably expect that willingness to provide protection would be significantly affected simply by switching from one regulatory level to another.[14] Instead, it rather seems plausible that the mechanisms of exclusion at the EU level today are the very same mechanisms that previously

10 See, however, Jürgen Bast, Frederik von Harbou, Janna Wessels, *Human Rights Challenges to European Migration Policy. The REMAP Study*, Nomos 2022, p. 15. In the same direction Evangelia (Lilian) Tsourdi, Cathryn Costello, „'Systemic Violations' in EU Asylum Law: Cover or Catalyst?", *German Law Journal* 24 (2023), p. 982–994, p. 993.

11 See only Violeta Moreno-Lax, „Must EU Borders have Doors for Refugees? On the Compatibility of Schengen Visas and Carriers' Sanctions with EU Member States' Obligations to Provide International Protection to Refugees", *European Journal of Migration and Law* 10 (2008), p. 315-364; Melanie Fink, *Frontex and Human Rights. Responsibility in 'Multi-Actor Situations' under the ECHR and EU Public Liability Law*, Oxford University Press 2018; Cathryn Costello, Itamar Mann, „Border Justice: Migration and Accountability for Human Rights Violations", *German Law Journal* 21 (2020), p. 311–334.

12 In this direction, but differentiated, Steve Peers, „Building Fortress Europe: The Development of EU Migration Law", *Common Market Law Review* 35 (1998), p. 1235-1272; Elspeth Guild, „The Europeanisation of Europe's Asylum Policy", *International Journal of Refugee Law* (2006), p. 630-652.

13 Armin von Bogdandy, *The Emergence of European Society through Public Law. A Hegelian and Anti-Schmittian Approach*, Oxford University Press 2024, p. 3 et seq.

14 As Barbara Grabowska-Moroz, Dimitry Vladimirovich Kochenov, „The Loss of Face for Everyone Concerned. EU Rule of Law in the Context of the 'Migration Crisis'" (fn. 7), p. 189 note 'politically and also legally, deep intolerenace to the migrant other became the new normal in the EU'.

operated at the member state level.[15] Seen from this perspective, the new role of the EU is nothing exceptional. The EU reacts to forced migration in the 21st century as most public actors in the Global North do. Its current role as a potential threat to refugee rights simply reflects that the relevant competences have been shifted to EU level with the Amsterdam Treaty, i.e., that the EU has become key to regulating forced migration to Europe.

Yet, the argument goes beyond the realm of asylum law: in fact, the ambivalence in the EU's new role is a very normal state of public law. Any public actor can guarantee and violate rights, and usually does both. This ambivalence is inherent in the relationship between public actors and individuals, and the fact that the EU is now becoming ambivalent, too, only reflects the 'normalisation' of the EU.[16] The point can be made with examples from every regulatory level, but the administrative context is perhaps the most obvious, as administrative activity inevitably comes with the risk of violating individual rights, and this risk is particularly high in contexts located at the EU external border.[17] When the EU acts as part of the integrated administration, it, hence, necessarily becomes an 'ordinary' public actor.

1.2 The EU as a Critical Actor in Asylum Administration

While the EU's role has shifted at all regulatory levels, its new role has become especially clear at the administrative level. For a long time, legislative

15 The transfer of exclusion mechanisms from member state to EU level becomes very clear in the case of EU citizenship. Moving beyond a mere transfer of 'nationalistic' ideas from member state to EU level would in fact require to reconceptualise EU citizenship as including, in some form, third-country-nationals see Dimitry Kochenov, „The Essence of EU Citizenship Emerging From Ten Years of Academic Debate: Beyond the Cherry Blossoms and the Moon?", *The International and Comparative Law Quarterly* 62 (2013), p. 97-136, p. 106 with further references.

16 Differently Armin von Bogdandy, „Grundprinzipien", in Armin von Bogdandy, Jürgen Bast (ed.), *Europäisches Verfassungsrecht. Theretische und dogmatische Grundzüge*, Springer 2009, p. 13-71, p. 56 who argues that the relation between Union and individual is only beneficial for the individiual: 'entwickelt der EuGh die Prinzipien in einer Weise, dass die den Einzelnen rechtlich grundsätzlich nur begünstigen, sie betreffen nicht die klassische Dialektik von Hoheitsgewalt und Freiheit.'.

17 Fundamental Rights Agency, Update of the 2016 Opinion on fundamental rights in the 'hotspots' set up in Greece and Italy, February 2019, p. 7: 'The processing of asylum claims in facilities at borders (...) brings along built-in deficiencies. (...) this approach creates fundamental rights challenges that appear almost unsurmountable.'.

integration has been conceptualised as key to the project of a Common European Asylum System (CEAS). At the latest since the 2015 crisis, however, administrative integration has moved into the focus. In fact, administrative cooperation has seen the most significant development in the past decade and, in this sense, constitutes the most recent step towards further integration.

To get a clear understanding of administrative cooperation in the asylum system, two forms of cooperation must be distinguished. First, there is horizontal cooperation among member states. The paradigm example here is cooperation between national asylum authorities in the context of the so-called 'Dublin procedure', i.e. to determine the member state responsible for conducting the asylum procedure. This horizontal form of cooperation, persisting practical difficulties notwithstanding, is largely consolidated.[18]

The second and much less consolidated form is vertical administrative cooperation between member states and EU bodies. This form of cooperation has exponentially gained relevance only since the early 2000s.[19] The initial step in this regard was the foundation of the European Asylum Support Office (EASO) in 2004.[20] Mandated to support member states with the implementation of EU asylum law, the agency provides training as well as general and concrete operational support, which obviously requires close administrative cooperation with member state authorities.[21] Similarly,

18 From the countless contributions on horizontal cooperation see only Jürgen Bast, „Transnationale Verwaltung des europäischen Migrationsraums: Zur horizontalen Öffnung der EU-Mitgliedstaaten", *Der Staat* 46 (2007), p. 1–32; Francesco Maiani, „The Dublin III Regulation: A New Legal Framework for a More Humane System?", in Vincent Chetail, Philippe De Bruycker, Francesco Maiani (ed.), *Reforming the Common European Asylum System*, 2016.

19 Council of the European Union, The Hague Programme: Strengthening Freedom, Security and Justice in the European Union, 13 December 2004, OJ C 53/1, 1.3., para 3 for the first time defines the creation of a 'European support office' as a political goal.

20 See Françoise Comte, „A New Agency Is Born in the European Union: The European Asylum Support Office", *European Journal of Migration and Law* 12 (2010), p. 373-405.

21 Regulation (EU) No 439/2010 of the European Parliament and of the Council of 19 May 2010 establishing a European Asylum Support Office (hereinafter: EASO Regulation); Regulation (EU) 2021/2303 of the European Parliament and of the Council of 15 December 2021 on the European Union Agency for Asylum and repealing Regulation (EU) No 439/2010 (hereinafter EUAA Regulation).

other EU agencies such as Frontex,[22] Europol, and Eurojust cooperate with national asylum administrations at both the supervisory and operational levels.[23] And finally, the European Commission is increasingly involved in administrative cooperation, too. Unlike the agencies, however, the Commission mainly operates at the supervisory level, setting administrative guidelines and coordinating administrative cooperation.[24] As will be argued in more detail below, vertical administrative cooperation has gained new momentum in the aftermath of the 2015 crisis, with the EU hotspots representing the most advanced state of administrative integration in the European asylum system today.[25]

To describe and analyse the complex web of administrative cooperation, this study relies on the well-established notion of an 'integrated European administration' and applies it to the context of the asylum system. The concept of an integrated administration, generally speaking, refers to a tension between separation in organisational terms and unification in functional terms.[26] Member state authorities and EU bodies share the same function, namely implementing EU law, while at the same time remaining distinct organisational units. In terms of structure, the European administration is thus characterised by elements of cooperation as well as of hierarchy.[27] In the specific context of the asylum administration, both the separating and the unifying elements are especially pronounced. This is so because, on the one hand, the limits of the Union's competences in the area of asylum and

---

22 Regulation (EU) 2019/1896 of the European Parliament and of the Council of 13 November 2019 on the European Border and Coast Guard and repealing Regulations (EU) No 1052/2013 and (EU) 2016/1624 (hereinafter Frontex Regulation).

23 In more detail on Europol's role see David Fernández-Rojo, *EU Migration Agencies. The Operation and Cooperation of FRONTEX, EASO and EUROPOL*, Edward Elgar 2021.

24 See below 3.3.

25 See below 2; chapter 2.

26 Herwig C. H. Hofmann, Alexander Türk, „The Development of Integrated Administration in the EU and its Consequences", *European Law Journal* 13 (2007), p. 253–271; Eberhard Schmidt-Aßmann, „Einleitung: Der Europäische Verwaltungsverbund und die Rolle des Europäischen Verwaltungsrechts", in Eberhard Schmidt-Aßmann, Bettina Schöndorf-Haubold (ed.), *Der Europäische Verwaltungsverbund. Formen und Verfahren der Verwaltungszusammenarbeit in der EU*, Mohr Siebeck 2005, p. 1–23.

27 Eberhard Schmidt-Aßmann, „Europäische Verwaltung zwischen Kooperation und Hierarchie. Festschrift für Helmut Steinberger", in Hans-Joachim Cremer (ed.), *Tradition und Weltoffenheit des Rechts*, Springer 2002, p. 1375-1399, p. 1399.

return are politically charged with the argument of national sovereignty,[28] and on the other hand, sincere cooperation is reinforced by the principles of mutual trust and solidarity.[29] As will become clear throughout this study, this reinforced tension lies at the root of the particular difficulties concerning the allocation of responsibility in the context of the EU hotspots and, at the same time, makes this case study so particularly instructive.

To understand the structure of vertical administrative cooperation, two points are of particular relevance. The first concerns the structure of the EU's administrative competences. Generally, the competence to implement EU law lies with member states, as follows from Art. 197 para 1 and Art. 291 para 1 TFEU. The EU can support member states in their implementation, for instance, through capacity building, as Art. 197 para 2 TFEU provides in general terms. With regard to the asylum system, the Treaties confer additional administrative competences upon the Union. These are enshrined in Art. 78 para 2 and Art. 74 TFEU, and, insofar as return decisions and deportations are concerned, in Art. 77 para 2 lit d and Art. 79 para 2 lit c TFEU. More specifically, Art. 78 para 2 TFEU allows the EU to provide support and supervise member states' authorities with regard to various aspects of the asylum administration, such as the provision of reception conditions and the conduct of asylum procedures. As will become clear throughout this study, the precise scope of the EU's competences is controversial, with dispute arising in particular on the question of whether the EU has the competence to issue administrative decisions towards individuals.

The second point concerns the relevant EU bodies that cooperate with national authorities. These include the agencies specifically mandated to implement EU asylum law, namely the EUAA and Frontex, as well as the agencies supporting them, such as inter alia the European Union Agency for Law Enforcement Cooperation (Europol), the EU Agency for Funda-

28 See only Guy S Goodwin-Gill, Jane McAdam, *The Refugee in International Law*, Oxford University Press 2007, p. 357: 'From the point of view of international law, therefore, the grant of protection to its territory derives from the State's sovereign competence, a statement of the obvious.'; Paul Kirchhof, „Staatliche Souveränität als Bedingung des Asylrechts", in Georg Jochum, Wolfgang Fritzemeyer, Marcel Kau (ed.), *Grenzüberschreitendes Recht - Crossing frontiers. Festschrift für Kay Hailbronner*, C.F. Müller 2013, p. 105-121, p. 114.

29 On solidarity see Art. 80 TFEU; on mutual trust see Court (Grand Chamber), judgment of 21 December 2011, N.S. v Secretary of State for the Home Department and M.E. and Others v Refugee Applications Commissioner and Minister for Justice, Equality and Law Reform, Joined cases C-411/10 and C-493/10, paras 78–83.

mental Rights (FRA), and the European Union Agency for the Operational Management of Large-Scale IT Systems in the Area of Freedom, Security and Justice (eu-LISA). Certainly, the agencies have become increasingly relevant for the functioning of the European asylum administration – a phenomenon that is often referred to as agencification.[30] The Commission's activities, however, are pivotal, too: they range from the provision of large sums of EU funding to administrative supervision on the ground to the provision of operational support, e.g. in the context of camp planning.[31]

1.3 The Failure to Regulate the EU's Responsibility

As a consequence, and this is the crucial point here, the regulatory requirements for EU law largely correspond to those for national law: EU law must define and hedge the responsibility of the EU itself, which includes allocating competences and enabling judicial protection. In the context of the asylum system, however, this regulatory task is not adequately fulfilled by EU law as it currently stands. Put bluntly, EU law continues to be conceived almost as if the EU were a human rights organisation, when in fact, it has since long acquired the legal competences and political powers to govern forced migration towards Europe. In this sense, European asylum law is largely characterised by a failure to regulate the EU's responsibility.[32] As a result, EU bodies often act without legal basis, and concerned individuals usually have no possibility to challenge the EU's conduct before a court.

This lagging behind of the law in relation to administrative reality can be traced back to several factors. One of the most obvious explanations has to do with the character of crisis response as an informal administrative experiment.[33] From a governmental perspective, the perpetuation of emergency instruments through belated legalisation reflects the function of crises as

30 See only Merijn Chamon, „Agencification in the United States and Germany and What the EU Might Learn From It", *German Law Journal* 17 (2016), p. 119-152; Miroslava Scholten, Marloes van Rijsbergen, „The Limits of Agencification in the European Union", *German Law Journal* 15 (2014), p. 1223-1255.

31 See below 3.3.

32 This regulatory gap cannot, of course, be filled by national law and also not by ECHR law, as long as the EU is not a party to the ECHR.

33 On informal governance prior to 2015 see for instance Maarten Vink, Claudia Engelmann, „Informal European Asylum Governance in an International Context", in Thomas Christiansen, Christine Neuhold (ed.), *International Handbook on Informal Governance*, Edward Elgar 2012, p. 534-553.

an opportunity for administrative experimentation.[34] This is particularly clearly visible in the area of asylum and migration, where the rights of non-citizens are at stake.[35] In this sense, the EU's increased involvement in the asylum system appears as outcome of a crisis-induced experiment.[36]

Historically, EU law has long not accounted for the EU as an ordinary public actor. The Treaty drafters did not conceive of either the EU agencies or of the Commission as actors that pose a potential threat to individual rights, let alone as administrative actors involved in procedures that have direct and severe effects on basic fundamental rights.[37] The Commission was originally conceived as a sort of governmental institution that would enforce EU law against member states, which implied the idea that it would act mainly in the interest of those persons to whom EU law grants individual rights.[38] EU agencies, in turn, were initially designed as regulatory bodies to assist and support member states in implementing EU law through activities such as coordination, training or funding.[39] Closely connected, European administrative law has historically developed in such a way that

34 Charles F. Sabel, Jonathan Zeitlin, „Experimentalist Governance", in David Levi-Faur (ed.), *The Oxford Handbook of Governance*, Oxford University Press 2012, p. 169-184; Jonathan Zeitlin, „EU experimentalist governance in times of crisis", *West European Politics* 39 (2016), p. 1073-1094.

35 Johannes Pollak, Peter Slominski, „Experimentalist but not Accountable Governance? The Role of Frontex in Managing the EU's External Borders", *West European Politics* 32 (2009), p. 904-924; Martina Tazzioli, „Refugees' Debit Cards, Subjectivities, and Data Circuits: Financial-Humanitarianism in the Greek Migration Laboratory", *International Political Sociology* 13 (2019), p. 392-408; Joanna Parkin, *The Difficult Road to the Schengen Information System II: The legacy of 'laboratories' and the cost for fundamental rights and the rule of law*, CEPS Policy Paper 2011, https://www.ceps.eu/ceps-publications/difficult-road-schengen-information-system-ii/.

36 Similarly David Fernández-Rojo, *EU Migration Agencies* (fn. 23), p. 149–157; Giuseppe Campesi, „Seeking Asylum in Times of Crisis: Reception, Confinement, and Detention at Europe's Southern Border", *Refugee Survey Quarterly* 37 (2018), p. 44-70, p. 53–56.

37 In addition, the prevailing narrative of the 'EU with a clean slate' might have been another factor.

38 It is symbolic in this regard that it was the European Commission who initiated the proposal for the EU's accession to the ECHR, see European Commission, Memorandum of 4 April 1979, Bulletin of the European Communities, Supp. 2/79. Until the late 1990s, the EU's human rights policies, insofar as they existed, largely fell within the institutional mandate of the European Commission, see Philip Alston, J. H. H. Weiler, „An 'Ever Closer Union' in Need of a Human Rights Policy" (fn. 4), p. 667.

39 Paul Craig, *EU Administrative Law*, Oxford University Press 2018, p. 153–155; Merijn Chamon, *EU Agencies. Legal and Political Limits to the Transformation of the EU Administration*, Oxford University Press 2016, p. 102–106.

the relationship between EU bodies and individuals is structurally under-regulated. Unlike national administrative law, which has always focused on the state-individual relationship, European administrative law has long focused on the state-state and state-EU relationship, thereby often losing sight of the concerned individual.[40]

Against this background, the crisis response would have required to explicitly regulate the EU's new legal responsibility. But the crisis measures largely failed to do so. In the immediate context of the 2015 crisis, new tasks were assigned to the Commission and the agencies in an ad hoc manner. In essence, the crisis response was introduced on the basis of policy papers, memoranda of understanding or similar political agreements among the involved stakeholders.[41] For instance, EASO and Frontex were de facto charged with tasks for which the then-applicable Regulations provided no legal basis,[42] and the Commission was entrusted with tasks that lacked definition in secondary law altogether.[43] This mode of operation persists until today. As the Commission's reaction to the burning of *Moria* in 2020 or to the Covid-19 crisis clearly shows, informal means of regulation still prevail.[44] Politically, these measures were often justified on the basis of an

---

40 Eberhard Schmidt-Aßmann, „Einleitung: Der Europäische Verwaltungsverbund und die Rolle des Europäischen Verwaltungsrechts" (fn. 26), p. 6–7.

41 See only Federico Casolari, „The unbearable lightness of soft law: on the European Unions recourse to informal instruments in the fight against irregular immigration", in Francesca Ippolito, Gianluca Borzoni, Federico Casolari (ed.), *Bilateral Relations in the Mediterranean. Prospects for Migration Issues*, Edward Elgar 2020, p. 215-228; Caterina Molinari, „EU Readmission Deals and Constitutional Allocation of Powers: Parallel Paths that Need to Cross?", in Eva Kassoti, Narin Idriz (ed.), *The Informalisation of the EU's External Action in the Field of Migration and Asylum*, Springer 2022, p. 15-35. See further below 3; chapter 2.

42 On the de facto expansion of EASO's mandate see Evangelia (Lilian) Tsourdi, „Bottom-Up Salvation? From Practical Cooperation Towards Joint Implementation Through the European Asylum Support Office", *European Papers* 1 (2017), p. 997–1031; on the de facto expansion of Frontex's mandate see David Fernández-Rojo, *EU Migration Agencies* (fn. 23), p. 63–77, 87–100. In some instances, the de facto extended competences were then later enshrined in secondary law; see in detail below 3.1 and 2; chapter 2.

43 See below 3.3; chapter 2.

44 An illustrative example is the establishment of the EU hotspots 2.0. on the basis of European Commission, Annex to the Commission Decision approving the Memorandum of Understanding between the European Commission, European Asylum Support Office, the European Border and Coast Guard Agency, Europol and the Fundamental Rights Agency, of the one part, and the Government of Hellenic Republic, of the other part, on a Joint Pilot for the establishment of a new Multi-Purpose

emergency narrative. Especially those measures that appeared particularly restrictive or strongly changed the EU's role were defended with the argument that they were necessary to prevent chaos or worse.[45]

1.4 The Challenge to Redefine the EU's Responsibility

In legal terms, however, such emergency argumentation cannot be convincing. To begin with, and quite apart from the fact that the structure of the argument as such is doubtful, it must be observed that hardly any emergency measure was withdrawn after the immediate crisis context. On the contrary, almost all measures, including those which were explicitly introduced only for a limited period of time, have been perpetuated in one way or another.[46] This holds true not only for those measures restricting asylum seekers' rights[47] but also for those expanding the EU's role. Consider, for instance, the crisis reaction to task EASO with providing operational support, including the examination of individual asylum claims,[48] although the then applicable EASO Regulation allowed for the deployment of asylum support teams only for 'a limited time' and excluded any 'direct or indirect powers' in relation to the taking of decisions on individual asylum claims;[49] or the similar tasking of Frontex without formal compe-

Reception and Identification Centre in Lesvos, Brussels 2 December 2020, C(2020) 8657 final (hereinafter: MoU Joint Pilot). See in more detail below 2.1.

45 See only Klaus Ferdinand Gärditz, „Territoriality, Democracy, and Borders: A Retrospective on the "Refugee Crisis"", *German Law Journal* 17 (2016), p. 907-922, p. 919: 'The general political atmosphere evoked connotations of a constitutional crisis. (...) Soon, rhetorical hysteria invoked emergency scenarios. An ominous Schmittian yearning to (...) declare the state of emergency regrettably exerts some intellectual fascination even today and inspires crisis rhetoric, which (...) relishes in the idea of a nearing apocalypse.'.

46 An exception in this regard is the relocation mechanism which was not perpetuated but to the contrary hardly implemented, see Thomas Matthies, *Relocation. Die Umsiedlung von Asylbewerbern in der Europäischen Union*, LIT Verlag 2021, p. 28–30. It hence appears that the tendency of perpetuation is limited to those crisis mechanisms that limit the rights of individuals and/or broaden the EU's competences.

47 For examples see Cathryn Costello, Minos Mouzourakis, „The Common European Asylum System. Where did it all go wrong?" (fn. 8), p. 298–294.

48 For details see EASO, *Archive of Operations*, available at: https://easo.europa.eu/archive-of-operations.

49 For the time limit see Art. 13 EASO Regulation. Note that the EUAA Regulation – again reflecting the process of belated legalisation – does no longer set a specific time limit. Instead, Art. 18 para 2 lit b merely requires to define 'the foreseeable

tence.[50] Once the immediate crisis context was over, the EU's increased administrative involvement was usually not withdrawn – which would have brought administrative practice again in line with legislative basis. In fact, the approach was often reversed: practices that were introduced as 'emergency instruments' were subsequently underpinned by a legislative basis and thereby perpetuated. EASO's and Frontex's crisis-induced increased involvement, for instance, was not scaled back but instead enshrined in secondary law through subsequent reforms.[51] In this manner, results gained through real-life administrative experiments on the ground were literally written into the law.

From a constitutional perspective, it is obvious that the approach of an administrative real-life experiment is deeply problematic. First, it implies the idea that a situation of crisis can justify administrative conduct without a formal legal basis, which runs counter to the very foundations of the rule of law as enshrined in Art. 2 TEU. In the specific context at hand, the question also arises as to whether such far-reaching measures without a legal basis would have been politically feasible vis-à-vis citizens, too, or whether the rights of non-citizens were not implicitly regarded as 'less worthy'. If this were the case, then not only the rule of law but also the principles of equality before the law and the prohibition of discrimination on the grounds of race and ethnic origin, as enshrined in Art. 21 para 1 ChFR, would have been at stake. Second, ex-post legalisation cannot, of course, legitimise the EU's conduct in retrospect. Third, the writing into

---

duration of the deployment'; similarly also Art. 20, in particular para 5 thereof. For the competence limit see recital 14, Art. 2 para 6 EASO Regulation.

50 Matthias Lehnert, *Frontex und operative Maßnahmen an den europäischen Außengrenzen. Verwaltungskooperation – materielle Rechtsgrundlagen – institutionelle Kontrolle*, Nomos 2014, p. 119–120.

51 For Frontex see only Vittoria Meissner, „The European Border and Coast Guard Agency Frontex After the Migration Crisis: Towards a 'Superagency'?", in Johannes Pollak, Peter Slominski (ed.), *The Role of EU Agencies in the Eurozone and Migration Crisis. Impact and Future Challenges*, Palgrave Macmillan 2021, p. 151-174. For the EUAA see Evangelia (Lilian) Tsourdi, „Beyond the 'Migration Crisis': The Evolving Role of EU Agencies in the Administrative Governance of the Asylum and External Border Control Policies", in Johannes Pollak, Peter Slominski (ed.), *The Role of EU Agencies in the Eurozone and Migration Crisis. Impact and Future Challenges*, Palgrave Macmillan 2021, p. 175–203; Salvatore F. Nicolosi, David Fernandez-Rojo, „Out of control? The case of the European Asylum Support Office", in Miroslava Scholten, Alex Brenninkmeijer (ed.), *Controlling EU Agencies. The Rule of Law in a Multi jurisdictional Legal Order*, Edward Elgar 2020, p. 177–195, in particular p. 187–186.

the law often remains deficient and incomplete. The reformed EUAA and Frontex Regulations, for instance, still define the agency's competences in a convoluted and vague manner, and fail to establish a strong independent complaints mechanism.[52] Fourth, the approach of belated legalisation has the effect that the asylum system operates in a perpetuated state of crisis.[53] At the administrative level, for instance, the involvement of the Commission and the agencies continue to be characterised by features and tools that were developed from a logic of crisis or even a state of emergency.

Thus, one of the central challenges in the European asylum system today is to redefine the EU's responsibility. More specifically, the challenge is to determine what exactly the EU is legally competent to do and how the EU can be held responsible before a court in case of alleged misconduct.[54]

As follows from the rule of law, especially the fundamental right to effective judicial protection enshrined in Art. 47 ChFR, and as the CJEU has consistently held since *Les Verts*, all public acts, including those issued by the EU itself, must be subject to judicial review.[55] The EU legal protection system, however, lags far behind administrative reality. It was not designed to address the challenges that arise when the EU operates at the administra-

52 It must be stressed that this process of belated legalisation often leads to deficient outcomes. The reformed Regulations on Frontex and the EUAA, for instance, remain vague concerning the agency's competences and fail to provide for sufficient safeguards for individuals. On the considerable delays in hiring fundamental rights monitors and connected failures, for instance, see Luisa Marin, „Frontex and the Rule of Law Crisis at EU Borders", Verfassungsblog of 05/09/2022.

53 Note, however, the Commission's explicit attempt to overcome the crisis rhetoric in its Communication on a New Pact on Migration and Asylum, Brussels 23/09/20, COM(2020) 609 final (hereinafter: New Pact on Migration).

54 Similarly for the case of the EUAA Salvatore F. Nicolosi, David Fernandez-Rojo, „Out of control? The case of the European Asylum Support Office" (fn. 51) who at p. 178 identify as central challenge the 'control over activities which might impact on individuals, namely asylum seekers, and undermine the Member States' competence as to the determination of refugee status', and at p. 187 argue that 'the control over the de facto expansion of (EASO's) competences is crucial because of the enormous impact of its activities on the individual situations of asylum seekers and also because of possible tensions with relevant domestic authorities in the field of asylum.'.

55 CJEU, Court, judgement of 23 April 1986, Parti écologiste 'Les Verts' v European Parliament, 294/83, para 23; CJEU, Court, judgement of 25 July 2002, Unión de Pequeños Agricultores v Council of the European Union, C-50/00 P, para 38–39: '[T]he European Community is, however, a community based on the rule of law in which its institutions are subject to judicial review of the computability of their acts with the Treaty and with the general principles of law which include fundamental rights. Individuals are therefore entitled to effective judicial protection (...)'.

tive level, including in areas that are especially sensitive to fundamental rights and in direct contact with concerned individuals. As a result, judicial protection against the EU is rather difficult to obtain. In the context of the European asylum administration – and specifically in the context of EU hotspots – the key question is hence not so much whether but rather *how* the EU can be held responsible for alleged misconduct.[56]

The challenge of finding a procedural way to hold the EU responsible is constitutional in nature. The root of the insufficient regulation of the EU's responsibility lies in primary law, which is still based on the anachronistic understanding that the EU would not be an ordinary public actor. Given the persisting regulatory deficits in secondary law, the key problem is that the EU's new role is not, or perhaps not yet, sufficiently reflected in the constitutional framework. Moreover, it is highly unlikely that EU secondary law will be reformed at any time soon in such a way that the EU's responsibility will be clearly defined. On the contrary, it currently seems more likely that ad hoc policy arrangements and informal governance will continue to prevail. Therefore, if a solution is to be found based on the law as it currently stands, the challenge must be addressed at the level of primary law.[57]

Finding ways to hold the EU responsible for its administrative conduct is important in many areas of law but remains of particular salience in the context of the asylum system. Certainly, the increasing reliance on agencies can also be observed in other policy fields, ranging from financial regulation to the medical market.[58] Also, the Commission's increasing involvement is a general tendency that can be observed in different policy fields, ranging from competition to the Eurozone.[59] And, of course, the

56 This follows from Art. 2 TEU, Art. 47 ChFR, as argued in more detail in Catharina Ziebritzki, *The EU's Responsibility in the Asylum Administration. Administrative Integration, Judicial Protection and the Case of the EU Hotspots,* Dissertation at Frankfurt University, Law Department, January 2024, p. 190 et seq.

57 In other words, the approach is to explore the potential inherent in EU constitutional law, see chapter 3.

58 See only Miroslava Scholten, Marloes van Rijsbergen, „The Limits of Agencification in the European Union" (fn. 30), p. 1225, 1229–1231; Merijn Chamon, „Agencification in the United States and Germany and What the EU Might Learn From It" (fn. 30).

59 John Peterson, „Juncker's political European Commission and an EU in crisis", *Journal of Common Market Studies* 55 (2017), p. 349-367; James D Savage, Amy Verdun, „Strengthening the European Commission's budgetary and economic surveillance capacity since Greece and the euro area crisis: a study of five Directorates-General", *Journal of European Public Policy* 23 (2015), p. 101-118.

increasing involvement of EU bodies in these policy fields also raises urgent questions concerning the EU's responsibility, including questions related to the competences of agencies,[60] and questions related to the EU's responsibility for fundamental rights violations by these and the European Commission.[61]

Yet, the challenge is particular in the asylum system.[62] The violation of fundamental rights is particularly likely because the relevant agencies interact directly with individuals in an especially vulnerable situation. The relevant EU bodies operate in a context that is especially sensitive to basic fundamental rights such as Art. 4, 6, 7 18, 19, 24, 41 ChFR.[63] These rights protect the essence of human life and the rule of law and thus form part of the constitutional core as defined in Art. 2 TEU.[64]

2 EU Hotspots as a Paradigm Example of the EU's New Role

The case of the EU hotspots constitutes a paradigm example of the EU's new role. It exemplifies both the EU's role as a critical administrative actor and the EU's ambivalence as both a guarantor of and a threat to the rights of asylum seekers. As will be shown in the following, the development

60 See CJEU, Court (Grand Chamber), judgement of 22 January 2014, UK and Northern Ireland v European Parliament and Council of the European Union (ESMA-Short-selling), C-270/12.

61 On the latter see CJEU, Court (Grand Chamber), judgement of 20 September 2016, Ledra Advertising Ltd et al v European Commission et al, Joined Cases C-8/15 P to C-10/15 P; in more detail chapter 3 to 5.

62 Similarly Sergio Carrera, Leonhard Den Hertog, Joanna Parkin, „The Peculiar Nature of EU Home Affairs Agencies in Migration Control: Beyond Accountability versus Autonomy?", *European Journal of Migration and Law* 15 (2013), p. 337–358, p. 337–339; Jorrit R Rijpma, „Hybrid Agencifiation in the Area of Freedom, Security and Justice and its inherent tension: The case of Frontex", in Madalina Busuioc, Martijn Groenleer, Jarle Trondal (ed.), *The Agency Phenomenon in the European Union. Emergence, Institutionalisation and Everyday Decision-Making*, Manchester University Press 2012, p. 84-102, p. 84, p. 92–94.

63 David Fernández-Rojo, *EU Migration Agencies* (fn. 23), p. 63–64.

64 For the understanding of Art. 2 TEU as the core of the EU's constitution Armin von Bogdandy, *The Emergence of European Society through Public Law* (fn. 13), p. 85 et seq. One step further Reijer Passchier, Maarten Stremler, „Unconstitutional Constitutional Amendments in European Union Law: Considering the Existence of Substantive Constraints on Treaty Revision", *Cambridge Journal of Internationa and Comparative Law* 5 (2016), p. 337-362, p. 356–359. On the agency's systemic interference with the cited fundamental rights in more detail chapter 2, 3.

of the EU hotspots from their establishment in the 2015 crisis to their current form under the so-called Joint Pilot of 2020 is a textbook example of a crisis-driven administrative experiment. Studying the integrated EU hotspot administration hence allows to better understand the European asylum administration more broadly.

As mentioned, the focus here lies on the EU hotspots in Greece, which are located on the Aegean islands of Lesvos, Chios, Kos, Samos and Leros. This is justified because the EU hotspots located in Italy function differently and do not appear as a testing ground for advanced administrative integration.[65] While the reasons for the location of the 'testing laboratory' in Greece remain understudied, one factor seems to lie in the close connection of the initial EU hotspot approach in Greece to the EU-Türkiye Statement.[66]

2.1 From Initial EU Hotspots to 'EU Hotspots 2.0'

The idea of establishing EU hotspots dates back to a feasibility study on Frontex published by the European Commission in 2014.[67] This study proposed the gradual supranationalisation of border control in three phases, with the second phase consisting of the limited transferral of executive powers upon Frontex only in so-called EU hotspots. Although the 2014 proposal was never realised, it is key in that it introduced the concept of EU hotspots and defined them as geographical areas subject to 'urgent and exceptional' migratory pressure where increased administrative cooperation would take place.[68]

Since then, EU hotspots are conceptualised as consisting of two elements. First, they are established in response to a 'crisis' caused by a relative increase in the number of asylum applications in a specific location at the EU's external border. Second, they are characterised by increased vertical

---

65 Given that the EU hotspots in Greece evolve rapidly and change frequently, it must be recalled that this study takes into account only developments from 2015 to 2022 (see already introduction, fn. 25).

66 In this direction also interviews with Commission representative 1 and Commission representative 2 conducted on 12 February 2021, and interview with Commission representative 4 conducted on 26 February 2021 (introduction, fn. 102).

67 See in more detail David Fernández-Rojo, *EU Migration Agencies* (fn. 23), p. 297.

68 Unisys, *Study on the Feasibility of the Creation of a European System of Border Guards to Control the External Borders of the Union (ESBG), conducted for the European Commission*, 2014, p. 7, 24.

cooperation between national authorities and EU bodies, with the latter exercising broader competences than in other contexts.

a *The Initial EU Hotspot Approach of 2015*

Against this background, it comes as no surprise that the Commission took up the idea of establishing EU hotspots in the context of the 2015 crisis. The Commission mentioned the EU hotspot approach already in its European Agenda on Migration published in May 2015.[69] Upon request of the Council to explain the approach in more detail, the Commission, together with the relevant EU agencies, and the designated host member states Italy and Greece, then worked out the approach in a non-public policy paper. This paper was entitled the 'EU hotspot explanatory note' and was sent to the member states' Interior Ministries and to the European Parliament in July 2015.[70] In September 2015, a shortened version of the explanatory note was published as annex to a communication by the Commission.[71]

According to the Commission's initial idea from 2015, the EU hotspots were conceived as platforms for the implementation of the relocation program.[72] As this program provided for the relocation of 160.000 asylum applicants from Greece and Italy to other member states, the idea was that these relocations would take place directly from the EU hotspots. Yet the

69 European Commission, Communication from the Commission to the European Parliament, the Council, the European Economic and Social Committee and the Committee of the Regions, A European Agenda on Migration, 13/05/2015, COM(2015) 240 final (hereinafter: European Agenda on Migration), p. 6.

70 European Commission, Explanatory Note on the 'Hotspot' Approach, available at: http://www.statewatch.org/news/2015/jul/eu-com-hotsposts.pdf (hereinafter: EU Hotspot Explanatory Note).

71 European Commission, Communication to the European Parliament, the European Council and the Council, Managing the Refugee Crisis: Immediate Operational, Budgetary and Legal Means under the European Agenda on Migration, 23/09/2015, COM(2015) 490 final, in particular Annex 2 on Migration Management Support Teams working in 'hotspot' areas.

72 The Relocation Programme was established by Council Decision (EU) 2015/1523 of 14 September 2015 and Council Decision (EU) 2015/1601 of 22 September 2015 resp. establishing provisional measures in the area of international protection for the benefit of Italy and of Greece (hereinafter: Relocation Decisions I and II). On the interconnections between the EU hotspot approach and the Relocation programme see Francesco Maiani, „Hotspots and Relocation Schemes: The Right Therapy for the Common European Asylum System?", eumigrationlawblog of 03/02/2016.

relocation program largely failed, with only less than 30.000 relocations implemented before the program expired in September 2017.[73] As widely known, this overall failure was due to strong political resistance from several member states, practical difficulties and conceptual flaws in the program itself.[74]

b *The EU-Türkiye Statement of March 2016: From Relocation to Return*

Insofar as the specific context of the EU hotspots in Greece is concerned, however, the failure of the relocation program is also due to another reason, namely the policies of the European Commission itself. The Commission ensured that relocation was suspended as from the day of the entry into force of the EU-Türkiye Statement.[75] This is remarkable because the Commission generally advocated for the implementation of the relocation program.

The background to the Commission's contradictory policies is that the entry into force of the EU-Türkiye Statement in March 2016[76] led to a complete overhaul of the function of the EU hotspots located in Greece. Literally overnight, the EU hotspots were transformed from relocation centres into return centres.[77] From the perspective of EU policymakers,

73 European Commission, Report from the Commission to the European Parliament, the European Council and the Council, Fifteenth Report on Relocation and Resettlement, 06/09/2017, COM/(2017) 465 final, p. 2.

74 See only Thomas Matthies, *Relocation* (fn. 46), p. 279–282.

75 European Commission, Communication from the Commission to the European Parliament, the European Council and the Council. First Report on the progress made in the implementation of the EU-Turkey Statement, 20 April 2016, COM(2016) 231 final, 5: 'With the support of the Commission and Frontex, the hotspots are being adapted to facilitate swift returns to Türkiye from the islands, and the integration of return and asylum officers in the infrastructure and workflow of the hotspots.'; European Commission, Report from the Commission to the European Parliament, the European Council and the Council. Second report on relocation and resettlement, 12 April 2016, COM(2016) 222 final, 2.2.: 'The nature of the hotspot work has significantly changed after the adoption of the EU-Turkey statement and currently provision of information on the relocation scheme in the Hotspot is suspended for migrants arriving after 20 March (2016).'.

76 European Council, Press Release, EU-Turkey statement, 18 March 2016, https://www.consilium.europa.eu/en/press/press-releases/2016/03/18/eu-Turkey-statement/.

77 Catharina Ziebritzki, Robert Nestler, „'Hotspots' an der EU-Außengrenze. Eine rechtliche Bestandsaufnahme", *MPIL Research Paper Series (SSRN)* 17 (2017), p. 17–20, 22–23.

this was only consequential. Given that the EU-Türkiye Statement aimed to 'end irregular migration from Türkiye to the EU', its implementation required a comprehensive return policy. The central idea was that all asylum applicants who entered the EU irregularly via the EU hotspots in the Greek Aegean should be swiftly deported, either back to Türkiye or to their country of origin.[78]

This fundamental change in the function of the EU hotspots obviously had a profound impact on the administrative procedure conducted in these centres. To begin with, it was politically considered necessary to keep asylum seekers on the relevant island during the entire procedure in order to facilitate their deportation. This was initially ensured through a general detention scheme,[79] which was soon replaced by a restriction of movement on some islands[80] and permanently remained in place on others.[81] In addition, the procedure was transformed into a border procedure under Art. 43 Asylum Procedures Directive allowing for restrictions in terms of individual procedural rights.[82] Further, and this is the central point, the EU hotspot procedure was redesigned to reject asylum applications with the least possible administrative burden. Although the understanding that asylum procedures serve, first and foremost, to reject applications perverts

78 EU-Turkey Statement (fn. 76), para 1.

79 Nora Markard, Helene Heuser, „'Hotspots' an den EU-Außengrenzen: Menschen- und europarechtswidrige Internierungslager", *Zeitschrift für Ausländerrecht und Ausländerpolitik* (2016), p. 165-172, p. 166–167; Maria Pichou, „Reception or Detention Centres? The detention of migrants and the EU 'Hotspot' Approach in the light of the European Convention on Human Rights", *Kritische Vierteljahresschrift für Gesetzgebung und Rechtswissenschaft* 99 (2016), p. 114-131, p. 116–118.

80 Catharina Ziebritzki, Robert Nestler, „Implementation of the EU-Turkey Statement: EU Hotspots and restriction of asylum seekers' freedom of movement", eumigrationlawblog of 22/06/2018. In the context of the outbreak of the Covid 19 pandemic, some EU hotspots were temporarily 'closed' again, see only Equal Rights Beyond Borders, Report of February 2023, Extraordinary Measures. How Greece Used the Covid-19 Pandemic as a Pretext for the Unlawful Detention of Asylum Seekers in Chios, https://www.equal-rights.org/resources/publications.

81 Equal Rights Beyond Borders, Report of 10 November 2021, Detained and Forgotten at the Gates of the EU: Detention of Migrants on the Island of Kos, https://www.equal-rights.org/resources/publications. See in more detail on the detention policy chapter 2, 31.

82 Art. 43 of Directive 2013/32/EU of the European Parliament and of the Council of 26 June 2013 on common procedures for granting and withdrawing international protection (recast) (hereinafter: Asylum Procedures Directive).

the very purpose of these procedures as such, this understanding is implicit in the political aim of return.[83]

Since March 2016, the EU hotspot procedure has been roughly structured as follows.[84] For applicants from countries of origin with low recognition rates, it is assumed that the application can be rejected as unfounded, so an interview on the merits is conducted. In the case of countries of origin with higher recognition rates, a rejection as unfounded seems unlikely from the outset.[85] Accordingly, the central idea is to reject asylum claims with the argument that the concerned persons should seek protection in Türkiye instead. This idea is operationalised on the basis of protection elsewhere clauses, i.e. the concepts of first country of asylum and safe third country, enshrined in Art. 35 and 38 Asylum Procedures Directive,[86] which allow the rejection of asylum applications regardless of whether or not the claim is substantiated. In practice, the focus of the procedure hence lies on the admissibility interview, which is conducted with the political aim of

83 This aim was defined in the EU-Turkey Statement (fn. 76) and was confirmed by European Commission, New Pact on Migration (fn. 53), p. 4.

84 See in more detail on the EU hotspot procedure and its development over the past years: Equal Rights Beyond Borders, December 2019, The Lived Reality of Deterrence Measures. Inhumane Camps at Europe's External Border, https://www.equal-rights.org/resources/publications; Equal Rights Beyond Borders, July 2021, Consequences of the EU-Turkey Statement. The Situation of Syrian Asylum Seekers on the Greek Aegean Islands, https://www.equal-rights.org/resources/publications; Equal Rights Beyond Boders, HIAS Greece, Refugee Support Aegean, September 2022, The State of the Border Procedure on the Greek Islands, https://rsaegean.org/en/border-procedure-greek-islands/.

85 In 2016, this concerned in particular applicants of Syrian nationality. Note, however, that applications submitted by Syrians has reduced considerably over the past five years: While in 2015, almost 60 % of applicants arriving to the EU hotspots were of Syrian nationality, the number fell to about 20 % in 2020, see UNHCR, Greece data snapshot, 26 December 2015, https://data2.unhcr.org/en/documents/details/46627; UNHCR, Sea Arrivals Dashboard of December 2020, 22 February 2021, available at: https://data2.unhcr.org/en/documents/details/85039.

86 While the first country of asylum concept (Art. 35 Asylum Procedures Directive) refers the person to a third state where they *had already* been granted protection prior to entering the EU, the safe third country concept refers to a third state with the argument that they *could potentially* seek and be granted protection in the third state (Art. 38 Asylum Procedures Directive). Art. 33 para 2 lit b and lit c Asylum Procedures Directive allows for the rejection of a claim for international protection as inadmissible on the basis of both concepts. Given that the safe third country concept is practically much more relevant, the following is limited to that concept.

considering Türkiye as safe and, on this basis, rejecting the application as inadmissible.[87]

c Political Insistence on a Non-Functional Return Policy

A crucial point for understanding the EU hotspots is that the politically envisaged return policy has never actually worked. Although the procedures were aligned with the return policy envisaged in the EU-Türkiye Statement, the implementation of this policy has failed. The idea of deporting all asylum seekers may have been politically effective in the sense that the EU-Türkiye statement was largely perceived as efficient, but it was never implemented in practice. In fact, the number of deportations to Türkiye has remained vanishingly small, with only about 2,000 deportations between March 2016 and March 2020.[88]

The main reasons for this were practical and legal obstacles to the return policy as such. Most importantly, the political assumption that Türkiye can be considered a safe third country has proven to be legally untenable in most cases.[89] Since March 2020, the implementation of the return policy

87 The non-refoulement principle requires an individual examination of each asylum claim. Hence, even where a country has adopted a list of safe countries, each individual must at least be heard and have the possibility to refute the assumption that the third country is safe for them, see only Stephen H Legomsky, „Secondary Refugee Movements and the Return of Asylum Seekers to Third Countries: The Meaning of Effective Protection", *International Journal of Refugee Law* 51 (2003), p. 567-677, p. 669 with further references. The obligation to examine each individual case is explicitly codified in the EU Asylum Procedures Directive, see Art 10 para 3 lit a, Art 33 para 2 lit b ('a first country of asylum *for the applicant*') and lit c ('a safe third country *for the applicant*'), Art 35 last sentence ('The applicant shall be allowed to challenge the application of the first country of asylum concept to his or her particular circumstances.'), Art 38 para 2 lit c ('rules in accordance with international law, allowing an individual examination of whether the third country concerned is safe for a particular applicant which, as a minimum, shall permit the applicant to challenge the application of the safe third country concept on the grounds that the third country is not safe in his or her particular circumstances.').

88 UNHCR, Returns from Greece to Turkey (in the framework of the EU-TUR Statement) as of 31 March 2020, https://data.unhcr.org/en/documents/details/75075.

89 Between January 2021 and February 2022, Greece has usually rejected between 11 and 25 % of applications for international protection as inadmissible, see https://migration.gov.gr/en/statistika/. Note that Greece invokes a lack of enforcement capacity as another reason for the low number of returns, see Ekathimerini, 14 Jan 2021, Greece submits request for return of 1,450 failed asylum seekers

has even come to a complete standstill. The reason for this is that Türkiye no longer accepts any readmissions, citing first the Covid-19 pandemic and then Greece's non-compliance with specific political demands.[90] Despite diplomatic efforts on the part of Greece, this situation has not changed until the end of 2023. For the past three years, there have thus been almost no deportations to Türkiye.

The EU hotspot procedure is thus characterised by a fundamental and persistent mismatch between the goal of a comprehensive return policy and the fact that the implementation of such policy is impossible due to practical, legal and political obstacles. Although it is clear that deportations cannot be carried out in the overwhelming majority of cases, the procedure is nevertheless designed to reject claims as swiftly as possible.[91] The politically intended function of the EU hotspots as deportation centres thus runs dry, and the EU hotspots function as containment centres instead.

d *The EU Hotspot Approach 2.0 of 2020*

Unsurprisingly, the non-functional return procedures and the de facto containment policy quickly led to severe deficiencies in the EU hotspot administration. As will be set out in more detail below, these include extreme overcrowding, inhumane living conditions, practices of systemic detention, systemically unlawful procedures, and eventually completely inadequate pandemic management. It was amid these circumstances that a fire broke out in the largest EU hotspot, *Moria,* on the island of Lesvos in September 2020. Unlike previous fires, this one did not remain confined to a small

to Turkey, https://www.ekathimerini.com/news/261208/greece-submits-request-for-return-of-1-450-failed-asylum-seekers-to-Turkey/.

90 EU Observer, 19 Jan 2021, *Turkey snubs Greece on migrant returnees*; interview with Commission representative 1, conducted on 12 February 2021 (introduction, fn. 102); European Commission, Communication from the Commission to the Council and the European Parliament. Sixth Annual Report on the Facility for Refugees in Türkiye, 24 May 2022, COM/2022/243 final, p. 3: Turkey demands Greece to stop push backs to Turkey, and to revoke its national list of safe third countries.

91 As will be explained in more detail in chapter 2, 3.2.c, the continued application of the safe third country concept despite the halt of readmissions is unlawful. This was recognised by the Commission, although belatedly, with EN P-000604/2021, 1 June 2021, Answer given by Ms Johansson on behalf of the European Commission, available at: https://www.europarl.europa.eu/doceo/document/P-9-2021-000604-ASW_EN.pdf.

section but burned down almost the entire camp, including administrative areas, leaving some 13,000 residents without shelter.[92]

The fire of *Moria* in September 2020 is emblematic. It not only led to the physical destruction of Europe's largest refugee camp but has also become a symbol of the disastrous living conditions. Some even speak of Europe's values having burned down with the fire.[93] Leaving aside the question of the adequacy of this metaphor, it can be observed in any case that the fire has brought the EU hotspots back into the consciousness of the European public, even though only for a very short time. This public attention, combined with the fact that the EU's new migration policy plan was due to be published in the fall of 2020 anyway, had the effect that the Commission, after years of a rather passive stance, eventually felt called upon to take concrete steps to improve conditions in the EU hotspots in Greece.

To this end, the Commission proposed to step up both EU funding and its own administrative involvement in the EU hotspot administration and to replace the previous Reception and Identification Centres (RIC) with so-called Multi-Purpose Reception and Identification Centres (MP-RIC). This proposal was labelled Joint Pilot and presented by the Commission in the context of its New Pact on Migration.[94] In December 2020, a Memorandum of Understanding on the Joint Pilot (MoU-JP) was then concluded between the Commission and the relevant agencies on one part and Greece on the other part.[95] While the MoU was formally limited to the island of Lesvos, it de facto also applied to the other islands. At the end of 2021, the construction of MP-RICs on Samos, Kos and Leros was already completed, whereas the works in Chios and Lesvos still remained stuck due to difficulties in finding a suitable site for the new camp.[96]

92 BBC, 9 September 2020, Moria migrants: Fire destroys Greek camp leaving 13,000 without shelter, https://www.bbc.com/news/world-europe-54082201.

93 Heinrich Boell Stiftung, 10 September 2020, Moria is burnt. Europe's values, too. Europe's double responsibility towards human dignity, https://www.boell.de/en/2020/09/10/moria-burnt-europes-values-too-europes-double-responsibility-towards-human-dignity.

94 European Commission, New Pact on Migration (fn. 53), p. 3.

95 European Commission, MoU Joint Pilot (fn. 44). For now, the Joint Pilot is framed by the Commission as a Greece-specific project, thereby reinforcing the already different development of the EU hotspots located in Greece and Italy respectively.

96 European Commission, Directorate-General HOME, Annual Activity Report 2021, p. 26; interview with Commission representative 4, conducted on 26 February 2021; interview with Commission representative 5, conducted on 7 April 2021 (introduction, fn. 102).

According to the Commission's plan, the main difference between the previous RIC and the new MP-RIC is that the latter shall have an increased capacity and provide for several additional social services. At the same time, however, the MP-RIC also include an adjacent detention area, which is de facto conceived as a closed centre.[97] Considering the combination of all these innovations and taking into account that a significant gap between policy plans and administrative reality is common in the context of the EU hotspots, it thus remains to be awaited whether the Joint Pilot will actually lead to substantial improvements in living conditions. Based on the current state of implementation in any case, it rather seems that the Commission's new plans entail increased detention practices.[98]

For the purpose of this study, the Joint Pilot is of particular interest not so much because of the promised improvements in reception conditions but mainly because it constitutes a new stage in the gradual process of increasing administrative integration. As will be set out in more detail below, the MoU strengthens the Commission's involvement at both the supervisory and the operational level, with the focus of these new competences being on ensuring adequate reception conditions.[99] In order to fulfil its new tasks, the Commission established a 'dedicated task force' in the fall of 2020, and the already existing Steering Committee was adapted accordingly.[100] The agencies are also increasingly involved under the Joint Pilot, especially

97 MoU Joint Pilot (fn. 44), p. 2–7. Tellingly, the Greek terminology refers to 'closed controlled centres'.

98 See only ECRE, 6 October 2020, Joint Statement: The Pact on Migration and Asylum: to provide a fresh start and avoid past mistakes, risky elements need to be addressed and positive aspects need to be expanded, https://ecre.org/the-pact-on-migration-and-asylum-to-provide-a-fresh-start-and-avoid-past-mistakes-risky-elements-need-to-be-addressed-and-positive-aspects-need-to-be-expanded; Equal Rights Beyond Borders, April 2024, Still Detained and Forgotten. Update on Detention Policies, Practices and Conditions on Kos 2023/24, https://equal-rights.org/resources/publications. For parallels to recent developments in US policies see UCLA School of Law, Center for Immigration Law and Policy and Equal Rights Beyond Borders, July 2024, Immigration Detention Across Borders, https://law.ucla.edu/news/amidst-rise-anti-immigrant-policies-across-globe-new-report-examines-treatment-migrants-seeking-protection-us-and-eu/.

99 See below 3; and chapter 2, 2.

100 See in more detail below 3.3.b; and chapter 2.

regarding reception-related activities.[101] Furthermore, the new centres are largely funded by the EU.[102]

2.2 Regulatory Framework: Crisis and Informality

As the outline of the historical developments has indicated already, the regulatory framework governing the EU hotspot administration is characterised by informality and a logic of crisis. This can be traced back to the fact that EU hotspots were initially conceived as a temporary mechanism. In the following years, the EU hotspot approach was perpetuated, and in this process, the legal framework was formalised to a certain extent. The belated legalisation, however, remains incomplete and deficient. As a result, informal rules remain central, and the crisis logic persists to this day.

a *Relevant Informal Rules as EU Soft Law*

Initially, the EU hotspots were established without a formal legal basis. In 2015, Greek law did neither provide for the instalment of asylum processing centres at the external borders, nor for the application of the safe third country concept in accelerated border procedures, nor for close administrative cooperation between national authorities and EU bodies.[103] EU law did not provide for a formal legal basis either: in 2015, there was neither provision for the establishment of EU hotspots nor for specific support by agencies or supervision by the Commission.

Instead, the initial framework consisted almost exclusively of informal rules that were adopted in an ad hoc manner by the Commission, the relevant agencies, and the concerned member states. These rules, enshrined for instance in policy papers, Operating Plans or Standard Operating Procedures, lacked formal legal force but nonetheless had the effect that EU hotspot centres were built, that agencies deployed their staff to work hand-in-hand with national authorities, and that asylum and deportation procedures were implemented as envisaged by the Commission.

---

101 See below 3.1 and 3.2; and chapter 2.

102 European Commission, Directorate-General HOME, Annual Activity Report 2021, p. 26: 'the Commission has granted € 276 million to Greece to build these five centres.'.

103 ECRE, Country Report Greece, 2018 Update, https://asylumineurope.org/reports/country/greece/, p. 31–32: 'legislative vacuum'.

Thus, it is argued here that these informal rules qualify as EU soft law. EU soft law is an intermediate category of rules that are not formally binding but nonetheless legally relevant. It is usually set by the executive and often not published. Consequently, internal administrative guidelines, i.e. rules that are set by the administration itself to regulate its own conduct, also qualify as EU soft law insofar as they address, at least inter alia, another authority than the one that has issued the guideline.

In the context of the EU hotspots, one can distinguish a more general and a more detailed level of EU soft law. While the general rules establish the basic framework, the detailed rules carve out the administrative details. At the general level, a central example is the so-called explanatory note on the EU hotspot approach. At the detailed level, typical examples include the Standard Operating Procedures (SOP), Terms of Cooperation (ToC) and staff working documents that are set up by involved administrative actors to regulate specificities such as the course of the EU hotspot procedure, or the operation of the main supervisory fora.[104] Arguably, Operational Plans (OP) also qualify as detailed EU soft law, as they are not legislative rules and are agreed upon by the EUAA or Frontex and the host member state to regulate the precise tasks of the respective agency.[105] However, it must be kept in mind that OPs are different from other means of EU soft law in that they have a legal basis in secondary law, which explicitly vests them with binding force.[106]

b *In Search for a Legal Basis in Primary Law*

Regulation by EU soft law always raises the question of an appropriate legal basis in primary law. Against this background, it is astonishing how vague

---

104 See in particular European Commission Staff Working Document, Best Practices on the implementation of the hotspot approach, accompanying the document: Report from the Commission to the European Parliament, the European Council and Council. Progress Report on the European Agenda on Migration, 15 November 2017, SWD(2017) 372 final (hereinafter: European Commission, SWD EU Hotspots 2017).

105 Similarly Roberto Cortinovis, „The Evolution of Frontex Governance: Shifting from Soft to Hard Law?", *Journal of Contemporary European Research* 11 (2015), p. 252-267, p. 260.

106 For the notion of soft law see introduction, fn. 85. For the difference between OPs and other means of EU soft law see Art. 18 para 2 EUAA Regulation; Art. 38 para 3 Frontex Regulation.

legal scholarship remains concerning the legal basis of the EU hotspot approach. While some have suggested the crisis competence under Art. 78 para 3 TFEU,[107] others have argued that the EU hotspot approach was adopted on the basis of Art. 78 para 3 TFEU in conjunction with the solidarity clause under Art. 80 TFEU.[108] Neither view is convincing. Art. 78 para 3 TFEU cannot constitute the correct legal basis already because it requires a Council decision, whereas the EU hotspot approach was introduced on the basis of policy papers by the Commission. Art. 80 TFEU, in turn, does not even qualify as a self-standing competence norm.[109] And even if it were, it cannot constitute an adequate legal basis because EU hotspots, at the latest since their transformation from relocation into return centres, have ceased to function as solidarity mechanisms.

Instead, it is argued here that the EU hotspot approach could only have been based on Art. 78 para 1, 2 TFEU in conjunction with Art. 17 para 1 TEU. As argued in detail elsewhere, Art. 78 TFEU confers upon the EU a comprehensive competence to involve itself in the administration of the asylum system, including in conduct of asylum procedures and management of reception centres.[110] Art. 17 TEU then regulates that the institutional competences to issue informal rules on these issues lies with the Commission, who is both guardian of the Treaties and administrative actor itself. Consequently, the adoption of rules on EU hotspots after consultation

107 Darren Neville, Amalia Rigon, Sarah Salome Sy, *On the frontline: the hotspot approach to managing migration, Study conducted for the European Parliament, Committee on Civil Liberties, Justice and Home Affairs*, 2016, p. 26.

108 Violeta Moreno-Lax, *Europe in Crisis: Facilitating Access to Protection, (Discarding) Offshore Processing and Mapping Alternatives for the Way Forward, Study for the Red Cross*, 2015, p. 12 with reference to the Council's view; David Fernández-Rojo, *EU Migration Agencies* (fn. 23), p. 114, 136–137; similarly also European Commission, Communication to the European Parliament, the Council, the European Economic and Social Committee and the Committee of the Regions, on the Delivery of the European Agenda on Migration, 27 September 2017, COM(2017) 558 final, p. 12.

109 Art. 80 TFEU does not confer additional competences upon the Union, but it must be taken into account when interpreting the EU's competences, see only Matthias Rossi, „Artikel 80 AEUV", in Christian Calliess, Matthias Ruffert (ed.), *EUV/AEUV. Kommentar*, C.H. Beck 2022, para 1; Daniel Thym, „Legal Framework for EU Asylum Policy", in Daniel Thym, Kay Hailbronner (ed.), *EU Immigration and Asylum Law. Article-by-Article Commentary*, C.H. Beck, Hart Publishing and Nomos 2022, p. 1129-1176, p. 1129–1176, para 43.

110 Catharina Ziebritzki, *The EU's Responsibility in the Asylum Administration* (fn. 56), p. 117 et seq. Still, the following is based on the prevailing opinion, according to which the EU's competences are limited to providing support.

with the relevant agencies or member states, or even a joint adoption by the Commission and agencies, can be considered to be based on primary law – as long as the doctrine of delegated powers is respected.[111]

This being said it is crucial to note that the Commission's administrative competence cannot go beyond the limits set by the legislator. In other words, the Commission's competence under Art. 17 TFEU is limited to interpreting and concretising EU secondary law. The Commission cannot, however, adopt informal rules that alter rules enshrined in secondary law. For the EU hotspot approach, this means that it disposes of a legal basis in primary law only insofar as it respects the limits set by secondary law.

In order to determine to what extent the EU hotspot approach is covered by primary law, one must hence distinguish between, firstly, informal rules that merely interpret or concretise secondary law and, secondly, informal rules that alter or override secondary law. The majority of informal rules establishing the EU hotspot approach indeed fall within the first category. Most relevant informal rules prescribe which provisions of EU secondary law shall be applied and how these are to be interpreted. This is well illustrated by the SOP on the EU hotspot procedure as adopted by EASO and the Greek asylum service in 2016.[112] The SOP prescribe that, in the EU hotspots, only certain legal provisions of the EU asylum acquis shall be applied and that these shall be interpreted in a particular manner. Inter alia, the SOP foresees that the clauses for protection elsewhere are enshrined in Art. 33, 35, 38 Asylum Procedures Directive shall be applied with regard to Türkiye and the possibility of restricting the freedom of movement of

111 From the vast literature on the delegation doctrine see only Merijn Chamon, *EU Agencies* (fn. 39), p. 175–298; Marta Simoncini, *Administrative Regulation Beyond the Non-Delegation Doctrine. A Study on EU Agencies*, Hart Publishing 2020, p. 14–47, passim.

112 EASO, Standard Operating Procedures for the implementation of the border asylum procedures in the context of the EU-Turkey Statement 18/03/2016, Version of 19 June 2019 (redacted), available at: https://fragdenstaat.de/anfrage/standard-operating-procedures-for-the-implementation-of-the-border-asylum-procedures/425864/anhang/SOPS_border_en_jointEASO_August16_190624redacted.pdf (hereinafter: SoP EU-Hotspots June 2019). A later version is only available in Greek: Standard Operating Procedures for the implementation of the Border asylum procedures in the context of the EU-Turkey Statement, instructions by the Greek Asylum Service for the management of applications submitted under the procedure of Art 90 para 3, version of December 2019 (redacted), on file with the author (hereinafter: SoP EU-Hotspots December 2019). The change in authorship is due to the so-called 'embedded model', see chapter 2, 1.3.b.

asylum under Art. 7 para 2 Reception Conditions Directive shall be used with the view of confining freedom of movement to the respective island.[113]

Then, there are some informal rules that have moved over time from the problematic second into the first category. A good example here are the rules governing the European Regional Task Force (EURTF), i.e. the main supervisory forum. As will be explained in more detail below, the EURTF was initially established without any written rules.[114] In 2017, however, after the European Court of Auditors (ECA) had criticised that the EURTF's tasks were not clearly defined,[115] the Commission called for enhanced internal administrative regulation,[116] which eventually led to the adoption of specific Terms of cooperation and Rules of procedure.[117] Subsequently, the Commission's supervisory competence has been formalised in secondary law with the reform of the Frontex Regulation and the EUAA Regulation. As a result, the EURTF is today governed by informal rules, which can be read as concretising the Commission's tasks established by secondary law.[118]

Lastly, there are also some rules that have always fallen and continue to fall within the second category and, accordingly, lack a legal basis in primary law. The most prominent example here concerns the cooperation of the then EASO with national authorities.[119] According to the relevant OP and SOP adopted in the context of 2015, the agency was tasked with

113 Art. 7 para of Directive 2013/33/EU of the European Parliament and of the Council of 26 June 2013 laying down standards for the reception of applicants for international protection (recast) (hereinafter: Reception Conditions Directive). See in more detail Catharina Ziebritzki, Robert Nestler, „Implementation of the EU-Turkey Statement: EU Hotspots and restriction of asylum seekers' freedom of movement“ (fn. 80).

114 See chapter 2, 2.6.a.

115 European Court of Auditors, Special Report No 06/2017, EU response to the refugee crisis: the 'hotspot' approach (report pursuant to Article 287(4), second subparagraph, TFEU), 25 April 2017: https://www.eca.europa.eu/en/Pages/DocItem.aspx?did=41222 (hereinafter: ECA Special Report 2017), p. 34–35.

116 European Commission, SWD EU Hotspots 2017 (fn. 104).

117 Terms of cooperation for European Union Regional Task Forces, Ref. Ares(2018)1622597 – 23/03/2018 (hereinafter: ToC-EURTF); Rules of procedure of the European Union Regional Task Force for migration management support to Greece as endorsed on 4 Oct 2018 (hereinafter: RoP-EURTF-GR). Both documents are on file with the author.

118 More precisely under Art. 40 para 3 Frontex Regulation; Art. 21 para 2 EUAA Regulation; in more detail see chapter 2, 2.6.

119 For examples of Frontex overstepping its competences see David Fernández-Rojo, *EU Migration Agencies* (fn. 23), p. 71 fn. 27; Sergio Carrera, Elspeth Guild, „'Joint Operation RABIT 2010'. FRONTEX Assistance to Greece's Border with Turkey:

conducting asylum interviews and drafting legal opinions recommending the acceptance or rejection of the asylum claim. As will be explained in more detail below, this practice necessarily entailed that EASO influenced individual asylum decisions.[120] According to the then applicable Regulation, however, the agency had no competences whatsoever in relation to individual asylum decisions.[121] The agency thus acted ultra vires, or in other words, the applicable secondary law was de facto overridden by informal rules.[122] While the European Ombudsman expressed genuine concerns in this regard already in 2018,[123] the administrative practice has not been brought back into the limits of EU secondary law until today. On the contrary, since 2020, the agency has operated under the so-called embedded model, which entails an even closer involvement in the taking of individual

Revealing the Deficiencies of Europe's Dublin Asylum System", *CEPS Liberty and Security in Europe* (2010), p. 7.

120 See chapter 2, 1.

121 Art. 2 para 6 EASO Regulation: 'The Support Office shall have no powers in relation to the taking of decisions by Member States' asylum authorities on individual applications for international protection.'; recital 14: 'The Support Office should have no direct or indirect powers in relation to the taking of decisions by Member States' asylum authorities on individual applications for international protection.' Not that the French ('ne dispose d'aucune compétence'), Spanish ('no tendrá competencia alguna') and German ('keine Befugnisse (...) Einfluss zu nehmen') version of Art. 2 para 6 EASO Regulation reflect recital 14 more clearly.

122 Evangelia (Lilian) Tsourdi, „Bottom-Up Salvation? From Practical Cooperation Towards Joint Implementation Through the European Asylum Support Office" (fn. 42), p. 1024; David Fernández-Rojo, *EU Migration Agencies* (fn. 23), p. 154–156: 'Until the future Regulation on the EUAA enters into force, the Agency's operational power to autonomously conduct the asylum interviews and draft an admissibility recommendation to the Greek Asylum Service will openly exceed the mandate of Regulation 429/2010 establishing EASO. (...) The experts deployed by EASO in the Greek hotspots were thus operating in a legal limbo (...)'.

123 European Ombudsman, Decision of 5 July 2018, on the European Asylum Support Office's' (EASO) involvement in the decision-making process concerning admissibility of applications for international protection submitted in the Greek Hotspots, in particular shortcomings in admissibility interviews, Case 735/2017/MDC, para 32–35: the Ombudsman acknowledged that 'EASO is being encouraged politically to act in a way which is, arguably, not in line with its existing statutory role' but refrained from further action because 'it is likely that EASO's founding Regulation will be amended in the near future to provide explicitly for the type of activity in which EASO is currently engaged, thus resolving the issue of EASO possibly operating outside of its statutory brief.' This argument is remarkable in that the Ombudsman implicitly sanctions the approach to make use of the EU hotspots for an administrative experiment without legal basis.

asylum decisions, while the legal basis has still not fully been adjusted to administrative reality.[124]

To conclude, the informal rules governing the EU hotspot approach are partially based on Art. 78 TFEU, Art. 17 TEU, namely insofar as they merely concretise secondary law. Insofar as the informal rules go beyond secondary law, however, they also lack a legal basis in primary law.

c *Belated Formalisation in National and EU Secondary Law*

In the years following 2015, and the political insistence on the idea of an 'emergency response' notwithstanding, the EU hotspot approach was perpetuated and has since become a permanent feature of the asylum system. This perpetuation has been brought about by several factors, including the consolidation of administrative practices and the repeated extension of the temporal scope of the application of informal rules. The most important factor, however, was the adoption of legal reforms that created, albeit belatedly, a formal legal basis for the operation of the EU hotspot administration.

This process of belated legalisation adapted the legislative framework to a pre-existing administrative reality and thereby ensured its persistence. Remarkably, this process took place both at national and at EU level.

At national level, the process of legalisation began in the immediate crisis context. Less than two weeks after the EU-Türkiye Statement took effect, the Greek asylum system was fundamentally reformed.[125] With Law 4375/2016, adopted in April 2016, the Asylum Procedures Directive and the Reception Conditions Directive were transposed in a manner that allowed for the implementation of the EU hotspot approach. Inter alia, the new law formally established the EU hotspot facilities as Reception and Identification Centres (RIC),[126] created the possibility to reject asylum applications as inadmissible based on the safe third country concept in the

124 See chapter 2, 1.3.b.

125 Law No. 4375 of 2016 on the organization and operation of the Asylum Service, the Appeals Authority, the Reception and Identification Service, the establishment of the General Secretariat for Reception, the transposition into Greek legislation of the provisions of Directive 2013/32/EC, 3 April 2016 (hereinafter: Greek Asylum Law 4375/2016), unofficial English translation available at: https://www.refworld.org/docid/573ad4cb4.html.

126 Art. 19 Greek Asylum Law 4375/2016.

context of so-called fast-track border procedures,[127] and vested operational cooperation with EASO with a legal basis.[128]

In the following years and until today, Greece has then continuously readjusted its asylum legislation with a view to implementing the EU hotspot approach as envisaged by the Commission.[129] The June 2016 reform provides an illustrative example. After it had become clear that the Appeals Committees under the Law of April 2016 mostly concluded that Türkiye could not be considered safe, the composition of the Committees was amended,[130] with the result that their decision-making practice was aligned to the Commission's opinion that Türkiye could generally be considered as a safe third country.[131]

Similarly, the fundamental reform of the Greek asylum law in November 2019, at least inter alia, served to align the Greek legal framework to the Commission's policies.[132] The considerable extension of the possibilities to detain asylum seekers,[133] for instance, corresponds to the Commission's recommendation to make returns more effective and increasingly rely on

127 Art. 54 to Art 5, Art 60 para 4 Greek Asylum Law 4375/2016.

128 In this regard, however, the April 2016 version of the law still lagged behind practical realities and was hence revised in June 2016 already. See Evangelia (Lilian) Tsourdi, „Bottom-Up Salvation? From Practical Cooperation Towards Joint Implementation Through the European Asylum Support Office" (fn. 42), p. 1023.

129 This adaptation at national level took place by means of administrative decrees specifying or amending the scope or manner of application of specific provisions, by means of legislative reform.

130 Previously consisting of one human rights expert, one UNHCR representative, and one representative of the Greek government, the Appeals Committee since the June 2016 amendment consists of two Greek administrative judges and one person that is proposed by UNHCR or the Greek human rights Committee; at the same time, the previous second hearing was limited to exceptional cases. See on this reform Mariana Gkliati, „The Application of the EU-Turkey Agreement: A Critical Analysis of the Decisions of the Greek Appeals Committee", *European Journal of Legal Studies* 10 (2017), p. 81-124, p. 84.

131 Catharina Ziebritzki, Robert Nestler, „'Hotspots' an der EU-Außengrenze" (fn. 77), p. 30. Note, however, that the recomposition changed the decision-making practice only in the short term, as shown by Mariana Gkliati, „The Application of the EU-Turkey Agreement" (fn. 130), p. 86, 115–116, 122.

132 Law No. 4636/2019, 'The International Protection Act' of 1 November 2019 (usually referred to as 'IPA'), https://www.hellenicparliament.gr/UserFiles/bcc26661-143b-4f2d-8916-0e0e66ba4c50/dietnis-prostasia-pap-aposp.pdf. The reform entered into force on 1 January 2020.

133 See in more detail Minos Mouzourakis, „All but last resort: The last reform of detention of asylum seekers in Greece", eumigrationlawblog of 18/11/2019.

detention for that purpose.[134] Another example is the repeal of the so-called vulnerability exemption. Under the law of 2016, and in accordance with the Asylum Procedures Directive, vulnerable asylum seekers were exempted from the EU hotspot procedure.[135] This exemption, despite its deficient implementation,[136] had the effect that vulnerable persons were at least legally pre-empted from return.[137] Against this background, the Commission had already in 2016 recommended abolishing the vulnerability exemption in order to increase returns.[138] Back then, the proposal was met with justified legal concerns of Greek authorities and EASO.[139] In November 2019, however, these concerns did not hinder the Greek legislator from implementing the Commission's proposals and abolishing the exemption.[140]

At EU level, the process of belated legalisation is even more obvious. The EU hotspot approach was never consolidated in a tailored 'EU hotspot Regulation'.[141] Instead, the Commission included some central regulatory elements in its proposals for the Frontex and the EUAA reforms. The first formal provisions reflecting administrative reality in the EU hotspots were thus enshrined in the 2016 Frontex Regulation, with the EUAA Regulation

134 European Commission, Communication from the Commission to the European Parliament, the European Council and the Council. Progress report on the Implementation of the European Agenda on Migration, 16 October 2019, COM(2019) 481 final; European Commission, Recommendation of 7 March 2017 on making returns more effective when implementing the Directive 2008/115/EC of the European Parliament and of the Council, C(2017) 1600 final, para 10 lit c, para 12.

135 Art. 14 para 8, Art. 60 para 4 lit f of Greek Asylum Law 4375/2016; Art. 43 para 3 Asylum Procedures Directive.

136 In practice, vulnerable persons often remained in the EU hotspots for several months before they were actually transferred to the mainland, see Catharina Ziebritzki, Robert Nestler, „'Hotspots' an der EU-Außengrenze" (fn. 77), p. 46.

137 Karin Aberg, „Examining the Vulnerability Procedure: Group-based Determinations at the EU Border", *Refugee Survey Quarterly* (2021), p. 1-27.

138 European Commission, Joint Action Plan on the Implementation of the EU-Turkey Statement, agreed upon between Greece and the EU coordinator for the implementation of the EU-Turkey Statement in Greece, December 2016 (on file with the author).

139 Catharina Ziebritzki, Robert Nestler, „'Hotspots' an der EU-Außengrenze" (fn. 77), p. 46.

140 The relevant reform was introduced with Law 4636/2019, enacted in January 2020, see Equal Rights Beyond Borders, July 2021, Consequences of the EU-Turkey Statement (fn. 84), p. 20.

141 See for criticism Darren Neville, Amalia Rigon, Sarah Salome Sy, *On the frontline: the hotspot approach to managing migration, Study conducted for the European Parliament, Committee on Civil Liberties, Justice and Home Affairs* (fn. 107), p. 9, 30.

following in 2021.[142] Arguably, the latest attempt to consolidate the EU hotspot approach in EU secondary legislation was made by the Commission with its 2020 New Migration Pact.[143] The Pact, providing for the comprehensive CEAS reform adopted in 2024, foresees a pre-entry screening and an expedited procedure geared towards return.[144] Although the reform package remained silent on where this procedure would be conducted, it can be inferred from the respective instruments that the procedures are to be carried out in the EU hotspots.[145] In essence, the 2024 reform thus amounts to consolidating the type of procedures that have already been conducted in the EU hotspots since March 2016.

d *Formalisation of Key Elements in EU Secondary Law and Remaining Regulatory Gaps*

Prior to the 2024 reform, however, the formalisation at EU level had already progressed so far that three central elements of the EU hotspot approach were laid down in secondary law: first, the definition of an EU hotspot, second, the specific form of administrative cooperation between agencies and national authorities and, third, the specific form of administrative supervision by the Commission.

---

142 See below 3.1. and 3.2.

143 In fact, the entire Pact largely proposes to belatedly legalise what is already administrative reality, see for the aspect of the agencies' involvement Evangelia (Lilian) Tsourdi, „The New Pact and EU Agencies: An Ambivalent Approach Towards Administrative Integration", eumigrationlawblog of 06/11/2020.

144 European Commission, Proposal for a Regulation of the European Parliament and of the Council introducing a screening of third country nationals at the external borders and amending Regulations (EC) No 767/2008, (EU) 2017/2226, (EU) 2018/1240 and (EU) 2019/81, 23 September 2020, COM(2020) 612 final, 2020/0278 (COD) (hereinafter: Screening Regulation Proposal); European Commission, Amended Proposal for a Regulation of the European Parliament and of the Council establishing a common procedure for international protection in the Union and repealing Directive 2013/32/EU, 23 September 2020, COM(2020) 511 final, 2016/0224 (COD) (hereinafter: Asylum Procedures Regulation Proposal); European Commission, Proposal for a Regulation of the European Parliament and of the Council addressing situations of crisis and force majeure in the field of migration and asylum, 23 September 2020, COM(2020) 613 final, 2020/0277 (COD) (hereinafter: Crisis Regulation Proposal).

145 European Commission, New Pact on Migration (fn. 53), p. 10; Screening Regulation Proposal (fn. 144), recital 20.

Regarding the first regulatory element, the 2016 Frontex Regulation and its successors, as well as the 2021 EUAA Regulation, define a 'hotspot area' as 'an area in which the host Member State, the Commission, relevant Union agencies and participating Member States cooperate, with the aim of managing an existing or potential disproportionate migratory challenge characterised by a significant increase in the number of migrants arriving at the external borders.' Remarkably, this definition abandons the notion that EU hotspots are limited in time to an acute crisis situation. Instead, the definition confirms that the characteristic feature of the EU hotspot administration is close cooperation between EU bodies and national authorities.[146] Regarding all other aspects, however, the definition remains rather vague.

Secondly, the Frontex and the EUAA Regulation provide for specific teams that shall be deployed to the EU hotspots in order to provide administrative support, namely the so-called migration management support teams (MMST).[147] The distinct feature of those teams lies in their composition. MMSTs are composed of experts from several EU agencies, including Frontex, Europol and the EUAA.[148] Again, it is worth noting that such inter-agency teams have been operating in the EU hotspots since 2016 already, so the Regulations merely consolidated an existing administrative practice.[149]

The third regulatory element concerns the Commission's supervision of the EU hotspot administration. Both the Frontex and the EUAA Regulations state that the Commission 'shall establish the terms of cooperation at the hotspot area and shall be responsible for the coordination of the activities of the migration management support teams'.[150] Unlike in the case of support, however, the Regulations do not provide a legal basis for the

146 Evangelia (Lilian) Tsourdi, „Bottom-Up Salvation? From Practical Cooperation Towards Joint Implementation Through the European Asylum Support Office" (fn. 42), p. 1015.

147 Art. 2 para 19, Art. 36 para 1 lit d, Art. 40 Frontex Regulation; Art. 16 para 2 lit l, 21 EUAA Regulation.

148 Art. 2 para 19 Frontex Regulation; in detail see chapter 2, 1.2.

149 Consequently, EASO staff operating in the EU hotspots prior to the EUAA proposal of 2021 must be considered as part of MMST; see chapter 2, 1.2.

150 Art. 40 para 3, recital 55 Frontex Regulation; Art. 21 para 2, recital 34 EUAA Regulation. Similarly, already Art. 18 para 3 Regulation (EU) 2016/1624 of the European Parliament and of the Council of 14 September 2016 on the European Border and Coast Guard and amending Regulation (EU) 2016/399 of the European Parliament and of the Council and repealing Regulation (EC) No 863/2007 of the European

specific institutional form in which the Commission shall exercise this task. Therefore, the European Regional Task Force (EURTF) to date remains governed solely by informal rules.[151]

This shows that the formalisation in secondary law still has important gaps. The most relevant gap arguably concerns the overall function of the EU hotspot administration. Both the Frontex and the EUAA Regulation define the function as 'the management of [a] [...] migratory challenge'. This formulation is so open that it allows for almost any concrete function to be assigned to the EU hotspot administration. This flexibility was explicitly intended by the Commission, which stressed in September 2015 that even though EU hotspots could facilitate relocation, the approach should also allow for the implementation of any other policies.[152] Consequently, the legal framework as laid down in secondary law allows political actors to specify the function of the EU hotspots in accordance with current policy objectives. In other words, the formalisation of the legal framework at the EU level has intentionally remained incomplete.

e *Persisting Relevance of Informal Rules and Logic of Crisis*

As a result, the regulatory framework is still strongly characterised by informality, even after the adoption of the 2024 CEAS reform.[153] For instance, the organisation of the Commission's supervisory forum, the course of the EU hotspot procedure, and the recently established EU hotspots 2.0 are still not regulated in formal legal terms. Crucially, the continuing focus on informality coincides with a perpetuated logic of crisis. When the Commis-

---

Parliament and of the Council, Council Regulation (EC) No 2007/2004 and Council Decision 2005/267/EC (hereinafter: Frontex 2016 Regulation).

151 This is even more remarkable considering that the establishment of an EURTF is not limited to Greece, but seems to be a general approach of the Commission to 'manage' the EU hotspot administration.

152 Chiara Loschi, Peter Slominski, „The EU hotspot approach in Italy: strengthening agency governance in the wake of the migration crisis?“, *Journal of European Integration* 44 (2022), p. 769-786.

153 Evangelia (Lilian) Tsourdi, „Bottom-Up Salvation? From Practical Cooperation Towards Joint Implementation Through the European Asylum Support Office“ (fn. 42), p. 158: '(...) the EU hotspot approach strengthened, like never before, the operational assistance and inter-agency cooperation of Frontex, EASO and Europol on the ground. Nonetheless, there is not yet a legally binding framework regulating and delimiting the tasks of these agencies and the competent national authorities in the hotspots.'.

sion relies on informal rules to regulate those aspects that are left open by secondary law, it tends to invoke the idea of emergency.

The persisting relevance of informal rules and crisis logic is well illustrated by the overall function of the EU hotspot administration. As mentioned above, EU hotspots were transformed from relocation into return centres in 2016. This shows that, although EU hotspots had already been defined in secondary law, the definition remained sufficiently open to allow for a complete overhaul of the function of EU hotspots without legislative reform. Given that the legislative definition remains open until today, EU hotspots could again be retransformed into relocation centres.[154] This option, however, remains rather theoretical, as the CEAS reform has instead reinforced the conceptualisation of EU hotspots as designated return centres.[155]

Another example of persisting informality concerns the kind of agency support. While EU secondary law regulates the composition of the teams deployed to the EU hotspots, it remains flexible concerning the agencies' exact tasks in the EU hotspots. Instead, the concrete tasks are defined in the relevant OPs.[156] The EASO-OP, for instance, regulates in much detail which support shall be provided by the agency and how it shall cooperate with the Greek Asylum Service (GAS), the First Reception and Identification Service (RIS), and the Hellenic Police. The same holds true for the relevant Frontex-OP.[157] In short, EU soft law remains central to the regulation of administrative cooperation between EU agencies and national authorities.

---

154 In 2020, some member states adopted national ad hoc relocation programs which were partly implemented in EU hotspots, see: EASO, Operating Plan 2021, p. 23, Measure EL-REL.

155 For an early analysis of the Commission's reform proposals see ECRE, *Reception, detention and restriction of movement at EU external borders*, Heinrich Böll Stiftung 2021, p. 38–47.

156 Since 2015, the support provided by EASO to the EU hotspot administration is defined in annual OPs which are published on the agency's website. For a different opinion see Evangelia (Lilian) Tsourdi, „Holding the European Asylum Support Office Accountable for its role in Asylum Decision-Making: Mission Impossible?", *German Law Journal* 21 (2020), p. 506–531; Gaia Lisi, Mariolina Eliantonio, „The Gaps in Judicial Accountability of EASO in the Processing of Asylum Requests in Hotspots", *European Papers* 4 (2019), p. 589–602, p. 516 who argues that the role of EASO is 'currently regulated exclusively by national administrative law'.

157 Frontex's support is defined the OP relevant to the Joint Operation Poseidon; Frontex Operating Plans are not published. The author's request for access to currently applicable OPs has been rejected by the agency with reference to Art. 4 para 1 lit a first indent of the Transparency Regulation. Therefore, reference is made in the following to the latest OP to which access has been granted, namely: Operating

The most recent and arguably the most relevant example of persisting informality and crisis logic concerns the establishment of the EU hotspots 2.0. As explained above, the EU hotspots 2.0 were introduced in reaction to the burning of Moria in 2020 on the basis of a Memorandum of Understanding alone. The Memorandum, albeit informal in nature, has brought about substantial changes in the EU hotspot administration, as it has changed decision-making structures and the character of administrative cooperation with a view to increasing the involvement of EU bodies. Again, the EU hotspot administration was fundamentally restructured through informal rules in the context of an immediate crisis. And again, the relevant informal rules conceive the changes as strictly limited to the period of emergency.[158] Experience, however, suggests that the innovations of the EU hotspots 2.0 are likely to be perpetuated, too.

2.3 EU Hotspots as a Testing Ground

Against this background, it becomes clear that the EU hotspots function as a testing ground for advanced administration integration and are, hence, the most suitable case to study the EU's new role as a central administrative actor in the asylum system.

In fact, EU hotspots have always served as testing laboratories, from their establishment in 2015 to their current form under the 2020 Joint Pilot.[159] The case clearly illustrates that the EU's new role is brought about through crisis-induced administrative experiments. As the Commission itself puts it, reform proposals often 'build on the hotspot approach' or 'draw on recent experience of crisis response'.[160] Typically, new forms of cooperation are introduced in an informal manner and usually as an emergency mechanism. Once some administrative experience is gathered, the intensified cooperation is then consolidated and partially formalised in secondary law

Plan to JO Poseidon 2019, Main Part including Annexes and Handbooks, 21 January 2019 (redacted version on file with the author; hereinafter: Frontex JO Poseidon OP 2019).

158 The MoU Joint Pilot (fn. 44) was initially limited to a period of two years.

159 Similarly Evangelia (Lilian) Tsourdi, „Bottom-Up Salvation? From Practical Cooperation Towards Joint Implementation Through the European Asylum Support Office“ (fn. 42), p. 1015 describing the EU hotspots as a 'breeding ground' for the integrated European asylum administration; David Fernández-Rojo, *EU Migration Agencies* (fn. 23), p. 149.

160 See only European Commission, New Pact on Migration (fn. 53), p. 10.

– although only to the extent that such formalisation is deemed politically desirable.

Obviously, the experimentalist approach endangers fundamental principles of the rule of law, including respect for fundamental rights, the principle of a legal basis, and the right to judicial protection. The costs for the testing results are thus unbearably high.[161] Given that decades of systemic fundamental rights violations are tolerated, one cannot help but suspect that the 'EU hotspot experiment' is possible only because it is the rights of third-country nationals, and not those of EU citizens, that are being violated.[162]

Yet, it is precisely the experimentalist character that makes the EU hotspots the best-suited case study. First, the EU hotspots must be studied because they represent the most advanced form of administrative cooperation in the entire European asylum system today. This concerns both vertical and inter-agency cooperation. Second, it seems likely that these intensified forms of administrative cooperation will, in the future, be extended to other contexts, such as, for instance, processing centres at internal borders or on the territory of third countries. This will raise even more complex questions about the EU's responsibility, the analysis of which presupposes a clear understanding of the EU's responsibility in the EU hotspots. Third, the systemic deficiencies as such argue in favour of focusing on the case of the EU hotspots. The question of whether the EU is responsible for the systemic deficiencies has become so pressing that it urgently requires an answer – for the sake of the rule of law and for the sake of the concerned individuals.

3 The EU's Main Administrative Actors

Any attempt to define the EU's responsibility presupposes a clear understanding of what exactly EU bodies do in the context of the EU hotspot

161 Five years of systemic violations of fundamental rights, leaving durable marks on the lives of ten thousands of people does not exactly seem an appropriate price to pay. Similarly Refugee Support Aegean (RSA), 'The "hotspots" experiment: removing human rights from the equation', 9 October 2018, available at: https://rsaegean.org/en/the-hotspots-experiment/.

162 Imagine, for instance, an administrative practice that allows for the detention of criminal suspects without legal basis, and in close cooperation with EU agencies. The outcry would be loud, and rightly so.

administration. This requires a precise understanding of the relevant EU bodies, their competences and internal decision-making structures.

The main argument here is that, at the latest since 2015, the EUAA, Frontex and the European Commission have become vital for the functioning of the European asylum administration. More precisely, it is argued that the EU's new political focus on operational support required an institutional strengthening of the agencies,[163] and that this in turn created new needs in terms of supervision which were essentially taken over by the Commission.

This argument comes with the caveat that the EU's role varies greatly from one member state to another, depending on the extent to which a national asylum system relies on EU support. This, in turn, depends on a complex interplay of a whole range of factors, including the member state's geographical location, the strength of its national asylum administration, its political willingness to accept EU support, and the interplay with other crises such as the Eurozone crisis[164] or the rule of law crisis.[165] This caveat does not weaken the main argument. On the contrary, the fact that some national subsystems, e.g. the Greek one,[166] depend almost entirely on EU support only confirms that the functioning of the European asylum system as a whole also depends on the EU. An isolated observation of national sub-systems does not lead any further. The European asylum system is only as functional as its weakest subsystems[167] and must hence be considered as a whole.

---

163 David Fernández-Rojo, *EU Migration Agencies* (fn. 23), p. 7–13; Cathryn Costello, „Administrative governance and the Europeanisation of asylum and immigration policy", in Herwig C.H. Hofmann, Alexander H. Türk (ed.), *EU Administrative Governance*, Edward Elgar 2006, p. 287–340, p. 305–309.

164 Notably in Greece, see Angeliki Dimitriadi, Antonia-Maria Sarantaki, „The refugee 'crisis' in Greece: politicisation and polarisation amidst multiple crises", *CEASEVAL Research on the Common European Asylum System* 11 (2018), http://ceaseval.eu/publ ications.

165 Notably in Hungary, see Barbara Grabowska-Moroz, Dimitry Vladimirovich Kochenov, „The Loss of Face for Everyone Concerned. EU Rule of Law in the Context of the 'Migration Crisis'" (fn. 7), p. 190 and passim.

166 Consequently, EU bodies have long played a much lesser role in Hungary or Germany than in Italy, Spain or Malta. Against this background, this section mainly refers to the example of Greece where, due to several factors, including the geopolitically difficult location as Türkiye's neighbour, the weakness of its national asylum system, and the Commission's consolidated role as a strong actor in the context of the financial crisis, EU support has been most extensive since 2015.

167 Remarkably, it is more often stated that 'the external border is as strong as its weakest link', see only Maarten Den Heijer, Jorrit R Rijpma, Thomas Spijkerboer,

3.1 The EU Asylum Agency (EUAA)

As mentioned above, the foundation for the EU's involvement in the asylum administration was laid with the establishment of agencies that were entrusted with implementing European asylum law.[168] In the following, these agencies became increasingly important, with the 2015 crisis being an important catalyst. The central agency here is the EU Asylum Agency (EUAA), founded in 2010 as the European Asylum Support Office (EASO) and mandated to support member states in implementing the EU asylum acquis. In the years following its establishment, EASO remained a small and largely unknown body.[169] This changed fundamentally with the 2015 crisis. In just one year, the agency developed from a rather insignificant office into one of the most important agencies. EASO has become essential to the functioning of the CEAS and, thus, of the Area of Freedom, Security and Justice more broadly.

Remarkably, this change in EASO's role was not brought about by legislative reform but by policy decisions. In the early 2010s, the agency was tasked mainly with information-gathering and coordination.[170] Since 2013, the scope of its operational support, its overall activities and its budget were significantly and steadily increased.[171] In response to the crisis, EASO immediately and significantly expanded its operational support as well as its information and training activities.[172] Crucially, this increased engagement was not scaled back after the crisis context but has been maintained since. This is clearly reflected in the agency's budget. After it had increased from only 8 to 15 million between 2011 and 2015, it was augmented to almost 60

„Coercion, prohibition, and great expectations. The continuing failure of the Common European Asylum System", *Common Market Law Review* 53 (2016), p. 607-642, p. 615.

168 In more detail David Fernández-Rojo, *EU Migration Agencies* (fn. 23), p. 21–62.

169 For an early account see Françoise Comte, „A New Agency Is Born in the European Union: The European Asylum Support Office" (fn. 20).

170 With the exception of Greece, where operational support was provided since 2011.

171 Therefore, Salvatore F. Nicolosi, David Fernandez-Rojo, „Out of control? The case of the European Asylum Support Office" (fn. 51), p. 180 date the fundamental shift in EASO's role to 2013 rather than to 2015.

172 Similarly, for the other agencies, David Fernández-Rojo, *EU Migration Agencies* (fn. 23), p. 63–113.

million in one fell swoop in 2016.[173] Since then, the budget has been steadily increased and amounts to about 180 million in 2023.[174]

After facts had been created, it took another five years until the legal basis was eventually adapted. Although the Commission had recognised in 2016 already that an adjustment of the legal basis was urgently required,[175] political negotiations turned out extremely controversial, so that the new EUAA Regulation did not enter into force until 2021.[176] The EUAA Regulation is, hence, a paradigm example of belated legalisation. In essence, the new Regulation codifies and legitimises practices that have been implemented already since 2016. In large part, the Regulation merely creates a legal basis for already existing practices and provides institutional safeguards in an ex-post manner. After EASO had considerably stepped up its operational support in the crisis, it operated without a concrete legal basis and without urgently required safeguards. With the EUAA Regulation, these crisis-induced practices were eventually vested with a legal basis and, at least on paper and at least partially, with institutional safeguards such as an individual complaints mechanism.[177]

a *The EUAA's Competences as a Political Compromise*

The EUAA Regulation thus reflects a political compromise. It adjusts the legal basis to the fact that the agency has become central to the asylum administration but decidedly refrains from establishing a 'true' decision-making EU asylum authority. This is important because the question of whether an EU agency should be vested with powers to decide on individu-

173 In more detail on the development of EASO's budget Evangelia (Lilian) Tsourdi, „Bottom-Up Salvation?" (fn. 42), p. 1006–1007.

174 EUAA, Statement of Revenues and Expenditures 2016, https://is.gd/2mgQ0q (30.05.2024); Statement of Revenues and Expenditures 2023, https://euaa.europa.eu/publications/budget-2023 (23.05.2024).

175 European Commission, Proposal for a Regulation of the European Parliament and of the Council on the European Union Agency for Asylum and repealing Regulation (EU) No 439/2010, 04/05/2016, COM/2016) 271 final.

176 EUAA Regulation (see introduction, fn. 39).

177 Art. 39 EUAA Regulation. On the modelling of the EUAA Regulation after the Frontex Regulation see Alexandra Tarzikhan, „The European Union Agency for Asylum: A Promising Improvement or Vestige of the European Asylum Support office?", *Refugee Law & Migration Studies Brief* 1 (2022), p. 1-10, p. 6.

al asylum claims creates an intractable tension in the agency's mandate.[178] Accordingly, the innovations of the EUAA reform are anything but groundbreaking. The reform is characterised by two main developments: firstly, an expansion of the agency's competences; and secondly, a reconfiguration of its institutional structure.[179]

As regards the first point, it should be recalled that the EUAA's competences can be roughly divided into three areas.[180] The first and oldest area of competences is the provision of knowledge-based support to member states. This includes the provision of training for national asylum authorities, the preparation and sharing of operational standards, guidelines or so-called best practices, and the gathering, analysing and sharing of information concerning, inter alia, the situation in countries of origin or in third countries, or the situation within the EU and at its external borders. Second, the agency is tasked with the provision of operational support to national authorities. This includes selection and deployment of staff and technical devices to specific areas, often located at the EU's external borders, where the deployed staff works hand-in-hand with national authorities on the ground in order to enhance the functioning of the concerned asylum system. Third, and this is the most recent area of competences, the agency is tasked with 'monitoring' the European asylum system. In this context, too, a particular focus lies on those national systems that have been identified as relatively weak, which often concerns member states located at the EU external border.

While the 2021 reform expanded the agency's competences in terms of operational support and in terms of monitoring, the following focuses on its operational competences.[181] The EASO Regulation had formulated that

---

178 Note that the question is not whether the EU can provide international protection (which is a difficult question, given that the idea underlying protection is to substitute a broken state-bond) but merely whether the EU can decide whether member states shall grant international protection.

179 In more detail on the EUAA reform David Fernández Rojo, „From EASO to the European Agency for Asylum: 'Business as Usual?'", eumigrationlawblog of 15/10/2018.

180 Similarly, with respect to EASO Evangelia (Lilian) Tsourdi, „Bottom-Up Salvation?" (fn. 42), p.1002 – 1003. For an enumeration of the EUAA's tasks see Art. 2 para 1 lit. a to s EUAA Regulation.

181 This is because the agency's monitoring activities are not yet clearly defined in practice, so that a discussion of the EU's legal responsibility for failure to adequately monitor the European asylum system would remain a rather hypothetical exercise. See further on EUAA's monitoring role David Fernández-Rojo, *EU Migration*

the agency shall have 'no direct or indirect powers' in relation to the 'taking of decisions by member states' asylum authorities on individual applications for international protection'.[182] Still, the crisis-induced soft law tasked EASO with conducting asylum interviews and issuing legal opinions recommending the acceptance or rejection of the claim. Since 2015, the agency had thus systemically overstepped the limits of its competences under the EASO Regulation.[183] Against this background, the EUAA Regulation reads as a failed attempt to adjust the legal basis as far as necessary, while at the same time accommodating political concerns against a 'true' EU asylum agency. It reflects both the need to codify crisis-induced practices, which, as a matter of fact, include EASO conducting asylum procedures, and the continuous political reluctance to make individual asylum decisions at EU level. The result is that the EUAA Regulation tones down the limits of the agency's competence to a considerable extent[184] and defines its operational tasks in remarkably fuzzy and convoluted terms.[185] Certainly, these compromise-like formulations do leave ample room for manoeuvre on the ground which appears to have been a central political aim. When it comes to defining the EU's responsibility in legal terms, however, the EUAA Regulation is hardly a step forward.

b *The EUAA's Internal Decision-Making Structure*

This leads to the second point of the EUAA reform that is of interest here, namely, the agency's internal decision-making structure. For in order to determine who is responsible for fundamental rights violations committed

---

Agencies (fn. 23), p. 102–104; Evangelia (Lilian) Tsourdi, „Monitoring and Steering through FRONTEX and EASO 2.0: The Rise of a New Model of AFSJ agencies?", eumigrationlawblog of 29/01/2018; Evangelia (Lilian) Tsourdi, „The New Pact and EU Agencies: An Ambivalent Approach Towards Administrative Integration" (fn. 143).

182 Recital 14, Art. 2 para 6 EASO Regulation.

183 See only Evangelia (Lilian) Tsourdi, „Bottom-Up Salvation?" (fn. 42), p. 1021–1026.

184 Stressing that all tasks of the agency are 'without prejudice' to the 'competence of national asylum authorities to decide on individual applications for international protection', see recital 17, 21, 66; Art. 11 para 3, Art. 18 para 2 lit. j, Art. 22 para 4 EUAA Regulation.

185 See only Art. 16 para 2 lit c which provides that 'the Agency shall (...) facilitate the examination by the competent national authorities of applications for international protection or provide those authorities with the necessary assistance in the procedure for international protection'.

by or with the contribution of EUAA staff, it is essential to have a precise picture of who knows what and who takes which decisions.

Generally, the internal structure of the EUAA is similar to that of other agencies. It consists of two main decision-making bodies, the Management Board and the Executive Director.[186] The Management Board is composed of one representative of each member state, two representatives of the Commission, and one non-voting representative of UNHCR. As its name indicates, the management board is responsible for the overall management of the agency. This includes the taking of general decisions related to the agency's budget and policy, as well as the issuance of more specific guidelines.[187] The Executive Director, on its part, is the agency's legal representative and responsible for its day-to-day administration. This includes inter alia, evaluating, approving and coordinating the agency's operational support and ensuring the implementation of the Operational Plans.[188] In principle, the office is designed as independent,[189] but a certain dependence on the Management Board cannot be denied: after all, the Executive Director is appointed by the Board, shall implement its decisions, and remains accountable to it.[190]

When it comes to the EUAA's operations on the ground, the Executive Director accordingly plays a key role. They decide on the deployment of asylum support teams (AST) or migration management support teams (MMST). Once the teams are deployed, the Executive Director delegates their supervisory power to one or several coordinating officers, formerly so-called Union contact points, who coordinate the work of the deployed teams and act as interface between the agency and the host member state. The coordinating officers are responsible for 'monitoring' compliance with the Operational Plan and EU law and, to this end, provide general instructions. At the same time, the host member state retains responsibility for detailed instructions concerning daily operations. In this sense, the regular AST are subject to a dual supervision structure. Supervision works slightly differently in the case of MMST. As will be set out in more detail below, MMSTs are subject to a two-layered supervision structure, with the first

186 Art. 39 EUAA Regulation.
187 Art. 40, 41 EUAA Regulation.
188 Art. 46, 47 EUAA Regulation.
189 Art. 47 para 2 EUAA Regulation.
190 Art. 47 para 1, para 2, para 3, para 5 lit b to f, lit h, lit o, lot r to s, lit x EUAA Regulation.

layer corresponding to the dual structure of the AST and the second layer consisting of supervision by the European Commission.[191]

In addition to the Management Board and Executive Director, the EUAA disposes of two complementary bodies that serve to improve the agency's fundamental rights record, namely the Fundamental Rights Office and the Consultative Forum.[192] Both have been introduced only with the EUAA Regulation and are modelled after the Frontex Regulation.[193] Their purpose is to secure the agency's overall compliance with fundamental rights and, in the event of a violation, strengthen its accountability. The Consultative Forum consists of representatives of civil society organisations and relevant stakeholders, including UNHCR, Frontex and FRA, and serves to maintain the agency's dialogue with these.[194] The task of the Fundamental Rights Office is formulated as 'ensuring' the agency's compliance with fundamental rights.[195] This, however, seems quite ambitious, if not unrealistic, considering that the actual competences of the Office are mainly advisory and consultative in nature. In most agency-internal procedures, such as the conclusion of operational plans and the adoption of the agency's code of conduct, the Fundamental Rights Officer must be consulted but cannot ensure that its advice is followed.[196] In addition, the Fundamental Rights Office is responsible for handling individual complaints under the new complaints mechanism.[197] Although this arguably is the core task of the Office, its position remains relatively weak even in this context because it is competent to review only the admissibility of the complaints, while the competence for reviewing the substance and ensuring follow-up lies with the concerned member state or the Executive Director.[198]

191 This is very simplified. For details see Art. 18–21, 25 EUAA Regulation. In more detail on the supervisory structure in the case of MMST see chapter 2, 1.2.

192 Art. 39 EUAA Regulation.

193 On the modelling of the EUAA Regulation after the Frontex Regulation see Alexandra Tarzikhan, „The European Union Agency for Asylum: A Promising Improvement or Vestige of the European Asylum Support office?“ (fn. 177), p. 6.

194 Art. 50 EUAA Regulation.

195 Art. 49 para 3 EUAA Regulation.

196 Art. 49 para 5 EUAA Regulation.

197 Art. 51 para 4 EUAA Regulation.

198 Art. 51 para 4 lit. a, c, d, para 6, para 8 EUAA Regulation. Note that the grounds for inadmissibility are defined in an extraordinarily broad and vague manner, as Art. 51 para 3 sentence 3: 'Complaints which are anonymous, abuse, malicious, frivolous, vexatious, hypothetical or inaccurate shall also be inadmissible.'.

3.2 The EU Border Agency (Frontex)

The EUAA cooperates with a considerable number of other agencies whose mandates are in one way or the other connected to the implementation of European asylum law. Out of those, Frontex is of particular importance and, for the purpose of this study, hence requires a closer look.

a *Inter-Agency Cooperation as a Defining Feature of the European Asylum Administration*

Inter-agency cooperation in the asylum system is so extensive that it has itself become a central feature of the European asylum administration.[199] The EUAA's most important cooperation partners are Frontex, Europol, Eurojust, the EU Fundamental Rights Agency (FRA) and the Agency for the Operational Management of Large-Scale IT Systems in the Area of Freedom, Security and Justice (eu-LISA).[200] Each of these agencies, in turn, cooperates with a whole range of other agencies. Frontex, for instance, cooperates with the EUAA, Europol, Eurojust, FRA, the European Fisheries Control Agency (EFCA), and the European Maritime Safety Agency (EMSA).[201]

Given that inter-agency cooperation is increasingly vital to the functioning of the asylum system, scholarly contributions have repeatedly argued for the establishment of a central EU migration agency.[202] Taking into account current political debates and the state of reform so far, however, such proposals are likely to remain within the realm of academic discussion for the time being. Instead, it seems much more realistic that cooperation between the existing agencies will be strengthened further.[203] The present study, hence, concentrates on analysing the allocation of responsibility in inter-agency cooperation as it currently exists. As will be explained in more detail below, the focus is on the example of the so-called migration

199 David Fernández-Rojo, *EU Migration Agencies* (fn. 23), p. 115–120, p. 121–133.
200 Art. 5, 8, 21, 29, 31, 32, 50, and in a general manner Art. 37 EUAA Regulation.
201 Art 10 para 1 lit. q to t Frontex Regulation.
202 See only Elspeth Guild, „Does the EU Need a European Migration and Protection Agency?", *International Journal of Refugee Law* 28 (2016), p. 585-600 with further references.
203 Similarly, David Fernández-Rojo, *EU Migration Agencies* (fn. 23), p. 119–120.

management support teams (MMST), which represent the most advanced form of inter-agency cooperation and operate in EU hotspots.[204]

Yet, this study is limited to the analysis of inter-agency cooperation between the EUAA and Frontex. This limitation is justified for three reasons. First, Frontex's mandate necessarily requires it to comply with, and sometimes even to proactively apply, asylum law.[205] This is increasingly reflected in EU secondary law: while the 2004 Frontex Founding Regulation[206] mentioned neither asylum nor refoulement, the 2019 Regulation puts particular emphasis on the agency's compliance with the EU asylum acquis, in particular the fundamental right to asylum and the non-refoulement principle.[207] Second, Frontex's close cooperation with the EUAA reflects the increasing securitisation of migration policy.[208] Seen from this perspective, Frontex's involvement in the asylum administration is problematic as such, which makes the analysis of its responsibility for misconduct even more pressing. Third, Frontex and the EUAA provide the bulk of operational support in individual asylum procedures and are therefore de facto most likely to be involved in fundamental rights violations.[209]

b *Frontex's Competences and Internal Decision-Making Structures*

Consequently, and with a view to the analysis in the following chapters, the remainder of this section provides a brief introduction to Frontex. As

---

204 Art. 2 para 19, Art. 40 Frontex Regulation, Art. 21 EUAA Regulation. See chapter 2, 1.2.

205 For instance, a denial of entry for non-compliance with visa requirements is permissible only if the non-refoulement principle is respected. See further Roberta Mungianu, *Frontex and Non-Refoulement*, Cambridge University Press 2016, in particular p. 129–135, 205–206.

206 Council Regulation (EC) No 2007/2004 of 26 October 2004 establishing a European Agency for the Management of Operational Cooperation at the External Borders of the Member States of the European Union.

207 See only recital 51, 84, 103, Art. 21 para 3 lit b, Art. 36 para 2, Art. 43 para 4, Art. 48 para 1, Art. 50 para 3, Art. 71 para 2, Art. 73 para 2, Art. 80, Art. 86 para 4 Frontex Regulation.

208 For the prevailing view see only Sarah Léonard, „EU border security and migration into the European Union: FRONTEX and securitisation through practices", *European Security* 19 (2010), p. 231-254. Challenging that view Andrew W Neal, „Securitization and Risk at the EU Border: The Origins of FRONTEX", *Journal of Common Market Studies* 47 (2009), p. 333-356.

209 See chapter 2.

in the case of the EUAA, the most important steps in the development of Frontex were taken in the aftermath of the crisis.[210] The 2016 reform significantly expanded the agency's mandate, granted it more autonomy vis-à-vis member states and, to this end, introduced the concept of 'shared' responsibility for border control.[211] Also, Frontex was renamed the European Border and Coast Guard Agency, but the use of its previous name remained common usage.[212] In comparison, the latest reform of 2019 seems rather modest.[213] Although the ambitious and perhaps unrealistic[214] goal of establishing a permanent corps of 10,000 operational staff attracted media attention, the 2019 innovations remain mainly quantitative. Qualitatively, the latest reform brings little new, as the idea of establishing a permanent corps with executive powers had in fact already been introduced with the 2016 reform.[215]

Overall, Frontex's legal competences as well as its factual involvement have continuously and substantially increased over the past decades. Again, this is clearly reflected in the agency's budget which has grown exponentially from 6 million in 2005 to 829 million in 2023.[216] An increase of this scale is indeed extraordinary; and a comparison with the EUAA, in terms of budgetary growth and numbers of legislative reforms, clearly shows that political agreement is apparently much easier reached when it comes to 'protecting' the EU's external borders against migrants than when it comes to protecting persons in need of international protection.[217]

---

210 Vittoria Meissner, „The European Border and Coast Guard Agency Frontex After the Migration Crisis: Towards a 'Superagency'?" (fn. 51), p. 159–168.

211 Frontex 2016 Regulation (fn. 150).

212 Art. 3 Frontex 2016 Regulation.

213 Frontex Regulation (introduction, fn. 39). See on that reform and its implications David Fernández-Rojo, *EU Migration Agencies* (fn. 23), p. 87–100.

214 Vittoria Meissner, „The European Border and Coast Guard Agency Frontex After the Migration Crisis" (fn. 51), p. 168.

215 Art. 20 para 5 Frontex 2016 Regulation.

216 Statista, Budget der Europäischen Agentur für die Grenz- und Küstenwache (Frontex) in den Jahren 2005 bis 2024, https://de.statista.com/statistik/daten/studie/1172183/umfrage/budget-der-europaeischen-agentur-fuer-die-grenz-und-kuestenwache-frontex/ (30.05.2024).

217 Note that the notion of 'protecting' instead of 'controlling' borders is based on the paradigm of 'migration as danger'. The terminological aberration is taken one step further with the idea of 'vulnerable' borders, see only Art. 32 Frontex Regulation on the 'vulnerability assessment' through which the agency 'shall assess (...) the Member States' capacity to carry out all border management tasks'.

Frontex's competences can be roughly divided into the same categories as those of the EUAA, namely knowledge-based support, operational support and monitoring.[218] As regards, first, knowledge-based support, Frontex conducts research, in particular on the use of advanced surveillance technology, develops technical standards for information exchange or equipment, promotes the interconnection of systems and networks, and supports the development of common minimum standards for external border surveillance. Second, in terms of operational support, the agency deploys different kinds of teams depending on the practical needs on the ground, and provides assistance in all areas related to border control, ranging from the provision of vessels and technical equipment to the registration of asylum seekers in EU hotspots and the coordination and organisation of deportations. Third, Frontex is tasked with monitoring all aspects of the European border administration[219] as well as member states border control capacities.[220] As in the case of the EUAA, these monitoring-based tasks have only recently been assigned to the agency, and yet remain to be defined in terms of both practical activities and legal obligations.

As in the case of the EUAA, the question of Frontex's competence limits is so contentious that the Frontex Regulation appears as an unsuccessful attempt to accommodate all views. Again, the political compromise comes at the expense of legal clarity, as vague formulations and convoluted regulatory structures show. For example, the Regulation provides that the performance of all tasks, and in particular 'those requiring executive powers, shall be subject to the authorisation of the home member state', while stressing at the same time that 'member states may authorise members of the (Frontex) teams to act on its behalf'.[221] Similarly, the 'use of force' shall in principle be exercised only in the 'presence of border guards of the host member state', which may, however, 'authorise members of the teams to use force on its territory in the absence of border guards of the host member state'.[222] Taking into account that Frontex operations usually take place in contexts characterized by quick decisions and actions on the part of public actors

218 For an overview see Art. 10 Frontex Regulation.

219 Similarly, the Frontex Regulation refers to the 'European Border and Coast Guard', see Art. 4 Frontex Regulation, and sometimes also to the 'integrated border management', see Art. 10 para 1 lit. a Frontex Regulation.

220 In particular Art. 10 para 1 lit. a to e Frontex Regulation.

221 Art. 82 para 2 and para 4 Frontex Regulation.

222 Art 82 para 8 Frontex Regulation; see further Art. 2 para 18, 19, 29, Art. 29, Art. 39, 40, 48, 52, and Art. 82 para 8 Frontex Regulation.

as well as by a lack of evidence on the part of the individuals concerned, provisions such as the cited ones necessarily lead to uncertainty as to whether a specific action was covered by the agency's mandate or not. In sum, the Frontex Regulation is at least as deficient in terms of regulating responsibilities as the EUAA Regulation.

The internal organisation of Frontex is very similar to that of the EUAA, too.[223] The agency disposes of a Management Board, an Executive Director who is responsible for the day-to-day administration, as well as a Fundamental Rights Office and a Consultative Forum.[224] As in the case the EUAA, the Fundamental Rights Office is structurally weak, and the recently created individual complaints mechanism works rather poorly.[225]

When it comes to the supervision of deployed support teams, there are three main differences between the EUAA and Frontex. Tellingly, all these differences seem to be due to the traditional understanding of border control as an inherently sovereign task, and concern, in particular, the use of force and the carrying of weapons. First, the home member state is involved to a much greater extent in the case of Frontex. While deployed Frontex teams, as deployed EUAA teams, are subject to supervision by the coordinating officers who act on behalf of the Executive Director, and by the host member state, they are also subject to closer control by the host member state. Second, the host member state is involved to a greater extent in the case of Frontex than in the case of the EUAA. Third, the Frontex Regulation explicitly vests the Executive Director with the power, and thus also the obligation, to unilaterally withdraw the agency's support in case of systemic and persistent fundamental rights violations. These agency-specific differences notwithstanding, the supervisory structure in the case of the inter-agency MMST, in which staff of both the EUAA and Frontex cooperate, is uniform insofar as the Commission is responsible for ensuring the overall legality of the agencies' operational support.[226]

---

223 Given that the EUAA has been built upon the model of Frontex, see fn. 193.

224 Art. 99 Frontex Regulation.

225 On the considerable delays in hiring fundamental rights monitors and connected failures see Luisa Marin, „Frontex and the Rule of Law Crisis at EU Borders“ (fn. 52).

226 Again, this is very simplified. For the supervisory structures on the different deployment types in detail see Art. 36–44, 46, 48–50, 52–53, 54–58, 82 Frontex Regulation. In more detail on the supervisory structure in the case of MMST see chapter 2, 1.2.

3.3 The European Commission

The European Commission has become a central administrative actor in the asylum system, too. While this development is often overlooked in legal scholarship, it is telling that the European Ombudsman has recently opened its first own-initiative inquiry against the Commission concerning its role in the asylum administration.[227] Whether it is a matter of far-reaching policy decisions, the funding of individual projects, the details of the implementation of single provisions of the EU asylum acquis, or the overall state of national asylum administrations: it is always the Commission that has the overview, keeps the relevant information, and takes the key decisions. When it comes to exercising public authority at EU level, all threads come together at the Commission. In this sense, the Commission acts as general supervisor of the European asylum administration. To exercise this supervisory role, it relies on a whole range of measures, out of which policy making, funding, operational instructions, and monitoring are of particular practical relevance.[228]

a *The Commission's Administrative Competences under Art. 17 para 1 TEU*

Unlike in the case of the agencies, the Commission's specific tasks are not bundled in one Regulation. Instead, its competences derive mainly from Art. 17 para 1 TEU and are then concretised in several Regulations, including the EUAA Regulation, the Frontex Regulation, and the AMIF Regulation.[229] Art. 17 para 1 TEU establishes the Commission's role as guardian of the Treaties, or more precisely as guardian of EU law. In a nutshell, it provides that the Commission shall ensure the application of primary and secondary law, oversee the application thereof, and exercise coordinating,

---

227 European Ombudsperson, How the European Commission ensures respect for fundamental rights in EU-funded migration management facilities in Greece, Case OI/3/2022/MHZ, opened 11/07/2022.

228 In more detail on these four categories see Catharina Ziebritzki, *The EU's Responsibility in the Asylum Administration* (fn. 56), p. 100 et seq.

229 Regulation (EU) No 516/2014 of the European Parliament and of the Council of 16 April 2014 establishing the Asylum, Migration and Integration Fund, amending Council Decision 2008/381/EC and repealing Decisions No 573/2007/EC and No 575/2007/EC of the European Parliament and of the Council and Council Decision 2007/435/EC (hereinafter: AMIF Regulation).

executive and management functions.[230] Arguably, the Commission's mandate as supervisor of the integrated European asylum administration, more precisely its competences related to policy making, funding, operational supervision and monitoring, thus follow from Art. 17 para 1 TEU.[231]

First, the Commission's competence to develop policies and issue guidelines on the interpretation of EU law follows, in particular, from sentence 1, 2 and 5 of Art. 17 para 1 TEU.[232] The crucial point here is that Art. 17 para 1 TEU enables the Commission to issue guidelines that interpret the EU asylum acquis, but not to create new rules. In practice, however, this distinction is often difficult to make. The EU hotspot approach of 2015, for instance, can be seen as a guideline on how to apply the then-existing EU asylum acquis. At the same time, the specific interpretative combination has the effect that an entirely new procedure is created, namely the EU hotspots procedure;[233] seen from this perspective, the Commission's guideline could also be qualified as going beyond the EU asylum acquis.

The second aspect of the Commission's competence, namely funding, is more straightforward. Art. 17 para 1 sentence 4 TEU is unequivocal in that the Commission is competent to administer EU funding which includes granting funds and evaluating EU funded projects. This must be read in conjunction with Art. 317 TFEU which provides that the Commission shall implement the budget in cooperation with member states and establishes the principle of sound financial management.[234] The Commission's specific

---

230 Art. 17 para 1 TEU provides that 'The Commission shall promote the general interest of the Union and take appropriate initiatives to that end. It shall ensure the application of the Treaties, and of measures adopted by the institutions pursuant to them. It shall oversee the application of Union law under the control of the Court of Justice of the European Union. It shall execute the budget and manage programmes. It shall exercise coordinating, executive and management functions, as laid down in the Treaties. With the exception of the common foreign and security policy, and other cases provided for in the Treaties, it shall ensure the Union's external representation. It shall initiate the Union's annual and multiannual programming with a view to achieving interinstitutional agreements.'.

231 On the Commission's competences related to external representation see Matthias Ruffert, „Artikel 17 EUV", in Christian Calliess, Matthias Ruffert (ed.), *EUV/AEUV. Kommentar*, C.H. Beck 2022, para 16.

232 'Policy-making' as understood here falls mainly under governmental or executive functions, and only exceptionally under administrative functions; on this distinction see Matthias Ruffert, „Artikel 17 EUV" (fn. 231), para 3.

233 See further chapter 2, 1.3. and 3.2.

234 Matthias Ruffert, „Artikel 17 EUV" (fn. 231), para 12. The principle of sound financial management, as established by Art. 317 TFEU, is defined in Art. 33 para of the

competences are then defined in several Funding Regulations.[235] These Regulations usually allow the Commission to withhold or withdraw funding in standard cases of non-compliance with EU law.[236] In grave cases of systemic and persisting fundamental rights violations, the Commission's possibilities to withdraw or withhold funding often go even further, as not only the Regulation on Common Provisions for Funds[237] but arguably also the Conditionality Regulation become applicable.[238] Although the latter was adopted with a view to 'classic' rule of law deficits, it appears to be applicable to rule of law deficits that are specific to the asylum administration, too.[239]

Financial Rules Regulation, see Regulation (EU, Euratom) 2018/1046 of the European Parliament and of the Council of 18 July 2018 on the financial rules applicable to the general budget of the Union (hereinafter: Financial Rules Regulation).

235 In particular: Regulation (EU) No 515/2014 of the European Parliament and of the Council of 16 April 2014 establishing, as part of the Internal Security Fund, the instrument for financial support for external borders and visa and repealing Decision No 574/2007/EC (hereinafter: ISF Regulation); Regulation (EU) 2021/1060 of the European Parliament and of the Council of 24 June 2021 laying down common provisions on the European Regional Development Fund, the European Social Fund Plus, the Cohesion Fund, the Just Transition Fund and the European Maritime, Fisheries and Aquaculture Fund and financial rules for those and for the Asylum, Migration and Integration Fund, the Internal Security Fund and the Instrument for Financial Support for Border Management and Visa Policy (hereinafter: Regulation on Common Provisions for Funds). See in particular Art. 14 para 5 AMIF Regulation.

236 Under Art. 10 para 2, 3 ISF Regulation which must be read in conjunction with Art. 3 para 4 thereof, the Commission may condition the approval of EU funding upon compliance with EU law, and especially with the ChFR. The same arguably follows from recital 33, Art. 3 para 1, Art. 19 para 2 AMIF Regulation read in conjunction with Art. 17 TEU. In general terms, Art. 9 para 1, Art. 15 para 1, para 6 Regulation on Common Provisions for Funds in conjunction with Annex III thereof provides that EU funding may be conditioned upon compliance with EU law, and especially with the ChFR.

237 Art. 96 and 97 Regulation on Common Provisions for Funds provide that the 'Commission may suspend all or part of payments' inter alia 'if (...) there is a serious deficiency' as defined in Art. 2 para 32 of that Regulation.

238 Regulation (EU, Euratom) 2020/2092 of the European Parliament and of the Council of 16 December 2020 on a general regime of conditionality for the protection of the Union budget (hereinafter: Conditionality Regulation).

239 Art. 2 lit a Conditionality Regulation defines the rule of law as the values enshrined in Art 2 TEU, including 'effective judicial protection, including access to justice, by independent and impartial courts, also as regards fundamental rights'; Art. 3 defines situations that are indicative of breaches of the principles of the rule of law and refers, in its lit c, to 'limiting the availability and effectiveness of legal remedies,

This leads to the third and fourth aspect of the Commission's competences, namely operational supervision and monitoring of the integrated European administration. Arguably, these competences follow in particular from sentences 1, 2 and 5 of Art. 17 para 1 TEU. The Commission's mandate as guardian of the Treaties comes with a broad competence to undertake all kind of appropriate initiatives in the realm of supervision, coordination and monitoring.[240] This broad interpretation is widely agreed upon in scholarship, if only because the functioning of the EU to an important extent depends on the Commission's comprehensive supervisory mandate.[241] Moreover, this broad reading is also shared by the co-legislators. In fact, EU secondary law confers upon the Commission far-reaching supervisory and monitoring competences, including in areas in which those are not explicitly laid down in the Treaties. As prominently illustrated with the example of the Eurozone,[242] supervising and monitoring the implementation of EU law is certainly one of the Commission's main tasks today.[243]

As far as the asylum system is concerned, this reading of Art. 17 para 1 TEU is confirmed by Art. 74 TFEU. This provision states, albeit rather incidentally, that national administrations, when implementing EU asylum

---

including through restrictive procedural rules'. Note that the European Parliament in its resolution of 7 February 2024 on the rule of law and media freedom in Greece (2024/2502(RSP) has called upon the European Commission 'to make full use of the tools available to it to address the breaches of the values enshrined in Article 2 TEU in Greece', including an 'assessment under the Rule of Law Conditionality Regulation' with reference to, inter alia, deficits in the context of asylum and migration.

240 Matthias Ruffert, „Artikel 17 EUV" (fn. 231), para 7–11; Gerard C. Rowe, „Administrative supervision of administrative action in the European Union", in Herwig Hofmann, Alexander Türk (ed.), *Legal Challenges in EU Administrative Law*, Edward Elgar 2009, p. 179-217, p. 185–186 with reference to 211 EC (the predecessor of Art 17 para 1 TEU) as a legal basis for the Commission's comprehensive supervisory powers.

241 Paul F Nemitz, „Artikel 17 EUV", in Ulrich Becker, Armin Hatje, Johann Schoo, Jürgen Schwarze (ed.), *EU-Kommentar*, Nomos 2019, para 41.

242 Michael W. Bauer, Stefan Becker, „The Unexpected Winner of the Crisis: The European Commission's Strengthened Role in Economic Governance", *Journal of European Integration* 36 (2014), p. 213-229, p. 217 noting that despite the Commission's competences granted by the European Financial Stabilization Mechanism, 'its old mandate of guarding the Treaties' continues to play a role.

243 Stefan Becker, Michael W. Bauer, „Die Europäische Kommission. Koordinationsbürokratie mit Regierungsanspruch", in Peter Becker, Barbara Lippert (ed.), *Handbuch Europäische Union*, Springer 2020, p. 369-389, p. 371–373.

law, shall cooperate with the Commission.[244] Although Art. 74 TFEU does clearly not extend the EU's substantial competences, it promotes formal and informal administrative cooperation between national administrations and EU bodies, notably including in areas where the EU does not have substantial decision-making competences.[245] In this sense, Art. 74 TFEU implicitly confirms that the Commission has a broad competence to supervise and monitor national asylum administrations.

b *The Commission's Internal Decision-Making Structures*

When it comes to determining the EU's responsibility for administrative misconduct, the Commission's internal decision-making structure is less decisive than that of the agencies. This is because when Commission staff violates EU law, it is clear that this act must be attributed to the Commission.[246] The Commission's internal decision-making structures are hence only of interest insofar as it must be determined what the Commission knew or should have known, and which measures it has taken or should have taken.[247]

The Commission is divided into several Directorates-General which operate under the ultimate responsibility of the respective Commissioners. In the context of 2015, the Commission, to a large extent, relied on its Structural Support and Reform Service (SSRS), i.e. today's DG Reform. For instance, the EU coordinator for the implementation of the EU-Türkiye Statement in Greece formed part of the SSRS. Subsequently, responsibilities were moved to DG Home Affairs (HOME) and DG European Civil Protection and Humanitarian Aid Operations (ECCHO). In particular, the EU's

---

244 Art 74 TFEU reads: 'The Council shall adopt measures to ensure *administrative cooperation between the relevant departments of the Member States* (...) as well as between those departments *and the Commission* (...).' (emphasis added). As here Matthias Rossi, „Artikel 74 AEUV", in Christian Calliess, Matthias Ruffert (ed.), *EUV/AEUV. Kommentar*, C.H. Beck 2022, para 1. Differently, however, Stephan Breitenmoser, Robert Weyeneth, „Artikel 74 AEUV", in Hans von der Groeben, Jürgen Schwarze, Armin Hatje (ed.), *Europäisches Unionsrecht*, Nomos 2015, para 25 arguing that the Commission's main role is not to cooperate with, but to supervise, national administrations, in particular via the infringement procedure.

245 Daniel Thym, „Artikel 74 AEUV", in Winfried Kluth, Andreas Heusch (ed.), *BeckOK Ausländerrecht*, C.H. Beck 2022, para 2.

246 On the attribution of conduct to the agencies see chapter 4.

247 On the relevant questions of causation see chapter 5.

supervisory fora established in Greece were operating under the responsibility of these.[248] In the meanwhile, the Commission's internal structure was adjusted to reflect the political focus on migration, and all matters related to the asylum system were moved within the responsibility of DG Migration and Home Affairs. Within this DG, the department for migration and asylum, that for home affairs funds, and the deputy Director-General who is also the head of the Task Force Migration Management, are of particular relevance for the purpose of this study.[249] Out of these, the Task Force Migration Management deserves particular attention here, as it has been created precisely to ensure the legality of the EU hotspot administration 2.0.[250]

When it comes to determining whether the Commission has knowledge about specific deficiencies in the integrated administration, the Commission's concrete supervisory fora established on the ground are crucial. In order to exercise its extensive administrative tasks, the Commission operates not only from Brussels but also on the ground, and increasingly so. In Greece, for instance, the Commission has established several supervisory fora such as the European Regional Task Force (EURTF) and Steering Committees. While the EURTF focuses on operational coordination, the Steering Committees serve to discuss all funding-related aspects of the asylum administration in Greece.[251] Furthermore, the Commission also deploys representatives that are closely involved at the operational level. Figuratively referred to as 'the Commission's eyes and ears on the ground', the representatives' main task is information-gathering and reporting.[252]

4 The EU's Main Forms of Administrative Cooperation

Having clarified which EU bodies perform the relevant conduct in the EU hotspots, this last section zooms into the main forms of administrative cooperation. With a view to this study's aim of defining the EU's responsibility in legal terms, the section has two specific objectives. First, it seeks

248 See chapter 2, 2.
249 For an organisational chart of DG Home see https://commission.europa.eu/about-european-commission/departments-and-executive-agencies/migration-and-home-affairs_en.
250 See chapter 2, 2.6.
251 See ibid.
252 See ibid.

to classify the forms of cooperation into the categories of European administrative law. Tthe approach here is to avoid reference to asylum-specific or policy-oriented categories such as 'joint' or 'assisted processing',[253] and instead to rely on the more consolidated categories of general European administrative law.[254] This reveals similarities between different areas of the integrated administration, and thus allows to transfer insights from areas such as competition law or the Eurozone to the asylum system.[255] Second, this section seeks to define the EU's legal responsibilities in the context of administrative cooperation in the EU hotspots. While the precise scope of the EU's obligations depends on the specific provision it stake, and hence cannot be determined in a generalised manner, this section provides some basic orientation, thereby preparing the ground for a more detailed doctrinal analysis in the following.[256]

4.1 Administrative Support

Support, for the purpose of this study, is understood as a form of cooperation in which one actor assists another in fulfilling its administrative task. In the context of the asylum administration, support in this sense is usually provided by the EUAA and Frontex to a member state.

253 Based on Helene Urth, Mathilde Heegaard Bausager, Hanna-Maija Kuhn, Joanne Van Selm, *Study on the Feasibility and legal and practical implications of establishing a mechanism for the joint processing of asylum applications on the territory of the EU, conducted for the European Commission*, 2013, most scholarly contributions refer to these categories. For an attempt to reconcile both terminologies see Evangelia (Lilian) Tsourdi, „Holding the European Asylum Support Office Accountable for its role in Asylum Decision-Making: Mission Impossible?" (fn. 156), p. 514–515 who differentiates between three categories of joint processing, namely assisted, common and EU-level processing, and argues that 'common processing essentially refers to "mixed" or "composite" administraive proceedings'.

254 Taking into account that it still holds true that the 'terminology used in the nascent field of EU administrative law is not yet established', as noted by Herwig Hofmann, Alexander Türk, „Legal challenges in EU administrative law by the move to an integrated administration", in Herwig Hofmann, Alexander Türk (ed.), *Legal Challenges in EU Administrative Law*, Edward Elgar 2009, p. 355-379, p. 358. Where appropriate, reference is made here to the Research Network on EU Administrative Law Model Rules on EU Administrative Procedure, Books I to VI, available http://www.reneual.eu/projects-and-publications/reneual-1-0 (hereinafter: ReNEUAL Model Rules).

255 For the transfer of the relevant case law see chapter 5.

256 See chapter 4 and 5.

a *Reception-Related and Procedure-Related Support*

As the main tasks performed by the European asylum administration are to conduct asylum procedures and to provide reception conditions during these procedures, a distinction can be made between procedure-related and reception-related support. In relation to reception conditions, the EU's support has long mainly consisted in the provision of knowledge. More precisely, the EUAA has supported national administrations with trainings, specific advice or counselling, sharing of expertise, and technical equipment. Only recently, the EUAA has extended the scope of its reception-related activities and now also provides operational assistance. In specific contexts, such as the EU hotspots 2.0, EUAA staff is since 2021 actively involved in designing, planning, and building of refugee camps including administrative structures and detention facilities.[257]

Procedure-related support, in turn, only partially consists in knowledge-based measures such as trainings, the provision of information on relevant countries of origin or third countries,[258] or the issuance of best practices and guidelines. The bulk of procedure-related support has always been provided through operational assistance. For instance, the EUAA supports with the conduct of asylum interviews and vulnerability assessments, the assessment of the obtained information in light of EU asylum law, and the issuance of legal opinions recommending to reject or accept the concrete asylum claim. Further, Frontex supports with first registration and identification measures, as well as with organising and carrying out deportations.[259]

For the purpose of this study, procedure-related operational support is more problematic and will hence be in the focus.[260] This is for two reasons. First, the agencies' operational competences are especially sovereignty-sensitive and hence especially controversial in the context of asylum and return procedures. Second, administrative reality over the past years has clearly shown that the EUAA and Frontex are involved in asylum and return

257 See in more detail chapter 2, 1.

258 EUAA (formerly EASO), Country of Origin Information (COI) Reports, partially available online: https://euaa.europa.eu/coi-publications.

259 See chapter, 2.1.

260 In fact, most scholarly contributions that discuss the EUAA's responsibility only on the basis of procedure-related support. Once the EU hotspots 2.0 will be built, however, the question of the EUAA's responsibility due to reception-related support will become relevant.

procedures that result in the systemic fundamental rights violations. The agencies' involvement in reception conditions, by contrast, is so new that its effects can hardly be determined yet.

b *Administrative Support and EU Responsibility*

In order to clarify which of several involved administrative actors bears responsibility for misconduct, it is helpful to rely on the categories of general European administrative law. This will show that, the distinction between reception-related and procedure-related support notwithstanding, cooperation between agencies and national authorities generally results in composite administrative procedures. A procedure is composite when EU bodies and member state authorities have distinct but inter-dependent functions, and therefore cooperate, each assuming a specific sub-task in an administrative procedure.[261] Composite procedures thus generally entail that one actor issues the administrative decision, whilst the other provides support.[262] General doctrine mainly refers to examples where support serves to prepare a decision, in particular support consisting in providing a legal interpretation or a particular information.[263] A closer look, however,

261 ReNEUAL Model Rules, Art I-4(3). Similarly Giacinto Della Cananea, „The European Union's Mixed Administrative Proceedings", *Law and Contemporary Problems* 68 (2004), p. 187-218, p. 208: 'these proceeding are composed of several phases, and these involve both the Community and the national administrations in different capacities and at different stages of the sequence.' For a more comprehensive definition see Herwig C.H. Hofmann, Gerard C. Rowe, Alexander H. Türk, *Administrative Law and Policy of the European Union*, Oxford University Press 2011, p. 406: 'multiple-step procedures with input from administrative actors from different jurisdictions, cooperating either vertically (between EU authorities and those of a Member State), horizontally (between authorities in two or more Member States), or in triangular relations (involving authorities of different Member States and of the EU).'.

262 Mariolina Eliantonio, „Judicial Review in an Integrated Administration: the Case of 'Composite Procedures'", *Review of European Administrative Law* 7 (2015), p. 65-102, p. 69, however, stressed that, unlike linked or complex procedings, composite procedures are characterised by 'decision-making (being) carried out at both national and European level'.

263 See only Filipe Brito Bastos, „Derivate Illegality in European Composite Administrative Procedures", *Common Market Law review* 55 (2018), p. 101-134, p. 103; Timo Rademacher, *Realakte im Rechtsschutzsystem der Europäischen Union*, Mohr Siebeck 2014, p. 274. Note that interpretative and informational support can either relate to an individual case or be generalised.

shows that support can also serve to enforce a decision, for instance when one authority assists the other in overcoming an individual's resistance against the execution of a decision.[264]

Applying these categories to the context at hand, it follows that the asylum and return procedures in which the EUAA or Frontex provide operational support qualify as composite procedures. The EUAA's support is mainly preparatory in nature, and contains interpretational and informational elements which cannot be clearly separated.[265] Frontex's support, by contrast, mainly consists in assistance with enforcement, and contains elements related to the use of force.[266]

At first glance, it hence appears that the EU's responsibility is limited to ensuring the legality of its own conduct. A closer look, however, reveals that things are not quite that simple. With a view to the case at hand, the decisive point is that the EU, through its support, typically predetermines the content of the national decision. As will be set out in more detail in the following chapters, national authorities usually adopt the non-formally binding guidelines, opinions and recommendations issued by the EUAA, Frontex and the European Commission.[267] This is not a mere empirical coincidence, but can be explained by the fact that the EU's conduct, despite its lack of formal bindingness, comes with strong normative force. As will be argued, this can usually be traced back to the EU's political power, to its technical expertise or knowledge advantage in relation to national authorities, or the EU's financial pressure upon the member state.[268]

In general terms, the key question can be formulated as to which actor bears legal responsibility when the supporting actor, i.e. the EU in the

264 The scholarly lack of attention seems due to the fact that one constellation, namely that a member state enforces an administrative decision taken at EU level is the standard situation under Art. 197 para 1 TFEU and Art. 291 para 1 TFEU, and thus usually not even classified as an instance of vertical administration cooperation; and the other constellation, namely that the EU is involved in the enforcement of an administrative decision taken at member state level, has emerged only recently, with Frontex's assistance in the context of deportations constituting a paradigm example. Note that ReNEUAL Model Rules also do not cover 'enforcement assistance', see Book V, C., V-1, para 3 recital 5.

265 See chapter 2, 1.

266 See only Herbert Rosenfeldt, *Frontex im Zentrum der Europäischen Grenz- und Küstenwache. Bestandsaufnahme, Unionsrechtmäßigkeit und Verantwortlichkeit*, Mohr Siebeck 2021, p. 86–102.

267 See chapter 2, 1.

268 See below 4.3 and chapter 2.

context at hand, determines the content of the decision, i.e. the administrative act issued by the member state. In such cases, the intricate legal question arises as to whether and under which conditions responsibility for an unlawful decision lies with the supporting actor. While this question obviously requires detailed doctrinal analysis that will be carried out in the following,[269] two basic arguments can be made here already. First, it is clear on the basis of European administrative law as it currently stands that the allocation of responsibility between the supporting and the decision-issuing actor depends on a whole set of circumstances and thus requires a careful analysis of each concrete case.[270] Second, it must certainly be avoided that the EU can exploit the structure of the integrated administration as a strategy to circumvent constitutional safeguards and evade its own legal responsibility. Thus, a very generalised answer arguing that 'legal responsibility presupposes the issuance of a formally-binding decision' cannot convince from the outset.

4.2 Administrative Supervision

Administrative supervision is understood here as a form of cooperation in which one actor is responsible for ensuring, at least to some extent, the legality of another actor's administrative conduct.[271] The degree to which the supervisor is responsible then depends on the form of supervision and on the supervisor's obligations in the specific context. Usually, the supervisor is not obliged to detect or even prevent every single breach of law, but only to identify, prevent or remedy widespread, persisting or even systemic issues.[272] In other words, the supervisor is typically responsible for misconduct on the part of the supervisee only insofar as it is systemic.

---

269 See chapter 5. As will be shown, the relevant issue appears as a doctrinal question of attribution and causation.

270 Gerard C. Rowe, „Administrative supervision of administrative action in the European Union" (fn. 240), p. 186. Even the ReNEUAL Model Rules book V, para 5 clarify that 'Supervisory powers will be regulated in sector-specific legislation (...)'.

271 Similarly Alberto Gil Ibáñez, *The Administrative Supervision and Enforcement in EC Law: Powers, Procedures and Limits*, Hart Publishing 1999, p. 16–17; H. Audretsch, *Supervision in European Community Law*, North-Holland 1986, p. 7.

272 A good example are the Commission's supervisory obligations in the context of EU funding, see above fn. 238 et seq.

Supervision can be internal or external in nature. It is internal when the supervisor and the supervisee form part of the same authority or body: for instance, the Frontex Executive Director bears an internal obligation to supervise the conduct of the teams deployed by the agency.[273] It is external when the supervisor is not part of the body that is supervised: for instance, the Commission bears an external obligation to supervise the migration management support teams (MMST) deployed to the EU hotspots.[274] Given that this study's main interest lies in allocating responsibility in contexts of administrative cooperation, its primary focus lies on external supervision.[275]

As regards supervisory practices, it must first be recalled that supervision encompasses practices of review and of correction. Accordingly, all four areas of conduct identified above, namely policy making, funding, operational supervision and monitoring can, in some sense and to some extent, serve to exercise supervision. For the purpose of this study, however, the latter two are of particular relevance. This is because the supervisory effect of policy making and funding is rather incidental,[276] whereas operational supervision and monitoring serve first and foremost exercise supervision.[277]

a *Operational Supervision as a Consolidated Form of Supervision*

Operational supervision is defined here as the more consolidated or conventional form of supervision – to be distinguished from monitoring as a more recently emerging form of supervision. In terms of concrete practices, a whole range of practices can qualify as operational supervision, from conducting an informal discussion to imposing conditionalities to initiating an infringement procedure.[278]

273 Art. 106 para 4 lit. b, j, l Frontex Regulation.

274 Art. 40 para 3 Frontex Regulation, Art. 21 para 2 EUAA Regulation; see further chapter 2, 1.2.

275 Internal supervision, however, is also relevant, especially in the context of attribution, see chapter 4, 2.2.

276 With the exception of instruments such as the Conditionality Regulation.

277 In more detail Catharina Ziebritzki, *The EU's Responsibility in the Asylum Administration* (fn. 56), p. 100 et seq.

278 For supervision via the infringement procedure see only Stine Andersen, *The Enforcement of EU Law: The Role of the European Commission*, Oxford University Press 2013; Kim Lane Scheppele, Dimitry Vladimirovich Kochenov, Barbara

This broad functional definition of operational supervision notwithstanding, two particularly common categories can be distinguished, namely coordinating the supervisees' conduct and ensuring its legality. Coordination becomes relevant, in particular, when one actor is entrusted with supervising several actors who cooperate with each other. In this case, ensuring the legality of the supervisees' conduct almost necessarily requires coordination of their cooperation. In the context at hand, agencification and inter-agency cooperation are required to coordinate the work of the growing number of actors. Given that the agencies themselves are able to coordinate their work only to a limited extent, especially because no agency disposes of all relevant information, it only seems consequential to assign the task of coordination to the Commission.[279] Ensuring legality, in turn, is understood here as a supervisory practice that primarily aims to guarantee that the conduct of either one or several supervisees complies with the applicable legal standard. While this understanding is disputed, with some differentiating enforcement from supervision,[280] it is argued here that enforcement activities clearly serve to ensure the legality of the supervisee's conduct and hence qualify as supervision. In the context at hand, the Commission's recommendations to remedy shortcomings identified through the EUAA's monitoring mechanism, for instance, qualify as a means to ensure the legality of the agency's conduct.[281]

A further distinction can be made between soft and hard forms of enforcement. Typically, the supervisor's choice between soft and hard measures will depend on its relation to the supervisee. For instance, when the supervisor depends on cooperation on the part of the supervisee or when its political and financial position suffices to make the supervisee comply, it is more likely to refrain from hard enforcement.[282] In the context

Grabowska-Moroz, „EU Values Are Law, after All: Enforcing EU Values through Systemic Infringement Actions by the European Commission and the Member States of the European Union", *Yearbook of European Law* 39 (2020), p. 2-21.

279 See Art. 40 para 2, para 3 Frontex Regulation, Art. 21 para 2 EUAA Regulation; further on the Commission's obligation to coordinate see chapter 2, 2.2.

280 Alberto Gil Ibáñez, *The Administrative Supervision and Enforcement in EC Law* (fn. 271), p. 16–17, however, differentiates supervision and enforcement and understands both as means to 'ensure the application of EC law'.

281 Art. 14 para 5 to 8 EUAA Regulation.

282 As a consequence, soft law is both a means of enforcement and enforced itself, see Oana Ştefan, „Soft Law and the Enforcement of EU Law", in András Jakab, Dimitry Kochenov (ed.), *The Enforcement of EU Law and Values: Ensuring Member States' Compliance*, Oxford University Press 2017, p. 202 with reference to Francis Snyder,

of the EU hotspot administration, the Commission depends on the host member state's willingness to cooperate and, therefore, largely refrains from making use of hard means of enforcement, such as, for instance, initiating an infringement procedure. Instead, the Commission mainly relies on non-formally binding guidelines to the relevant national authorities and agencies.[283]

This being said, it must be stressed that the distinction between supervision and support is not clear-cut. Some forms of cooperation are difficult to classify and could fall into either category. In the EU hotspots, the Commission's practice has evolved over time from operational supervision towards elements of operational support. Whereas the Commission has mainly exercised its supervisory obligations through coordination since 2016, it became obvious in 2021 that the Commission has structurally failed to ensure compliance with EU law. As a consequence, the Commission created the EU hotspot administration 2.0 and became more involved at the operational level.[284]

On this basis, the question of allocating responsibility can be addressed, albeit here, only in a prospective manner. Clearly, the supervisee, here the member state, is itself responsible for its own misconduct. The crucial question, then, is whether the supervisor, here in the EU, bears legal responsibility, too. While this will be analysed in detail in the following chapters, two general arguments can be made here already. First, and for the purpose of doctrinal precision, one should realise that the supervisor's responsibility can be construed in two different ways: either as a breach of the supervisory obligation as such or as a breach of the rule that the supervisee has violated. While the former alternative requires a more precise definition of what exactly the relevant supervisory obligation consists of and whether that obligation has been breached at all, the latter alternative raises intricate questions of causation.[285] Second, and based on general supervision doctrine, the argument that 'a supervising authority cannot bear legal responsibility because it does nothing but supervise' cannot persist.

„The Effectiveness of European Community Law: Institutions, Processes, Tools and Techniques", *The Modern Law Review* 56 (1993), p. 19-54.

283 This is deemed sufficient because the Commission's political and budgetary authority entails that its informal guidelines are usually complied with, see below 4.3 and chapter 2.

284 E.g. through creating a dedicated Task Force and a special Steering Committee, see chapter 2, 2.6.

285 See chapter 5.

As will be set out in more detail in the following chapters, it depends on a whole range of factors whether or not the supervisor bears legal responsibility for the violation of individual rights that occur as a result of misconduct on the part of the supervisor.[286]

b *Monitoring as an Emerging Form of Supervision*

As mentioned above, EU secondary law increasingly entrusts the agencies and the Commission with 'monitoring'.[287] The most prominent example is probably the so-called vulnerability assessment of Frontex and the monitoring mechanism of the EUAA. The aim of these mechanisms is for the agencies to assess the overall functioning of the border control and asylum administrations of the member states, in particular with regard to their capacity and readiness to face present and upcoming challenges.[288] Similarly, the Commission's monitoring tasks oblige it to gather information on and evaluate the overall development of the asylum system.[289]

In terms of general European administrative law, however, the notion of monitoring remains vague. While monitoring is generally understood to mean a sort of 'keeping track' of all relevant developments, identifying shortcomings, and 'following up' with the relevant stakeholders, the scope of the activity is not legally defined.[290] In particular, general doctrine does not clarify whether monitoring is a form of supervision, what the legal consequences are if a monitoring body fails to comply with its obligations, and whether monitoring-related measures impose legal obligations on the

286 See chapter 4 and 5.

287 The Frontex Regulation, for instance, refers 122 times to 'monitor' or 'monitoring'. See in more detail on this development Evangelia (Lilian) Tsourdi, „Monitoring and Steering through FRONTEX and EASO 2.0" (fn. 181); David Fernández-Rojo, *EU Migration Agencies* (fn. 23), p. 102–104; Herbert Rosenfeldt, *Frontex im Zentrum der Europäischen Grenz- und Küstenwache* (fn. 266), p. 64–67.

288 Art. 32 Frontex Regulation; Art. 14, 15 EUAA Regulation.

289 Art. 42 para 10 Frontex Regulation; Art. 14, 15 EUAA on cooperation between the agency and the Commission in the context of monitoring. Note that the Commission's monitoring role will be enhanced with the reform proposals, see only Art. 79 of the Regulation (EU) 2024/1351 of the European Parliament and of the Council of 14 May 2024 on asylum and migration management, amending Regulations (EU) 2021/1147 and (EU) 2021/1060 and repealing Regulation (EU) No 604/2013 (hereinafter: AMM Regulation).

290 Note that Evangelia (Lilian) Tsourdi, „Monitoring and Steering through FRONTEX and EASO 2.0" (fn. 181) speaks of 'monitoring-like' functions.

monitored body. This section is, hence, necessarily tentative in nature and developed inductively from the specific context of the asylum system.[291]

This being said, monitoring is defined, for the purpose of this study, as a reduced form of supervision. Unlike in the case of operational supervision, the monitoring body is not legally responsible for misconduct by the monitored body but only for a breach of its own monitoring obligations as such. This arguably follows from the regulatory structure of monitoring as conceived in EU asylum law. Monitoring obligations are generally designed to consist of a primary and a secondary obligation. The primary obligation of the monitoring body is to review the performance of the monitored body and to identify shortcomings. In case of shortcomings, the monitoring body has a secondary obligation to initiate an inter-administrative procedure vis-à-vis the monitored body, the goal of which is for the monitored body itself to correct its performance.

Due to their regulatory structure, monitoring obligations encompass the issuance of binding or non-binding measures. The primary aim of detecting shortcomings can largely be achieved through non-formally binding measures. When it comes to the secondary aim of inducing the monitored body to remedy these shortcomings, however, legal bindingness is, of course, a very useful tool. Accordingly, EU asylum law usually designs the inter-administrative monitoring procedure as consisting of several escalation steps, with non-binding measures at the beginning, followed by increasingly binding measures. The regulatory structure of monitoring obligations is well illustrated with Frontex's vulnerability assessment or the EUAA's monitoring mechanism.[292] In the first place, the agency is obliged to comprehensively review the member states' conduct. If the agency identifies shortcomings, its secondary obligation to conduct an inter-administrative procedure is activated, with the initial step being that the Executive Director shall make a recommendation to the member state concerned. If the member state fails to comply with this recommendation, the so-called 'follow-up' procedure is initiated.[293] This procedure, which involves the agency's Management Board, the Commission and the Council, consists of several escalation steps, the last option being to legally oblige the member

291 While this comes with the opportunity to further develop the general doctrine, the question of a possible generalisation is explicitly left open here.

292 Art. 32 Frontex Regulation; Art. 14, 15 EUAA Regulation.

293 Note 'following up' is even less defined than 'monitoring'.

state to adopt certain measures and to cooperate with the respective agency.[294]

As regards the difference between operational supervision and monitoring, it is key to realise that a monitoring body has, despite the potentially legally binding nature of its instructions, no way of actually ensuring that the monitored body corrects its performance. For instance, even when the respective agency's Executive Director or the Commission adopt a legally-binding decision, the concerned member state cannot be forced to comply therewith.[295] Unlike in the case of 'true' supervision, where the supervising authority can, as a last resort, enforce EU law by hard means, this is not possible in the case of monitoring. Therefore, it is argued here that a monitoring body is, in principle, responsible only for the breach of its own obligations.

Consequently, monitoring is, per se, external in nature, i.e., the monitoring body is always distinct from the monitored body.[296] The wording of the Frontex and the EUAA Regulation, however, is sometimes misleading on this point. This is clearly illustrated by Frontex's obligation to ensure that operational plans are correctly implemented: Although the Regulation refers to the obligation of the coordinating officer and the fundamental rights monitors to 'monitor' the correct implementation of the operational plan, including compliance with fundamental rights,[297] it is clear from the Regulation itself that this obligation actually requires operational supervision. For the Regulation requires that the Executive Director 'ensure' the correct implementation of operational plans and withdraw the agency's support if fundamental rights are seriously and persistently violated,[298] which implies that the agency itself bears legal responsibility for its involvement in the incorrect implementation of operational plans.

This being said, this study in the following focuses on operational supervision as defined here. One reason for this is that determining the EU's legal responsibility for breaches of its monitoring obligations would remain a

294 The escalation options differ between the EUAA and Frontex, see Art. 14 para 5 to 8 EUAA Regulation vs Art. 32 para 9 to 11, Art. 42 Frontex Regulation.

295 This confirms that the element of cooperation is never absent in the context of the integrated administration, see above fn. 27 et seq.

296 To the extent that so designated 'monitoring' obligations are internal, the monitoring body is actually responsible for unlawful conduct of the monitored body, which means that internal monitoring is simply tantamount to internal operational supervision.

297 Art. 44 para 3 lit b Frontex Regulation.

298 Art. 106 para 4 lit. j, Art. 46 para 3 and 4 Frontex Regulation.

rather hypothetical endeavour. The monitoring mechanism foreseen in the EUAA Regulation has not yet been established. In any case, failures by the agencies to adequately exercise their monitoring obligations are extremely difficult to prove. Another reason for the focus on supervision is that this study is concerned with the relationship between the EU and individuals. A failure of an EU body to adequately monitor a member state, however, affects individuals only indirectly. While a similar difficulty, of course, also arises in the context of supervisory obligations, the link between a breach of the EU's obligations and a violation of individual rights is arguably even more difficult to establish in the case of monitoring obligations than in the case of supervisory obligations. Therefore, it makes sense for this study to focus on the EU's responsibility for breaches in the context of operational supervision. On this basis, subsequent studies – to be conducted after the establishment of the EUAA mechanism – could then examine whether and how individuals can hold the EU responsible for breaches of its monitoring obligations.

4.3 'Determining Without Deciding'

Against the background of what has been presented throughout this chapter, it becomes clear that the EU's mode of operation – in the general context of the European asylum administration and in the specific context of the EU hotspot administration – can be described as 'determining without deciding'.[299] The notion of 'determining without deciding' is used here to describe that the EU's conduct, despite its lack of formal bindingsness, has a strong normative effect. From a strictly formal perspective, the EU merely provides non-formally binding support and supervision. The binding administrative decision towards the individual is always issued by a member state, so that the EU, at least formally, does not cross the line drawn by traditional sovereignty concerns. De facto, however, the EU guides and steers the course of the asylum administration. Despite the lack of formal bindingness, the EU prescribes crisis responses and policies, funds large parts of the asylum system, including the EU hotspot administration, and

299 This will facilitate the analysis in the following chapter. In more detail on 'determining without deciding' as a feature of the European asylum administration more generally see Catharina Ziebritzki, *The EU's Responsibility in the Asylum Administration* (fn. 56), p. 124 et seq.

is largely responsible for the supervision of its legality. Insofar as the EU is involved at the operational level, it even determines the outcome of individual asylum procedures.[300] In sum, the EU thus trumps its de jure weakness with its de facto strength.

a *Factual Conduct as a Strategy to Evade Judicial Review*

As argued above, informal regulation is particularly salient in times of crisis. While informalisation during a crisis can be traced back to a whole range of factors, two appear especially important in the context at hand.[301] First, EU soft law allows for more flexibility and faster reactions than formal legislation. Administrative bodies are typically quicker to react than legislative bodies, and informal rules allow to circumvent legislative procedures. As a result, the EU tends to rely on informal means, in particular when a situation of crisis seems to dictate the swift achievement of policy outcomes or in areas where it is especially difficult to reach a political agreement.[302] Second, EU soft law apparently has a relatively strong normative effect –

300 See chapter 2, 1.3.

301 See only Eva Kassoti, Narin Idriz, „The Informalisation of the EU's External Action in the Field of Migration and Asylum", in Eva Kassoti, Narin Idriz (ed.), *The Informalisation of the EU's External Action in the Field of Migration and Asylum*, Springer 2022, p. 1-12; Juan Santos Vara, Laura Pascual Matellám, „The Informalization of EU Return Policy: A Change of Paradigm in Migration Cooperation with Third Countries?", in Eva Kassoti, Narin Idriz (ed.), *The Informalisation of the EU's External Action in the Field of Migration and Asylum*, Springer 2022, p. 37–52; Sergio Carrera, „The 20 years anniversary of the Tampere programme: Securitization, intergovernmentalism and informalization", *Maastricht Journal of European and Comparative Law* 27 (2020), p. 3-9. For the period prior to 2015 see Maarten Vink, Claudia Engelmann, „Informal European Asylum Governance in an International Context" (fn. 33).

302 Oana Ştefan, „COVID-19 Soft Law: Voluminous, Effective, Legitimate? A Research Agenda", *European Papers* 5 (3 June 2020), p. 663–670, p. 663–665. Note the European Parliament, Working Document on Institutional and Legal Implications of the Use of 'Soft Law' Instruments, 14 February 2007, PE 384.581 v02–00, p. 6: 'Where the Community has legislative competence but the political will seems to be lacking to introduce legislation, use of soft law is liable to circumvent the influence of the other (democratic) instruments and may flow out the principles of democracy and legality.'.

especially in times of crisis.[303] This could be due to the fact that member states appear more likely to adopt EU instructions when they are administratively overburdened and politically disoriented.[304] In sum, informal rules combine swift policy reaction, circumvention of formal legislative procedures and relatively effective governance. As such, informal rules were particularly well suited to respond to the immediate crisis context of 2015: the situation required a quick response at the EU level, the EU legislator proved largely unable to reach an agreement, and national administrations, by and large, considered informal EU rules as the relevant standard.[305] Seen from this perspective, it cannot be surprising that the European Commission decided to address the 2015 crisis, insofar as the immediate response was concerned, mainly on the basis of informal regulation.

From a rule of law perspective, however, the EU's strategy of 'determining without deciding' is deeply problematic. One central problem is that 'determining without deciding' makes it overly difficult, and in many cases practically impossible, for concerned individuals to access judicial review against the EU. This has two main reasons. The first lies in the lack of legal bindingness. Until today, EU procedural law largely builds on the assumption that public authority manifests itself in formally-binding decisions. As a result, factual conduct continues to largely escape judicial review before the CJEU.[306] The second reason lies in the structure of administrative cooperation as such. The involvement of multiple actors in one procedure, eventually resulting in a violation of rights, makes it difficult to establish which actor bears legal responsibility.[307] Thus, judicial review is difficult in

303 Examples range from environmental law over public procurement to tax law. For examples see Linda Senden, „Soft Post-Legislative Rulemaking: A Time for More Stringent Control", *European Law Journal* 19 (2013), p. 57-75, p. 60.

304 This hypothesis is based on the concept of 'weak member states' developed by Michael Ioannidis, „Weak Members and the Enforcement of EU Law", in András Jakab, Dimitry Kochenov (ed.), *The Enforcement of EU Law and Values. Ensuring Member States' Compliance*, Oxford University Press 2017, p. 476-492, and requires further research.

305 Implementation deficits are not a counterargument because formally binding EU legislation was implemented in a deficient manner, too.

306 Further Timo Rademacher, *Realakte im Rechtsschutzsystem der Europäischen Union* (fn. 263); Timo Rademacher, „Factual Administrative Conduct and Judicial Review in EU Law", *European Review of Public Law* 30 (2017), p. 399–435.

307 For an analysis focusing on the issues related to the multitude of involved actors see Melanie Fink, *Frontex and Human Rights* (fn. 11).

the context of the integrated administration per se, even when the measures at stake are formally-binding.[308]

In the context of the European asylum administration, the combination of both factors – i.e. factual conduct and administrative cooperation – results in severely deficient legal protection against EU bodies. Although EU bodies have been cooperating closely with national authorities and relying mainly on non-formally binding conduct for almost a decade now, and although it is obvious that the EU's policies result in large-scale fundamental rights violations, EU bodies have so far not been held responsible for any of their informal measures before a court.[309] There have been only a few proceedings before the European Ombudsman, and most of these have been unsuccessful.[310] Complaints before international courts[311] or complaints bodies have been even rarer and even less successful.[312] Moreover, scholarship largely adopts an almost apologetic approach and concludes that the law as it currently stands does simply not provide for a remedy which would allow the involved EU bodies to be held responsible in a quasi-judicial forum or a court.[313] Scholars largely conclude that the EU legal protection system is not yet prepared to adequately deal with the challenges that arise when EU bodies operate at the operational level, let alone in an area that is particularly sensitive to fundamental rights.[314]

308 See only Alexander Türk, „Judicial review of integrated administration in the EU", in Herwig Hofmann, Alexander Türk (ed.), *Legal Challenges in EU Administrative Law: Towards an Integrated Administration*, Edward Elgar 2009, p. 218–256.

309 For a recent attempt see CJEU, General Court (Sixth Chamber), judgement of 6 September 2023, WS et al v Frontex, T-600/21.

310 In more detail on the role of the European Ombudsperson see chapter 3, 1.

311 For a recent attempt see Omer Shatz and Juan Branco, *EU Migration Policies in the Central Mediterranean and Libya (2014–2019). Communication to the Office of the Prosecutor of the International Criminal Court Pursuant to the Article 15 of the Rome Statute* (The Hague, 2019), https://www.statewatch.org/news/2019/jun/eu-icc-case-EU-Migration-Policies.pdf.

312 On the potential of international complaint bodies, however, see Başak Çalı, Cathryn Costello, Stewart Cunningham, „Hard Protection through Soft Courts? Non-Refoulement before the United Nations Treaty Bodies", *German Law Journal* 21 (2020), p. 355–384.

313 See introduction, fn. 64.

314 Mariolina Eliantonio, Nikos Vogiatzis, „Judicial and Extra-Judicial Challenges in the EU Multi- and Cross-Level Administrative Framework", *German Law Journal* 22 (2021), p. 315–324, p. 315–316 who base their argument on the 'premise that there may be decisions affecting natural and legal persons which cannot be easily reviewed judicially'. For further references see introduction, 5.

b *Ensuring Judicial Review by Unfolding the Potential of EU Constitutional Law*

The most obvious occasion to address these shortcomings in judicial protection against the EU would have been the CEAS reform. Developed in the aftermath of the 2015 crisis and adopted in several legislative steps between 2016 and 2024, the reform is based on the experience of the crisis and could have ensured the fundamental right to effective legal protection, for instance, by defining the EU's administrative competences more clearly, by creating a tailor-made remedy, or by writing into secondary law the doctrine that 'de facto' binding conduct is subject to judicial review. Reform proposals in this direction, however, would have required to define compliance with EU constitutional law as a central political objective – when instead, reducing the number of asylum seekers in the EU was defined as the main political aim.[315] Accordingly, neither the reformed Frontex Regulation nor the EUAA Regulation substantially improves the definition of the agencies' and the Commission's competences. The concept of 'shared responsibility' under the Frontex Regulation, while promising, falls short of its ambition, as it does not define how responsibility is shared in concrete terms between member states and the agency[316] and defines Frontex's responsibility in a circular manner.[317] Concerning judicial protection, the mentioned Regulation almost seem to conceptualise non-judicial accountability mechanisms as a substitute.[318] The remaining reform instruments are also in no way aimed at improving legal protection against the EU. On the contrary, the new Regulations only further restrict judicial protection against the member states, especially in border procedures and similarly

315 See fn. 2.

316 Art 7 para 1 Frontex Regulation provides that 'the European Border and Coast Guard shall implement European integrated border management as a shared responsibility of the Agency and of the national authorities responsible for border management, including coast guards to the extent that they carry out maritime border surveillance operations and any other border control tasks. Member States shall retain primary responsibility for the management of their sections of the external borders.' However, it remains unclear what primary responsibility, sole responsibility or shared responsibility entails in concrete terms.

317 Art. 7 para 4 Frontex Regulation in its last sentence provides that 'the Agency shall be fully responsible and accountable for any decision it takes and for any activity for which it is solely responsible under this Regulation.' In essence, this amounts to stating that the agency is responsible when it is responsible.

318 Thereby falling short of the constitutional standard, see chapter 3, 1.

precarious situations, and leave judicial protection against the EU largely unregulated.

Against this background, it is argued here that – for a proposal to be realistic and go beyond scholarly advocacy – the issue must be addressed at the level of EU primary law. Given that the EU legal protection system lacks a tailor-made remedy, this will require making creative use of the possibilities offered by the Treaties.

In doing so, the guiding question will not so much be whether but rather how judicial protection against the EU can be ensured. The key point here is that EU constitutional law requires that all public conduct, including factual conduct, is subject to judicial review. This follows from two aspects of the rule of law.[319] First, the fundamental right to an effective judicial remedy enshrined in Art. 47 ChFR guarantees that any conduct of EU bodies is subject to legal review.[320] Second, the effectiveness or *effet utile* of EU law requires that individuals can enforce their individual rights,[321] a mechanism that applies not only to member states but also to the EU, and that becomes particularly relevant in case of systemic deficiencies.[322] Seen from this perspective, the lack of judicial protection against EU bodies not only endangers the individual rights of concerned asylum seekers but also puts at risk the very nature of the Union as a community based on the rule of law. Finding ways to guarantee judicial protection against the EU's factual conduct is, hence, not a scholarly luxury but a very basic work of aligning administrative practice to constitutional requirements.

The process of finding ways to ensure judicial protection against the EU can hence be seen as a kind of 'doctrinal catch-up'. As will be argued in the following chapters, the EU legal protection system still lags behind administrative reality in the sense that those procedures that were traditionally

319 In detail on this argument see Catharina Ziebritzki, *The EU's Responsibility in the Asylum Administration* (fn. 56), p. 190 et seq.

320 CJEU, Court, judgement of 23 April 1986, Parti écologiste 'Les Verts' v European Parliament, 294/83, para 23; CJEU, Court, judgement of 25 July 2002, Unión de Pequeños Agricultores v Council of the European Union, C-50/00 P, para 38–39: '[T]he European Community is, however, a community based on the rule of law in which its institutions are subject to judicial review of the computability of their acts with the Treaty and with the general principles of law which include fundamental rights. Individuals are therefore entitled to effective judicial protection (...)'.

321 CJEU, Court, judgement of 5 February 1963, Van Gend & Loos, 26/62, p. 3, 12.

322 Armin von Bogdandy, Michael Ioannidis, „Systemic Deficiency in the Rule of Law: What it is, what has to be done, what can be done", *Common Market Law Review* 51 (2014), p. 59–96, p. 63.

central to ensuring judicial review largely fail to ensure review of the EU's 'determining without deciding' measures. Based on this insight, a thorough review of the EU legal protection system will show that the most suitable way to hold the EU accountable before court is through EU liability law.[323]

Put differently, the idea underlying this study is to make use of the rule of law as enshrined in Art. 2 TEU to counter problematic side-effects of administrative integration. As such, the approach of this study can also be described as unfolding or releasing the transformative potential inherent in EU constitutional law.

323 See chapter 3.

Chapter 2: The Integrated EU Hotspot Administration

The second chapter presents the operation of the integrated EU hotspot administration. In line with the aim of this study, the focus lies on activities of EU agencies and the European Commission. To get a clear picture of their role, a distinction is made between an operational level and a supervisory level. The first section sets out the EU's role at the operational level. Here, the competence to issue individual decisions lies with the host member state, while the EU's role is de jure limited to providing support (1).[1] The second section turns to the supervisory level, where the European Commission itself is in charge of coordinating and monitoring while the host member state provides support. The analysis shows that EU bodies determine the course of the relevant procedures without issuing binding administrative decisions: the EU hotspot administration thus clearly reflects the EU's mode to 'determine without deciding' (2).[2] The third section shows that the EU hotspot administration is systemically deficient. Fundamental rights of asylum seekers, including reception-related rights such as Art. 4, 6 ChFR and procedure-related rights such as Art. 41 ChFR, are violated on a regular basis. As the EU Fundamental Rights agency aptly put it, processing asylum claims in remote border locations comes with 'in-built deficiencies' so the EU hotspot approach 'creates fundamental rights challenges that appear almost unsurmountable' (3).[3] On this basis, and with a view to determining the EU's legal responsibility, the fourth section identifies the relevant types of misconduct on the part of the agencies and the Commission (4). The

1 On the basis of EU secondary law as it currently stands. EU primary law would allow for broader competences of EU agencies, see Catharina Ziebritzki, *The EU's Responsibility in the Asylum Administration. Administrative Integration, Judicial Protection and the Case of the EU Hotspots,* Dissertation at Frankfurt University, Law Department, January 2024, p. 117 et seq.

2 See chapter 1, 4.3.

3 European Union Agency for Fundamental Rights, Opinion 3/2019, Update of the 2016 Opinion on fundamental rights in the 'hotspots' set up in Greece and Italy, 4 March 2019, https://fra.europa.eu/en/publication/2019/update-2016-fra-opinion-fundamental-rights-hotspots-set-greece-and-italy (hereinafter: FRA, Opinion EU Hotspots 2019), p. 7: 'The processing of asylum claims in facilities are borders, particularly when these facilities are in relatively remote locations, although *per se* not unlawful, brings along in-built deficiencies. As almost three years of experience in Greece shows, this approach creates fundamental rights challenges that appear almost unsurmountable.'.

chapter closes by drawing conclusions on the EU's responsibility, thereby preparing the ground for the doctrinal analysis in the following chapters (5).

1 Operational Level

Between 2015 and 2021, roughly half of the staff operating in the EU hotspots were deployed by EU agencies.[4] These figures reflect the actual influence of Frontex and the EUAA clearer than a glance at their respective Regulation. While the Regulations limit the agencies to mere support, their support in practice is so considerable that Frontex and the EUAA effectively determine the course of the administration. As the analysis will show, the agencies issue recommendations and opinions in critical areas, and national authorities – even though not legally obliged to do so – routinely adopt these recommendations.[5]

1.1 A Multitude of Actors

To get a clear picture of the EU hotspot administration, it is necessary to start with a brief overview of all actors involved. The first type of actors are EU bodies. These include the European Commission and several EU agen-

4 FRA, Opinion EU Hotspots 2019 (fn. 3), p. 19 reporting that the operational agencies were 'significantly involved in the day-to-day administration'. The numbers of Frontex deployments is not publicly available. For the numbers of the EUAA's deployments of 2017 and 2018 see David Fernández-Rojo, *EU Migration Agencies. The Operation and Cooperation of FRONTEX, EASO and EUROPOL*, Edward Elgar 2021, p. 150–151; for 2019 to 2022 see the relevant Operational Plans, all availbale at: https://euaa.europa.eu/archive-of-operations?field_operation_year_value=2021&field_member_state_value=Greece&field_operation_type_value=All.

5 This chapter is limited to the argument that empirical data or the concerned EU bodies' own statements suggest that Greek authorities usually adopt the EU's non-formally binding recommendations and guidelines. On the basis, it will be argued in the fifth chapter that there is a causal link in the sense that the EU's non-formally binding conduct de facto predetermines the national authorities' decisions. As regards the compliance rate, it must be noted already here that the fact that not all non-formally binding acts are followed by Greece does not weaken the argument because legally binding acts do not entail a full compliance rate either, as extremely high non-compliance rates in the asylum system clearly confirm.

cies, namely the EUAA, Frontex, Europol,[6] and the Fundamental Rights Agency (FRA). As will be set out in more detail below, these agencies provide comprehensive support to national authorities concerning both camp management and asylum procedures and, to this end, cooperate closely with national authorities but also among themselves. The Commission, in turn, is charged with coordinating and supervising the entire construct of the EU hotspot administration.

Secondly, authorities of the host member state are involved. In Greece, these include the First Reception Service (RIS), the Asylum Service (GAS), the Hellenic Police, the Hellenic Army, and the Hellenic Centre for Disease Control and Prevention (KEELPNO). Out of these, the First Reception Service and the Asylum Service, which were created with the reforms of April 2016 and 2011, respectively,[7] are of central importance. In principle, the First Reception Service is responsible for camp management, and the Asylum Service is responsible for conducting the relevant procedures. The Hellenic Police, in turn, was in charge of asylum matters before the April 2016 reform and is since responsible mainly for matters related to first registration, camp security and deportation.[8] The Army has only temporarily been charged with camp management in the immediate crisis context.[9] The Hellenic Centre for Disease Control and Prevention has always had a rather marginal role, remarkably even during the outbreak of the Covid-19 pandemic.[10]

---

6 Note that Europol's involvement is particularly obscure, as Regulation (EU) 2016/794 of the European Parliament and of the Council of 11 May 2016 on the European Union Agency for Law Enforcement Cooperation (Europol) and replacing and repealing Council Decisions 2009/371/JHA, 2009/934/JHA, 2009/935/JHA, 2009/936/JHA and 2009/968/JHA (hereinafter: Europol Regulation) does not even provide for a legal basis for the deployment of operational Europol teams, see in more detail David Fernández-Rojo, *EU Migration Agencies* (fn. 4), p. 146–148. Yet, the focus here lies on Frontex and the EUAA, which is justified because their involvment is esesential to the operation of the EU hotspot administration, as evidenced by their function and reflected in numbers of deployment.

7 Hellenic Republic, Ministry of Migration and Asylum Service, About G.A.S, https://migration.gov.gr/en/gas/plirofories/.

8 ECRE, Country Report Greece, 2020 Update, https://asylumineurope.org/reports/country/greece/, p. 48. Note that in case of mass arrivals, the Police may be charged with conducting interviews.

9 Catharina Ziebritzki, Robert Nestler, „'Hotspots' an der EU-Außengrenze. Eine rechtliche Bestandsaufnahme", *MPIL Research Paper Series (SSRN)* 17 (2017), p. 9.

10 Equal Rights Beyond Borders, Report of February 2023, Extraordinary Measures. How Greece Used the Covid-19 Pandemic as a Pretext for the Unlawful Detention

The third type of actors involved in the EU hotspot administration are international organisations, specifically the United Nations High Commissioner for Refugees (UNCHR) and the International Organisation for Migration (IOM). The UNHCR is responsible for tasks related to information provision, the protection of vulnerable groups, and specific tasks in the area of camp management. The IOM also implements the so-called voluntary return program.[11] Unlike in many non-European countries, however, neither UNHCR nor IOM is in a position to steer the course of administration. Overall, the role of international organisations is rather marginal.[12]

A fourth type of actors are private entities. These include specialised NGOs that provide assistance ranging from medical services to legal aid and a security company whose tasks include safety inside the camp and assisting the Hellenic police with measures related to the confinement of residents.[13]

Considering the sheer number of actors, it becomes comprehensible why responsibility-shifting is such a key problem. In practice, involved actors tend to shift responsibilities around even for the smallest daily tasks. This attitude is clearly reflected at the political level: whenever the existing fundamental rights violations are discussed, Greek authorities argue that either the EU or international organisations are responsible; EU bodies blame Greece and international organisations; international organisations refer to the responsibility of Greece and the EU; and so on. The result is that nothing changes. It is precisely against this background that this study seeks to entangle the EU's involvement and determine its responsibilities.

---

of Asylum Seekers in Chios, https://www.equal-rights.org/resources/publications; Equal Rights Beyond Borders, November 2020, Update of the Report of May 2020. Abandoned and Neglected. The Failure to Prepare for a Covid-19 Outbreak in the Vial Refugee Camp, https://www.equal-rights.org/resources/publications.

11 Notably in Cooperation with the Commission, see European Ombudsman, Report on (i) the inspection of the European Commission's documents and (ii) the meeting of the European Ombudsman inquiry team with representatives of the European Commission, Inspection Report 9 March 2023, Case OI/3/2022/MHZ, para 11.

12 This corresponds to the marginal role of international organisations in the asylum administration more generally.

13 Catharina Ziebritzki, Robert Nestler, „'Hotspots' an der EU-Außengrenze" (fn. 9), p. 63; United Nations Human Rights Office of the High Commissioner (OHCHR), 20 December 2019, Concerns over States contracting private security companies in migration situations, https://www.ohchr.org/en/stories/2019/12/concerns-over-states-contracting-private-security-companies-migration-situations.

1.2 The 'Migration Management Support Teams'

Both the EUAA and Frontex deploy staff in the form of so-called migration management support teams (MMST). This EU-hotspot-specific type of deployment is regulated in Art. 40 Frontex Regulation and Art. 21 EUAA Regulation. In comparison to other deployment types, MMSTs have two distinctive features. First, the teams are characterised by close inter-agency cooperation. MMSTs are composed of staff deployed by Frontex, EUAA, Europol, as well as, optionally, FRA and other EU bodies.[14] Second, and as a result, the supervisory structure of MMSTs is distinct, with the main difference to regular EUAA or Frontex teams being that responsibility for coordination and supervision ultimately lies with the European Commission.[15]

Insofar as Frontex is concerned, there is no doubt that deployments to the EU hotspots have always taken place in the specific form of the MMST. Since the adoption of the 2016 reform, Frontex could deploy its staff to EU hotspots on the basis of the then Art. 18, the predecessor of Art. 40 of the current Regulation, which is the legal basis for the deployment of MMST.

As for the EUAA, the form of deployment has long not been unequivocally clear. This is because a specific legal basis for the deployment of MMST was introduced only with Art. 21 of the 2021 EUAA reform. Formally, the earlier deployments thus took place on the basis of Art. 13 EASO Regulation, i.e. as regular asylum support teams (AST).[16] Yet, it is argued here that the earlier deployments qualified as MMST. De facto, deployed EASO staff has been working hand-in-hand with staff of the other agencies, as if they were deployed as MMST, ever since 2016.[17] In conceptual terms, EASO itself differentiated between different kinds of operational support, one of which was described as dedicated specifically to the EU hotspot

14 Art. 2 para 19 Frontex Regulation.

15 Art. 40 para 3 Frontex Regulation, Art. 21 para 2 EUAA Regulation.

16 See for instance EASO, Operating Plan to Greece 2021, 2.1; EASO, Operating Plan to Greece 2022, 5.1.

17 EASO, Standard Operating Procedures for the implementation of the border asylum procedures in the context of the EU-Turkey Statement 18/03/2016, Version of 19 June 2019 (redacted), available at: https://fragdenstaat.de/anfrage/standard-operating-procedures-for-the-implementation-of-the-border-asylum-procedures/425864/anhang/SOPS_border_en_jointEASO_August16_190624redacted.pdf (hereinafter: SoP EU-Hotspots June 2019); interviews with EASO Union Contact Point conducted on 13 December 2019 and on 19 February 2021 (introduction, fn. 102).

approach.[18] Furthermore, and this is decisive, the Commission has, as a matter of fact, exercised its supervision also over EASO staff working in the EU hotspots, thereby implicitly considering them as part of the MMST. Therefore, it would have been formally correct to cite as a legal basis for the earlier deployments Art. 13 EASO Regulation in conjunction with Art. 18 of the former or Art. 40 of the 2019 Frontex Regulation.[19]

To disentangle the responsibilities of the agencies in the EU hotspot administration, it is indispensable to understand who decides what with regard to the MMSTs' operations. To get a clear picture, it must first be recalled that any teams deployed by Frontex or the EUAA consist of different types of staff.[20] The first type is national officers, often referred to as national experts, who are deployed for a short term or seconded for a long term to the agencies by the border guard or the asylum authority of the participating member states. The second type is statutory staff, i.e. the respective agency's own personnel. The third type, which is relevant only in the case of the EUAA, is the so-called interim staff, i.e. contracted staff that is hired to cover shortages.[21] Crucially, all types of MMST staff are subject to the same supervision structure. This also applies to seconded or deployed staff because, although they retain their status as civil servants of the home member state, that state cannot control their daily administrative activities.

The supervisory structure for MMST consists of two levels, with supervision at a first level resting with the host member state and the agency and at a second level with the Commission.[22] At the first level, the dual supervision is designed in a manner that differentiates between detailed

---

18 EASO, Work Programme 2016, Rev. 2, March 2016, p. 10–11; EASO, Operational Support, Types of Operations, available online: https://www.easo.europa.eu/operatio nal-support/types-operations (last accessed 2 August 2018).

19 Art. 13 EASO Regulation formulated the mandate of the asylum support teams so broadly that close cooperation with other agencies is not excluded, as long as this is provided for in the OP.

20 Art. 19 para 1 EUAA Regulation; formerly Art. 15, 16, 38 EASO Regulation; Art. 2 para 15, para 21, 22 Frontex Regulation.

21 According to interviews with EASO Union Contact Point conducted on 13 December 2019 and on 19 February 2021 (introduction, fn. 102), EASO has between 2019 and 2021 to an increasing extent relied on interim staff because member states' contributions were insufficient. EASO, Operating Plan to Greece, 6.3. differentiates in more detail and refers to six types of staff.

22 See Art. 21 EUAA Regulation; Art. 40 Frontex Regulation. In more detail on the Commission's supervisory role see below 2.

and general instructions. While the host member state issues detailed operations concerning daily operations, the agency ensures general compliance with EU law. On the part of the member state, the person in charge is determined by the responsible national authority. On the part of the agency, the person in charge is the coordinating officer, previously referred to as Union Contact Point under the EASO Regulation.[23] The coordinating officer represents the agency in the host member state and is responsible for the correct implementation of the Operational Plan, which includes ensuring that the agency generally complies with EU law. As the coordinating officer, in turn, is appointed by the Executive Director and reports to them, the supervisory competence ultimately lies with the Executive Director.[24] At the second level, supervision lies with the European Commission. As the Commission's supervisory obligations enshrined in Art. 40 para 3 Frontex and Art. 21 para 2 EUAA Regulation will be analysed in more detail below; suffice to note here that the scope of supervision differs between procedure-related and reception-related conduct.[25]

1.3 The Agencies' Procedure-Related Support

The distinction between procedure-related and reception-related conduct is key to conceptualising the MMSTs' operational support. As regards, first, conduct related to asylum and return procedures in the EU hotspots, the scope of support is aptly described as the agencies making full use of the competence limits set by the Treaties. The agencies respect traditional sovereignty concerns in the manner that they neither issue formal decisions towards individuals nor carry out deportations on their own. Yet, they provide extensive support in almost every procedural step, which results in the EU hotspot procedure qualifying as a composite administrative procedure.

23 Given the large number of staff deployed to Greece, the EUAA coordinating officer usually establishes a hierarchical system of team leaders and several mid-level coordinators under their authority, as confirmed in interviews with EASO Union Contact Point conducted on 13 December 2019 and on 19 February 2021 (introduction, fn. 102).

24 Art. 25 EUAA Regulation; formerly Art. 20 EASO Regulation; Art. 44 Frontex Regulation.

25 See below 2.3.

In order to set out the agencies' specific tasks in more detail, it is useful to go through the relevant steps of the EU hotspot procedure.[26]

a Identification and First Registration

The first procedural step takes place upon arrival of the asylum seekers to the respective island and consists of identification measures. These are carried out by the First Reception and Identification Service (RIS) and the Hellenic Police with the support of Frontex. Frontex's role here is to conduct a so-called debriefing aimed at detecting smuggling routes and, more importantly, for the purpose of this study, to register personal data.[27] More precisely, Frontex is responsible for nationality determination, age assessment, and the identification of vulnerable persons,[28] which involves the use of various methods such as verifying the authenticity of documents, visual inspection and, at least in theory, socio-psychological assessments. Frontex then communicates the determined nationality or age in a non-binding manner to national authorities, which register the person using a certain set of data.

The lack of bindingness of Frontex's recommendations notwithstanding, national authorities routinely register persons according to the data identified by Frontex.[29] For instance, if Frontex identifies a person as being minor or as being of a certain nationality, national authorities typically register the person as being of that age and of that nationality. This is crucial because, although registration may seem a minor issue at first sight, nationality and age, of course, have a fundamental impact on the entire asylum procedure. Thus, potential failures by Frontex during registration have far-reaching consequences for the concerned persons.[30]

---

26 See for a similar account of the role of Frontex, EASO and Europol in the EU hotspot procedure David Fernández-Rojo, *EU Migration Agencies* (fn. 4), p. 149–157.

27 Operating Plan to JO Poseidon 2019 (see chapter 1, fn. 157), 4.3.

28 Frontex JO Poseidon OP 2019 (fn. 27), p. 8.

29 Anecdotal evidence suggests that Frontex's recommendation is followed without further investigation in about 90 % of the cases, see interview with Commission representative 3, conducted on 16 February 2021 (introduction, fn. 102); own observation of the author (see introduction, fn. 103). Similarly, David Fernández-Rojo, *EU Migration Agencies* (fn. 4), p. 153 refers to 'Frontex' strong recommendatory powers', further p. 214–215.

30 If, for instance, a person who claims to be minor is registered as adult, this will also have the consequence that the person is not considered as eligible for family

b *Hearing and Examination of Claim*

The second step, and the centrepiece of the EU hotspot procedure, is the hearing and the subsequent examination of the claim. More precisely, the hearing consists of several elements, which are either conducted in one single interview or split up, depending on the country of origin of the concerned applicant.[31] The most important elements are the vulnerability assessment, the admissibility interview dedicated to assessing whether Türkiye is safe for the applicant, and the substantive interview dedicated to assessing whether the applicant is in need of international protection.

Since the hearing is particularly capacity-intensive, the EUAA provides extensive support in this context. The agency conducts asylum interviews and vulnerability assessments, provides interview transcripts, examines individual asylum claims, and drafts legal opinions recommending the rejection or acceptance of the claims.[32] As mentioned already, this practice clearly exceeded the agency's competences under the former EASO Regulation because it means that the agency influences individual asylum decisions; the practice has been vested with a legal basis only with the entry into force of the EUAA Regulation in 2021.[33]

The dispute on competences notwithstanding, the agency's involvement has been further intensified with the introduction of the so-called embed-

---

reunification under Art. 8 of Regulation (EU) No 604/2013 of the European Parliament and of the Council of 26 June 2013 establishing the criteria and mechanisms for determining the Member State responsible for examining an application for international protection lodged in one of the Member States by a third-country national or a stateless person (recast) (hereinafter: Dublin III Regulation). If, for instance, a person who identifies as Kuwaiti Bidoon is initially registered not as stateless, but as Iraqi national, this will have important effects on the assessment of their claim for international protection.

31 See 1.1.b.

32 SoP EU-Hotspots June 2019 (fn. 17), p. 25: 'the task of the EASO case officers during the interview is in the first place (...) to examine the claim for international protection'; European Union Agency for Fundamental Rights, Opinion on fundamental rights in the 'hotspots' set up in Greece and Italy, 29 November 2016, http://fra.europa.eu/en/publication/2018/fra-opinion-fundamental-rights-hotspots-set-greece-and-italy (hereinafter: FRA, Opinion EU Hotspots 2016), p. 17: 'Although (...) EASO is working side-by-side with colleagues from the Greek Asylum Service, EASO-deployed experts carry out the bulk of the fact-finding work for the determination of the asylum claim, thereby supporting first instance decision, which the Greek Asylum Service ultimately takes.'.

33 See chapter 1, 3.1.

ded model in 2020.[34] With this model, responsibility for daily instructions has been shifted from the agency's so-called 'team leader' to the Greek asylum service.[35] In addition, the legal opinions recommending to reject or accept the claim do no longer indicate the author, and on some islands, the opinions are not even included in the file anymore.[36] While this has made it much more difficult to identify the agency's contribution in practice, the shift towards the embedded model is of limited relevance from a legal perspective.[37] An operational shift cannot amend the internal decision-making and reporting structures as established by secondary law. In particular, the embedded model cannot absolve the coordinating officer from their responsibilities under the EUAA Regulation. Instead, the embedded model only means that the coordinating officer exercises their responsibility by delegating the day-to-day coordination to the national authority. This understanding is clearly reflected in administrative practice, as the coordinating officer still conducts quality-ensuring measures, organises coordination meetings, gives general instructions and reports to the Executive Director.[38] Ultimately, the responsibility for ensuring that the agency's staff generally complies with EU law and hence still lies with the Executive Director.

This being said the crucial point here is that in the vast majority of cases, the asylum service routinely adopts the agency's recommendation.[39] For instance, if the EUAA recommends rejecting the asylum claim of a certain applicant as inadmissible, arguing that the interview has shown that Türkiye could be considered safe for them, the Greek asylum service

34 Interviews with EASO Union Contact Point conducted on 13 December 2019 and on 19 February 2021 (introduction, fn. 102). Note that for practical reasons, the cooperation between EASO and the First Reception and Identification Service (RIS) has always been organised along the lines of the embedded model, without however being referred to as such.

35 In more detail EASO, Operating Plan to Greece 2021 (fn. 16), 5.3.

36 Interviews with EASO Union Contact Point conducted on 13 December 2019 and on 19 February 2021 (introduction, fn. 102); own observation of the author (see introduction, fn. 103).

37 From a procedural perspective, the main difference is that it has become more difficult to collect evidence for misconduct on the part of EUAA.

38 Interviews with EASO Union Contact Point conducted on 13 December 2019 and on 19 February 2021 (introduction, fn. 102).

39 Remarkably, no statistics presenting the percentage of compliance with EASO's recommendations are published, and EASO representatives do not disclose any figures either. Anecdotal evidence, collected over the past five years by the author (see introduction, fn. 103), however suggests that the Greek asylum service adopts EASO's opinion fully in about 85 % of the cases, and partly in the remaining 15 %.

will typically dismiss the claim as inadmissible without further inquiries, typically even adopting the reasoning and structure of the EUAA's recommendation.[40] This cannot surprise because the procedural arrangement necessarily requires that the national asylum service base its decision on the file compiled by the agency.[41] Furthermore, capacity constraints on the part of national authorities and the general assumption that the agency's recommendations are well-qualified contribute to the result that the agency's recommendations have a de facto binding effect.[42]

c *Administrative and Judicial Appeals*

The third procedural step, which becomes pertinent only in case of a rejection of the asylum claim at first instance, is administrative and judicial appeals. Administrative appeals can be made before the Appeals Committees. While the EUAA also assists in this second instance, the scope of its support is much more limited here.[43] Unlike in the first instance, the agency only has an auxiliary function. The so-called rapporteurs deployed by the EUAA compile files and provide country of origin information but do not make recommendations on how the individual case should be decided.[44] As a result, the influence of the EUAA at the Appeals Stage is much less concrete, which makes it, for now, very difficult to reconstruct the EU's responsibility in this context. Judicial appeals can be lodged before Greek

---

40 Equal Rights Beyond Borders, July 2021, Consequences of the EU-Turkey Statement. The Situation of Syrian Asylum Seekers on the Greek Aegean Islands, https://www.equal-rights.org/resources/publications, p. 13.

41 Based on anecdotal evidence, collected over the past five years by the author (see introduction, fn. 103), there are only a few case constellations in which, due to political disagreement between EU and national level, the asylum service systemically deviates from the agency's recommendation. Apart from these constellations, national authorities make use of their right to invite the applicant for another hearing only in very exceptional cases.

42 See in more detail chapter 5.

43 EASO, Operating Plan to Greece 2021 (fn. 16), p. 21.

44 It is telling that in the words of EASO, 'the agency, *unlike in the first instance*, is not involved in any decision-making in the second instance' (emphasis added), interviews with EASO Union Contact Point conducted on 13 December 2019 and on 19 February 2021 (introduction, fn. 102).

administrative courts.[45] In this context, EU bodies have not been involved so far.

d *Deportation Procedure*

In case of a final rejection of the asylum claim, the last step is the deportation procedure. This is where Frontex comes in again. While deportations are carried out under the competence of the national Police, Frontex provides support. Inter alia, the agency provides technical assistance such as vessels and other equipment, and supports through operational coordination, for instance by organising return flights. In addition, Frontex deploys specialised return escorts who accompany individual deportations.[46]

1.4 The Agencies' Reception-Related Support

With regard to reception conditions, the support provided by the MMST is much less comprehensive than the procedure-related support. Moreover, the focus here is on EUAA staff because Frontex has – at least according to the available information – not been entrusted with any substantial reception-related tasks so far.[47] This being said, a distinction must be made between the EUAA's support provided under the original EU hotspot approach and that provided under the EU hotspot approach 2.0.

45 In case of a rejection in second instance before the Appeals Committees, asylum seekers have, at least on paper, the possibility to initiate an annulment procedure, see ECRE, Country Report Greece, 2021 Update, https://asylumineurope.org/reports/country/greece/, p. 32. In practice, however, the annulment procedure is subject to manifold obstacles, as there is no free legal aid.

46 Frontex JO Poseidon OP 2019 (fn. 27), 4.3.9.

47 To the best of the author's knowledge. Note, however, that European Commission, Annex to the Commission Decision approving the Memorandum of Understanding between the European Commission, European Asylum Support Office, the European Border and Coast Guard Agency, Europol and the Fundamental Rights Agency, of the one part, and the Government of Hellenic Republic, of the other part, on a Joint Pilot for the establishment of a new Multi-Purpose Reception and Identification Centre in Lesvos, 2 December 2020, C(2020) 8657 final, Annex (hereinafter: MoU Joint Pilot), p. 11–12, 18–20 provides that Frontex shall provide support concerning design and planning services for the new camps, and remains unclear concerning some tasks such as provision and installation of appropriate equipment or the establishment of a reception qualify monitoring system, where reference is made only to 'agencies' in general.

Under the original approach, i.e. between 2015 and 2019, EASO's assistance mainly consisted in capacity-building and advice. This included the development of Standard Operating Procedures but also concrete tasks related to general reception, unaccompanied minors, vulnerable persons, communication and infrastructure planning.[48]

Under the EU hotspot approach 2.0, the EUAA's reception-related support has been stepped up considerably. Although the Memorandum of Understanding stresses that the enhanced assistance is 'without prejudice to the competences of the Greek authorities, e.g. for the site planning, design, construction and management' of the new camp[49], it foresees that the EUAA shall be closely involved in the development and construction of the new MP-RIC as well as in the maintenance of adequate reception conditions. Inter alia, the MoU provides that the EUAA shall support with the determination of the location of the new camp, design and planning services, provide experts, including engineers, and assist with the construction of the new camp comprising a reception facility and a closed detention centre, as well as with the provision of food and in-kind assistance to meet basic reception needs, the assessment of and adequate care for vulnerable persons, the provision of recreational and vocational training activities, and continuous information provision in the camp.[50]

Given this broad definition of the EUAA's reception-related support, it seems that the same applies here as for procedure-related support: Generally speaking, the scope of the support can be defined as making full use of the agency's competences as set in primary law.[51]

Yet, it has so far been very difficult to reconstruct the reception-related support of the EUAA as precisely as the procedural support. This is because reception-related support has just begun to increase and is not documented in files. Thus, if one wanted to analyse the EU's legal responsibility on the basis of the EUAA's reception-related support for the EU hotspots 2.0, one would first have to wait and see how the conditions in these new camps develop and then find out by means of access to documents requests to what extent exactly the EUAA provides support. For the purposes of

48 Interviews with EASO Union Contact Point conducted on 13 December 2019 and on 19 February 2021 (introduction, fn. 102).

49 MoU Joint Pilot (fn. 47), p. 1.

50 MoU Joint Pilot (fn. 47), p. 11–12, p. 18–20.

51 On the EU's administrative competences in the CEAS see in more detail Catharina Ziebritzki, *The EU's Responsibility in the Asylum Administration* (fn. 1), p. 114 et seq.

this study, however, the focus will be on the already more consolidated procedure-related support.[52]

2 Supervisory Level

At the supervisory level, the central actor is the European Commission. After the Commission had been charged with supervision in the immediate crisis context in an ad hoc manner, its obligations were subsequently consolidated in secondary law. Today, the Commission's mandate to coordinate and supervise the EU hotspot administration is enshrined in Art. 40 para 3 Frontex Regulation and Art. 21 para 2 EUAA Regulation, which must be read in light of Art. 17 para 2 TEU. As the purpose of this study requires a precise understanding of the Commission's involvement, the following provides a detailed reconstruction of its supervisory obligations and practices.

2.1 Belated Consolidation of the Commission's Supervision

The Commission's supervisory obligation is another example of an ad hoc crisis arrangement that was subsequently legalised in secondary law. As the 2015 EU hotspot approach required close operational cooperation between the host member state and several EU agencies, there was an obvious need for coordination and supervision. The Commission, as the initiator of the new policy, was the obvious candidate for this role and thus coordinated and supervised the implementation of the EU hotspot approach as of 2015. Inter alia, the Commission collected information on the ground through its deployed staff and organised meetings among the involved stakeholders to discuss and coordinate the implementation of the EU hotspot approach.[53]

The Commission's supervisory role was then reinforced with the entry into force of the EU-Türkiye Statement in March 2016. As the European Council[54] announced that the Commission would be responsible for coor-

52 See in more detail chapter 5.

53 Interview with Commission representative 4 conducted on 26 February 2021 (introduction, fn. 102).

54 Note the announcement by the Council although the Statement, according to the CJEU, was concluded by the member states, and not by the Council, see CJEU, General Court (First Chamber, Extended Composition), order of 28 February 2017, NF v European Council (EU-Turkey Statement), T-192/16.

dinating and organising the necessary structures to implement the Statement in Greece, the Commission reacted on the same day and created the new office of the EU coordinator.[55] This newly appointed EU coordinator, a Commission staff member, immediately established the European Regional Task Force (EURTF) and the Steering Committee as the central fora for coordinating the EU hotspot administration. In addition, the Commission henceforth issued regular reports on the implementation of the EU-Türkiye Statement, which also covered the implementation of the EU hotspot approach.[56] While the Commission had assumed all these tasks without a formal legal basis in the immediate crisis context, this changed in September 2016, when the reformed Frontex Regulation with its Art. 18 para 3 eventually codified pre-existing administrative practices and created a basis for the Commission's role as supervisor of the EU hotspot administration.[57]

Today, the almost identical successor provisions are enshrined in Art. 40 para 3 Frontex Regulation and Art. 21 para 2 EUAA Regulation. Both articles regulate, with only minor editorial differences in the wording, that 'the Commission shall, in cooperation with the host Member State and the relevant Union bodies, offices and agencies, establish the terms of cooperation at the hotspot area and be responsible for the coordination of the activities of the migration management support teams.' Both provisions must be read in light of the relevant recitals, respectively, providing that 'in hotspot areas, the Member States cooperate, under the coordination of the Commission, with relevant Union bodies, offices and agencies. Union bodies, offices and agencies are to operate in accordance with their respective mandates and powers. The Commission, in cooperation with the relevant Union bodies, offices, and agencies, ensures that activities in hotspot areas comply with relevant Union law.'[58]

---

55 European Commission, Press Release 18 March 2016: President Juncker appoints EU Coordinator to organise operational implementation in Greece, https://europa.eu/rapid/press-release_IP-16-942_en.htm. As the only measure of the Statement to be implemented in Greece was the return policy, the main responsibility of the EU coordinator was the coordination of the EU hotspot administration.

56 Regular reports were issued until November 2017. The reports are available at: https://ec.europa.eu/home-affairs/what-we-do/policies/european-agenda-migration/proposal-implementation-package_en (last accessed 23 March 2018).

57 Art. 18 para 3 Frontex 2016 Regulation (chapter 1, fn. 150): 'The Commission shall, in cooperation with the host Member State and the relevant agencies, establish the terms of cooperation at the hotspot area and be responsible for the coordination of the activities of the migration management support team.'.

58 Recital 55 Frontex Regulation; recital 34 EUAA Regulation.

2.2 Coordination and Ensuring Legality

The history and the wording of Art. 40 para 3 Frontex Regulation, Art. 21 para 2 EUAA Regulation clearly show that the Commission's supervisory mandate covers two aspects. The Commission has the duty, first, to coordinate the cooperation within the EU hotspot administration and, second, to ensure its legality, including compliance with fundamental rights.

As regards the first aspect, the scope of the Commission's obligation is easily clarified. Art. 40 para 3 Frontex Regulation and Art. 21 para 2 EASO Regulation are unequivocal in that the Commission is responsible for the coordination of the administrative cooperation. This includes both the coordination of inter-agency cooperation, in particular in the framework of the MMST, and vertical administrative cooperation between agencies and the host member state.[59]

The second aspect is more difficult: While recital 55 Frontex Regulation and recital 30 EUAA Regulation provide that the Commission is responsible for ensuring the legality of the EU hotpot administration,[60] that aspect is not explicitly mentioned in Art. 40 para 3 Frontex Regulation and Art. 21 para 2 EUAA Regulation. Yet, it is argued here that the wording of the legal provisions must be read in light of the relevant recitals, i.e. as meaning that the Commission is, in principle at least, responsible for ensuring the legality of the EU hotspot administration. This interpretation is supported by two main arguments.

First, the Commission itself interprets its obligations in this manner.[61] In fact, the Commission places a particular emphasis on ensuring fundamental rights compliance in the EU hotspot administration. Already in the immediate crisis context, the Commission argued that it had conducted a human rights impact assessment.[62] Since then, the Commission's supervi-

59 This understanding is clearly confirmed by recital 55, establishing that 'the member states should cooperate with the relevant Union agencies, which should act within their respective mandates and powers, under the coordination of the Commission'.

60 The German version 'sicherstellen' is as clear in this regard as the English version. The French version 'veiller', however, is less unequivocal 'veiller'.

61 European Ombudsman, Inspection Report 9 March 2023, Case OI/3/2022/MHZ (fn. 11), para 6: 'The Task Force seeks to *facilitate cooperation* with the different Greek authorities involved. It also aims to *ensure* the camps on the islands Lesvos, Chios, Samos, Leros and Kos *comply with EU standards*.' (emphasis added).

62 See European Ombudsman, 18 January 2017, Decision of the European Ombudsman in the joint inquiry into complaints 506–509–674–784–927–1381/2016/MHZ against

sory practice within the EURTF has put a particular focus on fundamental rights compliance. This is evident from the fact that the Fundamental Rights Agency (FRA) has been invited to participate permanently in the EURTF meetings.[63] Accordingly, Commission representatives explicitly emphasise that their task within the EURTF is to monitor compliance with EU law, especially with fundamental rights.[64] With the EU hotspot approach 2.0, this focus on fundamental rights has been reinforced. In fact, one of the main political objectives of the approach is to ensure that the new centres are built and managed in line with fundamental rights.[65] Consequently, Commission representatives themselves stress that their task within the newly created Steering Committee is to ensure not only coordination but also compliance with EU law, and especially with the Charter.[66]

Second, the Commission's own interpretation of its obligations under Art. 40 para 3 Frontex Regulation, Art. 21 para 2 EUAA Regulation corresponds to its duties under Art. 17 para 1 TEU. As the CJEU has consistently held, the Commission, as guardian of the Treaties, must not engage in any conduct that violates EU law or even fundamental rights.[67] In the present context, it is therefore crucial that the Commission itself forms part of the EU hotspot administration so that a failure to ensure the legality of the EU hotspot administration is necessarily tantamount to a failure to ensure the legality of its own conduct. In other words, if the Commission failed to ensure the legality of the EU hotspot administration, it would itself be

the European Commission concerning a human rights impact assessment in the context of the EU-Turkey Agreement, Case 506/2016/MHZ, para 11 to 15.

63 Interview with Commission representative 1, conducted on 12 February 2021 (introduction, fn. 102), FRA, Opinion EU Hotspots 2019 (fn. 3), p. 19; RoP-EURTF-GR, para I.1.

64 Interview with Commission representative 3 conducted on 16 February 2021 (introduction, fn. 102).

65 MoU Joint Pilot (fn. 47), p. 1: 'the swift creation of a new Multi-Purpose Reception and Identification Centre (MPRIC) on Lesvos, in line with relevant standards and Union law (...) has been outlined as a key priority'; p. 2: 'The implementation of the Joint Pilot, which is based on existing national and EU law, is setting an example (...) for a holistic approach to migration (...) ensuring respect of the EU Charter of Fundamental Rights (...)'.

66 MoU Joint Pilot (fn. 47), p. 1, 3–5; interviews with Commission representative, conducted on 26 February 2021; interview with Commission representative 5, conducted on 7 April 2021 (introduction, fn. 102).

67 See only CJEU, Court (Grand Chamber), judgement of 20 September 2016, Ledra Advertising Ltd et al v European Commission et al, Joined Cases C-8/15 P to C-10/15 P, para 57–59.

engaged in unlawful administrative conduct. Furthermore, 'the Commission has a duty to ensure that EU-funded initiatives uphold fundamental rights', as the European Ombudsman recalls in its own-initiative inquiry concerning how the Commission ensures respect for fundamental rights in the EU hotspots 2.0.[68] In light of Art. 17 para 1 TEU, Art. 40 para 3 Frontex Regulation and Art. 21 para 2 EUAA Regulation must thus be read to mean that the Commission is obliged to ensure the legality of its own cooperation with EU agencies and member states and, as a consequence, also the legality of the EU hotspot administration as a whole.

2.3 Procedure-Related vs. Reception-Related Supervision

That being said, a distinction must be made between procedure-related and reception-related supervision. In a nutshell, the Commission fulfils its procedure-related supervisory duty already when it instructs and urges agencies and host member state to conduct lawful procedures. With respect to reception conditions, however, its duties go much further. At the latest since the Commission's reception-related duties have been stepped up with the EU hotspot 2.0, it must, if required, itself ensure that the reception conditions comply with EU law.[69]

Again, this follows from an interpretation of Art. 40 para 3 Frontex Regulation, Art. 21 para 2 EUAA Regulation in light of Art. 17 para 1 TEU. While the Commission's obligations as guardian of the Treaties must generally be interpreted in a broad manner, the specific scope of its obligations in a given policy area depends on its competences. Depending on the competences and the context concerned, the Commission can either be obliged to follow a certain procedure and to ensure a certain outcome.[70]

---

68 European Ombudsman, How the European Commission ensures respect for fundamental rights in EU-funded migration management facilities in Greece, Case OI/3/2022/MHZ, opened on 11 July 2022, case description.

69 This is based on a distinction between supervisory duties to ensure the legality of the supervisee's conduct and duties to ensure the achievement of a certain outcome. In more detail on this distinction Gerard C. Rowe, „Administrative supervision of administrative action in the European Union", in Herwig Hofmann, Alexander Türk (ed.), *Legal Challenges in EU Administrative Law*, Edward Elgar 2009, p. 179–217, p. 208–209.

70 Similarly, Uwe Säuberlich, *Die außervertragliche Haftung im Gemeinschaftsrecht. Eine Untersuchung der Mehrpersonenverhaltnisse*, Springer 2005, p. 232–234 refers to 'Erfolgshaftung' v 'obligation de moyens'. In CJEU, judgement of 14 July 1967,

As regards, first, the Commission's procedure-related supervision, the key point is that the operational competence to conduct asylum and return procedures, according to the prevailing reading of the Treaties, lies with the host member state, to which the agencies provide support. The Commission's obligation is thus limited to giving instructions and can, in this sense, be described as a due diligence obligation. The concrete scope of its obligations, then, differs between the host member state and the agencies. With respect to the host member state, the Commission's supervisory obligation is rather broad. As the Commission's obligations under Art. 17 para 1 TEU include the duty to ensure that member states comply with EU law concerning EU-funded projects, the Commission is obliged to take all supervisory measures that remain below the threshold of issuing legally-binding instructions or acting in the place of the member state. In the case of the EU hotspots 2.0, this explicitly includes the option to withdraw or withhold EU funding.[71] With respect to the agencies, the Commission's supervisory obligation is comparatively narrow. The crucial point here is that the Commission must respect the agencies' independence.[72] Although the independence postulate as such is not entirely convincing insofar as the Commission forms part of the management boards of Frontex and the EUAA,[73] it aptly describes that the agencies do not directly report to the Commission and that the Commission, in turn, has no competence to issue binding instructions to the agencies. Accordingly, the Commission's

Kampffmeyer, Joined Cases 5, 7, and 13 to 22/66, p. 262, for instance, the court concluded that the specific provision obliged the Commission to ensure that the outcome of the administrative cooperation complies with EU law, whereas in its judgement of 10 May 1987, Société pour l'Exportation des Sucres, 132/77, in particular para 23, the court found that the specific provision obliged the Commission merely to follow the applicable procedural rules.

71 European Ombudsman, Inspection Report 9 March 2023, Case OI/3/2022/MHZ (fn. 11), para 15.

72 Note that Matthias Lehnert, *Frontex und operative Maßnahmen an den europäischen Außengrenzen. Verwaltungskooperation – materielle Rechtsgrundlagen – institutionelle Kontrolle*, Nomos 2014, p. 473 therefrom concludes that the Commission, based on the secondary law as it stood back then, did not have the competence to supervise Frontex's operational activities.

73 Note that both member states and the Commission participate in the agencies' management board. See on Frontex' and EASO's management boards David Fernández-Rojo, *EU Migration Agencies* (fn. 4), p. 176–182. For a critical account of the independence postulate see only Ellen Vos, „EU Agencies and Independence", in D Ritleng (ed.), *Independence and Legitimacy in the Institutional System of the European Union*, Oxford University Press 2016, p. 206-227.

supervisory obligation cannot go beyond urging the agencies to conduct procedures in compliance with EU law.

As regards, second, the Commission's reception-related supervision, it must be taken into account that the operational competence to provide reception conditions in the EU hotspots lies with the host member state which is supported, since the implementation of the Joint Pilot, by the Commission itself. Accordingly, the Commission fulfils its supervisory duty only if it ensures that reception conditions actually comply with EU law. If the host member state fails to implement the Commission's requests and informal instructions, the Commission is obliged to make use of its own operational competence and provide the required administrative support itself.[74] In this sense, the reception-related aspect of Art. 40 para 3 Frontex Regulation, Art. 21 para 2 EUAA Regulation can be described as an outcome obligation, i.e. an obligation to ensure that reception conditions in EU-funded centres which are co-managed by the Commission comply with EU law. The pertinence of this interpretation is underpinned by the Commission's current administrative practice. In the framework of the Joint Pilot, the Commission itself defines its task as ensuring that reception conditions comply with EU law and, in particular, with fundamental rights.[75] To this end, the Commission has not only adapted its internal organisational structure[76] but also provides considerable operational support. Inter alia, it is actively engaged in designing and planning the new infrastructure and finding a suitable site for the new camp.[77] The question of the continuity of these developments notwithstanding,[78] the Commission's current practice clearly confirms that it interprets its reception-related mandate under Art. 17 para 1 TEU, Art. 40 para 3 Frontex Regulation, Art. 21 para 2 EUAA Regulation as 'outcome obligation'.

---

74 While the Commission cannot act against the will of the concerned member state, it must do everything it can, within the limits of its competences, to ensure that the concerned member state agrees.

75 MoU Joint Pilot (fn. 47), p. 3–5; interviews with Commission representative 4, conducted on 26 February 2021; with Commission representative 5, conducted on 7 April 2021 (introduction, fn. 102).

76 See on the dedicated Task Force on Migration Management below 2.7.

77 MoU Joint Pilot (fn. 47), p. 4–5.

78 While the Commission stresses the temporary nature of these developments (see interviews with Commission representative 5, conducted on 7 April 2021 (introduction, fn. 102), note that the MoU Joint Pilot (fn. 47) is conceived as strictly limited to a period of two years), experience rather suggests that the Commission will not reduce its increased involvement.

2.4 Reduced Discretion in Case of Systemic Deficiencies

In order to determine whether the Commission has violated its supervisory obligations Art. 40 para 3 Frontex Regulation, Art. 21 para 2 EUAA Regulation, Art. 17 para 1 TEU, it must be taken into account that these are discretionary in nature. The Commission generally enjoys broad discretion when exercising its tasks as guardian of the Treaties,[79] especially when it comes to ensuring compliance with fundamental rights.[80] In principle, the Commission can thus decide *whether* it takes any supervisory measures and, if so, *which* measures it takes.

The Commission's discretion, however, is not unlimited. As a rule, discretionary limits depend on the specific circumstances of the individual case.[81] In the context of the EU hotspot administration, this case-by-case assessment is arguably guided by two general considerations.

First, the Commission must make use of its competences to the fullest extent possible in order to ensure that the EU hotspot administration complies with EU law. This doctrine of a 'maximum use of competences' is confirmed by Commission representatives themselves, who explain that their understanding is that the Commission is obliged 'to do everything it can, within the scope of its competences of course, to ensure the legality of the EU hotspot administration'.[82] The same follows from the CJEU's consistent case law, according to which the Commission must refrain from participating in behaviour that is in breach of EU law. As the CJEU has held both concerning supervisory obligations under secondary law and concerning Art. 17 para 1 TEU, the Commission's role as guardian of the Treaties implies that it must not participate in conduct that violates EU law. The Commission must hence use its competences to prevent breaches of EU law and, where this is not possible, at least 'insist' on national authorities to not continue their unlawful behaviour.[83] Applied to the context of the

79 Matthias Ruffert, „Artikel 17 EUV", in Christian Calliess, Matthias Ruffert (ed.), *EUV/AEUV. Kommentar*, C.H. Beck 2022, para 7–11.

80 Uwe Säuberlich, *Die außervertragliche Haftung im Gemeinschaftsrecht* (fn. 70), p. 228.

81 In more detail on discretion in EU law see Joana Mendes, „Bounded Discretion in EU Law: A Limited Judicial Paradigm in a Changing EU", *The Modern Law Review* 80 (2017), p. 443-472.

82 See only interview with Commission representative 2, conducted on 16 February 2021 (introduction, fn. 102).

83 CJEU (Grand Chamber), judgement of 20 September 2016, Ledra (fn. 67), para 57–59; CJEU, judgement of 26 February 1986, Krohn, 175/84, para 21.

integrated EU hotspot administration – where a violation of EU law necessarily has the consequence that the Commission, as the general supervisor, itself becomes entangled in unlawful conduct – this must mean that the Commission is obliged to do everything it can to prevent the occurrence of unlawful conduct in the first place. Therefore, Art. 40 para 3 Frontex Regulation, Art. 21 para 2 EUAA, Art. 17 para 1 TEU must be interpreted to mean that the Commission cannot rely on political considerations when deciding whether or not to exercise its supervisory powers, but that it must make use of these powers in the manner which most likely prevents the occurrence of the unlawful conduct, i.e. to the fullest possible extent.[84]

Second, and as a consequence, it is argued here that once the Commission is informed about systemic violations of fundamental rights in the EU hotspot administration, its discretion is reduced to 'how' to exercise supervision, i.e. to the choice of the most suitable measure. Again, the Commission itself appears to agree with this interpretation. When asked what they would do in case of systemic fundamental rights violations, Commission representatives emphasised that they would certainly not remain inactive but would choose those supervisory measures that can be expected to be most effective.[85] This understanding is also doctrinally consistent. While the Commission's discretion under Art. 17 para 1 TFEU, in principle, encompasses both the 'whether' and the 'how', it is well established that the more obvious and persistent the breach of a rule of EU law on the part of the supervisee, the more can be expected from the supervisor.[86] Also, there can be little doubt that the Commission's discretion is reduced when its supervisory obligation follows not only from Art. 17 para 1 TEU but is defined as specific obligations in secondary law.[87] Against this background, and given that the Commission must refrain from participating in conduct that constitutes a violation of EU law, it follows that the Commission, when it is informed that an administrative structure of which it forms part itself is systemically deficient, must not remain inactive. Mere inaction despite

84 The limit lies in Art. 258 TFEU in the context of which the Commission has political discretion, see chapter 3, 2.1.

85 Interview with Commission representative 3 conducted on 16 February 2021 (introduction, fn. 102).

86 Melanie Fink, „EU Liability for Contributions to Member States' Breaches of EU Law", *Common Market Law Review* 56 (2019), p. 1227–1264, p. 1256 with reference to the relevant case law.

87 Similarly Uwe Säuberlich, *Die außervertragliche Haftung im Gemeinschaftsrecht* (fn. 70), p. 237.

knowledge of systemic deficiencies in such case would amount, at least, to tacit approval. As a result, the Commission's discretion under Art. 40 para 3 Frontex Regulation, Art. 21 para 2 EUAA Regulation, Art. 17 para 1 TEU, in a case where it informed about systemic fundamental rights violations, must be reduced to the choice of the most suitable measure.

2.5 The Agencies' Obligation to Assist the Commission

So far, the wording of Art. 40 para 3 Frontex Regulation and Art. 21 para 2 EUAA Regulation has been considered only partially, as it has only been established that the Commission is responsible for administrative supervision. According to the relevant provisions, however, the Commission shall 'in cooperation with the host Member State and the relevant Union bodies, offices and agencies', establish the terms of cooperation at the hotspot area and be responsible for coordination. Similarly, the corresponding recitals provide that the Commission, 'in cooperation with the relevant Union agencies', should ensure that activities in hotspot areas comply with relevant Union law and fundamental rights.

To get a clear understanding of the EU's role at the supervisory level, it is hence required to consider the agencies' involvement in supervision, too.

Starting with the wording of the relevant provisions, the mere grammatical structure of Art. 40 para 3 Frontex Regulation and Art. 21 para 2 EUAA Regulation shows that the provisions must be read as meaning that the Commission, first and ' in cooperation with' the relevant agencies, shall establish the terms of cooperation at the hotspot area and, second, shall be responsible for the coordination of the migration management support teams.[88] Similarly, the relevant recitals provide that the Commission, 'in cooperation with' the relevant agencies, should ensure the legality of the EU hotspot administration while, at the same time, the agencies act 'under the coordination of the Commission'. The wording thus suggests that the agencies' role at the supervisory level is rather limited and that the agencies are themselves subject to supervision by the Commission, at least insofar as their conduct within the EU hotspots is concerned.

88 The English version is grammatically not entirely clear insofar as the addition that the Commission is responsible 'in cooperation with' the relevant Union bodies could be read as referring to the overall coordination. The German, French and Spanish version, however, make unequivocally clear that the qualification 'in cooperation with' refers to the establishment of the terms of cooperation alone.

Although this understanding obviously creates tension in the agencies' mandate, as they are both supervisors and supervisees, it is clearly confirmed by administrative practice. In fact, the main bulk of the supervisory work, i.e. coordinating and ensuring the legality of the EU hotspot administration, is exercised by the Commission. It is the Commission that publishes reports on the implementation of the EU hotspot approach, sets the agenda of the EURTF meeting, gathers information from all actors, in short, oversees the whole situation. Further, it is also the Commission that is in the position to control EU funds and, as a last resort, to initiate an infringement procedure.

The agencies assist at the supervisory level, namely with two specific tasks. First, the agencies assist the Commission with setting up the terms of cooperation. Frontex and the EUAA participate in drafting the general rules for cooperation; and this role of the agencies has been confirmed under the EU hotspot approach 2.0.[89] Second, the agencies provide the Commission with the information that it needs to effectively supervise the EU hotspot administration. Art. 40 para 3 Frontex Regulation and Art. 21 para 2 EUAA Regulation must hence be read as obliging the agencies to forward the relevant information to the Commission. If, for instance, the EUAA or Frontex take note of national authorities systemically violating EU law, and if the matter cannot be settled in a cooperative manner, the coordinating officer or the Executive Director is obliged to bring this information to the attention of the EURTF in order to enable the Commission to exercise its supervisory mandate.[90]

The administrative practice thus also clearly confirms that the agencies, insofar as their conduct in the EU hotspots is concerned, are themselves subject to supervision by the Commission. In case of misconduct or a dispute among administrative actors that cannot be settled at the operational level, the matter is brought to the EURTF for the Commission to solve the issue. Ultimately, it is hence the Commission that is responsible for co-

89 MoU Joint Pilot (fn. 47), p. 20; Terms of cooperation for European Union Regional Task Forces, Ref. Ares(2018)1622597 – 23/03/2018 (hereinafter: ToC-EURTF); Rules of procedure of the European Union Regional Task Force for migration management support to Greece as endorsed on 4 Oct 2018 (hereinafter: RoP-EURTF-GR); both documents are on file with the author.

90 In practice, the agencies usually settle issues with the national authorities without involving the Commission for reasons of 'keeping good communication channels', interviews with the interviews with EASO Union Contact Point conducted on 13 December 2019 and on 19 February 2021 (introduction, fn. 102).

ordinating the overall EU hotspots administration and ensuring its legality. Insofar as the Commission is concerned, this understanding is clearly conform with Art. 17 para 1 TEU. Insofar as the agencies are concerned, it might seem to contradict the independence postulate.[91] But this contradiction is only apparent: Quite apart from the doubts on the independence postulate as such, it must be kept in mind that the postulate is mainly established by secondary law, so that secondary law can, of course, also restrict it. In fact, Art. 40 para 3 Frontex Regulation and Art. 21 para 2 EUAA Regulation must be read as setting limits to the agencies' independence. Of course, these limits only concern the specific case of the MMST; any issues related to the agencies' internal organisation fall outside the scope of the Commission's mandate. The proposed interpretation is clearly reflected in the MMSTs' dual reporting structures: The EUAA coordinating officer reports to the agency's headquarters in Malta concerning issues relating to the agencies' internal organisation and to the EURTF in Athens concerning issues relating to the coordination or legality of the EU hotspot administration.

To conclude, responsibility for coordinating and monitoring the EU hotspot administration lies with the Commission. The agencies assist the Commission at the supervisory level, as they participate in setting up the terms of cooperation and gather the relevant information. At the same time, the agencies are subject to the Commission's supervision insofar as their conduct in the EU hotspots is concerned.

2.6 The Commission's Institutional Supervisory Structure

Having defined the Commission's supervisory obligations under Art. 40 para 3 Frontex Regulation, Art. 21 para 2 EUAA Regulation, Art. 17 para 2 TEU, this section focuses on the corresponding institutional structure. Since 2015, the Commission has essentially relied on three institutional pillars to exercise its supervision, namely the European Regional Task Force (EURTF), several Steering Committees, and deployed staff. With the introduction of the EU hotspot approach 2.0, the so-called Dedicated Task Force for Migration Management (Task Force) was established as an additional fourth pillar.

91 See fn. 73.

a *The European Regional Task Force (EURTF)*

The EURTF is the oldest institutional structure that serves to coordinate and monitor the EU hotspot administration.[92] As set out above, it has been established without legal basis in the immediate crisis context and is, until today, mainly regulated by EU soft law. Initially, it was conceived as a meeting between the Commission and EU agencies alone, but national authorities were soon added to the list of permanent participants.[93] The circle of participants was then gradually expanded so that by now, all EU and national actors involved in the EU hotspot administration take part in the EURTF.[94] In addition to the regular general meetings of all participants, several working groups have been established which focus on specific topics and meet more frequently.[95]

For the purpose of this study, the crucial point is that the EURTF, albeit formally conceived as a coordination meeting where all actors meet at eye level, functions as a forum for the Commission to exercise its supervision.[96] The EURTF was created by the European Commission and convened under its auspices. It is the Commission who sets the agenda, invites the participants, and chairs the general meetings.[97] Consequently, it is also the Commission that has the last word in case of disagreement among the participants. Although the written rules are not entirely clear on this point, providing both that the work of the EURTF is 'based on consensus' and that the Commission is in charge of 'ensuring' that all participants work

92 European Commission Staff Working Document, Best Practices on the implementation of the hotspot approach, accompanying the document: Report from the Commission to the European Parliament, the European Council and Council. Progress Report on the European Agenda on Migration, 15 November 2017, SWD(2017) 372 final (hereinafter: European Commission, SWD EU Hotspots 2017), p. 2; ToC-EURTF, Introduction, both referring to Art. 18 para 3 Frontex 2016 Regulation (chapter 1, fn. 150) as the predecessor of Art. 40 para 3 Frontex Regulation.

93 ECA Special Report 2017, para 60; interviews with Commission representative 1 and Commission representative 2 conducted on 12 February 2021; interview with Commission representative 3, conducted on 16 February 2021 (introduction, fn. 102).

94 ToC-EURTF; RoP-EURTF-GR; interviews with Commission representatives (as in fn. 93).

95 Interview with Commission representative 4, conducted on 26 February 2021 (introduction, fn. 102).

96 FRA, Opinion EU Hotspots 2019 (fn. 3), p. 19, note 37 and 38.

97 ToC-EURTF; RoP-EURTF-GR.

together,[98] practice shows that controversies among the participants are settled by the Commission.[99]

b *The Steering Committee*

Second, the Commission also makes use of a so-called Steering Committee to exercise its supervision. This forum is complementary to the EURTF in that the latter focuses on operational coordination, whereas the Steering Committee focuses on funding-related aspects.[100] Like the EURTF, the Steering Committee was initially set up without written rules and lacks formal regulation until today. Its main focus has then evolved over time. In 2016, the initial Steering was set up by the EU coordinator for the implementation of the EU-Türkiye Statement under the auspices of the Commission's Structural Reform and Support Service, the predecessor of DG REFORM.[101] In 2017, another Steering Committee was established under the auspices of DG Home and DG ECCHO for the purpose of financial planning and monitoring funding for Greece's asylum and migration in general.[102] In 2020, these two Committees were merged and replaced with the Steering Committee for Migration Management, which was established for the purpose of implementing the EU hotspot approach 2.0.[103] As a consequence, it appears that the Commission's focus has shifted from the EURTF to the Steering Committee as the primary supervisory forum.

98 RoP-EURTF-GR, para 7, para 28.

99 Interview with Commission representatives (as in fn. 95).

100 Note, however, that the EURTF and the Steering Committee are institutionally linked. All higher level staff participates in both meetings, and the Commission makes sure that its staff responsible for funding is on the same page as its staff responsible for operational aspects, see interviews with Commission representative 3, conducted on 16 February 2021; with Commission representative 4, conducted on 26 February 2021 (introduction, fn. 102).

101 Interview with Commission representative 4, conducted on 26 February 2021 (introduction, fn. 102).

102 The idea of that second Steering Committee was to monitor the implementation of the yearly financial plans, see interview with Commission representative 4, conducted on 26 February 2021 (introduction, fn. 102).

103 As a result, the current Steering Committee, while covering all funding-related issues, thus has a particular focus on the EU hotspots, see interview with Commission representative 4, conducted on 26 February 2021 (introduction, fn. 102).

c *Deployment of Staff to the Ground*

The third pillar of the Commission's supervisory structure is deployed staff. Since 2015, the Commission has apparently considered it necessary to deploy its own staff to the EU hotspots in order to adequately exercise its supervisory mandate. This is consequential because the Commission requires timely and correct information regarding all operational aspects, and this information is provided only partially by the agencies and national authorities.

Figuratively referred to as 'the Commission's eyes and ears on the ground', the representatives' main task is information-gathering and reporting.[104] Since 2015 and until today, the representatives have regularly sent their detailed reports to Brussels, covering every single aspect of the EU hotspot administration, including reception conditions, asylum procedures, and deportation.[105] The Commission thus always holds up-to-date information on conditions and incidents in each EU hotspot and can accordingly address misconduct and deficiencies in the EURTF and the Steering Committee. This is of particular importance for the purpose of this study, as the Commission cannot convincingly argue that it was not informed about misconduct by authorities and violations of EU law at any time since 2015.

d *The Dedicated Task Force Migration Management*

The fourth pillar is the Dedicated Task Force Migration Management, short Task Force. This forum was established in 2020 for the purpose of implementing the EU hotspot approach 2.0[106] and is formally integrated into the Commission's internal structure. The Commission itself describes

104 Interviews with Commission representatives 1 and 2, conducted on 12 February 2021; with Commission representative 3, conducted on 16 February 2021; with Commission representative 4, conducted on 26 February 2021 (introduction, fn. 102).

105 Interview with Commission representative 4, conducted on 26 February 2021 (introduction, fn. 102).

106 European Commission, Press Release of 23 September 2020, Migration: A European taskforce to resolve emergency situation on Lesvos; European Ombudsman, Inspection Report 9 March 2023, Case OI/3/2022/MHZ (fn. 11), para 4. See further European Commission, Task Force Migration Management, https://home-affairs.ec.europa.eu/policies/migration-and-asylum/migration-management/task-force-migration-management_en.

the Task Force in a rather obscure manner, stating that it is 'not a separate team dedicated to specific tasks' but rather 'a collaboration framework between many different people in different units that, through the Task Force, come together to further certain objectives.'[107] What is clear is that the Task Force is headed by a Deputy Director-General from the Commission's Directorate-General for Migration and Home Affairs (HOME), that it consists of several staff in Brussels, and that it is supported by several staff members permanently based in Greece, including some in Athens and some on the islands.[108] Further, it is clear that, although the Task Force monitors operations in several countries, it puts a clear emphasis on Greece.[109] Insofar as Greece is concerned, the work of the Task Force includes 'ad hoc meetings wherever needs arise' and participation in the reformed Steering Committee, which is, in fact, defined as consisting of the Task Force and national authorities.[110]

For the purpose of this study, the Task Force is of particular interest insofar as it is responsible for the implementation of the EU hotspot approach 2.0.[111] According to the Commission itself, the creation of the Task Force must be understood as a belated reaction to the deficiencies in the implementation of the original EU hotspot approach.[112] It operates both on the ground, thereby integrating the previous individual deployed staff members,[113] and at a policy level, thereby formalising the Commission's various practises to exert influence and pressure over the host member state. With the Task Force, the Commission has thus streamlined its previous practices and, at the same time, reinforced its involvement in the EU hotspot administration. In sum, the Task Force can be described as a manner of organising the Commission's internal structure in a way that

---

107 European Ombudsman, Inspection Report 9 March 2023, Case OI/3/2022/MHZ (fn. 11), para 4, 8.

108 Ibid., para 4, 6, 12.

109 Ibid., para 8, passim.

110 Ibid., para 7.

111 Another responsibility of the Task Force is the 'monitoring of the implementation of EU funds (...) in the area of border management', as formulated by the European Commission in its response to questions by the European Ombudsman in the case opened on 7 November 2023, How the European Commission monitors EU funds granted to Greece in the context of border management operations, Case 1418/2023/VS, p. 5.

112 European Ombudsman, Inspection Report 9 March 2023, Case OI/3/2022/MHZ (fn. 11), para 1–5.

113 Ibid., para 12.

allows it, inter alia, to effectively exercise its mandate to coordinate and supervise the integrated EU hotspot administration.

2.7 The Commission's Concrete Supervisory Measures

This last section presents some concrete measures that the Commission has as its disposal to exercise its supervisory mandate. This is necessary because the purpose of this study, namely to determine whether the EU bears responsibility for systemic deficiencies in the EU hotspots, requires to identify specific misconduct or omissions.

Generally speaking, the Commission's toolbox consists of a wide range of measures, including policy-making, funding, and operational instructions.[114] In fact, the first and temporally earliest possibility for the Commission to adequately exercise its supervisory mandate would have been to design the EU hotspot approach, from the outset, as a policy that complies with EU law. The Commission, however, even failed to conduct a correct fundamental rights assessment,[115] resulting in the 2015 EU hotspot approach being designed in a manner that its implementation almost inevitably results in systemic fundamental rights violations.[116]

The second way for the Commission to exercise its supervisory mandate relates to funding.[117] As explained above, the Commission could ensure legality either by dedicating funding to specific activities that serve to

114 Monitoring, as established in chapter 1, 4.2., is less important here because it refers to measures ensuring the legality of the entire asylum system; in more detail on these categories Catharina Ziebritzki, *The EU's Responsibility in the Asylum Administration* (fn. 1), p. 100 et seq.

115 European Ombudsman, 18 January 2017, Case 506/2016/MHZ (fn. 62), para 30.

116 FRA, Opinion EU Hotspots 2019 (fn. 3), p. 7; in detail below 3.

117 Note that both NGOs and UNHCR have recently taken increasing interest in the Commission's funding-related obligations, see for instance ECRE and UNHCR, Follow the Money. Assessing the Use of EU Asylum, Migration and Integration Fund (AMIF) funding at the national level, 2018, https://ecre.org/wp-content/uploads/2018/01/follow-the-money_AMIF_UNHCR_ECRE_23-11-2018.pdf; ibid., Follow the Money II, Assessing the Use of EU Asylum, Migration and Integration Fund (AMIF) funding at the national level 2014–2018, 2019, https://ecre.org/follow-the-money-ii-report/; and the subsequent reports; PICUM and ECRE, Fundamental Rights Compliance of Funding Supporting Migrants, Asylum Applicants and Refugees inside the European Union, Policy Note 2023, https://ecre.org/ecre-and-picum-policy-note-fundamental-rights-compliance-of-funding-supporting-migrants-asylum-applicants-and-refugees-inside-the-european-union/.

ensure compliance with EU law or through direct or indirect conditionalities.[118] Considering that the infrastructure and the administration of the EU hotspots have since 2015 been funded to a significant extent by the EU[119] and that the EU hotspots 2.0 are almost entirely EU-funded,[120] funding-related measures must appear as a promising way for the Commission to exert influence. Yet, the Commission has so far been reluctant to make use of this option. According to publicly available information,[121] the Commission has long not imposed explicit conditionalities, even though Greece has received about 3.15 billion of EU support in the area of asylum, migration and border policy between 2015 and 2021.[122] In the context of the EU hotspots 2.0, the Commission has still not considered it necessary to require a fundamental rights impact assessment, but at least reaffirmed its right to withdraw or withhold funding in case of persisting deficiencies.[123]

Third, the Commission could fulfil its obligations under Art. 40 para 3 Frontex Regulation, Art. 21 para 2 EUAA Regulation, Art. 17 para 1 TEU through operational instructions. This includes negotiation and soft instructions within the framework of the EURTF and the Steering Commit-

118 See chapter 1, 4.2.

119 Interviews with Commission representatives 1 and 2, conducted on 12 February 2021; with Commission representative 3, conducted on 16 February 2021; with Commission representative 4, conducted on 26 February 2021 (introduction, fn. 102).

120 European Ombudsman, Inspection Report 9 March 2023, Case OI/3/2022/MHZ (fn. 11), para 15.

121 See European Ombudsman, case opened on 7 November 2023, How the European Commission monitors EU funds granted to Greece in the context of border management operations, Case 1418/2023/VS; initial complaint letter on file with the author.

122 European Commission, Factsheet: Managing Migration. EU Financial Support to Greece, March 2021, https://ec.europa.eu/home-affairs/what-we-do/policies/european-agenda-migration/background-information_en.

123 European Ombudsman, Inspection Report 9 March 2023, Case OI/3/2022/MHZ (fn. 11), para 15: 'The MPRICs are funded under emergency assistance awarded to the Greek government through the Asylum, Migration and Integration Fund (AMIF). (...) Although the financial rules do not refer to the need for fundamental rights impact assessments, the grant agreement gives the Commission the right to *recover or stop payments* if the requirements of the grant agreement are not respected.' (emphasis added).

tee. As the Commission itself explains, these fora allow it to effectively 'guide' or 'steer' the conduct of national authorities and agencies.[124]

Again, the crucial point here is that national authorities usually follow the Commission's operational instructions, although these lack formal bindingness. This is confirmed by the Commission itself, which reports that it is able to effectively influence the host member state's legislative and executive branches.[125] In the context of the EU hotspots 2.0, for instance, the Commission reported that it 'ensured the adoption of a ministerial decision' in the context of the EU hotspots 2.0, and 'requested written assurances at the highest level concerning the openness of accommodation areas'.[126] Similarly, the Commission has also reported in other areas of the asylum system that it has been able to make use of its special position to persuade the host member state to enact certain laws, adopt certain resolutions, or implement certain administrative practices.[127] As will be argued below, this can be explained by the fact that the Commission's instructions come with implicit financial pressure, informational advantage and political authority and thus have a de facto binding effect on national authorities.

It arguably follows that the Commission has been obliged, since 2015, to negotiate, conclude, and implement a Memorandum of Understanding in order to ensure the legality of the EU hotspot administration. Certainly, the conclusion of an MoU presupposes the consent of the concerned member state. According to the doctrine of the maximum use of its competences,[128] however, the Commission was obliged to at least insist upon the member state to agree, if all other measures have proven insufficient. However, the Commission made use of this option only after a devastating fire destroyed

124 Interviews with Commission representative 3, conducted on 16 February 2021; with Commission representative 4, conducted on 26 February 2021 (introduction, fn. 102).

125 Interviews with Commission representatives, passim (introduction, fn. 102). There is no empirical data to support this claim already because the Commission gives its instructions in non-public fora.

126 European Ombudsman, Inspection Report 9 March 2023, Case OI/3/2022/MHZ (fn. 11), para 16.

127 For instance, the Commission's influence with regard to the composition of the Greek Appeals Committees (see chapter 1, fn. 130 et seq.) or with regard to the abolishment of the exemption of vulnerable persons from border procedures, see Catharina Ziebritzki, Robert Nestler, „'Hotspots' an der EU-Außengrenze" (fn. 9), p. 30, 46.

128 See above 2.4.

Moria. With a view to the EU's responsibility, the MoU Joint Pilot could thus become relevant in two variants. If the MoU keeps its promise, the argument could be made that the Commission has failed to fulfil its supervisory obligations by not doing everything to ensure the conclusion of such MoU already earlier. If the MoU fails to ensure that the new reception centres comply with EU law, which currently seems likely,[129] the argument could be made that the Commission has failed to fulfil its obligations by failing to implement the MoU in compliance with EU law.[130]

3 Systemic Deficiencies in the EU Hotspot Administration

Keeping in mind the EU's involvement as set out hitherto, the following argues that the EU hotspot administration is systemically deficient. The disastrous living conditions entail a risk of inhuman or degrading treatment, in particular for vulnerable persons, and risks resulting from systemic detention practices; procedure-related deficiencies include violations of the right to be heard, specific procedural guarantees for children and the prohibition of refoulement.

This being said, two preliminary remarks are in order. The first is that, in order to determine whether or not the EU bears legal responsibility for fundamental rights violations occurring in the EU hotspots, a distinction must be made between inherent and resulting violations.[131] Due to the EU's mode of determining without deciding, some fundamental rights violations are inherent in the EU's misconduct, whereas others are brought about by the ensuing national decision and, in this sense, only result from the EU's misconduct. Inherent violations are well illustrated with procedure-related deficiencies. For instance, when the EUAA fails to adequately interview an asylum seeker, the violation of the fundamental right to good administration is inherent in the agency's misconduct. Also, when Frontex conducts an age assessment based on visual inspection alone and, on this basis, wrongly registers a child as an adult, the violation of the fundamental rights of the child is inherent in the agency's misconduct. Resulting violations, in turn, are well illustrated with reception-related deficiencies. For instance, when a person is subject to reception conditions that amount to inhuman

129 See below 3.
130 See in more detail chapter 5.
131 See on the further consequences of this distinction chapter 4 and 5.

treatment, that violation is not inherent in the Commission's failure to adequately supervise the EU hotspot administration but results from it.[132]

The second preliminary note concerns the objective of this section. Although it is argued here that two sets of systemic deficiencies can be identified, the consequentiality of this study as a whole does not depend on whether specific fundamental rights are violated or not. This study is not primarily concerned with 'proving' a specific fundamental rights violation but rather with reconstructing the role of the EU in the EU hotspots and, on that basis, assessing whether the EU bears legal responsibility for fundamental rights violations. In other words, the interest of this study is not so much to determine whether fundamental rights are violated or not – for this is the task of the numerous reports cited in this section – but rather to assess which entity is responsible for fundamental rights violations, if they occur.

3.1 Reception-Related Deficiencies

While the powerful pictures of 2015, showing vast makeshift camps of flimsy tents drowning in mud and snow, have long disappeared from the media, the reception conditions in the EU hotspots to this day remain disastrous. In fact, the prohibition of inhuman or degrading treatment as enshrined in Art. 4 ChFR is largely violated, especially in case of vulnerable persons.

a *The Prohibition of Inhuman or Degrading Treatment (Art. 4 ChFR)*

As consistently and extensively documented during the past years by bodies of the UN, the Council of Europe and the EU, Greek national bodies, and NGOs,[133] living conditions in the EU hotspots remain dire. Ever since their establishment, basic requirements such as housing, food, medical and psychological services, schooling and social services are either absent or absolutely insufficient. During the Covid-19 pandemic, the situation has

132 'Resulting' is used here in an non-technical sense. With regard to the EU's responsibility, resulting violations raise intricate doctrinal questions of causation, as will be discussed in chapter 5.

133 For a few relevant reports see introduction, fn. 3.

been further aggravated, namely through confinement of asylum seekers to the camps and restricted access to public health care services.[134]

In fact, there can be no doubt that the standards of the Reception Conditions Directive[135] are hardly complied with in any respect. The main dispute then revolves around whether the conditions constitute a violation of Art. 3 ECHR respectively Art. 4 ChFR. This alone shows the scale of the problem. While no generalised assessment can be made in this regard because it depends on the individual case whether or not the minimum requirements are met, a brief account of the relevant standard helps to orient in the discussion.

The starting point here is the judgement of the ECtHR in the case *M.S.S. v Greece and Belgium*. The ECtHR held that even though Art. 3 ECHR does not oblige state parties to provide everyone within their jurisdiction with a home; it must be taken into account that asylum seekers, as such, are a particularly underprivileged and vulnerable population group in need of special protection and that EU member states are bound to comply with their own standards, namely the Reception Conditions Directive.[136] Based on its previous judgement in *Budina v Russia*,[137] the ECtHR, therefore, concluded that a situation of extreme material poverty amounts to a violation of Art. 3 ECHR where an applicant, in circumstances wholly dependent on State support, finds themselves faced with official indifference when in a situation of serious deprivation or want incompatible with human dignity.[138] With a view to the facts in the case *M.S.S.*, the ECtHR emphasised that the applicant found himself in a particularly difficult situation

134 Equal Rights Beyond Borders, Report of February 2023, Extraordinary Measures (fn. 10); Equal Rights Beyond Borders, November 2020, Update of the Report of May 2020. Abandoned and Neglected (fn. 10); Equal Rights Beyond Boders, HIAS Greece, Refugee Support Aegean, September 2022, The State of the Border Procedure on the Greek Islands, https://rsaegean.org/en/border-procedure-greek-islands/, p. 27–31.

135 The same holds true under Directive (EU) 2024/1346 of the European Parliament and of the Council of 14 May 2024 laying down standards for the reception of applicants for international protection (recast) (hereinafter: reformed Reception Conditions Directive) which lowers standards, but not the extent to legalise practices in the EU hotspots.

136 ECtHR, judgement of 21 January 2011, M.S.S. v Belgium and Greece, Application No 30696/09, para 250.

137 ECtHR, judgement of 18 June 2009, Budina v Russia, Application No 45603/05.

138 ECtHR, judgement of 21 January 2011, M.S.S. v Belgium and Greece (fn. 136), para 253.

for several months, in which his essential needs were not met, which was marked by prolonged uncertainty, and which aroused in him feelings of fear, anguish or inferiority capable of inducing desperation. Therefore, the ECtHR ruled that the national authorities were responsible, because of their inaction, for the situation, which had attained the level of severity required to fall within the scope of Art. 3 ECHR.[139] In its following case law, the ECtHR clarified that the standards are higher for asylum seekers who have additional vulnerabilities. In its case *Tarakhel v Switzerland*, for instance, the ECtHR held that for children asylum seekers, due to their extreme vulnerability, already a situation in which they 'may be left without accommodation or accommodated in overcrowded facilities without any privacy, or even in insalubrious or violent conditions', could amount to a violation of Art. 3 ECHR.[140]

The CJEU, interpreting Art. 4 ChFR in the context of the CEAS, has adopted the ECtHR's standard in its landmark judgement *N.S.* and the following jurisprudence.[141] More recently, the CJEU's judgement in *Jawo* and the following jurisprudence may raise doubts as to whether it is lowering the standard compared to that of the ECtHR.[142] Those doubts, however, are irrelevant here because the *Jawo* line of case law concerns recognised beneficiaries of international protection and not asylum seekers.

In the case law of the ECtHR dealing with the reception conditions in EU hotspots specifically, a change seems to be taking place. In its early judgements concerning the living conditions in the closed centres that were established in March 2016, the Court decided that Art. 3 ECHR was not violated.[143] In 2020, however, the ECtHR granted numerous interim measures concerning cases of vulnerable persons and requested Greece to

---

139 Ibid., para 263 and 264.

140 ECtHR, judgement of 4 November 2014, Tarakhel v Switzerland, Application No 29217/12, para 98, para 118 et seq.; ECtHR, judgement of 19 January 2012, Popov v France, Applications Nos 39472/07 and 39474/07, para 91 and 102.

141 Court (Grand Chamber), judgment of 21 December 2011, N.S. v Secretary of State for the Home Department and M.E. and Others v Refugee Applications Commissioner and Minister for Justice, Equality and Law Reform, Joined cases C-411/10 and C-493/10, para 88 et seq.

142 CJEU, judgement of 19 March 2019, Abubacarr Jawo v Bundesrepublik Deutschland, C-163/17, para 91 et seq., para 95 et seq. See Georgios Anagnostaras, „The Common European Asylum System: Balancing Mutual Trust Against Fundamental Rights Protection", *German Law Journal* 21 (2020), p. 1180-1197, 1192 et seq.

143 ECtHR, judgement of 25 January 2018, J.R. et al v Greece, Application no 22696/16; ECtHR, judgement of 21 March 2019, O.S.A. at al. v Greece, Application no

provide conditions in compliance with Art. 3 ECHR.[144] Similarly, the European Committee of Social Rights has, in a case concerning the situation of unaccompanied minors in EU hotspots, found a violation of the rights to housing, the rights of children and the right to protection of health.[145] It can, therefore, reasonably be expected that the ECtHR would also find a violation of Art. 3 ECHR in the remaining complaints currently pending before the Court.[146]

In sum, existing jurisprudence clearly confirms that EU hotspots structurally entail a risk of a violation of Art. 3 ECtHR, at least in case of vulnerable persons. This means that any person, at least any vulnerable person, seeking asylum in the EU hotspots is exposed to a structural risk of inhumane or degrading treatment due to inadequate reception conditions.

b *The Prohibition of Systemic Detention of Asylum Seekers (Art. 6 ChFR)*

Furthermore, asylum seekers in EU hotspots are exposed to a systemic risk of being subject to unlawful detention in breach of Art. 6 ChFR. While detention practices have evolved over time and differ between different islands, this section focuses on two practices that have occurred on the island of Kos, namely, first, the systemic detention of asylum seekers between 2020 and 2021 and, second, the systemic detention of unaccompanied mi-

---

39065/16; ECtHR, judgement of 3 October 2019, Kaak and Others v Greece, Application no 343215/16.

144 ECtHR, Decision on interim measure of 14 May 2020, A.B. v Greece, Application no. 19614/20; ECtHR, Decision on interim measures of 7 April 2020, M.A. v. Greece, Application no. 15782/20; ECtHR, Decision on interim measures of 26 March 2020, M.A. v. Greece, Application no. 15192/20; ECtHR, Decision on interim measure of 16 April 2020, E.I. and Others v Greece, Application No 16080/20 (available at: https://www.proasyl.de/news/egmr-urteil-fluechtlinge-aus-moria-muessen-menschenwuerdig-untergebracht-werden/). For further similar decisions, see Refugee Support Aegean (RSA), *European Court of Human Rights orders Greece to safeguard asylum seekers' life and limb on Lesvos, 24 September 2020*, available at: https://rsaegean.org/en/european-court-of-human-rights-orders-greece-to-safeguard-asylum-seekers-life-and-limb-on-lesvos/.

145 European Committee of Social Rights, Decision of 26 January 2021, International Commissions of Jurists (ICJ) and European Council for Refugees and Exiles (ECRE) v Greece, Complaint No. 173/2018.

146 ECtHR, M.A. and others v Greece, Application No. 16865/20 concerns the living conditions and medical treatment of the applicants in the EU hotspots of Lesvos, Chios and Samos as well as the Nea Kavala camp.

nors in the newly built MP-RIC in 2022. The choice of these examples is justified because the first is representative of similar systemic detention practices that have been applied earlier on other islands,[147] and the second shows in which direction policies tend to develop in the context of the implementation of the EU hotspot approach 2.0.

Detention practices in EU hotspots must be seen in the context of the general policy of immigration detention in Greece. In 2019, Greece expanded the grounds for administrative detention of asylum seekers, limited the examination of alternatives to detention and extended the duration of detention to up to three years.[148] As a result, administrative detention of irregular migrants, including asylum seekers, has increased sharply from 2016 to 2021.[149] In addition, detention policy increasingly reflects the general shift towards informalisation. Recent practices, such as the so-called '25-day ban' and measures taken in response to the Covid-19 pandemic, tend to replace explicitly designated detention with other forms of restriction of liberty that resemble detention or even qualify as such.[150]

Before setting out the two case examples in more detail, a brief account of the standard established by Art. 6 ChFR in the context of asylum and border policy is required. As the CJEU has recently recalled in its case law concerning the Hungarian transit zones, the Reception Conditions Directive defines 'detention' as 'confinement of an applicant by a Member

---

147 For instance, systemic detention scheme that was applied on all islands as from the entry into force of the EU-Türkiye Statement in March 2016, see Catharina Ziebritzki, Robert Nestler, „'Hotspots' an der EU-Außengrenze" (fn. 9), p. 34–41.

148 The main changes were brought about with the adoption of Law 4636/2019 (International Protection Act), in particular Art. 46 thereof. The most recent reform, adopted with Law 4939/2022 (Asylum Code), replacing Art. 46 IPA with Art. 50 Asylum Code, did not change much in terms of content. See in more detail Equal Rights Beyond Borders, February 2023, Still Detained and Forgotten. Update on Detention Policies, Practices and Conditions on Kos 2022/23, https://equal-rights.org/resources/publications, p. 8.

149 Oxfam, 16 November 2021, Briefing Paper, Detention as the Default: How Greece, with the support of the EU, is generalizing administrative detention of migrants, https://policy-practice.oxfam.org/resources/detention-as-the-default-how-greece-with-the-support-of-the-eu-is-generalizing-621307/, p. 6.

150 On recent forms of so-called 'de facto detention' or 'alternatives to detention' as well as on the legal distinction between restriction of movement and detention see Equal Rights Beyond Borders, February 2023, Still Detained and Forgotten (fn. 148), p. 37–43. On the restrictions related to Covid-19 see further Equal Rights Beyond Borders, Report of February 2023, Extraordinary Measures (fn. 10); Equal Rights Beyond Borders, November 2020, Update of the Report of May 2020. Abandoned and Neglected (fn. 10).

State within a particular place, where the applicant is deprived of their freedom of movement'. This means that detention is 'any coercive measure that deprives that applicant of his or her freedom of movement and isolates them from the rest of the population, by requiring them to remain permanently within a restricted and closed perimeter'.[151]

According to settled case law, Art. 6 ChFR prohibits detaining persons solely due to their status as asylum seekers.[152] The few cases in which detention is allowed are exhaustively listed in Art. 8 para 3 Reception Conditions Directive; now, the reformed Art. 10 para 4 Reception Conditions Directive.[153] Apart from pre-removal detention, detention is allowed only for specific reasons such as inter alia, the determination of identity, to counter a risk of absconding, and to protect national security or public order.[154] All detention grounds can be applied only as a last resort, and detention of minors is subject to even stricter preconditions.[155]

Noting that the 2024 CEAS reform broadens the grounds for detention in border procedures,[156] the following refers to the case study as defined

151 CJEU (Grand Chamber), judgement of 17 December 2020, European Commission v Hungary, C-808/18, para 159; CJEU (Grand Chamber), judgement of 14 May 2020, FMS et al v Országos Idegenrendészeti Főigazgatóság Dél-alföldi Regionális Igazgatóság et al, C-924/19 PPU and C-925/19 PPU, para 223. Note that the definition of 'detention' is now enshrined in Art. 2 para 12 Regulation (EU) 2024/1356 of the European Parliament and of the Council of 14 May 2024 introducing the screening of third-country nationals at the external borders and amending Regulations (EC) No 767/2008, (EU) 2017/2226, (EU) 2018/1240 and (EU) 2019/817 (hereinafter: reform Screening Regulation II) as follows: "detention' means the confinement of a person by a Member State within a particular place, where such person is deprived of freedom of movement.'.

152 As explicitly laid down in Art. 8 para 1 Reception Conditions Directive.

153 On the qualification of the list as exhaustive see CJEU, judgement of 17 December 2020, European Commission v Hungary, C-808/18 (fn. 151), para 168; CJEU, judgement of 14 May 2020, FMS, C-924/19 PPU et al (fn. 151), para 250.

154 CJEU, judgement of 17 December 2020, European Commission v Hungary, C-808/18 (fn. 151), para 175; CJEU (Fourth Chamber), judgment of 14 September 2017, K. v Staatssecretaris van Veiligheid en Justitie, C-18/16, para 48.

155 See Art. 11 Reception Conditions Directive; Article 17 of Directive 2008/115/EC of the European Parliament and of the Council of 16 December 2008 on common standards and procedures in Member States for returning illegally staying third-country nationals (hereinafter: Return Directive). For the corresponding provisions in Greek Law, see Art. 50 para 2 Law 4939/2022, Art. 31 para 1 Law 3907/2011.

156 See ECRE, ECRE Comments on the Directive (EU) 2024/1346 of the European Parliament and of the Council of 14 May 2024 laying down standards for the reception of applicants for international protection (recast), September 2024, p. 8 et seq.

above, i.e. the period between 2015 and 2022, and hence to the law as it stood before the reform.

In the context of EU hotspots, the detention ground enshrined in Art. 8 para 3 lit c Reception Conditions Directive is of particular relevance. It allows detention 'in order to decide (...) on the applicant's right to enter the territory' and is designed precisely to enable member states to detain asylum seekers in border procedures. Consequently, detention is only allowed within the limits of Art. 43 Asylum Procedures Directive, i.e. the period of detention is limited to a maximum of four weeks from the date of the application for international protection, and detention is allowed only to determine whether a claim is inadmissible or unsubstantiated for specific reasons.[157]

Against this background, it becomes clear that the two mentioned cases raise the risk of a systemic violation of Art. 6 ChFR. The first case concerns systemic detention in Kos between 2020 and 2021. Since January 2020, all asylum seekers, including vulnerable persons who had newly arrived on the island and those whose claims had been rejected in last instance, were subject to prolonged detention for a period of up to eighteen months.[158] Detention conditions were wholly inadequate, with overcrowding, maltreatment by police officers, inadequate nutrition, lack of healthcare, and poor hygienic conditions.[159] Procedural rights and remedies were severely deficient, including a limited number of legal aid providers, failure to inform applicants about reasons for their detention, and widespread failure to grant access to an effective remedy.[160] In September 2021, after NGOs had intervened and successfully challenged detention in a large number

157 Those reasons are enlisted in Art. 31 para 8 Asylum Procedures Directive. See CJEU, judgement of 17 December 2020, European Commission v Hungary, C-808/18 (fn. 151), para 178–183; CJEU, judgement of 14 May 2020, FMS, C-924/19 PPU et al (fn. 151), para 237–239, 241–245.

158 Equal Rights Beyond Borders, Report of 10 November 2021, Detained and Forgotten at the Gates of the EU: Detention of Migrants on the Island of Kos, https://www.equal-rights.org/resources/publications, p. 13–21; Equal Rights Beyond Boders, HIAS Greece, Refugee Support Aegean, September 2022, The State of the Border Procedure on the Greek Islands (fn. 134), p. 31–32.

159 All persons were detained in the so-called Pre-Removal Detention Centre (PRDC), regardless of the alleged grounds of detention. On the conditions in the PRDC see Equal Rights Beyond Borders, 10 November 2021, Detained and Forgotten at the Gates of the EU (fn. 158), p. 44–61.

160 Equal Rights Beyond Borders, 10 November 2021, Detained and Forgotten at the Gates of the EU (fn. 158), p. 25–32.

of cases, the practice was lifted to some extent[161] but immediately replaced with detention-like Covid-19 restrictions.[162]

The second case concerns the detention of unaccompanied minors in the EU hotspot 2.0 on Kos. As mentioned above, the Centre on Kos was among the first to be inaugurated at the end of 2021 and has been operational since August 2022.

In general terms, it is not yet entirely clear to what extent asylum seekers are subject to detention in the newly built MP-RIC. Concerned persons describe their situation of 'imprisonment',[163] and independent reports speak of 'prison-like' facilities, 'quasi-detention centres' or 'de facto detention'.[164] What can be said with certainty is that the structures feature barbed wire fences, including internal fencing, and surveillance systems to control entry and exit, including cameras, x-ray scanners, and magnetic doors.[165] Uncertainty remains, however, as to whether recent practices in the MP-RIC that severely restrict asylum seekers' liberty without constituting formal administrative detention under Greek law qualify as detention in the sense

161 Since October 2021, the usual duration of detenion was reduced to 12 months, and since March 2022, it was further reduced to 6 months, see Equal Rights Beyond Borders, February 2023, Still Detained and Forgotten (fn. 148), p. 9–10. The conditions in the PRDC, however, remain inadequate and the procedural remedies remain insufficient, see ibid, p. 20–35.

162 Equal Rights Beyond Borders, February 2023, Still Detained and Forgotten (fn. 148), p. 9.

163 Twitter, Account Samos Advocacy Collective, 22 November 2021, shared experiences from concerned asylum seekers, https://twitter.com/AdvocacySamos/status/1462769773104746500?s=20.

164 ECRE, 26 November 2021, Greece: Excessive Use of Detention, Shortcomings in Asylum Procedures, Food Crisis Develops as Assistance to Refugees and Asylum Seekers Halted, https://ecre.org/greece-excessive-use-of-detention-shortcomings-in-asylum-procedures-food-crisis-develops-as-assistance-to-refugees-and-asylum-seekers-halted/; Oxfam, 16 November 2021, Briefing Paper, Detention as the Default (fn. 149); I Have Rights, 23 February 2023, Report: The EU-Funded Closed Controlled Access Centre. The De Facto Detention of People Seeking Protection on Samos, https://ihaverights.eu/de_facto_detention_in_the_ccac/.

165 ECRE, 26 November 2021, Greece: Excessive Use of Detention, Shortcomings in Asylum Procedures, Food Crisis Develops as Assistance to Refugees and Asylum Seekers Halted (fn. 164); ECRE, 3 December 2021, Greece: Government Continues NGO Crackdown, Closed Controlled Centres Close in on Asylum Seekers, Significant Jump in Negative Decisions Since Turkey Declared Safe Third Country, https://ecre.org/greece-government-continues-ngo-crackdown-closed-controlled-centres-close-in-on-asylum-seekers-significant-jump-in-negative-decisions-since-Turkey-declared-safe-third-country/.

of EU law.[166] Tellingly, relevant Greek law refers to the MP-RIC as 'closed controlled centres'.[167]

Despite all this, the European Commission indicates on its website that all MP-RICS are open structures.[168] When confronted with the contradiction between its own description versus Greek legal terminology and independent reports, the Commission insisted that only one part of the camp is a pre-removal detention area, whereas the rest of the camp is an open structure.[169] Remarkably, however, the Commission did not further specify whether the open structure is also used as such and which practices of restriction of liberty are applied. Against this background, it is at least likely that the MP-RIC have already led and will further lead to an increase in systemic detention practices.[170]

These uncertainties concerning the general practice under the EU hotspot approach 2.0 notwithstanding, independent reports describe that unaccompanied minors are subject to systemic detention in the MP-RIC in Kos. Since August 2022, unaccompanied minors who seek asylum are obliged to stay in the so-called 'safe zone', which is a closed section inside the MP-RIC. The section is surrounded by barbed wire and guarded by security personnel around the clock. Minors cannot leave during their entire stay on the island, there is no procedure to request unguarded exit, and lawyers must have prior legal authorisation to enter. Applying the above

166 For analysis see Equal Rights Beyond Borders, February 2023, Still Detained and Forgotten (fn. 148), p. 46–47.

167 Art. 8 para 4 of Greek Law 4375/2016, as last amended by Law 4825/2021, describes the facilities as *'Κλειστές Ελεγχόμενες Δομές', i.e. 'closed controlled centres'.*

168 According to European Ombudsman, Inspection Report 9 March 2023, Case OI/3/2022/MHZ (fn. 11), para 17. As of 27 March 2023, the webpage accessible under European Commission, Migration and Home Affairs, New multi-purpose reception and identification centres on Samos, Kos and Leros, https://home-affairs.ec.europa.eu/new-multi-purpose-reception-and-identification-centres-samos-kos-and-leros_en, shows no more than 10 briefly commented pictures of the construction process.

169 European Ombudsman, Inspection Report 9 March 2023, Case OI/3/2022/MHZ (fn. 11), para 17.

170 The fact that the Commission funds and co-manages detention centres in Greece, while at the same time condemning similar centres in Hungary (see only CJEU, judgement of 17 December 2020, European Commission v Hungary, C-808/18 (fn. 151), para 155) reflects that the Commission is both an administrative and a political actor in the European asylum system; on the tensions arising from this dual role see chapter 3, 2.1.

definition, there can be no doubt that this systemically applied practice qualifies as detention.[171]

In sum, it follows that the administrative practice in the EU hotspots violates Art. 6 ChFR in a large number of similar cases, and thus systemically.

3.2 Procedure-Related Deficiencies

Albeit less media-effective than reception conditions, the procedures conducted in the EU hotspots entail systemic fundamental rights violations, too. Three cases are of particular relevance here. First, the EUAA's failures in the context of the hearing regularly; second, Frontex's mistakes in the context of age assessment; and third, the misconduct of both agencies consisting in a misapplication of the third country concept with regard to Türkiye. The first and the second case concerns inherent violations, whereas the third case concerns a resulting violation.

a *The Right to Good Administration (Art. 41 ChFR)*

According to Art. 41 ChFR, the right to good administration guarantees that 'every person has the right to have his or her affairs handled impartially, fairly and within a reasonable time' which, according to Art. 41 para 2 lit a and lit c ChFR, explicitly includes the 'right of every person to be heard, before any individual measure which would affect him or her adversely is taken' and 'the obligation of the administration to give reasons for its decisions'.

The right to good administration serves to ensure 'that any decision adversely affecting a person is adopted in full knowledge of the facts', and that the person concerned is enabled to submit all 'information relating to his personal circumstances as will argue in favour of the adoption or non-adoption of the decision, or in favour of its having a specific content'.[172]

171 Equal Rights Beyond Borders and Terre des Hommes, 23 February 2023, Unaccompanied Minors on Kos are Deprived of Their Liberty and Childhood, https://www.equal-rights.org/articles/101.

172 CJEU (Seventh Chamber), judgment of 4 June 2020, European External Action Service v Stéphane De Loecker, C-187/19 P, para 69 with further references to the case law.

Generally, the scope of the right is 'extremely broad' and of 'general application'.[173]

In the context of asylum procedures, the right to a hearing is of vital importance, as it guarantees that every person must be given the opportunity to explain their individual situation and the reasons for their claim for international protection, including particular vulnerabilities, and the possible application of protection elsewhere clauses.[174] Although Art. 41 ChFR is directly applicable,[175] the Asylum Procedures Directive guarantees specific procedural standards which appear as concretisation of the right to be heard, namely the right to a personal interview in full confidentiality and with the assistance of an interpreter if necessary.[176] Crucially, the purpose of Art. 41 ChFR in this context is to ensure that all persons concerned are granted appropriate status within the meaning of Art. 78 para 1 TFEU.[177]

Consequently, Art. 41 ChFR is violated when the concerned person is not heard by the relevant authority. This applies regardless of whether or not the concerned person can prove that, if they had been heard, the outcome of the procedure would have been different. As the CJEU has consistently held, a breach of Art. 41 ChFR requires only that the procedural error has possibly influenced the content of the decision.[178] In the context of asylum

173 See only Advocate General Yves Bot, Opinion delivered on 7 November 2013, H.N. v Minister for Justice, Equality and Law Reform, C-604/12, para 62–63 with further references to the case law.

174 CJEU (Grand Chamber), judgment of 25 July 2018, Serin Alheto v Zamestnik-predsedatel na Darzhavna agentsia za bezhantsite, C-585/16, para 125–128.

175 CJEU (First Chamber), judgement of 22 November 2012, M.M. v Minister for Justice, Equality and Law Reform and Others, C-277/11, para 86; Hans Jarass, „Art. 41 Recht auf eine gute Verwaltung", *Charta der Grundrechte der EU*, C.H. Beck 2021, para 10.

176 Art. 14–17 Asylum Procedures Directive. Note that in the context of the appeal the right to a hearing derives from Art. 47 ChFR, see CJEU, judgment of 25 July 2018, Alheto, C-585/16 (fn. 174), para 125.

177 Advocate General Yves Bot, Opinion delivered on 7 November 2013, H.N., C-604/12 (fn. 173), para 64.

178 CJEU (Eigth Chamber), judgment of 6 September 2012, August Storck KG v Office for Harmonisation in the Internal Market, C-96/11 P, para 80; CJEU (Fifth Chamber), judgement of 3 July 2014, Kamino International Logistics BVabdDatema Hellmann Worldwide Logistics BV v Staatssecretaris van Financiën, para 79: 'in particular the right to be heard, results in the annulment of the decision taken at the end of the administrative procedure at issue only if, had it not been for such an irregularity, the outcome of the procedure might have been different' with further references to the case law; Hans Jarass, „Art. 41 Recht auf eine gute Verwaltung" (fn. 175), para 5, para 19.

procedures, it follows from this doctrine that the right to be heard is violated in all cases of significant errors, such as for instance, the omission of an interview, a lack of confidentiality or interpretation, suggestive questions on the part of the interviewer, a failure to let the interviewee finish their answers, or a failure to ask follow-up questions where required. As the course of the entire asylum procedure up to the final decision by courts is, to a large extent, predetermined by the information contained in the very first interview transcript, any of the mentioned errors possibly influence the outcome of the relevant procedure.

Applying this standard to the case of the EU hotspots, it must be kept in mind that the EUAA typically fails to comply with procedural standards as laid down in secondary law[179] and systemically oversteps its competences. Due to the seriousness or accumulation of secondary law violations, it is argued here that these mistakes frequently amount to a violation of Art. 41 ChFR. Two constellations require particular attention.

First, the EUAA, in many cases, conducts the asylum interview in a deficient manner. Typical procedural mistakes include conducting the interview in non-private circumstances, a failure to provide adequate translation, inappropriate questions, ignoring relevant claims of applicants, mistakes in the interview transcript, or a failure to provide reasons for its recommendations.[180] Where several procedural mistakes occur in one procedure or where one particularly severe mistake occurs, the misconduct typically amounts to a violation of the right to good administration. All mentioned mistakes constitute clear violations of the procedural safeguards laid down in Art. 14 to 17 Asylum Procedures Directive, now Art. 8 to 14 reformed Asylum Procedures Regulation,[181] and thus result in a failure

179 As the EUAA assists member states in applying EU secondary law, it is consequently obliged to comply with the standards laid down in EU secondary law. Insofar as certain provisions explicitly refer to the member states, such as e.g. Art. 17 para 1 Asylum Procedures Directive and Art. 22 para 1 Reception Conditions, those provisions must hence be applicable by analogy.

180 European Center for Constitutional and Human Rights (ECCHR), April 2019, Case Report: EASO's involvement in Greek Hotspots exceeds the agency's competence and disregards fundamental rights, https://www.ecchr.eu/en/case/greek-hotspots-complaint-against-european-asylum-support-office-to-the-eu-ombudsperson/; own observation of the author (see introduction, fn. 103).

181 Regulation (EU) 2024/1348 of the European Parliament and of the Council of 14 May 2024 establishing a common procedure for international protection in the Union and repealing Directive 2013/32/EU (hereinafter: reformed Asylum Procedures Regulation).

to fully take into account the individual circumstances of the applicant. Consequently, the right to be heard under Art. 41 para para 2 lit a ChFR is usually violated. Where the EUAA relies on standard reasoning, it also fails to comply with its obligation under Art. 41 para 2 lit c ChFR to state reasons. Although the agency's recommendation is not legally binding and thus not technically a 'decision' within the sense of that provision,[182] it must nonetheless contain the relevant reasons for the rejection of the asylum claim. As the national asylum authority will issue its decision without ever having heard the applicant in person, it will necessarily have to adopt the reasons stated in the recommendation. The applicability of Art. 41 ChFR to the EUAA's recommendation thus follows from the purpose of the obligation to state reasons, which is 'a corollary of the principle of respect for the rights of the defence' and thus serves, first, to enable the person concerned to recognise whether a certain act is wrongful and to seek judicial protection if so and, second, to enable the responsible court to review the legality of the concerned act.[183]

Second, the EUAA often fails to conduct a correct vulnerability assessment. Typical mistakes range from a complete omission of the vulnerability interview to an incorrect legal evaluation of claims indicating vulnerability.[184] The failure to conduct a vulnerability assessment or mistakes in that assessment typically violate Art. 21 to 25 Reception Conditions Directive, now Art. 24 to 28 reformed Reception Conditions Directive, establishing special guarantees for particularly vulnerable groups. Where the mistakes are particularly serious, the misconduct typically also amounts to a violation of the fundamental right to good administration. This is because the vulnerability assessment is decisive for the further course of the asylum procedure, as it predetermines whether the person must be exempted from the border procedure and is also relevant to the claim for international pro-

182 Hans Jarass, „Art. 41 Recht auf eine gute Verwaltung“ (fn. 175), para 31 with further references to the case law on the notion of 'decision' in that context.

183 CJEU (Third Chamber), judgement of 15 November 2012, Council of the European Union v Nadiany Bamba, para 49; CJEU (Fifth Chamber), judgment of 21 April 2016, Council of the European Union v Bank Saderat Iran, para 70; Hans Jarass, „Art. 41 Recht auf eine gute Verwaltung“ (fn. 175), para 30.

184 European Center for Constitutional and Human Rights (ECCHR), April 2019, Case Report: EASO's involvement in Greek Hotspots exceeds the agency's competence and disregards fundamental rights, https://www.ecchr.eu/en/case/greek-hotspots-complaint-against-european-asylum-support-office-to-the-eu-ombudsperson/; Equal Rights Beyond Borders, July 2021, Consequences of the EU-Turkey Statement (fn. 40), p. 20–21; own observation of the author (see introduction, fn. 103).

tection as such.[185] Consequently, a failure to give the concerned person the possibility to express the reasons establishing their vulnerability amounts to a violation of the right to be heard under Art. 41 para 2 lit a ChFR.

Since 2016 already, systemic procedural errors on the part of EASO respectively the EUAA have been identified by non-state actors. Yet, there is so far no jurisprudence on the matter. There is only one decision by the European Ombudsman who in 2017 was called upon to decide whether EASO, first, systemically overstepped its competences by effectively determining the outcome of individual asylum procedures in the EU hotspots and, second, systemically failed to respect the right to be heard under Art. 41 ChFR.[186] As regards the first matter, the Ombudsman stressed that EASO's practice raised 'very serious concerns' because it exceeded the legal basis in secondary law, but also recognised that EASO is 'in a particularly difficult position' given that EU soft law confers tasks upon the agency for which it has no competence.[187] Therefore, the Ombudsman argued that the likely future reform of the EASO Regulation would belatedly vest the agency's activities with a legal basis and, on this basis, refrained from further action.[188] Regarding the second matter, i.e., the alleged systemic violation of the fundamental right to be heard, the Ombudsman took a similar stance. Although she acknowledged that 'there are genuine concerns about the quality of the admissibility interviews as well as about the procedural fairness of how they are conducted', she refrained from further inquiries, arguing that EASO has already 'made considerable efforts' and 'steps in the right direction' and that 'ultimate responsibility for decisions on asylum applications rests with the Greek authorities'.[189]

---

185 Art. 24 para 3 Asylum Procedures Directive provides that vulnerable persons must be exempted from the border procedure if their special needs, in terms of procedure and reception conditions, cannot be met within the framework of the border procedure. Note, however, that the general exemption for vulnerable persons under Law 4375/2016 has always been applied in a deficient manner, and has been abolished in 2019, see Equal Rights Beyond Borders, July 2021, Consequences of the EU-Turkey Statement (fn. 40), p. 5.

186 European Ombudsman, Decision of 5 July 2018, on the European Asylum Support Office's (EASO) Involvement in the Decision-Making Process Concerning Admissibility of Applications for International Protection Submitted in the Greek Hotspots, in particular Shortcomings in Admissibility Interviews, Case 735/2017/MDC.

187 Ibid., para 32–33.

188 Ibid., para 34–35.

189 Ibid., para 45–46. See further Salvatore F. Nicolosi, David Fernandez-Rojo, „Out of control? The case of the European Asylum Support Office", in Miroslava Scholten,

b *Specific Procedural Guarantees for Children (Art. 24 and Art. 41 ChFR)*

Similarly, Frontex typically fails to comply with the applicable procedural standards in the context of first registration. A frequent procedural error is to conduct an age assessment only on the basis of visual inspection. Frontex often ignores claims of applicants to be minors and refuses to accept as proof identity documents issued by certain states. As a result, unaccompanied minors are frequently registered as adults.[190]

This practice of assessing an applicant's age purely based on their physical appearance clearly violates the rights of the child as enshrined in the Charter. Art. 24 para 2 ChFR establishes that in all actions relating to children, the child's best interests must be a primary consideration. The provision must be interpreted in light of Art 3 para 1 of the Convention on the Rights of the Child (CRC)[191] and is reflected throughout the applicable EU secondary law.[192] As the Frontex Regulation emphasises, the agency shall, in all its activities, pay particular attention to children's rights.[193] This is of particular relevance in the context of the EU hotspot administration because, usually, unaccompanied minors must be exempt from the border procedure, and the safe third country concept cannot be applied.[194]

Alex Brenninkmeijer (ed.), *Controlling EU Agencies. The Rule of Law in a Multi-jurisdictional Legal Order*, Edward Elgar 2020, p. 177–195, p. 184–185.

190 Chatham House, 28 July 2022, Lesvos: How EU asylum policy created a refugee prison in paradise, https://www.chathamhouse.org/2022/07/lesvos-how-eu-asylum-policy-created-refugee-prison-paradise, fn. 10; euobserver, 10 May 2021, Frontex 'mislabelling minors as adults' on Greek islands, https://euobserver.com/migration/151784; own observation of the author (see introduction, fn. 103).

191 At least insofar as Frontex is concerned because according to Art. 80 para 1 Frontex Regulation, the agency must comply with both EU law and the CRC.

192 For instance, Art. 11 and 23 Reception Conditions Directive, Art. 25 para 6 Asylum Procedures Directive, Art. 20 para 5 of the Directive 2011/95/EU of the European Parliament and of the Council of 13 December 2011 on standards for the qualification of third-country nationals or stateless persons as beneficiaries of international protection, for a uniform status for refugees or for persons eligible for subsidiary protection, and for the content of the protection granted (recast) (hereinafter: Qualification Directive), Art. 6 Dublin III Regulation.

193 See only recital 103 and Art. 80 para 1 and 3 Frontex Regulation.

194 Art. 25 para 6 lit a and b Asylum Procedures Directive provides that the applications of unaccompanied minors can be examined in accelerated border procedures under Art. 31 para 8 Asylum Procedures Directive or the in border procedures under Art. 43 Asylum Procedures Directive only under very specific conditions. Furthermore, Art. 25 para 6 lit c Asylum Procedures Directive provides that the safe third country may only applied if this is in the best interest of the minor. In any case,

With regard to applicants who claim to be minors, it follows from Art. 24 para 2 ChFR that the estimation of their physical appearance as such is not even sufficient to justify a decision to undertake an age assessment. In case of substantial doubt about the age, the applicant's physical appearance can be taken into account, however, only in conjunction with several other criteria and only by qualified physicians.[195] Furthermore, the principle of the benefit of the doubt applies throughout the whole procedure, as Art 25 para 5 Asylum Procedures Directive, now Art. 25 para 2 reformed Asylum Procedures Regulation, explicitly provides.[196] This is especially important in situations of large numbers of arrivals where the responsible authorities' resources might be overstretched.[197]

In addition, estimating the age purely based on visual inspection frequently also violates the fundamental right to good administration, in particular, the right to be heard under Art. 41 para 2 lit a ChFR. According to Art. 24 para 1 ChFR, the child's views shall be taken into consideration on matters which concern them in accordance with their age and maturity. The right to be heard thus applies insofar as the concerned child is capable of forming their own views.[198] In case of doubt about the age, the child must at least be given the opportunity and time to explain any inconsistencies either orally or in writing.[199] Furthermore, age assessment which is purely based on sight can also violate the specific procedural rights inherent in the prohibition of refoulement as granted under Art. 4, 18, 19 ChFR. Insofar as age is a factor relevant to the claim for international protection, it namely follows from Art. 4 para 5 Qualification Directive that credible

---

Art. 11, 23 and 24 Reception Conditions Directive stress that member states must ensure a standard of living adequate for the minor's physical, mental, spiritual, moral and social development. As this is certainly not ensured in the EU hotspots, those provisions imply the obligation to exempt minors from the border procedure.

195 EASO, Practical Guide on Age Assessment, second edition, 2018, https://op.europa.eu/en/publication-detail/-/publication/ceefc444-a67e-11e8-99ee-01aa75ed71a1, p. 20, 23, 49–51, 55.

196 EASO, Practical Guide on Age Assessment (fn. 195), p. 22 formulates the principle as in dubio pro refugio or in dubio pro minore.

197 EASO, Practical Guide on Age Assessment (fn. 195), p. 24–25.

198 In case of doubt about the age, the child must at least be given opportunity and time to explain any inconsistencies either orally or in writing EASO, Practical Guide on Age Assessment (fn. 195), p. 28. Note Art 12 CRC as analysed by UN Committee on the Rights of the Child, General comment No. 12 (2009): The right of the child to be heard, 20 July 2009, CRC/C/GC/12, https://www.refworld.org/docid/4ae562c52.html.

199 EASO, Practical Guide on Age Assessment (fn. 195), p. 28.

oral statements about age must be accepted.[200] As it cannot be determined during the first registration whether child-specific protection needs arise, the benefit of the doubt must apply until an age assessment can be carried out at a later procedural stage.[201]

Despite the gravity of Frontex's systemic misconduct in the context of age assessment, there is so far no single decision by a court or Ombudsman on this issue.[202]

c *The Prohibition of Refoulement (Art. 4, 18, 19 ChFR)*

Lastly, the EU hotspot administration structurally entails a risk of refoulement in violation of Art. 4, 18, 19 ChFR. Although this specific risk of refoulement *through deportation from EU hotspots* to Türkiye has so far materialised only in relatively few cases, it will become relevant again as soon as Türkiye reinstates the readmission policy.[203] Unlike the other procedural errors, the violation of refoulement is not inherent to but results from the agencies' conduct. As will be set out in more detail in the following, the ultimate return decision is issued by Greece, while the EUAA routinely issues recommendations which incorrectly assume that Türkiye can be regarded as safe, and Frontex assists in deportations to Türkiye.

This being said a brief note on refoulement *through pushbacks* to Türkiye is in order. Pushback practices at the Greek land and sea borders, including pushbacks from the Aegean islands where the EU hotspots are located, have attracted increased media attention in recent years.[204] Indeed, evidence of

---

200 Art 4 para 5 lit a to 3 Qualification Directive, establishing that the statement is credible if the applicant has made genuine effort to substantiate the statement, submitted all relevant elements at their disposal and given a satisfactory explanation regarding any lack of other relevant elements, the statement is coherent and plausible, the applicant has applied for international protection at the earliest possible time or has demonstrated good reasons for not having done so, and the general credibility of the applicant is established.

201 This also follows from EASO, Practical Guide on Age Assessment (fn. 195), p. 22, 44–59 and annex 2 thereof.

202 To the best knowledge of the author.

203 See chapter 1, 2.1 on the extremely low numbers of return despite high rejection rates.

204 New York Times, 26 Nov 2020, E.U. Border Agency Accused of Covering Up Migrant Pushback in Greece, https://www.nytimes.com/2020/11/26/world/europe/frontex-migrants-pushback-greece.html; New York Times, 19 May 2023, Video Shows Greece Abandoning Migrants at Sea, https://www.nytimes.com/2023/05/19/world/europe/g

Frontex's involvement in systemic pushbacks was sufficient, in September 2022 already and still in July 2023, for the agency's own Fundamental Rights Officer to conclude that violations of fundamental rights or international protection obligations were of a serious nature or likely to persist and that the agency should therefore, according to Art. 46 para 4 Frontex Regulation, suspend or terminate its operations in Greece.[205] But that alarm call went largely unheard, and Frontex's operations at the Greek-Turkish borders continue. Nevertheless, and the gravity of these violations notwithstanding, the following does not address 'typical pushback practices', simply because they fall outside the scope of this study. Pushbacks usually take place before persons even arrive at the EU hotspot camps. However, it should be kept in mind that the following considerations on the EU's liability are not limited to the EU hotspot administration but can be transferred to pushback cases, too.

reece-migrants-abandoned.html; New York Times, 28 February 2024, Watchdog Finds E.U. Border Agency Too Weak to Prevent Migrant Disasters at Sea, https://www.nytimes.com/2024/02/28/world/europe/eu-migrant-boats-frontex.html; Der Spiegel, 27 April 2022, Frontex in illegale Pushbacks von Hunderten Flüchtlingen involviert, https://www.spiegel.de/ausland/frontex-in-illegale-pushbacks-von-hunderten-fluechtlingen-involviert-a-086f0e5a-0172-4007-b59c-7bced325cc75.

205 Frontex, 10 July 2023, Opinion by the Fundamental Rights Officer, Greece – advice to suspend or terminate Frontex operations in Greece in accordance with Article 46(4) of the EBCG Regulation (redacted version on file with the author), p. 1: 'In the last Opinion, from 1 September 2022, the Fundamental Rights Officer already advised the Executive Director to trigger the mechanism to withdraw the financing, suspend or terminate Frontex activities as provided for in Article 46 of the European Border and Coast Guard Regulation.', p. 2: 'Serious incidents in the pat indicated patterns of behaviour, the cumulation and nature of recent cases from Evros and the Greek Aegean islands now leads the Fundamental Rights Officer to conclude that pushbacks (with other associated fundamental rights violations) are complex, well-resourced and highly coordinated, covert operations conducted systematically, rather than isolated incidents.', p. 3: 'On these grounds, it must be concluded that Frontex support to Greece not only harms the reputation of the agency but also, at least indirectly, enables fundamental rights violations. For these reasons, and as stated at the Management Board meeting on 21 June 2023, the Fundamental Rights Officer considers it necessary to advise the Executive Director to trigger the mechanism to suspend or terminate Frontex activities as provided for in Article 46 of the European Board and Coast Guard Regulation and the corresponding Standard Operating Procedure.'.

i *Why Türkiye is Not a Safe Third Country*

To establish why deportation to Türkiye constitutes misconduct, it must first be argued why Türkiye cannot currently be regarded as a safe third country. For if it was, a deportation to Türkiye would not systemically violate Art. 4, 18, 19 ChFR.

The safe third country concept forms part of protection elsewhere clauses that serve to externalise responsibility for the provision of international protection. International refugee and human rights law sets limits to these externalisation practices. Thus, a third country must fulfil certain criteria in order to be considered as safe. Art. 38 Asylum Procedures Directive, now Art. 59 reformed Asylum Procedures Regulation,[206] codifies these standards and provides – simply put – that a country can be considered as safe only if deportation to that country does not amount to refoulement, i.e. if there is no risk of persecution in the sense of Refugee Convention or of serious harm in the sense of Art. 3 ECHR in the third country, if the third country itself respects the refoulement principle, i.e. if there is no risk of deportation to another non-safe country, and if the possibility exists in the third country to request refugee status and, if found to be a refugee, to receive protection in accordance with the Refugee Convention.[207]

Ever since 2015, it has been fiercely disputed among legal scholars, practitioners, and politicians whether Türkiye qualifies as a safe third country or not.[208] Applying Art. 38 Asylum Procedures Directive first requires a discussion of what it means that the third country must provide protection 'in accordance with' the Refugee Convention. This is of particular relevance because Türkiye is bound to the Convention only insofar as refugees

206 Regulation (EU) 2024/1348 of the European Parliament and of the Council of 14 May 2024 establishing a common procedure for international protection in the Union and repealing Directive 2013/32/EU (hereinafter: reformed Asylum Procedures Regulation). Considering the consequentiality of the case study, the following refers to the pre-reform Asylum Procedures Directive.

207 In more detail on Art. 38 Asylum Procedures Directive see CJEU (First Chamber), judgement of 19 March 2020, LH v Bevándorlási és Menekültügyi Hivatal, C-564/18, para 36–39.

208 Daniel Thym, „Why the EU-Turkey Deal is Legal and a Step in the Right Direction", Verfassungsblog of 09/03/2016; Roman Lehner, „The EU-Turkey-'deal': Legal Challenges and Pitfalls", *International Migration* 57 (2018), p. 176-185.

originating from Europe are concerned,[209] whereas refugees originating from Syria and all other relevant countries fall outside the scope of the Convention and instead receive, if at all, a form of temporary protection.[210] Some argue that Art. 38 must be interpreted as meaning that the third country must have ratified the Refugee Convention and thus conclude that Türkiye cannot be considered as a safe third country.[211] Others stress that the provision can also be understood as meaning that it is sufficient for the third country to provide a protection standard that is equivalent to what is required under the Refugee Convention.[212]

This dispute on Art. 38 Asylum Procedures Directive notwithstanding, the main point of discussion is whether the Turkish protection regime ensures a sufficient standard of protection, i.e. at least a standard equivalent to protection under the Refugee Convention.

The CJEU has not pronounced itself on that question yet. This can partly be explained by a political unwillingness on the part of national courts to provoke a decision by the CJEU on that matter.[213] The Greek Council of State, in the mentioned procedure, refrained from referring a preliminary question to the CJEU, arguing, albeit unconvincingly, that the legal question at stake was an acte clair.[214] Following this example, lower Greek administrative courts have since then refrained from making a reference to the CJEU. Courts of other member states are rarely concerned with the

---

209 UNHCR, Convention Relating to the Status of Refugees, States parties, including reservations and declarations, to the 1967 Protocol Relating to the Status of Refugees as of 4 October 1967, https://www.unhcr.org/5d9ed66a4, p. 4.

210 See only Meltem Ciger-Ineli, „Protecting Syrians in Turkey: A Legal Analysis", *International Journal of Refugee Law* 29 (2017), p. 555-579.

211 See, for instance, Administrative Court of Munich, interim decision of 17 July 2019, para 55; https://www.asylumlawdatabase.eu/de/case-law/germany-administrative-court-munich-17-july-2019-m-11-s-1950722-m-11-s-1950759-0.

212 In this direction Rainer Hofmann, Adela Schmidt, „Ist die Türkei für Asylantragsteller ein sicherer Drittstaat? – Das Urteil des Hellenischen Staatsrats vom 22.9.2017", *Zeitschrift für Ausländerrecht und Ausländerpolitik* 38 (2018), p. 1-6, p. 4 with further references including to European Commission, Communication from the Commission to the European Parliament and the Council on the State of Play of Implementation of the Priority Actions under the European Agenda on Migration, 10 February 2016, COM(2016) 85 final, p. 18.

213 See chapter 3, 2.2.

214 Greek Council of State, decision of 22 September 2017, 2347/2017. The assumption of an acte claire is unconvincing in light of CJEU, judgment of 6 October 1982, Srl CILFIT v Ministero della Sanità, C-283/91, para 16: 'Finally, the correct application of Community law may be so obvious as to leave no scope for any reasonable doubt as to the manner in which the question raised is to be resolved.'.

issue and have so far not been willing to refer either. To the remainder, the lack of case law is due to the CJEU's own political unwillingness to decide on the matter. When the CJEU had an occasion to pronounce itself on whether Türkiye qualified as safe, namely in the procedure concerning the action for annulment against the EU-Türkiye Statement, the CJEU dismissed the action as inadmissible with the consequence that the question of Art. 38 Asylum Procedures Directive fell outside the scope of its jurisdiction.[215]

The ECtHR, in the same vein but for different reasons than the CJEU, has so far also remained silent on the question of whether deportation to Türkiye amounts to refoulement. Unlike before the CJEU, however, this could change soon, as several individual complaints invoked a violation of Art. 3 ECHR due to deportation from Greece to Türkiye are pending.[216]

Yet, both the CJEU and the ECtHR have recently provided general guidance on the interpretation of the safe third country concept. Mainly in the context of cases concerning deportations from Hungary to Serbia, the CJEU has detailed its interpretation of Art. 38 Asylum Procedures Directive,[217] and the ECtHR, in turn, has specified its interpretation of Art. 3 ECHR in relation to protection elsewhere clauses.[218]

Amongst other things, the ECtHR emphasised that the assessment of the situation in the third country must necessarily take into account the factual situation and that it is the duty of the expelling state to seek all relevant information to substantiate the argument that the third country is safe for the concerned applicant.[219] In the words of the ECtHR in *Ilias and Ahmad*, 'the expelling state cannot merely assume that the asylum seeker will be treated in the receiving third country in conformity with the Convention

215 CJEU, orders of 28 February 2017, NF v European Council (EU-Turkey Statement), T-192/16 (fn. 54).

216 ECtHR, Communication of 18 May 2017, J.B. v Greece, Application No. 54796/16; ECtHR, Dana Ebrahimnezhad v Türkiye, Salih Braim Ahmed Ahmed v Türkiye, Application nos. 53614/19 and 56562/19.

217 See only CJEU, judgment of 25 July 2018, Alheto, C-585/16 (fn. 174); para 121–130; CJEU, Court (First Chamber), judgement of 19 March 202, LH v Bevándorlási és Menekültügyi Hivatal, C-564/18, para 36–47; CJEU, judgement of 14 May 2020, FMS, C-924/19 PPU et al (fn. 151), para 148–165.

218 ECtHR, judgement of 21 November 2019, Ilias and Ahmed v Hungary, Application No. 47287/15.

219 Ibid., para 65–78; ECtHR, judgement of 5 December 2013, Sharifi v Austria, Application No. 60104/08, para 31–32; ECtHR, judgement of 21 January 2011, M.S.S. v Belgium and Greece (fn. 136), para 359.

standards but, on the contrary, must first verify how the authorities of that country apply their legislation on asylum in practice.'[220]

Against this background, it is very problematic that the decision of the Greek Council for State, which has long been cited as confirming that Türkiye is generally safe for Syrian applicants, was based on the factual situation as presented by Turkish diplomats,[221] and stood in stark contradiction to the situation as presented by independent studies.[222]

Today, one of the central problems in assessing the situation in Türkiye is that, due to the increasing state repression of NGOs and lawyers in Türkiye, there are hardly any up-to-date independent situation reports.[223] While this as such speaks against considering Türkiye as safe, most assessments by the EUAA, formerly EASO, as well as decisions by the Greek Asylum Service simply rely on outdated information.[224]

This being said the scarce available and reliable information shows that Türkiye cannot be considered a safe third country under Art. 3 ECtHR, let alone under Art. 38 Asylum Procedures Directive. Several reliable sources

---

220 ECtHR, judgement of 21 November 2019, Ilias and Ahmed v Hungary (fn. 218), para 141. In addition to general information, the expelling state must also give 'sufficient opportunity' to the concerned person to demonstrate that the country in question is not safe in their particular case, see ibid. para 148.

221 Greek Council of State, decision of 22 September 2017, 2347/2017; Angeliki Tsiliou, „When Greek judges decide whether Turkey is a Safe Third Country without caring too much for EU law", eumigrationlawblog of 29/05/2018; Rainer Hofmann, Adela Schmidt, „Ist die Türkei für Asylantragsteller ein sicherer Drittstaat? – Das Urteil des Hellenischen Staatsrats vom 22.9.2017" (fn. 212), p. 3.

222 Orcun Ulusoy, Hemme Battjes, „Situation of Readmitted Migrants and Refugees from Greece to Turkey under the EU-Turkey Statement", *VU Migration Law Series* (2017); Ilse van Liempt, Maybritt Jill Alpes, Saima Hassan, Sevda Tunaboylu, Orcun Ulusoy, Annelies Zoomers, *Evidence-Based Assessment of Migration Deals. The case of the EU-Turkey Statement*, 2017, https://www.uu.nl/en/research/human-geography-and-planning/evidence-based-assessment-of-the-eu-Turkey-refugee-deal, p. 20 et seq.

223 See only the preface of ECRE, Country Report Türkiye, 2021 Update, https://ecre.org/aida-2021-update-turkiye/, noting that, while the original report and earlier update was drafted by Refugee Rights Turkey, 'the updates since 2017 have been researched and drafted by an independent consultant' and stressing that 'access to official information on the situation of persons under international or temporary protection in Turkey remains limited to date'. For instance, NGOs such as Mülteci-Der have retrieved most of their relevant publications from their website, with currently only one report on sexual and reproductive health being available in English, see https://multeci.org.tr/en/category/publications/.

224 Equal Rights Beyond Borders, July 2021, Consequences of the EU-Turkey Statement (fn. 40), p. 21–24.

report that readmitted persons are regularly subject to detention in Türkiye or to subsequent deportation to their country of origin, including Syria, often without the practical possibility to challenge these decisions before a court.[225] Further, there are numerous reports of severe discrimination, mistreatment or violent abuse on the part of Turkish authorities, of a lack of access to the temporary protection regime, and of a failure of Turkish authorities to provide emergency medical care, food, housing and further similarly basic rights.[226] Based on the factual situation as presented by independent sources, it can hence neither established that there is no risk of persecution in Türkiye, nor that Türkiye respects the non-refoulement principle, nor that Türkiye de facto grants protection that corresponds to protection under the Refugee Convention.

ii *The Administrative Practice in the EU Hotspots*

The practice in the EU hotspots concerning the application of the safe third country concept has evolved over time.[227] Between 2015 and 2019, the Greek asylum service has, in the overwhelming majority of cases, concluded that Türkiye could be considered a safe third country, but these decisions were routinely overturned on Appeal.[228] The arguments of the Appeals Committees were similar to those just presented in the application of the ECtHR's jurisprudence. As mentioned above, the Appeals Committees were then recomposed, which resulted in them generally considering Türkiye as a safe third country.[229]

225 EASO, Country of Origin Information Report, Syria Situation of returnees from abroad, 2021, p. 12–13 with further references; Amnesty International, 2019, Sent to a War Zone: Turkey's Illegal Deportations of Syrian Refugees, p. 5; Human Rights Watch, 24 October 2019, Turkey: Syrians being deported to danger, https://www.hrw.org/news/2019/10/24/Türkiye-syrians-being-deported-danger.

226 ECRE, Country Report Türkiye, 2021 Update (fn. 223), in particular p. 14–19, 26–49, 78–81, 114, 140; Equal Rights Beyond Borders, July 2021, Consequences of the EU-Turkey Statement (fn. 40), p. 14–19 with further references.

227 For a comprehensive case law report based on the analysis of 127 decisions see Greek Council for Refugees, HIAS, RSA, January 2021, Asylum Case Law Report, https://rsaegean.org/en/greek-asylum-case-law-report-issue1/ (available only in Greek).

228 Mariana Gkliati, „The Application of the EU-Turkey Agreement: A Critical Analysis of the Decisions of the Greek Appeals Committee", *European Journal of Legal Studies* 10 (2017), p. 81–124, p. 83.

229 See chapter 1, fn. 130 et seq.

Since the summer of 2020, the decision-making practice has changed again. This is due to a Joint Ministerial Decision (JMD), which classified Türkiye as a safe third country for persons originating from Afghanistan, Syria, Somalia, Bangladesh and Pakistan.[230] The issuance of the JMD immediately had the effect that asylum claims were frequently rejected as inadmissible based on the argument that Türkiye could be considered as safe.[231] The situation in Türkiye, however, had not substantially changed in the relevant period, nor had the information basis been improved.[232] In fact, most decisions were based on a template reasoning that combines standard sentences and references without, however, providing a single convincing argument as to why Türkiye should suddenly be considered safe.

It hence clearly appears that the Greek asylum service systemically misapplies the concept of a safe third country. For the purpose of this study, the crucial point is that both the EUAA and Frontex are involved in this systemic misapplication.

First, the EUAA typically recommends considering Türkiye as a safe third country. In fact, the agency often considers Türkiye as safe on the basis of standard reasoning and without taking sufficient account of the individual situation of the applicant concerned.[233] This practice, as such, violates Art. 38 Asylum Procedures Directive: for although the EUAA's recommendation is not formally binding upon the Greek asylum service,

230 ECRE, 3 December 2021, Greece: Government Continues NGO Crackdown, Closed Controlled Centres Close in on Asylum Seekers, Significant Jump in Negative Decisions Since Turkey Declared Safe Third Country (fn. 165); Equal Rights Beyond Boders, HIAS Greece, Refugee Support Aegean, September 2022, The State of the Border Procedure on the Greek Islands (fn. 134), p. 19–25. Note that the JMD was subject to review before the Council of State, see RSA, 8 October 2021, Decision declaring Turkey a "safe third country" brought before Greek Council of State, https://rsaegean.org/en/Turkey-a-safe-third-country-greek-council-of-state/.

231 Twitter, Account Minos Mouzourakis, 26 November 2021, Clear Signs of Impact of New Greek Safe Third Country Policy From Official EU Data, https://twitter.com/MinosMouz/status/1464209455726436355?s=20. See in more detail on the effects of the JMD: Equal Rights Beyond Borders, 28 February 2022, Submission to the Special Rapporteur on the Human Rights of Migrants, Human Rights Violations at International Borders: Trends, Prevention and Accountability, https://equal-rights.org/resources/publications, p. 4–5.

232 RSA, Common Statement by NGOs and civil society actors, 14 June 2021, Greece deems Turkey "safe", but refugees are not, https://rsaegean.org/en/greece-deems-Turkey-safe-but-refugees-are-not/#endnote-2.

233 Equal Rights Beyond Borders, July 2021, Consequences of the EU-Turkey Statement (fn. 40), p. 13–19; own observation of the author (see introduction, fn. 103).

it is certainly obliged to provide a legally correct recommendation. In addition, Art. 34 para 1 Asylum Procedures Directive, now Art. 59 para 4 lit. a reformed Asylum Procedures Regulation, is frequently violated, as it provides that applicants must be allowed to present their views with regard to the application of the safe third country concept in their particular circumstances.

At the same time, the EUAA's practice also violates the procedural dimension of the non-refoulement principle. It is an essential element of the right not to be refouled that an applicant can fully express all individual circumstances that might speak against the consideration of a particular third country as safe for them and that the responsible authority takes those circumstances into account.[234] The EUAA, however, often fails to give the applicant an effective opportunity to explain their individual experiences, often fails to assess those individual circumstances, and usually relies on outdated general information instead.[235] The agency thus typically violates the applicant's fundamental rights under Art. 4, 18, 19 ChFR too.

Remarkably, the EUAA has continued to consider Türkiye as safe even after readmissions to Türkiye were halted in March 2020.[236] This is problematic because the safe third country concept is based on the idea that the concerned person can effectively seek protection in the third country. With regard to a country that denies asylum seekers access to its territory, this rationale cannot apply. This is confirmed by Art. 38 para 4 Asylum Procedures Directive, which provides that a subsequent asylum procedure must be conducted if the third country does not permit the applicant to enter its territory.[237] In a situation in which it is already unequivocally clear at the time of the inadmissibility decision that the third country will not allow the applicant to enter its territory, it hence follows that this country cannot be considered as safe from the outset. Otherwise, the inadmissibility procedure would become a procedural step that merely delays the proce-

234 As expressly laid down in Art. 38 para 2 lit c Asylum Procedures Directive.

235 Equal Rights Beyond Borders, July 2021, Consequences of the EU-Turkey Statement (fn. 40), p. 21–24.

236 Ibid., p. 3–4, 14–15, 32.

237 Transposed in Art. 91 para 5 of the Greek Asylum Code which providing that 'where the third country in question does not allow the applicant to enter its territory, his application shall be examined on the merits by the Competent Examination Authority' (translation by Equal Rights Beyond Boders, HIAS Greece, Refugee Support Aegean, September 2022, The State of the Border Procedure on the Greek Islands (fn. 134), p. 21).

dure but is completely futile.[238] In sum, the EUAA's more recent practice violates Art. 33, 38 Asylum Procedures Directive, now 38, 59 reformed Asylum Procedures Regulation, and the non-refoulement principle already for the simple reason that Türkiye de facto refuses to take back asylum seekers.

Nonetheless, and second, Frontex supports the enforcement of deportations to Türkiye. Inter alia, the agency provides vessels, technical support, and personnel to accompany forcible returns.[239] Despite the low number of actual deportations, Frontex's misconduct in this context qualifies as systemic because the agency assists in all cases in which deportation actually occurs.

More precisely, Frontex's assistance is unlawful because enforcing deportations to a non-safe third country in itself constitutes a violation of the non-refoulement principle. Certainly, Frontex is not obliged to assess whether an individual deportation is unlawful or not. However, when Frontex becomes aware of indications that a deportation in which it provides assistance violates the non-refoulement principle, it is arguably obliged to inform the host member state and to recommend that the concrete deportation be halted. This follows from the Frontex Regulation which stresses that the agency must guarantee, within the limits of its competences of course, that the non-refoulement principle is granted.[240] This must mean that the agency is obliged to inform the host member state when it becomes aware of indications or evidence as to the unlawfulness of a concrete deportation in which it is assisting. Otherwise, the agency could provide support to unlawful deportations, which would be in breach of Art. 1 Frontex Regulation and Art. 51 para 1 ChFR.

To conclude, the EUAA's recommendation to consider Türkiye as safe, as well as Frontex's assistance in deportations to Türkiye, violates Art. 4, 18, 19 ChFR. The agencies thus engage in systemic misconduct, which results in fundamental rights violations.

---

238 For the Commission's opinion on that issue see Equal Rights Beyond Boders, HIAS Greece, Refugee Support Aegean, September 2022, The State of the Border Procedure on the Greek Islands (fn. 134), p. 21.

239 Frontex JO Poseidon OP 2019 (fn. 27), 4.1 – 4.3, and especially 4.3.9. on support of implementation of readmission activity.

240 Frontex Regulation, passim, in particular Art. 1, Art. 48 para 1 thereof.

3.3. Qualification as Systemic Deficiencies

It has been established that violations of Art. 4, 6, 24, 18, 19, 24 and 41 ChFR occur on such a regular basis and in such a large number of cases that these violations must be seen as 'built-in' to EU hotspots, in the sense that the construction of the integrated EU hotspot administration as such produces systemic fundamental rights violations. The following justifies the qualification of such deficiencies as 'systemic'.

The notion of systemic deficiencies, systemic deficits, or systemic breaches is an old and widespread one. Its main purpose is to set a threshold of gravity or seriousness beyond which a certain legal or political response becomes necessary.[241] In the context of EU law, there are two main strands of discourse on systemic deficiencies, one concerning the specific context of the asylum system,[242] and one concerning the more general context of the rule of law crisis.[243] While these two strands of discussion increasingly tend to overlap,[244] they are still not fully congruent in terms of structure, argument and telos.

Beginning with the specific context of the asylum system, the notion of systemic deficiencies was developed by the CJEU in its *N.S.* line of

241 On the history and general function Evangelia (Lilian) Tsourdi, Cathryn Costello, „'Systemic Violations' in EU Asylum Law: Cover or Catalyst?", *German Law Journal* 24 (2023), p. 982–994, p. 982 et seq.

242 And similar sub-systems based on mutual trust, see e.g. Anna Lübbe, „'Systemic Flaws' and Dublin Transfers: Incompatible Tests Before the CJEU and the ECtHR?", *International Journal of Refugee Law* 27 (2015), p. 135-140; Cathryn Costello, „Courting Access to Asylum in Europe: Recent Supranational Jurisprudence Explored", *Human Rights Law Review* 12 (2012), p. 287-339, p. 331; Evangelia (Lilian) Tsourdi, Cathryn Costello, „'Systemic Violations' in EU Asylum Law: Cover or Catalyst?" (fn. 241); Valsamis Mitsilegas, „The Limits of Mutual Trust in Europe's Area of Freedom, Security and Justice: From Automatic Inter-State Cooperation to the Slow Emergence of the Individual", *Yearbook of European Law* (2012), p. 319–372; also Koen Lenaerts, „La vie après l'avis: Exploring the Principle of Mutual (Yet Not Blind) Trust", *Common Market Law Review* 54 (2017), p. 805-840, p. 828 et seq.

243 Armin von Bogdandy, Michael Ioannidis, „Systemic Deficiency in the Rule of Law: What it is, what has to be done, what can be done", *Common Market Law Review* 51 (2014), p. 59–96; Armin von Bogdandy, „Principles of a Systemic Deficiencies Doctrine: How to Protect Checks and Balances in the Member States", *Common Market Law Review* 57 (2020), p. 705-740.

244 Evangelia (Lilian) Tsourdi, Cathryn Costello, „'Systemic Violations' in EU Asylum Law: Cover or Catalyst?" (fn. 241), p. 989 et seq.

jurisprudence,[245] which incorporated and adapted the ECtHR's *M.S.S.* line of jurisprudence to the EU legal order.[246] The main function of the notion of systemic deficiencies was to set a threshold for rebutting mutual trust in the context of intra-EU deportations or transfers.[247] As the CJEU put it in *N.S.*, the assumption of mutual trust between member states cannot hold when 'there are substantial grounds for believing that there are systemic flaws in the asylum procedure and reception conditions for asylum applicants in the Member State responsible, resulting in inhuman or degrading treatment, within the meaning of Article 4 of the Charter'.[248] Accordingly, systemic deficiencies in the asylum system are generally understood to mean particularly grave and widespread violations that are embedded in a national asylum system.[249]

With regard to the case at hand, however, this consolidated understanding is challenged insofar as it focuses on deficiencies at the national level. In the case of EU hotspots, the key question is whether breaches can be qualified as systemic even when they occur at the EU level or in the context of the integrated administration. In other words, the question is whether the fact that the EU is involved speaks against the conceptualisation of regular and grave fundamental rights violations as 'systemic'. While an in-depth discussion of this question would go beyond the scope of this chapter,[250] a few observations must suffice here. First, the focus of the consolidated

245 CJEU, judgment of 21 December 2011, N.S. et al, C-411/10 et al (fn. 141), para 86–106.

246 ECtHR, judgement of 21 January 2011, M.S.S. v Belgium and Greece (fn. 136). For the history of the concept's history in international human rights law see Evangelia (Lilian) Tsourdi, Cathryn Costello, „'Systemic Violations' in EU Asylum Law: Cover or Catalyst?" (fn. 241), p. 984–985, and for a convincing critique of the CJEU's adaption of the ECtHR's concept see ibid, 985–988 with further references to earlier literature, especially in fn. 16.

247 See CJEU, Court, Opinion of 18 December 2014 on the Accession of the European Union to the European Convention for the Protection of Human Rights and Fundamental Freedoms, 2/13, para 191–195; Bruno De Witte, Šejla Imamovic, „Opinion 2/13 on accession to the ECHR : defending the EU legal order against a Foreign Human Rights Court", *European Law Review* 40 (2015), p. 683-705.

248 CJEU, judgment of 21 December 2011, N.S. et al, C-411/10 et al (fn. 141), para 83–86.

249 Evangelia (Lilian) Tsourdi, Cathryn Costello, „'Systemic Violations' in EU Asylum Law: Cover or Catalyst?" (fn. 241), p. 983.

250 For a work in this direction see Evangelia (Lilian) Tsourdi, Cathryn Costello, „'Systemic Violations' in EU Asylum Law: Cover or Catalyst?" (fn. 241), p. 992: 'the CEAS that entails policies and practices that are nearly certain to expose protection-seekers to recurrent human rights violations', p. 993: 'Where the CEAS leads to systemic human rights violations, (…).', i.e. arguing that the CEAS 'facilitates' systemic breaches.

notion on the national level is not conceptually motivated but due to its historical genesis and doctrinal function.[251] Second, this chapter has shown empirically that the vertically integrated administration can result in the systemic violation of fundamental rights, including Art. 4 ChFR. Third, taking seriously the observation that the EU has become a threat to the fundamental rights of asylum seekers and refugees[252] necessarily implies that systemic deficiencies can occur at EU level. For the purpose of this study, it is hence concluded that the integrated asylum administration can be characterised by systemic deficiencies.

The second and more general strand of discussion on systemic deficiencies emerged in the context of the rule of law crisis in several EU member states and developed the notion as a significant threshold to trigger a specific legal and political response. In a nutshell, breaches of EU law are deemed 'systemic' when they constitute a persistent and significant deviation from the values enshrined in Art. 2 TEU.[253] Taking this argument one step further, and based on the understanding that there is a European society which is held together by its striving towards the realisation of the values enshrined in Art. 2 TEU,[254] it follows that systemic deficiencies in this broad sense must appear as grave deficits of the European society.

Applying this more general concept to the context at hand hence leads to the question of whether systemic deficiencies in the integrated asylum administration qualify as grave societal deficits. This is not a question for the ivory tower; it makes a decisive difference, in concrete political and legal terms, whether systemic deficiencies in the asylum system are understood as grave deficits of the European society or not.[255] Again, given the scope of this chapter, sketching a few points must suffice here. Clearly, systemic

251 See Evangelia (Lilian) Tsourdi, Cathryn Costello, „'Systemic Violations' in EU Asylum Law: Cover or Catalyst?" (fn. 241).

252 See chapter 1, 1.

253 Armin von Bogdandy, Michael Ioannidis, „Systemic Deficiency in the Rule of Law" (fn. 243).

254 Armin von Bogdandy, *The Emergence of European Society through Public Law. A Hegelian and Anti-Schmittian Approach*, Oxford University Press 2024, p. 3 et seq., on systemic deficiencies p. 162 et seq.

255 The answer to this question is relevant for the understanding of who forms part of the European society, but also for the understanding of EU law as a tool for transforming the European society. For instance, if systemic deficiencies were grave deficits of the European society, this would argue in favour of the applicability of rule of law mechanisms in this context; in this direction Evangelia (Lilian) Tsourdi, Cathryn Costello, „'Systemic Violations' in EU Asylum Law: Cover or Catalyst?" (fn.

violations of fundamental rights, including of Art. 4 ChFR, constitute a deviation from the EU's foundational values. Thus, an argument against qualifying systemic deficiencies in the asylum system as grave societal deficits would have to posit that it was a prerequisite for the latter that the violation of the values results primarily in the violation of the rights of EU citizens.[256] Put differently, only if violations of the fundamental rights of third-country nationals were less serious, in light of Art. 2 TEU, than similar violations affecting EU citizens, one could say that systemic deficits in the asylum system are not deficits of European society. Such an argument, however, could not be convincing. Art. 2 TEU does not establish a two-track system of values, nor does it provide for two versions of the rule of law,[257] which differ according to whether the persons affected by European public authority are EU citizens or not. Such reading would not only be a misinterpretation of Art. 2 TEU but would also reintroduce the long-overcome idea of migration law exceptionalism[258] through the back door. The values enshrined in Art. 2 TEU, by their very nature, must apply to any exercise of public authority within the EU, be it towards citizens or non-citizens.

Therefore, it is concluded here, for the purpose of this study, that systemic deficiencies in the vertically integrated asylum administration fall under the notion of 'systemic deficiencies' in the sense of the rule-of-law strand, too. The systemic violation of the fundamental rights of asylum seekers must be qualified as a deficiency of the European society as such. This is consistent not only from a doctrinal but also from a societal perspective: The normative standards of society are tested precisely when it comes to the treatment of those persons who do not or not yet have the

---

241), p. 989 et seq., albeit not referring to the specific context of the integrated administration.

256 Or distinguish on the basis of a similar membership marker, e.g. denizenship.

257 Barbara Grabowska-Moroz, Dimitry Vladimirovich Kochenov, „The Loss of Face for Everyone Concerned. EU Rule of Law in the Context of the 'Migration Crisis'", in V Stoyanova, S Smet (ed.), *Migrants' Rights, Populism and Legal Resilience in Europe*, Cambridge University Press 2022, p. 187–208, passim.

258 Migration law exceptionalism is understood here to refer to the idea that migration law escapes general constitutional principles or even human rights law. See with reference to the US American legal system: Peter H. Schuck, „The Transformation of Immigration Law", *Columbia Law Review* 84 (1984), p. 1-90, 1: 'Immigration has long been a maverick, a wild card, in our public law. Probably no other area of American law has been so radically insulated and divergent from those fundamental norms of constitutional right, administrative procedure, and judicial role that animate the rest of our legal system.'.

status of members. It is precisely in dealing with strangers that it becomes apparent whether a society lives up to its own standards. If the violation of Art. 4, 7, 8, 18, 19, 24, 41 ChFR in ten thousands cases would not constitute a grave deficiency of the society, then the promise of Art. 2 TEU would indeed be rather hollow.

4 Identifying Relevant Misconduct of EU Bodies

Having defined the agencies' and the Commission's involvement, as well as the systemic deficiencies in the EU hotspot administration, this section identifies the EU's specific misconduct. This is necessary because determining whether the EU is legally responsible for fundamental rights violations necessarily requires a precise definition of the misconduct in question. Put differently, only once it is clear what the misconduct is can it be discussed which procedure is best suited to address it before the CJEU.[259]

4.1 The EUAA's Misconduct at Operational Level

The EUAA systemically commits two procedural errors that amount to a violation of Art. 41 ChFR, and hence qualify as inherent violations. First, the agency often fails to conduct a correct vulnerability assessment, and second, it often makes mistakes during the conduct of the asylum interview. These mistakes are well illustrated in cases 1 and 2.

> *Case 1 – Sara Esmaili – Deficient vulnerability assessment (EUAA)*
> Although Ms Esmaili, being a pregnant single mother and a survivor of severe sexual and gender-based violence, clearly qualifies as vulnerable, the EUAA failed to identify and recognise her special needs. This constitutes a violation of Art. 22 para 1 Reception Conditions Directive, providing for the obligation to assess whether the applicant has special reception needs, and Art. 24 para 1 Asylum Procedures Directive, providing for the obligation to assess whether the applicant is in need of special procedural guarantees.[260] Due to the central importance of the

259 This will be discussed in the following chapters. On this basis, the following chapter will then discuss whether the identified instances of misconduct incur liability under Art. 41 para 3 ChFR, Art. 340 para 2 TFEU, or not.

260 Now Art. 25 para 1, 24 et seq. reformed Reception Conditions Directive.

vulnerability assessment to the asylum procedure in EU hotspots, the failure to give Ms Esmaili the opportunity to fully explain her particular situation also constitutes a violation of the right to be heard under Art. 41 para 2 lit a ChFR.

Case 2 – Magan Daud – Deficient asylum interview (EUAA)
In the case of Mr Daud, the EUAA conducted the interview in a semi-open space so that his answers could be easily overheard by the adjacent interviewee speaking the same language. This constitutes a breach of Art. 15 para 2 Asylum Procedures Directive which provides that the appropriate confidentiality must be granted.[261] Further, the EUAA provided an incomplete transcript, thereby violating Art. 17 para 1 Asylum Procedures Directive, according to which a thorough and factual report containing all substantive elements or a transcript shall be made of every personal interview.[262] Taking into consideration that the interview conducted by the EUAA is the only opportunity for Mr Daud to express the reasons for his claim for international protection, the failure to provide a complete transcript also violates his right to be heard under Art. 41 para 2 lit a ChFR because it deprives him of the possibility to review and, if necessary, complement his claim.
Moreover, the responsible EUAA caseworker conducted the admissibility interview in a manner that was primarily aimed at ending the interview quickly, asked standard questions only, and applied a template reasoning instead of analysing the specific circumstances of the individual case. In particular, she brushed aside Mr Daud's references to his experience of torture in Syria with the argument that this was an admissibility interview in which only the applicant's situation in Türkiye would be relevant. She thereby failed to allow Mr Daud to explain that he was tortured in Syria after Türkiye had returned him to his country of origin. This fact, however, was directly relevant to the admissibility interview because it clearly spoke against classifying Türkiye as a safe third country for him. Hence, ignoring the torture claims during the admissibility interview and recommending that Türkiye would be a safe third country for Mr Daud violates Art. 33, 34 para 1, 38 Asylum Procedures Directive, as well as his right to be heard under Art. 41 para 2 lit a ChFR.

261 Now Art. 7 reformed Asylum Procedures Regulation.
262 Now Art. 14 reformed Asylum Procedures Regulation.

Further, the EUAA is also involved in the systemic violation of the non-refoulement principle as granted by Art. 4, 18, 19 ChFR, as it typically misapplies the safe third country concept with regard to Türkiye, including in cases where readmission to Türkiye is de facto impossible due to the halt of the readmission policy.[263] In this constellation, the fundamental rights violation is not inherent in the EUAA's conduct but results from it, as illustrated by case 5.

> *Case 5 – Kareem Rashid – Misapplication of safe third country concept (EUAA)*
> In the case of Mr Rashid, the EUAA recommended considering Türkiye as a safe third country, thereby ignoring that the readmission policy had de facto been halted since March 2020. Mr Rashid's asylum claim was hence rejected as inadmissible, but he could obviously not be deported due to the halt of the readmission policy. While he had the right to lodge a subsequent application, he could not make use of that right because Greece had introduced high fees for subsequent applications.[264] As a result, he remained in Greece as a rejected asylum seeker and without access to any state support.

4.2 Frontex's Misconduct at Operational Level

Frontex typically commits two errors. First, it conducts the age assessment on the basis of visual inspection alone, and second, it provides personal and technical support to deportations to Türkiye, including in cases where Türkiye cannot be considered a safe third country. The respective failures are well illustrated with cases 3 and 4. In both cases, the violation of procedural rights is inherent to the agency's misconduct. At the same time, resulting violations come into consideration in both cases, too. As will become clear in the following, this concerns resulting violations relating to reception conditions, as in case 3, and relating to deportation to a non-safe third country, as in case 4.

---

263 See chapter 1, 2.1.

264 According to Art. 89 para 10 Law 4636/2019 (International Protection Act) as amended by Art. 23 Law 4825/04.09.2021, applicants must pay 100 Euro for every subsequent asylum application. See further ECRE, Country Report Greece, 2021 Update (fn. 45), p. 19, p. 134–135.

Case 3 – Daniat Kidane – Age assessment through visual inspection (Frontex)
In the case of Daniat Kidane, the responsible Frontex expert ignored her explicit claims to be minor. Instead, he exclusively relied on his subjective impression of Daniat's physical appearance and concluded that she was adult. The Frontex expert hence applied his estimation of the physical appearance as the only method for assessing the age. As established above, this constitutes a violation of the procedural rights of the child under Art. 24, 41 ChFR.

Case 4 – Nabeeh Al Badawi – Return to Türkiye (Frontex)
In the case of Mr Al Badawi, Frontex assisted the Hellenic Police in carrying out the unlawful deportation by providing the vessel and personnel to escort the deportation. Before Mr Al Badawi was handed over to Turkish authorities, he again mentioned that he had previously been returned from Türkiye to Syria and that he had subsequently been subject to torture there. He also expressed his fear of again being returned from Türkiye to Syria. The Frontex staff escorting the deportation asked for an interpreter and took note of Mr Al Badawi's concerns. He then informed Mr Al Badawi that he should have raised these concerns during the asylum procedure and that, in any case, Greece, and not Frontex, is responsible for assessing asylum claims. Accordingly, the staff member did not intervene or stop the deportation, nor did he later raise any concerns about the deportation towards the responsible coordinating officer.

4.3 The Commission's Misconduct at Supervisory Level

The Commission's typical misconduct can generally be described as a failure to adequately supervise the EU hotspot administration.[265] This concerns reception conditions as well as asylum and deportation procedures,

265 On the Commission's failure to enforce EU law in the context of the Greek asylum administration more generally, see European Parliament, Resolution of 7 February 2024 on the rule of law and media freedom in Greece, 2024/2502(RSP), para 17, where the Parliament 'calls on the Commission to assess the compliance with EU law of border surveillance systems using behavioural analytics, and *of the EU funding thereof*; condemns the Commission's *dramatic failure to enforce EU laws with regard to reception conditions, pushbacks and human rights*', and para 18, where the Parliament 'calls on the Commission to make *full use of the tools available to*

with the difference being that the Commission's reception-related obligations are broader than its procedure-related obligations. This being said, the Commission's failure to ensure adequate reception conditions – which means at least that basic needs are met and that there is no generic detention scheme – is well illustrated in cases 1, 5 and 6.

Case 1 – Sara Esmaili – Failure to provide humane reception conditions (Commission)
The case of Ms Esmaili and her daughter is representative insofar as the reception conditions in the camp amount to inhumane treatment under Art. 4 ChFR for vulnerable persons. Although this has been documented meticulously, the Commission apparently failed to comply with its obligation under Art. 40 para 3 Frontex Regulation, Art. 21 para 2 EUAA Regulation, Art. 17 TEU to prevent systemic deficiencies. From the outset, the Commission either failed to provide the necessary support or to adequately coordinate its cooperation with the host member state. Once the systemic deficiencies became apparent, the Commission obviously failed to effectively address the issue within the relevant supervisory fora, such as thc EURTF and the Steering Committee.

Case 5 – Kareem Rashid – Failure to address limbo situation (Commission)
Similarly, in the case of Mr Rashid, the crucial point is that his case reflects systemic malpractice on the part of the EUAA and Greek authorities since March 2020. The Commission, however, apparently failed to make appropriate usc of its competences within the relevant supervisory fora. Remarkably, it was only in June 2021 that the Commission publicly took note of the so-called limbo situation that arose due to the halt of readmissions and clarified that Art. 38 para 4 of the Asylum Procedures Directive was to be interpreted so as to allow asylum seekers affected by the limbo situation to submit a fresh claim for asylum, and that, in the meantime, applicants must be granted access to reception conditions in line with Union law.[266] While this answer can be interpreted as an expression of the Commission's role as a guardian of the Treaties in a

it to address the breaches of the values enshrined in Article 2 TEU in Greece (...)' (emphasis added).

266 Notably in a belated response to a priority question by a member of the European Parliament, see Answer given by Ms Johansson on behalf of the European Commission, EN P-000604/2021, 1 June 2021, available at: https://www.europarl.europa.eu/doceo/document/P-9-2021-000604-ASW_EN.pdf.

broad sense, it is not sufficient to comply with its concrete supervisory obligations under Art. 40 para 3 Frontex Regulation, Art. 21 para 2 EUAA Regulation. The Commission not only failed to take into account that the application of the safe third country as such is unlawful in a situation where the concerned third country generally refuses to accept readmissions but also acted in an ineffective manner, as shown by the fact that its intervention has not led to an adaption of the administrative practice in EU hotspots.

Case 6 – Reem Saeed – Failure to address the practice of prolonged detention (Commission)
In the case of Ms Saeed, it is again crucial that the violation of Art. 6 ChFR reflects a generic issue. And again, the Commission, despite its knowledge of the systemic malpractice in Kos, apparently failed to ensure that the host member state refrains from systemically detaining asylum seekers. Instead, the Commission continued to provide operational and financial support and thereby contributed to the maintenance of a general administrative practice that clearly qualifies as unlawful under EU law.

As regards asylum and deportation procedures, the Commission's typical failure to adequately exercise its supervisory obligations consists, in particular, in a failure to effectively address the EUAA's deficient interview practice and Frontex's deficient age assessment practice. These mistakes are well illustrated with cases 2 and 3.

Case 2 – Magan Daud – Failure to address the deficient interview practice (Commission)
As established above, the EUAA's malpractice in the context of asylum interviews is not limited to the case of Mr Daud, but of general nature. Accordingly, the Commission was obliged, under Art. 40 para 3 Frontex Regulation, Art. 21 para 2 EUAA Regulation, Art. 17 TEU, to address this issue in the framework of the EURTF and the Steering Committee. In particular, the Commission should have effectively exerted influence upon the EUAA to ensure that the agency does not systemically violate EU law.[267]

---

267 Despite the agencies' independence, the Commission is obliged to supervise the agencies' conduct in the EU hotspots. In concrete terms, the Commission could have urged the Executive Director and the coordinating officer to ensure that the agency does not systemically overstep its competences or engage in fundamental rights violations.

Case 3 – Daniat Kidane – Failure to address the deficient age assessment practice (Commission)
Again, as the agency's misconduct in the procedure of Daniat Kidane is an expression of a systemic malpractice, the Commission was obliged to address this issue. The Commission, however, apparently failed to address the issue through exerting influence on Frontex in the framework of the EURTF or the relevant Steering Committees, and thereby failed to comply with its supervisory obligation under Art 40. para 3 Frontex Regulation, Art. 21 para 2 EUAA Regulation, Art 17 TEU.

5 EU Responsibility for EU Hotspots?

In sum, this chapter has found that the EU, without issuing formally-binding decisions, de facto determines the course of the EU hotspot administration. There is no single aspect on which the EU does not have a major impact: The Commission has proposed and implemented the original EU hotpot approach in 2015, it has proposed and implemented the reformed EU hotspot approach 2.0 in 2021 and has throughout been responsible for overall coordination and supervision. EU agencies provide extensive operational support, including the adoption of guidelines, the provision of training, and also the conduct of asylum and deportation procedures in direct interaction with the concerned individuals. And the EU funds the centres to a considerable and increasing extent.

Against this background and in responding to recent calls by scholarship,[268] the remainder of this study will focus on judicial protection against the EU. The aim is to enable the CJEU, as the court responsible for safeguarding the rule of law in its EU dimension, to scrutinise the EU's involvement in the EU hotspot administration and to decide whether or to what extent the EU itself bears responsibility for fundamental rights violations. In doing so, the approach will be to make use of EU constitutional law as it currently stands and unfold the potential of the rule of law as enshrined in Art. 2 TEU – more precisely, of the fundamental right to effective judicial protection, the doctrine of a complete system of legal remedies, and the idea of vigilant individuals. As it follows from these guarantees that the EU's administrative conduct must necessarily be subject to judicial review,

268 See introduction, 5.

the question will not so much be whether but rather through which procedure the EU can be brought before the CJEU.

Chapter 3: The Potential of EU Liability Law

The third chapter argues that the EU's factual conduct in EU hotspots can be reviewed via the action for damages under Art. 41 para 3 ChFR, Art. 340 para 2 TFEU. The argument proceeds in four main steps. The first step is to provide a brief overview of non-judicial review mechanisms. This is necessary because, in practice, the so-far perceived lack of access to the CJEU has made non-judicial review increasingly relevant (1). The second step is to explain why, in the specific context of the EU hotspot administration, established pathways to the CJEU structurally fail. As will be shown, both enforcement from *above*, i.e. the infringement procedure under Art. 258 TFEU, and indirect enforcement from *below*, i.e. the preliminary reference procedure under Art. 267 TFEU fail because basic assumptions underlying these procedures are not fulfilled. As a result, the main discussion revolves around two options of direct enforcement from below: the action for annulment or failure to act under Art. 263, 265 TFEU, and the action for damages under Art. 340 para 2 TFEU (2). On this basis, the third argumentative step is to explain why and how the action for damages functions as a 'makeshift fundamental rights remedy'.[1] Although the action for damages was not originally conceived as a fundamental rights remedy, it has, for lack of procedural alternatives, acquired this function. At the same time, it comes with in-built deficiencies and, in this sense, remains a 'makeshift' solution (3). The fourth step, then, is to apply the argument to the specific case of the integrated EU hotspot administration. This requires defining the potential trigger for EU liability and the relevant legal basis for an action for damages against the Commission, the EUAA and Frontex, or the Union as such (4). The final part explains that the central doctrinal questions arise in the context of attribution and causation, clarifies these concepts, identifies the concrete doctrinal questions, and defines the relevant case law (5).

1 Relying on recent studies, including in particular Melanie Fink, *Frontex and Human Rights. Responsibility in 'Multi-Actor Situations' under the ECHR and EU Public Liability Law*, Oxford University Press 2018; Timo Rademacher, *Realakte im Rechtsschutzsystem der Europäischen Union*, Mohr Siebeck 2014. See in more detail chapter 4, 3.

1 Auxiliary Character of Non-Judicial Review

Clearly, non-judicial review mechanisms fall short of the standard enshrined in Art. 47 ChFR, already because neither an agency-internal forum nor the Ombudsman qualifies as an independent tribunal in the sense of that provision.[2] Still, it must be recognised that non-judicial remedies have an important function in practice. This is precisely due to the so-far prevailing opinion that there is no possibility of access to the CJEU: in fact, misconduct by EU bodies in the EU hotspot administration has so far been challenged only via non-judicial remedies. Scholarship, too, tends to place a clear emphasis on non-judicial review[3] and often prioritises questions of accountability in a broad sense over issues related to judicial redress in the sense of Art. 47 ChFR.[4]

As mentioned already, non-judicial review in the context of the EU hotspots consists of two main fora: agency-internal complaints mechanisms and the European Ombudsman. The main problem with agency-internal complaints mechanisms is their poor design. Frontex's complaints mechanism exemplifies the problems. Until today, it falls short of the basic requirements enshrined in Art. 41 ChFR.[5] First, it does not allow for review

---

2 See only Jürgen Bast, Frederik von Harbou, Janna Wessels, *Human Rights Challenges to European Migration Policy. The REMAP Study*, Nomos 2022, p. 138; Jorrit R Rijpma, *The Proposal for a European Border and Coast Guard: evolution or revolution in external border management? Study for the LIBE Committee*, European Parliament 2016, p. 30.

3 See for instance Sergio Carrera, Marco Stefan, „Complaint Mechanisms in Border Management and Expulsion Operations in Europe. Effective Remedies for Victims of Human Rights Violations?", *CEPS Policy Insights* (2018); ECRE, „Holding Frontex to Account. ECRE's Proposals for Strengthening Non-Judicial Mechanisms for Scrutiny of Frontex", *Policy Paper 7, May 2021* (2021).

4 Usually with the argument that judicial review of agency conduct before national courts is not possible, and without in-depth analysis of procedural ways reach the CJEU, see for instance, Evangelia (Lilian) Tsourdi, „Holding the European Asylum Support Office Accountable for its role in Asylum Decision-Making: Mission Impossible?", *German Law Journal* 21 (2020), p. 506–531, p. 252–530; Salvatore F. Nicolosi, David Fernandez-Rojo, „Out of control? The case of the European Asylum Support Office", in Miroslava Scholten, Alex Brenninkmeijer (ed.), *Controlling EU Agencies. The Rule of Law in a Multi-jurisdictional Legal Order*, Edward Elgar 2020, p. 177–195, p. 186–194.

5 Elspeth Guild, „The Frontex Push-Back Controversy: Lessons on Oversight (Part I)", eumigrationlawblog of 19/04/2021; Sergio Carrera, Marco Stefan, „Complaint Mechanisms in Border Management and Expulsion Operations in Europe. Effective Remedies for Victims of Human Rights Violations?" (fn. 3), p. 24–26; David Fernandez-Rojo,

by a truly independent body. While the fundamental rights officer shall be responsible for handling complaints, their competence is limited to reviewing the admissibility of a claim.[6] Substantial review is exercised by the executive director or, in case of complaints concerning deployed staff, by the home member state. In case of complaints concerning the agency's own staff, the outcome of a complaints procedure hence entirely depends on the discretion of the executive director.[7] Moreover, the fundamental rights officer is an ordinary employee and is thus required to report to the Frontex management board.[8] Second, the complaints mechanism is subject to a relatively high threshold of admissibility: complaints cannot be lodged anonymously, a complaint popularis is not allowed, and complaints can only be submitted in writing.[9] Due to these structural shortcomings, the mechanism is also of limited practical relevance: between 2016 and 2021, only 69 complaints had been lodged, out of which only 22 were deemed admissible.[10] As regards the EUAA, a legal basis for an internal complaints procedure was introduced only with the 2022 Regulation,[11] and the mechanism has not been established yet.[12] Given that it is modelled after the Frontex one, similar problems can be expected.

With regard to review by the Ombudsman, three points require mention here. First, and from a more theoretical perspective, it must be stressed that the Ombudsman holds an important constitutional function. It unites elements of the rule of law and democracy and, as such, constitutes an im-

„The introduction of an individual complaint mechanism within FRONTEX: two steps forward, one step back", *Tijdschrift voor Bestuurswetenschappen en Publiekrecht* 4 (2016), p. 225-234, p. 232–234.

6 See Art. 111 para 4 Frontex Regulation.

7 The fundamental rights officer can recommend appropriate measures to the executive director but the decision on which measures are taken lies with the latter, see Art. 111 para 6 Frontex Regulation.

8 Herbert Rosenfeldt, *Frontex im Zentrum der Europäischen Grenz- und Küstenwache. Bestandsaufnahme, Unionsrechtmäßigkeit und Verantwortlichkeit*, Mohr Siebeck 2021, p. 275 argues that this issue has been overcome with Art. 109 para 4 and 5 Frontex Regulation.

9 Art. 111 para 2 Frontex Regulation.

10 European Ombudsman, Decision of 15 June 2021, on the functioning of the European Border and Coast Guard Agency's (Frontex) complaints mechanism for alleged breaches of fundamental rights and the role of the Fundamental Rights Officer, Case OI/5/2020/MHZ.

11 EUAA Regulation (introduction, fn. 39).

12 As of 3 October 2024, to the best knowledge of the author, based on the information available on the EUAA's homepage.

portant complement to judicial review.[13] Second, and from a more practical perspective, it must be kept in mind that access to the Ombudsman in the asylum system is subject to important practical hurdles. The lack of legal aid and difficulties concerning the collection of evidence make it practically very difficult to lodge a complaint.[14] In fact, Ombuds-complaints depend on comprehensive support by strategic litigants and thus remain rare.

Third, the relevance of Ombuds-review in the asylum context largely depends on the officeholder's own political approach. In this regard, it appears that their approach has developed from a rather cautious position in 2016 to a rather proactive stance in 2022. This is well illustrated by the Ombudsman's positioning towards the EUAA: In the context of the 2015 EU hotspot approach, they refrained from opening an own initiative inquiry against EASO. And when a complaint was eventually lodged in 2017, they still adopted a rather deferent attitude: although they agreed with the applicants that the agency systemically overstepped its competences, they nonetheless concluded that further inquiries were not required.[15] In a similar decision concerning a complaint from 2018, they found a significant procedural error but merely asked the agency to explain how it would avoid such errors in the future.[16] Things seem to have changed; however, in 2022, the Ombudsman decided to open their first own inquiry initiative against the EUAA and proactively looked into compliance with fundamental rights obligations and accountability for potential fundamental rights violations.[17]

The Ombudsman's approach towards the Commission has been subject to a similar development. In the context of the 2015 EU hotspot approach, they still avoided confronting the Commission and refrained from opening

13 Anne Peters, „The European Ombudsman and the European Constitution", *Common Market Law Review* 42 (2005), p. 697-743.

14 Sergio Carrera, Marco Stefan, „Complaint Mechanisms in Border Management and Expulsion Operations in Europe. Effective Remedies for Victims of Human Rights Violations?" (fn. 3), p. 35.

15 European Ombudsman, Decision of 5 July 2018, on the European Asylum Support Office's (EASO) Involvement in the Decision-Making Process Concerning Admissibility of Applications for International Protection Submitted in the Greek Hotspots, in particular Shortcomings in Admissibility Interviews, Case 735/2017/MDC.

16 European Ombudsman, Decision of 30 September 2019, on the Conduct of Experts in Interviews with Asylum Seekers Organised by the European Asylum Support Office, Case 1139/2018/MDC.

17 European Ombudsman, Decision of 23 February 2023 on how the EU Asylum Agency complies with its fundamental rights obligations and ensures accountability for potential fundamental rights violations, SI/4/2022/MHZ.

an own-initiative inquiry, notably although the European Court of Auditors had found severe misconduct.[18] Concerning a complaint from 2016 against the Commission's failure to conduct a human rights assessment in the context of the implementation of the EU-Türkiye Statement, they merely suggested that the Commission deal more explicitly with human rights implications in its future reports.[19] Since 2022, however, they appear increasingly aware of the Commission's problematic involvement in the asylum administration and opened a first own-initiative inquiry concerning the Commission's misconduct related to the management of funds concerning the Croatian border management system[20] and a second concerning the Commission's mismanagement in the context of the EU hotspot approach 2.0.[21] These inquiries are remarkable because they show that the Ombudsman now assumes, unlike in earlier decisions,[22] that – even when the competence for formally-binding administrative decisions lies with the member state – EU bodies are, in principle, responsible for their own misconduct. In terms of outcome, however, the decisions remain relatively restrained. In the case concerning the EU-funded border management system in Croatia, the Ombudsman 'identified significant shortcomings', notably as regards the monitoring of fundamental rights compliance, but ultimately considered the steps taken by the Commission to address these shortcomings as sufficient and hence refrained from issuing formal recommendations. Similarly, in the case concerning the EU hotspots 2.0, they closed their inquiry with some 'suggestions for improvement', which, in essence, were

18 European Court of Auditors, Special Report No 06/2017, EU response to the refugee crisis: the 'hotspot' approach (report pursuant to Article 287(4), second subparagraph, TFEU), 25 April 2017: https://www.eca.europa.eu/en/Pages/DocItem.aspx?did=41222 (hereinafter: ECA Special Report 2017), p. 34–35.

19 European Ombudsman, 18 January 2017, Decision of the European Ombudsman in the joint inquiry into complaints 506–509–674–784–927–1381/2016/MHZ against the European Commission concerning a human rights impact assessment in the context of the EU-Turkey Agreement, Case 506/2016/MHZ.

20 European Ombudsman, Decision of 22 February 2022, How the European Commission ensures that the Croatian authorities respect fundamental rights in the context of border management operations financed by EU funds, Case 1598/2020/VS.

21 European Ombudsman, Decision of 11 June 2023, How the European Commission ensures respect for fundamental rights in EU-funded migration management facilities in Greece, Case OI/3/2022/MHZ.

22 European Ombudsman, Decision of 5 July 2018, Case 735/2017/MDC (fn. 15), para 32.

limited to increasing transparency regarding the Commission's work and conducting a fundamental rights impact assessment.[23]

2 Structural Failure of Established Pathways to the CJEU

Concerning judicial review, the decisive question is which procedure is best suited to hold the EU responsible for its non-formally binding administrative conduct.

Laying the ground for the following argument in favour of the action for damages, this section shows that judicial review via more established pathways to the CJEU largely fails. The main problem is that the EU legal protection system is based on the traditional assumption that public power is exercised only through formally-binding decisions. Until today, the system has not yet been sufficiently adapted to challenges that arise when EU bodies exercise public power through factual conduct – let alone at the operational level and in an area that is particularly sensitive to fundamental rights. Neither the Treaties nor the CJEU's interpretation thereof takes into account recent developments in the European asylum administration. In this sense, the EU legal protection system lags behind administrative reality.

To substantiate this argument, this section goes through the various procedures that lead towards the CJEU and examines which would allow – or not – to challenge the EU's factual conduct. A distinction is made between enforcement from *above*, i.e. enforcement by the European Commission via the infringement procedure under Art. 258 TFEU; and enforcement from *below*, i.e. enforcement by individuals. Concerning the latter, a further distinction is made between *indirect* enforcement from below, i.e. enforcement of individual rights via the preliminary reference procedure under Art. 267 TFEU; and *direct* enforcement from below, i.e. enforcement of individual rights via the annulment procedure and the action for failure to act under Art. 263, 265 TFEU, or via the action for damages under Art. 41 para 3 ChFR, Art. 340 para 2 TFEU.

23 European Ombudsman, Decision of 22 February 2022, Case 1598/2020/VS (fn. 20); European Ombudsman, Decision of 11 June 2023, Case OI/3/2022/MHZ (fn. 21).

2.1 Failure of Enforcement From Above (Art. 258 TFEU)

When assessing the infringement procedure in the context of the EU hotspot administration, it must first be clarified whether this procedure is suitable at all to address misconduct by the EU itself. Clearly, Art. 258 TFEU requires that 'a member state' has failed to fulfil its obligations under EU law, and the CJEU's verdict is directed only to the concerned member state. Still, it would arguably be possible for the CJEU to assess the EU's conduct in a procedure under Art. 258 TFEU. If the Commission launched an infringement procedure against the member state involved in the integrated administration, here Greece, the CJEU could argue that the member state's responsibility for a breach of EU law was limited because the EU itself also bears part of the responsibility. In this manner, the CJEU could incidentally examine the legality of the EU's conduct.[24]

This being said the key point with regard to the infringement procedure is that its legislative conception is based on the assumption that the European Commission has a political interest in enforcing EU law – and hence, structurally fails where this is not the case. Put bluntly, the infringement procedure only works insofar as the Commission wants it to work. If, however, the Commission has strong political incentives to refrain from initiating infringement proceedings – e.g. in cases involving potential misconduct by its own staff or by staff deployed by EU agencies – the mechanism appears to fail. This requires some explanation.

a *The Commission's Unequal Enforcement Policy*

To evaluate the potential of the infringement procedure in the context of the asylum administration, it must be noted that the Commission's approach differs strongly among member states. The matter is well illustrated with the differences between its approach towards Greece and that towards Hungary. Whereas the Commission has initiated several infringement procedures to ensure Hungary's compliance with the EU asylum acquis, it has for over a decade refrained from doing the same in the case of Greece, with the first formal letters of notice having been sent only in January 2023.[25]

24 To the best of the author's knowledge, the CJEU did so far not make this argument.

25 It was only in January 2023 that the Commission opened infringement proceedings against Greece for its failure to fully transpose the Reception Conditions Directive

Remarkably, the Commission's unequal approach even extends to areas that are only politically related to the EU asylum acquis, as the example of anti-NGO campaigns shows. While both Greece and Hungary have, in the late 2010s, enacted legislation that severely restricted the work of NGOs and lawyers in the area of migration and asylum,[26] the Commission has initiated infringement proceedings in this regard only against Hungary.[27]

---

and the Qualification Directive by sending formal letters of notice, see European Commission, 26 January 2023, January Infringements package: key decisions, section 3. According to media reports, the Commission's letters of notice focused on failures to comply with EU law in the context of detention and social benefits, see ECRE, 3 February 2023, Greece: Infringement Letters from the European Commission, NGOs Urge More Oversight on Greek Islands, Joint Civil Society Rule of Law Submission, Hundreds of Thousands 'Prevented' Entry, with further reference to https://www.efsyn.gr/ellada/dikaiomata/376712_apologoymeni-gia-zitimata-prosfygon-i-ellada.

26 For Hungary see only Heinrich Böll Stiftung, News of 29 December 2017 by Nóra Köves, Hungary 2017: Detained refugees, persecuted NGOs, lack of legal certainty, https://www.boell.de/en/2018/01/03/hungary-2017-detained-refugees-persecuted-ngos-lack-legal-certainty. For Greece see the legislative amendments introduced with Law 4986/2020 and with the Joint Ministerial Decision 10616/2020; for comment see ECRE, 29 October 2021, Greece: Criminalisation of Rescuers, Death for People on the Move, Impunity for Vigilantes, States Persist with Dublin Take-Back Requests Despite Risks and Deficiencies, https://ecre.org/greece-criminalisation-of-rescuers-death-for-people-on-the-move-impunity-for-vigilantes-states-persist-with-dublin-take-back-requests-despite-risks-and-deficiencies/; ECRE, 3 December 2021, Greece: Government Continues NGO Crackdown, Closed Controlled Centres Close in on Asylum Seekers, Significant Jump in Negative Decisions Since Türkiye Declared Safe Third Country, https://ecre.org/greece-government-continues-ngo-crackdown-closed-controlled-centres-close-in-on-asylum-seekers-significant-jump-in-negative-decisions-since-Türkiye-declared-safe-third-country/; and more recently European Parliament, Resolution of 7 February 2024 on the rule of law and media freedom in Greece, 2024/2502(RSP), para 18: '(the European Parliament) (i)s concerned by the attacks against civil society and, in particular, smear campaigns and judicial harassment by Greek authorities targeting human rights activists; is alarmed by the recent trials against humanitarian workers and people who provide humanitarian assistance to migrants and refugees; calls on the Greek authorities to drop all charges immediately and ensure that humanitarian workers and volunteers can provide assistance safely and freely'.

27 CJEU, Court (Grand Chamber), judgment of 16 November 2021, European Commission v Hungary (Incrimination de l'aide aux demandeurs d'asile), C-821/19. Concerning developments in Greece, the Commission remained silent, leaving it to the UN to react to the criminalisation of NGOs in that member state, see the UN Special Rapporteur on the rights to freedom of peaceful assembly and of association, the Special Rapporteur on the situation of human rights defenders, and the Special Rapporteur on the human rights of migrants in a letter of 31 March 2021 conclude that the amendments '*unnecessarily and disproportionally restrict the right to freedom of association*, as provided by Article 22 of the International Covenant of Civil and Polit-

The differing approach becomes particularly clear in case of refugee camps at external borders. Although EU law has since 2015 been systemically violated in this context in both Greece and Hungary, the Commission has made use of Art. 258 TFEU only against Hungary. In fact, the Commission has swiftly initiated a series of infringement procedures concerning the so-called transit zones in Hungary, thereby effectively improving compliance with EU law.[28] In the case of Greece, by contrast, the Commission chose to refrain from making use of Art. 258 TFEU and instead increased its own administrative involvement by setting up the EU hotspots 2.0.[29]

Seen from a strictly formal perspective, the Commission's practice is legal. Art. 258 TFEU leaves the Commission unfettered discretion and allows it to take into account both legal and political considerations.[30] This is clearly reflected in the CJEU's case law, which establishes that individuals who have brought a particular issue to the attention of the Commission cannot challenge its decision not to initiate infringement proceedings before the court.[31] In fact, the only option is a kind of mitigated plausibility check before the Ombudsman.[32] According to the CJEU, the Commission is

ical Rights (ICCPR)' and therefore urge the Greek government 'to undertake a review of (those amendments) to ensure that they are in accordance with Greece's international human rights obligations.' Letter available at: https://www.equal-rights.org/articles/61.

28 Although deficiencies the Hungarian asylum system persist, the infringement procedure was effective in improving compliance with EU law in the concrete case. After the CJEU had found several violation of EU law, Hungary responded and remedied the situation insofar as the transit zones were abolished, see ECRE, 22 May 2020, Hungary: Abolishment of Transit Zone Following CJEU Ruling, https://ecre.org/hungary-abolishment-of-transit-zone-following-cjeu-ruling/.

29 As described above, this strategy, although arguably intended to improve the application of EU law, actually only led to the Commission becoming entangled in the systemic violations of fundamental rights, see chapter 2, 2 and 3.

30 According to Art. 258 TFEU, the Commission 'shall' deliver a reasoned opinion when it considers that a member state has breached EU law, but merely 'may' bring the matter before the CJEU, even in case of persisting non-compliance.

31 For instance, via Art. 340 para 2 TFEU. For earlier case law see CJEU, decision of 25 May 2005, Retecal et al v COM, T-44/03, para 44 et seq.; CJEU, decision of 14 January 2004, T-202/02, Makedoniko Metro et al v Commission, para 43; judgement of 18 December 2009, Arizmendi, T-440/03 et al, para 62. More recently see the dismissal as inadmissible of similar actions in the Hungarian context CJEU, order of 22 March 2019, T-566/18, PITEE Fogyasztóvédelmi Egyesület, para 9 to 11; confirmed by order of 26 September 2019, C-358/19 P, PITEE Fogyasztóvédelmi Egyesület, para 16.

32 More precisely, the Ombudsman reviews whether the Commission has complied with its own guidelines enshrined in European Commission, Commission communication

not even obliged under Art. 258 TFEU to treat several member states who are in a comparable situation alike. As the court argues, the principle of equal treatment under Art. 4 para 2 TEU cannot be brought forward by member states to justify their own failures in a procedure under Art. 258 TFEU. The Commission is, hence, free to make political decisions about which member states to sue and which ones not. As long as the Commission does not engage in a manifest abuse of its discretion, i.e. as long as it can advance some kind of 'neutral and objective criterion', its choices will not be reviewed by the CJEU.[33]

b *Why the Commission's Practice is Problematic from a Broader Constitutional Perspective*

From a broader constitutional perspective, however, the Commission's practice of unequal enforcement is problematic.[34] When the Commission sues only some member states for their systemic violations of asylum law and fundamental rights but looks away when other member states do the same, it creates a system in which it depends on political and administrative

---

to the European Parliament and the European Ombudsman on relations with the complainant in respect of infringements of Community law, COM(2002) 141 final. See European Ombudsman, Decision of 30 January 2001, on complaint 995/98/OV against the European Commission, Mekedoniko Metro; European Ombudsman, Decision of 27 February 2014, closing the inquiry into complaint 230/2012/ER against the European Commission; Decision of 2 March 2018, in case 425/2017/ANA on the European Commission's alleged failure to enforce EU law on online gambling services in certain Member States; and in more detail Anne Peters, „The European Ombudsman and the European Constitution" (fn. 13), p. 717–721; Nikos Vogiatzis, *The European Ombudsman and Good Administration in the European Union*, Palgrave Macmillan 2018, p. 86–107.

33 Advocate General Eleanor Sharpston, Opinion delivered on 31 October 2019, European Commission v Republic of Poland, Republic of Hungary and Czech Republic, Joined Cases C-715/17, C-718/17, C- 719/18, paras 107–121; CJEU, judgement of 2 April 2020, European Commission v Republic of Poland, Republic of Hungary and Czech Republic (Relocation Decisions), Joined Cases C-715/17, C-718/17, C- 719/18 para 75–82; CJEU, Court (Fourth Chamber), judgement of 3 March 2016, European Commission v Republic of Malta, C-12/14, para 25; CJEU, Court (Fifth Chamber), judgement of 11 July 2018, European Commission v Belgium, C-356/15, para 106.

34 The European Parliament in its Resolution of 7 February 2024 on the rule of law and media freedom in Greece (fn. 26), para 17 'condemns the Commission's dramatic failure to enforce EU laws with regard to reception conditions, pushbacks and human rights, and believes that infringement proceedings are more appropriate than the Commissioner's praise'.

relations of member states to the Commission whether or not their failure to comply with EU law will be brought before the CJEU. Ultimately, the Commission's practice creates a two-tier rule of law in the sense that the effectiveness of asylum law falls far behind the effectiveness of, say, competition law.

To make sense of the Commission's unequal approach, it must be taken into consideration that the use of the infringement procedure as such has strongly decreased in the past decade.[35] Moreover, the Commission generally tended to focus on technical issues related to the internal market, while being rather reluctant to address issues related to fundamental rights and other areas that are traditionally considered as sovereignty-sensitive.[36]

Insofar as the Commission ignores systemic violations of fundamental rights, its approach in the asylum system thus seems to fit into its general approach. In fact, the Commission has adopted this approach with regard to several aspects of the asylum system, with the deficient implementation of the 'Dublin system' being a prominent example. Even when member states intentionally and explicitly circumvented EU law through bilateral agreements and thereby systemically deprived third-country nationals of their rights under the Dublin III Regulation, the Commission refrained from intervening[37] and instead left the matter to be addressed by vigilant individuals.[38]

35 Daniel Kelemen, Tommaso Pavone, „Where Have the Guardians Gone? Law Enforcement and the Politics of Supranational Forbearance in the European Union", *SSRN* (2021) observe a decrease at the latest since 2014; Melanie Smith, „Enforcement, monitoring, verification, outsourcing: the decline and decline of the infringement process", *European Law Review* 33 (2008), p. 777-802.

36 This well illustrated with the example of some member states' severe restrictions on media freedom and systemic disregard for minority protection in the early 2010s, where, although there was no doubt the Charter was systemically violated in several member states, the Commission refrained from initiating infringement procedures, see Armin von Bogdandy, Matthias Kottmann, Carlino Antpöhler, Johanna Dickschen, Simon Hentrei, Maja Smrkolj, „Reverse Solange – Protecting the Essence of Fundamental Rights Against EU Member States", *Common Market Law Review* 49 (2012), p. 489-520, p. 489–490 with further references espeically in fn. 2 and fn. 8.

37 See Hannah Bru, Aikaterini Anastasopoulou, Heini Hyrkkö, „The Circumvention of the Dublin III Regulation Through the Use of Bilateral Agreements to Return Asylum Seekers to Other Member States", in European Council on Refugees and Exiles (ECRE) (ed.), *Research Paper Ghent University* 2019, p. 22 deemed it 'questionable' whether the Commission would act inter alia 'due to the political climate'.

38 Robert Nestler, Vinzent Vogt, „Dublin-III-reversed. Ein Instrument zur Familienzusammenführung", *Zeitschrift für Ausländerrecht und Ausländerpolitik* 37 (2017), p. 21-29.

Insofar as the Commission differentiates between member states, however, its approach requires further explanation. While several hypothesis have been proposed in this regard,[39] it is argued here that the Commission's approach can be explained with three inter-related factors that are all primarily politically motivated, namely forbearance, outcome-orientation and avoidance of self-indictment.

Forbearance refers to the deliberate under-enforcement of the law in order to secure the political support of those against whom the law ought to be enforced.[40] Applied to the Commission, this means that its increasing reluctance to use Art. 258 TFEU is due to its fear that judicial confrontation would lead to decreasing political support by member state governments.[41] The Commission's decision whether or not to initiate an infringement procedure no longer depends on the scope or gravity of the breach of EU law but rather on how the Commission estimates the political cost of activating Art. 258 TFEU. The Commission is, hence, likely to refrain from making use of Art. 258 TFEU when it considers that this would make cooperation with the concerned national government more difficult or lead to decreased political support for the Commission's policy agenda in the concerned or another area of EU law.

The practice of forbearance explains the general decrease in infringement proceedings. As empirical research has shown, the decline is neither due to improved compliance rates[42] nor increased reliance on enforcement from below nor the Commission's increased use of non-judicial strategies[43]

39 Daniel Thym, „Muddy Waters: A Guide to the Legal Questions surrounding 'Push-backs' at the External Borders at Sea and at Land", eumigrationlawblog of 06/07/2021, for instance, argued that the Commission's choices are related to procedural risks.

40 Alisha C Holland, „Forbearance", *American Political Science Review* 110 (2016), p. 232-246.

41 Daniel Kelemen, Tommaso Pavone, „Where Have the Guardians Gone? Law Enforcement and the Politics of Supranational Forbearance in the European Union" (fn. 35), p. 3.

42 In this direction, however, Tanja A Börzel, Ulrich Sedelmeier, „Larger and More Law Abiding? The Impact of Enlargement on Compliance in the European Union", *Journal of European Public Policy* 24 (2016), p. 197-215, although they argue that compliance has been improved only in some member states and only in relative terms.

43 In this direction, however, Gerda Falkner, „A Causal Loop? The Commission's New Enforcement Approach in the Context of Non-Compliance with EU Law After CJEU Judgements", *Journal of European Integration* 40 (2018), p. 769-784, p. 773.

but to its politics of forbearance.[44] Forbearance also explains the Commission's decidedly unequal approach in context of asylum and migration matters. As the Commission is strongly concerned with safeguarding political support of national governments for the project of a Common European Asylum System as such, it seems ready to pay a particularly high price in terms of lack of enforcement. In fact, it appears that in the area of EU asylum law, the Commission has almost entirely sacrificed its role as guardian of the Treaties and has instead largely subscribed to its role as the 'motor of integration'.[45]

This leads to the second and most closely connected factor informing the Commission's decision. In fact, it seems that a particularly relevant factor in the Commission's decision-making process is the degree of functionality of the concerned national administration. For instance, if Greece or any other member state located at the external border that has a particularly weak national administration refused to cooperate with EU bodies, other member states would probably be faced with rising numbers of asylum applications very soon. If, however, Hungary or any other member state with a relatively strong national administration refuses to cooperate with EU bodies, the Commission can nonetheless trust these countries to effectively seal their borders – albeit at a high cost, namely that of accepting systemic breaches of EU law and fundamental rights. Hence, it seems that the Commission's approach is outcome-oriented in the sense that it tends to initiate infringement proceedings against those member states from which it can expect that they will implement a court decision. If a member state has a functional national asylum administration and generally complies with CJEU decisions, such as Hungary, the infringement procedure is a promising instrument of enforcement. If, however, a member state has either explicitly stressed its unwillingness to respect EU asylum law in a certain situation[46]

44 Daniel Kelemen, Tommaso Pavone, „Where Have the Guardians Gone? Law Enforcement and the Politics of Supranational Forbearance in the European Union“ (fn. 35), p. 4–7 with counterarguments to the theories quoted in fn. 42 to 43, p. 11–29 with quantative and qualitative emprical evidence for the theory of forbearance.

45 ECRE, Weekly Bulletin of 21 January 2022, https://us1.campaign-archive.com/?u=8e3ebd297b1510becc6d6d690&id=d9e4b1cb08, Editorial by Catherine Woollard, Asylum Mini-Package: Derogations Through the Backdoor, with further references.

46 For the example of Poland, Lithuania and Latvia in the context of the Belarus crisis see ECRE, 8 October 2021, EU Eastern Borders: Poland Ignores Commission Pressure for Frontex Deployment, Eastern States Move to 'Legalise' Pushbacks, Belarus Suspends Return Agreement, https://ecre.org/eu-eastern-borders-poland-ignores-co

or if a member state has such weak national administration that it is barely able to enforce its own national legislation,[47] an infringement procedure would be de facto vain. In short, the less functional the national administration is, the less willing the Commission seems to adopt a confrontational approach.[48]

The third factor in the Commission's decision-making process arguably is the aim to avoid self-indictment. The Commission seems to shy away from infringement proceedings when these would result in the CJEU looking into alleged misconduct of the agencies or the Commission itself. Obviously, making use of Art. 258 TFEU against Greece would mean that light is shed on the fact that the Commission and the agencies themselves contribute to the systemic violation of EU law, including fundamental rights. The Commission's willingness to initiate infringement proceedings thus appears to decrease to the degree that either itself or EU agencies are actively involved in the concerned member state's administration. In sum, the Commission seems to focus either on cooperative or confrontational enforcement strategies and to resort to the infringement procedure only in the latter cases.

Against this background, it becomes evident that the Commission's practice is problematic in the context of the broader constitutional architecture. For when the Commission acts as a central administrative and also political actor, its own interests come into conflict with its role as guardian of the Treaties. Ultimately, this conflictual role results in a weakening of the effectiveness, or even the normative force, of EU law.

The Commission's dual role and the conflicts inherent therein are particularly pronounced in the case of EU hotspots. As set out above, the Commission is a central actor at the administrative and political level. At the same time, it is supposed to function as the guardian of EU law, i.e., as an external supervisor, similar to an independent prosecutor.[49] Interestingly

mmission-pressure-for-frontex-deployment-eastern-states-move-to-legalise-pushbacks-belarus-suspends-return-agreement/.

47 For the example of Greece see Michael Ioannidis, „Weak Members and the Enforcement of EU Law", in András Jakab, Dimitry Kochenov (ed.), *The Enforcement of EU Law and Values. Ensuring Member States' Compliance*, Oxford University Press 2017, p. 476–49, p. 485–492.

48 This is not empirically proven, but very plausible, based on the most relevant cases in the context of the asylum system.

49 Remarkably, the Commission itself partially describes its work as similar to that of a 'prosecutor', see Daniel Kelemen, Tommaso Pavone, „Where Have the Guardians

enough, both roles are ultimately based on Art. 17 TEU. And yet, the dual role obviously leads to major conflicts of interest. When asked how to react to systemic violations of fundamental rights in EU hotspots, Commission representatives had no clear answer. On the one hand, they focused on the Commission's role as an administrative actor and emphasised their attempt to encourage or persuade the member state to comply with EU law at the administrative level, for instance, within the EURTF or the Steering Committees.[50] On the other hand, they did mention the option of initiating infringement proceedings; however, only to relativise in the same breath that this remained a 'rather theoretical' option due to 'political sensitivities' of asylum and migration matters and that a confrontation before the CJEU could jeopardise the cooperative approach on which the Commission has relied so far.[51]

This is problematic because it destabilises the constitutional architecture. When the Commission does not live up to its role as guardian, this creates an enforcement vacuum which cannot adequately be compensated by any other actor. While the European Parliament tries to fill the void,[52] it obvi-

---

Gone? Law Enforcement and the Politics of Supranational Forbearance in the European Union" (fn. 35), p. 19, 60, 76.

50 See chapter 2, 2.

51 Interview with Commission representative 4, conducted on 16 February 2021 (introduction, fn. 102): 'the Commission could initiate an infringement procedure (...). But the truth is that (...) this is an option that we use with parsimony. But basically, the mechanism is there: We ask, the member state answers. If we are not satisfied, we ultimately have the option to bring them to court. This is the normal procedure. But, as I said, with the specificity here that we are dealing with migration that is a politically very sensitive issue.'.

52 European Parliament, Resolution of 7 February 2024 on the rule of law and media freedom in Greece (fn. 26); European Parliament, Report on the Commission's 21st and 22nd Annual reports on monitoring the application of Community law (2003 and 2004), A6-0089/2006, para 13 calling on the Commission to place the principle of the rule of law and citizens' experience above purely economic criteria and evaluations, urging the Commission to monitor carefully the respect of the fundamental freedoms and general principles of the Treaty as well as the respect of regulations and framework directives, and inviting the Commission to use secondary legislation as a criterion for determining whether there has been an infringement of fundamental freedoms. On the role of the European Parliament in the case of media freedom (fn. 36) see European Parliament, Resolution of 10 March 2011 on media law in Hungary, P7_TA(2011)0094. On the European Parliament's role in the case of the asylum system more generally see Ariadna Ripoll Servent, „Failing under the 'shadow of hierarchy': explaining the role of the European Parliament in the EU's 'asylum crisis' ", in Edoardo Bressanelli, Nicola Chelotti (ed.), *The European Parliament in the Contested Union. Power and Influence Post-Lisbon*, Routledge 2020, p. 29-47.

ously lacks the competence to effectively enforce EU law. If anyone had the competence to act as guardian of the Treaties, it would be member states themselves, as they could initiate infringement proceedings under Art. 259 TFEU. But this possibility remains rather theoretical, too. Member states generally avoid enforcing EU law against each other, and given the current political constellations in the asylum system, it seems utterly unrealistic for member states to confront each other before the CJEU.[53] The Commission's negligence in its role as guardian of the Treaties thus results not only in its own involvement in systemic deficiencies but also weakens the effectiveness of EU law.[54] As a result, the rule of law in the asylum system is severely jeopardised already today.

2.2 Failure of Indirect Enforcement From Below (Art. 267 TFEU)

Given that enforcement from above largely fails, the focus necessarily is on enforcement from below. The first procedure that comes into consideration here is the infringement procedure as the central – albeit indirect – means of enforcement from below. The preliminary reference procedure constitutes a cornerstone of the EU legal protection system and is pivotal to ensuring the *effet utile* of EU law.[55] In addition, and unlike enforcement from above, it also ensures the right to an effective remedy under Art. 47 ChFR.[56] Yet, and this is the key point of this section, the preliminary reference procedure is inappropriate to address the EU's conduct in the

53 This being said, it seems worth to explore whether the argument for a revival of Art. 259 TFEU in the context of the rule of law crisis, as put forward by Dimitry Kochenov, „Biting Intergovernmentalism: The Case for the Reinvention of Article 259 TFEU to Make It a Viable Rule of Law Enforcement Tool", *Hague Journal on the Rule of Law* 7 (2015), p. 153-174.

54 The Council of Europe has been called upon to assist the Commission in the rule of law crisis, see Jörg Polakiewicz, Julia Katharina Kirchmayr, „Sounding the Alarm: The Council of Europe As the Guardian of the Rule of Law in Contemporary Europe", in Armin von Bogdandy, Piotr Bogdanowic, Iris Canor, Christoph Grabenwarter, Maciej Taborowski, Matthias Schmidt (ed.), *Defending Checks and Balances in EU Member States*, Springer 2021, p. 361-382, but obviously cannot replace it in its role as guardian of EU law.

55 CJEU, Court, judgement of 5 February 1963, Van Gend & Loos, 26/62, p. 12 CJEU, Court, Opinion of 18 December 2014 on the Accession of the European Union to the European Convention for the Protection of Human Rights and Fundamental Freedoms, 2/13, para 176.

56 On the – belated – recognition of the legal protection function in scholarship see Jürgen Bast, „Handlungsformen und Rechtsschutz", in Armin von Bogdandy, Jürgen

context at hand because it is based on the assumption that national courts cooperate. When, however, national courts refuse to refer the relevant questions, individuals have no means to access judicial protection before the CJEU.

Assessing the potential of the preliminary reference procedure in the context at hand again requires clarifying whether this procedure is suitable at all to address administrative misconduct by the EU itself.[57] Certainly, the idea underlying Art. 267 TFEU is that individuals may invoke before national courts the rights that are granted to them by EU law but denied by the national administration. The question, hence, is whether the mechanism also works when rights granted by EU law are denied by administrative bodies of the EU itself. This, in turn, depends on whether individuals can challenge unlawful administrative conduct by EU bodies before national courts. In this regard, it is argued here that – the jurisdiction rule of Art. 274 TFEU notwithstanding[58] – the preliminary reference procedure offers the possibility of incidental review. For instance, a national administrative court could be confronted with a claim to annul an administrative decision that was issued by a national authority, but the content of which has de facto been determined by an EU body. Such a claim would be directed against the national administration, but the public conduct of the EU would incidentally be subject to the dispute pending before the national court, which could hence refer the matters relating to EU law under Art. 267 TFEU.[59] In this manner, the preliminary reference procedure would even allow for the challenge of non-formally binding administrative

---

Bast (ed.), *Europäisches Verfassungsrecht. Theoretische und dogmatische Grundzüge*, Springer 2009, p. 489-557, p. 497–501.

57 For the reviewability of EU soft law and non-formally binding administrative conduct via Art. 267 TFEU see Giulia Gentile, „Ensuring Effective Judicial Review of EU Soft Law via the Action for Annulment before the EU Courts: a Plea for a Liberal-Constitutional Approach", *European Constitutional Law Review* (2020), p. 466–492, p. 484–486 with reference, inter alia, to Court (Grand Chamber), judgement of 16 June 2015, Peter Gauweiler and others v Deutscher Bundestag, para 23, in which the CJEU reviewed the legality of a Press Release in great detail, thereby dismissing the argument submitted by several member states that the procedure would be inadmissible because a Press Release is not a legal measure. For the limits and shortcomings of review of soft law via Art. 267 TFEU see ibid, p. 486–487.

58 See Catharina Ziebritzki, *The EU's Responsibility in the Asylum Administration. Administrative Integration, Judicial Protection and the Case of the EU Hotspots*, Dissertation at Frankfurt University, Law Department January 2024, p. 232 et seq.

59 Taking the example of an action for annulment, the national court would inter alia have to assess whether it is competent to annul an administrative decision although

conduct such as operational plans, non-binding recommendations or similar conduct of EU bodies.[60]

a *Greek Courts' Failure to Refer Relevant Questions to the CJEU*

The functioning of the preliminary reference procedure as an indirect or incidental way to challenge the EU's administrative conduct before the CJEU obviously depends on cooperation on the part of national courts.[61] Art. 267 TFEU is entirely built on the idea of judicial dialogue, and presumes loyalty and institutional cooperation between national and EU courts.[62]

In the context of the asylum system more broadly, the cooperative mechanism of Art. 267 TFEU works rather well. The courts of most member states make regular use of the preliminary reference procedure. The CJEU's most important judgements on the EU asylum acquis, including fundamental rights, have been brought about by asylum seekers claiming their rights before national courts.[63]

When it comes to vertical cooperation between national administrations and EU bodies, however, judicial cooperation appears to fail. Although several EU agencies and the Commission have been operating in the European asylum administration for almost two decades, and although fundamental rights in this context have been meticulously documented,

---

that decision was de facto determined by the EU, or whether Art. 274 TFEU must be interpreted so as to preclude its jurisdiction.

60 Elspeth Guild, Sergio Carrera, Leonhard Den Hertog, Joanna Parkin, *Implementation of the EU Charter of Fundamental Rights and its Impact on EU Home Affairs Agencies. Frontex, Europol and the European Asylum Support Office. Study for the LIBE Committee*, European Parliament 2011, p. 82–84; Mariana Gkliati, Herbert Rosenfeldt, „Accountability of the European Border and Coast Guard Agency: Recent developments, legal standards and existing mechanisms", *RLI Working Paper* 30 (2018), p. 10.

61 Eric Stein, „Lawyers, Judges, and the Making of a Transnational Constitution", *American Journal of International Law* 75 (1981), p. 1-27, p. 1.

62 This holds true especially in the context of fundamental rights, see Marta Cartabia, „Europe and Rights: Taking Dialogue Seriously", *European Constitutional Law Review* 5 (2009), p. 5-31, p. 23–31.

63 See only Court (Grand Chamber), judgment of 21 December 2011, N.S. v Secretary of State for the Home Department and M.E. and Others v Refugee Applications Commissioner and Minister for Justice, Equality and Law Reform, Joined cases C-411/10 and C-493/10; Court (Grand Chamber), judgement of 19 March 2019, Abubacarr Jawo v Bundesrepublik Deutschland, C-163/17.

national courts have not referred a single question on that issue to the CJEU.[64] This is especially striking in the case of Greece, where vertical administrative cooperation is most advanced, and at the same time raises numerous fundamental questions concerning EU primary and secondary law.[65]

b *The Illegality of the Non-Referral Practice under Art. 267 para 3 TFEU*

The most prominent case in this context is certainly the decision of the Council of State – Greece's highest administrative court – of September 2017 to not refer a question on the interpretation of the safe third country concept in the context of the EU-Türkiye Statement.[66] The Council justified its decision with the *acte claire* doctrine. This doctrine, however, cannot provide a valid justification, as indicated already by the fact that only a slight majority of 13 out of 25 judges voted against a referral to the CJEU.[67] Yet, the Council of State has since then in all major cases failed to identify and refer complex questions of EU law, including in cases concerning

64 As noted also by Herbert Rosenfeldt, *Frontex im Zentrum der Europäischen Grenz- und Küstenwache* (fn. 8), p. 326.

65 It can be left open here whether the failure of Greek courts to refer relevant questions to the CJEU is connected to structural weaknesses in terms of the rule of law more generally. This connection, however, seems likely, see Michael Ioannidis, „Weak Members and the Enforcement of EU Law" (fn. 47); Evangelia (Lilian) Tsourdi, Cathryn Costello, „'Systemic Violations' in EU Asylum Law: Cover or Catalyst?", *German Law Journal* 24 (2023), p. 982–994, p. 990 et seq.

66 Greek Council of State, judgement of 22 September 2017, 2347/2017 and 2348/2017, para 63: 'the Court ruled, with a majority 13/12, that, in view of the above, there is no reasonable doubt on the meaning of Art. 38 of the APD or the validity or interpretation of acts of organs of the EU and, thus, there is no reason to submit an application for a preliminary ruling to the CJEU according to Art. 267 TFEU'; non-official abbreviated English translation available at: https://www.refworld.org/cases,GRC_CS,5b1935024.html.

67 Angeliki Tsiliou, „When Greek judges decide whether Türkiye is a Safe Third Country without caring too much for EU law", eumigrationlawblog of 29/05/2018. The so-called *CILFIT* criteria were clearly not met. As the ongoing scholarly discussion on how to interpret the safe country concept clearly shows, the correct application of EU law was anything but obvious: According to CJEU, judgement of 6 October 1982, CILFIT v Ministry of Health et al, 283/81, para 16–20, the *acte claire* doctrine requires, inter alia, that 'the correct application of Community law may be so obvious as to leave no scope for any reasonable doubt as to the manner in which the question raised is to be resolved.'.

cooperation of national authorities with EASO, concerning restrictions on freedom of movement in the EU hotspots,[68] and more recently in pilot proceedings on judicial review in asylum procedures[69] as well as in proceedings challenging the anti-NGO campaigns.[70]

In sum, it appears that the Greek judiciary undermines the central mechanism of the EU legal protection system in the area of the integrated asylum administration simply by refraining from making use of it. Insofar as the Council of State is concerned, this practice constitutes a violation of Art. 267 para 3 TFEU. However, individuals cannot challenge this denial of access to the CJEU before national courts because the Greek system does not provide for a remedy of this kind.[71]

2.3 Failure of Direct Enforcement From Below via Annulment (Art. 263, 265 TFEU)

As the central mechanisms of Art. 258 TFEU and Art. 267 TFEU largely fail, one must turn towards direct remedies before the CJEU. Direct remedies are construed precisely to review the conduct of EU bodies and are therefore from the outset much better suited to ensuring judicial review of the administrative activities of Frontex, the EUAA and the European Commission.

In fact, the main discussion today revolves around whether the action for annulment under Art. 263 TFEU[72] or rather the action for damages

68 For instance, Council of State, judgement of 17 April 2018, 805/2018, which raised intricate questions concerning Art. 6 and Art. 45 para 2 ChFR and concerning the Reception Conditions Directive. See further Catharina Ziebritzki, Robert Nestler, „Implementation of the EU-Turkey Statement: EU Hotspots and restriction of asylum seekers' freedom of movement“, eumigrationlawblog of 22/06/2018 with a non-official abbreviated English translation of the judgement by Evita Armouti.

69 These questions were essentially determined by an interpretation of Art. 47 ChFR and the Asylum Procedures Directive. For the relevant procedures Refugee Support Aegean, The Council of State pilot procedure on judicial review in the asylum procedure, 1 February 2021, available at: https://rsaegean.org/en/the-council-of-state-pilot-procedure-on-judicial-review-in-the-asylum-procedure/.

70 These questions raised questions related to Art. 12, 16, 21 para 2 and 41 ChFR as well as to the interpretation of relevant secondary law. For the relevant procedure see Equal Rights Beyond Borders, 4 December 2022, NGO Law at the Greek Council of State, https://www.equal-rights.org/articles/87.

71 To the best knowledge of the author.Corrections are very welcome.

72 Respectively the action for failure to act under Art. 265 TFEU.

under Art. 340 TFEU are better suited in this context.[73] While earlier scholarship advocates for the former approach, more recent contributions tend to favor the latter.[74] Here, it will be argued that, although Art. 263 and Art 265 TFEU are capable of providing access to the CJEU in some specific case constellations, their overall relevance in the context of the integrated asylum administration necessarily remains limited. Again, this is because the core assumption of the legislative conception is not fulfilled. While Art. 263 and Art. 265 TFEU are based on the assumption that the EU acts in formally-binding manner, and thus provide protection only against formal administrative acts or the omission thereof, the EU's conduct in the asylum system is characterised by informality.

To make this point clear, it must first be recalled that the criteria for admissibility under Art. 263, 265 TFEU – as has been criticised many times – are extremely narrow.[75] The 'admissibility bottleneck' is due to two criteria. First, the act in question must be a legislative act or an act intended to produce legal effects vis-à-vis third parties. Second, the act must have a certain link to the concerned person which, since the Lisbon Treaty, can take three different forms: either the act is addressed to the concerned person, or it is of direct and individual concern to them, or it is a regulatory act which is of direct concern to them and does not entail implementing measures.[76]

---

73 On the respondent in the context of Art. 263 TFEU see Herbert Rosenfeldt, *Frontex im Zentrum der Europäischen Grenz- und Küstenwache* (fn. 8), p. 318 with further references; on the respondent in the context of Art. 340 para 2 TFEU see below 4.3. On Art. 277 TFEU see Giulia Gentile, „Ensuring Effective Judicial Review of EU Soft Law via the Action for Annulment before the EU Courts: a Plea for a Liberal-Constitutional Approach" (fn. 57), p. 484; Alexander H. Türk, „Liability and Accountability for Policies Announced to the Public and for Press Releases", *ECB Legal Conference 2017. Shaping a new legal order for Europe: a tale of crises and opportunities,* https://www.ecb.europa.eu/pub/pdf/other/ecblegalconferenceproceedings201712.en.pdf, p. 53.

74 See only Melanie Fink, *Frontex and Human Rights* (fn. 1); Melanie Fink, „The Action for Damages as a Fundamental Rights Remedy: Holding Frontex Liable", *German Law Journal* 21 (2020), p. 532–548.

75 See only Paul Craig, „Standing, Rights, and the Structure of Legal Argument", *European Public Law* 9 (2003), p. 493-508.

76 Based on CJEU, Court, judgement of 15 July 1963, Plaumann & Co. v Commission of the European Economic Community, 25/62. In more detail Steve Peers, Marios Costa, „Judicial Review of EU Acts after the Treaty of Lisbon; Order of 6 September 2011, Case T-18/10 *InuitTapiriit Kanatami and Others v. Commission* & Judgment of 25 October 2011, Case T-262/10 *Microban v. Commission*", *European Constitutional Law Review* 8 (2012), p. 82-104.

a *The Very Limited Potential of the Annulment Procedure and the Action for Failure to Act*

Still, there are three case constellations in which Art. 263, 265 TFEU could provide access to the CJEU. The first is when individuals seek to challenge a formally-binding decision of an agency-internal complaints mechanism.[77] In such cases, the criteria of formal bindingness and of the direct link in the sense of Art. 263 TFEU are fulfilled so that the admissibility bottleneck would not pose an obstacle.[78] Yet, the possibility to appeal a decision of an internal complaints mechanism via Art. 263 para 1, 4 TFEU cannot significantly enhance judicial protection against Frontex or the EUAA. As the internal complaints mechanisms as such are dysfunctional, they are rarely used in practice – and in any case, cannot function as a quasi-pre-judicial procedure.

The second constellation in which Art. 263 para 1, 4 TFEU or Art. 265 TFEU could work are the rare cases when the agencies act through formally-binding decisions. The most important example in this regard is probably a decision of Frontex's Executive Director to withdraw agency support under Art. 46 para 3 Frontex Regulation. In fact, one of the first actions that have been filed against Frontex sought to challenge its failure to withdraw from an operation via Art. 265 TFEU.[79] While it had seemed that the main doctrinal issue in this case concerned the criterion of the direct link,[80] the CJEU dismissed the action as inadmissible on another ground. Frontex had, upon invitation of the applicants under Art. 265 para 2 TFEU, reaffirmed and provided reasons for its position to not withdraw its support. The CJEU hence concluded that an action for failure to act was

77 Jürgen Bast, Frederik von Harbou, Janna Wessels, *Human Rights Challenges to European Migration Policy. The REMAP Study* (fn. 2), p. 139–142; Herbert Rosenfeldt, *Frontex im Zentrum der Europäischen Grenz- und Küstenwache* (fn. 8), p. 322–323; Mariana Gkliati, Herbert Rosenfeldt, „Accountability of the European Border and Coast Guard Agency: Recent developments, legal standards and existing mechanisms" (fn. 60), p. 11–12.

78 In detail Catharina Ziebritzki, *The EU's Responsibility in the Asylum Administration* (fn. 58), p. 240 et seq.

79 CJEU, order of 7 April 2022, SS and ST v European Border and Coast Guard Agency, T-282/21. For the argument of the applicants see https://www.front-lex.eu/court-case-frontex.

80 Herbert Rosenfeldt, *Frontex im Zentrum der Europäischen Grenz- und Küstenwache* (fn. 8), p. 321 therefore sceptical as to the success of that action which was still pending at the time of his writing.

no longer the appropriate remedy because Art. 265 TFEU 'concerns failure to act by failing to take a decision or to define a position'. Instead, the CJEU argued, the applicants should have submitted an action for annulment under Art. 263 TFEU, which they had not done.[81] The doubts as to the consistency of the CJEU's interpretation of Art. 265 TFEU notwithstanding,[82] an action under Art. 263 TFEU also meets a number of hurdles. The main problem in this regard is the admissibility bottleneck, which applies in the context of Art. 265 TFEU, too,[83] and would be extremely difficult to fulfil here.[84] In the case concerning a decision to withdraw agency support, for instance, the required link between the act and the applicant is typically very difficult or even impossible to establish.[85] This is not a coincidence, but results from the very structure of the integrated administration. After all, the agency's tasks are structurally limited to assisting and supporting, while the relevant decisions towards individuals are always issued by the member states.[86]

The third possibility to challenge formally-binding conduct of EU bodies via Art. 263 TFEU would be to rely on its second paragraph, i.e. an application by so-called privileged applicants. In this case, the criterion of

81 CJEU, order of 7 April 2022, SS and ST v European Border and Coast Guard Agency, T-282/21 (fn. 79), para 21–33, in particular para 32.

82 The argument is formalistic: As the applicants challenged the failure to withdraw, reinforcing the position to not withdraw still appears as a failure to act, and thus an omission.

83 Although the wording of that provision differs from that of Art. 263 para 4 TFEU, the CJEU held that the admissibility criteria correspond, see CJEU, General Court (Fourth Chamber), order of 17 November 2010, Fernando Marcelino Victoria Sánchez v European Parliament and European Commission, T-61/10, para 28; CJEU, General Court (Sixth Chamber), order of 27 November 2012, H-Holding AG v European Parliament, T-672/11, para 16. However, it is not yet clear whether this also applies to the third variant of Art. 263 para 4 TFEU, see Oliver Dörr, „Art. 263 AEUV", in Eberhard Grabitz, Meinhard Hilf, Martin Nettesheim (ed.), *Das Recht der Europäischen Union*, C.H. Beck 2023, para 19.

84 As this applies regardless of the quality of the concerned team members, and hence also to statutory staff (see on the different kinds of staff see chapter 2, 1.2), addressing misconduct by the latter via Art. 263 TFEU is not as simple as Herbert Rosenfeldt, *Frontex im Zentrum der Europäischen Grenz- und Küstenwache* (fn. 8), p. 359 suggests.

85 Herbert Rosenfeldt, *Frontex im Zentrum der Europäischen Grenz- und Küstenwache* (fn. 8), p. 320–321.

86 Elspeth Guild, Sergio Carrera, Leonhard Den Hertog, Joanna Parkin, *Implementation of the EU Charter of Fundamental Rights and its Impact on EU Home Affairs Agencies* (fn. 60), p. 83–84.

the link between the act and the applicant is not required. The practical relevance of this option, however, is limited from the outset because privileged applicants cannot challenge non-formally binding conduct either, so that the vast majority of acts in the asylum administration fall outside the scope of Art. 263 para 2 TFEU. In addition, one should keep in mind that Art. 263 para 2 TFEU is an instrument of enforcement from above, and can hence ensure the *effet utile* of EU law but not the fundamental right to an effective remedy. As individuals have no rights under Art. 263 para 2 TFEU, they entirely depend on political discretion of privileged applicants.[87] These limitations notwithstanding, it has been proposed that individuals or NGOs could submit formal complaints to the Commission, the Parliament, the Council or a member state which could then decide to pursue the case.[88] Theoretically, this construction is conceivable. In practice, however, it seems rather unlikely that privileged applicants would be willing to bring alleged misconduct of Frontex, the EUAA or even the Commission before the CJEU. Given the political sensitivities and complex disputes in the context of the asylum system, neither member states, including those governed by leftist parties, nor the Council seem to have any political interest in addressing systemic misconduct at the EU's external borders. Obviously, the Commission itself does not have such interest either, as its unwillingness to initiate infringement proceedings clearly shows. Not even the Parliament, which is at least partially acting as if it were the guardian of the Treaties in the context of the asylum system,[89] has so far shown any sign of considering an action under Art. 263 para 2 TFEU.

87 Mariana Gkliati, Herbert Rosenfeldt, „Accountability of the European Border and Coast Guard Agency: Recent developments, legal standards and existing mechanisms" (fn. 60), p. 10 noting that an individual could 'lobby' before an EU institution to lodge an action under Art. 263 para 4 TFEU.

88 In fact, the Parliament has already in 2011 been called upon to make use of Art. 263 para 2 TFEU, see Liora Lazarus, Cathryn Costello, Nazila Ghanea, Katja S. Ziegler, „The Evolution of Fundamental Rights Charters and Case Law. Report for the European Parliament Directorate-General for Internal Policies", *SSRN* (2011), https://ssrn.com/abstract=2210448, p. 82.

89 On the role of the European Parliament see 2.1.b.

b *Challenging Non-Formally Binding Conduct via Art. 263, 265 TFEU?*

As challenging formally-binding conduct is of very limited practical relevance,[90] the central point of discussion is whether Art. 263, 265 TFEU – despite their wording and established doctrine – allow to challenge non-formally binding conduct. Taking into account that the EU increasingly acts in a non-formally binding manner,[91] and based on the argument that Art. 47 ChFR requires individual legal protection against all forms of EU conduct, some scholarly contributions indeed seek to broaden the interpretation of Art. 263, 265 TFEU in this respect. While the core idea always is to re-interpret the notions of 'legislative acts' and 'acts intended to produce legal effects vis-à-vis third parties',[92] three specific doctrinal approaches can be distinguished.

The first approach is to develop the notion of a 'tacit decision'.[93] The second is to broaden the notion of the reviewable act in the sense of Art. 263, 265 TFEU. In essence, the argument is that the CJEU has by now adopted an 'substance over form' approach.[94] A closer look at the jurisprudence that is cited in support, however, shows that these proposals cannot convince, especially not in the specific context of the EU hotspot administration.[95]

A third proposal is to abandon the bindingness-requirement under Art. 263 TFEU altogether. This proposal would require for the CJEU to give up its doctrine insofar as it presupposes 'legally binding effects' in the formal sense of the term.[96] Advocacy in this direction stresses that the EU's increasing reliance on soft law and factual administrative conduct makes this step necessary.[97] Quite apart from the doubts as to whether it would be possible to overcome the bindingness-criterion in that manner, such reform

90 Melanie Fink, *Frontex and Human Rights* (fn. 1), p. 8.

91 See chapter 1, 4.

92 As laid down in Art. 263 para 1 TFEU.

93 On the first and the second approach see Herwig Hofmann, Morgane Tidghi, „Rights and Remedies in Implementation of EU Policies by Multi-Jurisdictional Networks", *European Public Law* (2014), p. 147–164, p. 155.

94 Notion borrowed from Giulia Gentile, „Ensuring Effective Judicial Review of EU Soft Law via the Action for Annulment before the EU Courts: a Plea for a Liberal-Constitutional Approach" (fn. 57), p. 477.

95 In detail Catharina Ziebritzki, *The EU's Responsibility in the Asylum Administration* (fn. 58), p. 245 et seq.

96 A similar result could be achieved via secondary law reform.

97 In this direction Oliver Dörr, „Art. 263 AEUV" (fn. 83), para 114, noting that it would be possible to broaden the admissibility criteria of the action for annulment with

seems currently highly unlikely. In any case, further scholarly advocacy calling on the CJEU to broaden the admissibility criteria of Art. 263, 265 TFEU seems a rather futile – at least if the aim is to enable those affected by systemically unlawful conduct of EU bodies to obtain legal protection as soon as possible.

For the purpose of this study, pragmatic considerations hence speak against further pursuing the third approach. In light of ongoing systemic fundamental rights violations, advocacy for a reform of the CJEU's doctrine – albeit conceptually appealing – is simply not sufficient. The crucial point is that, so far, there are no signs whatsoever that the scholarly calls for reform are being heard by the CJEU. On the contrary, rather than relaxing or even abandoning the bindingness-criterion, more recent case law points to a development in the opposite direction.[98] To date, the CJEU is apparently entirely unwilling to broaden its interpretation of Art. 263, 265 TFEU so as to allow for review of non-formally binding acts.[99]

Furthermore, it must be taken into account that even if the CJEU did broaden its interpretation of the bindingness-criterion, the problem of the admissibility bottleneck would still persist. For, even if non-formally binding conduct by EU bodies was, in principle, open to review via Art. 263, 265 TFEU, the relevant non-formally conduct such as e.g. opinions by Frontex, the EUAA or the Commission, would still be addressed to national authorities, and not to the concerned individuals. In the vast majority of cases, the inadmissibility hurdles related to the criterion of the direct link would hence persist. In order for Art. 263, 265 TFEU to function as an effective remedy in the asylum administration, it would thus be required for the CJEU to broaden not only its understanding of the bindingness-criterion but also of the direct link.[100] The CJEU's recent case law on the direct link,

regard to specific agencies because Art. 263 para 5 TFEU allows to deviate from its para 1.

98 This is well illustrated with the CJEU's more recent jurisprudence which sets a particularly high threshold for the bindingnes-criterion Departing from earlier jurisprudence. This is also pointed out also by Giulia Gentile, „Ensuring Effective Judicial Review of EU Soft Law via the Action for Annulment before the EU Courts: a Plea for a Liberal-Constitutional Approach“ (fn. 57), p. 479–483, however, using this as an argument for the need to reform the doctrine.

99 In detail Catharina Ziebritzki, *The EU's Responsibility in the Asylum Administration* (fn. 58), p. 249 et seq.

100 Elspeth Guild, Sergio Carrera, Leonhard Den Hertog, Joanna Parkin, *Implementation of the EU Charter of Fundamental Rights and its Impact on EU Home Affairs Agencies* (fn. 60), p. 83.

however, also points to the opposite direction. After the CJEU had stressed, in its earlier case law, that the criterion of the direct link must be interpreted in light of the rule of law,[101] and after this critique was incorporated with the Lisbon reform of Art. 263 para 4 TFEU, the CJEU has recently become increasingly reluctant to further broaden the interpretation of the direct link.[102]

3 Potential of the Action for Damages (Art. 340 para 2 TFEU)

It is against this background that this study argues for exploring the potential of the action for damages instead. As has become clear already, this choice is mainly justified by pragmatic considerations. Scholarly proposals to reconceptualise Art. 263, 265 TFEU, to introduce a specialised procedure that allows judicial review of agency acts, or even an EU fundamental rights complaint,[103] of course have their merits. The aim of this study, however, is to contribute to addressing systemic deficiencies in the asylum administration. Given the persistence and severity of these violations, and taking into account the current political climate, the approach here is to make use of EU law as it currently stands.

More precisely, and building on recent scholarship,[104] it is argued that the action for damages functions as a 'makeshift fundamental rights reme-

101 CJEU, Court of First Instance (Eighth Chamber), judgement of 8 October 2008, Sogelma v AER, T-411/06, para 37, arguing that 'it cannot be acceptable, in a community based on the rule of law, that such acts escape judicial review'.

102 Michael Rhimes, „The EU Courts Stand Their Ground: Why Are the Standing Rules for Direct Actions Still so Restrictive?", *European Journal of Legal Studies* (2016), p. 103-172.

103 In this direction Christoph-David Munding, *Das Grundrecht auf effektiven Rechtsschutz im Rechtssystem der Europäischen Union*, Duncker & Humblot 2010, p. 562–571. Critical Christina Last, *Garantie wirksamen Rechtsschutzes gegen Maßnahmen der Europäischen Union. Zum Verhältnis von Art. 47 Abs. 1, 2 GRCh und Art. 263 ff. AEUV*, Mohr Siebeck 2008, p. 274–279 with further references to literature.

104 In particular, Melanie Fink, *Frontex and Human Rights* (fn. 1), p. 180–316; Melanie Fink, „EU Liability for Contributions to Member States' Breaches of EU Law", *Common Market Law Review* 56 (2019), p. 1227–1264; Timo Rademacher, *Realakte im Rechtsschutzsystem der Europäischen Union* (fn. 1), p. 260–303, 373–386. Similarly, Mariana Gkliati, Herbert Rosenfeldt, „Accountability of the European Border and Coast Guard Agency: Recent developments, legal standards and existing mechanisms" (fn. 60), p. 13 evaluating the action for damages, despite its difficulties, as 'the most appropriate litigation route'; Herwig Hofmann, Morgane Tidghi, „Rights and

dy'. This notion makes clear that making use of the action for damages in the context of the asylum administration is a double-edged sword. On the one hand, it has great potential insofar as it allows to hold the EU responsible for fundamental rights violations, even when the EU's conduct is 'only' factual in nature. On the other hand, it comes with certain pitfalls because the action for damages was not conceptualised as a fundamental rights remedy, but as an action for monetary compensation, which results in in-built doctrinal shortcomings. In other words, the action for damages is today the best of many bad options to ensure judicial review in the integrated asylum administration – but that is already quite a lot.[105]

Remarkably, the CJEU itself has recently confirmed the potential of the action for damages as a fundamental rights remedy with its judgement in *WS et al. v Frontex.*[106] Contrary to what is often assumed,[107] the judgement

Remedies in Implementation of EU Policies by Multi-Jurisdictional Networks" (fn. 93), p. 156 noting that 'currently, the only way to review the legality of factual conduct is (...) the action for damages'. Remarkably, even Giulia Gentile, „Ensuring Effective Judicial Review of EU Soft Law via the Action for Annulment before the EU Courts: a Plea for a Liberal-Constitutional Approach" (fn. 57), p. 483 concedes that the action for damage offers the possibility to claim compensation for damages caused by EU soft law. Differently, however, Herbert Rosenfeldt, *Frontex im Zentrum der Europäischen Grenz- und Küstenwache* (fn. 8), p. 326 and 327. It is worth noting here that the scholarly trend to focus on Art. 340 para 2 TFEU is endorsed also by EU institutions: The European Parliament has proposed in 2015 already to make use of the action for damages to hold Frontex to account, see European Parliament, Resolution on the special report of the European Ombudsman in own-initiative inquiry OI/5/2012/BEH-MHZ concerning Frontex, 2014/2215(INI), 2 December 2015, para C: 'whereas even today Frontex coordination activity cannot in practice be dissociated from the member state activity carried out under its coordination, so that Frontex (and thereby the EU through it) could also have a direct or indirect impact on individuals' rights and trigger, at the very least, the EU's extra-contractual responsibility (see Court of Justice Judgement T-341/07, Sison III).' Similarly, the European Commission has noted that in its submissions in the context of CJEU, opinion of 18 December 2014, 2/13 (fn. 55) that in case of acts that do not produce binding legal effects, the only remedy available is the action for damages, see ibid, para 99.

105 Considering that, according to Winston Churchill '(...) democracy is the worst form of Government except for all those other forms that have been tried from time to time.' Quote of 11 November 1947, https://winstonchurchill.org/resources/quotes/the-worst-form-of-government/.

106 CJEU, General Court (Sixth Chamber), judgement of 6 September 2023, WS et al v Frontex, T-600/21.

107 For instance, Christopher Paskowski, „Verwaltung ohne Verantwortung. Zur Abweisung der ersten Schadensersatzklage gegen Frontex durch das EuG", Verfassungs-

constitutes as a milestone towards fundamental rights protection.[108] The ruling concerned one of the first actions for damages against Frontex in which applicants claimed compensation for damages suffered due to unlawful deportation.[109] In 2016, WS and several other Syrian nationals had arrived in Greece and expressed their intention to apply for international protection. Only eleven days after their arrival, their deportation to Türkiye was carried out in a joint return operation by Greek authorities together with Frontex. With their complaint, the deported applicants sought compensation for their rights under Art. 18, 19, 4, Art. 24, and Art. 41, 47 ChFR. Now, the crucial point is that the General Court found the applicants' complaint under Art. 340 para 2 TFEU to be admissible. This in itself is a great success. Even though the applicants lost the case in first instance and even though the General Court has fallen for a standard sham argument in the context of causation,[110] the judgment represents an important step towards the protection of fundamental rights. As the General Court leaves no doubt that the action for damages is a suitable way to address factual misconduct by Frontex before the CJEU, *WS et al.* has paved the way for similar claims to be pursued via the action for damages.[111]

3.1 Preconditions, Potentials and Pitfalls

Art. 340 para 2 TFEU provides that 'in the case of non-contractual liability, the Union shall, in accordance with the general principles common to the laws of the Member States, make good any damage caused by its institutions or by its servants in the performance of their duties.' That provision must be read in connection with the almost identical Art. 41 para 3 ChFR

blog of 27/09/2023; Joyce De Coninck, „Shielding Frontex. On the EU General Court's "WS and others v Frontex"", Verfassungsblog of 09/09/2023.

108 The following is based on Catharina Ziebritzki, „A Hidden Success. Why the EU General Court's Frontex Judgment is Better Than it Seems", Verfassungsblog of 13/10/23.

109 Prakken d'Oliveira, News of 2021, 'EU agency Frontex charged with illegal pushbacks', https://www.prakkendoliveira.nl/en/news/news-2021/eu-agency-frontex-charged-with-illegal-pushbacks; Front-Lex, Press Release of March 2022, 'For the First Time: Syrian Refugee Who Was a Victim of 'Pushback' Sues Frontex For Half a Million Euro', https://www.front-lex.eu/alaa-hamoudi.

110 In detail on this criticism see chapter 5, 1.2.

111 As Mariana Gliakti has put it in der Spiegel, 9 September 2023, Syrische Geflüchtete scheitern mit Klage gegen Grenzschutzagentur Frontex, the main success of this case is that it has paved the way for further proceedings of its kind.

according to which 'every person has the right to have the Community make good any damage caused by its institutions or by its servants in the performance of their duties, in accordance with the general principles common to the laws of the Member States.'

Liability under Art. 340 para 2 TFEU arises under the same conditions as under Art. 41 para 3 ChFR.[112] Since both provisions refer to the general principles common to the laws of the member states, the concrete preconditions for Union liability are established by the CJEU's case law.[113] The CJEU's interpretative approach can be described as a combination of evaluative comparison and autonomous interpretation.[114] The CJEU primarily bases its interpretation on an evaluative comparison of the member states' laws on state liability,[115] and complements this with considerations relating to the particularities of the Union's legal and administrative structure.[116]

Based on this method, the CJEU has established in consolidated jurisprudence that the EU incurs public liability when unlawful conduct of its bodies, qualifying as a sufficiently serious breach of a rule conferring rights on individuals, has caused a damage. EU liability hence arises upon three main conditions: first, a qualified unlawful conduct of the Union, second a damage, and third a causal link between the unlawful conduct and the damage. Crucially, the first element is qualified in two respects: the

112 Paul Craig, „Article 41", in Steve Peers, Tamara Hervey, Jeff Kenner, Angela Ward (ed.), *The EU Charter of Fundamental Rights. A Commentary*, Nomos 2021, p. 1125-1152, 1130–1131.

113 As the predecessors of Art 340 para 2 TFEU were phrased in the same manner, see Art. 215 para 2 EC Treaty (Maastricht Treaty, consolidated version) and Art. 288 para 2 EC Treaty (Nice Treaty, consolidated version), the CJEU's earlier jurisprudence still applies.

114 Philipp Dann, „Thoughts on a Methodology of European Constitutional Law", *German Law Journal* 6 (2005), p. 1453-1474, p. 1446 with reference to Art. 288 para 2 EC: 'Hence, it is not a simple transfer of national rules onto European law, but the development of common European standards.'.

115 Kathleen Gutman, „The Evolution of the Action for Damages Against the European Union and Its Place in the System of Judicial Protection", *Common Market Law Review* 48 (2011), p. 695-750, p. 709–710, and in more detail on the CJEU's 'comparative role' p. 738–749.

116 Ton Heukels, Alison McDonnell, „The Action for Damages in a Community Law Perspective: Introduction", in Ton Heukels, Alison McDonnell (ed.), *The Action for Damages in Community Law*, Wolters Kluwer 1997, p. 3.

unlawful conduct must consist, firstly, in a sufficiently serious breach of a rule that, secondly, confers rights upon individuals.[117]

As explained already, the potential of the action for damages mainly lies in the fact that EU liability does not presuppose formal-bindingness of the conduct at stake.[118] As the CJEU put it in *Bourdouvali*, 'in the system of legal remedies established by the FEU Treaty, actions for non-contractual liability pursue a compensatory purpose, intended in particular to guarantee effective judicial protection to an individual also against acts and conduct of the institutions of the European Union (...) which cannot be subject of an action for annulment under Article 263 TFEU.'[119] Today, it is thus consolidated jurisprudence that, in principle, *any* form of administrative conduct, be it formally-binding or factual, be it inter-administrative or directed towards individuals, can incur liability.[120] As a result, the action for damages today is – in the vast majority of cases – the only way to exercise the right to an effective remedy vis-à-vis the EU's conduct in the integrated asylum administration.[121]

At the same time, however, the action for damages comes with several pitfalls. The main problem is that – due to the twofold qualification of the criterion unlawfulness, i.e. the requirement of a sufficiently serious breach of a rule conferring rights upon individuals – the threshold for liability is rather high. This is obviously problematic insofar as the action for damages has become the sole remedy available. As the CJEU has also consistently held, Art. 47 ChFR in principle requires a remedy for each and every breach of EU law.[122] While the criterion of individual rights can arguably

117 See only CJEU, Court (Grand Chamber), judgement of 20 September 2016, Ledra Advertising Ltd et al v European Commission et al, Joined Cases C-8/15 P to C-10/15 P, para 64–65.

118 For detailed argument see chapter 5.

119 CJEU, General Court (Fourth Chamber), judgement of 13 July 2018, Eleni Pavlikka Bourdouvali v Council of the European Union, European Commission, European Central Bank, Euro Group and European Union, T-786/14, para 105–110, in particular 107.

120 See only Alexander Türk, *Judicial Review in EU Law*, Edward Elgar 2009, p. 241; Timo Rademacher, *Realakte im Rechtsschutzsystem der Europäischen Union* (fn. 1), p. 264. See in more detail chapter 5.

121 Similarly, Melanie Fink, „EU Liability for Contributions to Member States' Breaches of EU Law" (fn. 104), concluding at p. 1231: 'Hence, the action for damages is often the only action available to a private party to challenge EU contributions to Member State breaches of EU law.'.

122 Herwig Ch Hofmann, Liisa Holopainen, Elina Paunio, Laurent Pech, Clara Rauchegger, Debbie Sayers, Angela Ward, „Article 47", in Steve Peers, Tamara

be justified with reference to procedural efficiency or the exclusion of an actio popularis,[123] the criterion of a sufficiently serious breach is extremely difficult to uphold in light of Art. 47 ChFR.[124] From the perspective of the concerned individual who has no other remedy available than an action for damages, it cannot make a difference whether EU law is breached in a sufficiently serious manner or whether it is simply breached.[125] In practice, this problem is further aggravated by the lack of doctrinal clarity on when a breach is sufficiently serious,[126] which in turn entails a lack of predictability for the applicant, as well as the particularly high standard of proof.[127]

To fully unlock the potential of the action for damages as a remedy against factual conduct, it is hence key to realise that its pitfalls are mainly due to historical origins. The original idea was to differentiate between two levels of legal protection: individuals should be able to seek, at a first level, annulment of an unlawful act via Art. 263 TFEU, and at a second level, monetary compensation for damages resulting from unlawful acts via Art. 340 para 2 TFEU.[128] The action for damages was originally conceived as a subsidiary remedy, meaning that an individual would first have to lodge another action to establish the illegality of a certain measure before then lodging an action for damages.[129] Based on the assumption that all relevant conduct was formally-binding and could hence be addressed at the first level, it seemed consequential to limit the possibility to claim

Hervey, Jeff Kenner, Angela Ward (ed.), *The EU Charter of Fundamental Rights. A Commentary*, Nomos 2022, p. 1268.

123 As here Timo Rademacher, *Realakte im Rechtsschutzsystem der Europäischen Union* (fn. 1), p. 382–383.

124 Herwig Hofmann, Morgane Tidghi, „Rights and Remedies in Implementation of EU Policies by Multi-Jurisdictional Networks" (fn. 93), p. 156 with reference to the relevant case law.

125 Timo Rademacher, *Realakte im Rechtsschutzsystem der Europäischen Union* (fn. 1), p. 383.

126 Kathleen Gutman, „The Evolution of the Action for Damages Against the European Union and Its Place in the System of Judicial Protection" (fn. 115), p. 723 with further references.

127 Isabel Rooms, Ariti Skarpa, „An Insurmountably High Standard for Damage Claims against the EU? Case T-834/17, UPS v Commission", *Journal of European Competition Law & Practice* 13 (2022), p. 487–489.

128 On the gradual development of the action or damages into a self-standing remedy see Catharina Ziebritzki, *The EU's Responsibility in the Asylum Administration* (fn. 58), p. 2576 et seq.

129 CJEU, judgement of 15 July 1963, Plaumann, 25/62 (fn. 76), p. 108.

monetary compensation to cases of particularly severe misconduct.[130] The high threshold for liability seemed legitimate because it was considered to strike a fair balance between the interests of the concerned individual, the interests of taxpayer and the effective functioning of the administration. Limiting monetary compensation seemed necessary to avoid a situation in which every single misconduct burdens the EU's budget,[131] and to avoid paralyzing administrative action due to the concern of being required to pay compensation even for minor errors.[132]

Against this background, it becomes clear that the high threshold for liability is legitimate only because – and thus only as long as – the action for damages functions, first, as a subsidiary remedy and, second, allows for monetary compensation alone.[133] The key question that will guide the following analysis thus is whether this conceptualisation is still convincing, and if not, which doctrinal consequences this entails.

As regards the first aspect, i.e. the subsidiarity, the answer is rather straightforward. With the judgements in *Lütticke* and *Schöppenstedt* of 1971, already, the idea of subsidiarity has been overcome. Departing from earlier doctrine, the CJEU reconceived the action for damages as an autonomous form of action that is no longer conditional upon a prior action for annulment or action for failure to act.[134] Since then, the CJEU has consistently confirmed that the action for functions as a self-standing or 'independent'

130 See only Marc Jacob, Matthias Kottmann, „Art. 340 AEUV", in Eberhard Grabitz, Meinhard Hilf, Martin Nettesheim (ed.), *Das Recht der Europäischen Union* C.H. Beck 2023, para 94 with further references also to comparative analysis.

131 Ibid., para 17–18.

132 Timo Rademacher, *Realakte im Rechtsschutzsystem der Europäischen Union* (fn. 1), p. 383 with further references; very clear also CJEU, General Court (First Chamber), judgement of 25 November 2014, Safa Nicu Sepahan Co. v Council of the European Union (Safa Nicu I), T-384/11, para 51.

133 The 'and' is cumulative, not alternative.

134 CJEU, Court, judgement of 28 April 1971, Alfons Lütticke GmbH v Commission of the European Communities, 4/69, para 6; CJEU, Court, judgement of 2 December 1971, Aktien-Zuckerfabrik Schöppenstedt v Council of the European Communities, 5/71, para 3. Interestingly, the CJEU's departure from the subsidiarity doctrine is a return to the Founding Treaties, which included the then principle of Community liability to ensure that the transfer of powers to the Community level would not lead to reducing the individual's right to individual legal protection, see Francette Fines, „A General Analytical Perspective on Community Liability", in Ton Heukels, Alison McDonnell (ed.), *The Action for Damages in Community Law*, Wolters Kluwer 1997, p. 24.

legal remedy.[135] The relation between Art. 340 para 2 TFEU and Art. 263, 265 TFEU is hence clear: applicants are not required to lodge the latter as a precondition to the former.[136]

The second aspect, i.e. the focus on monetary compensation, requires more discussion. To begin with, it must be established that a situation in which Art. 340 para 2 TFEU is the only remedy available but at the same time allows for monetary compensation alone, falls short of Art. 47 ChFR. Unlike the ECtHR,[137] the EU legal order considers legal protection as effective only if it allows to annul the relevant act, or at least to declare the relevant act as unlawful. This follows from four considerations.[138] First, the CJEU requires member states' courts to grant primary legal protection,[139] and Art. 47 ChFR does not allow for double standards, in the sense that the same standard must also apply to the Union. Second, the CJEU's jurisprudence on legal protection before the CJEU itself increasingly stresses the need for primary remedies – at least in those cases where the nature of the breach is such that is has led to irreversible immaterial damage.[140] Third,

135 See only CJEU, Court of First Instance, judgement of 4 October 2006, Hans-Martin Tillack v Commission of the European Communities, T-193/04, para 97, 117; Court (Full Court), judgement of 23 March 2004, European Ombudsman v Frank Lamberts, C-234/02 P, para 59; CJEU, judgement of 13 July 2018, Bourdouvali, T-786/14 (fn. 119), para 105 with further references.

136 Timo Rademacher, *Realakte im Rechtsschutzsystem der Europäischen Union* (fn. 1), p. 274. For exceptions to this rule in case of an 'abuse' of the action for damages see Kathleen Gutman, „The Evolution of the Action for Damages Against the European Union and Its Place in the System of Judicial Protection“ (fn. 115), p. 703–708.

137 On the ECtHR's doctrine of 'acquiesce and liquidate' see Sacha Prechal, Rob Widdershoven, „Redefining the Relationship between 'Rewe-effectiveness' and Effective Judicial Protection“, *Review of European Administrative Law* 4 (2011), p. 31-50, p. 49; Nasiya Daminova, „'Access to Justice' and the Development of the Van Gend en Loos Doctrine: The Role of Courts and of the Individual in EU Law“, *Baltic Journal of Law & Politics* 10 (2017), p. 133-153, p. 139 with references to the relevant case law.

138 This paragraph draws extensively on the work of Timo Rademacher. In more detail on the first three Timo Rademacher, *Realakte im Rechtsschutzsystem der Europäischen Union* (fn. 1), p. 185–208.

139 Ibid., p. 188–191 with further references to the relevant case law and literature.

140 Ibid., p. 191–194. Note that the CJEU's case law is not entirely unequivocal on this point. In some cases, such as CJEU, Court of First Instance (Second Chamber), judgement of 15 January 2003, Philip Morris International et al v Commission of the European Communities, Joined Cases T-377/100 et al, para 123, the CJEU argues that secondary protection is sufficient where the Treaties do not foresee more. In other cases, such as CJEU, General Court (Second Chamber), judgement of 12 November 2013, Deutsche Post AG v European Commission, T-570/08 RENV, para 60; CJEU, Court (Fifth Chamber), judgement of 23 September 1986, AKZO Chemie

the fact that Art. 41 para 3 ChFR regulates the action for damages separately from Art. 47 ChFR shows that the Charter conceives secondary protection as complementary to effective protection, which accordingly must mean primary protection.[141] Fourth, it must be taken into consideration that the CJEU, in its seminal judgements *Les Verts* and *Union de Pequenos Agricultores*, considered the 'complete system of remedies' to consist of the annulment procedure, the preliminary reference procedure and the collateral review procedure,[142] thereby implying that the action for damages - notably in its original form as a secondary remedy - does not constitute an equivalent full element of the system of remedies. It follows from this understanding that a remedy which at its maximum results in monetary compensation must, at least in principle, be considered to fall short of the constitutional standard.[143]

On this basis, the remainder of this chapter will show that the original doctrine on the action for damages has undergone considerable development, and that the CJEU's current interpretation brings it closer to a primary remedy in the sense of Art. 47 ChFR - namely by conceptualising it more and more as a form of declaratory relief. Moreover, it will be argued that Art. 340 para 2 TFEU - due to its decidedly open wording - holds potential for further doctrinal development in this direction.

3.2 Interpreting in Light of the Constitutional Standard

To better understand the function of the action for damages within the EU legal protection system, this section briefly assesses its doctrine in light of the two relevant constitutional standards: the fundamental right to an effective remedy and the doctrine of vigilant individuals.

BV and AKZO Chemie UK Ltd v Commission of the European Communities, 5/85, para 29, the CJEU stressed that secondary remedies do not meet the standard of the right to an effective remedy.

141 Timo Rademacher, *Realakte im Rechtsschutzsystem der Europäischen Union* (fn. 1), p. 195–196.

142 Now Art. 277 TFEU.

143 For detailed argument with references to the relevant case law see Timo Rademacher, *Realakte im Rechtsschutzsystem der Europäischen Union* (fn. 1), p. 185–198. Note that this does not deny that for damages is 'indispensable to uphold the (...) right to an effective remedy', as argued by Herwig Ch Hofmann, Liisa Holopainen, Elina Paunio, Laurent Pech, Clara Rauchegger, Debbie Sayers, Angela Ward, „Article 47" (fn. 122), p. 1316.

a *The Legal Protection Gap Argument: A Broad Reading of Art. 340 para 2 TFEU*

The fundamental right to an effective remedy constitutes both yardstick and inspiration for the interpretation of Art. 340 para 2 TFEU.[144] On the one hand, Art. 47 ChFR establishes a constitutional standard in which the action for damages in its current form appears deficient.[145] On the other hand, Art. 47 ChFR also strongly influences the doctrine on the action for damages in the sense that the action for damages strives towards the constitutional standard. The CJEU, in fact, interprets the action for damages in light of Art. 47 ChFR – precisely in order to make it an effective remedy.[146]

The argument that Art. 340 para 2 TFEU must be interpreted broadly in order to avoid gaps in the EU legal protection system is referred to here as the 'legal protection gap argument'. It is a concrete expression of the CJEU's general approach to interpreting the procedures laid down in primary law in light of the requirements of Art. 47 ChFR.[147] Ever since *Les Verts*, the CJEU has consistently justified broad interpretations of the procedures laid down in primary law with reference to the rule of law and the right to an effective remedy.[148] This holds true for both admissibility and substantial criteria.[149]

144 Hans Jarass, „Art. 47 Recht auf einen wirksamen Rechtsbehelf und ein unparteiisches Gericht", *Charta der Grundrechte der EU*, C.H. Beck 2021, para 31–33.

145 On the pitfalls see above 3.1.

146 Kathleen Gutman, „The Evolution of the Action for Damages Against the European Union and Its Place in the System of Judicial Protection" (fn. 115), p. 750; Hans Jarass, „Art. 47 Recht auf einen wirksamen Rechtsbehelf und ein unparteiisches Gericht" (fn. 144), para 4, 32–33.

147 See only CJEU, Court (Fourth Chamber), judgment of 6 June 2013, MA, BT and DA v Secretary of State for the Home Department, C-548/11, para 50; CJEU, Court (Fourth Chamber), judgement of 29 January 2009, Migrationsverket v Edgar Petrosian and Others, C-19/08, para 34.

148 Mariana Gkliati, Herbert Rosenfeldt, „Accountability of the European Border and Coast Guard Agency: Recent developments, legal standards and existing mechanisms" (fn. 60), p. 9.

149 As the reconstruction of the CJEU's argument by Giacomo Rugge, „The Euro Group's informality and *locus standi* before the European Court of Justice: *Council v. K. Chrysostomides & Co. and Others*", *Zeitschrift für ausländisches öffentliches Recht und Völkerrecht (Heidelberg Journal of International Law)* (2021), p. 917-936, p. 923 shows, both General Court and Court agree that the lack of access to legal protection is an argument in favour of attribution to the Union if, otherwise, the applicants would be deprived of legal protection altogether.

The validity of this argument can be called into question with two basic objections. First, one could contend that Art. 19 TEU requires member states to fill gaps in the EU legal protection system, so that it would not be necessary for Art. 340 para 2 TFEU to function as gap-filler.[150] This argument, however cannot persist because member states are not capable to provide judicial protection against the EU's own administrative conduct.[151]

Another objection might be that the legal protection gap argument must apply equally to all procedures enshrined in primary law and not only to Art. 340 para 2 TFEU. In this regard, it is, of course, true that the standard of Art. 47 ChFR applies to all remedies and has, inter alia, led to a broadening of annulment procedure. Yet, it is argued here that the legal protection gap argument is of a particular quality and salience in the context of Art. 340 para 2 TFEU. This is because the action for damages functions as *the* gap filler in the EU legal protection system.[152] Unlike Art. 263, 265 TFEU, the wording of Art. 340 para 2 TFEU is sufficiently open and flexible to function as a fall-back option when no other remedy is available.[153] Further, Art. 41 para 3 TFEU grants a fundamental right to claim compensation from the Union and thus speaks in favour of a broad interpretation of the action for damages.[154] For if an individual was denied legal protection under Art. 340 para 2 TFEU that would violate not only Art. 47 ChFR but also Art. 41 para 3 ChFR.

The understanding of Art. 340 para 2 TFEU as the gap-filler in the EU legal protection system is reflected in the CJEU's jurisprudence.[155] In the case of *Lesieur*, for instance, the CJEU held that an action for damages

150 As mentioned above, some argue that Art. 19 TEU prescribes that gaps in the EU legal protection system must be filled by member states, so that Art. 47 ChFR cannot justify a broad interpretation of Art. 340 para 2 TFEU, see only Hans Jarass, „Art. 47 Recht auf einen wirksamen Rechtsbehelf und ein unparteiisches Gericht" (fn. 144), para 32.

151 As here Herwig Hofmann, Morgane Tidghi, „Rights and Remedies in Implementation of EU Policies by Multi-Jurisdictional Networks" (fn. 93), p. 156.

152 As here, Timo Rademacher, *Realakte im Rechtsschutzsystem der Europäischen Union* (fn. 1), p. 373–387.

153 Uwe Säuberlich, *Die außervertragliche Haftung im Gemeinschaftsrecht. Eine Untersuchung der Mehrpersonenverhaltnisse*, Springer 2005, p. 56–59.

154 Similarly, Melanie Fink, „The Action for Damages as a Fundamental Rights Remedy: Holding Frontex Liable" (fn. 74), p. 536.

155 On the advances of the Treaty of Lisbon in this regard see Kathleen Gutman, „The Evolution of the Action for Damages Against the European Union and Its Place in the System of Judicial Protection" (fn. 115), p. 701.

is to be considered admissible if, otherwise, no legal protection would be granted because it was not possible for the applicants to lodge their claims before national courts.[156] In Bank Refah Kargaran, the court even expanded the scope of the application of Art. 340 para 2 TFEU to the area of the CFSP 'in order to avoid a lacuna in the judicial protection of the natural or legal persons concerned'.[157]

Taking this idea one step further, it is argued here that an action for damages is admissible when legal protection at the member state level is systemically excluded.[158] The reason for this is well illustrated in the case of the EU hotspots. When individuals staying in EU hotspots do not have access to an effective remedy against the national administration, it is either due to extreme delays in national procedures, which amount to a violation of Art. 47 ChFR, or because national courts systemically refuse to refer the relevant questions to the CJEU – the action for damages against the Union becomes the only remedy available to review compatibility with EU law, and for this reason alone, must be considered as admissible. In other words, where both a member state and the Union are involved in a specific administrative misconduct, and where the member state systemically fails to grant Art. 47 ChFR, the Union must fill in that gap and allow for judicial review. As no other remedy comes into consideration, the action for damages must function as a gap-filler in this regard.

The CJEU's approach to interpreting the action for damages broadly in light of Art. 47 ChFR is particularly well illustrated with the jurisprudential turn brought about in the cases of *Brasserie* and *Bergaderm*.[159] With the *Schöppenstedt* doctrine of 1971, the CJEU had established quite narrow criteria for EU liability: it required a breach of a superior rule of law and made a strict distinction between legislative and administrative action, and it had

156 CJEU, Court, judgement of 17 March 1976, Lesieur Cotelle et Associés SA and others v Commission of the European Communities, Joined cases 67/75 et al, para 14–16.

157 CJEU, Court (Grand Chamber), judgement of 6 October 2020, Bank Refah Kargaran v Council of the European Union, C-134/19 P, para 39. Critical of the interpretation defended here Giacomo Rugge, „The Euro Group's informality and *locus standi* before the European Court of Justice" (fn. 149), p. 933.

158 Even further Giacomo Rugge, ibid., p. 929 who argues in favour of a general presumption of admissibility.

159 CJEU, judgement of 5 March 1996, Brasserie du Pêcheur SA v Federal Republic of Germany et al and the Queen v Secretary of State for Transport, C-46/93 and C-48/93; CJEU, Court, judgement of 4 July 2000, Laboratoires pharmaceutiques Bergaderm SA and Jean-Jacques Goupil v Commission of the European Communities, C-352/98 P, para 40–45.

then, over the years, interpreted these criteria in an increasingly narrow manner.[160] In the 1990s, this narrowing of the action for damages led to fierce criticism from scholars,[161] and even judges of the CJEU themselves noted that it had become practically almost impossible to hold the Union liable.[162] The prevailing opinion back then was that the criteria were too strict and that the action for damages failed to live up to its promise to protect individual rights.[163]

Eventually, the CJEU reacted and loosened the criteria for Union liability. This doctrinal change was brought about in two steps. The first was taken with the judgement in *Brasserie du Pêcheur* of 1996, a case concerning member state liability, where the Court stated that the criteria for EU liability and member state liability 'in the absence of particular justification' should not be different.[164] The second step was taken with the *Bergaderm* decision of 2000, in which the CJEU applied its new approach to EU liability: it ruled that EU liability would arise under the same conditions as those established in *Brasserie du Pêcheur* and thereby departed explicitly from its previous narrow *Schöppenstedt* approach.[165] Since then, EU liability no longer presupposes a breach of a superior rule of law but instead only a sufficiently serious breach of a rule of law conferring rights upon individuals.

Obviously, the argument underlying this jurisprudential turn is that the right to an effective remedy establishes a yardstick with which the EU legal protection system should comply and that the action for damages functions as a gap-filler in this regard. Further, it seems no coincidence that the

160 See only CJEU, Court, judgement of 13 March 1992, Industrie-en Handelsonderneming Vreugdenhil BV v Commission of the European Communities, C-282/90.

161 See only Francette Fines, „A General Analytical Perspective on Community Liability" (fn. 134), p. 21–24; Ian Ward, *A Critical Introduction to European Law*, LexisNexis Buttersworths 1996, p. 64.

162 For instance judge at the CJEU Federico Mancini, *Democracy and Constitutionalism in the European Union*, Hart Publishing 2000, p. 46–48 noted that there were to areas in which 'the Court of Justice has let the individual down', naming the action for damages against the Union and access to the action for annulment.

163 See Pekka Aalto, *Public Liability in EU Law. Brasserie, Bergaderm and Beyond*, Hart Publishing 2011, p. 86–87, noting that 'The case law was there to support the institutions, not the individuals.'.

164 CJEU, judgement of 5 March 1996, Brasserie du Pêcheur, C-46/93 (fn. 159), para 42; in the same direction CJEU, judgement of 8 October 1996, Dillenkofer et al v Federal Republic of Germany, C-178/94 et al, para 25.

165 CJEU, judgement of 4 July 2000, Bergaderm, C-352/98 P (fn. 159), para 40–45.

turn occurred in the context of the adoption of the ChFR, which renewed the emphasis on individual rights and fundamental-right-ized the action for damages.[166] In fact, the CJEU's main argument for departing from its earlier doctrine was based on the function of the action for damages as a means of individual legal protection. It namely argued that the 'protection of the rights which individuals derive from Community law cannot vary depending on whether a national authority or a Community authority is responsible for the damage.'[167] At the same time, the CJEU introduced the criterion of a sufficiently serious breach,[168] thereby recalibrating the balance between individual rights and the effective functioning of the administration in favour of the former.[169] At the latest since this 2000 *Brasserie-Bergaderm*-turn,[170] it is hence unequivocally clear that the CJEU conceives the action for damages as a means to ensure the right to an effective remedy and is, at least in principle, willing to adjust its doctrine on Art. 340 para 2 TFEU accordingly.

b *The Action for Damages as a Mechanism for Vigilant Individuals*

As to the second element of the constitutional standard, namely the idea of vigilant individuals, it is argued here that Art. 340 para 2 TFEU, just as any other remedy, functions as a mechanism of enforcement from below. The argument essentially builds on case law in which the CJEU has held that member-state liability serves the principle of effective judicial protection.[171] After the CJEU had, in its very early case law, ruled that member state liability only has a subjective dimension,[172] it has since the 1990s held that

166 On the importance of Art. 41 para 3 ChFR see Kathleen Gutman, „The Evolution of the Action for Damages Against the European Union and Its Place in the System of Judicial Protection" (fn. 115), p. 702–703.

167 CJEU, judgement of 5 March 1996, Brasserie du Pêcheur, C-46/93 (fn. 159), para 42.

168 Ibid., para 55–57.

169 See in more detail Pekka Aalto, *Public Liability in EU Law* (fn. 163), p. 91–96 tracing this argument in several opinions of Advocates Generals from 1976 to 2000.

170 For a detailed account of the *Brasserie-Bergaderm*-turn see Pekka Aalto, ibid.

171 See only Court, judgement of 30 September 2003, Gerhard Köbler, C-244/01, para 34; and further Sacha Prechal, Rob Widdershoven, „Redefining the Relationship between 'Rewe-effectiveness' and Effective Judicial Protection" (fn. 137), p. 36.

172 CJEU, judgement of 24 October 1973, Merkur v Commission, 43/72, para 4: 'The action for damages seeks (...) satisfaction solely for the benefit of the applicant.'.

member state liability has both a subjective and an objective dimension.[173] In *Frankovich,* for instance, the CJEU stated explicitly that the action for damages against member states serves both to ensure 'the full effectiveness of Community rules' and to 'protect the rights which they confer on individuals'.[174] As the action for damages against the Union builds upon and thus has the same telos as the action for damages against member states, it follows that Art. 340 para 2 TFEU also serves both subjective and objective legal protection.[175]

Some, however, dispute this reading and argue that the rhetoric of *Frankovich* notwithstanding, member state liability, in fact, does no more than compensate private parties.[176] To support this understanding, reference is made, in particular, to the statistically relatively low success rate and to the requirement that the rule in breach must confer rights upon individuals. On this basis, it is then concluded that member state liability is only a subjective dimension and that the same must, hence, be true for Union liability.[177]

Whereas the dispute concerning member state liability need not be decided here, the arguments allegedly refuting the objective dimension, in any case, do not apply to EU liability. First, as regards the relatively low financial compensation, it must be noted that this, as such, is not an argument against an objective dimension. In fact, even those who contest the dual purpose concede that the action for damages might serve general prevention,[178] which cannot be clearly distinguished from objective legal protection.[179] Second, the political impact of a CJEU decision should not be underestimated. Even though Art. 340 para 2 TFEU does not allow for

173 As follow from CJEU, judgement of 5 March 1996, Brasserie du Pêcheur, C-46/93 (fn. 159), para 72–74. Futher Marek Safjan, Dominik Düsterhaus, „A Union of Effective Judicial Protection: Addressing a Multi-level Challenge through the Lens of Article 47 CFREU", *Yearbook of European Law* 33 (2014), p. 3–40, p. 37.

174 CJEU, Court, judgement of 19 November 1991, Andrea Frankovich et al v Italy, C-6/90 and C-9/90, para 32–33.

175 Marc Jacob, Matthias Kottmann, „Art. 340 AEUV" (fn. 130), para 13.

176 Tobias Lock, „Is Private Enforcement of EU Law Through State Liability a Myth? An Assessment 20 Years After Frankovich", *Common Market Law Review* 49 (2012), p. 1675-1702.

177 Ibid., p. 1702 referring to Art 340 TFEU as a procedure 'the chief purpose of which is the protection of individual rights', without further justifying this understanding.

178 Ibid., p. 1700.

179 Uwe Säuberlich, *Die außervertragliche Haftung im Gemeinschaftsrecht* (fn. 153), p. 50–56.

erga omnes judgments, cases such as *Ledra* show that it can reasonably be expected that a CJEU decision stating that the EU is liable for fundamental rights violations has effects beyond the individual case.[180] Third, lower financial compensation could also indicate that the action for damages evolves towards declaratory relief. Seen from this perspective, less compensation speaks in favour, not against, a function of the action for damages as a mechanism for enforcement from below.

3.3 A Makeshift Fundamental Rights Remedy

Since the action for damages serves both individual legal protection and the *effet utile* of EU law, it is obviously of particular importance when fundamental rights are at stake.[181] Yet, the claim that the action for damages functions as a proper fundamental rights remedy requires further argument. For the claim to hold on the basis of the law as it currently stands, it must be shown that, in case of a fundamental rights violation, the high threshold for liability is met. Specifically, it must be argued that fundamental rights qualify as individual rights,[182] that breaches of fundamental rights as such qualify as sufficiently serious, and that fundamental rights violations as such constitute immaterial damage.

To avoid misunderstandings, the claim made here is not that the action for damages is the only procedure which functions as a fundamental rights remedy. Certainly, other procedures, such as the action for annulment, can also serve to address fundamental rights violations. Due to its gap-filling function, however, the action for damages holds a special place within the range of procedural options, as Art. 41 para 3 ChFR confirms. In fact, a large part of severe fundamental rights violations are brought about

---

180 Although the CJEU's judgement in Ledra (fn. 117) concerned one specific austerity measure, it was largely understood as setting a general standard for the legality of austerity measures under EU law.

181 Melanie Fink, „The Action for Damages as a Fundamental Rights Remedy: Holding Frontex Liable“ (fn. 74), p. 534–536; Angela Ward, „Damages under the EU Charter of Fundamental Rights“, *ERA Forum* 12 (2012), p. 589–611, p. 590–593; Nina Półtorak, „Action for Damages in the Case of Infringement of Fundamental Rights by the European Union“, in Ewa Bagińska (ed.), *Damages for violations of human rights. A comparative study of domestic legal systems*, Springer 2016, p. 427–441, p. 427–441, p. 434–436.

182 The argument here is limited those fundamental rights that are most relevant in the context of the EU hotspot administration.

through factual or inter-administrative conduct and hence escape the scope of the action for annulment. Even before the entry into force of the ChFR, individuals thus mainly relied on the action for damages in case of fundamental rights violations.[183]

a *The Relevant Fundamental Rights as Individual Rights*

The first matter, i.e. the qualification of fundamental rights as individual rights, concerns the relation between 'rights and freedoms guaranteed by the law of the Union' in the sense of Art. 47 ChFR and 'rules conferring rights upon individuals in the sense of Art. 340 para 2 TFEU. Generally, the CJEU interprets the individual rights criterion in the context of Art. 340 para 2 TFEU rather broadly and applies a purpose test. According to this test, it is not required that the provision in question has a direct effect or that it grants subjective rights. Instead, it is sufficient that the provision *inter alia* serves to protect the individual.[184]

183 CJEU, Court of First Instance (Fifth Chamber), AFCon Management Consultants, Patrick Mc Mullin and Seamus O'Grady v Commission of the European Communities, judgment of 17 March 2005, T-160/3; CJEU, Court of First Instance (Fourth Chamber), judgement of 11 July 2007, Schneider Electric SA v Commission of the European Communities (Schneider I), T-351/03; CJEU, Court (Second Chamber), judgement of 4 July 1989, Benito Francesconi and others v Commission of the European Communities, 326/86 and 66/88, in particular para 4–5; CJEU, Court, judgement of 30 September 1988, Portuguese Republic v Council of the European Union (Coldiretti), T-149/96, in particular para 67–79. See further Nina Półtorak, „Action for Damages in the Case of Infringement of Fundamental Rights by the European Union" (fn. 181), p. 434; Angela Ward, „Damages under the EU Charter of Fundamental Rights" (fn. 181), p. 596–597; for the context of the Eurozone see Anastasia Poulou, „Financial Assistance Conditionality and Human Rights Protection: What is the Role of the EU Charter of Fundamental Rights?", *Common Market Law Review* 54 (2017), p. 991-1026.

184 Pekka Aalto, *Public Liability in EU Law* (fn. 163), p. 111–132, 158–176; Melanie Fink, „EU Liability for Contributions to Member States' Breaches of EU Law" (fn. 104), note 100 with further reference to the relevant case law. Note that the CJEU, General Court (Second Chamber) in its judgement of 23 November 2011, Jose Maria Sison v Council of the European Union (Sison III), T-341/07, para 33 explicitly clarified that the different expressions used in the jurisprudence, such as a rule of law 'intended to confer rights on individuals', a rule of law 'for the protection of the individual' or a rule of law 'intended to protect individuals' are 'mere variations of a single legal concept'.

When applying this purpose test to fundamental rights, two considerations are of particular importance. The first concerns the interpretative method. Generally, the CJEU's doctrine on how to determine the purpose of a particular rule remains rather thin. The CJEU usually refers to contextual interpretation, and its conclusions then seem to be based on jurisprudential intuition.[185] However, regarding the interpretation of the Charter, Art. 52 para 3 and para 4 ChFR provide some more concrete guidance by establishing that both the constitutional traditions of the member states and the ECtHR's jurisprudence must be taken into account.[186] In particular, Art. 52 para 4 ChFR provides the basis for the argument that those rights which have been interpreted as absolute by the ECtHR also qualify as conferring rights upon individuals. This follows from the notion of absolute rights. Contrary to conventional wisdom, the ECtHR does not conceive all absolute rights as non-derogable in a strict sense: the prohibition of non-refoulement, for instance, is considered 'less absolute' than the prohibition of torture, although both are enshrined in Art. 3 ECHR.[187] This is strongly criticized, and rightly so.[188] Yet, it must be acknowledged here that the ECtHR apparently determines the quality of a right as absolute according to whether it is judged as particularly important, in the sense that it protects goods and interests that are so central to the life and living of individuals that infringements can be justified, if at all, only with very important arguments and only in very exceptional circumstances.[189] Consequentially, these rights, *per definition,* qualify as rights that serve the interest of the individual.

185 Angela Ward, „Damages under the EU Charter of Fundamental Rights“ (fn. 181), p. 594.

186 Ibid., p. 599.

187 Hemme Battjes, „In Search of a Fair Balance: The Absolute Character of the Prohibition of Refoulement under Article 3 ECHR Reassessed“, *Leiden Journal of International Law* 22 (2009), p. 583-621, in particular p. 595–599; Steven Greer, „Is the Prohibition against Torture, Cruel, Inhuman and Degrading Treatment Really 'Absolute' in International Human Rights Law?“, *Human Rights Law Review* 15 (2015), p. 101-137, p. 118.

188 Natasa Mavronicola, Francesco Messineo, „Relatively Absolute? The Undermining of Article 3 ECHR in Ahmad v UK“, *The Modern Law Review* 76 (2013), p. 589-619; Natasa Mavronicola, „Is the Prohibition Against Torture and Cruel, Inhuman and Degrading Treatment Absolute in International Human Rights Law? A Reply to Steven Geer“, *Human Rights Law Review* 17 (2017), p. 479-498.

189 Similarly Hemme Battjes, „In Search of a Fair Balance: The Absolute Character of the Prohibition of Refoulement under Article 3 ECHR Reassessed“ (fn. 187), p. 618–619.

The second consideration concerns the distinction made in the Charter between rights and principles. As follows from Art. 51 para 1, Art. 52 para 1, 2, 5 ChFR, principles are distinct from rights in that principles do not grant subjective rights.[190] This does not mean, however, that principles cannot, at least amongst other things, serve to protect individual rights in the sense of Art. 340 para 2 TFEU. This is well illustrated with Art. 25 ChFR: although this norm is generally qualified as a principle, it can hardly be denied that it serves, at least inter alia, to protect the rights of elderly people.[191] Whether or not a principle serves to protect individual rights cannot, therefore, be answered in general terms but can only be determined by interpreting the provision in question. This is different in the case of rights. Since rights are defined as provisions conferring subjective rights, they qualify per se as rules that serve to protect individual rights within the meaning of Art. 340 para 2 TFEU.[192]

Based on these considerations, the purpose test can be applied to those fundamental rights that are at stake in the context of the integrated EU hotspot administration. As established above, these are, in particular, the prohibition of refoulement granted by Art. 4, 18, 19 ChFR, the right to good administration enshrined in Art. 41 ChFR, the specific procedural guarantees for children granted by Art. 24 and 41 ChFR, the prohibition of inhuman and degrading treatment enshrined in Art. 4 ChFR, and the right to liberty under Art. 6 ChFR.[193]

---

190 On the distinction between rights and principles see Hans Jarass, „Art. 52 Tragweite und Auslegung der Rechte und Grundsätze", *Charta der Grundrechte der EU*, C.H. Beck 2021, para 69a, 72 arguing that the qualification depends on contextual interpretation; slightly differently Thorsten Kingreen, „Artikel 52 EU-GRCharta", in Christian Calliess, Matthias Ruffert (ed.), *EUV/AEUV. Kommentar*, C.H. Beck 2022, para 16 arguing that all those provisions which are directed only to the Union qualify as principles.

191 As here for instance Hans Jarass, „Art. 25 Rechte älterer Menschen", *Charta der Grundrechte der EU*, C.H. Beck 2021, para 3; differently Thorsten Kingreen, „Artikel 25 EU-GRCharta", in: Christian Calliess, Matthias Ruffert (ed.), *EUV/AEUV. Kommentar*, C.H. Beck 2022, para 1.

192 Explanations relating to the Charter of Fundamental Rights, OJ 2007 C 303/30 of 14 December 2007 (hereinafter: Charter Explanations), p. 17–35, Article 52 para 1 ChFR.

193 Further, the right to personal data as now enshrined in Art 8 ChFR and the right to private life as now enshrined in Art 7 ChFR. See Angela Ward, „Damages under the EU Charter of Fundamental Rights" (fn. 181), p. 596–599.

Art. 4, 6, 41 and 24 ChFR qualify as rights in the sense of Art. 51, 52 ChFR,[194] and thus also as norms conferring rights upon individuals in the sense of Art. 340 para 2 TFEU. The same holds true for the absolute rights enshrined in Art. 4 ChFR. Concerning Art. 41 ChFR, the CJEU has explicitly pronounced itself on its qualification in the context of EU liability. Whereas earlier case law concluded that a breach of the obligation to give reasons could not incur liability,[195] more recent judgements establish that the principle of sound administration confers rights upon individuals where it constitutes the expression of specific rights such as the right to have affairs handled impartially, fairly and within reasonable time, the right to be heard, the right to have access to files, or the obligation to give reasons for decisions.[196] Concerning the right to asylum, the CJEU has not explicitly pronounced itself yet, and scholarship remains divided over the question of whether Art. 18 ChFR qualifies as right or principle, with the prevailing opinion arguing for the latter.[197] For the question at stake, however, that dispute is largely irrelevant. This is because the right to asylum as granted by Art. 18 ChFR consists of several components, and the component corresponding to the protection granted by Art. 3 ECHR is certainly absolute and must hence be understood as conferring individual rights.[198] This is even confirmed by the prevailing opinion which accepts that the non-refoulement principle as granted under the ChFR is subjective

194 See Charter Explanations (fn. 192), Explanations on the cited articles.

195 See for instance CJEU, Court of First Instance (Third Chamber), judgement of 6 December 2001, Emesa Sugar (Free Zone) NV v Council of the European Union, T-43/98.

196 CJEU, judgement of 4 October 2006, Tillack, T-193/04 (fn. 135), in particular para 127; CJEU, judgement of 23 November 2011, Sison III, T-341/07 (fn. 184); CJEU, Court (Grand Chamber), order of 9 June 2010, European Commission v Schneider Electric SA (Schneider II), C-440/07 P. As here Angela Ward, „Damages under the EU Charter of Fundamental Rights“ (fn. 181), p. 596–597; in more detail on the contradictions in the CJEU's case law see Pekka Aalto, *Public Liability in EU Law* (fn. 163), p. 121–125.

197 For the minority opinion see María-Teresa Gil-Bazo, „The Charter of Fundamental Rights of the European Union and the Right to be Granted Asylum in the Union's Law“, *Refugee Survey Quarterly* 27 (2015), p. 33-52.

198 This is ultimately a technical question of doctrinal reconstruction: In the alternative, one could also argue that the individual-rights-granting component is enshrined exclusively in Art. 19 para 2 and Art. 4 ChFR.

in nature,[199] thereby implying that Art. 18 ChFR qualifies as subjective right insofar as it prohibits non-refoulement.

To conclude, the purpose-test leads to the conclusion that all relevant fundamental rights fulfil the individual-rights criterion in the sense of Art. 340 para 2 TFEU.

b *A Fundamental Rights Violation as a Sufficiently Serious Breach*

The second question is whether violations of fundamental rights per se qualify as sufficiently serious breaches. When discussing this, it should be kept in mind that the sufficiently-serious-breach criterion is often decisive for whether or not the Union is liable.[200] This is because the balancing of private interests with the effective functioning of the administration, which lies at the heart of public liability law, is mainly carried out in the context of this criterion.[201] At the same time, the criterion is particularly problematic because it not only sets quite a high threshold but also lacks legal certainty – notably to such an extent that some have argued that the effectiveness of legal protection is endangered.[202]

This being said, the CJEU's test on whether a breach is sufficiently serious can be described as an evaluation of the relevant breach in light of several factors, which in sum amounts to a comprehensive due-dili-

199 See, for instance, Daniel Thym, „Legal Framework for EU Asylum Policy", in Daniel Thym, Kay Hailbronner (ed.), *EU Immigration and Asylum Law. Article-by-Article Commentary*, C.H. Beck, Hart Publishing and Nomos 2022, para 55a and b, para 60.

200 In more detail on the CJEU's doctrine on the 'sufficiently serious breach' see Kathleen Gutman, „The Evolution of the Action for Damages Against the European Union and Its Place in the System of Judicial Protection" (fn. 115), p. 712–724; Melanie Fink, „EU Liability for Contributions to Member States' Breaches of EU Law" (fn. 104), p. 1253–1257.

201 CJEU, judgement of 23 November 2011, Sison III, T-341/07 (fn. 184), para 34: 'This requirement of a sufficiently serious breach (...) is intended (...) to avoid the risk of having to bear the losses claimed by the persons concerned obstructing the institution's ability to exercise to the full its power in the general interest (...) without however thereby leaving individuals to bear the consequences of flagrant and inexcusable misconduct.'.

202 Jill Wakefield, *Judicial Protection through the Use of Article 288(2) EC*, Wolters Kluwer 2002, p. 147.

gence-test.[203] The decisive question, according to the CJEU, is whether the relevant breach would also have occurred had the competent authority exercised due diligence and care; if that is not the case, the breach qualifies as sufficiently serious. As the CJEU formulated in *Sison III*, 'only the finding of an irregularity that an administrative authority, exercising ordinary care and diligence, would not have committed in similar circumstances, can render the Community liable'.[204]

In applying this test, discretion remains a central factor.[205] In concrete terms, where the 'institution in question has only considerably reduced, or even no, discretion, the mere infringement of Community law may be sufficient to establish the existence of a sufficiently serious breach.'[206] When there is more than none or narrow discretion, a breach is sufficiently serious if Union bodies 'manifestly and gravely disregard the limits on their discretion'.[207] This being said, the determination of the degree of discretion, of course, requires an interpretation of the specific provision rather than general considerations about the degree of discretion enjoyed in a particular policy area.[208]

203 The sufficiently-serious-breach criterion thus partly overlaps with the individual-rights criterion, Angela Ward, „Damages under the EU Charter of Fundamental Rights" (fn. 181), p. 600–601.

204 CJEU, judgement of 23 November 2011, Sison III, T-341/07 (fn. 184), para 39.

205 In its earlier case law, the CJEU distinguished between administrative acts where Union bodies must exercise 'ordinary care' and legislative acts where liability would only arise if the Union bodies 'manifestly and gravely disregarded the limits on the exercise of its powers' see CJEU, judgement of 25 May 1978, Bayerische HNL, Joined cases 83 and 94/76, 4, 15 and 40/77, para 6. Since the *Bergaderm* turn, the decisive criterion is no longer the legislative or administrative nature of the act in question but rather the margin of available discretion. This '*Bergaderm* approach' is often described as the 'new', the 'discretion-centred' approach, see in more detail Chris Hilson, „The Role of Discretion in EC Law on Non-Contractual Liability", *Common Market Law Review* 42 (2005), p. 681 – 685.

206 CJEU, judgement of 4 July 2000, Bergaderm, C-352/98 P (fn. 159), para 40–46.

207 See only CJEU, judgement of 12 July 2005, CEVA Santé Animale SA, C-198/03 P, para 65; CJEU, judgement of 19 April 2007, Holcim (Deutschland) v COM, C-282/05, para 47.

208 Opinion of Advocate General Stix-Hackl, 28 November 2002, Fresh Marine, C-472/00 P, para 78; CJEU, 10 July 2003, Fresh Marine, C-472/00 P, para 26; CJEU, judgement of 10 December 2002, C-312/00 P, COM v Camar and Tico, para 58.

In addition, several further factors are taken into consideration.[209] Among these are the severity[210] and the reprehensibility of the violation, i.e. whether the breach was intentional or inexcusable.[211] Further, the complexity of the situation and difficulties or uncertainties in the interpretation of the legislation must be taken into account.[212] In this context, it is decisive whether there are authoritative assessments of a certain conduct as unlawful. If jurisprudence or other reliable legal sources have already established that specific conduct is unlawful, the relevant authority cannot excuse its behaviour with reference to situational complexity or interpretational uncertainty; instead, the breach must then be considered as sufficiently serious.[213] The CJEU has made this argument with regard to its own judgements[214] to legal opinions expressed by the Fundamental Rights Agency, the European Parliament, the European Commission,[215] or UN bodies.[216] The same applies to ECtHR judgements: for once the ECtHR has found

209 Kathleen Gutman, „The Evolution of the Action for Damages Against the European Union and Its Place in the System of Judicial Protection“ (fn. 115), p. 716; Angela Ward, „Damages under the EU Charter of Fundamental Rights“ (fn. 181), p. 600; Nina Półtorak, „Action for Damages in the Case of Infringement of Fundamental Rights by the European Union“ (fn. 181), p. 427–441, 433.

210 This is so already because the purpose of the criterion is balancing public and private interests, see Advocate General Lagrange, Opinion of 7 June 1961, Meroni, Joined cases 14, 16, 17, 20, 24, 26 and 27–60 and 1–61, p. 174: 'On the other hand it is true that the required degree of seriousness varies according to the nature of the service, the extent of the difficulty encountered in guaranteeing it, and, on the other hand, to the extent of the protection which the interests which have suffered damage deserve. In each case a balance must be struck between the public interest and private interest'. Note that Chris Hilson, „The Role of Discretion in EC Law on Non-Contractual Liability“ (fn. 205), p. 694 criticises the Bergaderm formula for not making this explicit.

211 CJEU, judgement of 23 November 2011, Sison III, T-341/07 (fn. 184), para 37 to 39, 40, 58. Johannes Saurer, *Der Einzelne im europäischen Verwaltungsrecht*, Mohr Siebeck 2014, p. 173 hence understands the sufficiently-serious-breach criterion as equivalent to the reprehensibility-criterion as required under German public liability law.

212 CJEU, judgement of 4 July 2000, Bergaderm, C-352/98 P (fn. 159), para 43;; CJEU, judgement of 19 April 2007, Holcim (Deutschland) v COM, C-282/05 (fn. 207), para 50; CJEU, 10 July 2003, Fresh Marine, C-472/00 P (fn. 208), para 24.

213 Angela Ward, „Damages under the EU Charter of Fundamental Rights“ (fn. 181), p. 602.

214 CJEU, judgement of 23 November 2011, Sison III, T-341/07 (fn. 184), para 37–40, 58.

215 Angela Ward, „Damages under the EU Charter of Fundamental Rights“ (fn. 181), p. 602.

216 CJEU, judgement of 23 November 2011, Sison III, T-341/07 (fn. 184), para 60–77; CJEU, judgement of 3 September 2008, Yassin Abdullah Kadi and Al Barakaat

that a particular conduct violates human rights, an administrative authority exercising ordinary care would henceforth refrain from performing that conduct.

On this basis, it is argued here that fundamental rights violations qualify as sufficiently serious – at least when the violations are systemic in nature, or when there is authoritative opinion evaluating the situation as violating fundamental rights.[217] This holds true all the more when it comes to the rights that constitute basic elements of the rule of law such as those granted by Art. 4, 6, 18, 19, 24 and 41 ChFR.[218]

This understanding is convincing already at a conceptual level because fundamental rights hold a special place in the EU legal order, as made clear by Art. 2 TEU, and breaches thereof, let alone systemic breaches, should not remain unaddressed.[219] In addition, the fact that the determination of the violation of a fundamental right as such requires a balancing exercise speaks in favour of omitting another balancing exercise to determine the sufficient seriousness of the breach.[220]

Further, this understanding reconciles two strands of case law, namely judgements in cases such as *Staelen*,[221] *Ledra Advertising*[222] or *Bocchi*,[223] in which it was held that fundamental rights violations were per se sufficiently serious breaches, on the one hand,[224] and judgements in cases such as *Sison*

International Foundation v Council and Commission, C-402/05 P and C-415/05 P, para 361–363.

217 These two conditions depend on each other because: For if the invoked fundamental rights violation affects a large number of individuals in the same situation, it is more likely that authoritative assessments of the situation exist.

218 Similarly, Melanie Fink, *Frontex and Human Rights* (fn. 1), p. 226–227 who focuses on 'core' fundamental rights; similarly, also Angela Ward, „Damages under the EU Charter of Fundamental Rights" (fn. 181), p. 601.

219 Thus, where Art. 340 para 2 TFEU is the only remedy available, this as such speaks in favour of the qualification of the relevant breach as sufficiently serious, see Melanie Fink, *Frontex and Human Rights* (fn. 1), p. 226.

220 Melanie Fink, *ibid.*, p. 227.

221 General Court (Fourth Chamber), judgement of 29 April 2015, Claire Staelen v European Ombudsman (Staelen I), T-217/11, para 86.

222 CJEU, judgement of 20 September 2016, Ledra, C-8/15 P et al (fn. 117), para 69–70. See further chapter 5, 4.2.

223 CJEU, Court of First Instance (Fifth Chamber), judgement of 20 March 2001, Bocchi Food Trade International GmbH v Commission of the European Communities, T-30/99, para 80.

224 Melanie Fink, *Frontex and Human Rights* (fn. 1), p. 224–225 with reference to further similar case law in note 248 and 249.

III,[225] *Schneider*[226] and *Safa Nicu*,[227] in which it was held that fundamental rights violations were sufficiently serious due to the complexity of the situation and interpretational uncertainty, on the other hand. Stressing that the latter strand implies that 'simple' violations of fundamental rights are not sufficiently serious, some have interpreted the two lines of jurisprudence as contradicting each other.[228] For the purpose of this study, however, the crucial point is that both strands concur insofar as those breaches qualify as sufficiently serious which are systemic, authoritatively documented, or concern fundamental rights that are 'core' to the rule of law. If one or several of these criteria are met, the CJEU concludes that fundamental rights violations qualify as sufficiently serious breaches.[229]

This is consequential because – and this is the most important argument in favour of the understanding proposed here – it follows from the due-diligence test as set out above. Violations of fundamental rights are always especially severe and always inexcusable. An exemplary authority exercising ordinary care might make a mistake and might perhaps even fail to prevent the violation of fundamental rights in exceptional and isolated cases. However, such authority would certainly not systemically and continuously violate fundamental rights, let alone core fundamental rights, in a situation

225 CJEU, judgement of 23 November 2011, Sison III, T-341/07 (fn. 184), para 75–82.

226 CJEU, Court of First Instance (Fourth Chamber), judgement of 11 July 2007, Schneider I, T-351/03 (fn. 183), para 154–156; CJEU, order of 9 June 2010, Schneider II, C-440/07 P (fn. 196), para 173.

227 CJEU, judgement of 25 November 2014, Safa Nicu I, T-384/11 (fn. 132), para 32–36, 60–67.

228 Melanie Fink, *Frontex and Human Rights* (fn. 1), p. 224–226.

229 On the one hand, in CJEU, judgement of 29 April 2015, Staelen I, T-217/11 (fn. 221) the fundamental right concerned was the right to good administration, i.e. a right that is 'core' to the rule of law; in CJEU, judgement of 20 September 2016, Ledra, C-8/15 P et al (fn. 117), the breach was systemic insofar as the measures at stake led a large number of similar fundamental rights violations; in CJEU, judgement of 20 March 2001, Bocchi, T-30/99 (fn. 223) none of the three conditions is met, but the CJEU still found the breach to be sufficiently serious, which confirms the conclusion because the list of conditions is not exhaustive. On the other hand, in CJEU, judgement of 23 November 2011, Sison III, T-341/07 (fn. 184), para 41, the fundamental rights concerned are the right to respect for private life and for property and the CJEU found the breach to be not sufficiently serious; in CJEU, order of 9 June 2010, Schneider II, C-440/07 P (fn. 196), the concerned fundamental rights were the rights of defence; in CJEU, judgement of 25 November 2014, Safa Nicu I, T-384/11 (fn. 132), para 59–69, the fundamental right at stake was the right to effective judicial protection.

which has already been evaluated by authoritative opinion as breaching the Charter.[230]

c *A Fundamental Rights Violation as a Damage*

The third issue concerns the notion of damage,[231] specifically the question of whether the violation of a fundamental right as such constitutes damage.[232]

To begin with, it must be recalled that the CJEU defines the notion of damage in a broad manner. In principle, any impairment of a legally protected good or interest constitutes damage.[233] Provided that the damage is actual and certain,[234] it can be material or non-material.[235] The notion of non-material harm in itself is quite broad and has been interpreted by the CJEU as encompassing pain or physical suffering,[236] harm to emotional well-being or career,[237] reputational harm,[238] similar harm to personality

230 Angela Ward, „Damages under the EU Charter of Fundamental Rights" (fn. 181), p. 601.

231 See on this question also Melanie Fink, *Frontex and Human Rights* (fn. 1), p. 228–231.

232 On the question at which relevant point in time a damage must be manifest, see Catharina Ziebritzki, *The EU's Responsibility in the Asylum Administration* (fn. 58), p. 269 et seq.

233 See only Katri Havu, „Damages Liability for Non-Material Harm in EU Case Law", *European Law Review* 44 (2019), p. 492-514, p. 492–514, 492, 495 with extensive reference to the relevant case law; Timo Rademacher, *Realakte im Rechtsschutzsystem der Europäischen Union* (fn. 1), p. 288–289.

234 Kathleen Gutman, „The Evolution of the Action for Damages Against the European Union and Its Place in the System of Judicial Protection" (fn. 115), p. 735.

235 Paul Craig, *EU Administrative Law*, Oxford University Press 2018, p. 248.

236 CJEU, judgement of 3 March 2004, François Vainker and Brenda Vainker v European Parliament, T-48/01, para 178; CJEU, judgement of 27 March 1990, Alfredo Grifoni v European Atomic Energy Community, C-308/87, para 2, 7.

237 CJEU, General Court (Sixth Chamber), judgement of 16 December 2015, Randa Chart v European External Action Service, T-138/14, para 149–150; CJEU, Court (Grand Chamber), judgement of 4 April 2017, European Ombudsman v Claire Staelen, C-337/15 P (Staelen II), para 129.

238 See only CJEU, General Court (Fourth Chamber), judgement of 6 April 2006, Manel Camós Grau v European Commission, T-309/03, para 162. See on the distinction of reputational harm and material economic damage Katri Havu, „Damages Liability for Non-Material Harm in EU Case Law" (fn. 233), p. 508–513.

rights,[239] or even discomfort created by a prolonged state of uncertainty.[240] The most important limit to the notion of non-material harm is that 'normal inconvenience' does not constitute damage.[241] For instance, the CJEU has considered damage the psychological harm experienced because of the way in which the European Ombudsman dealt with a complaint.[242] Typical cases of reputational harm are staff cases and so-called sanctions list cases, and typical cases of prolonged state of uncertainty are cases concerning excessive duration of court or administrative proceedings in competition matters.[243] The broadness of the notion of immaterial harm is particularly well illustrated with the case of *Camós Grau,* in which the CJEU qualified as immaterial damage the impairment of the applicant's 'honour and professional reputation' and 'difficulties in his living conditions' resulting from a publication of a report by OLAF.[244]

Based on this jurisprudence, it follows that any fundamental rights violation entails immaterial damage in the sense of Art 340 para 2 TFEU. There are two alternative lines of argument to support this conclusion. One is that any violation of fundamental rights as such constitutes immaterial damage.[245] This understanding might be surprising from the perspective of legal systems such as the German one, which make a strict distinction between the breach of a right and the ensuing damage, but is firmly rooted in the French legal tradition.[246]

---

239 See only CJEU, Court, judgement of 7 March 1995, Fiona Shevill et al v Press Alliance SA, C-68/93, para 23; CJEU, Court of First Instance (Fourth Chamber), judgement of 9 July 1999, New Europe Consulting, T-231/97, para 53–54.

240 Both of natural persons and of companies, see only CJEU, Court (Third Chamber), judgement of 23 April 2002, Anna Maria Campogrande v European Commission, C-62/01 P, para 21; CJEU, Court (Sixth Chamber), judgement of 14 May 1998, Council of the European Union v Lieve de Nil and Christiane Impens, C-259/96 P, para 25.

241 CJEU, Court (Second Chamber), judgment of 25 March 2010, Sviluppo Italia Basilicata SpA v European Commission, C-414/08 P, para 139–142; CJEU, judgement of 4 April 2017, Staelen II, C-337/15 P (fn. 237), para 91–95; CJEU, General Cort (First Chamber), order of 13 January 2017, Idromacchine Srl et al v European Commission, T-88/09 DEP, para 91–93.

242 CJEU, judgement of 4 April 2017, Staelen II, C-337/15 P (fn. 237), para 129.

243 See Katri Havu, „Damages Liability for Non-Material Harm in EU Case Law" (fn. 233), p. 496–499.

244 CJEU, judgement of 6 April 2006, Camós Grau, T-309/03 (fn. 238), para 162–163.

245 Melanie Fink, *Frontex and Human Rights* (fn. 1), p. 228–232; Herbert Rosenfeldt, *Frontex im Zentrum der Europäischen Grenz- und Küstenwache* (fn. 8), p. 285.

246 Timo Rademacher, *Realakte im Rechtsschutzsystem der Europäischen Union* (fn. 1), p. 377–378 with further references.

An alternative line of argument is that the violation of fundamental rights qualifies as damage because a it per definitiom goes beyond normal inconvenience and necessarily amounts to immaterial harm. According to this reasoning, the immaterial damage i.e. the physical or psychological suffering is inherent in the fundamental rights violation.[247] This is well illustrated with the fundamental rights identified as particularly relevant to the asylum administration. A violation of Art. 4 ChFR, for instance, presupposes[248] and thus necessarily entails severe psychological and physical suffering. The same is true concerning violations of Art. 41 ChFR: a failure to conduct a hearing in private circumstances, a failure to conduct a correct age assessment, or delays in the asylum procedure, for instance, typically cause severe psychological distress or even disease, harm to personality rights, and feelings of anxiety due to a prolonged state of uncertainty.[249] Similar considerations apply to violations of Art. 6 ChFR, Art. 18, 19 ChFR and the procedural dimension of Art. 24 ChFR. As all these fundamental rights protect interests that are fundamental for psychological and physical wellbeing of human beings, it follows in reverse that a violation of these rights necessarily constitutes immaterial damage.

3.4 Towards Declaratory Relief

This last section addresses the conceptual weaknesses of Art. 340 para 2 TFEU identified above, namely that it is traditionally conceived as a means for monetary compensation with a particularly high threshold for liability. The problem with this understanding is that, while the action for damages by now occupies a central place in the EU legal protection system and even functions as fundamental rights remedy in critical areas of EU law, monetary compensation alone is not sufficient to meet the standard of Art. 47 ChFR, and the precondition of a sufficiently serious breach is difficult to reconcile with the requirement that each and every breach of EU law requires judicial redress. Hence, the question to be discussed is whether

247 Melanie Fink, *Frontex and Human Rights* (fn. 1), p. 228–231.

248 ECtHR, judgement of 21 January 2011, M.S.S. v Belgium and Greece, Application No 30696/09; CJEU, judgment of 21 December 2011, N.S. et al, C-411/10 et al (fn. 63), para 106; CJEU, judgement of 19 March 2019, Jawo, C-163/17 (fn. 63), para 85.

249 This holds true all the more in situations in which the concerned person is exposed to living conditions violating Art. 4 ChFR during the entire procedure.

Art. 47 ChFR allows, or even requires, to interpret Art. 340 para 2 TFEU as a primary remedy.

The CJEU has recognised the issue and, in cases of immaterial harm, indeed attaches less and less importance to monetary compensation. Instead, it increasingly grants restitution in kind under Art. 340 para 2 TFEU, and in some cases even considers the recognition of the unlawfulness as such as appropriate compensation. The function of the action for damages is thus shifting towards a form of declaratory relief. This, in turn, argues for a lowering of the threshold for liability. Once Art. 340 para 2 TFEU functions as declaratory relief, it would be conceptually consequential to lower the threshold to a simple breach of EU law.[250] The CJEU, however, has so far stuck to its traditional sufficiently-serious-breach criterion – thereby creating a remedy that unjustifiably makes the mere finding of illegality dependent on a particular gravity of the violation.

a *Towards Restitution in Kind and Recognition of Unlawfulness*

For long, the action for damages has been conceived exclusively as a means for monetary compensation.[251] When it comes to immaterial damage, the CJEU thus traditionally quantifies that damage and then awards material compensation.[252] Concerning the amount of monetary compensation, the CJEU conducts an evaluation on a case-by-case basis, referring to a 'fair evaluation ex aequo et bono' or fixing an amount 'on an equitable basis'.[253] In some cases, mainly concerning reputational harm, the CJEU has indeed granted quite considerable sums.[254] In *Camós Grau* of 2006, for instance,

250 The action for damages would then no longer be 'makeshift' but instead a fully-fledged primary remedy in its own right.

251 As becomes clear from the doctrine on Art. 340 para 2 TFEU (see above 3.1), this is not due to the wording of the provision but rather due to a certain concept of state liability in the law of most member states.

252 See only Melanie Fink, *Frontex and Human Rights* (fn. 1), p. 228–229 with further references to the case law.

253 In detail Katri Havu, „Damages Liability for Non-Material Harm in EU Case Law" (fn. 233), p. 506–511 with further references.

254 CJEU, Court (Grand Chamber), judgement of 30 May 2017, Safa Nicu Sepahan Co. v Council of the European Union (Safa Nicu II), C-45/15 P, para 47–53, 86–92, 101–107; CJEU, Court of First Instance (Eighth Chamber) judgement of 24 September 2008, M v Ombudsman, T-412/05, para 146, granting compensation of 10,000 Euro for reputational harm; CJEU, General Court (First Chamber), judgement of 10

the CJEU considered that the applicant had 'his honour and professional reputation impaired' and 'suffered difficulties in his living conditions' due to the publication of a report by the EU agency OLAF and thus ordered the Union to pay 10,000 Euro as compensation.[255] Another example is the judgement in *Safa Nicu* of 2017 in which 50,000 Euro were granted as compensation for reputational harm.[256]

Yet, compensation under Art. 340 para 2 TFEU is not necessarily limited to monetary compensation. In fact, the CJEU goes beyond monetary compensation in two respects. First, monetary compensation is often replaced with restitution in kind; and second, the amount of monetary compensation is often reduced with the argument that the recognition of the unlawfulness as such constitutes appropriate compensation.

The first reasoning is based on the understanding that 'making good damage' in the sense of Art. 340 para 2 TFEU means to put the concerned person in the situation they would have been in if the unlawful conduct had not been committed.[257] In *Galileo,* and similarly also in *Systran*, for instance, the CJEU has argued that nothing in the Treaties precludes the grant of compensation in kind, and that therefore, it has the 'power to impose on the Community any form of reparation that accords with the general principles of non-contractual liability common to the laws of the Member States, including, if it accords with those principles, compensation in kind, if necessary in the form of an injunction to do or not to do something'.[258] Consequently, where monetary compensation is insufficient to fully rectify the damage, the CJEU tends to grant restitution in kind, and to prevent the occurrence of any further damages.[259]

June 2004, Jean-Paul François v European Commission, T-307/01, para 111, granting compensation of 8,000 Euro.

255 CJEU, judgement of 6 April 2006, Camós Grau, T-309/03 (fn. 238), para 162–163.

256 CJEU, judgement of 25 November 2014, Safa Nicu I, T-384/11 (fn. 132), para 78 to 92.

257 Paul Craig, *EU Administrative Law* (fn. 235), p. 748 with reference to the relevant case law in note 138.

258 CJEU, General Court (Second Chamber), judgement of 10 May 2006, Galileo International Technology LLC and Others v European Commission, T-279/03, para 62–73, in particular para 63. Similarly, CJEU, General Court (Third Chamber), judgement of 16 December 2010, Systran SA et al v European Commission, para 120–123. Further on preventive judicial protection via Art. 340 para 2 TFEU see Timo Rademacher, *Realakte im Rechtsschutzsystem der Europäischen Union* (fn. 1), p. 384–386.

259 Timo Rademacher, *ibid.*, p. 191–194.

In the context of the integrated asylum administration, this doctrine raises difficulties because the EU might, in some cases, not have the competence to do what is required to grant restitution in kind. For instance, if unlawful conduct of Frontex had resulted in a person being refouled to Türkiye, the CJEU would not be able to oblige the EU to bring back that person to EU territory because competences to issue the relevant administrative decisions to allow re-entry lie with member states.[260] In these cases, granting restitution in kind would hence mean to oblige the EU to do everything – within its competences – to make sure that the person is put in the situation in which it would have been had the mistake not occurred; which would include exerting influence on the responsible national authorities.[261]

The second argument with which the CJEU goes beyond monetary compensation is to understand it as superfluous where the declaration of illegality as such constitutes appropriate compensation. This reasoning is closely connected to the first one: for if unlawful conduct as such constitutes the damage, the declaration of illegality as such constitutes a form of restitution in kind.

This argument is firmly anchored in established doctrine. Generally, when considering what is 'adequate' monetary compensation for immaterial harm, the CJEU takes into account whether, and if so to what extent, the declaration of illegality as such provides relief.[262] It is hence only consequential to considerably reduce the amount of monetary compensation, sometimes even to a symbolic i.e. a negligible amount, where the recognition of the unlawfulness of the contested act as such constitutes adequate relief.[263] In the 1990 judgement of *Culin*, for instance, the CJEU applied this reasoning and accordingly granted a symbolic amount of only one

260 In detail on the EU's administrative competences Catharina Ziebritzki, *The EU's Responsibility in the Asylum Administration* (fn. 58), p. 114 et seq.

261 The verdict could be formulated similarly to those of German administrative courts which obliged German authorities to do everything they can, within their competence, to ensure that authorities of other member states would accept their take-charge requests under the Dublin III Regulation, see fn. 39. This is consequential because it would transfer the jurisprudence on horizontal administrative cooperation to vertical administrative cooperation.

262 Similarly, Katri Havu, „Damages Liability for Non-Material Harm in EU Case Law" (fn. 233), p. 503.

263 CJEU, Court (Grand Chamber), judgment of 28 May 2013, Abdulbasit Abdulrahim v Council of the European Union and European Commission, C-239/12 P, para 71–72; CJEU, judgement of 25 November 2014, Safa Nicu I, T-384/11 (fn. 132), para

Franc.[264] In *Abdulrahim* and *Safa Nicu* of 2013, however, the CJEU also found that the recognition of the unlawfulness of the contested measure as such could constitute 'a form of reparation for the non-material harm', and still granted considerable sums of compensation.[265] In sum, the CJEU seems to consider the declaration of illegality as sufficient only in some cases of immaterial harm, and in others complements the declaration of illegality with monetary compensation.

b *From the Function of Compensation to Declaratory Relief*

These ambiguities notwithstanding, the CJEU's case law clearly shows that the action for damages increasingly functions as a form of declaratory relief.[266] This argument also concerns the relation between Art. 340 para 2 TFEU and Art. 263 TFEU because conceptualising the former as declaratory relief approximates its effects to the latter.

In fact, the aim of applicants lodging an action for damages is often not exclusively, and not even primarily, to receive monetary compensation. This holds true not only in cases where the applicants state from the outset that their main interest is to have the EU's conduct declared unlawful, but also in those cases where the applicants seek monetary compensation in addition to, or as a confirmation of the unlawfulness of the relevant conduct. Arguably, the quest for the recognition of unlawfulness becomes particularly salient in those cases where EU bodies systemically violate EU law and where fundamental rights are at stake. This is well illustrated with *Ledra* and similar cases emerging from the context of the Eurozone. The applicants had sought to have the EU's conduct scrutinised via Art. 263 TFEU and via Art. 340 para 2 TFEU, and once the former was dismissed as inadmissible, the latter de facto became the procedure in which the legality

86. Further Katri Havu, „Damages Liability for Non-Material Harm in EU Case Law" (fn. 233), p. 501.

264 CJEU, Court (Fourth Chamber), judgement of 7 February 1990, Annibale Culin v Commission of the European Communities, C-343/87, para 26–29.

265 CJEU, judgment of 28 May 2013, Abdulbasit Abdulrahim, C-239/12 P (fn. 263), para 71–72.

266 As here Herbert Rosenfeldt, *Frontex im Zentrum der Europäischen Grenz- und Küstenwache* (fn. 8), p. 285; in more detail Timo Rademacher, *Realakte im Rechtsschutzsystem der Europäischen Union* (fn. 1), p. 295–304; similarly Herwig Hofmann, Morgane Tidghi, „Rights and Remedies in Implementation of EU Policies by Multi-Jurisdictional Networks" (fn. 93), p. 156.

of the EU's conduct in the Eurozone crisis more generally was discussed.[267] The function of the action for damages hence clearly goes beyond individual monetary compensation and instead focuses on the recognition of the illegality as such.

The most important objection to this understanding concerns the remaining difference to the action for annulment. Certainly, the use of the action for damages as a declaratory relief must not become a way of circumventing the narrow admissibility requirements of the action for annulment. Upon closer inspection, however, it becomes clear that there is not risk of undermining Art. 263 TFEU at all, for Art. 340 para 2 TFEU does not lead to an annulment of the act erga omnes, but only establishes the unlawfulness of the act with effect vis-à-vis the applicant. To the contrary, the wording and context of Art. 340 para 2 TFEU speak in favour of understanding it as a form of declaratory relief. The open formulation of obliging the Union to 'make good damages' clearly allows for restitution in kind and declaratory relief.[268] In fact, the widespread understanding of Art. 340 para 2 FEU as focused on monetary compensation simply stems from the fact that the law on state liability of most member states traditionally only provided for 'acquiesce and liquidate'. If one were to hold on to this understanding, however, one would overlook that, by now, most national state liability laws have been modernised and allow for declaratory judgements.[269]

This reasoning is clearly confirmed by the General Court's judgment in *WS et al.*[270] Concerning the admissibility of the claims of WS et al., Frontex had argued that the applicants should have lodged an action for annulment against the latest response letter of the agency's Fundamental Rights Office within the relevant time limit, and that therefore, their later action for damages was inadmissible. The General Court took the occasion to recall and specify the relation between Art. 263 TFEU and Art. 340 para 2 TFEU. Although the action for damages is a self-standing form of action in the EU system of remedies, it must be declared inadmissible 'where

267 CJEU, judgement of 20 September 2016, Ledra, C-8/15 P et al (fn. 117).

268 Similarly, Herwig Hofmann, Morgane Tidghi, „Rights and Remedies in Implementation of EU Policies by Multi-Jurisdictional Networks“ (fn. 93), p. 156 who come to the same conclusion based on the principle of 'qui peut le plus, peut le moins'.

269 Timo Rademacher, *Realakte im Rechtsschutzsystem der Europäischen Union* (fn. 1), p. 220–237, 376.

270 CJEU, judgement of 6 September 2023, WS et al v Frontex, T-600/21 (fn. 106). The following paragraph is based on Catharina Ziebritzki, „A Hidden Success“ (fn. 108).

it is actually aimed at securing withdrawal of an individual decision'.[271] Nonetheless, the General Court then continued, 'it would be contrary to the autonomy of an action for damages, and to the effectiveness of the system of remedies' to consider an action for damages inadmissible 'on the sole ground that it might lead to a result comparable to the results of an action for annulment'.[272] Therefore, the General Court held, 'an action for damages may also be able to nullify the legal effects of a decision which has become final where the applicant seeks greater benefit, but including that which it could obtain from an annulling judgement'.[273] Remarkably, the General Court did not even object to the applicants not only seeking compensation for their material and immaterial damage but also requesting the Court to 'find that Frontex engaged in improper conduct with regard to them'.[274] Dedicating only a few paragraphs to this issue, it considered it 'clear' that the present action for damages 'does not have the same purpose or the same effect as an action for annulment' as the maximum effect of an action for annulment would have been a fresh examination by Frontex's Fundamental Rights Office and, on this basis, deemed the action for damages admissible.[275]

c *Lowering the Threshold for Liability: A Project De Lege Ferenda*

The understanding of the action for damages as declaratory relief has the consequence that the main justification for the high threshold of liability is no longer valid. As explained above, the high threshold is justified only because, and hence only as long as, the action for damages primarily serves to grant monetary compensation. The fact that the action for damages functions as declaratory relief hence speaks in favour of lowering the threshold for liability.

Several proposals have been made on how this could be achieved. Some, for instance, have argued that the threshold for liability should be lowered at least where the action for damages is the only remedy available and

271 CJEU, judgement of 6 September 2023, WS et al v Frontex, T-600/21 (fn. 106), para 24.
272 Ibid., para 25.
273 Ibid., para 26.
274 Ibid., para 17.
275 Ibid., para 27 to 29.

where fundamental rights are at stake. More specifically, this argument goes, the CJEU should not require a sufficiently serious breach in these cases.[276] Others, instead, have proposed to adapt the criteria for liability in relation to the applicant's request.[277] According to this proposal, the application of the individual-rights criterion and the sufficiently-serious-breach criterion should depend on whether the applicant primarily seeks monetary compensation or the recognition of the unlawfulness of the contested act. Clearly, such scaled interpretation would be compatible with the wording of Art. 340 para 2 TFEU, and has the advantage that it allows to flexibly adapt the doctrine of the action for damages. At the same time, however, this proposal might lead to legal uncertainty and comes with the difficulty that it is not always clear from the outset – and sometimes not even for the applicants themselves – whether the declaration of illegality is the primary or only a complementary aim of the action.

For the purpose of this study, this discussion on which proposal would be preferably *de lege ferenda* need not be decided, because the approach here is to determine the EU's responsibility on the basis of EU law as it currently stands. And *de lege lata*, the CJEU applies the high threshold – regardless of what is the subjective aim as defined by the applicants, and regardless of what the CJEU decides in the operative part of its judgement. When it comes to assessing whether the EU is liable for fundamental rights violations under Art. 340 para 2 TFEU as it currently stands, one must hence operate with the high threshold for pragmatic reasons, be it conceptually convincing, or not.[278]

4 The Action for Damages and the EU Hotspot Administration

On this basis, the remainder of this study analyses whether the EU or its bodies incur liability for their administrative misconduct in the specific context of EU hotspots. This requires to clarify three preliminary points.

---

276 See for instance Angela Ward, „Damages under the EU Charter of Fundamental Rights" (fn. 181), p. 607–609.

277 This scaled system was proposed by Timo Rademacher, *Realakte im Rechtsschutzsystem der Europäischen Union* (fn. 1), p. 383–384.

278 See chapter 5.

4.1 Defining the Potential Trigger for EU Liability

First, the potential trigger for EU liability for must be defined more precisely. In doing so, two points must be kept in mind: first, the relevant misconduct as identified in the second chapter,[279] and second, that EU liability can be triggered only by a sufficiently serious breach of a rule conferring rights upon individuals.[280] The specific problems differ between the agencies on the one hand and the Commission on the other.

In the case of the agencies, the main question concerns which of several instances of misconduct are defined as liability trigger. This issue arises because the agencies' misconduct results from failures at several hierarchical levels. Case 1 illustrates the point.

> *Case 1 – Sara Esmaili – Deficient vulnerability assessment (EUAA's misconduct at two levels)*
> In the case of Ms Esmaili, the EUAA staff in charge failed to identify and recognise her special needs and thus wrongly registered her as non-vulnerable, thereby breaching her obligations under the EUAA Regulation and the ChFR. Considering, however, that this is not an isolated case, but a general malpractice, the instance can also be reconstructed as a failure of the responsible EUAA coordinating officer to adequately supervise their staff, i.e. as a violation of their supervisory obligations under the EUAA Regulation. Further, the instance could also be understood as a failure of the EUAA's Executive Director to address systemic malpractices at a structural level and to ensure that the practices of its agency generally comply with EU secondary and primary law, i.e. as a violation of their supervisory obligations.[281]

This issue arises in all cases concerning the agencies. At the lowest hierarchical level, the responsible staff fail to adequately conduct a vulnerability assessment, or an interview, or to adequately react to the information that a deportation is unlawful. The crucial point, however, is that these malpractices occur systemically, and should therefore have been addressed at a higher hierarchical level. Each failure at the lower hierarchical level thus corresponds to a failure at a higher hierarchical level. In concrete terms, the responsible coordinating officers fail to issue adequate instructions to

279 See chapter 2, 4.
280 See above 3.1, 3.3.
281 On the EUAA's internal supervisory obligations see chapter 4, 3.

the team members, and the respective Executive Director fails to ensure through internal guidelines that fundamental rights are not systemically violated, or to withdraw from an operation that systemically exceeds the agency's competences or violates fundamental rights.[282]

Consequently, there are two different ways to construct the agency's liability. One could consider either the misconduct at the lower or at the higher hierarchical level as potential trigger for liability.[283] Doctrinally, both approaches are equally convincing. If one focuses on the lower hierarchical level, the sufficiently serious breach of a rule conferring rights upon individuals is clearly established because the responsible caseworker or expert disregard fundamental rights.[284] If one focuses on the higher hierarchical level, the same holds true: First, the provisions obliging the coordinating officers and the Executive Director qualify as rules conferring rights upon individuals because they primarily serve to ensure compliance with fundamental rights, and because they serve to ensure, in an area interfering with the exercise of fundamental rights, that the agency acts within the limits of its competences.[285] Second, the breach of internal supervisory obligations must be considered as sufficiently serious when it consists in a failure to prevent systemic and authoritatively documented breaches of 'core' fundamental rights.

From a practical perspective, however, it appears more promising to focus on the agency's misconduct at the lower hierarchical level. From the outset, it is more difficult to establish a breach of internal supervisory obligations at a higher hierarchical level because the content and scope of

---

282 On the supervision structure of the Migration Management Support Teams (MMSTs) see chapter 2, 1.2.

283 In the direction of the latter Sergio Carrera, Leonhard Den Hertog, Joanna Parkin, „The Peculiar Nature of EU Home Affairs Agencies in Migration Control: Beyond Accountability versus Autonomy?", *European Journal of Migration and Law* 15 (2013), p. 337–358, p. 344; Andreas Fischer-Lescano, Timo Tohidipur, „Europäisches Grenzkontrollregime. Rechtsrahmen der europäischen Grenzschutzagentur Frontex", *Zeitschrift für ausländisches öffentliches Recht und Völkerrecht* 67 (2007), p. 1219-1276, p. 1266.

284 At least in the cases concerning inherent violations; on the questions arising in cases concerning resulting violations see chapter 5.

285 Regardless of whether fundamental rights are violated in a specific case, the very fact that interference is only permissible under certain conditions is sufficient to qualify the provisions on competence limits as conferring rights upon individuals, see CJEU, judgement of 23 November 2011, Sison III, T-341/07 (fn. 184), para 50. Insofar as the agencies systemically overstep their competence limits, they interfere with fundamental rights without legal basis.

these obligations is not yet fully clarified.[286] Further, and more importantly, it would be quite difficult, for a concerned asylum seeker as potential applicant under Art. 340 para 2 TFEU, to prove that the agency has violated its internal supervisory obligations. Making this argument would require access to the agency's internal procedures and meetings, including the minutes of personal instructions and informal supervisory rounds – which is almost impossible in practice. Therefore, the agency's liability is construed here on the basis of the agency's misconduct at the lower hierarchical level.[287]

In the case of the Commission, determining the relevant trigger for EU liability comes with another difficulty. Here, the main question concerns the precise definition of the Commission's failure to supervise, i.e. of its omission to act. The issue is well illustrated with case 1, too.

Case 1 – Sara Esmaili – Failure to provide humane reception conditions (Commission's omission to act)

As stressed several times, the case of Ms Esmaili and her daughter is a typical case. Insofar as the breach of Art. 4 ChFR by providing inhumane reception conditions is concerned, this violation concerns – at least – all those asylum seekers who qualify as vulnerable.[288] However, and despite extensive, authoritative and publicly available reports, the Commission apparently failed to prevent these systemic deficiencies, thereby failing to comply with its supervisory obligations under Art. 40 para 3 Frontex Regulation, Art. 21 para 2 EUAA Regulation, Art. 17 TEU. But the crux of the matter now lies in the detail: from the perspective of potential applicants under Art. 340 para 2 TFEU, it will be almost impossible to determine what exactly the Commission failed to do, i.e. whether it failed to provide the necessary support, or to adequately coordinate its cooperation with the host member state, or to effectively address the issue within the relevant supervisory fora such as the EURTF and the Steering Committee, or to take any other measure that would have ensured com-

286 In more detail see Evangelia (Lilian) Tsourdi, „Monitoring and Steering through FRONTEX and EASO 2.0: The Rise of a New Model of AFSJ agencies?", eumigrationlawblog of 29/01/2018.

287 This being said, it should be kept in mind that defining the misconduct at the lower hierarchical level as trigger for liability does not mean that the misconduct at the higher level becomes irrelevant. As will be shown below, the failure to adequately exercise internal supervisory obligations remains decisive in the context of attribution, see chapter 4.

288 On the standards of Art. 4 ChFR for reception conditions see chapter 2, 3.

pliance with Art. 4 ChFR, such as e.g. concluding a Memorandum of Understanding with the concerned host member state.

In principle, the CJEU requires applicants under Art. 340 para 2 TFEU to clearly define the defendant's omission.[289] In the case at hand, however, this would most likely not be feasible for concerned applicants because the Commission has a vast range of measures at its disposal, some of which are not even publicly known.[290] Moreover, the minutes of the meetings in the relevant supervisory fora are not publicly available. In sum, it will be almost impossible for applicants to determine in concrete terms what the Commission has done, what it has not done, and what it could and should have done to prevent a specific fundamental rights violation.

But this problem is only apparent, as the CJEU has already recognised it and provided a solution. Considering that this advance in knowledge on the part of the Commission is relevant in many policy areas, the CJEU's approach in such cases is rather generous towards the applicants. In fact, it is sufficient for them to state a bundle of measures, or acts and omissions as a whole, that have allegedly caused damage. In *Bourdouvali*, for instance, the applicants simply invoked 'various forms of conduct' and, even more generally, unlawful 'conduct related to the adoption' of the Memorandum of Understanding in question.[291] Therefore, an action for damages would arguably be sufficiently substantiated already if it firstly sets out, in a general manner, the measures which the Commission has as its disposal and secondly, shows that the EU hotspot administration has been systemically deficient since 2015, and that the Commission has been informed about the deficiencies ever since, which indicates that the Commission has not sufficiently made use of its options in terms of policy making, funding and operational assistance to remedy that situation.

---

289 As the burden of proof lies with the applicant, see only CJEU, Court, judgement of 4 March 1980, Richard Pool v Council of the European Communities, 49/79; CJEU, Court of First Instance (Fifth Chamber), judgement of 1 February 2001, T. Port GmbH & Co. KG v Commission of the European Communities, T-1/99, para 55 with further references.

290 In more detail on the Commission's options see chapter 2, 2.

291 CJEU, judgement of 13 July 2018, Bourdouvali, T-786/14 (fn. 119), para 200; similarly, CJEU, Court of First Instance (Third Chamber), judgement of 24 October 2000, Fresh Marine Company AS v Commission of the European Communities, T-178/98, para 55: 'The applicant submits that the Commission's decision (…) must be regarded (…) as a bundle of administrative acts (…).'.

4.2 A Sufficiently Serious Breach and Individual Rights

For the defined misconduct to trigger EU liability under Art. 340 para 2 TFEU, it must qualify as a sufficiently serious breach of a rule of law conferring rights upon individuals. With a view to the six typical cases at hand, two questions must be differentiated here.

The first is whether the fundamental rights violations at stake – i.e. the violations of Art. 4, 6, 18, 19, 24, 41 ChFR – qualify as sufficiently serious breach of a rule of law conferring rights upon individuals. Based on what was said above on the function of the action for damages as a fundamental rights remedy, this question is easily answered. As established above, all mentioned fundamental rights qualify as rules conferring rights upon individuals. As also established above, fundamental rights violations qualify as sufficiently serious breaches at least when 'core' fundamental rights are at stake, when the fundamental rights violations are systemic in nature, or when the fundamental rights violations have been authoritatively documented in publicly available reports.[292] Further, and closely related to the latter point, knowledge on the part of the supervisor about the violation of individual rights is decisive in determining the sufficient seriousness of the breach.[293] On this basis, and taking into account the circumstances as described in the six typical cases, the relevant fundamental rights violations qualify as sufficiently serious breaches in the sense of Art. 340 para 2 TFEU.

The second question is more specific and requires more discussion: it concerns the qualification of the Commission's misconduct as a sufficiently serious breach of a rule of law conferring rights upon individuals within the meaning of Art. 340 para 2 TFEU. Since the Commission's misconduct consists in a failure to adequately exercise its supervisory obligation, two rules come into consideration: either the supervisory obligation as such, i.e. Art. 40 para 3 Frontex Regulation, Art. 21 para 2 EUAA Regulation, Art. 17 TEU, or the relevant fundamental right, i.e. Art. 4, 6, 18, 19 24 and 41 ChFR. As the latter constitutes the supervisory standard compliance with

---

292 See above 3.3.

293 See, for instance, CJEU, Court, judgement of 4 July 1989, Francesconi, 326/86 and 66/88 (fn. 183), para 23–24, where the court stressed that at the relevant point in time, the Commission 'had insufficient facts at its disposal' to require a review of the Italian monitoring measures; CJEU, Court, judgement of 30 September 1998, Coldiretti, T-149/96 (fn. 183), para 84, where the Commission refers to reports issued by the World Health Organisation to support its claim that its supervision was sufficient.

which must be ensured, the question can be formulated as to whether the relevant breach in the sense of the Art. 340 para 2 TFEU is the breach of the supervisory obligation or that of the supervisory standard.[294]

As will be shown in more detail below, the CJEU's approach to this matter has shifted over time. Whereas in its earlier case law, the CJEU considered the breach of the supervisory obligation as trigger for liability, its more recent case law rather focuses on the breach of the supervisory standard.[295]

Yet, the choice is irrelevant here if both the supervisory obligation and the supervisory standard fulfil the individual-rights criterion and the sufficiently-serious-beach-criterion. As regards the supervisory standard, it has been shown already that this is the case, because the standard consists in fundamental rights. As regards the supervisory obligation, more comprehensive argumentation is required. Concerning, first, the individual-rights criterion, it is argued here that a rule establishing supervisory obligations fulfils that criterion if the purpose of the supervision is, at least inter alia, to ensure compliance with individual rights.[296] This follows from the CJEU's general doctrine as set out above. As regards supervisory obligations more specifically, further case law supports this conclusion: Whereas the CJEU's 1992 decision in *Cato* could be read to suggest that the Commission's supervisory obligations as such must be understood as serving solely member states' compliance with EU law,[297] the 1992 judgement in *Vreugdenhil* and the 2012 decision in *Artegodon* clarify that this argumentation applies only to rules that are primarily intended to ensure the division of competences.[298] As regards supervision in the context of the integrated administration, the CJEU has consistently held that a super-

294 This is due to the structure of supervisory obligations. Assume A has a supervisory obligation x to ensure that B's conduct complies with the standard y. A's obligation can be formulated as x, y. Imagine A fails to adequately supervise B which results in B breaching y. The failure of A can be formulated either as breach of the obligation to supervise x or as a breach of the supervisory standard y.

295 See chapter 5, 3.

296 In detail on that matter see Uwe Säuberlich, *Die außervertragliche Haftung im Gemeinschaftsrecht* (fn. 153), p. 208–232.

297 CJEU, Court, judgment of 8 April 1992, James Joseph Cato v Commission of the European Communities, C-55/90, para 23.

298 CJEU, judgement of 13 March 1992, Industrie- en Handelsonderneming Vreugdenhil BV v Commission of the European Communities, C-282/90, para 20 to 22; CJEU, judgement of 19 April 2012, Artegodan GmbH v European Commission, C-221/10 P, para 81–82, 96.

visory obligation confers rights upon individual rights if the supervisory standard serves, at least inter alia, to protect individuals.[299] Since its 1967 judgement in *Kampffmeyer*, the CJEU has interpreted supervisory obligations established by secondary law in light of the objective of the relevant Regulation or Directive, and has considered the individual-rights criterion as fulfilled if the Regulation or Directive as such serves to protect, at least inter alia, the applicant's interests.[300] Moreover, the CJEU has established in its 2011 judgement in *Sison III* that provisions on the division of competences must be considered as conferring rights upon individuals if the EU's conduct at stake amounts to an interference with the exercise of the fundamental rights of the persons concerned.[301] It therefrom follows, a fortiori, that the same must be true for supervisory obligations in the context of the integrated administration,[302] in particular where the relevant administrative conduct interferes with the exercise of fundamental rights, as in the area of freedom, security and justice. Applying this test to Art. 40 para 3 Frontex Regulation, Art. 21 para 2 EUAA Regulation, Art. 17 TEU leads to the conclusion that these qualify as rules conferring rights upon individuals. The relevant administrative activity interferes with the exercise of fundamental rights; the relevant recitals in the Frontex and the EUAA Regulation explicitly stress that Commission must ensure that activities in the EU hotspots comply with relevant Union law and fundamental rights; and the Commission itself, in defining its supervisory obligation, puts a particular emphasis on fundamental rights compliance.[303]

299 Notably regardless of whether the supervisory obligation at the same time regulates the division of competences, and regardless of whether the interests protected by the supervisory standard are of general nature.

300 CJEU, Court, judgement of 14 July 1967, Firma E. Kampffmeyer et al v Commission of the European Economic Community, Joined Cases 5/66 et al, p. 262–263. This case is particularly remarkably because the court considered the very fact that the secondary law establishing the single market serves the interests of producers in the member states as sufficient to consider the Commission's supervisory obligations as conferring rights upon individuals, explicitly regardless of the fact that these interests are of a general nature.

301 CJEU, judgement of 23 November 2011, Sison III, T-341/07 (fn. 184), para 49–52.

302 The provisions establishing the integrated administration regulate both the relation of the administrative actors among each other and the relation of these to the concerned individuals. The legality of the administration is hence not an end in itself. Rather, administrative supervision, in principle, serves to ensure the legality of the integrated administration, precisely because this is necessary to protect the rights of the concerned individuals.

303 See chapter 2, 2.

Concerning, second, the sufficiently-serious-breach criterion, it is argued here that a breach of a supervisory obligation qualifies as sufficiently serious if it results in systemic fundamental rights violations and if the obligation has the purpose of ensuring compliance precisely with those fundamental rights that are systemically violated. Again, this already follows from the CJEU's general doctrine. To briefly recall: According to the CJEU, a breach is sufficiently serious if the relevant breach would also have occurred had the competent authority exercised due diligence and care. Inter alia, the CJEU takes into account the severity of the individual rights violation, the reprehensibility of the breach, and whether there have been authoritative assessments of a situation as unlawful. Discretion on the part of the supervisor must be taken into consideration but is reduced to 'how' to react in the case of systemic deficiencies.[304] Applying this test to the Commission's breach of its supervisory obligation under Art. 40 para 3 Frontex Regulation, Art. 17 TEU shows that the breach is sufficiently serious. As established above, the relevant fundamental rights violations are systemic in nature, authoritatively documented, and known to the Commission. The Commission's discretion is accordingly reduced to the choice of an appropriate measure. Further, Art. 40 para 3 Frontex Regulation, Art. 21 para 2 EUAA Regulation, and Art. 17 TEU serve precisely to ensure compliance with those fundamental rights that are violated.[305] In short, as an administrative authority exercising ordinary care and diligence would have exhausted all its possibilities to address the well-documented systemic fundamental rights violations,[306] the Commission's failure to do so qualifies as a sufficiently serious breach of its supervisory obligations.

Therefore, the dispute as to whether the supervisory obligation or the supervisory standard constitutes the relevant liability trigger need not be decided here. In any case, the Commission's failure to exercise its supervisory obligations, as described in the cases above, qualifies as a potential trigger for EU liability.

---

304 See chapter 2, 2.4.

305 See chapter 2, 2.

306 Note that in 2016 already, the European Ombudsman urged the Commission to carry out an appropriate human rights assessment, see European Ombudsman, 18 January 2017, Case 506/2016/MHZ (fn. 19).

4.3 Legal Basis in Case of the Agencies

Having defined the relevant triggers for EU liability, and having established that these fulfil the qualification-criterion, the remainder of this first section defines the legal basis for an action for damages more precisely. In the case of the Commission, it is clear that EU liability arises on the basis of Art. 340 para 2 TFEU, Art. 41 para 3 ChFR. In the case of the agencies, however, the relation between these general provisions and the specific provisions for non-contractual liability enshrined in the EUAA and the Frontex Regulation requires clarification. Three points must be made here.

First, there can be no doubt that the EU is liable for misconduct by its agencies under Art. 340 para 2 TFEU, Art. 41 para 3 ChFR. Both articles provide that the Union is liable for damages caused by 'its institutions'. That term must be interpreted broadly: it is not limited to institutions in the sense of Art. 13 TEU but instead includes all bodies established within the legal system of the Union.[307] As the CJEU has recently confirmed, this follows from the rule of law principle. If the term 'institutions' was interpreted narrowly, this would allow the Union to escape liability under primary law and thus avoid judicial review simply by establishing new bodies under secondary law.[308] Hence, there is a broad consensus that agencies qualify as institutions under Art. 340 para 2 TFEU, Art. 41 para 3 ChFR.[309]

307 See only CJEU, Court, judgement of 2 December 1992, SGEEM et al v European Investment Bank, C-370/98, para 16; Paul Craig, *EU Administrative Law* (fn. 235), p. 736–737.

308 CJEU, judgement of 13 July 2018, Bourdouvali, T-786/14 (fn. 119), para 110, remarkably with regard even to the Eurogroup: 'Any contrary solution would clash with the principle of the Union based on the rule of law, in so far as it would allow the establishment, within the legal system of the European Union itself, of entities whose acts and conduct could not result in the European Union incurring liability.'.

309 This conclusion is shared by most contributions, although the arguments in detail differ. See Timo Rademacher, *Realakte im Rechtsschutzsystem der Europäischen Union* (fn. 1), p. 244–245 for an argument, albeit in the context of Art. 263 TEU, based on CJEU, judgement of 8 October 2008, Sogelma v EAR, T-411/06, para 37; Merijn Chamon, *EU Agencies. Legal and Political Limits to the Transformation of the EU Administration*, Oxford University Press 2016, p. 355–357 for an argument based, inter alia, on CJEU, judgement of 12 July 1962, L Worms v High Authority of the European Coal and Steel Community, 18/60; Sergio Carrera, Leonhard Den Hertog, Joanna Parkin, „The Peculiar Nature of EU Home Affairs Agencies in Migration Control: Beyond Accountability versus Autonomy?" (fn. 283), p. 352 for an argument *e contrario* from Art 340 para 3 TFEU. For a different opinion see Alexander Türk, *Judicial Review in EU Law* (fn. 120), p. 243.

Second, it is also clear that the EUAA and Frontex each incur public liability for their own misconduct under conditions equivalent to those of Art. 340 para 2 TFEU. This follows from Art. 97 para 4 Frontex Regulation and Art. 66 para 3 EUAA Regulation, which regulate the non-contractual liability of the respective agency.[310] The wording of these provisions corresponds to Art. 340 para 2 TFEU, with the only difference being that, instead of the Union, now 'the Agency shall, in accordance with the general principles common to the laws of the member states, make good any damage caused by its departments or by its staff in the performance of their duties'. Both provisions must thus be understood to refer to the CJEU's established doctrine.[311] Crucially, staff in the sense of Art. 97 para 4 Frontex Regulation and Art. 66 para 3 EUAA Regulation includes statutory staff as well as seconded or deployed staff.[312]

This understanding is compatible with the provisions on civil liability of the agency's team members, namely Art. 84 Frontex Regulation and Art. 26 EUAA Regulation.[313] In this regard, it is crucial to distinguish between the non-contractual liability of the agency on the one hand and the liability of the agency's team members, which is then transferred to the host member state, the home member state or the agency, on the other hand. Keeping this in mind, it becomes clear that Art. 84 para 1 Frontex Regulation, and accordingly Art. 26 para 1 EUAA Regulation, establish that, as a rule, the host member state shall incur liability in accordance with its national law for any damage caused during agency operations. Para 2 of the cited provisions then provides for a transfer of liability in cases of gross negligence or wilful misconduct: if the concerned team member is seconded or deployed, the host member state may request reimbursement from the home member state; and if they are a statutory member of staff, reimbursement may be requested from the agency. Regarding the latter case, Art. 84 para 2 Frontex Regulation explicitly clarifies that this is without prejudice to Art. 98, which

310 Prior to the entry into force of the EUAA Regulation: Art 45 para 3 EASO Regulation.

311 For Frontex see Melanie Fink, *Frontex and Human Rights* (fn. 1), p. 184; Herbert Rosenfeldt, *Frontex im Zentrum der Europäischen Grenz- und Küstenwache* (fn. 8), p. 286.

312 The respective Regulations consistently refer to 'staff' as including seconded and deployed as well as statutory staff. Where the Regulations exclusively refer to statutory staff, this is always made explicit. This becomes particularly clear in Art. 95 Frontex Regulation and Art. 38 EASO Regulation.

313 Formerly Art. 21 EASO Regulation.

in turn refers to the agency's non-contractual liability under Art. 97 para 4 Frontex Regulation. This clearly shows that, as far as the agency's liability is concerned, Art. 84 is lex specialis to Art. 97 para 4, Art. 98 Frontex Regulation.[314] As regards the EUAA Regulation, the same argument applies.

Thus, Art. 97 para 4 Frontex Regulation and Art. 66 para 3 EASO Regulation are applicable to cases of misconduct during agency operations despite the applicability of Art. 84 Frontex Regulation and Art. 26 EUAA Regulation to these cases. Otherwise, the former provisions would be rendered void of purpose. Misconduct during operations is precisely the main case where agency liability becomes relevant, as the reference of Art. 84 para 2 to Art. 98 Frontex Regulation clearly confirms. As a matter of course, this does not mean that a person can claim compensation for one damage twice. This, however, is a question of procedural, not of substantial, concurrence between agency liability and member state liability.[315] Clearly, liability of the host member state under Art. 84 Frontex Regulation or Art. 26 EUAA Regulation does not exclude agency liability in terms of substance.[316] Otherwise, the fact that agency liability under Art. 97 para 4 Frontex Regulation and Art. 66 para 3 EUAA Regulation does not require guilt would be undermined: as the host member state is liable only in accordance with its national law, guilt on the part of the team members might be a precondition.

The third point concerns the relationship between Union liability under Art. 340 para 2 TFEU, on the one hand, and agency liability under Art. 97

314 Daniel Thym, *European Migration Law*, Oxford University Press 2023, p. 220, however, considers the relation between these provisions to remain uncertain.

315 In more detail on the complex questions of concurrence see only Peter Oliver, „Joint Liability of the Community and the Member States", in Ton Heukels, Alison McDonnell (ed.), *The Action for Damages in Community Law*, Wolters Kluwer 1997, p. 285–309; Maartje de Visser, „The Concept of Concurrent Liability and Its Relationship with the Principle of Effectiveness: A One-Way Ticket into Oblivion", *Maastricht Journal of European and Comparative Law* 11 (2004), p. 47-70. As procedural concurrence is not relevant to the question of whether the Union is liable in substance, this issue will not be dealt with here. Prima facie, it seems that the question is parallel to that of the relation between Union liability under Art. 340 para 2 TFEU and member state liability under the Frankovich doctrine. Therefrom, it would follow that, where a claim for compensation by a member state is pending or has been granted, a claim for compensation by the agency for that same damage must be inadmissible. Crucially, however, the concerned person is not prevented from approaching the agency first.

316 Even if one disagrees, the Union would be liable for the agency's conduct under Art. 340 para 2 TFEU anyways.

para 4 Frontex Regulation and Art. 66 para 3 EUAA Regulation, on the other hand. As will be argued, agency liability is subsidiary to Union liability – however, and this is crucial, only in procedural terms.

To begin with, agency liability is not lex specialis to Union liability in the sense that the applicability of Art. 97 para 4 Frontex Regulation and Art. 66 para 3 EUAA Regulation would generally preclude Union liability. Art. 340 para 2 TEU simply regulates a distinct matter. While Art. 340 para 2 TFEU regulates under which conditions the Union incurs liability for the misconduct of its agencies, Art. 97 para 4 Frontex Regulation and Art. 66 para 3 EUAA Regulation regulate under which conditions the agencies themselves incur liability for their own misconduct.[317]

However, it would obviously be contrary to the telos of public liability law if a person could claim compensation for one damage twice. This shows that the main issue is procedural in nature: the question is whether a claimant must approach the Union or the agency, or whether they are simply free to choose.

In this regard, it is argued here that Union liability is procedurally subsidiary to agency liability.[318] A claimant must, hence, first seek compensation from the concerned agency. The agency is closer to its own misconduct than the Union as such. Also, if a claimant was obliged to first approach the Union, Art. 97 para 4 Frontex Regulation and Art. 66 para 3 EUAA Regulation would become practically irrelevant. Hence, a claim under Art. 340 para 2 TFEU is inadmissible insofar as a claim under Art. 97 para 4 Frontex Regulation and Art. 66 para 3 EUAA Regulation is admissible. Obviously, this solution must not lead to a situation in which a claimant is left without compensation because the agency is not able to pay, for instance, because it is not solvent. In this case, the Union is thus obliged to pay compensation as a default guarantor for the agency, so to speak.[319]

317 See only Alexander Türk, *Judicial Review in EU Law* (fn. 120), p. 243.

318 As here Herbert Rosenfeldt, *Frontex im Zentrum der Europäischen Grenz- und Küstenwache* (fn. 8), p. 286.

319 And hence arguably on the basis of Art. 97 para 4 Frontex Regulation or Art. 66 para 3 EUAA Regulation. As here in substance but considering Art. 340 para 2 TFEU as the correct legal basis Ino Augsberg, „Art. 340 AEUV (ex-Artikel 288 EGV)", in Hans von der Groeben, Jürgen Schwarze, Armin Hatje (ed.), *Europäisches Unionsrecht. Vertrag über die Europäische Union, Vertrag über die Arbeitsweise der Europäischen Union, Charta der Grundrechte der Europäischen Union*, Nomos 2015, para 19; Merijn Chamon, *EU Agencies* (fn. 309), p. 355–357. This would, however, require the applicant to conduct another procedure. Taking into consideration the telos of Art. 47 para 3 ChFR, the solution proposed here appears preferable.

To conclude, the Union is liable for the misconduct of its agencies under Art. 340 para 2 TFEU, Art. 41 para 3 ChFR. At the same time, the EUAA and Frontex are themselves liable for their own misconduct under Art. 97 para 4, Art. 98 Frontex Regulation and Art. 66 para 3 EUAA Regulation, respectively. Union liability is procedurally subsidiary to agency liability unless the agency is insolvent. This being said, the following largely refers only to Art. 340 para 2 TFEU for the sake of simplicity. While this simplified form of citation is imprecise insofar as it does neither make explicit that the right to claim damages from the Union is a fundamental right nor that Art. 340 para 2 TFEU is procedurally subsidiary to Art. 97 para 4 Frontex Regulation and Art. 66 para 3 EUAA Regulation, it is still legally correct because agency liability does not materially exclude Union liability.

5 Doctrinal Approach

Having established the relevant liability trigger as well as the legal basis, this last part prepares the ground for the substantial analysis that will be conducted in the following chapters. The decisive doctrinal questions will arise in the context of attribution and causation.

5.1 Concepts of Attribution and Causation

The concepts of attribution and causation need clarification. The CJEU's approach in this regard is inconsistent. The court refers to attribution, causation and imputation interchangeably and discusses attribution and causation sometimes in the context of admissibility and sometimes in the context of the substance of the claim, apparently depending on the arguments of the parties in the individual case.[320]

Given the lack of conceptual clarity in the jurisprudence, legal scholarship has developed different definitions.[321] Based on these, attribution is defined here as denoting the link between a certain conduct and a certain

320 CJEU, judgement of 13 July 2018, Bourdouvali, T-786/14 (fn. 119), para 97: 'In the present case, in the light in particular of the parties' arguments (...), the Court considers that it is necessary to examine the question of attribution in the context of the examination of the Court's jurisdiction.'.

321 The following definition are based, in particular, on the work of Melanie Fink.

actor. It thus defines in whose name a certain administrative conduct is performed, or in other words, who is the author of a certain act.[322] For instance, when a German asylum service officer is seconded to the EUAA and is then deployed by the agency to an EU hotspot located in Greece, and if that officer then fails to respect the right to good administration as enshrined in Art. 41 ChFR, attribution gives an answer to the question of whether that misconduct shall be considered an act of Germany, of Greece, or of the agency.

Causation, by contrast, is defined here as denoting the link between conduct and certain damage and, hence, defines whether certain misconduct is to be considered as the fault that led to the damage.[323] For instance, when the European Commission fails to adequately exercise its obligation to supervise the EU hotspot administration, and when this then results in Greek authorities providing reception conditions which constitute inhumane treatment, causation gives an answer to the question of whether the violation of Art. 4 ChFR shall be considered as the result of Greece's or the Union's misconduct.

Obviously, the concepts of attribution and causation are closely connected. This is because both form part of the broader concept of imputation, which is the very basis of liability law.[324] If there was no imputation, every person would bear the full risk for all damages to their legally protected rights and interests, regardless of how or by whom the damage was brought about. Simply put, imputation serves to ensure that damages are borne by the actor who can be reproached for the occurrence of the damage. Consequentially, reprehensibility is the most important common feature of attribution and causation. Both the assessment of whether certain misconduct is to be attributed to a certain actor and of whether certain damage is to be considered as having been caused by certain misconduct ultimately depends on a balancing exercise, in the context of which the essential issue is always which entity shall be 'accused' for having brought about the

322 Melanie Fink, *Frontex and Human Rights* (fn. 1), p. 15–16. For the notion of the 'author' see CJEU, judgement of 13 July 2018, Bourdouvali, T-786/14 (fn. 119), para 79.

323 Melanie Fink, *Frontex and Human Rights* (fn. 1), p. 15–16; Martin Weitenberg, *Der Begriff der Kausalität in der haftungsrechtlichen Rechtsprechung der Unionsgerichte*, Nomos 2014, p. 317.

324 Francette Fines, „A General Analytical Perspective on Community Liability" (fn. 134), p. 16–18; Uwe Säuberlich, *Die außervertragliche Haftung im Gemeinschaftsrecht* (fn. 153), p. 31–33.

damage. Thus, although guilt is not a precondition for Union liability, the CJEU's interpretation of both attribution and causation is clearly shaped by considerations related to reprehensibility.[325]

5.2 Imputation and the 'Normative Bridge Function'

All questions of imputation – i.e. both attribution and causation – become particularly relevant and complicated where several actors are involved. For instance, in a case where the EU has provided non-formally binding support to a member state or where it has failed to adequately supervise a member state, and where this leads to the member state adopting a formally-binding decision which then results in damage, the concept of imputation serves to answer whether the damage must be reproached to the EU, despite the fact that it has acted only in non-formally binding form. In this sense, the concept of imputation has the function of 'normatively bridging' the factual gap between the conduct of one actor and the occurrence of the damage. As both causation and attribution are informed by reprehensibility considerations and only together flesh out the concept of imputation, the bridge function can be assigned to either criterion.

Consequently, the question of whether the damage that was ultimately brought about by an administrative decision of a member state will trigger liability of the Union can be reconstructed either as a question of attribution or as a question of causation.

As the CJEU's jurisprudence is not clear on this point either,[326] legal scholarship has developed different doctrinal approaches. The traditional approach assigns the bridge function mainly to the causation criterion.[327] The question of whether actor B, here the Union, incurs liability for the formally binding conduct of actor A, here the host member state, is thus mainly discussed in the context of causation. As a consequence, the concept of attribution is defined narrowly, i.e. to denote the link between the conduct and the actor, strictly speaking. Seen from this perspective, the central

325 As Francette Fines, ibid., p. 13 explains, the reason for this is that the doctrine of Art. 340 para 2 TFEU is influenced by French law, which differentiates between 'faute the service' and 'faute personnelle'.

326 See fn. 320.

327 See Paul Craig, *EU Administrative Law* (fn. 235), p. 746–748; Martin Weitenberg, *Der Begriff der Kausalität in der haftungsrechtlichen Rechtsprechung der Unionsgerichte* (fn. 323), passim, in particular p. 316.

questions at stake here – i.e. whether the fundamental rights violations that are ultimately brought about by the member state's formally-binding decisions must nonetheless be reproached to the EU because the EU has predetermined the decision through its non-formally binding recommendations or failure to supervise – appear as questions of causation. Only the question of whether the conduct of a certain staff member must be attributed to the host member state, to the home member state or to the Union appears as a question of attribution.

A recently proposed alternative approach, by contrast, assigns the bridge-function mainly to the attribution criterion.[328] The disputed question of whether or not actor B is liable on the basis of a formally binding act of A is accordingly discussed in the context of attribution. What is crucial about this alternative approach is that, from its specific perspective, the CJEU's doctrine appears to draw a distinction between primary and associated liability. Primary liability, in this sense, denotes the liability of A for its own administrative decision, while associated liability denotes the liability of B for its support to A or for its failure to adequately supervise A.[329] Certainly, this clear terminological distinction between the primary liability of A and the associated liability of B is appealing in terms of conceptual clarity.

Yet, the following builds on the traditional approach and assigns the bridge function to the concept of causation. There are several reasons for this. To begin with, a closer inspection shows that the alternative approach assigns the bridge function only partially to attribution. According to the alternative approach, B may still incur primary liability for the provision of non-formally binding support or the breach of supervisory obligations, and, to this extent, the disputed questions are still discussed as questions of causation. It is only insofar as the associated liability of B is concerned that the disputed questions are addressed as questions of attribution.[330] The gain in conceptual clarity is, therefore, not as significant as it seems at first glance.

328 Melanie Fink, *Frontex and Human Rights* (fn. 1), p. 233–237; Melanie Fink, „EU Liability for Contributions to Member States' Breaches of EU Law“ (fn. 104), p. 1234–1239.

329 Melanie Fink, „EU Liability for Contributions to Member States' Breaches of EU Law“ (fn. 104), further differentiates between two sub-approaches to establish associated liability: Associated liability can be established either as 'truly associated', i.e. based on the primary liability, or as 'associated light', i.e. based on the administrative support as such.

330 Melanie Fink, ibid.

Further, the political aim of the alternative approach can be achieved on the basis of the traditional approach, too. In fact, the alternative approach has been developed to account for the integration of the administration, and has the aim of increasing the possibility of holding actor B, here the Union, liable, despite the fact that the formally-binding administrative decision was ultimately issued by actor A, here the host member state. This result, however, can also be achieved in the framework of the traditional approach. As will be shown throughout this chapter, assigning the bridge function to causation also allows the Union to be held liable for the provision of administrative support or for a failure to adequately supervise the host member state.

Moreover, the innovative approach assimilates the doctrine of Union liability to the international rules on state liability as established by the Draft Rules on the Responsibility of States and International Organisations (DARS/DARIO).[331] This, however, is at odds with the understanding of the integrated administration as a structure that is genuinely characterised by EU law. The relations among the involved public actors, namely the member states and the Union, as well as between these and the concerned individuals, fundamentally differ from those relations under international law. As a consequence, attribution in the context of the integrated administration is not governed by DARS/DARIO, and there is, hence, no reason to assimilate the rules of EU public liability law to the rules applicable under international law.[332]

Lastly, and this is decisive here, pragmatic considerations speak in favour of the traditional approach. While the alternative approach develops a conceptually appealing reconstruction of the case law, the traditional approach stays closer to the CJEU's usual manner of argument. For instance, the CJEU itself does not distinguish between primary and associated liability. Therefore, and the conceptual strength of the alternative approach notwithstanding, it seems rather unlikely that the CJEU would adopt a claimant's argument that is based exclusively on the distinction between primary and associated liability. As the aim of this chapter is to develop an argument that could be used by potential applicants to enforce their fundamental rights before the CJEU on the basis of the law as it currently stands, the traditional

331 The concept of associated liability is similar to responsibility on the basis of 'aid or assistance' under Art. 16 DARS, Art. 14 DARIO (see introduction, fn. 44).

332 See below 5.4. For detailed analysis see Catharina Ziebritzki, *The EU's Responsibility in the Asylum Administration* (fn. 58), p. 37 et seq., p. 58 et seq.

approach is adopted here. Consequently, the bridge function is assigned here mainly to the concept of causation. The doctrinal challenges that arise in the context of attribution are hence limited to the definition of the link between certain conduct and the actor, strictly speaking.

5.3 Specific Doctrinal Questions

Having defined the meaning of attribution and causation eventually allows to precisely formulate the specific doctrinal questions that need to be discussed in the following. In this context, the distinction between inherent and resulting violations becomes central again.[333]

As this section will argue, a closer look leads to the following conclusions. First, concerning liability on the basis of the agencies' misconduct: as regards inherent violations, the main doctrinal problem lies at the level of attribution (*attribution*), whereas concerning resulting violations, attribution is also relevant, but the main doctrinal problem lies at the level of causation (*causation I*). Second, concerning liability on the basis of the Commission's misconduct, as regards both inherent and resulting violations, the main doctrinal issue lies at the level of causation, with the specific question differing from that in the case of the agencies (*causation II*). Yet, the distinction is relevant because inherent violations are mainly procedure-related, while resulting violations are mainly reception-related; and the Commission's procedure-related competences are narrower than its reception-related competences.[334] Therefore, the Commission's failure to supervise asylum procedures raises slightly different questions of causation (*causation IIa*) than its failure to supervise reception conditions (*causation IIb*).[335]

333 See chapter 2, 3.
334 See chapter 2, 2.3 and 3.
335 Based on this doctrinal framework, the question of attribution will be discussed in chapter 4, and the questions of causation I and II will be discussed in chapter 5.

		Operational Level		**Supervisory Level**
Misconduct	Damage	Formal Decision	Support	Coordination and Ensuring Legality
Conduct of Asylum Procedures	**Inherent Violations**	Host member state	EUAA Frontex *Question: Attribution*	Commission *Question: Causation IIa*
Provision of Reception Conditions	**Resulting Violations**	Host member state	EUAA Frontex *Question: Attribution and Causation I*	*Question: Causation IIb*

Table 1: Typical Misconduct of EU Bodies in the Integrated EU Hotspot Administration and the Respective Concrete Doctrinal Questions

a *The Agencies' Liability for Inherent Violations: A Question of Attribution*

As established above, the agencies' typical misconduct at the operational level consists in procedural mistakes. Hence, a first type of damage consists in the violation of procedural fundamental rights such as Art. 41 ChFR, the procedural dimension of Art. 24 ChFR, and the procedural dimension of Art. 4, 18, 19 ChFR.

Concerning these inherent damages, causation, i.e. the link between the conduct and the damage, is not difficult to establish because the fundamental rights violation as such constitutes the damage.[336] For instance, where an EUAA caseworker fails to comply with Art. 41 ChFR, it is clear that the procedural mistake as such constitutes the violation of fundamental rights and, hence, the damage. Similarly, where a Frontex officer fails to comply with the procedural dimension of Art. 24 ChFR, the damage is inherent in the misconduct.

Instead, the main doctrinal question arises in the context of attribution. As explained above, attribution gives an answer to the question in whose name a certain act is performed. Usually, this is quite easy to answer. For in-

336 See above 3.3.c.

stance, if a staff member of a national authority performs unlawful conduct, that act is obviously attributed to the member state. If a statutory member of staff from an EU agency breaches EU law, the author of that conduct is obviously the Union. With respect to the cases at hand, where the relevant misconduct is performed by staff members of a migration management support team (MMST), things are less straightforward. As explained above, MMSTs consists of different kinds of staff: Statutory staff of the EUAA and Frontex, usually acting as coordinating staff; a few staff members permanently seconded by member states to the agency; and staff that are provided by member states to the agency for the purposes of short-term deployment. It is with regard to this latter category of staff that attribution is difficult. This is because the MMSTs work under a complex supervision structure. Whereas each staff member remains embedded in the internal structures of their respective agency, they also remain connected to their home member state, and daily instructions are issued by the host member state.[337] It is hence not obvious, from the outset, whether the relevant misconduct must be attributed to the respective agency, to the home member state, or to the host member state. This is well illustrated with cases 2 and 3.[338]

Case 2 – Magan Daud – Deficient asylum interview – Art. 41 ChFR (EUAA: question of attribution)
In the case of Mr Daud, it is clear that the deficient interview as such constitutes a violation of his rights under Art. 41 ChFR. It is also clear that the violation of fundamental rights as such constitutes damage in the sense of Art. 340 para 2 TFEU. What requires further discussion, however, is whether the misconduct of the EUAA caseworker must be considered as an act on the part of the host member state, the home member state, or the agency. This is because the caseworker has been deployed to the EUAA by the German asylum service and is now working as part of the MMST under a dual supervision structure, receiving instruction from both the EUAA and the Greek asylum service.

Case 3 – Daniat Kidane – Age assessment through visual inspection – Art. 41 ChFR (Frontex: question of attribution)
Similarly, in the case of Daniat Kidane, it is clear that the unlawful age assessment constitutes a violation of her procedural rights under

337 See chapter 1, 3.1 and chapter 2, 1.2.

338 These examples are not exhaustive. The question of attribution become relevant in all cases where MMST are involved, i.e. also in cases 1, 4 and 5.

Art. 24 and 41 ChFR and that this violation, as such, constitutes damage under Art. 340 para 2 TFEU. What is questionable, however, is whether the procedural misconduct performed by the Frontex officer is to be considered as an act on the part of Greece, Germany or Frontex. Again, this is because the Frontex officer has been deployed to Frontex by the German federal police and is now working as part of the MMST under a dual supervision structure, receiving instructions from both Frontex and from the Hellenic police.

This being said it must be stressed that the question of attribution only arises because the approach adopted here is to construct liability on the basis of the misconduct at the lower hierarchical level.[339] As explained, it is the particular legal position of deployed MMST members that raises the question of whether their conduct is attributable to the host member state, the home member state or the agency. If one chooses to construct liability on the basis of misconduct at the higher hierarchical level, the question of attribution will not arise because there is no doubt that the conduct of the coordinating officer or the Executive Director is attributable to the agency. This is important to keep in mind because it means that disagreement with the following argument on attribution does not, per se, exclude agency liability. If one were to disagree on that point, one would have to consider the higher hierarchical level and examine the concrete doctrinal question of whether a failure on the part of the coordinating officer or the Executive Director constitutes the cause of a concrete breach at the operational level. Without going into details here, it seems likely that the answer to this question will be positive, at least insofar as operational misconduct is systemic in nature, because the very purpose of internal supervision is to prevent systemic misconduct at the operational level.

b *The Agencies' Liability for Resulting Violations: A Question of Causation I*

As explained above, the procedural mistakes by the agencies typically result in further, usually substantial, fundamental rights violations. This is so because the administrative support provided by the agency is the basis for the administrative decision issued by the member state. Where the support is deficient, the decision is usually also deficient. For instance, where the

339 See above 4.1.

EUAA provides an unlawful recommendation to reject an asylum claim as inadmissible, the Greek asylum service usually adopts that recommendation and issues the decision rejecting the asylum claim to the asylum seeker.[340] In the same vein, where Frontex conducts an unlawful age assessment and concludes that the concerned applicant is an adult, the Greek first reception service usually follows Frontex's advice and registers the date of birth determined by Frontex, which means that the concerned applicant will hence not be exempt from the border procedure.[341] As a result, the concerned applicant will then be obliged to stay in the EU hotspot camp. This will, depending on the specific camp, typically result in the violation of their rights under Art. 4 ChFR or Art. 6 ChFR.[342]

As the relevant misconduct in these cases is also performed by MMST members, establishing the link between the conduct and the actor is as difficult as in the case of inherent violations. The question of attribution hence remains the same.

In addition, however, establishing the link between the conduct and the damage is difficult, too. For instance, it is not obvious whether the procedural mistakes made by the EUAA or Frontex can be considered as the cause of the violation of the resulting violations of Art. 4 or Art. 6 ChFR. In general terms, the decisive question here is under which conditions non-formally binding conduct by the agencies can be considered as causal, despite the fact that a later administrative decision issued by the member state is the last element in the sequence of events leading to the occurrence of the damage.

The question of causation is hence closely related to the fact that the EU's mode of operation is to determine without deciding. This is crucial because what has been said above on this mode of operation *prima facie* speaks in favour of causation. As argued above, the EU's choice to rely on non-formally binding conduct appears as a strategy to circumvent constitutional rules while at the same time making sure that it can steer and guide the course of the administration.[343] The point is clearly illustrated by the EUAA's recommendation. Although that recommendation is non-formally binding, it is usually followed by the Greek authorities. When the EUAA recommends rejecting an asylum claim, this will regularly result in

340 See chapter 2, 1 and 3.
341 See chapter 2, 1 and 3.
342 See chapter 2, 3.1.b.
343 See chapter 1, 1.

the person being subject to an expulsion procedure.[344] This suggests that the content of the EUAA's recommendation predetermines the resulting fundamental rights violation. Of course, such considerations cannot replace doctrinal analysis based on the CJEU's case law – which will be conducted in the following chapters. But, as doctrinal analysis is never free from considerations of equity, especially not in the context of EU public liability law, it is important to keep these arguments concerning the EU's mode of operation in mind.

The question of causation arises in all cases where the agencies determine at the preparatory level without issuing the binding decision. This is well illustrated with cases 1 and 3.[345]

> *Case 1 – Sara Esmaili – Deficient vulnerability assessment – Art. 4 ChFR (EUAA: question of causation I)*
> In the case of Ms Esmaili and her daughter Ayla, the EUAA caseworker failed to correctly conduct the vulnerability assessment and thus recommended qualifying them as non-vulnerable. As usual, the Greek Asylum Service rubber-stamped that opinion. As a result, Ms Esmaili and her daughter were obliged to remain in the EU hotspot camp during the entire asylum procedure, under reception conditions amounting to a violation of their rights under Art. 4 ChFR. The most difficult legal questions arise with regard to causation, as the link between the EUAA's unlawful recommendation and the violation of Art. 4 ChFR is not evident.

> *Case 3 – Daniat Kidane – Age assessment through visual inspection – Art. 4 ChFR (question of causation I)*
> In the case of Daniat Kidane, the Frontex officer estimated her age based on her physical appearance and came to the conclusion that she was an adult. As is usual practice, the Greek first reception service followed Frontex's opinion without any further inquiries, and registered Daniat Kidane as an adult. As a result, she was obliged to stay in the EU hotspot camp, where she was subject to reception conditions that violated her rights under Art. 4 ChFR. When discussing whether Frontex is liable for the violation of Art. 4 ChFR, further analysis is obviously required to determine whether the damage can be considered as having been caused by the unlawful age assessment.

---

344 As mentioned above, this is not always the case. Due to the halt of readmissions, the concerned persons usually remain in a legal limbo, see chapter 1, 2.1.c.

345 The question of causation I also arises in cases 2, 4 and 5.

Lastly, it must be stressed again that the concrete question of causation, as defined here, is a result of the approach to construct liability on the basis of the misconduct at the lower hierarchical level.[346] If one were to construct liability on the basis of misconduct at a higher hierarchical level, the decisive question in the context of causation would be whether the agency's failure to adequately supervise the member state's conduct is to be considered causal for the resulting fundamental rights violation. Given that the scope and content of the agencies' relatively new monitoring obligations is not yet entirely clear,[347] this would require further investigation.[348]

c *The Commission's Liability for Resulting Violations: A Question of Causation II*

Concerning the Commission's misconduct, attribution is easily established. As explained above, the Commission exercises its supervision mainly in the framework of the EURTF and different Steering Committees.[349] These fora are not institutionally consolidated to the extent that one could speak of misconduct on the part of the fora as such, and in any case, do not qualify as institutions in the sense of Art. 340 para 2 TFEU, because they are clearly not bodies established by the Treaties and do not have competences of their own.[350] Instead, the EURTF and the Steering Committees are regular meetings under the auspices of the Commission. There can thus be no doubt that the supervisory conduct on the part of the Commission's representatives, who act within the framework of the EURTF and the Steering Committee, is to be attributed to the Commission itself.

Establishing causation, however, is more difficult. As all damages for which individuals might claim compensation from the Commission are ultimately brought about by other actors, the link between the Commis-

346 See above 4.1.

347 See Evangelia (Lilian) Tsourdi, „Monitoring and Steering through FRONTEX and EASO 2.0: The Rise of a New Model of AFSJ agencies?" (fn. 286).

348 In this direction Andreas Fischer-Lescano, Timo Tohidipur, „Europäisches Grenzkontrollregime. Rechtsrahmen der europäischen Grenzschutzagentur Frontex" (fn. 283), p. 1266, however, without detailed doctrinal analysis.

349 See chapter 2, 2.6.

350 On these criteria see CJEU, Court, judgement of 16 December 2020, Council of the European Union v Dr. K. Chrysostomides and Co. LLC et al, Joined Cases C-597/18 P, para 78–90; and further Giacomo Rugge, „The Euro Group's informality and *locus standi* before the European Court of Justice" (fn. 149), p. 917–936.

sion's misconduct at the supervisory level and the damage requires further discussion. In general terms, the doctrinal question can be formulated as to whether, and if so, under what circumstances, the breach of a supervisory obligation is to be considered as the cause of a fundamental rights violation, where that violation ultimately results from a formally-binding decision by the supervisee.

In concrete terms, a distinction must be made between fundamental rights violations inherent in the agencies' procedural mistakes, in particular Art. 41 ChFR, and violations brought about by the host member state, in particular Art. 4 ChFR. As mentioned above, the reason for this is that the Commission's supervisory obligation under Art. 40 para 3 Frontex Regulation, Art. 21 para 2 EUAA Regulation, Art. 17 TEU is narrower concerning asylum procedures than concerning reception conditions. Whereas the Commission's procedure-related obligations are limited to due diligence, its reception-related obligations encompass the duty to ensure the legality of reception conditions, if necessary, by providing the required support.[351]

It therefrom follows that, concerning procedure-related damages, the decisive question is whether the Commission's failure to adequately supervise can be considered as causal despite the fact that the Commission only has the competence to urge the agencies in non-formally binding manner to comply with EU law. This question is well illustrated, for instance, with case 3.[352]

> *Case 3 – Daniat Kidane – Age assessment through visual inspection – Art. 41 ChFR (Commission: question of causation IIa)*
> The wrongful age assessment conducted in the case of Daniat Kidane represents systemic malpractice on the part of Frontex. The Commission must, therefore, have known about the issue and was obliged, under Art. 40 para 3 Frontex Regulation, Art. 21 para 2 EUAA Regulation, Art. 17 para 1 TEU to do everything it can to ensure that Frontex complies with EU law. Yet, it is not obvious that the Commission's failure to adequately supervise was causal for the breach of Art. 41 ChFR in the specific case of Daniat Kidane. The link between the Commission's misconduct at the supervisory level and the violation of the fundamental rights inherent in Frontex's conduct hence requires further discussion.

351 See chapter 2, 2.3.

352 The question of causation IIa arises in all cases where the agencies breach procedure-related obligations, i.e. also in cases 1, 2, 4.

Concerning reception-related damages, in turn, it must be taken into consideration that the Commission has the competence to provide administrative support itself and must do everything it can to ensure that the host member state accepts this support.[353] The doctrinal questions in this regard are well illustrated with case 1, 5 and 6.

Case 1 – Sara Esmaili – Art. 4 ChFR (Commission: question of causation IIb)
In the case of Sara Esmaili, which is representative of systemic malpractice, the Commission failed to comply with its supervisory obligation under Art. 40 para 3 Frontex Regulation, Art. 21 para 2 EUAA Regulation, Art. 17 TEU because it failed to ensure that the reception conditions generally comply with EU law. Yet, the individual administrative decision obliging Ms Esmaili and her daughter to stay in the camp where their right under Art. 4 ChFR was violated was issued by Greek authorities. The link between the Commission's failure at the supervisory level and the violation of Art. 4 ChFR thus requires further discussion.

Case 5 – Kareem Rashid – Art. 4 ChFR (Commission: question of causation IIb)
Similarly, the case of Mr Rashid reflects systemic misconduct. Here, the Commission failed to adapt the general operating procedures to the fact that Türkiye had halted the readmission policy since March 2020, thereby violating its supervisory obligation. Again, however, the individual administrative decision which rejected Mr Rashid's asylum claim and thus excluded him from access to any kind of state support was issued by Greek authorities. Thus, the main legal question is whether the link between the Commission's breach of its supervisory obligations under Art. 40 para 3 Frontex Regulation, Art. 21 para 2 EUAA Regulation, Art. 17 TEU and the violation of Art. 4 ChFR can be established in the concrete case.

Case 6 – Reem Saeed – Art. 6 ChFR (Commission: question of causation IIb)
In the case of Ms Saeed, the decision ordering her prolonged detention was issued by the host member state. At the same time, the Commission failed to exercise its competences at the supervisory level so as to prevent the systemic malpractice of the general detention of asylum seekers on

353 See chapter 2, 2 and in more detail Catharina Ziebritzki, *The EU's Responsibility in the Asylum Administration* (fn. 58), p. 117 et seq.

the island of Kos. With regard to Union liability on the basis of the Commission's misconduct, it thus requires further doctrinal analysis whether a causal link can be established between the Commission's failure to adequately supervise and the violation of Art. 6 ChFR in the concrete case of Ms Saeed.

As in the case of the agencies, these doctrinal questions of causation are closely related to the EU's mode of determining without deciding. Again, what has been said above on this mode of operation *prima facie* speaks in favour of causation. The point is well illustrated by the Commission's failure to adequately supervise the reception-related aspects of the EU hotspot administration. Although the Commission's instructions are non-formally binding, they are usually followed by the host member state.[354] The following doctrinal analysis notwithstanding, this suggests that the Commission's failure to issue the relevant instructions and provide the necessary support predetermines the resulting violations of fundamental rights.

Lastly, a pragmatic consideration must be taken into account. One might wonder whether there is a shortcut around the question of causation because the CJEU, in its more recent jurisprudence, considers the infringement of the supervisory standard as the relevant breach for the purposes of Art. 340 para 2 TFEU.[355] In adopting that approach, one might argue that if the violation of Art. 4 and Art. 6 ChFR is considered as the relevant breach, causation is easily established because the Commission's infringement as such constitutes the damage for which compensation is claimed under Art 340 para 2 TFEU. This argument, however, cannot be convincing. A closer look at the jurisprudence shows that the CJEU presupposes a breach of the supervisory obligation, and only then proceeds to examine whether the supervisory standard fulfils the individual-rights criterion and the sufficiently-serious-breach criterion. This means that, for the purposes of establishing causation, the breach of the supervisory obligation remains decisive. As will be explained in more detail below, the CJEU's more recent doctrine thus splits the rule of law into two aspects. While requiring that the supervisory standard meets the individual-rights criterion and the suf-

354 See chapter 2, 2; for detailed doctrinal argument see chapter 5, 5.2.
355 See chapter 5, 3.2.

ficiently-serious-breach criterion, it is still the breach of the supervisory obligation that must be the cause of the damage.[356]

5.4 Non-Applicability of DARS and DARIO

Before delving into the doctrinal intricacies of the CJEU's case law on attribution and causation eventually, it must be stressed that the international rules on attribution, i.e. the Draft Articles on State Responsibility and on the Responsibility of International Organisations (DARS and DARIO),[357] are not applicable to the case of EU hotspots, nor to any other case in the integrated asylum and border administration.[358] While the CJEU's jurisprudence is certainly inspired by those rules,[359] the CJEU has developed a genuine EU law doctrine on attribution and causation. This is consequential because the relation between the agencies and the involved member states is fundamentally distinct from that between an international organisation and its member states, and the relation between EU member states is fundamentally distinct from that among other states. In a nutshell, the

356 The question remains whether the supervisory standard must also fulfil the individual-rights criterion and the sufficiently-serious-breach criterion. While the CJEU's earlier approach rather seems to require this, its more recent approach leaves the question open because the breach of the supervisory standard was already denied. For the purposes of this study, though, the question must not be decided because, as demonstrated, both the supervisory standard and the supervisory obligation meet the individual-rights criterion and the sufficiently-serious-breach criterion.

357 See fn. 335.

358 For an application of DARS/DARIO to cooperation in the framework of Frontex, however, see Roberta Mungianu, *Frontex and Non-Refoulement. The International Responsibility of the EU*, Cambridge University Press 2016, p. 60; Mariana Gkliati, „The first steps of Frontex accountability: Implications for its Legal Responsibility for Fundamental Rights Violations", eumigrationlawblog of 13/08/2021; André Nollkaemper, Dov Jacobs, „Shared Responsibility in International Law: A Conceptual Framework", *Michigan Journal of International Law* 34 (2013), p. 359-438, p. 362 with further references in note 8. As here Melanie Fink (fn. 74); and also Andreas Fischer-Lescano, Timo Tohidipur, „Europäisches Grenzkontrollregime. Rechtsrahmen der europäischen Grenzschutzagentur Frontex" (fn. 283), p. 1250–1253, who apply DARS only with regard to the relation between member states and third states.

359 Note that Advocate General Juliane Kokott, Opinion delivered on 17 November 2005, A.G.M.-COS.MET, C-470/03, para 84–85, extensively referred to international law. The CJEU, however, refrained from referring to international law, although it adopted her conclusions.

structure of the integrated European administration is governed by EU law, not by international law.[360]

5.5 Case Law Relevant to the Doctrine on EU Liability

The doctrinal questions concerning attribution and causation can be answered only on the basis of the CJEU's jurisprudence. The case law, however, is extremely vast, concerns a wide range of constellations, and has developed considerably over the past decades. Analysing whether the Union is liable in a particular case hence requires determining which case law is relevant to the present analysis. Two points must be made in this regard.

The first is that case law concerning other areas of law is applicable to the context at hand. This is of particular relevance because the vast majority of jurisprudence concerns competition law,[361] agricultural subsidies,[362] and the Eurozone,[363] while there is no case law concerning the asylum system as yet. Certainly, most judgements refer to case law from the same policy area.[364] A closer look at the case law, however, shows that the doctrine of Union liability is consistent across different areas of law, and the CJEU's more recent judgments even explicitly rely on competition law cases to establish liability in the Eurozone.[365] This is consequential because the Treaties conceive Art. 340 para 2 TFEU as one general rule that is applicable to all areas of EU law.[366]

360 Catharina Ziebritzki, *The EU's Responsibility in the Asylum Administration* (fn. 58), p. 37 et seq., p. 58 et seq.

361 Francette Fines, „A General Analytical Perspective on Community Liability" (fn. 134), p. 29–30.

362 In the words of Pekka Aalto, *Public Liability in EU Law* (fn. 163), p. 112, it is all about 'milk quotas, bananas, maize grits, starch and cotton'.

363 Most prominently CJEU, judgement of 20 September 2016, Ledra, C-8/15 P et al (fn. 117).

364 Melanie Fink, „EU Liability for Contributions to Member States' Breaches of EU Law" (fn. 104), p. 1231.

365 For instance, CJEU, judgement of 13 July 2018, Bourdouvali, T-786/14 (fn. 119), para 80 relies on CJEU, Court, judgement of 26 February 1986, Krohn & Co. Import-Export v Commission of the European Communities, 175/84, insofar as the causal link is concerned.

366 Crucially, this does not ignore structural differences between the internal market and the area of freedom, security and justice. For instance, the fact that function of the action for damages as a fundamental rights remedy is of particular practical

The second point concerns the question of whether and to what extent the CJEU's earlier jurisprudence is still applicable. The decisive development here is the 2000 *Brasserie-Bergaderm*-turn, with which the CJEU lowered the preconditions for Union liability by aligning it to member state liability.[367] Thus, that matter is closely connected to the question of whether the case law on member state liability, as established with the Frankovich line,[368] is relevant to the interpretation of Art. 340 para 2 TFEU.

The crucial point here is that the convergence between Union liability and member-state liability is not complete. Two important differences remain. First, the convergence was limited from the outset to the individual-rights criterion and the sufficiently-serious-breach criterion. This is consequential because the purpose of the alignment was to address the criticism of the narrow definition of qualified unlawful conduct. The doctrine, hence, remains differentiated insofar as the notions of causation and damage are concerned.[369] Second, the convergence finds its limits where specific characteristics of the Union or the member states determine the respective liability doctrine. For instance, if the CJEU, in a case on member state liability, relies on national sovereignty as a main argument against liability, this argument cannot be transferred to a case on Union liability, or at least not without further justification. In the same vein, the specific characteristics of the Union and the function of the action for damages in the system of legal protection against the EU must be decisive considerations when interpreting Art. 340 para 2 TFEU.[370]

It thus follows that pre-*Bergaderm* case law on Union liability is relevant to the current doctrine on Union liability only insofar as the causation criterion and the damage criterion are concerned. Further, post-*Brasserie* case law on member state liability is relevant insofar as the individual-rights criterion and the sufficiently-serious-breach criterion are concerned, and

---

relevance in the area of freedom, security and justice can be taken into account within the framework of the established doctrine.

367 See fn. 159 et seq.

368 CJEU, judgement of 19 November 1991, Frankovich, C-6/90 (fn. 174).

369 Pekka Aalto, *Public Liability in EU Law* (fn. 163), p. 10–11; Uwe Säuberlich, *Die außervertragliche Haftung im Gemeinschaftsrecht* (fn. 153), p. 16–29.

370 Hence, the accession of the EU to the ECHR could lead to the convergent doctrine moving apart again because the ECHR requirements would then be decisive considerations for the interpretation of Art. 340 para 2 TFEU, see Advocate General Léger, Opinion of 8 April 2003, Köbler, C-224/01, para 94.

provided that the interpretation of Art. 340 para 2 TFEU takes into consideration the specificities of the Union's legal structure.

Chapter 4: Attribution of Conduct to the EU

The last two chapters of this study test the argument developed in the previous chapters and confirm that the action for damages functions as a makeshift fundamental rights remedy against the EU. The present chapter discusses questions of attribution before the following chapter turns to the issue of causation. Specifically, this chapter seeks to answer under which conditions administrative conduct that is performed by staff working for Frontex or the EUAA in EU hotspots, i.e. as members of the so-called migration management support teams (MMST), is to be attributed to the agency themselves.[1] To do so, the first section provides a detailed reconstruction of the CJEU's emerging attribution doctrine (1). This will show that two criteria are decisive: the external appearance of the relevant conduct towards a reasonable addressee and the internal competences (2). Based on these two criteria, the last section shows that and why the administrative conduct of MMST staff – including deployed, statutory and contracted staff – is to be attributed to the EUAA and Frontex, respectively. As a consequence, fundamental rights violations that are inherent in the MMST members' conduct can be challenged via the action for damages under Art. 340 para 2 TFEU (3).

1 Emerging Doctrine on Attribution

As mentioned above, the CJEU has not yet explicitly pronounced itself on the specific matter of attribution to agencies. Existing scholarly analysis remains limited to regular Frontex teams deployed for the purpose of border protection. Concerning these, most contributions conclude, albeit with varying arguments, that the conduct of deployed staff is attributable to the host member state or, under specific circumstances, to the home member state.[2]

1 As explained in previous chapter, this question arises because MMSTs consist of staff deployed by member states, statutory staff of the agencies and contracted staff.

2 See Matthias Lehnert, *Frontex und operative Maßnahmen an den europäischen Außengrenzen. Verwaltungskooperation – materielle Rechtsgrundlagen – institutionelle Kon-*

The specific case of MMSTs deployed for the purpose of support in EU hotspots, however, has not been discussed yet.[3] Therefore, the present argument is developed on the basis of the CJEU's general doctrine on attribution as it currently stands. Considering the scarcity of the jurisprudence on this matter, the analysis necessarily remains tentative.

The CJEU has addressed the question of attribution in two different contexts. First, attribution became pertinent in the context of alleged ultra vires conduct. In judgements such as *Sayag v Leduc*[4] and *A.G.M.-COS-MET*,[5] the Court had to decide whether the relevant conduct was to be considered as an act of a Union body or whether it was ultra vires and, hence, a private act of the staff in question. Second, attribution was discussed in the context of the conclusion of international agreements or memoranda of understanding. In judgements such as *ERTA*[6] and the orders in *NF et al. v Council*, the Court had to decide whether the relevant agreement was concluded by the Union or by the member states, which depended on whether it was the Council or the member states who had acted. Similarly, in judgements such as *Bourdouvali*,[7] the Court had to decide whether the conduct in the context of the sovereign debt crisis was attributable to the Eurogroup or to the European Stability Mechanism (ESM), which again depended on to whom the relevant conduct was to be attributed.

---

trolle, Nomos 2014, p. 319–332 arguing on the basis of the German concept of 'Organleihe'; Anna Mrozek, *Grenzschutz als supranationale Aufgabe. Der Schutz der europäischen Außengrenzen unter der Beteiligung der Bundespolizei*, Nomos 2013, p. 244–245 applying the criteria of Art. 263 TFEU; Roberta Mungianu, *Frontex and Non-Refoulement. The International Responsibility of the EU*, Cambridge University Press 2016, p. 68–87 arguing on the basis of DARS/DARIO (see chapter 3, fn. 358).

3 To the best knowledge of the author. Melanie Fink, *Frontex and Human Rights. Responsibility in 'Multi-Actor Situations' under the ECHR and EU Public Liability Law*, Oxford University Press 2018, p. 35 makes explicit that she does not discuss the specific case of MMST.

4 CJEU, Court, judgement of 10 July 1969, Claude Sayag et al v Jean-Pierre Leduc et al, 9/69.

5 CJEU, Court, judgement of 17 April 2007, A.G.M.-COS-MET Srl v Suomen valtio, Tarmo Lehtinen et al, C-470/03.

6 CJEU, Court, judgement of 31 March 1971, Commission of the European Communities v Council (ERTA), 22/70.

7 CJEU, General Court (Fourth Chamber), judgement of 13 July 2018, Eleni Pavlikka Bourdouvali v Council of the European Union, European Commission, European Central Bank, Euro Group and European Union, T-786/14.

1.1 Public Conduct vs. Ultra Vires Conduct

In the case *Sayag v Leduc*, the question which is of interest here was whether certain conduct by Mr Claude Sayag, an official of the European Atomic Energy Community, was attributable to the Community or whether it was his private act because he had acted ultra vires. Mr Sayag, while driving his private car from Brussels to Mol, had caused an accident in which two persons were injured. As Mr Sayag was in possession of a travel order which provided for the use of his own car, he argued that he had acted in performance of his professional duties and that, accordingly, the Community was liable for the damage resulting from the accident.[8]

The CJEU found that attribution to the Union presupposes an internal and direct relationship between the conduct and the tasks entrusted to the institution so that the conduct appears as a necessary extension of those tasks.[9] While the preconditions for such an internal and direct relationship are not explicitly clarified, it becomes apparent from the Court's reasoning that the decisive factor is the internal administrative structure. In the case of Mr Sayag, the CJEU concluded that a direct relationship did not exist because the travel order was merely intended to enable reimbursement of travel expenses and that the conduct in question could thus not be attributed to the Union.[10] The court hence considered the conduct of EU staff attributable to the Union only insofar as it qualifies as a performance of their duties as defined in the relevant institution's competences.

The facts in *A.G.M.-COS.MET* were similar. Here, the case concerned a dispute between AGM, an Italian company selling vehicle lifts, and Mr Lehtinen, an official of the Finnish Ministry of Social Affairs and Health. Mr Lehtinen had publicly expressed his opinion that AGM's products did not meet the safety standards required by EU legislation. While the head of the Ministry had also publicly made clear that these were Mr Lehtinen's personal views, the AGM sought damages not only from Mr Lehtinen but also from the Finnish State. The national court referred several questions to the CJEU, including whether Mr Lehtinen's statements were attributable to Finland.[11]

8 CJEU, Court, judgement of 10 July 1969, Sayag v Leduc, 9/69 (fn. 4), p. 331.
9 Ibid., para 7–8.
10 Ibid., para 9–12.
11 CJEU, Court, judgement of 17 April 2007, A.G.M.-COS-MET, C-470/03 (fn. 5), para 40.

Remarkably, and despite the similarity in terms of facts, the CJEU did not rely on its previous jurisprudence. Instead, it considered decisive whether the persons to whom the statements were addressed could reasonably suppose, in the given context, that the official expressed the relevant positions with the authority of his office.[12] In this assessment, the CJEU took into account, inter alia, whether the official letterhead of the competent institution was used, whether TV interviews were given on the institution's premises, whether the staff themselves qualified their statements as personal or as official, and whether the institution publicly distanced itself from the relevant statement.[13] In sum, the CJEU hence held that attribution depends on how the statements in question may have been perceived by a reasonable addressee.

With a view to applying these findings to the case of the agencies operating in EU hotspots, two points require clarification. First, the pertinence of the judgement in *A.G.M.-COS.MET* appears to require justification because that case concerned attribution of conduct to a member state, whereas the case at hand concerns attribution of conduct to the Union.[14] In this regard, it suffices to recall that the criteria for Union liability and member-state liability are largely aligned.[15] It is, therefore, not a uniform notion of attribution but, instead, a distinction that would require justification. Such justification, however, is not apparent. From the outset, there is no plausible reason why the conditions for establishing a link between a certain conduct and a certain actor should depend on whether that actor is a member state or the Union. Instead, the fact that the structure of the integrated administration is determined by EU law speaks in favour of a uniform notion of attribution.

Second, it must be noted that both *Sayag v Leduc* and *A.G.M.-COS.MET* concern the demarcation of public from private conduct, whereas the question in the case at hand concerns the demarcation of member state

12 Ibid., para 56–58.

13 Having clarified the preconditions for attribution, the CJEU then left the application of these criteria to the referring national court. The relevance of these factors, however, follows from the facts of the case, see CJEU, Court, judgement of 17 April 2007, A.G.M.-COS-MET, C-470/03 (fn. 5), para 27–36.

14 Melanie Fink, *Frontex and Human Rights* (fn. 3), p. 239, for instance, argues that this case is not particularly relevant in the context of Union liability because it concerns the liability of member states.

15 See chapter 3, fn. 160 et seq.

conduct from Union conduct.[16] This difference, however, is less relevant than it might seem at first glance. In both cases, the decisive question is whether a certain act can be attributed to the Union or not. The fact that the alternative actor is a member state in one case and a private person in the other case cannot justify a difference in the attribution criteria. Otherwise, it would be entirely unpredictable for EU staff who are deployed by member states under what circumstances their conduct is attributable to the Union.

1.2 Union Conduct vs. Intergovernmental Conduct

In its *ERTA* judgement, the CJEU pronounced itself further on the conditions under which certain conduct is attributable to the Union. The case concerned a dispute between the Commission and the Council of the then European Communities on the European Agreement on Road Transport (ERTA). In 1967, negotiations for the revision of the ERTA were resumed within the UN Economic Commission for Europe, and the agreement was made available for signature by the member states in 1970. Meanwhile, the Commission had undertaken similar work, which in 1969 resulted in a Regulation on those issues. Against this background, the Commission sought from the CJEU the annulment of the Council's proceedings relating to the conclusion of the ERTA. The Council submitted that the application was inadmissible because the proceedings were nothing more than a coordination of policies amongst member states within the framework of the Council.[17]

The Court, in deciding whether the Council was the author of the conduct in question, explicitly considered decisive the division of competences. The test established by the Court was whether, at the date of the proceedings in question, power to negotiate and conclude the ERTA was vested in the Community or in the member states. The core argument was that a matter falling within the competence of the Community could not be regulated by member states. On this basis, the court concluded that the proceedings in question, which potentially deviated from the Treaty proce-

16 Many thanks to Melanie Fink for this remark.

17 CJEU, Court, judgement of 31 March 1971, ERTA, 22/70 (fn. 6), para 36.

dure on the conclusion of agreements with third countries, were indeed authored by the Council and thus subject to legal review by the CJEU.[18]

The case of *NF et al. v Council* was very similar to *ERTA* – at least in terms of facts. The CJEU was called upon to decide whether the EU-Türkiye Statement was attributable to the Council or to the member states who had been meeting, allegedly for practical reasons alone, in the Council's building. Again, the decisive question was whether it was the Union or the member states who had concluded the relevant agreement with the third country.[19]

Astonishingly, however, the court's reasoning in *NF et al. v Council* differed considerably from *ERTA*. Instead of applying the competence test, the court focused on an analysis of the external appearance of the relevant conduct to a reasonable addressee. More precisely, the court assessed the presentation of the conduct, taking into account the location of the meeting and official documents relating to the meeting, such as press releases, working programmes and time schedules.[20] On this basis, the CJEU then concluded that the EU-Türkiye Statement could not be regarded as a measure adopted by the European Council or, moreover, by any other institution, body, office or agency of the European Union, but instead, be considered as an act of the member states.[21] The applicant's claim was accordingly dismissed as inadmissible.[22]

The court's argument in *NF et al. v Council* was met with fierce criticism, and rightly so. In particular, the decision was considered doctrinally unconvincing because the CJEU departed from its previous *ERTA* doctrine without even mentioning that decision.[23] Instead, the CJEU introduced the external appearance criterion with reference to its 1993 judgement *Parlia-*

18 Ibid., para 3–5, 52, 54–55.

19 CJEU, General Court (First Chamber, Extended Composition), order of 28 February 2017, NF v European Council (EU-Turkey Statement), T-192/16, para 47.

20 Ibid., para 47–70.

21 Ibid., para 71.

22 Ibid., para 53–60, 71. The applicants' appeals to the Court were dismissed as manifestly inadmissible, see CJEU, Court, order of 12 September 2018, NF, NG and NM v European Council, Joined Cases C-208/17 P to C-210/17 P.

23 Jürgen Bast, „Scharade im kontrollfreien Raum: Hat die EU gar keinen Türkei-Deal geschlossen?", Verfassungsblog of 03/03/2017; Rainer Hofmann, Adela Schmidt, „'EU-Türkei-Deal' ohne Beteiligung der EU? – Die Beschlüsse des EuG zur Erklärung EU-Türkei vom 18. März 2016", *Europäische Grundrechte-Zeitschrift* 44 (2017), p. 317-327.

ment v Council and Commission.[24] This reference, however, is misleading because that judgement corresponds to the ERTA doctrine insofar as the starting point of the assessment is the division of competences.[25] Even based on the external appearance criterion, the reasoning in *NF et al. v Council* still cannot convince, as the Statement had been pre-negotiated by the Commission, the relevant meeting took place in the Council's building, the Statement was published on the homepage of the Council and was clearly designated and publicly communicated as an agreement between the EU and Türkiye.[26] In sum, the decision in *NF et al. v Council* can only be understood as an avoidance strategy which allowed the CJEU to remain silent on the highly controversial and politicised questions concerning the quality and legality of the EU-Türkiye Statement.[27] This criticism – while entirely justified – is not the main point here.

The main point here is that the decision in *NF et al. v Council* shows that the CJEU considers the external appearance of the relevant conduct as decisive for the question of attribution. Just as the judgement in *ERTA*, the decision in *NF et al. v Council* established criteria for distinguishing Union conduct from member state conduct and hence forms part of the CJEU's emerging doctrine on attribution.

Seen from this perspective, the CJEU's *Bourdouvali* judgment then appears to combine the two different approaches from *NF* and *ERTA*. The case concerned the Cypriot bank restructuring. During the first months of 2012, certain banks established in Cyprus encountered severe financial difficulties in context of the sovereign debt crisis. The Republic of Cyprus thus considered it necessary for them to be recapitalised and submitted

---

24 CJEU, orders of 28 February 2017, NF v European Council (EU-Turkey Statement), T-192/16 (fn. 19), para 42, 44–45, 52, referring to CJEU, Court, judgment of 30 June 1993, European Parliament v Council of the European Communities, Joined Cases C-181/91 and C-248/91, para 12–14.

25 CJEU, Court, judgment of 30 June 1993, Parliament v Council, Joined Cases C-181/91 (fn. 24), para 15–25, in particular 16: 'it should be pointed out that the Community does not have exclusive competence in the field of humanitarian aid, and that consequently the Member States are not precluded from exercising their competence in that regard collectively in the Council or outside it.'.

26 Catharina Ziebritzki, Robert Nestler, „'Hotspots' an der EU-Außengrenze. Eine rechtliche Bestandsaufnahme", *MPIL Research Paper Series (SSRN)* 17 (2017), p. 13–14.

27 Enzo Cannizzaro, „Denialism as the Supreme Expression of Realism. A Quick Comment on NF v. European Council", *European Papers* (2017), p. 215-257; Sergio Carrera, Leonhard Den Hertog, Marco Stefan, „It wasn't me! The Luxembourg Court Orders on the EU-Turkey Refugee Deal", *CEPS Policy Insights* (15/04/2017).

a request to the Eurogroup for financial assistance. In June 2012, the Eurogroup declared that such assistance would be granted through the European Stability Mechanism (ESM), subject to the conditionalities of a macro-economic adjustment programme to be defined in a memorandum of understanding (Mou) between Cyprus and the ESM. Ms Eleni Pavlikka Bourdouvali, along with other applicants, argued that the bank restructuring had caused damages to her and hence sought compensation from the Union. More precisely, the applicants submitted that the damages had occurred as a result of several acts, including formally binding decisions and non-formally binding conduct of the ECB, the Council, the Commission, and the Eurogroup.[28]

While the *Bourdouvali* judgment is instructive in many respects, the point that is of interest here is the court's argument concerning the attribution of conduct in the context of the claim against the Eurogroup. Based on the assumption that the latter qualified as an institution in the sense of Art. 340 para 2 TFEU,[29] the court examined whether the conclusion of the MoU must be attributed to the Eurogroup as an EU body or to the ESM as an international financial institution. To begin with, the CJEU considered it decisive that member states had conferred the competence to conclude the MoU to the ESM and not to the Eurogroup.[30] It hence relied on the division of competences and insofar returned to its *ERTA* doctrine. At the same time, the CJEU also took into account that the member states had clearly stated that the relevant conduct was governed by international law and not by EU law and thus followed the rules and procedures provided for by the ESM treaty and not by the Eurogroup.[31] Hence, it also relied on the external appearance of the conduct in question towards reasonable addressees and, insofar applied its *NF* doctrine. As both approaches led to the same result,

28 CJEU, judgement of 13 July 2018, Bourdouvali, T-786/14 (fn. 7), para 73.

29 Note that this assumption is no longer valid. CJEU, Court, judgement of 16 December 2020, Council of the European Union v Dr. K. Chrysostomides and Co. LLC et al, Joined Cases C-597/18 P, para 78–90 found that the Eurogroup does not qualify as an institution in the sense of Art 340 para 2 TFEU. See, for a critical analysis, Giacomo Rugge, „The Euro Group's informality and *locus standi* before the European Court of Justice: *Council v. K. Chrysostomides & Co. and Others*", *Zeitschrift für ausländisches öffentliches Recht und Völkerrecht (Heidelberg Journal of International Law)* (2021), p. 917–936.

30 CJEU, judgement of 13 July 2018, Bourdouvali, T-786/14 (fn. 7), para 124–128.

31 Ibid., para 122–124.

the court then concluded that the conduct at issue was to be attributed to the ESM.[32]

Remarkably, the decisions in *ERTA*, *NF*, and *Bourdouvali* are rarely considered relevant to the attribution of conduct to EU agencies. Therefore, the reading proposed here and their application to the EU hotspots case requires justification.

Two points need to be considered. First, *ERTA* and *NF* concern actions for annulment under Art. 263 TFEU, whereas the case at hand concerns an action for damages under Art. 340 para 2 TFEU. In this regard, it suffices to recall that the question of who the author of a certain conduct is cannot depend on the action at stake. Otherwise, one single act could be attributable to the Union for the purpose of one action and to a member state for the purpose of another action. This would not only be illogical but also endanger the coherence of legal protection. The criteria for attribution must hence be coherent across the EU legal protection system. Second, the conduct at stake in *ERTA*, *NF* and *Bourdouvali* does not qualify as administrative conduct. Instead, these cases concern the attribution of conduct related to the conclusion of international agreements or memoranda of understanding. In this regard, a similar argument applies. The nature of the relevant conduct cannot be decisive for attribution. As the court made clear in *NF*, it is rather the other way round: the question of who has acted is prior to the question of the nature of the act.[33]

This being said it becomes apparent that the questions of attribution in *ERTA*, *NF* and *Bourdouvali* are indeed very similar to the questions of attribution in the case at hand. Specifically, both *ERTA* and *NF* deal with the question of whether certain conduct adopted in the framework or the premises of the Council is attributable to the Council or whether it must be qualified as an act of the member states instead. Similarly, the question in *Bourdouvali* was whether certain conduct is attributable to the Eurogroup as an EU body or to the ESM as an international institution established among member states. In the case of EU hotspots, the decisive question is whether certain conduct, which is performed by MMST members who are deployed by a member state and who act within the framework of an EU agency, is attributable to that agency or to the member state instead. The legal question is parallel because the institutional structure of the

32 Ibid., para 101–114, in particular 113, 115–129.

33 CJEU, orders of 28 February 2017, NF v European Council (EU-Turkey Statement), T-192/16 (fn. 19), para 44, passim.

Council is arguably quite similar to that of EU agencies insofar as both are supranational bodies with intergovernmental elements. In this sense, a German or French asylum officer who is deployed as an MMST member and acts in the EU hotspots is comparable to a member state representative who acts in the Council premises.

2 Internal Competence and External Appearance

The case law analysis has shown that the CJEU considers decisive for establishing attribution, first, the internal competences of the actor in question and, second, the external appearance of the conduct at stake. This is conceptually convincing because the criteria correspond to the structural principles of the European administration. The external appearance criterion corresponds to the principle of a functionally unified administration insofar as the integrated administration appears as a uniform entity against which legal protection must be granted. The competence criterion corresponds to the principle of separation insofar as individual legal protection must be sought from the competent actor. The following section takes a closer look at the respective criteria and discusses their relation.

2.1 External Appearance Criterion

The external appearance criterion was introduced with the judgement in *A.G.M.-COS.MET*, and then prominently spelt out in the orders on *NF et al. v Council*. The CJEU considers decisive whether the persons to whom the relevant conduct is addressed could reasonably suppose that it was undertaken with the authority of the relevant office, and to this end, provides a detailed analysis of the external appearance of the relevant conduct towards a reasonable addressee, including a whole range of factors ranging from press releases and locations to letterheads and explicit statements.[34]

In general terms, the external appearance test can hence be formulated to ask whether a reasonable addressee would perceive certain conduct as the conduct of the Union, i.e. here of the respective agency. In order to establish whether this is the case, the concrete circumstances must be com-

34 CJEU, Court, judgement of 17 April 2007, A.G.M.-COS-MET, C-470/03 (fn. 5), para 56–58; CJEU, orders of 28 February 2017, NF v European Council (EU-Turkey Statement), T-192/16 (fn. 19), para 53–60, 71.

prehensively assessed, including factors such as the appearance of offices, uniforms, public statements, and official reports.

2.2 Internal Competence Criterion

The internal competence criterion was established in *Sayag v Leduc*, where the CJEU held that attribution presupposes an internal and direct relationship between the conduct and the tasks entrusted to the institutions. Whereas it became apparent from the CJEU's reasoning in that case already that such a relationship depends on the relevant institutions' competences,[35] this was clearly spelt out in the judgement on *ERTA*. Here, the CJEU explicitly considered decisive whether the power to negotiate and conclude the relevant international agreement was vested in the Community or in the member states.[36] In *Bourdouvali*, the CJEU then confirmed this approach, arguing that attribution depended on which institution had the competence to conclude the relevant memorandum of understanding.[37]

In general terms, the CJEU hence considers decisive which institution has the competence to perform the conduct in question. This formulation, however, is not sufficiently precise because it does not provide a clear answer in two constellations that are key to the case of EU hotspots, namely when an agency's misconduct consists in an omission to act,[38] or when it systematically exceeds its competences.[39]

A more precise formulation of the competence test requires a better understanding of the underlying idea. It follows from the CJEU's jurisprudence that the competence criterion serves to concretise the concept of imputation. Imputation, in turn, serves to determine which entity shall bear responsibility for a certain damage and thus requires a risk assessment. In

35 The officer's conduct is attributable to the Community only if it qualifies as a performance of his duties as defined in the internal administrative structure. In the case of Mr Sayag, the CJEU concluded that a direct relationship was absent because the relevant travel order was merely intended to enable a reimbursement of travel expenses, see CJEU, Court, judgement of 10 July 1969, Sayag v Leduc, 9/69 (fn. 4), para 7–12.

36 CJEU, Court, judgement of 31 March 1971, ERTA, 22/70 (fn. 6), para 36, para 3–5, 52, 54–55.

37 CJEU, judgement of 13 July 2018, Bourdouvali, T-786/14 (fn. 7), para 122–128.

38 This becomes especially relevant in the case of the Commission, as its main misconduct in an omission to adequately exercise supervisory obligations.

39 Both the agencies' and the Commission's misconduct is systemic in nature, see chapter 2, 1 to 3.

this context, it is not only decisive how the course of action actually was but also how the course of action should have been according to the legal order. It is precisely this twofold dimension of imputation that explains why the competence criterion is decisive. At the first level, the competence criterion ensures that the actor who actually determined the course of action incurs liability. This is well illustrated with *Sayag v Leduc*, where the CJEU, in essence, held that the Union should not be liable for damages resulting from a purely private decision to undertake the harmful conduct. At a second level, the competence criterion also ensures that the actor who should have acted according to the legal order incurs liability. This is well illustrated with *ERTA*, where the CJEU held that responsibility should lie with the actor who bears the risk for misconduct because it should have acted according to the Treaties.

It follows that the competence test can be formulated as to whether the respective entity, in the concrete case, has made use of its competences to determine the actual unlawful course of action, or whether it should have made use of its competences to bring about an alternative lawful course of action.[40] This formulation is still not sufficiently precise insofar as it leads to ambiguous and inadequate results in the case of omissions.[41] The test could mean that the conduct must be attributed to the entity which has the competence to prevent the occurrence of unlawful conduct in general terms. This interpretation would lead to an overly broad concept of attribution, as omissions on the part of member states were attributable to the agencies already if the agency could have ensured, e.g. through better training, that the error did not occur. In the alternative, the test could mean that the conduct is attributable to the entity which could have carried out the required concrete lawful conduct. This understanding would lead to an overly narrow definition of the attribution criterion, as the agencies would not be liable even if they had breached their duty to inform the member state about certain circumstances in their sphere of knowledge and the member state had, therefore, issued an unlawful decision.

For the attribution criterion to be meaningful also in the context of omissions, the test must hence be formulated as to which entity could have prevented the specific unlawful omission in the circumstances of the

40 In case of shared administrative competences within an integrated administration, this might require to take into account the internal division of tasks.

41 Many thanks to Melanie Fink for this remark.

concrete case.[42] Accordingly, an unlawful omission is attributable to an agency if it has the competence either to carry out the specific required lawful conduct itself or to ensure that the relevant member state does so.

The consequentiality of this formulation is confirmed by the fact that it leads to unequivocal and adequate results also in cases of systemic ultra vires conduct. According to the formulated test, the decisive question is whether the agency had the competence to prevent specific unlawful conduct. Where the unlawful ultra vires act is an exceptional case, one might wonder whether it was the private decision of a staff member to exceed the competence limits. However, when the ultra vires act represents a systemic practice, it is clear that the relevant supervisory staff must have been informed and thus had not only the competence but even the duty to prevent the occurrence and persistence of the practice.[43] Otherwise, EU agencies could evade the EU legal protection system simply by exceeding their competences. Put differently, it is the principle of estoppel which prevents an agency as a defendant in the context of Art. 340 para 2 TFEU from invoking the exceeding of its competences as an argument against attribution, where it at the same time presents that conduct as its own towards potential addressees.[44] The competence test thus shows that a systemic overstepping of competences per se speaks in favour of attribution to the respective agency.[45]

2.3 Relationship Between the Criteria

Having said this, the relationship between the two criteria requires clarification. The CJEU applies the criteria alternatively, and the reasons for the court's choice of one or the other criterion are not apparent. This becomes problematic when the application of either criterion leads to differing results – which occurs, in particular, where the external appearance deviates structurally from the internal competences, i.e. where it systemi-

42 For a similar approach, albeit in the context of causation see Uwe Säuberlich, *Die außervertragliche Haftung im Gemeinschaftsrecht. Eine Untersuchung der Mehrpersonenverhaltnisse*, Springer 2005, p. 236.

43 This follows from the agency's internal supervisory obligations, see in detail below 3.3.

44 At least to the extent that the unlawfulness results from the exceeding of the agency's competences.

45 Many thanks to Anna Lübbe for suggesting to base the argument on the structural incongruence between internal competences and external appearance.

cally appears that the Union acts although it does not have the required competence.

In order to solve such cases, one must first be aware of the telos underlying each criterion. As regards the competence criterion, it has been shown that its rationale is to ensure that the actor who was responsible according to the Treaties to do things correctly incurs liability if things are not done correctly. As regards the external appearance criterion, in turn, the case law shows that the underlying rationale is to empower concerned persons to sue the actor they have faced.[46] This is particularly important in the case of the European asylum administration. As the European Ombudsman put it, 'persons affected by Frontex operations are typically under stress and vulnerable, and it cannot possibly be expected from them to investigate what is undoubtedly a complex allocation of responsibility'.[47] In a nutshell, the main idea underlying the internal competence criterion is a formal understanding of the rule of law, whereas the main idea underlying the external competence criterion is a substantial understanding of the rule of law.

Second, one must also be aware of the telos of the action for damages. As argued above, it serves, at least inter alia, to ensure that individuals can exercise their right to an effective remedy against the Union.[48]

Consequently, it is argued here that, in case of conflicting results, the criterion that is better suited to ensure judicial protection in the sense of Art. 47 ChFR should prevail. This conclusion is supported by the reasoning in *Bourdouvali,* where the CJEU made explicit that ensuring judicial protection is a central consideration in the context of attribution.[49]

46 Although the CJEU put the focus on the other side of the coin, namely on the fact that it must not adjudicate on matters that fall outside its jurisdiction (see CJEU, orders of 28 February 2017, NF v European Council (EU-Turkey Statement), T-192/16 (fn. 19), para 44), it becomes clear from the CJEU's list of criteria (see ibid., para 47–70; CJEU, Court, judgement of 10 July 1969, Sayag v Leduc, 9/69 (fn. 4), para 9–12) that the purpose of the assesment is to determine who was perceived as the 'author' of the conduct in question by a reasonable addressee.

47 European Ombudsperson, Decision of 12 November 2013, closing own-initiative inquiry concerning the European Agency for the Management of Operational Cooperation at the External Borders of the Member States of the European Union (Frontex), case OI/5/2012/BEH-MHZ, para 16–18, 23, 31–41, summary.

48 See chapter 3, 3.

49 CJEU, judgement of 13 July 2018, Bourdouvali, T-786/14 (fn. 7), para 107, albeit in the context of the interpretation of the term institution in the sense of Art 340 para 2

Which criterion prevails thus depends on the concrete circumstances of the case. But two general observations can be made. On the one hand, the external appearance criterion bears particular weight where the internal competence order is overly complex and regulated in non-public or informal inter-administrative agreements, or when EU bodies structurally overstep their competences. In such circumstances, the competence criterion would frustrate the very purpose of individual legal protection.[50] For in order to determine which body is competent, applicants would have to delve into the complexities of internal decision-making structures which in turn would require several access to documents requests and comprehensive empirical and legal research.[51] De facto, it would hence become almost impossible for applicants to determine to whom certain conduct must be attributed and thus against whom to lodge an action for damage. Crucially, the point here is not to say that the law must be so simple that any layperson must be able to determine the correct respondent of an action for damages in every case. However, when even specifically trained lawyers experienced in the field who spend a reasonable part of their resources on this issue are unable to determine to whom an alleged fundamental rights violation should be attributed, then the application of the competence criterion seems disproportionate in light of the function of the action for damages.[52]

On the other hand, the internal competence criterion is of particular significance where the external appearance structurally misleads reasonable

TFEU. Similarly, CJEU, judgement of 16 December 2020, Chrysostomides, C-597/18 P (fn. 29), para 92–94.

50 Jens Hofmann, *Rechtsschutz und Haftung im Europäischen Verwaltungsverbund*, Duncker & Humblot 2004, p. 380 noting that the external-appearance-criterion would mean maximal clarity and simplicity with regard to the choice of the correct legal procedure, and proposing a similar solution with reference to the Opinion of Advocate General Mancini, 19 November 1985, Krohn & Co. Import-Export v Commission of the European Communities, 175/84.

51 The present study, for instance, required several access to documents requests, many of which remained unanswered, several years of observation of the administrative practice on the ground, several semi-structured qualitative interviews with representatives of the European Commission and EUAA (introduction, fn. 102), only to understand, first, which actor is competent to do what, and second, which actor does what within the integrated EU hotspot administration. Further on the method see introduction, 7.

52 As here, Jens Hofmann, *Rechtsschutz und Haftung im Europäischen Verwaltungsverbund* (fn. 50), p. 379 arguing that 'the individual cannot be expected to rummage through every nook and cranny of the procedure' (translation by author).

addressees in the sense that the conduct of a Union body structurally appears as the conduct of a member state authority.[53] In such a situation, the application of the external competence criterion would de facto preclude individual legal protection because applicants would typically assume that member states have acted and thus turn towards national courts for review. The internal competence criterion thus serves to prevent a situation in which Union bodies blur or alter their external appearance to the extent that they de facto escape judicial review.[54]

3 Conclusions on Attribution

This last section applies the findings on the CJEU's attribution doctrine to the case of EU hotspots. This will lead to the conclusion that the conduct of all MMST members, notably including deployed staff, is attributable to the EUAA and Frontex, respectively.

3.1 Attribution of Conduct to the EUAA

First, applying the criterion of external appearance, the key question is how a reasonable addressee would perceive the conduct of EUAA staff operating in the EU hotspots. This analysis must take into account the manner in which the EUAA itself presents its operations to the public, to the cooperating national authority, and particularly to the concerned asylum seeker.

Several factors indicate that a reasonable observer would perceive the conduct of EUAA MMST members as the conduct of the agency itself. EUAA staff wear EUAA uniforms and badges during deployment[55] and present themselves as EUAA representatives to asylum seekers.[56] Moreover,

---

53 An illustrative example in the context of administrative cooperation is the so-called embedded model, which structurally conceals conduct of the EUAA, see chapter 2, 1.3.b. For the parallel problem in the context of international agreements see Sergio Carrera, Leonhard Den Hertog, Marco Stefan, „It wasn't me! The Luxembourg Court Orders on the EU-Türkiye Refugee Deal" (fn. 27).

54 This was the core of the critique on the judgement in CJEU, orders of 28 February 2017, NF v European Council (EU-Turkey Statement), T-192/16 (fn. 19), see the literature cited above in fn. 23.

55 Unlike in the case of deployed Frontex staff, the respective home member state cannot be identified from the external appearance of deployed EUAA staff.

56 Own observation of the author (see introduction, fn. 103).

the EUAA depicts the MMST's actions as the agency's conduct in public reports and on its homepage.[57]

As regards further circumstances, one must distinguish between the period before and after the introduction of the so-called embedded model in 2020.[58] Prior to 2020, asylum applicants were usually informed that EUAA, then EASO, was in charge of conducting the interview, and the emblem of the agency was usually the only official sign in the offices where agency staff worked. Also, the interview transcripts and legal opinions prepared by agency staff were clearly identifiable as such. Furthermore, agency staff could be recognised because they spoke English instead of Greek, unless in exceptional cases, and hence also relied on interpreters translating from the applicant's language to English.[59] A reasonable addressee would hence have perceived agency staff as 'officers of the EU asylum agency'. Since 2020, however, it has become more difficult to identify agency staff on the basis of their external appearance. Usually, they now also speak Greek, and it can no longer be discerned from the interview transcript whether the agency or the Greek Asylum Service conducted the interview. Still, agency staff remains identifiable as such from a badge that distinguishes them from national staff.[60] Considering all circumstances together, it is hence still likely – although not certain anymore – that a reasonable addressee would perceive the conduct of agency staff as the conduct of the agency.

Applying the second criterion, the internal competence test, requires determining whether the EUAA had the competence to determine unlawful conduct or to prevent unlawful omission in the specific circumstances of the case. This requires a detailed examination of the supervisory structure of the MMSTs and the EUAA's role within it. As explained above, MMSTs are subject to supervision by the host member state and the respective agency at the first level and by the Commission at the second level. Since the introduction of the embedded model, the first level has been organised

---

57 EASO, *EASO Asylum Report 2021. Annual Report on the Situation of Asylum in the European Union*, p 59–61; EASO, *EASO Annual General Report 2020*, p 9–10, 25–31; EASO, *EASO's support to Greece*, available online: https://www.easo.europa.eu/operational-support/types-operations.

58 The embedded model differs from the previous mode of cooperation insofar as daily instructions to EASO staff are now mainly given by the Greek Asylum Service, see chapter 2, 1.3.b.

59 Own observation of the author (see introduction, fn. 103).

60 On some islands, the EUAA has during some periods even refrained from issuing a written recommendation, own observation of the author (see introduction, fn. 103).

in such a manner that the host member state is responsible for day-to-day instructions, and the EUAA is responsible for more general compliance of its operations with EU law. This general supervision is carried out by the EUAA through its coordinating officers, who are appointed by and report to the Executive Director.[61]

Thus, defining what the EUAA can or should have done to prevent concrete unlawful conduct or omission requires a precise understanding of the tasks and competences of the coordinating officer and the Executive Director respectively.

The coordinating officer's mandate is defined in Art. 25 EUAA Regulation.[62] Inter alia, they are responsible for monitoring the correct implementation of the operational plan and reporting to the Executive Director when the operational plan is not adequately implemented. As regards the supervisory standard, the implementation can only be 'correct' in that sense when it complies with EU law, and especially with the ChFR.[63] The supervisory measures follow the coordinating officer's mandate that they must be able, at least, to issue instructions to the EUAA team members. Otherwise, it would be impossible for the coordinating officer to ensure that the operational plan is implemented in compliance with EU law.

Crucially, the introduction of the embedded model cannot absolve the coordinating officer from their obligations under Art. 25 EUAA Regulation.[64] Although the embedded model has shifted responsibility for issuing daily instructions from the coordinating officer to the host member state,[65] decision-making and reporting structures, as established by secondary law, remain intact. As the embedded model was introduced via operational plans only, it cannot amend supervisory structures under the EUAA Regulation. The shift of responsibility for daily instructions must hence be understood as meaning that the coordinating officer exercises their responsibility under Art. 25 EUAA Regulation by delegating the daily coordination to the national authority. This understanding is clearly reflect-

61 See chapter 2, 1.2.

62 The coordinating officer was formerly called 'Union contact point', but the tasks were similar, see Art. 20 para 2 EASO Regulation.

63 As follow from an interpretation of Art. 25 EUAA Regulation in light of Art. 51 ChFR.

64 Especially Art. 25 para 3 EUAA.

65 In practice, the EASO coordinating officer usually appointed EASO team leaders who then issued instructions towards the staff, interviews with the EASO Union Contact Point (i.e. the predecessor of the coordinating officer) conducted on 13 December 2019 and on 19 February 2021 (introduction, fn. 102).

ed in administrative practice. In fact, the coordinating officer continues to conduct quality-ensuring measures, organise coordination meetings, issue general instructions and report to the Executive Director on all aspects of the deployment,[66] thereby clearly exercising their tasks under Art. 25 EUAA Regulation.

Ultimately, responsibility for supervision lies with the Executive Director. This is consequential because their mandate, as defined in Art. 46, 47 EUAA Regulation is sufficiently broad to actually ensure the legality of the agency's practice. For instance, when the coordinating officer's instructions are not sufficient, the Executive Director could step in and arguably, at least as an interim measure, even give direct instructions to the team members.[67] When misconduct is performed only by a particular staff member, the Executive Director could exercise its powers related to staffing,[68] and when misconduct arises due to conceptual deficiencies in the operational plan, the Executive Director could amend that plan, albeit only in agreement with the host member state.[69] As a last resort, the Executive Director could arguably even withdraw the agency's support. While the EUAA Regulation does not explicitly regulate the matter, notably unlike the Frontex Regulation,[70] it is obvious that the agency cannot be obliged to violate EU law. Therefore, the Executive Director's obligations relating to the day-to-day administration and the implementation of operational plans as defined in Art. 47 para 5 lit a, lit u EUAA Regulation must be interpreted as enabling them, at least in case of persisting and systemic fundamental rights violations, to unilaterally terminate a deployment.

Against this background, the crucial point here is that the identified typical misconduct on the part of EUAA is systemic in nature. While it cannot reasonably be expected from the Executive Director and the coor-

66 Ibid., stressing that EASO staff is still supervised by the coordinating officer, also in the context of the embedded model (see fn. 53).

67 Art. 7, 17–21, 25, 46–47 EUAA Regulation, especially Art. 47 para 5 lit m, according to which the Executive Director is responsible for taking all decisions relating to the management of the agency's internal structures; previously Art. 18 para 1 lit d, Art 20 para 2 lit a and b, para 3, Art 31 para 6 lit a and i EASO Regulation. This must hold true at least when giving direct instructions is the only way to prevent public liability of the agency for fundamental rights violations.

68 Art. 47 para 5 lit k, 60 EUAA Regulation; previously Art. 31 para 6 lit g, Art 38 EASO Regulation.

69 Art 18 para 5 EUAA Regulation.

70 Art. 46 para 4 Frontex Regulation, see in more detail below fn. 97.

dinating officer to prevent every single or exceptional misconduct,[71] they are certainly obliged under Art. 25, 47 EUAA Regulation to ensure that the agency's operations generally comply with EU law. What is more, the Executive Director and the coordinating officer even have the duty to make use of their supervisory competences to ensure that systemic malpractice is remedied and that the agency's practice is generally realigned with EU law. As the interpretation of Art. 25, 47 EUAA Regulation in light of Art. 51 para ChFR confirms that neither the Executive Director nor the coordinating officer can be allowed to ignore the agency's involvement in systemic fundamental rights violations. In such cases, their supervisory discretion is hence reduced to the question of how to act.[72]

Therefore, to the extent that a specific misconduct is an expression of a systemic deficiency, the agency – namely its Executive Director and the coordinating officer – is obliged to prevent the occurrence of that specific misconduct by preventing the systemic issue. In other words, the agency has not only the competence but even the duty to prevent specific misconduct insofar as it constitutes an expression of systemic malpractice.

With regard to the case at hand, this means that because the typical misconduct identified above reflects systemic deficiencies, the EUAA's coordinating officer and Executive Director were competent and obliged to prevent the occurrence of that misconduct. This is well illustrated, for instance, with the EUAA's misconduct relating to deficient asylum interviews or the misapplication of the safe third country concept.

In the case of deficient asylum interviews, the Executive Director should arguably have refrained from concluding the operating plan in the first place, as it was clear that this plan required the agency to assess individual asylum claims which meant systemically overstepping its competences as defined under the former EASO Regulation.[73] Further, the coordinating officer should have correctly monitored the implementation of the operating plan so as to ensure that the agency's conduct generally complies with EU law. In particular, the coordinating officer should have made use of its monitoring competence to instruct the EUAA staff to either not conduct

71 Especially where it results from unlawful daily instructions on the part of the host member state.

72 This is further supported by the telos of Art. 46 para 4 and 5 Frontex Regulation. For a parallel argument concerning the Commission's supervisory discretion see chapter 2, 2.4.

73 See chapter 1, fn. 186 et seq.

interviews with asylum seekers or to conduct these interviews in a lawful manner. These mistakes are well exemplified in case 2.

> *Case 2 – Magan Daud – Deficient asylum interview – Art. 41 ChFR (attribution to EUAA)*
> In the case of Mr Daud, the responsible EUAA caseworker conducted the asylum interview in a deficient manner. Crucially, the malpractices described were not limited to individual cases but of a general nature. There can thus be no doubt that the responsible coordinating officer and the Executive Director were aware of the ongoing malpractices. In addition, the misconduct in the individual case of Mr Daud was even brought to the attention of the agency via the internal complaints mechanism. Thus, the coordinating officer and the Executive Director were obliged to make use of their respective competences to ensure that interviews were generally conducted in compliance with EU law. The EUAA coordinator officer and the Executive Director thus had the competence, and even the duty, to prevent the misconduct in the case of Mr Daud.

As regards the misapplication of the safe third country concept, the Executive Director and the coordinating officer should have taken into consideration since March 2020 already that Türkiye no longer accepts readmissions. When it became obvious that asylum seekers could no longer be returned to Türkiye, the Executive Director and the coordinating officer were obliged to amend the operating plan, as well as the corresponding standard operating procedures and similar instructions, so as to ensure that the agency would no longer recommend the rejection of asylum applications on the basis of the argument that Türkiye could be considered as safe. These failures become relevant in case 5.

> *Case 5 – Kareem Rashid – Limbo situation – Art. 41 ChFR (attribution to EUAA)*
> In the case of Mr Rashid, the EUAA caseworker recommended the rejection of his asylum claim as inadmissible, arguing that Türkiye could be considered a safe third country for him. The reason for this misconduct on the part of the individual caseworkers was that the Executive Director had failed to adapt the operating plan to the changed circumstances and that the coordinating officer had failed to instruct his team members to refrain from applying the safe third country concept since March 2020. In this sense, the Executive Director and the coordinating officer had the

competence, and even the duty, to prevent the occurrence of the concrete misconduct that appears as an expression of a systemic issue.

In sum, the application of the external appearance test and the internal competence test as established by the CJEU hence shows that the identified typical misconduct on the part of EUAA staff must be attributed to the agency itself. While the external appearance is not entirely unequivocal, as the agency's staff tends to appear as staff of the host member state since the introduction of the embedded model in 2020, the internal competence test clearly shows that, insofar as misconduct is systemic, the EUAA is competent and obliged to prevent it. As regards the remaining doubts concerning the agency's external appearance, it must be taken into consideration that the embedded model structurally blurs legal responsibilities, thereby concealing which entity exercises public authority. The crucial point here is that the EUAA itself has changed its outward appearance so as to not be identifiable by reasonable applicants – and that, therefore, it cannot be allowed to argue in a procedure under Art. 340 para TFEU that is not the correct defendant, as this would not only be abusive and contradictory but also go to the detriment of the telos of Art. 47 ChFR. The concrete circumstances of the case, hence, suggest that the internal competence test must prevail.

3.2 Attribution of Conduct to Frontex

The application of the attribution doctrine to Frontex largely corresponds to the reasoning on the EUAA. Firstly, in applying the external appearance criterion, again, several and partly contradictory circumstances must be considered. To begin with, and unlike in the case of the EUAA, some factors suggest that Frontex's team members appear as staff of their respective home member states. In particular, the Frontex vessels bear the flag of the home state,[74] and Frontex team members usually wear the uniform of their home member state.[75] Other factors, however, as in the case of the EUAA, refer to the host member state. For instance, Frontex team members usually

74 Remarkably, Frontex has not been obliged to disclose under which flag specific vessels are operating, see CJEU, judgement of 27 November 2019, Luisa Izuzquiza and Arne Semsrott v Frontex, T-31/18.

75 Art 82 para 6 Frontex Regulation. Note that the new Frontex standing corps wears Frontex uniforms (see https://frontex.europa.eu/careers/standing-corps/about/) which alters the external appearance significantly.

operate in the presence of Greek authorities, and one might also argue that a reasonable addressee arriving in Greece would expect to encounter Greek officials.

The overwhelming number of factors, however, suggest that a reasonable addressee would perceive the administrative conduct of Frontex team members as the conduct of the agency itself. All deployed Frontex staff are clearly identifiable as working for Frontex and wear a visible personal identification and a blue armband with the insignias of the EU and of the agency.[76] Frontex vessels, albeit under the flag of the home Member States, bear the insignia of the agency, and Frontex offices are clearly marked as such.[77] Further, although the rule is that Frontex should operate in the presence of Greek authorities, the latter may authorise Frontex to act in its absence, notably including the use of force and the carrying and use of weapons,[78] and this option is often used in practice. As regards the operation of Frontex in EU hotspots, it must further be taken into account that asylum seekers will find an EU flag at the entrance of the camp.[79]

A reasonable addressee is hence regularly confronted with an officer who wears the uniform of any member state but presents itself as Frontex and acts independently of Greek authorities, including the use of force. On this basis, a reasonable addressee must assume that public power is exercised towards them by Frontex itself. Although the officers' uniform indicates the home member state, it cannot be expected from reasonable addressees to be able to identify uniforms of all EU member states. Also, anecdotal evidence suggests that reasonable addresses are generally informed that they would be 'checked and controlled' by 'Frontex officers' upon arrival to the EU; asylum seekers arriving at the EU external border are not always aware of which member state they find themselves in, but they are mostly aware of having entered the EU and would, hence, reasonably expect to encounter Frontex.

Lastly, Frontex itself presents the conduct of its teams in the EU hotspots as the agency's conduct and is therefore prevented from invoking that reasonable addressees would perceive it otherwise.[80] Frontex not only de-

76 Art. 82 para 6 Frontex Regulation.
77 Own observation of the author (see introduction, fn. 103).
78 Art. 82 para 4 and para 8 Frontex Regulation.
79 Own observation of the author (see introduction, fn. 103).
80 On the principle of estoppel in EU law see only CJEU, General Court (Second Chamber), judgement of 5 September 2014, Éditions Odile Jacob v Commission, T-471/11, para 52.

picts its conduct as the agency's on its homepage and in public reports. It also presents itself as 'Frontex' in its daily contact with asylum seekers and proactively informs asylum seekers that the conduct of its teams is to be challenged through the 'Frontex' complaints mechanism.[81] Against this background, not even lawyers working in EU hotspots would regularly notice which home member state a particular Frontex officer stems from. Even a legally trained addressee would perceive Frontex staff simply as 'Frontex' – and nothing else can be expected from a reasonable asylum seeker.

Concerning, second, the internal competence criterion, it must be determined whether Frontex, in the specific circumstances of the individual case, had the competence to determine the unlawful conduct or to prevent the unlawful omission at stake.

As mentioned above, the prevailing opinion in legal scholarship stresses that the internal supervisory structure – albeit only concerning regular Frontex deployments – is such that deployed staff, as a general rule, acts under the concrete instructions of the host member state.[82] In practice, however, the exception to that general rule is applied so often that deployed Frontex staff regularly acts without concrete instructions and in the absence of the host member state's authority, notably including the use of force. And in any case, the supervisory structure of the MMST differs from regular teams, so that the reasoning of the prevailing opinion cannot apply.

This being said the decisive point here is that the identified typical misconduct of Frontex in EU hotspots is systemic in nature. As in the case of the EUAA, the key argument is that Frontex – more precisely, the responsible coordinating officer and the Executive Director – are obliged to ensure that Frontex's operations generally comply with EU law. Notwithstanding the host member state's competence to issue daily instructions, systemic fundamental rights violations must be prevented or remedied by Frontex itself. Thus, Frontex has not only the competence but even the obligation to determine a specific misconduct or prevent a specific omission insofar as it appears as an expression of systemic malpractice.

81 Frontex Fundamental Rights Office regularly visits the islands and informs asylum seekers that they should contact the Frontex complaints mechanism in case of misconduct by any Frontex team member, own observation of the author (see introduction, fn. 103).

82 See the literature cited in fn. 2. This conclusion is supported by Art. 43 para 1, Art. 82 para 4 sentence 1 and para 8 sentence 2 Frontex Regulation.

This requires some explanation. The Frontex Regulation clearly formulates that the agency shall 'ensure' the legality of its conduct.[83] Art. 80 para 1 provides that Frontex 'shall guarantee the protection of fundamental rights',[84] and Art. 82 para 3 provides that 'while performing their tasks and exercising their powers, members of the teams shall fully ensure respect for fundamental rights.'[85] Frontex is thus obliged, under Art. 40, 43, 44, 46, 106, 1, 80 Frontex Regulation, Art. 51 para 1 ChFR, to do everything it can within its competences to ensure that the agency complies with EU law.

The competences to exercise the required internal supervision lie with the Executive Director and the coordinating officer, whose tasks and competences largely correspond to those of the EUAA. The Executive Director appoints the coordinating officer who is in charge of monitoring the correct implementation of the operational plan and reports to the Executive Director on this.[86] The coordinating officer supervises the Frontex staff of the MMSTs together with the host member state. The division of tasks between

83 See only Art. 1 para 1, Art 10 para 1 lit s; Art. 38 para 3 lit l; Art 44. para 1and para 3 lit b; Art. 50 para 3 sentence 1 and 2; Art. 80 para 2 and 3 Frontex Regulation: 'In the performance of its tasks, the European Border and Coast Guard shall *ensure* that no person, in contravention of the principle of non-refoulement, be forced to disembark in, forced to enter, or conducted to a country, or be otherwise handed over or returned to the authorities of a country (...). The European Border and Coast Guard shall in all its activities pay particular attention to children's rights and ensure that the best interests of the child are respected.'; Art. 106 para 4 lit b, lit j: The Executive Director shall 'take all necessary steps, including the adoption of internal administrative instructions and the publication of notices, to *ensure* the day-to-day administration and functioning of the Agency in accordance with this Regulation (...) and *ensure* the implementation of the operational plans (...).' (emphasis added).

84 Art. 80 para 1 Frontex Regulation reads: 'The European Border and Coast Guard shall *guarantee* the protection of fundamental rights in the performance of its tasks under this Regulation in accordance with relevant Union law, in particular the Charter, and relevant international law, including the 1951 Convention relating to the Status of Refugees, the 1967 Protocol thereto, the Convention on the Rights of the Child and obligations related to access to international protection, in particular the principle of non-refoulement.' (emphasis added).

85 Art. 81 para 3 Frontex Regulation reads: 'While performing their tasks and exercising their powers, members of the teams shall *fully ensure* respect for fundamental rights and shall comply with Union and international law and the national law of the host Member State.' (emphasis added).

86 Art. 44 Frontex Regulation. Insofar as monitoring fundamental rights compliance is concerned, the coordinating officer shall coordinate closely with the fundamental rights officer, see. Art 44 para 3 lit b. In more detail on the tasks of the coordinating officer see David Fernández-Rojo, *EU Migration Agencies. The Operation and Cooperation of FRONTEX, EASO and EUROPOL*, Edward Elgar 2021, p. 71.

the host member state and the coordinating officer is similar to the case of the EUAA, with the main difference being that the host member state remains involved to some extent.

Crucially, the fact that the host member state and the home member state are involved in the supervisory structure cannot absolve the coordinating officer from its obligations under the Frontex Regulation. As in the case of the EUAA, the coordinating officer is responsible for monitoring the correct implementation of the operational plan, which includes the responsibility to ensure the protection of fundamental rights during Frontex operations.[87] The home member state, in turn, retains the competence to exercise disciplinary power towards seconded or deployed staff and may also receive complaints via the complaints mechanism,[88] but it cannot directly determine the conduct of its deployed staff.[89] Instead, daily instructions are issued by the host member state. These instructions, however, are subject to implicit or explicit approval by the agency: from the outset, the host member state must take into account and follow the agency's views as communicated by the coordinating officer to the greatest extent possible.[90] If the host member state's instructions are not in compliance with the operational plan or violate EU law, the coordinating officer shall immediately inform the Executive Director.[91] The Executive Director shall then assess the situation and, in case the operational is not respected by the host member state, may even unilaterally decide to withdraw the financing or suspend or terminate the operational plan.[92]

Ultimately, responsibility for ensuring that Frontex generally complies with EU law, hence, lies with the Executive Director. According to their mandate as defined in Art. 106, 107 Frontex Regulation, they are responsible for the management of the agency, including for taking decisions related to the operational activities of the agencies, and have the last word on

87 Art. 44 para 1 and 3 Frontex Regulation.

88 See Art. 2 para 21, Art. 43 para 5, Art. 111 para 4, para 7 Frontex Regulation.

89 Except in cases where large vessels are involved, where the home member state retains some control of the vessel's use, see Melanie Fink, *Frontex and Human Rights* (fn. 3), p. 57–58, 70–71.

90 Art. 43 para 2, Art. 44 Frontex Regulation.

91 Art. 43 para 3 Frontex Regulation.

92 Art. 46 para 3 Frontex Regulation: 'The executive director *may*, after informing the Member State concerned, *withdraw the financing of an activity or suspend or terminate it if the operational plan is not respected* by the host Member State.' (emphasis added).

any decisions related to the conduct of Frontex staff in the EU hotspots.[93] In fact, the Executive Director can enforce compliance with EU law in a top-down manner: They instruct the coordinating officer to act in line with EU law and exercise staffing authority, if necessary.[94] Where this is not sufficient, the Executive Director can amend the operational plan, albeit subject to agreement by the host member state,[95] or suspend the implementation of the operational plan as mentioned.[96] In case of serious or persisting fundamental rights violations, the Executive Director can unilaterally suspend or terminate the deployment, according to Art. 46 para 4 Frontex Regulation.[97] In making that decision, the Executive Director shall take into account the opinion of the Fundamental Rights Officer, but they do not depend on the host member state's agreement.

The agency thus has not only the competence but even the obligation to prevent or address systemic malpractice. With regard to the case at hand, this means that the agency – namely its Executive Director and the coordinating officer – is obliged to prevent the occurrence of the identified specific misconduct by preventing breaches at a systemic level. This is well illustrated by Frontex's failures in the context of age assessment and deportations to Türkiye.

As described above, Frontex staff generally conducts age assessment in the context of initial registrations on the basis of visual inspection alone, thereby breaching relevant standards of child protection. Given that this deficient practice is applied systemically, both the coordinating officer and the Executive Director were obliged to address it. As provided for in Art. 80 para 3 Frontex Regulation, Frontex shall take into account the special needs of children and unaccompanied minors and shall pay particular attention to children's rights and ensure that the best interests of the child are respected. Accordingly, the agency is obliged to ensure that its statutory staff receives adequate training, including guidelines for addressing the special

93 As follows from Art. 40, 43, 44, 46, 106 Frontex Regulation.
94 Art. 106 para 4 in particular lit a, lit b, lit j, lit l Frontex Regulation.
95 Art. 38 para 4 Frontex Regulation.
96 Art. 46 para 4 Frontex Regulation, see fn. 70.
97 Art. 46 para 4 Frontex Regulation: 'The executive director *shall*, after consulting the fundamental rights officer and informing the Member State concerned, *withdraw the financing for any activity by the Agency, or suspend or terminate any activity by the Agency*, in whole or in part, if he or she considers that there are *violations of fundamental rights or international protection obligations* related to the activity concerned that are *of a serious nature or are likely to persist*.' (emphasis added).

needs of children, including unaccompanied minors, and to draw up a code of conduct laying down procedures with a particular focus on vulnerable persons, including children and unaccompanied minors.[98] In case that instructions issued by the host member states are unlawful, the coordinating officer is obliged to report to the Executive Director, who must then take the appropriate action.[99] If possible, the Executive Director must settle the matter in cooperation with the host member state, and in case of persisting and serious violations of Art. 24, 41 ChFR, they should decide to withdraw the agency's support. The agency's failures in this regard are well illustrated in case 3.

> Case 3 – Daniat Kidane – Age assessment through visual inspection (attribution to Frontex)
> As established above, Frontex's prima facie age assessments, resulting in the incorrect registration of minors as adults, is not an isolated phenomenon but a systemic flaw in the EU hotspot administration. The malpractice of the agency is widely known and has been brought to the attention of the agency. Therefore, the agency's failure to put an end to this unlawful practice constitutes a failure of the internal supervisory obligations of the Executive Director and the coordinating officer under Art. 106, 1, 44, 46, 80 Frontex Regulation. Insofar as the specific misconduct in the case of Daniat Kidane represents systemic malpractice, Frontex was hence not only competent but, in fact, obliged to prevent the occurrence of that mistake.

Similarly, Frontex also failed to address the issue of unlawful deportations to Türkiye. As follows from Art. 51 para 1 ChFR, and as specified in Art. 1, Art. 43 para 4, Art. 48 para 1, Art. 50 para 1 Frontex Regulation, Frontex is obliged to ensure the performance of return assistance with full respect to fundamental rights and pay particular attention to the rights of vulnerable persons. Accordingly, the Executive Director and the coordinating officer are obliged to ensure that the agency does not provide support with regard to deportation practices that are systemically unlawful. The agency's failures in this regard are well illustrated in case 4.

> *Case 4 – Nabeeh Al Badawi – Return to Türkiye (attribution to Frontex)*
> Mr Al Badawi was returned to Türkiye despite the fact that Türkiye cannot generally be considered a safe third country for asylum seekers

98 Art. 62 para 2, Art. 81 para 1 Frontex Regulation.
99 Art. 43 para 3 and Art. 44 para 3 lit d Frontex Regulation.

and despite the fact that Mr Al Badawi had raised specific concerns substantiating his reasonable fear, based on his previous experience of being deported from Türkiye to Syria, to be subject to chain refoulement in Türkiye. As established above, this was not an exceptional case, but in fact, representative of systemic malpractice, of which Frontex was informed due to previous complaints by other concerned persons through the agency's internal complaints mechanism. Insofar as Frontex's conduct is representative of systemic malpractice, the coordinating officer and the Executive Director were hence obliged to prevent the occurrence of that typical mistake in the case of Mr Al Badawi. In concrete terms, the relevant staff member should have informed the coordinating officer, who then should have raised the matter towards the Executive Director.

In sum, the application of the CJEU's doctrine on attribution hence shows that the identified typical misconduct on the part of Frontex staff operating as part of MMSTs is attributable to the agency itself. As set out, the competence criterion leads to the conclusion that misconduct, insofar as it reflects general malpractice, can and must be prevented by the agency itself. Also, a balanced consideration of all factors relating to the external appearance of Frontex's team members suggests that a reasonable addressee would perceive them as officials of the agency.

3.3 The Agencies' Liability for Inherent Violations

To conclude, the argument made in this chapter has shown that the agencies incur liability for those fundamental rights violations that are inherent in their conduct.

First, both the EUAA's and Frontex's external appearance is such that their conduct must be perceived by a reasonable addressee as the conduct of the respective agency. In the case of the EUAA, doubts remain insofar as the introduction of the embedded model in 2020 has blurred the EUAA's external appearance to the extent that it may now appear as the conduct of the host member state Greece – this, however, cannot be decisive already because the agency could otherwise absolve itself from liability by concealing its outward appearance.

Second, both the EUAA's and Frontex's internal competences are such that the agencies are not only competent but even obliged to prevent systemic malpractice, especially when it consists of systemic and persisting fundamental rights violations. More precisely, the EUAA's respective Frontex's internal supervisory duties, as enshrined in the respective Regulations[100] and ultimately based on Art. 51 para 1 ChFR, oblige the respective coordinating officers and Executive Directors to do everything they can within their competence to ensure that the operations of the respective agency generally comply with EU law. This includes, in case of serious or persisting deficiencies, withdrawing the agency's support.[101] If the respective agency fails to exhaust its options, this constitutes a breach of internal supervisory obligation.

As a result, misconduct of EUAA's and Frontex's staff must be attributed to the respective agency, at least insofar as it is representative of systemic malpractice. Provided that the remaining conditions of public liability are met, the agencies are hence liable under Art. 97 para 4, Art. 98 Frontex Regulation and Art. 66 para 3 EUAA Regulation, respectively. In case the agencies are not solvent, damages can be claimed directly from the Union under Art. 340 para 2 TFEU. The agencies' liability for inherent violations becomes relevant in all cases where their misconduct as such is unlawful, i.e. in cases 1, 2, 3, 4 and 5.

> *Case 1 – Sara Esmaili – Deficient vulnerability assessment – Art. 41 EUAA (liability of the EUAA)*
>
> In the case of Ms Esmaili, the responsible EUAA staff failed to conduct a correct vulnerability interview, and on this basis qualified her and her 9-year-old daughter Ayla as non-vulnerable. Due to the central importance of the vulnerability assessment to the asylum procedure in the EU hotspots, the failure to give Ms Esmaili the opportunity to fully explain her particular situation constitutes not only a violation of her rights under the Asylum Procedures Directive[102] but also a violation of her fundamental right to be heard under Art. 41 para 2 lit a ChFR.
>
> Ms Esmaili's claim for compensation of immaterial damages against the EUAA, and in the alternative against the Union, is successful. The

100 Art. 44, 46, 106, 1, 80 Frontex Regulation; Art. 7, 16–21, 25–29, 46–47, 1 EUAA Regulation; formerly Art. 20, 31, 1 EASO Regulation.

101 Enshrined explicitly in Frontex Regulation Art. 46 para 3, 4 Frontex Regulation; and arguably implicit in Art. 1, 4, 46–47 EUAA Regulation: for the EUAA Executive Director cannot be obliged to command their agency to participate in systemic fundamental rights violations, as this would not only run counter Art. 51 para 1 ChFR but also defeat the very purpose of the existence of the agency.

102 Now the reformed Asylum Procedures Regulation.

violation of Art. 41 ChFR qualifies as misconduct of the agency because, first, the conduct of the relevant staff must have been perceived as conduct of the agency,[103] and second, the agency's coordinating officer and Executive Director were competent and obliged to prevent the agency systemically conducted vulnerability assessments in a deficient manner. The violation of Art. 41 ChFR constitutes a sufficiently serious breach of a rule conferring rights upon individuals.[104] The question of causation does not arise because the violation of the fundamental rights itself constitutes the damage. Thus, the CJEU would have to find that the EUAA has breached fundamental rights. The CJEU could either consider monetary compensation as necessary and oblige the EUAA, and in the alternative, the Union, to pay an appropriate amount of monetary compensation to the applicant, or it could consider the finding of illegality as such as sufficient to remedy the immaterial harm and thus grant a symbolic amount of monetary compensation or even no monetary compensation at all.[105]

Case 2 – Magan Daud – Deficient asylum interview – Art. 41 ChFR (liability of the EUAA)

In the case of Mr Daud, the responsible EUAA staff failed to identify him as vulnerable and also failed to give him sufficient opportunity to express his reasons for seeking international protection. Given the gravity of these procedural errors, not only the rights under the Asylum Procedures Directive but also the right to be heard Art. 41 ChFR para 2 lit. a ChFR is violated.

Mr Daud's claim for compensation against the EUAA, and in the alternative against the Union, is successful. The misconduct must be attributed to the EUAA and constitutes a sufficiently serious breach of a rule of law conferring rights upon individuals. As the violation of the fundamental rights constitutes the damage, the link between misconduct and damage is established. The CJEU would hence have to establish that the EUAA's conduct was unlawful and, optionally, grant appropriate or symbolic monetary compensation.

---

103 The case took place in 2018, i.e. prior to introduction of embedded model (see fn. 53).

104 See chapter 3, 3.3.

105 See chapter 3, 3.4.

Case 3 – Daniat Kidane – Age assessment through visual inspection – Art. 24, 41 ChFR (liability of Frontex)
In the case of Daniat Kidane, the Frontex staff responsible for first identification failed to conduct a correct age assessment, which amounted to a violation of her fundamental rights under Art. 24, 41 ChFR.
Her claim for compensation against Frontex, and in the alternative against the Union, is successful. The misconduct must be attributed to Frontex because, first, the conduct of the relevant staff must have been perceived as the conduct of the agency by a reasonable addressee, and second, the agency's coordinating officer and Executive Director were competent and obliged to prevent that the agency systemically engages in unlawful age assessment practices. As the misconduct consists in a fundamental rights violation, it qualifies as a sufficiently serious breach of a rule of law. The fundamental rights violation constitutes the damage so that the question of causation does not arise. The CJEU would hence have to establish that Frontex's conduct was unlawful and, depending on whether monetary compensation is deemed necessary, grant appropriate, symbolic or even no monetary compensation.

Case 4 – Nabeeh Al Badawi – Return to Türkiye – Art. 4, 18, 19 ChFR (liability of Frontex)
In the case of Mr Al Badawi, the Frontex staff responsible for escorting deportations failed to intervene during the process of deportation or to raise his concerns about the legality of the deportation to his coordinating officer. Considering the gravity of these procedural mistakes, which resulted directly in a violation of the non-refoulement principle, Frontex's failures constitute a violation of Mr Al Badawi's procedural rights under Art. 4, 18, 19 ChFR.
Mr Al Badawi's claim for compensation against Frontex, in the alternative against the Union, is successful. As the misconduct reflects systemic malpractice, it must be attributed to Frontex. The fundamental rights violation qualifies as a sufficiently serious breach of a rule of law and constitutes damage. The CJEU would hence have to establish that Frontex's conduct was unlawful and, optionally, grant appropriate or symbolic compensation.

Case 5 – Kareem Rashid – Limbo situation – Art. 41 ChFR (liability of the EUAA)
In the case of Mr Rashid, the EUAA staff responsible for conducting asylum interviews failed to take into account that readmissions to Türkiye

had been halted. Instead, they applied a standard reasoning and on this basis considered Türkiye as safe for Mr Rashid. Given the gravity of these procedural mistakes, the failure to apply the safe third country concept correctly constitutes a violation of Mr Rashid's rights under Art. 41 ChFR.

His claim for compensation against the EUAA, and in the alternative against the Union, is successful. The misconduct must be attributed to the EUAA and constitutes a sufficiently serious breach of a rule of law conferring rights upon individuals. The fundamental rights violation constitutes the damage so that the link between misconduct and damage is established. The CJEU would hence have to establish that the EUAA's conduct was unlawful and, optionally, grant appropriate or symbolic monetary compensation.

Chapter 5: Causation of Fundamental Rights Violations by the EU

This last chapter continues the application of the action for damages to the case of the EU hotspots and addresses the doctrinal matters related to causation. The main question here is under which conditions the EU's administrative misconduct – i.e. the EUAA's and Frontex's informal recommendation or the European Commission's failure to adequately exercise its supervisory obligations – is causal for resulting fundamental rights violations. The first section explains why causation is difficult to establish in multi-actor settings (1). The second and third sections then provide a detailed analysis of the relevant case law. This shows that the CJEU's case law has developed from a binding/non-binding dichotomy towards a more flexible approach. Regarding administrative support, the 1994 judgement in the case of *KYDEP* represents the decisive turning point.[1] With this judgement, the CJEU established that the EU's administrative support is causal when it meets a certain threshold of bindingness (2). Regarding administrative supervision, the CJEU similarly held in its 2016 judgment in *Ledra*[2] that the EU's supervisory measures are causal when they are sufficiently binding (3). The fourth section defines the threshold of bindingness more precisely. Based on the case law analysis, it shows that the required 'bindingness-threshold' is met when the EU's conduct is 'de facto binding' upon national authorities: In these cases, the EU predetermines the national decision (4). The last section applies these findings to the case at hand, leading to the conclusion that the relevant conduct by the EUAA, Frontex and the Commission reaches the threshold of de facto bindingness. In sum, the chapter argues that the EU and its bodies incur liability for fundamental rights violations in the EU hotspots that result from the agencies' or the Commission's misconduct (5).

---

1 CJEU, Court, judgement of 15 September 1994, Koinopraxia Enoseon Georgikon Synetairismon Diacheiriseos Enchorion Proionton *(KYDEP)* v Council of the European Union, C-146/91.

2 CJEU, Court (Grand Chamber), judgement of 20 September 2016, Ledra Advertising Ltd et al v European Commission et al, Joined Cases C-8/15 P to C-10/15 P.

1 Causation in Multi-Actor Situations

To substantiate its argument, this chapter conducts a detailed analysis of the case law on causation.

1.1 Failure of the Conventional Causation Criterion

This is necessary because, in the specific context of the integrated administration, the CJEU's well-established general formula does not lead to unequivocal results. According to this formula, causation requires that the conduct is a *condition sine qua non* to the damage and that there is a sufficiently direct link between the conduct and the damage.[3] Where several actors are involved, however, the conduct of each involved actor typically constitutes a *condition sine qua non* to the damage. The criterion of the sufficiently direct link leaves ample room for interpretation already where only one actor is involved and is – as such – simply too vague to determine the contribution of which of several involved actors shall be considered as causal.[4] These shortcomings of the conventional causation test are well illustrated in case 1.

> *Case 1 – Sara Esmaili – Futile Application of the Conventional Causation Test*
> In the case of Ms Esmaili and her daughter, the failure of the EUAA to conduct a correct vulnerability assessment clearly constitutes a *condition sine qua non* for their subsequent stay in the EU hotspots, i.e. for the resulting violation of Art. 4 ChFR. The same, however, holds true for the Commission's failure to adequately supervise as well for the host member state's decision to consider Ms Esmaili as non-vulnerable. If the

3 See only CJEU, Court (Fourth Chamber), judgement of 18 March 2010, Trubowest Handel GmbH and Viktor Makarov v Council of the European Union and European Commission, C-419/08 P, para 53. For a detailed analysis see Martin Weitenberg, *Der Begriff der Kausalität in der haftungsrechtlichen Rechtsprechung der Unionsgerichte*, Nomos 2014, p 317 referring to these two criteria as establishing factual and juridical causation.

4 Uwe Säuberlich, *Die außervertragliche Haftung im Gemeinschaftsrecht. Eine Untersuchung der Mehrpersonenverhaltnisse*, Springer 2005, p. 76–79; similarly A.G. Toth, „The Concepts of Damage and Causality as Elements of Non-Contractual Liability", in Ton Heukels, Alison McDonnell (ed.), *The Action for Damages in Community Law*, Wolters Kluwer 1997, p. 179-198, p. 191–198. On the function of the sufficiently-direct-link criterion in the context of multi-actor situations see below fn. 161 et seq.

EUAA had acted correctly, if the Commission had adequately exercised supervision, or if the host member state had issued a correct vulnerability decision, Ms Esmaili would not have been exposed to the reception conditions in the EU hotspot camp so that her right under Art. 4 ChFR would not have been violated. At the same time, all three contributions have a sufficiently direct link to the damage. The conventional definition of the causation criterion does hence not lead any further.

The legal question that must be analysed can hence be formulated more precisely as to whether the causal link between an earlier non-formally binding administrative support issued by one actor, e.g. a recommendation to take a certain decision, is 'broken' by a later formally-binding decision issued by the other actor.

Given that the CJEU's jurisprudence on that matter is extensive and partly contradictory, an extensive discussion has emerged in legal scholarship, which essentially aims to develop a coherent doctrine on causation by making sense of the case law.[5] Contributing to that discussion, the following argues that the CJEU has developed its approach to causation in multi-actor constellations in two major steps. In the first step, the strict binding/non-binding dichotomy was abandoned. While earlier jurisprudence considered bindingness as a precondition for certain conduct to be causal, the CJEU has gradually let go of that requirement.[6] The second step, then, was to replace the bindingness-criterion with a more flexible approach according to which causation requires a certain degree or threshold of bindingness.

5 See only Timo Rademacher, *Realakte im Rechtsschutzsystem der Europäischen Union*, Mohr Siebeck 2014, p. 264–288; Melanie Fink, „EU Liability for Contributions to Member States' Breaches of EU Law", *Common Market Law Review* 56 (2019), p. 1227–1264; Uwe Säuberlich, *Die außervertragliche Haftung im Gemeinschaftsrecht* (fn. 4), p. 31–37, 72–181, and passim; Mariolina Eliantonio, „Judicial Review in an Integrated Administration: the Case of 'Composite Procedures'", *Review of European Administrative Law* 7 (2015), p. 65–102.

6 Insofar, the reading proposed here is in line with the prevailing interpretation. Although some contributions interpret more recent case law as a return to the strict non-binding/binding dichotomy (see fn. 80 et seq.), most contributions agree that bindingness is no longer a precondition for causation. The currently most prominent version of this opinion is probably Melanie Fink, „EU Liability for Contributions to Member States' Breaches of EU Law" (fn. 5). While her contribution is based on the alternative approach adopting a broad understanding of attribution (see chapter 3, 5.2.), the following shows that an analysis based on the traditional approach leads to the same conclusion.

1.2 Why *WS et al. vs. Frontex* is No Counterargument

The following reconstruction of the CJEU's case law will show that the General Court's recent decision in the case of *WS et al.* is not convincing insofar as the court's argument on causation is concerned.[7] The General Court, in essence, repeats the standard answer of Frontex itself to allegations of misconduct. The point is as commonplace as it is inconsistent, suggesting that the causal link between Frontex's conduct and the resulting damage is not established because Frontex 'only assists'. In other words, the argument is that Frontex does not have the competence to issue return decisions, and therefore, its operations cannot be considered causal for damages resulting from the execution of the deportations.

Based on the CJEU's own doctrine, as established in more detail in the following, the General Court's argument is not tenable.[8] The court made two basic mistakes. First, it failed to define Frontex's misconduct. Instead of beginning its assessment with the identification of what exactly Frontex did wrong, the General Court jumped directly to the criterion of the causal link[9] and based its assessment of causation on a general reference of 'Frontex misconduct before, during and after the deportation'.[10] This is problematic because a meaningful evaluation of causation necessarily presupposes a precise definition of the conduct at stake. Although the conditions for EU liability are cumulative, as the General Court rightly stresses,[11] it seems logically impossible to assess the causal link between

7 CJEU, General Court (Sixth Chamber), judgement of 6 September 2023, WS et al v Frontex, T-600/21. The following paragraph is based on Catharina Ziebritzki, „A Hidden Success. Why the EU General Court's Frontex Judgment is Better Than it Seems", Verfassungsblog of 13/10/23. As argued in chapter 3, 3, *WS et al* is convincing insofar as it deems the action for damages admissible. When it comes to the merits, however, the judgment remains doctrinally weak – this is the part of the judgement that justifies the harsh scholarly criticism.

8 As shown by Joyce De Coninck, „Shielding Frontex. On the EU General Court's "WS and others v Frontex"", Verfassungsblog of 09/09/2023; Christopher Paskowski, „Verwaltung ohne Verantwortung. Zur Abweisung der ersten Schadensersatzklage gegen Frontex durch das EuG", Verfassungsblog of 27/09/2023.

9 CJEU, judgement of 6 September 2023, WS et al v Frontex, T-600/21 (fn. 7), para 55.

10 Ibid., para 57.

11 Ibid., para 53.

the conduct and the damage without prior identification of the relevant conduct.[12]

Second, the General Court started its analysis of causation with the wrong question. Instead of asking whether Frontex's conduct properly defined was causal for the resulting damage, the General Court implicitly asked which conduct was causal for the resulting damage.[13] It then concluded that the national decision to reject the applicants' asylum claims and to issue their deportation orders was causal for the deportation.[14] While this statement is correct in itself, it ignores what has been explained above: there can be multiple causes for one result, i.e., both a national administrative decision and EU administrative support can be causal for the resulting damage. Based on its wrong assumption, however, the General Court then observed that Frontex was not competent to issue the relevant administrative decisions and, from this, concluded that Frontex's conduct could hence not have been causal.[15] Again, the argument here misses the point. While it is, of course, true that Frontex's competences are limited, this, as such, does not say anything about whether its factual conduct is causal for the resulting damage.

As WS et al. have appealed the General Court's decision, it will now be up to the Court of Justice to make things right.[16] The Court of Justice will have to first clearly define Frontex's relevant conduct. Second, it will have to ask the right question on causation, namely whether Frontex's participation in the process of deportation was causal for the damage resulting from the deportation. This question will have to be answered on the basis of an extensive case law analysis, which – as this chapter shows – should lead to the conclusion that Frontex's conduct is causal for the resulting damage as soon as it is de facto binding on national authorities.

---

12 This is why this study proceeds as it does: firstly, to define the relevant conduct, and then, secondly, assess the questions of causation.

13 CJEU, judgement of 6 September 2023, WS et al v Frontex, T-600/21 (fn. 7), para 62.

14 Ibid., para 64 and 65.

15 Ibid., para 66.

16 As Gareth Davies, „The General Court finds Frontex not liable for helping with illegal pushbacks: it was just following orders", europeanlawblog of 11 Sept 2023 put it, 'things do not look good for Frontex' and 'the Court of Justice must now sort out this mess on appeal'.

2 Doctrine on Causation I: Lessons from KYDEP

As regards non-formally binding administrative support provided here by the EUAA and Frontex, the key question is whether support can be considered causal for resulting fundamental rights violations and hence trigger EU liability under Art. 340 para 2 TFEU, despite the fact that the relevant violations are ultimately evoked by formally-binding decisions of national authorities.

This question actually consists of two. The first is whether the EU can incur liability for administrative *support*, i.e., inter-administrative conduct. This question relates to the tension between the separation principle and administrative integration and arises whenever the Union leaves it to a member state to issue the formally-binding decision towards an individual. The second question is whether the EU can incur liability for acts that are *non-formally binding*. This question relates to the broader issue of legal protection against factual acts,[17] and arises whenever the Union refrains from issuing formally-binding decisions but nonetheless determines the outcome of an administrative procedure. While these two issues are obviously closely interrelated, keeping the distinction in mind is useful for the sake of a clear argument.

The CJEU's doctrine on both aspects has evolved considerably in recent decades. In its earlier jurisprudence, the CJEU excluded liability for administrative support as well as for non-formally binding conduct. While this approach provided legal clarity,[18] it was increasingly at odds with administrative reality and hindered individual judicial protection. Taking into account scholarly criticism, the CJEU hence gradually adjusted its jurisprudence. In a first step, it recognised that administrative support, at least when formally-binding, can trigger liability. In a second step, with its landmark decision in the 1994 judgement on *KYDEP*,[19] it recognised that this also applies when administrative support is non-formally binding. In a third step, the CJEU then confirmed with more recent judgements, such as

17 On this question in detail Timo Rademacher, „Factual Administrative Conduct and Judicial Review in EU Law", *European Review of Public Law* 30 (2017), p. 399–435; Napoleon Xanthoulis, „Administrative factual conduct: Legal effects and judicial control in EU law", *Review of European Administrative Law* 12 (2019), p. 39-73.

18 Daniel Thym, European Migration Law, 2023, p. 219 still stresses that 'judges have held repeatedly that preparatory acts are controlled at a subsequent stage, when reviewing the legality of the final outcome of the procedure'.

19 CJEU, judgement of 15 September 1994, *KYDEP*, C-146/91 (fn. 1).

Ledra and *Bourdouvali*, that the '*KYDEP* doctrine', as it is called here, is still applicable today.

2.1 Liability for Administrative Support

In its early case law, the CJEU applied the separation principle in a strict manner and argued that inter-administrative conduct by EU bodies could not incur EU liability already due to the lack of external legal effects towards an individual. This doctrine was prominently spelt out in the judgement of *Sucrimex* of 1980.[20] *Sucrimex* forms part of a series of similar cases concerning the regulation of the sugar and milk market. *Interagra* of 1982[21] and *Société pour l'Exportation des Sucres* of 1987[22] also form part of this series, to mention only the most prominent examples.[23] In all these cases, import-export companies had applied to national authorities for export refunds. The national authorities rejected these applications based on instructions that the European Commission had sent via telex. As a result, the companies suffered financial losses. They then claimed damages from

20 CJEU, judgement of 27 March 1980, Sucrimex S. A. and Westzucker GmbH v Commission of the European Communities, 133/79.

21 CJEU, Court, judgement of 10 June 1982, Compagnie Interagra S.A. v Commission of the European Communities, 217/81.

22 CJEU, Court, judgement of 10 May 1987, Société pour l'Exportation des Sucres S.A. v Commission of the European Communities, 132/77.

23 Timo Rademacher, *Realakte im Rechtsschutzsystem der Europäischen Union* (fn. 5), p. 266–267 refers to these judgements as a 'first generation' of case law. For further similar cases see Melanie Fink, „EU Liability for Contributions to Member States' Breaches of EU Law" (fn. 5), p. 1240. It must be noted here that also *IBM* (CJEU, Court, judgment of 11 November 1981, International Business Machines Corporation (IBM) v Commission of the European Communities, 60/81) and *Borelli* (CJEU, Court, judgement of 3 December 1992, Oleificio Borelli SpA v Commission of the European Communities, C-97/91) are often cited as landmark cases for the CJEU's early doctrine of a strict binding/non-binding dichotomy. A closer look, however, shows that these judgements do not form part of the *Sucrimex* doctrine as understood here. The CJEU's main argument in these cases was that once the Commission's letter at stake had left its sphere of influence, the Commission might still change its opinion before the issuance of the actual decision and that *therefore*, the letter did not have binding effects on the national authority (see only CJEU, IBM, para 9). This shows that the CJEU's reasoning in *IBM* already departs from *Sucrimex* insofar as the CJEU argues that a lack of formal bindingness does not per se lead to a lack of bindingness.

the Union, arguing that the Commission's telex had caused the damage.[24] In all these cases, the CJEU rejected the claim for damages as inadmissible, arguing that 'internal co-operation between the Commission and the national bodies (...) as a general rule (...) cannot make the Community liable to individuals'.[25] Instead, the CJEU argued that the concerned companies should seek legal protection against the national administrative decision before national courts.[26]

In the late 1980s, the *Sucrimex* doctrine was met with fierce scholarly criticism. In a nutshell, the doctrine was seen as insufficient in light of the principle that any Union conduct must be subject to legal review, as spelt out in *Les Verts* in 1986.[27] More precisely, the critique focused on the two aspects mentioned above. The first point of critique was that inter-administrative conduct should be considered as a potential trigger for liability. The CJEU's interpretation of the separation principle was criticised as overly formalistic. The *Sucrimex* doctrine was seen as inappropriate given the increasing integration of the administration,[28] as the traditional judicial habit of focusing on formal administrative decisions impaired the right to an effective remedy in the context of an integrated administration.[29] The second aspect of the criticism was that non-formally binding conduct should be considered as a potential trigger for liability. In this regard, the main argument was that the CJEU attached too much importance to the criterion of legal bindingness. In particular, the *Sucrimex* doctrine was considered inappropriate in cases in which non-formally binding support reduced the room for manoeuvre of the decision-issuing actor in a legally relevant manner, thereby de facto determining the decision.[30]

---

24 CJEU, Court, judgement of 27 March 1980, Sucrimex, 133/79 (fn. 20), para 9; CJEU, Court, judgement of 10 May 1987, Exportation des Sucres, 132/77 (fn. 22), para 7–9.

25 CJEU, Court, judgement of 27 March 1980, Sucrimex, 133/79 (fn. 20), para 22; CJEU, Court, judgement of 10 June 1982, Interagra, 217/81 (fn. 21), para 8.

26 CJEU, Court, judgement of 27 March 1980, Sucrimex, 133/79 (fn. 20), para 24.

27 CJEU, Court, judgement of 23 April 1986, Parti écologiste 'Les Verts' v European Parliament, 294/83, para 23.

28 Filipe Brito Bastos, „Derivate Illegality in European Composite Administrative Procedures", *Common Market Law review* 55 (2018), p. 101–134, note 57 to 60 with further references to contributions criticizing the CJEU's early approach.

29 Quoted literally from Giacinto Della Cananea, „The European Union's Mixed Administrative Proceedings", *Law and Contemporary Problems* 68 (2004), p. 187–218, p. 210 with reference to *Borelli.*

30 Astrid Czaja, *Die außervertragliche Haftung der EG für ihre Organe*, Nomos 1996, p. 139–132. By contrast Peter Oliver, „Joint Liability of the Community and the

Both points of critique were addressed by the CJEU. As regards the response to the first criticism, the landmark case was the 1986 judgement in *Krohn*.[31] With *Krohn,* the CJEU partially overturned its *Sucrimex* doctrine and henceforth applied the separation principle in a less strict manner. Departing from its earlier jurisprudence, the CJEU now held that inter-administrative conduct as such can incur liability.[32] The new *Krohn* doctrine was confirmed in subsequent judgements such as *Emerald Meats* of 1993.[33]

This change in the CJEU's doctrine is remarkable because the facts of *Krohn* are very similar to those of the *Sucrimex* cases. The judgment concerned a dispute between the import-export company Krohn and the Commission. Krohn sought compensation for damages incurred as a result of the refusal of the national authority to grant import licences. Compensation was sought from the Commission because national authorities were acting upon instruction by the Commission.[34] As elaborated by Advocate General *Mancini* in his opinion on the admissibility of the claim, the court had two options: it could either stick to its formal understanding of the separation principle or adopt a more substantial understanding and determine whether the fault actually lies with the Commission or the national authority. While Mancini acknowledged the scholarly criticism of the former option as overly formalistic, he argued that, for the sake of legal clarity, this approach should nonetheless be given preference.[35] The CJEU instead opted for the substantial approach. Unlike Mancini, the court stressed that the national body had acted in order to ensure the implementation of Community rules. It further held that if the unlawful conduct is 'in fact

Member States", in Ton Heukels, Alison McDonnell (ed.), *The Action for Damages in Community Law*, Wolters Kluwer 1997, p. 306 justifies the judgements in *Sucrimex* and *Interagra* with the argument that the actual loss was borne by the pertinent EU fund anyways. Obviously, this argument does not persist in the context of a violation of fundamental rights.

31 CJEU, judgement of 26 February 1986, Krohn, 175/84.

32 Thereby transferring the doctrine developed in the context of legislative acts, namely, that the actor from which the unlawfulness emanates shall be liable (see for instance CJEU, Court, judgement of 19 May 1992, J.M. Mulder et al v Council of the European Communities et al, Joined Cases C-104/89 and C-37/90, para 16), to the context of administrative acts.

33 CJEU, Court, judgement of 20 January 1993, Emerald Meats Limited v Commission of the European Communities, Joined Cases C-106/90, C-317/90 and C-129/91, in particular para 35–38.

34 CJEU, Court, judgement of 26 February 1986, Krohn, 175/84 (fn. 31), para 1–14.

35 Opinion of Advocate General Mancini, 19 November 1985, Krohn, 175/84 (fn. 31), p. 760–761.

the responsibility of a community institution', the Union's support, and not the national decision, ought to be considered as causal to the damage.[36] In applying this new doctrine to the case at hand, the court then argued that the national authority was legally bound to comply with the Commission's instructions and that, therefore, the Commission's conduct was to be considered as relevant misconduct.

Krohn thus overturned *Sucrimex* only insofar as inter-administrative conduct is formally binding upon the national authority. In other words, *Krohn* addressed only the first point of criticism. It did take into account the increasing integration of the administration, but left the overemphasis on the criterion of legal bindingness intact.[37]

2.2 Liability for Non-Formally Binding Conduct

With its judgement in *KYDEP* of 1994, the court eventually addressed the second criticism and held that non-formally binding inter-administrative conduct could also trigger liability, thereby fully overturning its *Sucrimex* doctrine. This turn in case law was consequential, given that the CJEU had, in previous years, gradually turned away from its overemphasis on legal bindingness. Since the 1970s, the CJEU has consistently ruled that factual acts of the Union towards individuals can trigger liability[38] and thereby

36 CJEU, Court, judgement of 26 February 1986, Krohn, 175/84 (fn. 31), para 19: 'Where, as in this case, the decision adversely affecting the applicant was adopted by a national body acting in order to ensure the implementation of Community rules, it is necessary, in order to establish the jurisdiction of the Court, to *determine whether the unlawful conduct* alleged (...) *is in fact a responsibility of a Community institution* and cannot be attributed to the national body.' (emphasis added). Given the CJEU's inconsistent terminology, it is not decisive that reference is made here to attribution instead of to causation, see chapter 3, 5.1.

37 For the case at hand, however, the second point is of particular importance because the EU's conduct in the EU hotspots generally lacks formal bindingness, see chapter 1, 4; chapter 2, 1 and 2.

38 CJEU, Court, judgement of 28 May 1970, Denise Richez-Paris et al v Commission of the European Communities, Joined Cases 16/69 et al, para 32; CJEU, Court, judgement of 9 July 1970, Fiehn, 23/69, para 19 et seq. (failure to provide information as legally required); CJEU, Court, judgement of 10 July 1969, Claude Sayag et al v Jean-Pierre Leduc et al, 9/69, para 5, 11; CJEU, judgement of 7 November 1985, Adams, 145/83 (non-compliance with duty of confidentiality); CJEU, judgement of 8 October 1986, Leussink, Joined cases 169/83 and 136/84, para 15 et seq. (mistakes in maintenance of the service vehicle); CJEU, Court, judgement of 17 March 1993, Moat

recognised that legal bindingness is not a prerequisite for causation. With its *Grimaldi* judgement of 1989, the CJEU also recognised that non-formally binding support could have legal effects on the national judiciary.[39]

With *KYDEP*, the recognition of the legal relevance of non-formally binding conduct was then extended to the specific context of the integrated administration. Again, this change in the doctrine is particularly remarkable because the facts in *KYDEP* were parallel to the *Sucrimex* cases in that the applicant sought compensation from the Union for damages suffered allegedly as a result of non-formally binding inter-administrative conduct by the Commission. The dispute in *KYDEP* arose in the aftermath of the Chernobyl disaster in April 1986. *KYDEP* was a cooperative established under Greek law for the purpose of buying large quantities of cereals and vegetables for stocking and reselling. The Community, in reaction to the Chernobyl disaster, had progressively adopted rules concerning maximum radioactivity tolerances: In May 1986, a Regulation governing imports from third countries was adopted. As regards exports, however, a Regulation was adopted only in November 1988. Thus, at the time of the 1986 harvest, no Community rule was in place governing exports of agricultural products originating in the member states. Therefore, the Commission sent a telex to member states, pointing out that the common rules for export refunds were to be interpreted in light of the May 1986 Regulation so that refunds by the European Agricultural Guarantee Fund would not be granted for products which are not merchantable owing to an elevated level of radioactivity. As a consequence, Hellenic authorities refused to grant refunds to *KYDEP*,

---

v Commission, T-13/92; CJEU, judgement of 11 October 1995, Baltsavias, Joined Cases T-39/93 and T-554/93 (both mistakes in personal files); CJEU, Court, judgement of 19 October 1995, Dieter Obst et al, T-562/93 (mistakes in the preparation and implementation of an appointment decision).

39 CJEU, Court, judgement of 13 December 1989, Salvatore Grimaldi v Fonds des maladies professionnelles, C-322/88, para 19. Note that the combination of *Grimaldi* and *Sucrimex* led to a problematic legal protection gap. According to *Sucrimex*, it was for national courts to provide legal protection against a national decision, also when this decision was issued on the basis of the Commission's instructions. Now, according to *Grimaldi*, national courts were obliged to assume that the Commission's legal opinion is correct, which means that the action against the national decision will most likely be rejected. This result is highly problematic and arguably even amounts to a violation of the right of an effective remedy as enshrined in Art. 13 ECHR and Art. 47 ChFR, see Timo Rademacher, *Realakte im Rechtsschutzsystem der Europäischen Union* (fn. 5), p. 267; Astrid Czaja, *Die außervertragliche Haftung der EG für ihre Organe* (fn. 30), p. 130.

meaning that *KYDEP*, had to bear the financial losses resulting from the buying in of the contaminated 1986 harvest. *KYDEP*, then sought damages from the Union, arguing that the Commission's telex was unlawful and had caused the financial losses.[40]

The CJEU began its argument by clarifying that the telex does not constitute a formally-binding administrative decision.[41] However, the CJEU then continued that the member states were at risk of reduced access to EU funding had they ignored the Commission's interpretation in the telex. For this reason, the court considered it 'necessary to examine the alleged incompatibility of the Commission's telex with Community law'.[42] In the concrete case, the CJEU came to the conclusion that the Commission's conduct was lawful and, therefore, dismissed the applicant's claim for compensation.[43] The crucial point here is that the CJEU in *KYDEP* finally departed from the traditional habit of focusing on formal bindingness and instead provided a more appropriate understanding of individual legal protection in the context of the integrated administration. In order to determine whether the Union's inter-administrative conduct is causal for the resulting damage, the CJEU assessed to what extent the Union's conduct is binding upon the national authority. In this assessment, the court took into consideration the factual and legal circumstances of the individual case and emphasised that financial incentives can have effects similar to bindingness. With *KYDEP*, the court thus fully replaced its earlier strict binding/non-binding dichotomy with the understanding of bindingness as a matter of degree.[44]

Lastly, and with a view to the case at hand, it is worth noting that the facts in the case of *KYDEP* bear remarkable parallels to the case of the EU hotspots. Both cases stem from a crisis context in which the Union legislator was not yet able to react; and in both cases, the Commission stepped in with non-formally binding instructions effectively guiding member states' conduct, including through financial pressure.[45]

---

40 CJEU, judgement of 15 September 1994, *KYDEP*, C-146/91 (fn. 1), para 1–8.

41 Ibid., para 23–25.

42 Ibid., para 26–30.

43 Ibid., para 81.

44 Similarly, albeit only with regard to interpretative communications by the Commission, Timo Rademacher, *Realakte im Rechtsschutzsystem der Europäischen Union* (fn. 5), p. 37 with further references in note 126.

45 See chapter 3, in particular 2.3.

2.3 Confirmation of the '*KYDEP* Doctrine'

Having shown that the CJEU has recognised in *KYDEP* that non-formally binding inter-administrative conduct by EU bodies can trigger EU liability, the remainder of this section argues that this doctrine is still good law. This claim is relatively uncontroversial only insofar as a first post-*KYDEP* generation is concerned.[46] As regards the further development of the case law, there is quite some discussion. While some argue that it is yet to be awaited whether the CJEU will confirm *KYDEP*,[47] others argue that the CJEU has already returned to the strict binding/non-binding dichotomy.[48] Here, it is argued instead that the CJEU has consistently confirmed the *KYDEP* doctrine with a second and a third post-*KYDEP* generation.[49] As will be shown, the case law is indeed consistent insofar as the CJEU considers inter-administrative conduct as a potential trigger for liability, provided that the conduct meets the threshold of de facto bindingness.[50]

---

46 Uwe Säuberlich, *Die außervertragliche Haftung im Gemeinschaftsrecht* (fn. 4), p. 8 raises doubts, referring to CJEU, Court of First Instance, judgment of 15 September 1998, Oleifici Italiani SpA et al v Commission, T-54/96, para 67, which leads him to conclude that the jurisprudence is contradictory.

47 Werner Berg, „Art. 340 AEUV", in Ulrich Becker, Armin Hatje, Johann Schoo, Jürgen Schwarze (ed.), *EU-Kommentar*, Nomos 2019, para 25.

48 Timo Rademacher, *Realakte im Rechtsschutzsystem der Europäischen Union* (fn. 5), p. 271–274.

49 Note that, in terms of results, the interpretation proposed here agrees with the interpretation proposed by Melanie Fink insofar as the case law is read as establishing that the Union can incur liability for non-formally binding inter-administrative conduct. The difference only lies in the doctrinal reconstruction (see chapter 3, 5). From the perspective of the alternative approach, *KYDEP* appears as an 'anormal' exception. Consequentially, the third post-*KYDEP* generation, in particular *Bourdouvali*, is considered as a return to the 'normal' binding/non-binding dichotomy – however, and this is crucial, in the context of *primary* liability (see Melanie Fink, „EU Liability for Contributions to Member States' Breaches of EU Law" (fn. 5), p. 1242–1243, 1277 – however noting at p. 1244 that *Bourdouvali* 'somewhat left the door ajar' to consider 'factually binding conduct' for the purpose of attributing conduct to the EU body; ibid, *Frontex and Human Rights. Responsibility in 'Multi-Actor Situations' under the ECHR and EU Public Liability Law*, Oxford University Press 2018, p. 10, 256–257). From the perspective of the traditional approach adopted here, however, *KYDEP* and also *Bourdouvali* appear as confirming the rule.

50 As here Martin Gellermann, „Art. 340 AEUV ", in Rudolf Streinz (ed.), *EUV/AEUV*, C.H. Beck 2018, para 16; Matthias Ruffert, „AEUV Art. 340 (ex-Art. 288 EGV)", in Matthias Ruffert, Christian Calliess (ed.), *EUV/AEUV*, C.H. Beck 2022, para 11 (explicitly welcoming that development); Marc Jacob, Matthias Kottmann, „Art. 340 AEUV", in Eberhard Grabitz, Meinhard Hilf, Martin Nettesheim (ed.), *Das Recht der*

a *The First Post-KYDEP Generation – from Geotronics to Camós Grau*

The first post-*KYDEP* generation consists of judgements such as *Geotronics* of 1994,[51] *Oleifici Italiani* of 1998,[52] *New Europe Consulting* of 1999,[53] *Malagutti-Vezinhet* of 2004[54] and *Camós Grau* of 2006.[55] This first generation is important because it shows that the judgement in *KYDEP* was not exceptional crisis jurisprudence in the specific context of the Chernobyl disaster but instead represented a genuine change in the CJEU's doctrine.

In *Geotronics*, the CJEU, for the first time, applied the *KYDEP* doctrine to a non-crisis context. The dispute arose in the context of the so-called PHARE program that provided subsidies to Hungary and Poland.[56] Just as in *KYDEP*, the national administration, upon instructions by the Commission, issued a decision to the detriment of the applicant, and the applicant sought damages from the Union. In line with *KYDEP*, the CJEU examined the legality of the Commission's telex, remarkably, without even considering the argument that the telex could not have caused the damage due to a lack of formal bindingness.[57]

With its judgement in *Oleifici Italiani*, the CJEU again confirmed the *KYDEP* doctrine and specified how the degree of bindingness is to be determined. The case arose in the context of the Community's financial support for olive oil production. The applicants were entrusted by the Italian intervention agency with storage and carrying out intervention operations on the Italian oil market. Between 1991 and 1993, the applicants stored several thousand tons of olive oil. According to the Community support system in

Europäischen Union C.H. Beck 2023, para 65; Foroud Shirvani, „Haftungsprobleme im Europäischen Verwaltungsverbund", *Europarecht* 46 (2011), p. 619-635, p. 619.

51 CJEU, Court of First Instance, judgement of 26 October 1995, Geotronics SA v Commission of the European Communities (Geotronics I), T-185/94; confirmed by Court, judgement of 22 April 1997, Geotronics SA v Commission of the European Communities (Geotronics II), C-395/95 P.

52 CJEU, judgment of 15 September 1998, Oleifici Italiani, T-54/96 (fn. 46).

53 CJEU, Court of First Instance, judgement of 9 July 1999, New Europe Consulting Ltd v Commission of the European Communities, T-231/97.

54 CJEU, Court of First Instance, judgement of 10 March 2004, Malagutti-Vezinhet SA v Commission of the European Communities, T-177/02.

55 CJEU, Court of First Instance, judgement of 6 April 2006, Manel Camós Grau v Commission of the European Communities, T-309/03.

56 CJEU, judgement of 26 October 1995, Geotronics I, T-185/94 (fn. 51), para 1–16.

57 Ibid., para 37. As in *KYDEP*, the action was dismissed because the Commission's support was lawful, see CJEU, judgement of 26 October 1995, Geotronics I, T-185/94 (fn. 51), para 57.

place, the national intervention agency was to be refunded by the European Agricultural Fund. In the case of Oleifici Italiani, however, the Agricultural Fund found that a large percentage of the oil was not of the declared quality. Therefore, the Commission notified Italy that its expenditures would not be refinanced. As a consequence, a legal dispute between Oleifici Italiani and the national intervention agency unfolded before Italian courts and the agency was ultimately ordered to pay the sums due to the applicants. The agency, however, refused to pay, arguing that the Commission had already made clear in a letter of 1996 that expenditures would not be refinanced.[58] In these circumstances, the applicants sought compensation for the harm resulting from the allegedly unlawful decision contained in the 1996 letter.[59]

The CJEU confirmed that the degree of bindingness of the measure at stake is decisive for establishing the causal link and specified that it must be taken into account how a reasonable addressee would have perceived the measure.[60] On this basis, the CJEU then concluded that the Commission's letter involved no decisional element and was a purely informal opinion that did not bind the Italian authorities in any manner whatsoever.[61] While the CJEU's assessment of the concrete circumstances is not convincing insofar as the concerned member state would indeed have faced financial disadvantages if it had ignored the Commission's letter, its argument clearly confirms the *KYDEP* doctrine.[62] The CJEU's detailed interpretation of the letter's effects, despite the fact that the letter was non-formally binding, clearly confirms the assumption that, in principle, non-formally binding conduct can trigger liability.

58 CJEU, judgment of 15 September 1998, Oleifici Italiani, T-54/96 (fn. 46), para 12–31.

59 More precisely, the applicants lodged two actions against the Commission, seeking the annulment of the decision allegedly contained in the 1996 letter, and compensation of the resulting financial harm, see CJEU, judgment of 15 September 1998, Oleifici Italiani, T-54/96 (fn. 46), para 36.

60 CJEU, judgment of 15 September 1998, Oleifici Italiani, T-54/96 (fn. 46), para 49. Note the similarity to the Court's approach in the context of attribution (see above 3.1 and 2). This is consequential because the requirement of effective individual legal protection requires to take into account the external appearance of the relevant conduct towards the individual.

61 CJEU, judgment of 15 September 1998, Oleifici Italiani, T-54/96 (fn. 46), para 54, 57, 58 and 67.

62 If the CJEU had adopted the opinion that only formally-binding conduct can incur liability, it would simply have dismissed the action for damages on the same grounds that led to the inadmissibility of the action for annulment, namely with the argument that the letter was no formally-binding decision.

In *New Europe Consulting*, the application of the *KYDEP* doctrine for the first time resulted in the liability of the Union for unlawful non-formally binding administrative support. The case also concerned the PHARE program.[63] The Commission had informed the responsible national authorities of its view that the company New Europe Consulting was in financial difficulties and hence strongly recommended that national authorities not consider any application by that company.[64] When the concerned company sought damages from the Union, the CJEU applied the *KYDEP* doctrine and argued that the Commission's telex had caused the national administration's decision.[65] Consequently, the court examined the legality of the telex, concluded that it was in breach of the principle of sound administration, and thus ordered the Union to pay compensation.[66]

The court's argument in *Malagutti-Vezinhet* then shows that *KYDEP* had already become a consolidated doctrine. The case concerned a dispute between the fruit import-export company Malagutti-Vezinhet SA and the Commission. Malagutti suffered financial loss because the Commission had issued a rapid alert message notifying the presence of pesticide residues in apples from France and giving the applicant's name as the relevant exporter.[67] The company sought damages from the Union, arguing that the Commission's email at stake had caused its financial losses. The Commission argued, remarkably still relying on the *Sucrimex* doctrine, that the communication took place in the context of internal cooperation and that such cooperation cannot cause the Community to incur liability.[68] This argument was plainly dismissed by the CJEU, which stated that 'in that connection, suffice to say that the unlawful conduct complained of by the applicant in the present case is that of the Commission and cannot be regarded as attributable to the national agencies'.[69]

63 CJEU, judgement of 9 July 1999, New Europe Consulting, T-231/97 (fn. 53), para 1–8.
64 Ibid., para 5.
65 Ibid., para 30–43, in particular para 43.
66 Ibid., para 44–49.
67 CJEU, judgement of 10 March 2004, Malagutti-Vezinhet, T-177/02 (fn. 54), para 1–20.
68 Ibid., para 27.
69 Ibid., para 29. The action was dismissed because the CJEU considered the Commission's support as lawful, see ibid, para 60–67.

With its judgement in *Camós Grau* of 2006, the CJEU, for the first time, applied the *KYDEP* doctrine to the conduct of an EU agency.[70] The case concerned an action lodged by Manel Camós Grau, an official of the Commission, who was involved in the management of the Institute for European-Latin American Relations. Due to budgetary and accounting irregularities at that Institute, the European Anti-Fraud Office (OLAF) initiated an investigation regarding, inter alia, Mr Camós Grau. In the ensuing report, OLAF criticised the management of the Institute and the role assumed by the Commission in that regard. In particular, the report recommended that disciplinary proceedings be initiated against Mr Camós Grau. Even though OLAF's report was an internal document, a newspaper shortly after published an article on the issue and mentioned the applicant by name. The Commission then carried out further investigations and, unlike OLAF, concluded that no misbehaviour of Mr Camós Grau could be found. Thus, Mr Camós Grau lodged several complaints and actions against OLAF. With regard to his claim for compensation, Mr Camós Grau argued that OLAF had breached, inter alia, the right to a fair hearing, the principle of sound administration, and the rule of impartiality.[71] As in *Malagutti-Vezinhet,* the CJEU considered the causal link as entirely unproblematic. Although the agency's report was an internal document with no bindingness and no external legal effects,[72] the CJEU discussed the question of causation only very briefly[73] and instead examined in detail only its lawfulness.[74] The judgement in *Camós Grau* hence clearly shows that the *KYDEP* doctrine has become a permanent and stable element of the CJEU's doctrine on causation – that must apply, as a matter of course, also to the conduct of EU agencies.

---

70 The action was filed against the Commission as a consequences of the administrative and budgetary attachment of OLAF to the Commission, see CJEU, judgement of 6 April 2006, Camós Grau, T-309/03 (fn. 55), para 66.

71 CJEU, judgement of 6 April 2006, Camós Grau, T-309/03 (fn. 55), para 18, 20, 25, 83–89, 160.

72 Ibid., para 24–58. All actions for annulment were dismissed because OLAF's conduct was without binding effects.

73 Ibid., para 141: 'such an infringement constitutes a fault capable of giving rise to liability on the part of the Community, since there is a direct and causal link between the wrongful behaviour and the damage claimed.'.

74 Ibid., para 104–141.

b *The Second Post-KYDEP Generation – Tillack and Arizmendi*

The second post-*KYDEP* generation consists of the 2006 judgement in *Tillack*[75] and the 2009 judgement in *Arizmendi*.[76] As mentioned above, some have interpreted these judgements as a return to the earlier *Sucrimex* doctrine.[77] Instead, it is argued here that the second generation must be read as an application and precision of the *KYDEP* doctrine to very specific case constellations. In *Tillack*, the national authority in question was a public prosecutor, while in *Arizmendi*, the Union conduct in question was a reasoned opinion in an infringement procedure. As will be shown, the CJEU confirmed that non-formally binding support could trigger Union liability and merely clarified the implications of the *KYDEP* doctrine in these specific constellations.

The case of *Tillack* concerns a dispute between OLAF and a journalist, Mr Hans-Martin Tillack. OLAF conducted investigations into alleged irregularities in the Commission's services and drew up a confidential note. Shortly after, Mr Tillack published articles which were based on the OLAF note. OLAF obtained information that Mr Tillack had paid somebody within the EU institutions for access to the confidential note and forwarded this information to judicial authorities in Brussels and Hamburg. These accordingly opened investigations into alleged corruption, and the Belgian police carried out search and seizure measures in the applicant's home and office. Mr Tillack, supported by the International Federation of Journalists, then filed several actions against the Commission.[78] Inter alia, he sought compensation for non-material harm suffered as a result of OLAF's complaint to the national judicial authorities.[79]

What is of interest here is the CJEU's argument concerning the bindingness of OLAF's note. Those who interpret the judgment as a return to

75 CJEU, Court of First Instance, judgement of 4 October 2006, Hans-Martin Tillack v Commission of the European Communities, T-193/04.

76 CJEU, General Court, judgement of 18 December 2009, Jean Arizmendi et al v Council of the European Union and European Commission, Joined Cases T-440/03 et al.

77 Timo Rademacher, *Realakte im Rechtsschutzsystem der Europäischen Union* (fn. 5), p. 271–274, referring to these cases as 'third generation' contradicting the 'second generation'.

78 CJEU, judgement of 4 October 2006, Tillack, T-193/04 (fn. 75), para 34–40.

79 See on the further damages for which compensation was claimed, see ibid., para 126–136.

the *Sucrimex* doctrine[80] usually rely on one paragraph in particular, where the court held that the forwarding of information by OLAF was 'in no way binding' upon the national judicial authorities and that, therefore, the applicant's harm was caused by the conduct of national authorities.[81] A reading of the judgment as a whole, however, shows that the CJEU did not depart from the *KYDEP* doctrine. To begin with, the judgement clearly confirmed that formal legal bindingness is not a precondition for Union liability. The CJEU explicitly emphasised that the admissibility of Art. 263 and Art. 340 para 2 TFEU are to be assessed independently of each other, and considered the action for damages admissible, notably although OLAF's conduct lacked formal bindingness.[82] In fact, the CJEU clearly distinguished between a measure which is 'not (...) a legally binding measure'[83] and a measure which is 'in no way binding' and applied the latter criterion in the context of the assessment of causation under Art. 340 para 2 TFEU.[84] The CJEU's conclusion, then, is due to the particular circumstances of the case. As the Court explains, the note by OLAF could not determine the relevant national decision to initiate criminal proceedings because the national authority in question was a public prosecutor. The court hence applied the *KYDEP* doctrine and merely clarified that the assessment of the degree of bindingness must take into consideration that national public prosecutors are independent in their decision-making.[85]

The case of *Arizmendi* concerned the liberalisation of the port business. A few years after the EU adopted a liberalisation Regulation, the French monopoly for ship brokers was still in place. The Commission hence issued a reasoned opinion under the predecessor of Art. 258 TFEU, to which the French legislator reacted by abolishing the monopoly. Mr Jean Arizmendi, a shipbroker himself, along with many of his colleagues, then claimed compensation from the Community for the harm caused by the abolition of the

80 Timo Rademacher, *Realakte im Rechtsschutzsystem der Europäischen Union* (fn. 5), p. 273–274.

81 CJEU, judgement of 4 October 2006, Tillack, T-193/04 (fn. 75), para 121–125.

82 His action for annulment, as in *Camós Grau*, was rejected as inadmissible with the argument that OLAF's did not issue legally binding measures, see CJEU, judgement of 4 October 2006, Tillack, T-193/04 (fn. 75), para 66–82.

83 CJEU, judgement of 4 October 2006, Tillack, T-193/04 (fn. 75), para 81–82.

84 Ibid., para 100.

85 Ibid., para 70 and 122, 142.

monopoly.[86] When assessing the action for damages, the court argued that a causal link between the Commission's reasoned opinion and the damage was not established because the opinion, due to the 'absence of any binding effect',[87] could not determine the conduct of member states.[88] Again, an isolated reading of this passage might suggest that the Court overturned the *KYDEP* doctrine.[89] A comprehensive reading in context, however, shows that such an interpretation is not very plausible. As in *Tillack*, the CJEU held that the action for damage was admissible and that, insofar as it was considered irrelevant, the reasoned opinion was not a measure intended to produce binding legal effects.[90] The CJEU's substantial argument, then, is clearly tailor-made to the specific case of infringement proceedings. The lack of a causal link was, in fact, only an auxiliary argument.[91] The main consideration underlying the CJEU's decision instead seems to be that the EU cannot incur liability for issuing reasoned opinions under Art. 258 TFEU because this would mean that the EU would pay compensation for 'damages' that arise due to the correct implementation of EU law. This alone shows that *Arizmendi* must not be understood as a general return to *Sucrimex* but instead as a clarification of the *KYDEP* doctrine in the specific context of infringement proceedings.

c *The Third Post-KYDEP Generation – Ledra and Bourdouvali*

This reading is further supported by the fact that the CJEU has recently again confirmed the *KYDEP* doctrine with its jurisprudence in the context

86 The CJEU limited its assessment to the question whether the loss was caused by the Commission's reasoned opinion, CJEU, judgement of 18 December 2009, Arizmendi, Joined Cases T-440/03 et al (fn. 76), para 56.

87 CJEU, judgement of 18 December 2009, Arizmendi, Joined Cases T-440/03 et al (fn. 76), para 93.

88 Ibid., para 86 to 87.

89 Timo Rademacher, *Realakte im Rechtsschutzsystem der Europäischen Union* (fn. 5), p. 273 note 271.

90 CJEU, judgement of 18 December 2009, Arizmendi, Joined Cases T-440/03 et al (fn. 76), para to 69–71.

91 Ibid., para 77–79.

of the Eurozone crisis. In this sense, *Ledra* of 2016[92] and *Bourdouvali* of 2018[93] constitute the third-post *KYDEP* generation.

Both disputes arose in the context of the Cypriot bank restructuring in the aftermath of the sovereign debt crisis. To briefly recall: After certain banks had encountered severe financial difficulties, the Republic of Cyprus submitted a request to the Eurogroup for financial assistance. That support was granted, subject to the conditionalities of a macro-economic adjustment programme as set out in a memorandum of understanding (MoU) between Cyprus and the ESM, which provided, among other things, for large Cypriot banks to be resolved. This was implemented by Cyprus in 2013 on the basis of a parliamentary law and several decrees. Ledra Advertising Ltd, a Cypriot company, and the other applicants had funds on deposit at the resolved banks. As the restructuring measures led to a substantial reduction in the value of these deposits, Ledra and others claimed compensation from the Union. The applicants' main argument was that the Cypriot measures merely implemented the conditionalities defined in the MoU and that, therefore, the financial losses were actually caused by the Union. More precisely, the applicants argued that their damages resulted, inter alia, from misconduct on the part of the Commission.[94]

The Commission, in fact, had a central role in the restructuring process. Although the ESM was established as an international financial institution among member states, the Commission was entrusted with two important tasks, namely, negotiating and signing the MoU on behalf of the ESM and monitoring compliance with the conditionalities as laid down in the MoU. More precisely, the Commission was supposed to conduct the negotiations and the monitoring as part of the so-called Troika, i.e. in liaison with the European Central Bank (ECB) and, wherever possible, the International Monetary Fund (IMF).[95] Against this background, the applicants submitted that the Commission should have refrained from signing the MoU because it contained certain paragraphs that allegedly violated EU law. In essence, the applicants hence argued that their damages resulted from the

92 CJEU, judgement of 20 September 2016, Ledra, C-8/15 P et al (fn. 2).

93 CJEU, General Court (Fourth Chamber), judgement of 13 July 2018, Eleni Pavlikka Bourdouvali v Council of the European Union, European Commission, European Central Bank, Euro Group and European Union, T-786/14.

94 CJEU, judgement of 20 September 2016, Ledra, C-8/15 P et al (fn. 2), para 1, para 42–47.

95 Ibid., para 9.

Commission's failure to ensure that the MoU was in conformity with EU law.[96]

The Court, therefore, had to assess whether the Commission's misconduct was causal for the damage, notably despite the fact that the temporally latest condition for the occurrence of the damage had been set by the member state and despite the fact that the Commission's conduct was not formally binding upon the member state.[97] The Court, however, did not even discuss this question in detail – and this is precisely the point. In fact, the CJEU's entire argumentation is based on the implicit assumption that non-formally binding conduct can, as a matter of course, trigger Union liability. This becomes clear from the course of the argumentation: The judgement begins with recalling that the Commission was not entrusted with making legally binding decisions in the context of the ESM and that the activities pursued by the Commission commit the ESM alone.[98] Although this was one of the main reasons for the General Court to dismiss Ledra's action,[99] the Court did not deal further with the lack of legal bindingness. Instead, it examined whether the Commission had 'contributed' to the breach of fundamental rights[100] and, in this regard, succinctly stated that the Commission had failed to provide adequate technical expertise, legal advice and guidance in the context of the negotiation and the monitoring of the MoU, and thereby had failed to fulfil its obligations as the guardian of the Treaties.[101] Subsequently, the Court entered into a detailed assessment of whether the Cypriot bank restructuring, as foreseen in the MoU, violated

---

96 Ibid., para 63.

97 It is that particular question, and not the probably most prominent question of whether the Commission was bound to the Charter although it was acting outside the realm of EU law, that is of interest here. See on the latter matter only Anastasia Poulou, „Financial Assistance Conditionality and Human Rights Protection: What is the Role of the EU Charter of Fundamental Rights?", *Common Market Law Review* 54 (2017), p. 991–1026.

98 CJEU, judgement of 20 September 2016, Ledra, C-8/15 P et al (fn. 2), para 51.

99 CJEU, General Court, judgement of 10 November 2014, Ledra Advertising et al v European Commission and European Central Bank, T-289/13, para 45–46, para 51–55, arguing that a causal link between the Commission's failure to ensure compliance with EU law and the damage could not be established because the reduction in the share of the applicant's deposit resulted from the entry into force of the Cypriot decree.

100 CJEU, judgement of 20 September 2016, Ledra, C-8/15 P et al (fn. 2), para 68.

101 Ibid., para 52.

the applicants' fundamental right to property, concluded that this was not the case, and hence dismissed the action for that reason.[102]

The Court's argument in *Ledra* hence clearly shows that it considered the economic pressure attached to the Commission's conduct as sufficient to establish causation in the sense of Art. 340 para 2 TFEU.[103] Otherwise, there would have been no reason for the Court to discuss the politically charged and doctrinally intricate questions of whether the fundamental right to property was applicable and violated. It was perfectly clear and undisputed that the Commission's conduct was not formally binding upon Cyprus. Thus, if the Court had considered the lack of legal bindingness as preventing the causal link, invoking that argument would have been a much simpler and less disputed way to reject Ledra's claim. The fact that the Court, notably unlike the General Court,[104] did not dismiss Ledra's action on that basis but instead discussed the difficult questions related to the Charter of Fundamental Rights unequivocally indicates that the Court did not consider the lack of legal bindingness as a relevant argument in the context of causation.

This reading is confirmed by the textbook-like *Bourdouvali* judgement issued by the General Court in 2009. As in *Ledra*, the applicants, among them Ms Bourdouvali, claimed compensation from the Union for a reduction of the value of their deposits with the resolved Cypriot banks.[105] The General Court started its argument by recalling the separation principle.[106] It then went on to remind that, nonetheless, the Union may incur liability in two constellations, namely: first, if the damage must be considered as having been caused by the EU because the national authorities de facto had no discretion in the implementation of EU measures,[107] or second, on

102 Ibid., para 65–76.

103 Differently René Repasi, „Judicial protection against austerity measures in the euro area: Ledra and Mallis", *Common Market Law Review* 54 (2017), p. 1123-1156, p. 1135 who argues that the Court did not pronounce itself on the existence of a causal link because it dismissed the action already on the ground of lawfulness of the conduct at stake.

104 CJEU, General Court, judgement of 10 November 2014, Ledra, T-289/13 (fn. 99), para 51–55.

105 CJEU, judgement of 13 July 2018, Bourdouvali, T-786/14 (fn. 93), para 47–48, 73.

106 Ibid., para 79.

107 Ibid., para 80, 97–192, remarkably with reference to Krohn 'by analogy', but not to *KYDEP*. Note that judgement's terminology is not only inconsistent but also unusual insofar as it differentiates between acts which are attributable 'formally' and those which are attributable 'in reality' to the Union, para 82–83, 89, 95. In the

the basis of non-formally binding conduct related to the EU's negotiation and monitoring tasks.[108] Whereas the *Ledra* judgement had already established that legal bindingness is not a precondition in the second case, the *Bourdouvali* judgement now clarified that legal bindingness is also not a precondition in the first case.[109]

Certainly, the General Court ultimately focused on a formally binding decision by the Council to establish that Cyprus had no margin of discretion.[110] This focus, however, was due to the facts of the case and must not be misunderstood to indicate that legal bindingness is a precondition to establishing causation.[111] Quite to the contrary, the *Bourdouvali* judgment is exceptionally unequivocal in that not only legal bindingness but also financial pressure is sufficient to establish causation within the sense of Art. 340 para TFEU. The General Court not only examined whether the contested EU acts were obligatory but also took into account the economic and financial pressure to which the Republic of Cyprus was confronted and, on this basis, concluded that the Cypriot authorities de facto had no choice but to implement the Union's conditionalities.[112]

In sum, the judgements in *Ledra* and *Bourdouvali* clearly show that the CJEU consistently considers the degree of bindingness of the Union's conduct decisive for establishing causation.

Yet, one last objection must be considered. The reading of *Ledra* and *Bourdouvali* as confirming the *KYDEP* doctrine requires justification insofar as the third post-*KYDEP* generation, unlike the first and the second one, which concerned factual conduct in the context of the integrated administration, concerned factual conduct in the context of international agreements. There are two ways to justify the reading proposed here.

The first argument is that Eurozone judgements must be read as extending the *KYDEP* rationale from administrative to legislative acts. Seen from

---

terminology adopted here (see chapter 3, 5), 'formal' attribution means causation on the basis of formal legal bindingness; attribution 'in reality' means causation on the basis of de facto legal bindingness.

108 CJEU, judgement of 13 July 2018, Bourdouvali, T-786/14 (fn. 93), para 81, 193–206.

109 Note that the second case can also be formulated as a sub-category of the first case, and vice versa. Seen from this perspective, *Ledra* already establishes the relevant doctrine, which *Bourdouvali* then only makes explicit.

110 CJEU, judgement of 13 July 2018, Bourdouvali, T-786/14 (fn. 93), para 182–190.

111 For such reading see Melanie Fink, as cited in fn. 49, albeit with doubts, from the perspective of the alternative approach.

112 After having examined several other relevant measures by Union bodies, in CJEU, judgement of 13 July 2018, Bourdouvali, T-786/14 (fn. 93), para 101–170.

this perspective, *Ledra* and *Bourdouvali* appear not only as applications of the *Les Verts* rationale to factual conduct but also as consequential applications of the *KYDEP* rationale to administrative and legislative conduct.[113] In other words, the *KYDEP* doctrine today follows a fortiori from the Eurozone jurisprudence. If financial pressure is sufficient to establish that a member state was de facto obliged to adopt a certain legislative act, it a fortiori must also be sufficient to establish that a member state was de facto forced to adopt a certain administrative decision.[114]

The second argument is specific to the case of the EU hotspots. As argued above, the EU hotspot administration can at least partially be understood as forming part of the Commission's implementation of the EU-Türkiye Statement.[115] If one adopts this understanding, the EU hotspots case bears remarkable parallels to the *Ledra* case. Both cases arose from a crisis context.[116] In both cases, member states concluded an agreement on common crisis management outside the scope of Union law.[117] In both cases, the Commission, assisted by other agencies or institutions, was entrusted with implementing that agreement, including monitoring compliance with EU law, which entails that the Commission exercised an important influence on how the agreement was implemented without however issuing formally binding decisions. It is hence only consequential that the Commission, in both cases, must exercise its tasks in compliance with its role as guardian of the Treaties and that a failure to do so can trigger EU liability.[118]

---

113 This understanding is supported by the CJEU's reference to Krohn 'by analogy', see fn. 107 above.

114 If legal bindingness is not even required when it comes to legislative acts of the member states, legal bindingness can also not be required when it comes to merely administrative acts of the member states.

115 See chapter 1, 2.

116 For a comparison see Franz Schimmelpfennig, „European integration (theory) in times of crisis. A comparison of the euro and Schengen crises", *Journal of European Public Policy* 25 (2018), p. 969-989; Felix Biermann, Nina Guérin, Stefan Jagdhuber, Berthold Rittberger, Moritz Weiss, „Political (non-)reform in the euro crisis and the refugee crisis: a liberal intergovernmentalist explanation", *Journal of European Public Policy* (2019), p. 246-266. Note, however, that the present study contradicts the cited literature insofar as it argues that the crisis of the asylum system has increased integration, too.

117 The ESM Treaty respectively the EU-Türkiye Statement.

118 CJEU, judgement of 20 September 2016, Ledra, C-8/15 P et al (fn. 2), para 56; CJEU, judgement of 13 July 2018, Bourdouvali, T-786/14 (fn. 93), para 196–197, 200–203.

3 Doctrine on Causation II: Lessons from Ledra

Based on the case law analysis conducted so far, this third section examines whether non-formally binding administrative supervision, more precisely the Commission's failure to adequately supervise, can be considered as causal for resulting fundamental rights violations and hence trigger EU liability under Art. 340 para 2 TFEU, despite the fact that these violations are ultimately evoked by formally-binding decisions of national authorities. Insofar as the question relates to the fact that supervisory measures are *non-formally binding*, the second section has shown already that such conduct can be causal if the threshold of de facto bindingness is met. What remains to be discussed here are, hence, only those elements of the question that arise due to the specific nature of administrative *supervision* in contrast to administrative support.

To this end, the following provides an overview of the case law dealing with breaches of the Commission's supervisory obligations specifically. The analysis starts with the court's earlier jurisprudence in the context of competition law and then moves on to the more recent jurisprudence in the context of the Eurozone crisis. This will show that the CJEU's doctrine on causation is largely consistent. Certainly, there are important differences between the two strands of jurisprudence – in particular, that, in the context of competition law, the Commission's supervisory duties arise from secondary law and the relevant breach for the purpose of Art. 340 para 2 TFEU is defined as the supervisory obligation, whereas, in the context of the Eurozone crisis, the Commission's supervisory duties arise from Art. 17 TEU and the relevant breach is defined as the supervisory standard, i.e. for instance, the concerned fundamental rights.[119] Yet, the case law is consistent insofar as the CJEU considers it decisive, irrespective of the context concerned, whether the supervisory measures at stake bear a sufficient degree of bindingness. In other words, the CJEU's case law on liability in the context of administrative supervision confirms the *KYDEP* doctrine in that de facto binding measures – or the lack thereof – can be considered as causal for resulting damages.[120]

---

119 On the implications for the individual-rights criterion and the sufficiently-serious-breach criterion see chapter 3, 3.3.

120 On the Commission's supervisory duties more generally see Sabino Cassese, „European Administrative Proceedings", *Law and Contemporary Problems* 86 (2004), p. 21-36, p. 21 with further references; Gerard C. Rowe, „Administrative supervision of

3.1 Liability for Breach of Supervisory Obligation

One of the CJEU's earliest judgments on Union liability for the Commission's breach of its supervisory obligations is *Kampffmeyer* of 1967.[121] The case concerns the common cereal market. Germany had suspended the issue of import licences for certain cereals for which the import levy was fixed at equal to zero, and the Commission then issued a decision authorising the German government to keep those protective measures in force. After the Commission's decision had been annulled by the Court of Justice, the applicants claimed compensation, arguing that the Commission had failed to adequately exercise its obligation to supervise national authorities, as established under the relevant secondary law. The Commission submitted that a breach of supervisory duties cannot, under a general principle common to the laws of the member states, incur public liability, except in the case of gross malfeasance.[122] The CJEU, however, plainly dismissed the Commission's argument as irrelevant; it instead interpreted the Commission's duties under the relevant Regulation and concluded that the Commission was obliged to comprehensively examine the national protective measures. Therefore, the court held, the Commission bears independent responsibility for the retention of a protective measure.[123] While the claim in the specific case was dismissed due to the speculative nature of the damage invoked by the applicant, the *Kampffmeyer* ruling is fundamental in that it established that a breach of a supervisory duty on the part of the Commission could, in principle, trigger Union liability. Until today, *Kampffmeyer* is one of the central references for applicants substantiating such claims before the CJEU.[124]

The chronologically next relevant judgements, it is argued here, were *Sucrimex* of 1980 and the related cases as set out above.[125] This reading is justified already because the facts in *Sucrimex* and *Kampffmeyer* are

---

administrative action in the European Union", in Herwig Hofmann, Alexander Türk (ed.), *Legal Challenges in EU Administrative Law*, Edward Elgar 2009, p. 179–217, p. 190–209.

121 CJEU, Court, judgement of 14 July 1967, Firma E. Kampffmeyer et al v Commission of the European Economic Community, Joined Cases 5/66 et al.

122 Ibid., p. 254.

123 Ibid., p. 262.

124 For instance, the applicants' argument in CJEU, judgement of 13 July 2018, Bourdouvali, T-786/14 (fn. 93), para 195.

125 See 2.1.

quite similar: Both cases concerned inter-administrative measures of the Commission to ensure the legality of member states' activities. The main difference is only that *Kampffmeyer* is concerned with an omission, while Sucrimex is concerned with an act on the part of the Commission. Yet, both strands are hardly read together.[126] In the context of supervisory duties, most arguments refer only to cases in which the misconduct consisted of a failure to act. Whereas this is understandable insofar as, in cases of omission, it is especially obvious that the misconduct consisted in a violation of supervisory duties, the measures taken in cases such as *Sucrimex*, e.g. in the form of letters or telexes to the national authorities, also serve to ensure the legality of the member state's activities, and in this sense also qualify as supervisory measures. From this perspective, *Sucrimex* appears to be a step back. Whereas in *Kampffmeyer*, the court did not even call into question that the Commission's inter-administrative conduct could trigger liability, this implicit assumption was revoked with *Sucrimex*, where it found that inter-administrative conduct cannot per se trigger Union liability.[127]

Consequentially, the 1986 *Krohn* judgment also forms part of the jurisprudence relevant to supervisory duties.[128] As set out above, *Krohn* partially overturned *Sucrimex* insofar as the CJEU held that inter-administrative instructions by the Commission can trigger Union liability, provided that those instructions are formally-binding upon the national authority issuing the administrative decision. Now, seen in the context of the earlier case law, *Krohn* appears as a partial return to the earlier *Kampffmeyer* doctrine.

On this basis, the 1994 *KYDEP* judgement and the first post-*KYDEP* generation, ranging from *Geotronics* to *Malagutti-Vezinhet*, are relevant here, too. Again, this case law now appears as confirming the *Kampffmeyer* insofar as non-formally binding supervisory conduct can be considered as

126 *Kampffmeyer* is often cited as a reference for supervisory duties of the Commission, and *Sucrimex* as a reference for the exclusion of liability for inter-administrative action.

127 As was confirmed with CJEU, Court, judgement of 10 June 1982, Interagra, 217/81 (fn. 21), and CJEU, Court, judgement of 10 May 1987, Exportation des Sucres, 132/77 (fn. 22).

128 As confirmed with CJEU, judgement of 20 January 1993, Emerald Meats, C-106/90 et al (fn. 33).

causal for resulting damages, even when these are ultimately evoked by national decision, and hence trigger EU liability.[129]

Further, the judgements in *Francesconi* of 1989 and *Coldiretti* of 1998[130] are of particular interest in the context of supervisory duties. Unlike in earlier cases, the applicants here claimed compensation for damages to interests that are protected by fundamental rights. Consequentially, these are the first judgements in which the CJEU established supervisory duties directly on the basis of fundamental rights.[131]

Francesconi is one of the very few cases where compensation was claimed from the Union for human death. The applicants, among them Benito Francesconi, invoked damages suffered as a result of the presence of adulterated Italian wine on the market.[132] They complained of bad management and a failure to supervise the market on the part of the Commission, which allegedly failed to ensure the proper implementation of the applicable rules governing the wine market.[133] In concrete terms, the applicants argued that their losses resulted from the Commission's failure to take action to prevent the presence of adulterated wine on the market and its failure to disclose information concerning that matter in a particular press conference. The judgment of *Francesconi* is insightful for two reasons. First, the court established the Commission's supervisory duties on the basis of the fundamental right to human health. More specifically, it held that the Commission is obliged to intervene where member states do not sufficiently comply with their obligations to protect health, although the applicable secondary law does not provide for such obligation.[134] The second instructive point is that the court does not rule out, at least not in principle, that the Commission's failure to supervise member state authorities is causal for resulting

129 CJEU, judgement of 15 September 1994, *KYDEP*, C-146/91 (fn. 1); CJEU, judgement of 26 October 1995, Geotronics I, T-185/94 (fn. 51); CJEU, judgement of 10 March 2004, Malagutti-Vezinhet, T-177/02 (fn. 54).

130 CJEU, Court, judgement of 30 September 1988, Portuguese Republic v Council of the European Union (Coldiretti), T-149/96.

131 In detail on this Uwe Säuberlich, *Die außervertragliche Haftung im Gemeinschaftsrecht* (fn. 4), p. 225–228.

132 The applicants consisted of, first, dealers, restaurateurs and producers of Italian wine claiming damages for financial loss consisting in a reduction of export of Italian wine, and second, persons who claimed damages for a loss of a member of their family who died from wine containing methanol.

133 CJEU, Court (Second Chamber), judgement of 4 July 1989, Benito Francesconi and others v Commission of the European Communities, 326/86 and 66/88, para 5.

134 Ibid., para 12.

fundamental rights violations, although the formally-binding decision that ultimately evoked these damages was issued by the member state. This follows from the course of the argumentation: If the court had considered causation to be excluded in principle, it could have dismissed the claims on this basis alone. Instead, however, the court examined in detail the scope of the supervisory duties and whether the Commission had complied with these. More specifically, it found that the Commission had adopted all required measures in relation to the management of the wine market and stressed that the Commission had insufficient facts at its disposal to require a review of the Italian monitoring measures.[135] The court, therefore, rejected the actions on the grounds that the applicants had failed to establish unlawful conduct on the part of the Commission.[136]

The case of *Coldiretti* is similar in that it also concerns damages to human health. The Italian trade organisation Coldiretti, along with more than one hundred Italian farmers, claimed compensation for the damage allegedly suffered as a result of acts and omissions of the Council and the Commission following the outbreak of BSE, a deadly disease affecting cattle. In particular, the applicants argued that the Commission, even though it was informed from 1989 onwards of the discovery of the BSE outbreak in the UK, failed to exercise its supervisory powers in order to ensure that member states took the necessary steps to prevent the epidemic from spreading. In particular, the applicants complained that the Community institutions had not adopted already in 1990 the measures they adopted in 1996, namely a ban on sales of beef from the UK to continental Europe.[137] The *Coldiretti* judgment focused specifically on causation. Unlike in *Francesconi,* the CJEU started its assessment with a detailed examination of the causal link, ultimately denied causation, and therefore refrained from discussing the scope of the Commission's supervisory obligations in much detail. As regards causation, the court recalled its doctrine in the context of omission, namely that one must assess the hypothetical situation if the measure at stake would have been taken.[138] The court also noted that conducting this assessment is particularly difficult due to the specific circumstances of the case. Having said this, however, it held that the applicants did not

135 Ibid., para 10–19, 22.

136 Ibid., para 24 to 26.

137 CJEU, judgement of 30 September 1998, Coldiretti, T-149/96 (fn. 130), para 67, 70–71, 79.

138 Ibid., para 115–123.

submit any indication whatsoever in support of their argument concerning causation. Rather, the court inferred from the applicants' submission that their losses were, in fact, due to alarmist media reports. Consequentially, the court considered it unlikely that the adoption of a sales ban in 1990 could have prevented losses of cattle farmers in Italy.[139] As no causal link could be established, the action was dismissed.[140] Hence, the court did not even examine the concrete scope of the Commission's supervisory duties. Nonetheless, it is clear from the judgement that the court assumed that supervisory duties can, at least in principle, arise from fundamental rights.[141]

3.2 Liability for Breach of Supervisory Standard

Based on this earlier jurisprudence, the doctrine of liability for breach of supervisory obligations was then fully unfolded with the case law in the context of the Eurozone crisis. Out of the many cases, *Ledra* of 2016[142] and *Bourdouvali* of 2018[143] deserve particular attention.[144] As established above, the applicants argued that the Commission had breached its supervisory obligations relating to the conclusion and the implementation of a memorandum of understanding (MoU). Remarkably, the CJEU agreed with the applicants insofar as it established relatively far-reaching supervisory obligations of the Commission on the basis of Art. 17 TEU. The respective claims under Art. 340 para 2 TFEU were dismissed only because the CJEU concluded that the fundamental right to property of the applicants was not violated in the specific cases.[145] As has been shown above already, *Ledra* and *Bourdouvali* established the degree of bindingness of the Union's conduct as the decisive factor in the context of causation; only

139 Ibid., para 115, 108–118, 122.

140 Ibid., para 123.

141 Ibid., para 77, 123.

142 CJEU, judgement of 20 September 2016, Ledra, C-8/15 P et al (fn. 2).

143 CJEU, judgement of 13 July 2018, Bourdouvali, T-786/14 (fn. 93).

144 For an overview see Anastasia Karatzia, „An Overview of Litigation in the Context of Financial Assistance", *Hungarian Yearbook of International Law and European Law* (2016), p. 573-590. Note that CJEU, Court, judgement of 20 September 2016, Konstantinos Mallis et al v European Commission et al, C-105/15 P et al. is less relevant here because it concerns only an action for annulment.

145 CJEU, judgement of 20 September 2016, Ledra, C-8/15 P et al (fn. 2), para 75; CJEU, judgement of 13 July 2018, Bourdouvali, T-786/14 (fn. 93), para 359.

two points concerning the specificities of supervisory obligations remain to be discussed, namely, first, the doctrinal shift from supervisory obligations under secondary law to those under Art. 17 TEU, and second, the shift from the focus on the supervisory obligation to the focus on the supervisory standard.

a *The Doctrinal Shift From Supervisory Obligations Under Secondary Law to Art. 17 TEU*

The *Ledra* doctrine is often read as a fundamental innovation or even as a surprise.[146] Seen in context with the earlier *Kampffmeyer* doctrine, however, it rather appears as a consequential development thereof. In fact, *Ledra* is not innovative in that the Union may incur liability for the Commission's breach of supervisory obligations.

What is innovative is only the legal basis for the supervisory obligation. Whereas the earlier jurisprudence established the Commission's supervisory obligations solely on the basis of the relevant secondary law, *Ledra* and *Bourdouvali* established the Commission's obligations on the basis of Art. 17 TEU. Although the CJEU also relied on the relevant provisions of the ESM Treaty, the decisive argument was that Art. 17 TEU defined the Commission's role as the guardian of the Treaties.[147] Referring to its earlier jurisprudence in *Pringle*, the court recalled that the Commission is obliged under Art. 17 TEU to promote the general interest of the Union and to oversee the application of Union law.[148] It then stressed that the Commission had retained this role within the framework of the ESM Treaty and that it must, therefore, exercise its obligations in that context, namely to negotiate and to sign the conclusion of the MoU between the ESM and the concerned member state as well as to monitor the implementation thereof, in compliance with Art. 17 TEU. In concrete terms, the Commission was

146 See only René Repasi, „Judicial protection against austerity measures in the euro area: Ledra and Mallis" (fn. 103), p. 1154.

147 CJEU, judgement of 20 September 2016, Ledra, C-8/15 P et al (fn. 2), para 57–59; CJEU, judgement of 13 July 2018, Bourdouvali, T-786/14 (fn. 93), para 200–203.

148 CJEU, Court (Full Court), judgement of 27 November 2012, Thomas Pringle v Government of Ireland et al, C-370/12, para 163.

hence obliged to refrain from signing an MoU whose consistency with EU law it doubts.[149]

The argumentative continuity, as well as the innovation relating to Art. 17 TEU, becomes particularly clear from the court's reasoning in *Bourdouvali.* The applicants supported their argument that the Commission's inadequate monitoring was capable of incurring Union liability with reference to *Kampffmeyer.* Adopting that argument in principle, the court then introduced a distinction, namely between the Commission's mere approval and its authorisation of certain national measures. According to the court, *Kampffmeyer* is concerned with the latter category, which means that the mere approval of certain measures is not sufficient to incur Union liability. Crucially, however, the court then argued that the Commission's supervisory obligations as guardian of the Treaties go beyond mere approval and that a breach of Art. 17 TEU can trigger liability, too.[150]

This new focus on Art. 17 TEU is remarkable because that provision defines the role of the Commission and thus establishes a normative programme but does not define the concrete duties of the Commission in a given context. With a view to an action for damages, however, it is indispensable to identify a specific misconduct. Art 340 para 2 TFEU thus requires the concretisation of the Commission's obligations under Art. 17 TEU. The CJEU solves this problem through contextual interpretation: In *Ledra* and *Bourdouvali,* for instance, it identified the concrete duties of the Commission by interpreting Art. 17 TEU in conjunction with the ESM Treaty. In similar judgements, it also relied on the Commission's obligations under secondary law, which must be understood as ultimately arising from Art. 17 TEU, even though the CJEU did not always make this explicit.[151]

While this approach is convincing in terms of substance, it also carries a procedural risk. As the applicants bear the burden of proof, they must be able to identify the scope of the Commission's duties in a given context. If, however, the applicants do not know what exactly the Commission's obligations are under Art. 17 TEU, it is very difficult to determine whether a certain failure constitutes unlawful conduct within the meaning of Art. 340

149 CJEU, judgement of 20 September 2016, Ledra, C-8/15 P et al (fn. 2), para 57–59; CJEU, judgement of 13 July 2018, Bourdouvali, T-786/14 (fn. 93), para 200.

150 CJEU, judgement of 13 July 2018, Bourdouvali, T-786/14 (fn. 93), para 195, 197–203, 219–225.

151 CJEU, judgement of 20 September 2016, Ledra, C-8/15 P et al (fn. 2), para 57–59; CJEU, judgement of 13 July 2018, Bourdouvali, T-786/14 (fn. 93), para 200–203; CJEU, judgement of 14 July 1967, Kampffmeyer, 5/66 et al (fn. 121), p. 260–267.

para 2 TFEU. This problem is further aggravated in contexts – such as the Eurozone crisis or the asylum administration – where applicants do not have sufficient insights into the Commission's workings to even prove what exactly the Commission did or did not do.[152]

As mentioned above, the CJEU seems to have recognised and mitigated that risk by a certain generosity regarding the definition of unlawful conduct. In fact, the court considers it sufficient for an applicant to state a bundle of measures, or acts and omissions as a whole, that has allegedly caused damage.[153] The CJEU's approach, hence, is to examine whether the invoked bundle of acts and omissions constitutes a breach of the Commission's supervisory obligations, thereby both identifying the relevant conduct and specifying the obligations under Art. 17 TEU at the same time.[154]

b *The Doctrinal Shift From the Supervisory Obligation to the Supervisory Standard*

The second innovative point of the *Ledra* doctrine is that the court does not consider the breach of the supervisory obligation, i.e. here of Art. 17 TEU, as the breach triggering liability under Art. 340 para 2 TFEU, but instead focuses on the breach of the supervisory standard, i.e. here, the fundamental rights with which the Commission must ensure compliance.

After the court had established in *Ledra* and *Bourdouvali* that the Commission had breached its supervisory obligations under Art. 17 TEU, one would now expect that Art. 17 TEU is the relevant rule that must qualify as conferring rights upon individuals, and the breach of which must be sufficiently serious. Instead, however, the court went on to examine whether the Commission, by not complying with its supervisory obligations, had violated the fundamental rights invoked by the applicants, inter alia Art. 17 ChFR and Art. 41 ChFR,[155] and defined these fundamental rights as the rel-

---

152 Note that in the case of the EU hotspots, the minutes of the relevant meetings in the responsible supervisory fora are not published. For the relevant fora see chapter 2, 2.6.

153 CJEU, judgement of 13 July 2018, Bourdouvali, T-786/14 (fn. 93), para 200–201; see fn. 30.

154 CJEU, judgement of 20 September 2016, Ledra, C-8/15 P et al (fn. 2), para 51–60, 65–73.

155 Ibid., para 47, 66–75; CJEU, judgement of 13 July 2018, Bourdouvali, T-786/14 (fn. 93), para 247, 247 to 508.

evant rules the breach of which triggers liability, and which must accordingly fulfil the individual-rights criterion and the sufficiently-serious-breach criterion.[156] The supervisory obligation enshrined in Art. 17 TEU hence merely serves as a bridging argument. Although the breach thereof was established, the court dismissed the actions in *Ledra* and *Bourdouvali* on the grounds that the applicants' fundamental rights were not violated.[157] This is particularly noteworthy because the court, at the same time, considered the breach of Art. 17 TEU as decisive in the context of attribution and causation.

Hence, the *Ledra* doctrine introduced a split in the liability doctrine. Whereas the breach of the supervisory obligation, i.e. Art 17 TEU, must be attributed to the Commission and constitutes the conduct that must be causal for the damage, the breach of the relevant fundamental right must fulfil the individual-rights criterion and the sufficiently-serious-breach criterion.[158] Unlike under the *Kampffmeyer* doctrine, the qualified unlawfulness in the sense of Art. 340 para 2 TFEU is hence not established by the breach of the supervisory obligation but by the breach of the supervisory standard.

From a practical perspective, however, this development is of limited relevance. Although one might think at first sight that the *Ledra* doctrine increases the threshold for Union liability by requiring applicants to prove a breach of both the supervisory obligation and the supervisory standard, a closer look shows that this is actually not correct. The *Ledra* doctrine does not make it more difficult for an applicant to successfully claim damages from the Union. This is because the breach of the supervisory obligation and the supervisory standard are inextricably linked. In fact, it can only be said that the Commission has breached its obligations under Art. 17 TEU once it is established that its failure resulted in a fundamental rights violation. For the same reason, the qualification of the supervisory obligation depends on the qualification of the supervisory standard. It is, therefore, actually easier for an applicant to establish a qualified breach of the supervisory standard, in particular where that standard consists of fundamental rights.

---

156 CJEU, judgement of 20 September 2016, Ledra, C-8/15 P et al (fn. 2), para 65–68.

157 Ibid., para 74; CJEU, judgement of 13 July 2018, Bourdouvali, T-786/14 (fn. 93), para 247–508.

158 Note that the fundamental rights violation as such constitutes the damage, see chapter 3, 3.3.c.

In any event, the doctrinal shift from *Kampffmeyer* to *Ledra* is practically irrelevant in cases where both the supervisory obligation and the standard fulfil the individual-rights criterion and the sufficiently-serious-breach criterion – and, as established above, the case of the EU hotspot administration falls within this category.[159]

4 *The* De Facto *Bindingness Threshold*

The case law analysis has shown that non-formally binding administrative conduct by a Union body is to be considered causal, provided that it is *de facto binding* upon the decision-issuing national authority. In order to apply this doctrine to the case of the EU hotspot administration, three points require clarification. First, the theoretical considerations underlying the CJEU's case law must be made explicit because this facilitates the application of the doctrine to new constellations. Second, the required degree of bindingness must be defined with regard to the specific case in which the misconduct consists of an omission to act.[160] Third, the concrete circumstances establishing *de facto* bindingness must be defined more precisely.

4.1 Degree of Bindingness as Decisive Factor

To understand why the degree of bindingness is a decisive factor for establishing causation, it is useful to start from the function of the causation criterion.[161] In general terms, causation serves to establish whose fault has led to the damage.[162] For a more precise understanding of this function in the specific context where several administrative actors are involved, consider the following example. Imagine a case in which actor A provides administrative support, such as, e.g. information or interpretative guidelines, with the content n, towards another actor B, who then issues an

159 See chapter 3, 4.2.

160 As set out in chapter 3, 4.1, the Commission's misconduct typically consists in an omission to act.

161 For a similar approach see Uwe Säuberlich, *Die außervertragliche Haftung im Gemeinschaftsrecht* (fn. 4), p. 75–97. He however makes a different argument, and comes to the conclusion that de facto binding support cannot trigger liability, see ibid., p. 97.

162 See chapter 3, 5.1.

administrative decision with the content n1 towards an individual who, as a result, suffers damage. Assuming that the individual claims damages from A, the decisive question is whether n is causal for the damage. As set out above, the CJEU's general formula on causation requires that the conduct is a *condition sine qua non* to the occurrence of the damage and that there is a sufficiently direct link between the conduct and the damage.[163] In multi-actor situations, where both the conduct n of actor A and conduct n1 of actor B constitute a *condition sine qua non*, the sufficiently direct link becomes the decisive criterion. In other words, the function of the sufficiently-direct-link criterion is to determine whether the contribution n of A, or rather the contribution n1 of B, is to be considered as the fault which has led to the damage.[164] In light of this function, it follows that the closeness of n to the damage is decisive for establishing a sufficiently direct link. Crucially, closeness must not be understood in terms of the chronological order of events but rather in substantive terms. The more A has contributed to the occurrence of the damage, the more speaks in favour of considering n as having a sufficiently direct link to the damage. Taking into account that n1 occurs chronologically later than n, it therefrom follows that the stronger n determines n1, the more speaks in favour of considering A as having caused the damage.

In other words, the sufficiently-direct-link criterion has the function of setting a *threshold of determinacy*.[165] This has three important implications for the argument of bindingness in the context of causation. First, the determinacy function is the very reason why legal bindingness is an argument for establishing causation. If the support provided by A, as in *Krohn* and *Emerald Meats,* is legally binding upon B, n fully determines n1, and

163 See fn. 3.

164 It must be kept in mind here that A and B could also be jointly liable. As defined above, this question and the ensuing complicated issues regarding the relation of A's and B's liability, however fall outside the scope of this study. See further Wouter P. J. Wils, „Concurrent liability of the Community and a Member State", *European law review* 17 (1992), p. 191-206; Peter Oliver, „Joint Liability of the Community and the Member States" (fn. 30); Georgios Anagnostaras, „The Common European Asylum System: Balancing Mutual Trust Against Fundamental Rights Protection", *German Law Journal* 21 (2020), p. 1180–1197.

165 Similarly, Melanie Fink, „EU Liability for Contributions to Member States' Breaches of EU Law" (fn. 5), p. 1240 who, from the perspective of the alternative approach focusing on attribution instead of causation, refers to 'the *threshold* required to attribute conduct of member state authorities to the Union' (emphasis added).

therefore, A is to be considered as having caused the damage.[166] If, however, as in *Tillack* and *Oleifici Italiani,* the support provided by A is in no way binding upon B, n does not determine n1 at all, and therefore, A cannot be considered as having caused the damage.[167] Second, and this is crucial, the determinacy function also shows that legal bindingness is not an argument in itself. The legal bindingness of n matters only because it has the effect that n determines n1. As legal bindingness matters only insofar as it reflects the determinacy function, a lack of legal bindingness does not per se speak against establishing causation. Therefore, the argument that A shall not be liable simply because n is not legally binding upon B cannot persist. Third, and instead, the determinacy function shows that the *degree* of bindingness is decisive for establishing causation. As n can determine n1 to a lesser or stronger extent, n can be said to be more or less binding upon B. Indeed, administrative reality shows that attaching legal bindingness to n is not the only way for A to make sure that n determines n1. Another option for A to make sure that n1 corresponds to n is to announce financial disadvantages for B in case of non-correspondence. Also, A could rely on its political authority or technical expertise, meaning that B routinely issues n1 in line with n because it trusts in A's assessment. Yet another option to ensure that n1 corresponds to n would be to rely on limits in terms of practical feasibility. For instance, if B does not have the capacity to double-check whether n is correct, B would generally issue n1 in line with n. All these scenarios show that the legal bindingness of n is not a precondition for n to determine n1.[168] Instead, whether or not the administrative support n determines n1 depends on the extent to which it is binding upon the actor B issuing the administrative decision n1. In this sense, the degree of the

166 See fn. 31 and fn. 33.

167 See fn. 75 and fn. 46.

168 Similarly Filipe Brito Bastos, „Derivate Illegality in European Composite Administrative Procedures" (fn. 28), p. 106, 114, stressing that where the decision-issuing actor has sufficient room for manoeuvre to make a lawful choice, it cannot be said that the supporting actor has caused the damage. Similarly, in terms of the approach, also Uwe Säuberlich, *Die außervertragliche Haftung im Gemeinschaftsrecht* (fn. 4), p. 86–93, although he concludes that the relevant criterion is the 'legal room for manouevre' and that, therefore, factual conduct cannot trigger liability. Similarly, in terms of result, also Melanie Fink, *Frontex and Human Rights* (fn. 49), p. 256–257 and Melanie Fink, „EU Liability for Contributions to Member States' Breaches of EU Law" (fn. 5), p. 1236, 1242 who argues that 'non-binding guidance does not limit the room for manoeuvre of the 'guided' authority', therefore establishes associated liability in these cases.

bindingness of n is the decisive factor in establishing the sufficiently direct link and, thus, causation.[169]

4.2 Degree of Bindingness in Case of Omission

In order to illustrate the specific questions arising in the case of omission to act, consider the following example. Imagine that actor A is responsible for supervising the conduct of supervisee B and that A fails to perform its supervisory task n, resulting in B issuing an unlawful decision n1, which results in damage to the interests of a concerned individual. The required conduct n is of a non-formally binding nature, which means that A would not have been able, also if it had complied with its supervisory obligations, to legally oblige B to issue a lawful decision n1. The question now is under which conditions A's failure to perform n is to be considered as causal for the resulting damage. As both the omission of n and n1 constitute a sine qua non to the damage, the decisive criterion, again, must be that of the sufficiently direct link.

Since causation in cases of omission involves an assessment of the consequences of actions that did not take place, it is obvious that probability plays a key role. In essence, causation depends on the level of certainty with which a certain damage would not have occurred if a certain action had been taken.[170]

The crucial question in determining the sufficiently direct link is hence with which level of certainty the performance of n would have prevented the damage, more specifically, whether it is sufficient to establish that the risk of the occurrence of the damage would have been reduced, or whether it is required to establish that the damage would certainly not have occurred if n had been performed. What is discussed in particular in this context is whether A's liability is excluded if B could have, despite the lack of adequate supervision, still have issued a lawful decision n1, or in other

169 If one adopts a narrow understanding of 'bindingness' as meaning only 'legal bindingness', one could also speak of the degree of 'influence' on the decision. This term is however not less ambiguous, as 'influence' is also sometimes defined as presupposing 'legal bindingness', see e.g. Opinion of Advocate General Ruiz-Jarabo Colomer, 7 September 2004, Portuguese Republic v Commission, C-249/02, para 44.

170 See Melanie Fink, „EU Liability for Contributions to Member States' Breaches of EU Law" (fn. 5), p. 1257–1259 with further references to the relevant case law.

words, whether discretion or room for manoeuvre to act lawfully on the part of B excludes the liability of A.

Some argue that an omission can only be said to be causal for damage if the required conduct would have prevented the occurrence of the damage with a level of probability close to certainty.[171] According to this opinion, any discretion on the side of B excludes A's liability. If B has the option to issue a lawful decision n1, regardless of the content of n, it cannot be said with certainty that the performance of n would have prevented the occurrence of the damage. Others correctly note that such understanding, in combination with the rules on the burden of proof,[172] would have the consequence that the supervising authority would almost never be held responsible for any omission to adequately supervise. Some of the latter authors conclude that the probability criterion is unsuitable for establishing causation and propose a competence criterion instead. According to this proposal, it should be decisive which body has the legal competence to prevent the occurrence of the damage.[173] While this approach is generally useful, it does not lead much further in the case of non-formally binding conduct. Where n is non-formally binding in nature, it cannot be said with certainty that A could have prevented the damage, so the application of the competence test would still require an assessment of the level of probability with which A could have prevented the occurrence of the damage.[174]

Therefore, it is argued here that in order to establish causation in the case of omission, a *reasonable* level of certainty is required.[175] This understanding is conceptually sound and plausible in light of administrative reality. If A's supervisory measure consists of issuing a legally binding decision n towards B, it is appropriate to consider A's omission as causal because

171 Astrid Czaja, *Die außervertragliche Haftung der EG für ihre Organe* (fn. 30), p. 112; Uwe Säuberlich, *Die außervertragliche Haftung im Gemeinschaftsrecht* (fn. 4), p. 236.

172 See fn. 152.

173 Uwe Säuberlich, *Die außervertragliche Haftung im Gemeinschaftsrecht* (fn. 4), p. 236 with reference to Opinion of Advocate General Gand, 19 April 1967, Kampffmeyer, Joined cases 5/66 et al, p. 361, 376.

174 For a similar approach in the context of attribution see chapter 4, 2.2. In that context, the approach based on a competence to prevent is sufficient because the relevant conduct is formally-binding.

175 Similarly, Opinion of Advocate General Dutheillet de Lamothe, 17 February 1971, Lütticke, 4/69, p. 346–347 who refers to 'sufficient causality' and argues that the Union's conduct can only be considered as causal in this sense if it is 'indissociable' from the national conduct.

it is certain that the issuance of that decision would have prevented the occurrence of the damage.[176] If A's supervision consists of a conduct n that is in no manner whatsoever binding upon B, it is appropriate to consider A's omission as non-causal because it is almost certain that the performance of that conduct, which is basically irrelevant to B, would not have prevented the damage. In administrative practice, however, most constellations are not that clear-cut. Usually, the supervising actor A does not act in formally-binding form, but nonetheless effectively determines the conduct of B. As set out above, in all cases from *KYDEP* to *Bourdouvali*, the Commission, if adequately exercising its supervision, would have acted in a non-formally binding form but would nonetheless have been able to effectively determine the content of n1.

The reasonable level of certainty hence depends on the degree of bindingness of the omitted conduct. The decisive question is whether A's supervisory conduct n, the omission of which is reproached in the context of Art. 340 para 2 TFEU would have been sufficiently binding upon B to conclude that it would have led B to issue a lawful decision n1. In other words, the sufficiently direct link between A's failure to adopt the supervisory measure n and the resulting damage is established if n would have been sufficiently binding upon B to conclude, with reasonable certainty, that the performance of that conduct would have resulted in B acting lawfully. Crucially, and in line with the argument set out above, this does not require formal legal bindingness. Supervisory measures that are de facto binding upon B have a similar effect to formally-binding measures in that B's discretion is effectively reduced. Therefore, de facto bindingness of n is sufficient to establish, with reasonable certainty, that B would have complied with n.

This understanding is implicit in the CJEU's jurisprudence. In *Kampffmeyer*, for instance, the court held that the Commission's failure to approve of certain national measures is not sufficient to establish causation.[177] This is consequential because the mere approval would not have been de facto binding upon national authorities. In similar cases, the court also held that the Commission's failure to authorise certain national measures is sufficient to establish causation, notably regardless

176 Of course assuming that B acts in line with legally binding measures, which – considering the grave implementation deficits in the EU legal order, and especially in the asylum system – is self-evident only in theory.

177 CJEU, judgement of 14 July 1967, Kampffmeyer, 5/66 et al (fn. 121).

of whether that authorisation would have been formally-binding or not.[178] This is also consequential because the Commission's authorisation, in the relevant administrative contexts, would have been de facto binding upon the national authorities so that it could be said, with reasonable certainty, that the Commission's authorisation would have prevented the occurrence of the damage. Similarly, in *Ledra* and *Bourdouvali*, the court found that the Commission's failure to exercise its supervisory obligations was, in principle, to be considered as causal for the resulting damage, although it was clear that the Commission's supervisory measures would not have been formally binding upon the concerned member states.[179] The court hence considered the omission of de facto binding conduct as sufficient to establish causation.

4.3 Decisive Criteria Establishing *De Facto* Bindingness

In order to establish, in a concrete case, whether a particular conduct of an EU body is de facto binding upon national authorities, the CJEU conducts a comprehensive analysis and takes into account all relevant circumstances of the case. Three factors recur across different case constellations and are of particular weight in the assessment. These are, first, financial incentives or pressure on the member state, second, superior technical expertise or information on the part of the EU body, and third, political authority on the part of the EU body.[180] As will be shown, this is consequential because these three factors have the effect that a non-formally binding measure issued by an EU body, for instance an informal recommendation or a guideline, is almost as 'compulsory' on the concerned national authority as if it was formally binding. In other words, financial pressure, superior expertise or political authority can have a normative effect that comes very close to that of formal bindingness.

178 See above 2.2 and 2.3.

179 CJEU, judgement of 13 July 2018, Bourdouvali, T-786/14 (fn. 93); CJEU, judgement of 20 September 2016, Ledra, C-8/15 P et al (fn. 2).

180 Similarly, Astrid Czaja, *Die außervertragliche Haftung der EG für ihre Organe* (fn. 30), p. 131.

a *Financial Incentives or Pressure*

First, attaching financial incentives or pressure to the supporting conduct n has a relatively strong effect on B because non-compliance with n would lead to considerable or severe disadvantages for the member state. Hence, the relevant EU conduct must be considered as de facto binding upon the member state, i.e. as sufficiently binding so as to establish causation.

This reasoning is clearly reflected in the Court's case law. In *KYDEP* already, the CJEU held that financial incentives provided by A are sufficient to consider the support n as sufficiently binding upon B.[181] Similarly, in *New Europe Consulting*, the Court argued that serious financial consequences are comparable to formal legal bindingness insofar as procedural guarantees become applicable.[182] *Ledra* and *Bourdouvali,* then, clearly confirm the similarity of financial incentives or pressure to formal legal bindingness. As has been widely discussed in that context, conditionalities attached to Union funding are an effective means of achieving member state compliance.[183] It is hence only consequential that the CJEU considered economic or financial pressure on the member state to adopt a certain measure as sufficient to consider the Union's non-formally binding conduct as triggering liability.[184]

When transferring this argument to the asylum system, one additional consideration must be taken into account. Unlike in the context of the internal market or in the Eurozone, EU support in the context of the asylum system encompasses both funding and administrative capacity. Where the Union provides administrative capacity, however, the host member

181 CJEU, judgement of 15 September 1994, *KYDEP*, C-146/91 (fn. 1), para 25–26.

182 CJEU, judgement of 9 July 1999, New Europe Consulting, T-231/97 (fn. 53), para 43. While the situation was different in that case insofar as the financial disadvantage arose on the part of the applicants, the argument nonetheless applies here insofar as the court argues that serious financial disadvantages have effects similar to formal legal bindingness.

183 See only Scott Greer, „Structural adjustment comes to Europe: Lessons for the Eurozone from the conditionality debates", *Global Social Policy* 14 (2013), p. 51-71; Kevin Featherstone, „External conditionality and the debt crisis: the 'Troika' and public administration reform in Greece", *Journal of European Public Policy* 22 (2015), p. 295-314.

184 CJEU, judgement of 13 July 2018, Bourdouvali, T-786/14 (fn. 93); CJEU, judgement of 20 September 2016, Ledra, C-8/15 P et al (fn. 2).

state is usually truly dependent on that support.[185] The withdrawal of the Union's administrative support would lead to severe difficulties on the part of the concerned member state in upholding a functioning administration.[186] Seen from this perspective, it does not make a substantial difference whether the member state depends on monetary or administrative support from the Union. The reasons that have led the CJEU to consider the provision of EU funding as a relevant factor in the context of causation also apply to the provision of administrative capacity. Hence, not only explicit financial pressure, e.g. in the form of conditionalities, but also implicit financial pressure, e.g. in the form of dependency on the Union's administrative capacity, are decisive factors for establishing de facto bindingness.

b *Political Authority*

Second, political authority is a factor to be taken into account in assessing the legal effects of the Union's recommendations or advice. This becomes relevant, in particular, in the case of the Commission. Due to the its role as guardian of the Treaties, the Commission's measures, including informal 'advice' or 'guidelines', bear a particular political weight which makes it difficult for national authorities to disregard them. In general terms, it is particularly likely for a member state B to adopt an EU body's recommendation n and issue a decision n1 towards an individual where the relevant EU body is the Commission. In this sense, political authority can establish de facto bindingness.

The particular weight of the Commission's measures is generally recognised in scholarship but usually not analysed in much depth. Most authors simply observe that the Commission's recommendations factually determine national conduct.[187] Some identify psychological and political

185 This follows already from the applicable EU secondary law, according to which the Union provides administrative support precisely when the national asylum system is systemically deficient to an extent that it jeopardises the functioning of the Common Asylum System as a whole, see e.g. Art. 14–15, 22 EUAA Regulation.

186 This holds true especially in the case of 'weak members' as defined by Michael Ioannidis, „Weak Members and the Enforcement of EU Law", in András Jakab, Dimitry Kochenov (ed.), *The Enforcement of EU Law and Values. Ensuring Member States' Compliance*, Oxford University Press 2017, p. 476–492.

187 Timo Rademacher, *Realakte im Rechtsschutzsystem der Europäischen Union* (fn. 5), p. 37 with further references.

pressure on national decision-makers as decisive factor.[188] A closer look, however, shows that it is not the psychological effect as such that is decisive for the threshold of bindingness but rather the political authority that generates this effect.

While it might sound counterintuitive at first sight to consider political authority as relevant to establishing de facto bindingness in a legal sense, it can hardly be denied that, in practice, the Commission's political authority makes it difficult for member states to not follow its opinions and guidelines.[189] At the same time, however, the Commission's authority alone cannot be considered as sufficient to establish de facto bindingness. For if that were so, every supervisory measure of the Commission's would have to be considered as de facto binding upon member states; and this understanding would certainly be too broad.

Conceptually, the derivation of legal effects from political authority is closely related to the concept of mutual trust. As well established concerning horizontal relations among member states, trust in the legal correctness and appropriateness of decisions taken by other authorities have hard legal consequences. Simply put, the principle of mutual trust establishes that one authority's trust that another authority works well, in general terms, has the result that the latter authority's decisions have legally binding effects for the former authority.[190] Transferring this idea from horizontal to vertical relations, it is only consequential that member states' trust in the Commission and their recognition of the Commission's role as guardian of the Treaties has the result that the Commission's informal advice has legal consequences. In other words, the Commission's informal measures have particular normative weight and are usually adopted precisely because the Commission is perceived by member states as political authority the opinions of which matter and are usually correct.

---

188 Astrid Czaja, *Die außervertragliche Haftung der EG für ihre Organe* (fn. 30), p. 131.

189 Ibid., p. 206.

190 CJEU, Court (Grand Chamber), judgment of 21 December 2011, N.S. v Secretary of State for the Home Department and M.E. and Others v Refugee Applications Commissioner and Minister for Justice, Equality and Law Reform, Joined cases C-411/10 and C-493/10, para 83–86; CJEU, Court, Opinion of 18 December 2014 on the Accession of the European Union to the European Convention for the Protection of Human Rights and Fundamental Freedoms, 2/13, para 168, 191.

c *Superior Technical Expertise or Information*

Third, superior technical expertise or an information monopoly are decisive in establishing de facto causation.[191] For when the Union body A holds superior technical expertise or information that is required to make the decision n1, it is particularly likely that B will issue n1 in accordance with the recommendation n. In this sense, an advantage in terms of expertise and information has effects similar to legal bindingness and must, therefore, be considered sufficient to establish causation.[192]

Again, this argument is clearly reflected in the CJEU's case law. In *Ledra,* for instance, the CJEU put a particular emphasis on the 'technical expertise' of the Commission and the ECB and the fact that they 'gave advice and provided guidance' to national authorities.[193] In *Bourdouvali,* the CJEU stressed that the ECB was dependent on information provided to it by national authorities.[194]

Unsurprisingly, the argument of superior expertise or advice is of particular importance in cases where EU agencies are involved, as these *per definitionem* hold superior information and expertise in one particular area.[195] Some even argue that, in the case of agencies, 'boundaries between scientific advice and decision-making become lost in practice' and that, as a result, 'the final decision de facto belongs to the agency'.[196] With regard to Frontex, more specifically, it has been noted several times that the agency's comprehensive information and expertise in the area of border control

191 As here Melanie Fink, „The Action for Damages as a Fundamental Rights Remedy: Holding Frontex Liable", *German Law Journal* 21 (2020), p. 532–548.

192 Ibid., p. 539: 'Even though the Member Sate is, legally speaking, free to disregard the advice, it may be difficult to do so in practice, especially when the EU body has more expertise than the national authority.'.

193 CJEU, judgement of 20 September 2016, Ledra, C-8/15 P et al (fn. 2), para 52, albeit here in the context of attribution, and to make the argument that they acted within the limits of their competences.

194 CJEU, judgement of 13 July 2018, Bourdouvali, T-786/14 (fn. 93), para 137–139, 383.

195 See on the conception of agencies as experts providing specialised knowledge in areas of growing complexity, see European Commission, Communication from the Commission to the European Parliament and the Council, European agencies – The way forward, 11 March 2008, COM(2008) 135 final.

196 As here Madalina Busuioc, *European Agencies: Law and Practices of Accountability*, Oxford University Press 2013, p. 192–193, arguing that the legality of non-binding acts should be reviewed because otherwise there would be an insurmountable gap in the accountability of the 'de facto operative decision maker.'.

makes it especially difficult for national authorities to ignore the agency's non-formally binding advice.[197]

On this basis, and with a view to applying the criterion of superior expertise or information to the context at hand, it should be noted that a combination of financial pressure and expertise is particularly likely to establish de facto causation, and that this combination occurs, in particular, in the context of systemic deficiencies. When the national administration, due to systemic deficiencies, depends on the Union's support, national authorities will usually not have the capacity to obtain or verify the information and assessment provided by EU bodies. As a result, the national authority will be de facto left with no option but to trust in the Union bodies' expertise, rely on the information obtained by them, and adopt their recommendations.

5 Conclusions on Causation

Having reconstructed the doctrine of causation, this section now applies the findings to the case at hand. This will lead to the conclusion that the EUAA's and Frontex's procedural misconduct must, depending on the circumstances of the concrete case, be considered as causal for the fundamental rights violations that result from the reception conditions in the EU hotspot camps, i.e. in particular Art. 4 and Art. 6 ChFR. More precisely, it will be argued that the effects of the agencies' recommendations are so close to legal bindingness that the threshold of de facto bindingness is reached. This is due to implicit financial pressure upon the host member state, as well as superior technical expertise and information on the part of the agencies.

For similar reasons, the Commission's failure to adequately supervise must be considered as causal both for fundamental rights violations related to the reception conditions, as well as for infringements of Art. 41 ChFR

---

197 See only Melanie Fink, „The Action for Damages as a Fundamental Rights Remedy: Holding Frontex Liable" (fn. 191), p. 541: 'given Frontex's accesss to relevant information, its expertise in the area of border management (...) national authorities may find themselves in a situation where it is difficult in practice to disregard a piece of 'advice' provided by the agency'; Mariana Gkliati, Herbert Rosenfeldt, „Accountability of the European Border and Coast Guard Agency: Recent developments, legal standards and existing mechanisms", *RLI Working Paper* 30 (2018), p. 12: Frontex's 'advice, although not formally binding, would be hard to disregard due to the research and technical expertise of the agency'.

that occur due to systemic malpractice on the part of the agencies. As will be argued, the Commission's superior expertise and political authority in combination with financial pressure have the effect that the Commission's non-formally binding supervisory measures are de facto binding upon agencies and host member state.

5.1 The Agencies' Individual Recommendations

There are three main reasons which together have the effect that the agencies' recommendations are de facto binding upon the host member state.[198]

The first is that the agencies' recommendations come with implicit financial pressure. In order to understand the relevance of this kind of pressure, it must be recalled that the Greek asylum system heavily depends on Union support, both in terms of funding and in terms of administrative capacity.[199] As set out above, this holds true, especially for the EU hotspots, in which about half of the administrative staff is provided by agencies, and national staff is also partly seconded by the EUAA and partly funded by the Union. Considering that, even with the considerable support provided by the Union, the EU hotspot administration is at the edges of its capacity, and lacks all kind of equipment, from offices to paper, there can be little doubt that, without Union support, it would simply not be functionable.[200]

Against this background, it becomes clear that practical needs and capacity limits often leave the Greek administration with no choice but to routinely adopt the agencies' recommendations. This is well illustrated with the EUAA's procedural support. Overturning the EUAA's recommendations to accept or reject an individual claim would require the asylum service to schedule another interview, assess the claim and write the decision from scratch. Given the permanent time pressure and the high caseload, such

198 Differently, Herbert Rosenfeldt, *Frontex im Zentrum der Europäischen Grenz- und Küstenwache. Bestandsaufnahme, Unionsrechtmäßigkeit und Verantwortlichkeit*, Mohr Siebeck 2021, p. 321 stressing – albeit with reference to regular Frontex teams, and not with reference to MMST teams – that an action for damages is doomed to fail because Frontex cannot instruct national authorities in a legally binding manner.

199 Similarly for the Greek administration more generally Michael Ioannidis, „Weak Members and the Enforcement of EU Law" (fn. 186), p. 485–487; Evangelia (Lilian) Tsourdi, Cathryn Costello, „'Systemic Violations' in EU Asylum Law: Cover or Catalyst?", *German Law Journal* 24 (2023), p. 982–994, p. 990.

200 See chapter 2, 1 to 3.

review procedure is simply not feasible on a regular basis. It is hence only consequential that the Greek asylum service in the vast majority of cases follows the comprehensive recommendation, thereby essentially limiting its additional work to translation.[201]

In the case of Frontex's procedural support, the same logic applies. The first registration of asylum applicants in the EU hotspots is usually a very hasty process, and the caseload is usually very high. Hellenic authorities rely on Frontex precisely for those procedural steps that are particularly time-consuming and require particular expertise and equipment. Once these tasks are taken over by Frontex, it appears counterproductive, from the perspective of the Hellenic authorities concerned with speeding up the registration process, to question Frontex's assessment. And when Frontex comes to the conclusion that a particular applicant is an adult, national authorities have an additional incentive to adopt that recommendation. Given that there is not sufficient room to adequately host minors,[202] it might even appear as a practical advantage, again from the perspective of national authorities, that a person is considered an adult.

Second, national authorities routinely adopt the agencies' recommendations because these are based on an information advantage. As the agencies' legal opinions are necessarily based on factual information obtained during an interview or a less formal form of personal interaction with the applicant, national authorities usually lack the factual knowledge to even cast doubt on the accuracy of the legal evaluation.[203] In the case of the EUAA, the asylum service has only so much information about the facts of the case as contained in the interview transcript provided by the agency. Thus, if the information and the legal assessment provided by the EUAA are coherent, the Greek asylum service has no indication to initiate a review. In practice, it is therefore very unlikely that the Greek asylum service would challenge the agency's recommendation.[204]

Similarly, in the case of Frontex, national authorities usually base their decisions on the case file. For example, if Frontex estimates an applicant's age solely on visual inspection alone, Frontex's estimate is nonetheless accepted by national authorities in the vast majority of cases. In fact, national

201 Since the implementation of the embedded model (see chapter 2, 1.3.b), not even a translation is required because the opinion is now usually drafted in Greek.

202 See chapter 2, 3.

203 Many thanks to Anne Pertsch for stressing this aspect in our discussions.

204 See chapter 2, 1.3.

authorities review the agency's recommendation only when the concerned applicant is represented by a lawyer willing to devote considerable capacity to the matter. And even in these cases, it is still extremely rare for Hellenic authorities to overturn a Frontex recommendation.[205]

Third, and closely related, the agencies' recommendations come with particular weight due to their particular professional expertise, or at least the perception thereof. The significant shortcomings in the agencies' administrative conduct notwithstanding, they are generally considered as experts in their specific areas of support. This perception is based on the fact that agency staff receive special trainings, for instance, on vulnerability in the case of the EUAA, or on document verification in the case of Frontex. In addition, the EUAA and Frontex provide trainings for national authorities, issue practical guidelines on how to apply EU asylum and border law, and publish comprehensive reports including legal evaluations.

Against this background, it is obvious that, for instance, a case officer of the national asylum authority who disagrees with an EUAA assessment will have to present a specific and well-reasoned argumentation to justify why they would not use the comprehensive recommendation of the expert agency and instead create additional workload for their own authority. Remarkably, the increasing institutional intertwinement between the EUAA and the Greek asylum authority makes the agency's knowledge advantage and professional expertise even more relevant. This is because the main reason for earlier divergences, namely the different policies of the two bodies,[206] disappears when the EUAA and the national asylum service work according to the same guidelines.

To conclude, the EUAA's and Frontex's recommendations are de facto binding upon Greek authorities. Therefore, the agency's recommendations must, in principle, be considered as causal for the violations of individual rights resulting from the national administrative decision that is based on the agency's recommendation. This is well illustrated with cases 1 and 3.[207]

Case 1 – Sara Esmaili – Inhumane reception conditions – Art. 4 ChFR (causation by the EUAA)

In the case of Ms Esmaili and her daughter Ayla, the EUAA officer failed in the winter of 2018 to conduct a correct vulnerability assessment and thus recommended considering them as non-vulnerable. National

205 Ibid.

206 See chapter 2, fn. 43.

207 Again, this list is not exhaustive.

authorities adopted that opinion without further assessment and accordingly obliged them to stay in the EU hotspot camp, where they were exposed to inhuman reception conditions – whereas, under the applicable law, vulnerable persons were to be exempt from the border procedure and transferred to the mainland. Regarding the causal link between the EUAA's misconduct and the resulting violation of Art. 4 ChFR, the crucial point is that the Greek authorities were de facto bound by the EUAA's recommendation. The EUAA is considered an expert on issues related to vulnerability. Greek authorities operate only on the basis of the information obtained by the EUAA and have regularly no reason to cast doubt on the agency's assessment. What is more, none of the Greek authorities involved actually have the capacity to double-check whether the EUAA's recommendation is correct, which leaves them with no choice but to adopt the EUAA's recommendation. Therefore, the EUAA's recommendation must be considered as causal for the resulting violation of Art. 4 ChFR.

Case 3 – Daniat Kidane – Inhumane Reception Conditions – Art. 4 ChFR (causation by Frontex)

In the case of Daniat Kidane, the Frontex officer assessed her age alone through visual inspection and, on this basis, concluded that she was an adult. Responsible national authorities adopted that opinion, again without further assessment, and hence obliged Daniat Kidane to stay in the EU hotspot camp, where she was subject to substandard reception conditions in breach of Art. 4 ChFR – although minors, according to the applicable law, were to be housed in special centres where the particular needs can be met.[208] Regarding the causal link between Frontex's misconduct and the exposure of Daniat Kidane to inhumane reception conditions, the main considerations are similar to those in the EUAA case. First, that Greek authorities are subject to implicit financial pressure in the sense that national authorities cannot 'afford' to not adopt Frontex's recommendations because they do not have the additional capacity to conduct another correct age assessment. Second, Frontex's recommendation is based on superior information. As national authorities are informed only about the outcome of Frontex's assessment, they have regularly no reason to doubt the accuracy of the agency's recommendation. Third, Frontex's recommendation comes with particular weight because the agency is,

208 See Art. 23–24 Reception Conditions Directive.

in practice, perceived as 'the expert' on age assessment. As a result, the agency's recommendation is de facto binding upon Greek authorities and must therefore be considered as causal for the resulting violation of Art. 4 ChFR.

5.2 The Commission's Failure to Supervise

For similar reasons, the Commission's supervisory measures must also be considered as de facto binding upon national authorities. As will be shown, this reasoning applies to those fundamental rights violations that are ultimately evoked by the misconduct of the agencies, i.e., in particular, violations of Art. 41 ChFR, and with regard to those that are ultimately evoked by the misconduct of the host member state, i.e. in particular, violations of Art. 4 and 6 ChFR.[209]

As a preliminary point, it must be stressed that the following argument applies only to systemic misconduct on the part of the host member state and the agencies, respectively. As established above, the Commission is obliged, under Art. 40 para 3 Frontex Regulation, Art. 21 para 2 EUAA Regulation, Art. 17 TEU, to ensure that the EU hotspot administration *generally* complies with EU law. Thus, and while it does not have the competences to ensure that each individual decision of the host member state and of the agencies is lawful, it can ensure that the host member state's and the agencies' practices are generally in line with EU law. In fact, the Commission's supervisory fora, especially the EURTF and the Steering Committees, were established precisely to ensure this compliance in general terms.[210]

This being said, there are three main factors which together have the effect that the Commission's supervisory measures have a de facto binding effect. First, the Commission's supervisory measures always come with implicit, and sometimes even with explicit, financial pressure. Given that Greece's whole asylum system, and in particular the EU hotspots, heavily depend on EU funding, the Commission's position in coordination fora such as the EURTF or the Steering Committees always comes with the powerful 'money argument'. Put bluntly, every participant knows that the

209 See on the distinction between procedure-related and reception-related violations see chapter 2, 3.

210 See chapter 2, 2.

Commission has the last word on EU funding.[211] As a result, the Commission's position can be challenged only with very strong arguments. Not following the Commission's instructions is potentially expensive.

Especially in contexts of immediate crisis, the sheer amount of EU financial support often leaves Greek authorities with no choice but to adopt the Commission's policies. This is well illustrated with the 2015 EU hotspot approach. As Greece's asylum system had been systemically deficient since the early 2010s and was about to collapse in the crisis, it would have been politically untenable to refuse the Commission's hotspot approach, which promised operational as well as financial support from the Union. Today, implicit financial pressure is particularly obvious in the context of the EURTF and the Steering Committee Migration Management. In 2023, the functioning of Greece's asylum administration still largely depended on EU funding. In addition, Greece strongly depended on EU funding also in other policy areas. Although financial support in one area cannot be made formally dependent upon policy implementation in another area, Greece's general dependence on EU money de facto leads to a further increase in the negotiating power of the Commission.[212] As a result, the Commission's negotiating power and leverage within the EURTF and the Steering Committee is indeed considerable.[213]

Second, the Commission's guidelines come with a specific knowledge advantage. As the Commission chairs the relevant coordination meetings and gathers all relevant information from the numerous participants, it has access to a unique factual basis and is, hence, in a particularly advantageous position to make decisions about the overall course of the EU hotspot administration. As a consequence, it is particularly difficult for other participants, especially for national authorities, to challenge the Commission's recommendations. As in the case of the agencies, the knowledge advantage is so significant that it results in the Commission's measures being de facto binding.

211 Interview with Commission representative 2 conducted on 12 February 2021 (introduction, fn. 102).

212 James D Savage, Amy Verdun, „Strengthening the European Commission's budgetary and economic surveillance capacity since Greece and the euro area crisis: a study of five Directorates-General", *Journal of European Public Policy* 23 (2015), p. 101–118; Michael W. Bauer, Stefan Becker, „The Unexpected Winner of the Crisis: The European Commission's Strengthened Role in Economic Governance", *Journal of European Integration* 36 (2014), p. 213–229.

213 Interview wirh Commission representative 2 conducted on 12 February 2021 (introduction, fn. 102).

The third reason why the Commission's supervisory measures are regularly adopted lies in the Commission's political authority and its perceived professional expertise. Again, this is well illustrated with the implementation of the 2015 EU hotspot approach. As explained above, the Commission's role in this regard is closely connected to its responsibility to implement the EU-Türkiye Statement.[214] This means that all member states had agreed to entrust the Commission with the implementation of the return policy. Greece, as the country where that policy would be implemented, could hence not easily object to the administrative guidelines issued by the responsible Commission representative. Again, a comparison to the Eurozone crisis supports the argument. Greece's position in the asylum crisis was arguably very similar to that of Cyprus in the Eurozone crisis. In both cases, the Commission was entrusted with the implementation of an informal agreement in a relatively weak member state,[215] and in both cases, that member state, albeit itself part of the agreement, de facto had no option but to comply with the Commission's implementing guidelines.

Lastly, it must be recalled that the fact that the Commission's instructions are not always followed does not argue against their de facto binding nature. Non-compliance occurs also in case of formally-binding rules, and is not per se an argument against the normative force of these. Therefore, the Commission's complaints about a lack of compliance on the part of the member state only confirms that compliance is the rule, i.e. that the Commission's instructions are usually adopted and hence de facto binding.

To conclude, the Commission's supervisory measures under Art. 40 para 3 Frontex Regulation, Art. 21 para 2 EUAA Regulation, Art. 17 TEU have de facto binding force on the host member state and the agencies insofar as their general compliance with EU law is concerned. Thus, the Commission's failure to undertake, or to correctly implement, the required supervisory measures must be considered as causal for the resulting violations of fundamental rights, especially of Art. 4, 6 and Art. 41 ChFR. Insofar as reception-related deficiencies are concerned, this is well illustrated with

---

214 See chatper 2, 2.1.

215 On the state of the rule of law in Greece see European Parliament, Resolution of 7 February 2024 on the rule of law and media freedom in Greece, 2024/2502(RSP), para 27, where the Parliament calls upon the Commission 'to make full use of the tools available to it to address the breaches of the values enshrined in Article 2 TEU in Greece'; further on the rule of law in Greece and Hungary, in the specific context of asylum, see Evangelia (Lilian) Tsourdi, Cathryn Costello, „'Systemic Violations' in EU Asylum Law: Cover or Catalyst?" (fn. 199), p. 991 et seq.

case 1, and insofar as procedure-related deficiencies are concerned, this is well illustrated with case 3.[216]

Case 1 – Sara Esmaili – Inhumane reception conditions – Art. 4 ChFR (causation by the Commission due to failure to adequately supervise host member state)
As established above, Greece's failure to provide adequate reception conditions is not limited to the case of Ms Esmaili. Vulnerable persons staying in the EU hotspots camps are systemically exposed to conditions below the standard of Art. 4 ChFR. Therefore, the violation of Art. 4 ChFR must be considered as having been caused by the Commission's failure to adequately exercise its supervisory obligations under Art. 40 para 3 Frontex Regulation, Art. 21 para 2 EUAA Regulation, Art. 17 TEU. While the Commission was informed about the conditions in the EU hotspots and thus obliged, according to the cited provisions, to ensure the overall legality of the EU hotspot administration, it failed to adequately exercise its supervisory powers. In particular, the Commission failed to make use of its possibilities within the EURTF and the Steering Committee to ensure that the living conditions generally meet the minimum requirements of Art. 4 ChFR, let al.one the minimum standards required under EU secondary law. Further, the Commission apparently failed to attach formal conditionalities to the funding provided by the Union. Due to implicit and explicit financial pressure, the Commission's perceived superior expertise, and its political authority as guardian of the Treaties, these measures would have been de facto binding upon Greece. Therefore, the Commission's failure to undertake these measures is to be considered as causal for the systemic violation of Art. 4 ChFR, and thus also of the violation of the rights of Ms Esmaili and her daughter, insofar as these violations reflect systemic deficiencies.

Case 3 – Daniat Kidane – Age assessment through visual inspection – Art. 24, 41 ChFR (causation by the Commission due to failure to adequately supervise Frontex)
Similarly, the case of Daniat Kidane reflects Frontex's systemic malpractice in conducting age assessments purely based on visual inspection. Therefore, the Commission's failure to adequately exercise its supervisory obligations must be considered as causal for the violation of Art. 24, 41 ChFR, as well as in the case of Daniat Kidane. Although the Commission

216 Again, this list is not exhaustive.

does not have the competence to issue binding instructions towards Frontex, it is obliged to ensure, under Art. 40 para 3 Frontex Regulation, Art. 21 para 2 EUAA Regulation, Art. 17 TEU, that Frontex's practices in the EU hotspots generally comply with EU law, especially with fundamental rights. To this end, the Commission should have made use of its positions in Frontex's internal decision-making bodies as well as in the EURTF and the Steering Committees. Given that the Commission's measures within these fora are de facto binding upon Frontex, its failure to adequately exercise supervision must be considered as causal for the resulting fundamental rights violations.

5.3 The EU's Liability for Resulting Violations

To conclude, liability of the agencies and of the Commission for fundamental rights violations resulting from their misconduct can be established. In brief, the argument is summarised as follows: As regards, first, recommendations and advice issued by the EUAA and Frontex, the crucial point is that the national administration is systemically deficient and notoriously overburdened. Therefore, national authorities strongly depend on support from the agencies. This, in combination with the fact that the agencies base their recommendations on information to which national authorities regularly do not have access and that the agencies are in practice considered as the experts, has the effect that national authorities are de facto obliged to regularly adopt the agencies' opinions without further assessment. In other words, the agencies' recommendations and advice are de facto binding upon national authorities.

Concerning, second, the Commission's guidelines and supervisory measures or lack thereof, a similar argument applies. To be precise, a distinction must be made here between the host member state and the agencies.

Insofar as the relationship between the Commission and Greece is concerned, it is again central that the functioning of the Greek asylum system heavily depends on EU funding. Although the Commission can, of course, not withdraw funding simply because its opinions are not followed by national authorities, the fact that it is in charge of EU funding as such has the effect that national authorities are in a structurally weaker position. This, together with the fact that the Commission's recommendations are based on superior knowledge and that the Commission has a particular political authority due to its role as guardian of the Treaties, has the effect that the Commission's guidelines have the facto binding force upon both national authorities.

Insofar as the relation between the Commission and the agencies is concerned, the crucial point is that the agencies' conduct in the EU hotspots – where their staff operates as part of migration management support teams (MMST) – is subject to supervision by the Commission. Notwithstanding the agencies' general independence, the Commission thus has the competence to ensure that the agencies' operations in the EU hotspots generally comply with EU law. In practice, the agencies regularly follow the Commission's opinions and guidelines without further assessment. In this sense, the Commission's supervisory measures are de facto binding upon the agencies.

As a result, misconduct on the part of Frontex, the EUAA and the Commission must be considered as causal for resulting fundamental rights violations – i.e. those which are ultimately evoked by decisions of national authorities – at least insofar as these violations are representative of systemic malpractice. Provided that the remaining preconditions of public liability are met, the agencies are hence liable under Art. 97 para 4, Art. 98 Frontex Regulation and Art. 66 para 3 EUAA Regulation, respectively; and in case of their insolvency, damages can be claimed directly from the Union under Art. 340 para 2 TFEU. This becomes relevant in all cases where the agencies' de facto binding conduct results in fundamental rights violations, i.e. in cases 1, 3, 4 and 5. The Commission, in turn, incurs liability under Art. 340 para 2 TFEU for fundamental rights violations that result from systemic misconduct of Frontex and the EUAA, and for those that result from systemic misconduct of the host member state. The Commission's failure to adequately supervise the host member state and the agencies becomes relevant in cases 1, 2, 3, 4, 5 and 6.

Case 1 – Sara Esmaili – Inhumane reception conditions – Art. 4 and 41 ChFR (liability of the EUAA and the Commission)

In the case of Ms Esmaili and her daughter Ayla, the EUAA has failed to conduct a correct vulnerability assessment. As established above, the EUAA hence incurs liability for the breach of Art. 41 ChFR that is inherent in its misconduct.[217]

Further, the EUAA also incurs liability for the resulting violation of Art. 4 ChFR. As shown above, the relevant misconduct performed by

217 See chapter 3, 5.a, and chapter 4, 3.1.

an MMST member must be attributed to the agency. As also shown, the breach of Art. 41 respectively Art. 4 ChFR constitutes a sufficiently serious breach of a rule conferring rights upon individuals.[218]

The question of causation remains, i.e., whether the EUAA's failure to conduct a correct vulnerability assessment is causal for the resulting violation of Art. 4 ChFR. As explained above, Ms Esmaili and her daughter were exposed to inhumane living conditions in the EU hotspots only because they were qualified as non-vulnerable. While the binding decision classifying them as non-vulnerable was formally issued by national authorities, the national authority merely rubberstamped the EUAA's opinion without further assessment. De facto, the national decision is predetermined by the EUAA's opinion. As empirical data shows, the EUAA's predetermination of national decisions is structural.[219] This structural determination is due to three factors in particular: First, the Greek administration factually depends on EU support and thus lacks the capacity to regularly double-check EUAA's opinions. Second, the Greek administration had no reason to cast doubt on the correctness of the EUAA's opinion because that opinion was based on the EUAA's interview with Ms Esmaili and, hence, on information that the national authority could not easily verify. Third, the EUAA was generally perceived as an expert on vulnerability assessments, so the Greek administration trusted in the correctness of the EUAA's opinions. In short, the EUAA's opinions are de facto binding on national authorities. According to the CJEU's established jurisprudence, the agency's opinions must hence be considered as causal for the resulting violations of Art. 4 ChFR.

Ms Esmaili's claim for compensation of immaterial damage against the EUAA, in the alternative against the Union, is successful. The CJEU would thus have to find, first, that the EUAA has breached Art. 4 ChFR. Second, the CJEU could either oblige the EUAA and, in the alternative, the Union, to pay an appropriate amount of monetary compensation to the applicant or consider the finding of illegality as such as sufficient to remedy the immaterial harm and thus grant a symbolic amount of monetary compensation or even no monetary compensation at all.[220]

As regards Ms Esmaili's claim under Art. 340 para 2 TFEU against the Commission, a similar reasoning applies. As established above, the Com-

218 See chapter 3, 3.3.
219 See chapter 2, 1.3.
220 See chapter 3, 3.4.

mission's misconduct was its failure to adequately exercise its supervisory obligations under Art. 40 para 3 Frontex Regulation, Art. 21 para 2 EUAA Regulation, Art. 17 TEU. As also follows from what has been argued above, the Commission's failures qualify as a sufficiently serious breach of a rule conferring rights upon individuals.[221]

Again, remains only the question of causation, i.e. whether the Commission's failure to adequately supervise the host member state and the agencies is causal for the resulting violations of Art. 4 and 41 ChFR. In this regard, it must first be stressed that the Commission, while not obliged to prevent every single breach of EU law, has the obligation to ensure that the host member state and the agencies generally comply with EU law. In other words, the Commission's supervisory obligation is to prevent that the EU hotspot administration becomes systemically deficient. Precisely this, however, is the case. Both the EUAA's breaches of Art. 41 ChFR through deficient vulnerability assessments and the host member state's breaches of Art. 4 ChFR through the provision of inhumane reception conditions are systemic in nature.

Against this background, the decisive point is that the Commission would have been able to ensure the legality of the EU hotspot administration via de facto binding guidelines. Although the Commission does not have the competence to issue formally-binding decisions towards host member states and agencies, it can de facto oblige them to comply with EU law. The de facto bindingness of the Commission's guidelines is due to its superior information, political authority and the host member state's dependence on EU funding. Further, the adoption of the EU hotspot approach 2.0 clearly confirms that the Commission has the competences and practical possibilities to exert influence upon the host member state through a combination of policy and funding in a manner that can actually ensure that the host member state provides reception conditions that are in compliance with EU law.[222] Thus, it can be established with a reasonable degree of certainty that if the Commission had issued guidelines and made maximum use of its competence within the relevant supervisory fora, such as the EURTF and the Steering Committees, it could have de facto obliged member state and agencies to comply with EU law. According to the CJEU's doctrine on causation in the case of omission, as set out above, the Commission's failure to adequately

221 See chapter 3, 4.2.

222 See chapter 1, 2.1.d and chapter 2, 2.

supervise the EU hotspot administration must hence be considered as causal for the resulting systemic violations of Art. 41 and 4 ChFR. With regard to the case of Ms Esmaili, this means that the fundamental rights violations must be considered as having been caused by the Commission insofar as they reflect systemic malpractice.

Ms Esmaili's claim under Art. 340 para 2 TFEU against the Commission, in the alternative against the Union, is hence successful. The CJEU would have to find that the Commission is responsible for the breaches of Art. 4 and 41 ChFR and, depending on the remaining circumstances of the case, either grant appropriate monetary compensation, a symbolic amount, or even no monetary compensation at all.[223]

Case 2 – Magan Daud – Deficient asylum interview – Art. 41 ChFR (liability of the Commission)

In the case of Mr Daud, the EUAA has conducted the asylum interview in a deficient manner and hence wrongly recommended to reject his asylum claim. As established above, the EUAA hence incurs liability for the violation of Art. 41 ChFR that is inherent in its procedural misconduct.[224] What remains to be discussed here is whether the Commission's failure to adequately supervise the EUAA also gives rise to liability under Art. 340 para 2 TFEU. As set out above, the Commission's obligation under Art. 40 para 3 Frontex Regulation, Art. 21 para 2 EUAA Regulation, Art. 17 TEU to supervise the EU hotspot administration encompasses the obligation to effectively exert influence upon the EUAA, especially in the framework of the EURTF and the Steering Committee, so as to ensure that the agency does not systemically violate EU law.[225] As also established already, the failure to ensure general compliance with Art. 41 ChCR constitutes a sufficiently serious breach of a rule conferring rights upon individuals, notably regardless of whether the supervisory obligation, i.e. Art. 40 para 3 Frontex Regulation, Art. 21 para 2 EUAA Regulation, Art. 17 TEU, or the supervisory standard, i.e. Art. 41 ChFR, is considered as decisive.

The decisive question is, hence, whether the Commission's failure to adequately supervise was causal for the breach of Art. 41 ChFR in the case of Mr Daud. The crucial point here is that the Commission's supervisory measures, especially in the framework of the EURTF and the Steering

223 See chapter 3, 3.4.
224 See chapter 3, 5.a, and chapter 4, 3.1.
225 See chapter 2, 2.

Committee, are de facto binding upon the EUAA. First, the Commission, as the overall coordinator and supervisor of the EU hotspot administration, has access to information from all authorities and bodies involved and can thus base its guidelines on superior information. Second, the Commission is in charge of EU funding, which ultimately affects the operations of the EUAA and hence gives particular weight to its guidelines and directions. Third, the Commission, as the guardian of the Treaties, has the political authority to effectively guide and steer the EUAA's conduct in the EU hotspots. Notwithstanding the fact that the agencies are generally independent of the Commission, Art. 40 para 3 Frontex Regulation and Art. 21 para 2 EUAA Regulation clearly establish that, in the specific context of the EU hotspots, the Commission is responsible for ensuring that the cooperation of the agencies with national authorities generally complies with EU law. Therefore, it can be established with a reasonable degree of certainty that if the Commission had made maximum use of its competences, it could have ensured the legality of the EUAA's practices via de facto binding measures. In this sense, the Commission's failure to adequately supervise the EU hotspot administration was causal for the EUAA's systemic malpractice, and hence also for the EUAA's misconduct in the concrete case of Mr Daud insofar as it reflects systemic practice.

Ms Daud's claim under Art. 340 para 2 TFEU against the Commission, in the alternative against the Union, is hence successful. The CJEU would have to find that the Commission is responsible for the violation of Art. 41 ChFR and, depending on the remaining circumstances of the case, either grant appropriate monetary compensation, a symbolic amount, or no monetary compensation at all.[226]

Case 3 – Daniat Kidane – Age assessment through visual inspection – Art. 24, 41 and 4 ChFR (liability of Frontex and the Commission)

In the case of Daniat Kidane, Frontex has conducted the age assessment on the basis of visual inspection alone. As established above, Frontex hence incurs liability for the violation of Art. 24, 41 ChFR that is inherent in its misconduct.[227]

What remains to be discussed here is, first, whether Frontex, and in the alternative the Union, incurs liability also for the resulting violation of Art. 4 ChFR. As explained above, this violation occurred because

226 See chapter 3, 3.4.

227 See chapter 3, 5.a, and chapter 4, 3.1.

Daniat Kidane was wrongly qualified as an adult and hence exposed to inhumane reception conditions in the camp instead of being transferred to adequate housing for unaccompanied minors. Second, it must be discussed whether the Commission incurs liability for the violation of Art. 41 ChFR and Art. 4 ChFR respectively.

First, regarding Frontex, it has already been established that its procedural misconduct constitutes a sufficiently serious breach of a rule conferring rights upon individuals. What remains to be discussed here is whether Frontex's procedural misconduct was causal for the resulting violation of Art. 4 ChFR. In this regard, the decisive point is that Frontex's misconduct was de facto binding upon national authorities. As set out above, Frontex's recommendations to register a certain age are regularly adopted by national authorities without further assessment. This is because Frontex is perceived as the expert on age assessment, because its recommendations are based on information to which national authorities usually do not have access and because the national administration heavily depends, in terms of capacity, on Frontex's support. These circumstances have the effect that Frontex's recommendations are de facto binding upon national authorities. Therefore, it can be established with a reasonable degree of certainty that if Frontex had recommended registering Daniat Kidane as a minor, she would have been registered as such and, hence, not have been exposed to inhumane living conditions in the camp. In this sense, Frontex's misconduct was causal for the resulting violation of Art. 4 ChFR. Daniat Kidane's claim for compensation against Frontex, and in the alternative against the Union, is hence successful.

Second, regarding the Commission, it has already been established that the Commission's misconduct consists in its failure to ensure that Frontex's practice in the context of age assessment in the EU hotspots generally complies with EU law.[228] It has also been established that this misconduct constitutes a sufficiently serious breach of a rule of law conferring rights upon individuals. As regards the decisive question of causation, the argument set out regarding case 2 applies respectively. It can hence be established with a reasonable degree of certainty that, if the Commission had made maximum use of its competences, especially in the framework of the EURTF and the Steering Committee, it could have ensured that Frontex conducts age assessments in compliance with EU

228 See chapter 2, 4.3.

law. As a consequence, the rights of Daniat Kidane under Art. 41 ChFR would not have been violated.

Further, it has also been established that the Commission failed to ensure that the host member state provides reception conditions that are generally compliant with EU law, including Art. 4 ChFR. Again, it has also been established that this misconduct constitutes a sufficiently serious breach of a rule of law conferring rights upon individuals. As regards the decisive question of causation, the argument set out regarding case 1 applies respectively. Due to the Commission's superior expertise, information and political authority, its guidelines, especially in the context of the EURTF and the Steering Committee, are de facto binding upon the host member state. It can hence be established with a reasonable degree of certainty that, if the Commission had made maximum use of its competences, it could have ensured that the host member state provides adequate reception conditions. The Commission's failure to do so was hence causal for the violation of Daniat Kidane's rights under Art. 4 ChFR, at least insofar as the violation reflects systemic malpractice. As a result, Daniat Kidane's claim under Art. 340 para 2 TFEU against the Commission for failure to adequately exercise supervisory obligations is successful concerning both, the resulting violation of Art. 41 ChFR and that of Art. 4 ChFR.

Case 4 – Nabeeh Al Badawi – Return to Türkiye – Art. 4, 18, 19 ChFR (liability of the Commission)

In the case of Nabeeh Al Badawi, Frontex has failed to intervene during the process of deportation to Türkiye. As a result, Mr Al Badawi was deported to Türkiye, despite the fact that Türkiye could not be considered as safe third country for him. As established above, Frontex hence incurs liability for the violation of the procedural dimension of the non-refoulement principle as enshrined in Art. 4, 18, 19 ChFR.[229]

What remains to be discussed here is whether Mr Al Badawi can claim compensation for breach of his procedural rights under Art. 4, 18, 19 ChFR also from the Commission. Clearly, the basis of this claim is the Commission's failure to adequately supervise the EU hotspot administration. On this basis, a distinction must be made between the Commission's supervision of Frontex and that of the host member state.

229 See chapter 3, 5.a, and chapter 4, 3.1.

As regards the supervision of Frontex, the crucial point is that Frontex is not responsible for issuing recommendations to deport or not deport specific applicants. Instead, Frontex only assists in the process of deportation. The Commission could hence only have prevented the violation of procedural rights in the case of Mr Al Badawi if Frontex's failure to intervene consisted of systemic malpractice. This, however, could only be established if the applicant could prove that deportees regularly raise their concerns against deportation to Türkiye towards accompanying Frontex staff and that Frontex staff regularly ignores these complaints. As this is not the case based on available information, the Commission's failure to adequately supervise Frontex's practice to accompany deportations cannot be considered as causal for the resulting violations of Art. 4, 18, 19 ChFR.

As regards the Commission's supervision of the host member state, however, the matter is different. The Commission has clearly supported, since 2015 and still in the context of the EU hotspot 2.0, that Greece would regularly reject asylum applications as inadmissible and deport the concerned persons to Türkiye. Crucially, the Commission still argued in favour of this solution when it was already clear that Türkiye could, in the vast majority of cases, not be considered a safe third country, even when Türkiye halted the readmission policy. This is decisive because, for the reasons set out above in the context of case 1, the Commission's instructions in the context of the EU hotspot administration have de facto binding force on the host member state. It is hence established with reasonable certainty that, if the Commission had urged the host member state, especially in the context of the EURTF and the Steering Committee, to stop the readmission policy, Greece would have responded to that guideline and generally halted readmissions. Insofar as the deportation of Mr Al Badawi represents systemic malpractice, the violation of Art. 4, 18, 19 ChFR in his case was hence caused by the Commission's failure to adequately supervise the EU hotspot administration. Therefore, Mr Al Badawi's claim for compensation for the violation of the non-refoulement principle against the Commission is successful.

Case 5 – Kareem Rashid – Limbo situation – Art. 4 and 41 ChFR (liability of the Commission)

In the case of Mr Rashid, the EUAA misapplied the safe third country concept and on this basis concluded that his asylum claim should be rejected as inadmissible, thereby ignoring the halt of the readmission policy since March 2021. As established above, the EUAA thus incurs liability for the breach of Art. 41 ChFR that is inherent in its procedural misconduct.[230]

What remains to be discussed here is Mr Rashid's claim for compensation, first, against the EUAA insofar as it is based on a violation of Art. 4 ChFR due to inhumane reception conditions, and second, against the Commission insofar as it is based on violations of Art. 4 and 41 ChFR respectively.

As regards the claim against the EUAA, the crucial point is that, unlike in case 1, the Greek asylum service was not de facto bound by the EUAA's opinion. The main reason for this is that the Greek asylum service was well informed about the halt of the readmission policy, and was therefore in a position to overrule the EUAA's opinion. In this specific case, the EUAA did not have a relevant information advantage, nor would it have cost the Greek asylum service much capacity to issue a decision stating that the claim cannot be rejected as inadmissible because Türkiye halted the readmission policy. Thus, and although the EUAA is generally perceived as expert, its recommendation to reject asylum claims as inadmissible despite the fact that deportations could not be carried out cannot be considered as de facto binding upon national authorities. Mr Rashied, hence, cannot claim compensation for the violation of Art. 4 ChFR from the EUAA.

As regards his claim against the Commission, however, the argument is parallel to cases 1 and 2. As established above, the Commission failed to exercise its supervisory powers so as to ensure that the EUAA would adapt its recommendation practice and that the host member state would adapt its deportation practice to the fact that readmissions had been halted by Türkiye since March 2020.[231] As also established above, this constitutes a sufficiently serious breach of a rule conferring rights upon individuals. As regards the question of causation, the decisive point is that the Commission would have been able to de facto oblige the EUAA and the host member state to adapt their respective practices. As in cases 1 and 2, the Commission, due to superior information, expertise and political authority, could have issued instructions towards the EUAA and the host member state, especially in the context of the EURTF and the Steering Committee, to halt readmissions, and it is established

230 See ibid.

231 See chapter 1, 2.c; chapter 2, 4.3.

with reasonable certainty that this would have led the EUAA and the host member state to adapt their practices. It is hence established that the Commission's failure to address the halt of readmissions and the resulting limbo situation at the supervisory level was causal for systemic breaches of Art. 4 and 41 ChFR. Hence, Mr Al Badawi's claim for compensation for violations of Art. 4 and 41 ChFR is successful against the Commission, at least insofar as it reflects systemic malpractice.

Case 6 – Reem Saeed – Prolonged detention – Art. 6 ChFR (liability of the Commission)

Reem Saeed claims compensation from the Commission, and in the alternative from the Union, for the breach of Art. 6 ChFR that occurred due to prolonged detention on the island of Kos. As established above, the Commission's failure to address the practice of generic detention on the island of Kos constitutes a breach of its supervisory obligations under Art. 40 para 3 Frontex Regulation, Art. 21 para 2 EUAA Regulation, Art. 17 TEU.[232] The Commission, albeit informed about the fact that asylum seekers are generally detained in the EU hotspot on that island, failed to undertake concrete measures to remedy that situation and to ensure that the EU hotspot administration generally complies with EU law. As also established, the Commission's misconduct constitutes a sufficiently serious breach of a rule of law conferring rights upon individuals. What remains to be discussed here is hence only whether the Commission's failure to adequately supervise the host member state's detention practices in the EU hotspots was causal for the application of the generic detention scheme in Kos. As in case 1 and 2, the crucial point here is that the Commission is capable to ensure the legality of the EU hotspot administration via de facto binding measures in the framework of the EURTF and the Steering Committee. Due to its superior information, expertise and political authority, it could have instructed the host member state to refrain from systemically detaining all new arrivals on the island of Kos and from holding them in detention for a prolonged period. As a last resort, the Commission could have withdrawn EU funding or urged the agencies to withdraw their operational support. Against this background, it is established with a reasonable degree of certainty that, if the Commission had made maximum use of its competences, it could have prevented that the host member state applies a generic

232 See chapter 2, 4.3.

detention scheme in the EU hotspot in Kos. The Commission's failure to adequately supervise and issue de facto binding guidelines towards the host member state was causal for the violation of Art. 6 ChFR in the concrete case of Ms Saeed, at least insofar as it reflects general malpractice. Hence, Ms Saeed's claim for compensation under Art. 340 para 2 TFEU against the Commission is successful.

Conclusion

1 Doctrinal Analysis in a Politicised Context

This study has shown that applying the CJEU's doctrine on EU public liability leads to the conclusion that Frontex, the EUAA, and the Commission incur liability under Art. 340 para 2 TFEU for systemic fundamental rights violations in the EU hotspots.[1] This includes in particular, liability for reception-related violations of Art. 4 and 6 ChFR and procedure-related violations of Art. 41, 24 and 4, 18, 19 ChFR.

Yet, it would be naïve to ignore that the topic of EU hotspots is a highly politicised one and that politicisation is an important factor in determining the outcome of court proceedings, including before the CJEU.[2] In the context of externalization policies more broadly, the CJEU has so far tended to shy away from confronting the EU's own administrative bodies. In similarly politicised cases, the CJEU has adopted a very restrictive stance, bringing its approach closer to that of the ECtHR. Prominent examples include the cases of *NF et al. v Council* concerning the legality of the EU-Türkiye Statement and of *X and X v Belgium* concerning the denial of humanitarian visas to Syrian war survivors.[3] In both cases, the CJEU refrained from making substantive decisions and instead argued that the EU was not involved or that EU law was not applicable and, on this basis, dismissed the actions. Crucially, the CJEU decided to proceed this way, although the claims in both cases were based on a doctrinally sound and constitutionally convincing argument, and although the individuals concerned were left with no avenue to enforce their fundamental rights in both cases. To avoid judgments on politically contentious matters, it hence appears that the

---

1 And respectively under the corresponding provisions in the agencies' Regulations, see chapter 3, 4.3.

2 For different perspectives see Carolyn Moser, Berthold Rittberger, „The CJEU and EU (de-)constitutionalization: Unpacking jurisprudential responses", *International Journal of Constitutional Law* 20 (2022), p. 1038-1070; Michael Blauberger, Dorte Sindbjerg Martinsen, „The Court of Justice in times of politicisation: 'law as a mask and shield' revisited", *Journal of European Public Policy* 27 (2020), p. 382-399.

3 CJEU, General Court (First Chamber, Extended Composition), order of 28 February 2017, NF v European Council (EU-Turkey Statement), T-192/16; Court (Grand Chamber), judgment of 7 March 2017, X and X v Belgium, C-638/16 PPU.

CJEU has not only been willing to compromise its role as a supranational constitutional court but also to sacrifice the doctrinal coherence of its own case law.

2 Why WS et al. vs. Frontex *Should Not Discourage*

In the specific context of EU liability for fundamental rights violations at the EU's external borders, however, the CJEU's approach has so far been more ambivalent. As mentioned, the only such case that has been decided so far is *WS et al. v Frontex.*[4] To briefly recall: the case concerned an unlawful pushback from Greece to Türkiye with Frontex involvement. The applicants' claim for damages against Frontex was based on the argument that Frontex's contribution was causal for the resulting violation of their fundamental rights. The General Court, which decided the case in September 2023, has found that the claims under Art. 340 para 2 TFEU were admissible – but argued that causation was not established and, on this basis, dismissed them as unfounded. The applicants' appeal before the Court of Justice is still pending.[5]

As established in more detail above, the General Court's argument has confirmed one major point of this study, namely that the action for damages under Art. 340 para 2 TFEU is a suitable remedy to address the EU's factual conduct at external borders, including when it results in fundamental rights violations.[6] On another major point of this study, namely the question of causation, however, the General Court disagreed. While this study has argued that the EU's factual contribution is causal for a resulting fundamental rights violation when it is *de facto* binding upon the national authorities that are responsible for issuing the formally-binding decision, i.e. when the EU *determines* the formally-binding decision, the General Court denied the causal link with simple reference to the fact the EU's conduct lacks formal bindingness, thereby ignoring long-standing case law of the CJEU itself.[7]

4 CJEU, General Court (Sixth Chamber), judgement of 6 September 2023, WS et al v Frontex, T-600/21.

5 Appeal brought on 14 November 2023 by WS et al. against the judgment of the General Court (Sixth Chamber) delivered on 6 September 2023 in Case T-600/21, WS and Others v Frontex, Case C-679/23 P.

6 See chapter 3, 3.4.

7 Chapter 5, 1.b.

Against this background, it is not unlikely that the General Court would dismiss an action construed along the proposal of this study – even if this would come at the cost of departing from established case law. Potential applicants who wish to ascertain their fundamental rights against the EU itself should be aware that there is a certain risk that the CJEU, and especially the General Court, would not hold Frontex, the EUAA or the Commission responsible. The actors driving forward such actions, most likely international networks of NGOs and scholars, should be aware that convincing legal arguments will perhaps not suffice to hold the EU responsible for its misconduct at the EU's external borders.

Assuming that the CJEU would not entirely refrain from engaging with its own case law, the easiest way for it to dismiss an action for damages in the context of the EU hotspots would probably be a return to its earlier *Sucrimex* doctrine.[8] Such a reversal of established case law could be done either silently or expressly. Alternatively, the CJEU could establish an exception from its *KYDEP* doctrine,[9] e.g. by arguing that the context of the European asylum system is particular and hence requires an exception from general doctrinal principles. Of course, such an argument would openly embrace the idea of immigration law exceptionalism and, as such, be not only anachronistic but also entirely unconvincing in constitutional terms.[10] Still, it cannot be entirely ruled out that the CJEU would take this route.

3 *Why Claiming Damages From the EU is Worth a Try*

Nevertheless, or precisely because of this, the approach developed in this study should be put to the test. It is not only worth a try but urgently necessary. Three points might help convince the sceptics. First, the CJEU's case law has almost never developed straightforwardly. Losing a case such as *WS et al.* in the first instance should certainly not discourage. It is very usual for the CJEU's case law to develop slowly and incrementally, with one step backwards every here and then. Examples include the CJEU's progressive extension of its jurisdiction in the context of the EU's Foreign and Security Policy and its progressive conceptualisation of the action for

8 See chapter 5, 2.1.
9 See chapter 5, 2.2 and 2.3.
10 See chapter 2, fn. 262.

damages as a form of declaratory relief.[11] Against this background, there can be no doubt that bringing several similar cases concerning the EU's involvement in fundamental rights violations at external borders before the CJEU is important. Otherwise, the CJEU would not even have the opportunity to overthink and potentially overrule its approach to causation in this context.

Second, the overall risk is manageable. Losing a case before the CJEU would have three types of consequences. Doctrinally, an overturn of long-established doctrine would certainly be a loss. A decision according to which the EU cannot incur liability for factual misconduct would be a clear step backwards; the EU's system of legal protection would become less complete than it already was, and the guarantee of Art. 47 ChFR would become even more fragmentary. Politically, a ruling stating that the EU is not responsible for its own misconduct in the EU hotspots – or that the EU's conduct in the EU hotspots is not reviewable before the CJEU – would be a major discursive defeat. But in terms of the situation on the ground, in terms of hard facts affecting the people concerned, things would most likely not get worse than they already are. There is no risk that strategic litigation could be perverted. Litigation, as proposed in this study, cannot become an end in itself, nor can it go to the detriment of those affected.

Third, the price for not trying to hold the EU responsible before the CJEU is simply too high. In a Union founded on the rule of law, it cannot be tolerated that the EU systemically disregards its own law and violates individual rights without being held responsible. If one decides not to take the risk of losing some cases, this would mean giving up and abandoning the understanding of the EU as enshrined in Art. 2 TEU. If the relevant actors, including NGOs, lawyers and other strategic litigators, decided not to even try to support those affected by the EU's externalisation policies in their legitimate wish to hold the EU responsible, this would be tantamount to admitting that the EU itself is de facto not bound by the rule of law. The EU's approach of creating overly complex administrative structures to evade judicial responsibility would have been successful. This, of course, would be a great loss for the affected asylum seekers, who would be permanently denied their rights under the Charter of Fundamental Rights. It would also be a loss for EU citizens – at least for those among them who

11 See chapter 3, 3.4.

still consider the EU's 'rule of law' to mean something other than closing borders, building walls and tacitly approving illegal pushback practices. In short, litigation, as proposed in this study, is worth a try from the perspective of all those who believe that the promise enshrined in Art. 2 TEU should be more than just empty words.[12]

12 On the transformative potential of EU law, especially of Art. 2 TEU, see Armin von Bogdandy, *The Emergence of European Society through Public Law. A Hegelian and Anti-Schmittian Approach*, Oxford University Press 2024, p. 3 et seq., p. 78 et seq., p. 157 et seq., p. 242 et seq.

Bibliography

Pekka Aalto, *Public Liability in EU Law. Brasserie, Bergaderm and Beyond*, Hart Publishing 2011

Karin Aberg, „Examining the Vulnerability Procedure: Group-based Determinations at the EU Border“, *Refugee Survey Quarterly* (2021), p. 1–27

Philip Alston, J. H. H. Weiler, „An 'Ever Closer Union' in Need of a Human Rights Policy“, *European Journal of International Law* 9 (1998), p. 658–723

Georgios Anagnostaras, „The Common European Asylum System: Balancing Mutual Trust Against Fundamental Rights Protection“, *German Law Journal* 21 (2020), p. 1180–1197

Stine Andersen, *The Enforcement of EU Law: The Role of the European Commission*, Oxford University Press 2013

H. Audretsch, *Supervision in European Community Law*, North-Holland 1986

Ino Augsberg, „Art. 340 AEUV (ex-Artikel 288 EGV)“, in Hans von der Groeben, Jürgen Schwarze, Armin Hatje (ed.), *Europäisches Unionsrecht. Vertrag über die Europäische Union, Vertrag über die Arbeitsweise der Europäischen Union, Charta der Grundrechte der Europäischen Union*, Nomos 2015

Jürgen Bast, „Scharade im kontrollfreien Raum: Hat die EU gar keinen Türkei-Deal geschlossen?“, Verfassungsblog of 03/03/2017

Jürgen Bast, „Transnationale Verwaltung des europäischen Migrationsraums: Zur horizontalen Öffnung der EU-Mitgliedstaaten“, *Der Staat* 46 (2007), p. 1–32

Jürgen Bast, „Handlungsformen und Rechtsschutz“, in Armin von Bogdandy, Jürgen Bast (ed.), *Europäisches Verfassungsrecht. Theoretische und dogmatische Grundzüge*, Springer 2009, p. 489–557

Jürgen Bast, Frederik von Harbou, Janna Wessels, *Human Rights Challenges to European Migration Policy. The REMAP Study*, Nomos 2022

Filipe Brito Bastos, „Derivate Illegality in European Composite Administrative Procedures“, *Common Market Law review* 55 (2018), p. 101–134

Hemme Battjes, „In Search of a Fair Balance: The Absolute Character of the Prohibition of Refoulement under Article 3 ECHR Reassessed“, *Leiden Journal of International Law* 22 (2009), p. 583–621

Michael W. Bauer, Stefan Becker, „The Unexpected Winner of the Crisis: The European Commission's Strengthened Role in Economic Governance“, *Journal of European Integration* 36 (2014), p. 213–229

Zygmunt Baumann, *Strangers at Our Door*, Polity Press 2016

Stefan Becker, Michael W. Bauer, „Die Europäische Kommission. Koordinationsbürokratie mit Regierungsanspruch“, in Peter Becker, Barbara Lippert (ed.), *Handbuch Europäische Union*, Springer 2020, p. 369–389

Werner Berg, „Art. 340 AEUV“, in Ulrich Becker, Armin Hatje, Johann Schoo, Jürgen Schwarze (ed.), *EU-Kommentar*, Nomos 2019

Felix Biermann, Nina Guérin, Stefan Jagdhuber, Berthold Rittberger, Moritz Weiss, „Political (non-)reform in the euro crisis and the refugee crisis: a liberal intergovernmentalist explanation“, *Journal of European Public Policy* (2019), p. 246–266

Michael Blauberger, Dorte Sindbjerg Martinsen, „The Court of Justice in times of politicisation: 'law as a mask and shield' revisited“, *Journal of European Public Policy* 27 (2020), p. 382–399

Armin von Bogdandy, „The European Union as a Human Rights Organization? Human Rights and the Core of the European Union“, *Common Market Law Review* 37 (2000), p. 1307–1338

Armin von Bogdandy, „Grundprinzipien“, in Armin von Bogdandy, Jürgen Bast (ed.), *Europäisches Verfassungsrecht. Theretische und dogmatische Grundzüge*, Springer 2009, p. 13–71

Armin von Bogdandy, „Principles of a Systemic Deficiencies Doctrine: How to Protect Checks and Balances in the Member States“, *Common Market Law Review* 57 (2020), p. 705–740

Armin von Bogdandy, *The Emergence of European Society through Public Law. A Hegelian and Anti-Schmittian Approach*, Oxford University Press 2024

Armin von Bogdandy, Michael Ioannidis, „Systemic Deficiency in the Rule of Law: What it is, what has to be done, what can be done“, *Common Market Law Review* 51 (2014), p. 59–96

Armin von Bogdandy, Matthias Kottmann, Carlino Antpöhler, Johanna Dickschen, Simon Hentrei, Maja Smrkolj, „Reverse Solange – Protecting the Essence of Fundamental Rights Against EU Member States“, *Common Market Law Review* 49 (2012), p. 489–520

Armin von Bogdandy, Pál Sonnevend (ed.), *Constitutional Crisis in the European Constitutional Area. Theory, Law and Politics in Hungary and Romania*, Nomos 2015

Tanja A Börzel, Ulrich Sedelmeier, „Larger and More Law Abiding? The Impact of Enlargement on Compliance in the European Union“, *Journal of European Public Policy* 24 (2016), p. 197–215

Mark Bovens, „Analysing and Assessing Accountability: A Conceptual Framework“, *European Law Journal* 13 (2007), p. 447–468

Stephan Breitenmoser, Robert Weyeneth, „Artikel 74 AEUV“, in Hans von der Groeben, Jürgen Schwarze, Armin Hatje (ed.), *Europäisches Unionsrecht*, Nomos 2015

Hannah Bru, Aikaterini Anastasopoulou, Heini Hyrkkö, „The Circumvention of the Dublin III Regulation Through the Use of Bilateral Agreements to Return Asylum Seekers to Other Member States“, in European Council on Refugees and Exiles (ECRE) (ed.), *Research Paper Ghent University* 2019

Madalina Busuioc, *European Agencies: Law and Practices of Accountability*, Oxford University Press 2013

Başak Çalı, Cathryn Costello, Stewart Cunningham, „Hard Protection through Soft Courts? Non-Refoulement before the United Nations Treaty Bodies", *German Law Journal* 21 (2020), p. 355–384

Giuseppe Campesi, „Seeking Asylum in Times of Crisis: Reception, Confinement, and Detention at Europe's Southern Border", *Refugee Survey Quarterly* 37 (2018), p. 44–70

Enzo Cannizzaro, „Denialism as the Supreme Expression of Realism. A Quick Comment on NF v. European Council", *European Papers* (2017), p. 215–257

Iris Canor, „My brother's keeper? Horizontal solange: 'An ever closer distrust among the peoples of Europe'", *Common Market Law Review* 50 (2013), p. 383–422

Sergio Carrera, „The 20 years anniversary of the Tampere programme: Securitization, intergovernmentalism and informalization", *Maastricht Journal of European and Comparative Law* 27 (2020), p. 3–9

Sergio Carrera, Leonhard Den Hertog, Joanna Parkin, „The Peculiar Nature of EU Home Affairs Agencies in Migration Control: Beyond Accountability versus Autonomy?", *European Journal of Migration and Law* 15 (2013), p. 337–358

Sergio Carrera, Leonhard Den Hertog, Marco Stefan, „It wasn't me! The Luxembourg Court Orders on the EU-Turkey Refugee Deal", *CEPS Policy Insights* (15/04/2017)

Sergio Carrera, Elspeth Guild, „'Joint Operation RABIT 2010'. FRONTEX Assistance to Greece's Border with Turkey: Revealing the Deficiencies of Europe's Dublin Asylum System", *CEPS Liberty and Security in Europe* (2010)

Sergio Carrera, Marco Stefan, „Complaint Mechanisms in Border Management and Expulsion Operations in Europe. Effective Remedies for Victims of Human Rights Violations?", *CEPS Policy Insights* (2018)

Marta Cartabia, „Europe and Rights: Taking Dialogue Seriously", *European Constitutional Law Review* 5 (2009), p. 5–31

Federico Casolari, „The EU's Hotspot Approach to Managing the Migration Crisis: A Blind Spot for International Responsibility?", *Italian Yearbook of International Law* 25 (2015), p. 109–134

Federico Casolari, „The unbearable lightness of soft law: on the European Unions recourse to informal instruments in the fight against irregular immigration", in Francesca Ippolito, Gianluca Borzoni, Federico Casolari (ed.), *Bilateral Relations in the Mediterranean. Prospects for Migration Issues*, Edward Elgar 2020, p. 215–228

Sabino Cassese, „European Administrative Proceedings", *Law and Contemporary Problems* 86 (2004), p. 21–36

Andrés Delgado Casteleiro, *The International Responsibility of the European Union. From Competence to Normative Control*, Cambridge University Press 2016

Mariavittoria Catanzariti, Alexander H. Türk, „EU agencies and the rise of a mixed administration in the EU multi-jurisdictional setting: facing the challenges of the rule of law", in Miroslava Scholten, Alex Brenninkmeijer (ed.), *Controlling EU Agencies. The Rule of Law in a Multi-jurisdictional Legal Order*, Edward Elgar 2020, p. 18–38

Merijn Chamon, „Agencification in the United States and Germany and What the EU Might Learn From It", *German Law Journal* 17 (2016), p. 119–152

Merijn Chamon, *EU Agencies. Legal and Political Limits to the Transformation of the EU Administration*, Oxford University Press 2016

B. S. Chimni, „The Geopolitics of Refugee Studies: a View from the South", *Journal of Refugee Studies* 11 (1998), p. 350–374

Meltem Ciger-Ineli, „Protecting Syrians in Turkey: A Legal Analysis", *International Journal of Refugee Law* 29 (2017), p. 555–579

Françoise Comte, „A New Agency Is Born in the European Union: The European Asylum Support Office", *European Journal of Migration and Law* 12 (2010), p. 373–405

Roberto Cortinovis, „The Evolution of Frontex Governance: Shifting from Soft to Hard Law?", *Journal of Contemporary European Research* 11 (2015), p. 252–267

Cathryn Costello, „Administrative governance and the Europeanisation of asylum and immigration policy", in Herwig C.H. Hofmann, Alexander H. Türk (ed.), *EU Administrative Governance*, Edward Elgar 2006, p. 287–340

Cathryn Costello, „Courting Access to Asylum in Europe: Recent Supranational Jurisprudence Explored", *Human Rights Law Review* 12 (2012), p. 287–339

Cathryn Costello, Itamar Mann, „Border Justice: Migration and Accountability for Human Rights Violations", *German Law Journal* 21 (2020), p. 311–334

Cathryn Costello, Minos Mouzourakis, „The Common European Asylum System. Where did it all go wrong?", in Maria Fletcher, Ester Herlin-Karnell, Matera Claudio (ed.), *The European Union as an Area of Freedom, Security and Justice*, Routledge 2017, p. 263–299

Paul Craig, „Standing, Rights, and the Structure of Legal Argument", *European Public Law* 9 (2003), p. 493–508

Paul Craig, *EU Administrative Law*, Oxford University Press 2018

Paul Craig, „Article 41", in Steve Peers, Tamara Hervey, Jeff Kenner, Angela Ward (ed.), *The EU Charter of Fundamental Rights. A Commentary*, Nomos 2021, p. 1125–1152

Astrid Czaja, *Die außervertragliche Haftung der EG für ihre Organe*, Nomos 1996

Nasiya Daminova, „'Access to Justice' and the Development of the Van Gend en Loos Doctrine: The Role of Courts and of the Individual in EU Law", *Baltic Journal of Law & Politics* 10 (2017), p. 133–153

Philipp Dann, „Thoughts on a Methodology of European Constitutional Law", *German Law Journal* 6 (2005), p. 1453–1474

Gareth Davies, „The General Court finds Frontex not liable for helping with illegal pushbacks: it was just following orders", europeanlawblog of 11 Sept 2023

Joyce De Coninck, „Shielding Frontex. On the EU General Court's "WS and others v Frontex"", Verfassungsblog of 09/09/2023

Maartje de Visser, „The Concept of Concurrent Liability and Its Relationship with the Principle of Effectiveness: A One-Way Ticket into Oblivion", *Maastricht Journal of European and Comparative Law* 11 (2004), p. 47–70

Bruno De Witte, Šejla Imamovic, „Opinion 2/13 on accession to the ECHR : defending the EU legal order against a Foreign Human Rights Court", *European Law Review* 40 (2015), p. 683–705

Giacinto Della Cananea, „The European Union's Mixed Administrative Proceedings", *Law and Contemporary Problems* 68 (2004), p. 187–218

Maarten Den Heijer, Jorrit R Rijpma, Thomas Spijkerboer, „Coercion, prohibition, and great expectations. The continuing failure of the Common European Asylum System", *Common Market Law Review* 53 (2016), p. 607–642

Angeliki Dimitriadi, Antonia-Maria Sarantaki, „The refugee 'crisis' in Greece: politicisation and polarisation amidst multiple crises", *CEASEVAL Research on the Common European Asylum System* 11 (2018)

Oliver Dörr, „Art. 263 AEUV", in Eberhard Grabitz, Meinhard Hilf, Martin Nettesheim (ed.), *Das Recht der Europäischen Union*, C.H. Beck 2023

ECRE, „Holding Frontex to Account. ECRE's Proposals for Strengthening Non-Judicial Mechanisms for Scrutiny of Frontex", *Policy Paper 7, May 2021* (2021)

ECRE, *Reception, detention and restriction of movement at EU external borders*, Heinrich Böll Stiftung 2021

Hanna Eklund, „Peoples, Inhabitants and Workers: Colonialism in the Treaty of Rome", *The European Journal of International Law* 34 (2023), p. 831–854

Mariolina Eliantonio, „Judicial Review in an Integrated Administration: the Case of 'Composite Procedures'", *Review of European Administrative Law* 7 (2015), p. 65–102

Mariolina Eliantonio, Nikos Vogiatzis, „Judicial and Extra-Judicial Challenges in the EU Multi- and Cross-Level Administrative Framework", *German Law Journal* 22 (2021), p. 315–324

Gerda Falkner, „A Causal Loop? The Commission's New Enforcement Approach in the Context of Non-Compliance with EU Law After CJEU Judgements", *Journal of European Integration* 40 (2018), p. 769–784

Kevin Featherstone, „External conditionality and the debt crisis: the 'Troika' and public administration reform in Greece", *Journal of European Public Policy* 22 (2015), p. 295–314

David Fernandez-Rojo, „The introduction of an individual complaint mechanism within FRONTEX: two steps forward, one step back", *Tijdschrift voor Bestuurswetenschappen en Publiekrecht* 4 (2016), p. 225–234

David Fernández-Rojo, *EU Migration Agencies. The Operation and Cooperation of FRONTEX, EASO and EUROPOL*, Edward Elgar 2021

David Fernández Rojo, „From EASO to the European Agency for Asylum: 'Business as Usual?'", eumigrationlawblog of 15/10/2018

Francette Fines, „A General Analytical Perspective on Community Liability", in Ton Heukels, Alison McDonnell (ed.), *The Action for Damages in Community Law*, Wolters Kluwer 1997

Melanie Fink, *Frontex and Human Rights. Responsibility in 'Multi-Actor Situations' under the ECHR and EU Public Liability Law*, Oxford University Press 2018

Melanie Fink, „EU Liability for Contributions to Member States' Breaches of EU Law", *Common Market Law Review* 56 (2019), p. 1227–1264

Melanie Fink, „The Action for Damages as a Fundamental Rights Remedy: Holding Frontex Liable", *German Law Journal* 21 (2020), p. 532–548

Andreas Fischer-Lescano, Timo Tohidipur, „Europäisches Grenzkontrollregime. Rechtsrahmen der europäischen Grenzschutzagentur Frontex", *Zeitschrift für ausländisches öffentliches Recht und Völkerrecht* 67 (2007), p. 1219–1276

Thomas Gammeltoft-Hansen, James C. Hathaway, „Non-refoulement in a World of Cooperative Deterrence", *Columbia Journal of Transnational Law* 53 (2015), p. 235–284

Klaus Ferdinand Gärditz, „Territoriality, Democracy, and Borders: A Retrospective on the 'Refugee Crisis'", *German Law Journal* 17 (2016), p. 907–922

Martin Gellermann, „Art. 340 AEUV ", in Rudolf Streinz (ed.), *EUV/AEUV*, C.H. Beck 2018

Giulia Gentile, „Ensuring Effective Judicial Review of EU Soft Law via the Action for Annulment before the EU Courts: a Plea for a Liberal-Constitutional Approach", *European Constitutional Law Review* (2020), p. 466–492

María-Teresa Gil-Bazo, „The Charter of Fundamental Rights of the European Union and the Right to be Granted Asylum in the Union's Law", *Refugee Survey Quarterly* 27 (2015), p. 33–52

Alberto Gil Ibáñez, *The Administrative Supervision and Enforcement in EC Law: Powers, Procedures and Limits*, Hart Publishing 1999

Mariana Gkliati, „The first steps of Frontex accountability: Implications for its Legal Responsibility for Fundamental Rights Violations", eumigrationlawblog of 13/08/2021

Mariana Gkliati, „The Application of the EU-Turkey Agreement: A Critical Analysis of the Decisions of the Greek Appeals Committee", *European Journal of Legal Studies* 10 (2017), p. 81–124

Mariana Gkliati, Herbert Rosenfeldt, „Accountability of the European Border and Coast Guard Agency: Recent developments, legal standards and existing mechanisms", *RLI Working Paper* 30 (2018)

Matthias Goldmann, „Dogmatik als rationale Rekonstruktion: Versuch einer Metatheorie am Beispiel völkerrechtlicher Prinzipien", *Der Staat* 53 (2014), p. 373–399

Guy S Goodwin-Gill, Jane McAdam, *The Refugee in International Law*, Oxford University Press 2007

Barbara Grabowska-Moroz, Dimitry Vladimirovich Kochenov, „The Loss of Face for Everyone Concerned. EU Rule of Law in the Context of the 'Migration Crisis'", in V Stoyanova, S Smet (ed.), *Migrants' Rights, Populism and Legal Resilience in Europe*, Cambridge University Press 2022, p. 187–208

Scott Greer, „Structural adjustment comes to Europe: Lessons for the Eurozone from the conditionality debates", *Global Social Policy* 14 (2013), p. 51–71

Steven Greer, „Is the Prohibition against Torture, Cruel, Inhuman and Degrading Treatment Really 'Absolute' in International Human Rights Law?", *Human Rights Law Review* 15 (2015), p. 101–137

Elspeth Guild, „The Frontex Push-Back Controversy: Lessons on Oversight (Part I)", eumigrationlawblog of 19/04/2021

Elspeth Guild, „The Europeanisation of Europe's Asylum Policy", *International Journal of Refugee Law* (2006), p. 630–652

Elspeth Guild, „Does the EU Need a European Migration and Protection Agency?“, *International Journal of Refugee Law* 28 (2016), p. 585–600

Elspeth Guild, Sergio Carrera, Leonhard Den Hertog, Joanna Parkin, *Implementation of the EU Charter of Fundamental Rights and its Impact on EU Home Affairs Agencies. Frontex, Europol and the European Asylum Support Office. Study for the LIBE Committee*, European Parliament 2011

Kathleen Gutman, „The Evolution of the Action for Damages Against the European Union and Its Place in the System of Judicial Protection“, *Common Market Law Review* 48 (2011), p. 695–750

Peo Hansen, Stefan Jonsson, *Eurafrica: The Untold History of European Integration and Colonialism*, Bloomsbury Academic 2014

James C. Hathaway, „The Emerging Politics of Non-Entrée“, *Refugees* 91 (1992), p. 40

Katri Havu, „Damages Liability for Non-Material Harm in EU Case Law“, *European Law Review* 44 (2019), p. 492–514

Ton Heukels, Alison McDonnell, „The Action for Damages in a Community Law Perspective: Introduction“, in Ton Heukels, Alison McDonnell (ed.), *The Action for Damages in Community Law*, Wolters Kluwer 1997

Chris Hilson, The Role of Discretion in EC Law on Non-Contractual Liability, Common Market Law Review 42 (2005), p. 677-695

Herwig Hofmann, Morgane Tidghi, „Rights and Remedies in Implementation of EU Policies by Multi-Jurisdictional Networks“, *European Public Law* (2014), p. 147–164

Herwig Hofmann, Alexander Türk, „Legal challenges in EU administrative law by the move to an integrated administration“, in Herwig Hofmann, Alexander Türk (ed.), *Legal Challenges in EU Administrative Law*, Edward Elgar 2009, p. 355–379

Herwig Ch Hofmann, Liisa Holopainen, Elina Paunio, Laurent Pech, Clara Rauchegger, Debbie Sayers, Angela Ward, „Article 47“, in Steve Peers, Tamara Hervey, Jeff Kenner, Angela Ward (ed.), *The EU Charter of Fundamental Rights. A Commentary*, Nomos 2022

Herwig C.H. Hofmann, Gerard C. Rowe, Alexander H. Türk, *Administrative Law and Policy of the European Union*, Oxford University Press 2011

Herwig C. H. Hofmann, Alexander Türk, „The Development of Integrated Administration in the EU and its Consequences“, *European Law Journal* 13 (2007), p. 253–271

Jens Hofmann, *Rechtsschutz und Haftung im Europäischen Verwaltungsverbund*, Duncker & Humblot 2004

Rainer Hofmann, Adela Schmidt, „‘EU-Türkei-Deal’ ohne Beteiligung der EU? – Die Beschlüsse des EuG zur Erklärung EU-Türkei vom 18. März 2016“, *Europäische Grundrechte-Zeitschrift* 44 (2017), p. 317–327

Rainer Hofmann, Adela Schmidt, „Ist die Türkei für Asylantragsteller ein sicherer Drittstaat? – Das Urteil des Hellenischen Staatsrats vom 22.9.2017“, *Zeitschrift für Ausländerrecht und Ausländerpolitik* 38 (2018), p. 1–6

Alisha C Holland, „Forbearance“, *American Political Science Review* 110 (2016), p. 232–246

Michael Ioannidis, „Weak Members and the Enforcement of EU Law", in András Jakab, Dimitry Kochenov (ed.), *The Enforcement of EU Law and Values. Ensuring Member States' Compliance*, Oxford University Press 2017, p. 476–492

Marc Jacob, Matthias Kottmann, „Art. 340 AEUV", in Eberhard Grabitz, Meinhard Hilf, Martin Nettesheim (ed.), *Das Recht der Europäischen Union* C.H. Beck 2023

András Jakab, Dimitry Kochenov (ed.), *The Enforcement of EU Law and Values. Ensuring Member States' Compliance*, Oxford University Press 2017

Hans Jarass, „Art. 25 Rechte älterer Menschen", *Charta der Grundrechte der EU*, C.H. Beck 2021

Hans Jarass, „Art. 41 Recht auf eine gute Verwaltung", *Charta der Grundrechte der EU*, C.H. Beck 2021

Hans Jarass, „Art. 47 Recht auf einen wirksamen Rechtsbehelf und ein unparteiisches Gericht", *Charta der Grundrechte der EU*, C.H. Beck 2021

Hans Jarass, „Art. 52 Tragweite und Auslegung der Rechte und Grundsätze", *Charta der Grundrechte der EU*, C.H. Beck 2021

Anastasia Karatzia, „An Overview of Litigation in the Context of Financial Assistance", *Hungarian Yearbook of International Law and European Law* (2016), p. 573–590

Eva Kassoti, Narin Idriz, „The Informalisation of the EU's External Action in the Field of Migration and Asylum", in Eva Kassoti, Narin Idriz (ed.), *The Informalisation of the EU's External Action in the Field of Migration and Asylum*, Springer 2022, p. 1–12

Daniel Kelemen, Tommaso Pavone, „Where Have the Guardians Gone? Law Enforcement and the Politics of Supranational Forbearance in the European Union", *SSRN* (2021)

Thorsten Kingreen, „Artikel 25 EU-GRCharta", in Christian Calliess, Matthias Ruffert (ed.), *EUV/AEUV. Kommentar*, C.H. Beck 2022

Thorsten Kingreen, „Artikel 52 EU-GRCharta", in Christian Calliess, Matthias Ruffert (ed.), *EUV/AEUV. Kommentar*, C.H. Beck 2022

Paul Kirchhof, „Staatliche Souveränität als Bedingung des Asylrechts", in Georg Jochum, Wolfgang Fritzemeyer, Marcel Kau (ed.), *Grenzüberschreitendes Recht – Crossing frontiers. Festschrift für Kay Hailbronner*, C.F. Müller 2013, p. 105–121

Karl E Klare, „Legal Culture and Transformative Constitutionalism", *South African Journal on Human Rights* 14 (1998), p. 146–188

Dimitry Kochenov, „The Essence of EU Citizenship Emerging From Ten Years of Academic Debate: Beyond the Cherry Blossoms and the Moon?", *The International and Comparative Law Quarterly* 62 (2013), p. 97–136

Dimitry Kochenov, „Biting Intergovernmentalism: The Case for the Reinvention of Article 259 TFEU to Make It a Viable Rule of Law Enforcement Tool", *Hague Journal on the Rule of Law* 7 (2015), p. 153–174

Christina Last, *Garantie wirksamen Rechtsschutzes gegen Maßnahmen der Europäischen Union. Zum Verhältnis von Art. 47 Abs. 1, 2 GRCh und Art. 263 ff. AEUV*, Mohr Siebeck 2008

Liora Lazarus, Cathryn Costello, Nazila Ghanea, Katja S. Ziegler, „The Evolution of Fundamental Rights Charters and Case Law. Report for the European Parliament Directorate-General for Internal Policies", *SSRN* (2011)

Stephen H Legomsky, „Secondary Refugee Movements and the Return of Asylum Seekers to Third Countries: The Meaning of Effective Protection", *International Journal of Refugee Law* 51 (2003), p. 567–677

Roman Lehner, „The EU-Turkey-'deal': Legal Challenges and Pitfalls", *International Migration* 57 (2018), p. 176–185

Matthias Lehnert, *Frontex und operative Maßnahmen an den europäischen Außengrenzen. Verwaltungskooperation – materielle Rechtsgrundlagen – institutionelle Kontrolle*, Nomos 2014

Koen Lenaerts, „La vie après l'avis: Exploring the Principle of Mutual (Yet Not Blind) Trust", *Common Market Law Review* 54 (2017), p. 805–840

Sarah Léonard, „EU border security and migration into the European Union: FRONTEX and securitisation through practices", *European Security* 19 (2010), p. 231–254

Gaia Lisi, Mariolina Eliantonio, „The Gaps in Judicial Accountability of EASO in the Processing of Asylum Requests in Hotspots", *European Papers* 4 (2019), p. 589–602

Tobias Lock, „Is Private Enforcement of EU Law Through State Liability a Myth? An Assessment 20 Years After Frankovich", *Common Market Law Review* 49 (2012), p. 1675–1702

Chiara Loschi, Peter Slominski, „The EU hotspot approach in Italy: strengthening agency governance in the wake of the migration crisis?", *Journal of European Integration* 44 (2022), p. 769–786

Anna Lübbe, „'Systemic Flaws' and Dublin Transfers: Incompatible Tests Before the CJEU and the ECtHR?", *International Journal of Refugee Law* 27 (2015), p. 135–140

Francesco Maiani, „Hotspots and Relocation Schemes: The Right Therapy for the Common European Asylum System?", eumigrationlawblog of 03/02/2016

Francesco Maiani, „The Dublin III Regulation: A New Legal Framework for a More Humane System?", in Vincent Chetail, Philippe De Bruycker, Francesco Maiani (ed.), *Reforming the Common European Asylum System*, 2016

Federico Mancini, *Democracy and Constitutionalism in the European Union*, Hart Publishing 2000

Itamar Mann, „Maritime Legal Black Holes: Migration and Rightlessness in International Law", *The European Journal of International Law* 29 (2018), p. 347–372

Luisa Marin, „Frontex and the Rule of Law Crisis at EU Borders", Verfassungsblog of 05/09/2022

Nora Markard, Helene Heuser, „'Hotspots' an den EU-Außengrenzen: Menschen- und europarechtswidrige Internierungslager", *Zeitschrift für Ausländerrecht und Ausländerpolitik* (2016), p. 165–172

Thomas Matthies, *Relocation. Die Umsiedlung von Asylbewerbern in der Europäischen Union*, LIT Verlag 2021

Natasa Mavronicola, „Is the Prohibition Against Torture and Cruel, Inhuman and Degrading Treatment Absolute in International Human Rights Law? A Reply to Steven Geer", *Human Rights Law Review* 17 (2017), p. 479–498

Natasa Mavronicola, Francesco Messineo, „Relatively Absolute? The Undermining of Article 3 ECHR in Ahmad v UK", *The Modern Law Review* 76 (2013), p. 589–619

Vittoria Meissner, „The European Border and Coast Guard Agency Frontex After the Migration Crisis: Towards a 'Superagency'?", in Johannes Pollak, Peter Slominski (ed.), *The Role of EU Agencies in the Eurozone and Migration Crisis. Impact and Future Challenges*, Palgrave Macmillan 2021, p. 151–174

Joana Mendes, „Bounded Discretion in EU Law: A Limited Judicial Paradigm in a Changing EU", *The Modern Law Review* 80 (2017), p. 443–472

Valsamis Mitsilegas, „The Limits of Mutual Trust in Europe's Area of Freedom, Security and Justice: From Automatic Inter-State Cooperation to the Slow Emergence of the Individual", *Yearbook of European Law* (2012), p. 319–372

Caterina Molinari, „EU Readmission Deals and Constitutional Allocation of Powers: Parallel Paths that Need to Cross?", in Eva Kassoti, Narin Idriz (ed.), *The Informalisation of the EU's External Action in the Field of Migration and Asylum*, Springer 2022, p. 15–35

Jörg Monar, „Der Raum der Freiheit, der Sicherheit und des Rechts", in Armin von Bogdandy, Jürgen Bast (ed.), *Europäisches Verfassungsrecht. Theoretische und Dogmatische Grundzüge*, Springer 2009, p. 749–797

Violeta Moreno-Lax, „Must EU Borders have Doors for Refugees? On the Compatibility of Schengen Visas and Carriers' Sanctions with EU Member States' Obligations to Provide International Protection to Refugees", *European Journal of Migration and Law* 10 (2008), p. 315–364

Violeta Moreno-Lax, *Europe in Crisis: Facilitating Access to Protection, (Discarding) Offshore Processing and Mapping Alternatives for the Way Forward, Study for the Red Cross*, 2015

Violeta Moreno-Lax, Mariagiulia Giuffré, „The Rise of Consensual Containment: From 'Contactless Control' to 'Contactless Reponsibility' for Forced Migration Flows", in Satvinder Singh Juss (ed.), *Research Handbook on International Refugee Law*, Edward Elgar 2019, p. 82–108

Carolyn Moser, *Accountability in EU Security and Defence. The Law and Practice of Peacebuilding*, Oxford University Press 2020

Carolyn Moser, Berthold Rittberger, „The CJEU and EU (de-)constitutionalization: Unpacking jurisprudential responses", *International Journal of Constitutional Law* 20 (2022), p. 1038–1070

Minos Mouzourakis, „All but last resort: The last reform of detention of asylum seekers in Greece", eumigrationlawblog of 18/11/2019

Anna Mrozek, *Grenzschutz als supranationale Aufgabe. Der Schutz der europäischen Außengrenzen unter der Beteiligung der Bundespolizei*, Nomos 2013

Christoph-David Munding, *Das Grundrecht auf effektiven Rechtsschutz im Rechtssystem der Europäischen Union*, Duncker & Humblot 2010

Roberta Mungianu, *Frontex and Non-Refoulement. The International Responsibility of the EU*, Cambridge University Press 2016

Andrew W Neal, „Securitization and Risk at the EU Border: The Origins of FRONTEX", *Journal of Common Market Studies* 47 (2009), p. 333–356

Paul F Nemitz, „Artikel 17 EUV", in Ulrich Becker, Armin Hatje, Johann Schoo, Jürgen Schwarze (ed.), *EU-Kommentar*, Nomos 2019

Robert Nestler, Vinzent Vogt, „Dublin-III-reversed. Ein Instrument zur Familienzusammenführung", *Zeitschrift für Ausländerrecht und Ausländerpolitik* 37 (2017), p. 21–29

Darren Neville, Amalia Rigon, Sarah Salome Sy, *On the frontline: the hotspot approach to managing migration, Study conducted for the European Parliament, Committee on Civil Liberties, Justice and Home Affairs*, 2016

Salvatore F. Nicolosi, David Fernandez-Rojo, „Out of control? The case of the European Asylum Support Office", in Miroslava Scholten, Alex Brenninkmeijer (ed.), *Controlling EU Agencies. The Rule of Law in a Multi-jurisdictional Legal Order*, Edward Elgar 2020, p. 177–195

André Nollkaemper, Jean d'Aspremont, Christiane Ahlborn, Berenice Boutin, Nataša Nedeski, Ilias Plakokefalos, Dov (collaboration) Jacobs, „Guiding Principles on Shared Responsibility in International Law", *European Journal of International Law* 31 (2020), p. 15–72

André Nollkaemper, Dov Jacobs, „Shared Responsibility in International Law: A Conceptual Framework", *Michigan Journal of International Law* 34 (2013), p. 359–438

John E. Noyes, Brian D. Smith, „State Responsibility and the Principle of Joint and Several Liability", *Yale Journal of International Law* 132 (1988), p. 225–267

Peter Oliver, „Joint Liability of the Community and the Member States", in Ton Heukels, Alison McDonnell (ed.), *The Action for Damages in Community Law*, Wolters Kluwer 1997, p. 285–309

Joanna Parkin, *The Difficult Road to the Schengen Information System II: The legacy of 'laboratories' and the cost for fundamental rights and the rule of law*, CEPS Policy Paper 2011

Christopher Paskowski, „Verwaltung ohne Verantwortung. Zur Abweisung der ersten Schadensersatzklage gegen Frontex durch das EuG", Verfassungsblog of 27/09/2023

Reijer Passchier, Maarten Stremler, „Unconstitutional Constitutional Amendments in European Union Law: Considering the Existence of Substantive Constraints on Treaty Revision", *Cambridge Journal of Internationa and Comparative Law* 5 (2016), p. 337–362

Steve Peers, „Building Fortress Europe: The Development of EU Migration Law", *Common Market Law Review* 35 (1998), p. 1235–1272

Steve Peers, Marios Costa, „Judicial Review of EU Acts after the Treaty of Lisbon; Order of 6 September 2011, Case T-18/10 *InuitTapiriit Kanatami and Others v. Commission* & Judgment of 25 October 2011, Case T-262/10 *Microban v. Commission*", *European Constitutional Law Review* 8 (2012), p. 82–104

Anne Peters, „The European Ombudsman and the European Constitution", *Common Market Law Review* 42 (2005), p. 697–743

John Peterson, „Juncker's political European Commission and an EU in crisis", *Journal of Common Market Studies* 55 (2017), p. 349–367

Max Pichl, *The 'Moria Complex'. Irresponsibility, Incompetence and Disenfranchisement Five Years After the EU-Turkey Accord and Launch of the Hotspot System. A Study for medico international*, 2021

Maria Pichou, „Reception or Detention Centres? The detention of migrants and the EU 'Hotspot' Approach in the light of the European Convention on Human Rights", *Kritische Vierteljahresschrift für Gesetzgebung und Rechtswissenschaft* 99 (2016), p. 114–131

Jörg Polakiewicz, Julia Katharina Kirchmayr, „Sounding the Alarm: The Council of Europe As the Guardian of the Rule of Law in Contemporary Europe", in Armin von Bogdandy, Piotr Bogdanowic, Iris Canor, Christoph Grabenwarter, Maciej Taborowski, Matthias Schmidt (ed.), *Defending Checks and Balances in EU Member States*, Springer 2021, p. 361–382

Johannes Pollak, Peter Slominski, „Experimentalist but not Accountable Governance? The Role of Frontex in Managing the EU's External Borders", *West European Politics* 32 (2009), p. 904–924

Nina Półtorak, „Action for Damages in the Case of Infringement of Fundamental Rights by the European Union", in Ewa Bagińska (ed.), *Damages for violations of human rights. A comparative study of domestic legal systems*, Springer 2016, p. 427–441

Anastasia Poulou, „Financial Assistance Conditionality and Human Rights Protection: What is the Role of the EU Charter of Fundamental Rights?", *Common Market Law Review* 54 (2017), p. 991–1026

Sacha Prechal, Rob Widdershoven, „Redefining the Relationship between 'Rewe-effectiveness' and Effective Judicial Protection", *Review of European Administrative Law* 4 (2011), p. 31–50

Timo Rademacher, *Realakte im Rechtsschutzsystem der Europäischen Union*, Mohr Siebeck 2014

Timo Rademacher, „Factual Administrative Conduct and Judicial Review in EU Law", *European Review of Public Law* 30 (2017), p. 399–435

René Repasi, „Judicial protection against austerity measures in the euro area: Ledra and Mallis", *Common Market Law Review* 54 (2017), p. 1123–1156

Michael Rhimes, „The EU Courts Stand Their Ground: Why Are the Standing Rules for Direct Actions Still so Restrictive?", *European Journal of Legal Studies* (2016), p. 103–172

Jorrit R Rijpma, „Hybrid Agencifiation in the Area of Freedom, Security and Justice and its inherent tension: The case of Frontex", in Madalina Busuioc, Martijn Groenleer, Jarle Trondal (ed.), *The Agency Phenomenon in the European Union. Emergence, Institutionalisation and Everyday Decision-Making*, Manchester University Press 2012, p. 84–102

Jorrit R Rijpma, *The Proposal for a European Border and Coast Guard: evolution or revolution in external border management? Study for the LIBE Committee*, European Parliament 2016

Ariadna Ripoll Servent, „Failing under the 'shadow of hierarchy': explaining the role of the European Parliament in the EU's 'asylum crisis'", in Edoardo Bressanelli, Nicola Chelotti (ed.), *The European Parliament in the Contested Union. Power and Influence Post-Lisbon*, Routledge 2020, p. 29–47

Isabel Rooms, Ariti Skarpa, „An Insurmountably High Standard for Damage Claims against the EU? Case T-834/17, UPS v Commission", *Journal of European Competition Law & Practice* 13 (2022), p. 487–489

Herbert Rosenfeldt, *Frontex im Zentrum der Europäischen Grenz- und Küstenwache. Bestandsaufnahme, Unionsrechtmäßigkeit und Verantwortlichkeit*, Mohr Siebeck 2021

Matthias Rossi, „Artikel 74 AEUV", in Christian Calliess, Matthias Ruffert (ed.), *EUV/AEUV. Kommentar*, C.H. Beck 2022

Matthias Rossi, „Artikel 80 AEUV", in Christian Calliess, Matthias Ruffert (ed.), *EUV/AEUV. Kommentar*, C.H. Beck 2022

Gerard C. Rowe, „Administrative supervision of administrative action in the European Union", in Herwig Hofmann, Alexander Türk (ed.), *Legal Challenges in EU Administrative Law*, Edward Elgar 2009, p. 179–217

Matthias Ruffert, „AEUV Art. 340 (ex-Art. 288 EGV)", in Matthias Ruffert, Christian Calliess (ed.), *EUV/AEUV*, C.H. Beck 2022

Matthias Ruffert, „Artikel 17 EUV", in Christian Calliess, Matthias Ruffert (ed.), *EUV/AEUV. Kommentar*, C.H. Beck 2022

Giacomo Rugge, „The Euro Group's informality and *locus standi* before the European Court of Justice: *Council v. K. Chrysostomides & Co. and Others*", *Zeitschrift für ausländisches öffentliches Recht und Völkerrecht (Heidelberg Journal of International Law)* (2021), p. 917–936

Charles F. Sabel, Jonathan Zeitlin, „Experimentalist Governance", in David Levi-Faur (ed.), *The Oxford Handbook of Governance*, Oxford University Press 2012, p. 169–184

Marek Safjan, Dominik Düsterhaus, „A Union of Effective Judicial Protection: Addressing a Multi-level Challenge through the Lens of Article 47 CFREU", *Yearbook of European Law* 33 (2014), p. 3–40

Juan Santos Vara, Laura Pascual Matellám, „The Informalization of EU Return Policy: A Change of Paradigm in Migration Cooperation with Third Countries?", in Eva Kassoti, Narin Idriz (ed.), *The Informalisation of the EU's External Action in the Field of Migration and Asylum*, Springer 2022, p. 37–52

Uwe Säuberlich, *Die außervertragliche Haftung im Gemeinschaftsrecht. Eine Untersuchung der Mehrpersonenverhaltnisse*, Springer 2005

Johannes Saurer, *Der Einzelne im europäischen Verwaltungsrecht*, Mohr Siebeck 2014

James D Savage, Amy Verdun, „Strengthening the European Commission's budgetary and economic surveillance capacity since Greece and the euro area crisis: a study of five Directorates-General", *Journal of European Public Policy* 23 (2015), p. 101–118

Kim Lane Scheppele, Dimitry Vladimirovich Kochenov, Barbara Grabowska-Moroz, „EU Values Are Law, after All: Enforcing EU Values through Systemic Infringement Actions by the European Commission and the Member States of the European Union", *Yearbook of European Law* 39 (2020), p. 2–21

Franz Schimmelpfennig, „European integration (theory) in times of crisis. A comparison of the euro and Schengen crises", *Journal of European Public Policy* 25 (2018), p. 969–989

Eberhard Schmidt-Aßmann, „Europäische Verwaltung zwischen Kooperation und Hierarchie. Festschrift für Helmut Steinberger", in Hans-Joachim Cremer (ed.), *Tradition und Weltoffenheit des Rechts*, Springer 2002, p. 1375–1399

Eberhard Schmidt-Aßmann, „Einleitung: Der Europäische Verwaltungsverbund und die Rolle des Europäischen Verwaltungsrechts", in Eberhard Schmidt-Aßmann, Bettina Schöndorf-Haubold (ed.), *Der Europäische Verwaltungsverbund. Formen und Verfahren der Verwaltungszusammenarbeit in der EU*, Mohr Siebeck 2005, p. 1–23

Miroslava Scholten, Marloes van Rijsbergen, „The Limits of Agencification in the European Union", *German Law Journal* 15 (2014), p. 1223–1255

Peter H. Schuck, „The Transformation of Immigration Law", *Columbia Law Review* 84 (1984), p. 1–90

Linda Senden, „Soft Post-Legislative Rulemaking: A Time for More Stringent Control", *European Law Journal* 19 (2013), p. 57–75

Foroud Shirvani, „Haftungsprobleme im Europäischen Verwaltungsverbund", *Europarecht* 46 (2011), p. 619–635

Marta Simoncini, *Administrative Regulation Beyond the Non-Delegation Doctrine. A Study on EU Agencies*, Hart Publishing 2020

Melanie Smith, „Enforcement, monitoring, verification, outsourcing: the decline and decline of the infringement process", *European Law Review* 33 (2008), p. 777–802

Francis Snyder, „The Effectiveness of European Community Law: Institutions, Processes, Tools and Techniques", *The Modern Law Review* 56 (1993), p. 19–54

Francis Snyder, „Soft Law and Institutional Practice in the European Community", in Stephen Martin (ed.), *The Construction of Europe. Essays in honour of Emile Noël*, Springer 1994, p. 197–227

Oana Ştefan, „Soft Law and the Enforcement of EU Law", in András Jakab, Dimitry Kochenov (ed.), *The Enforcement of EU Law and Values: Ensuring Member States' Compliance*, Oxford University Press 2017

Oana Ştefan, „European Competition Soft Law in European Courts: A Matter of Hard Principles?", *European Law Journal* 14 (2008), p. 753–772

Eric Stein, „Lawyers, Judges, and the Making of a Transnational Constitution", *American Journal of International Law* 75 (1981), p. 1–27

Alexandra Tarzikhan, „The European Union Agency for Asylum: A Promising Improvement or Vestige of the European Asylum Support office?", *Refugee Law & Migration Studies Brief* 1 (2022), p. 1–10

Martina Tazzioli, „Refugees' Debit Cards, Subjectivities, and Data Circuits: Financial-Humanitarianism in the Greek Migration Laboratory", *International Political Sociology* 13 (2019), p. 392–408

Fabien Terpan, „Soft Law in the European Union. The Changing Nature of EU Law", *European Law Journal* 21 (2015), p. 68–96

Daniel Thym, „Muddy Waters: A Guide to the Legal Questions surrounding 'Push-backs' at the External Borders at Sea and at Land", eumigrationlawblog of 06/07/2021

Daniel Thym, „Why the EU-Turkey Deal is Legal and a Step in the Right Direction", Verfassungsblog of 09/03/2016

Daniel Thym, „Artikel 74 AEUV", in Winfried Kluth, Andreas Heusch (ed.), *BeckOK Ausländerrecht*, C.H. Beck 2022

Daniel Thym, „Legal Framework for EU Asylum Policy", in Daniel Thym, Kay Hailbronner (ed.), *EU Immigration and Asylum Law. Article-by-Article Commentary*, C.H. Beck, Hart Publishing and Nomos 2022, p. 1129–1176

Daniel Thym, *European Migration Law*, Oxford University Press 2023

A.G. Toth, „The Concepts of Damage and Causality as Elements of Non-Contractual Liability", in Ton Heukels, Alison McDonnell (ed.), The Action for Damages in Community Law, Wolters Kluwer 1997, p. 179–198

Angeliki Tsiliou, „When Greek judges decide whether Turkey is a Safe Third Country without caring too much for EU law", eumigrationlawblog of 29/05/2018

Evangelia (Lilian) Tsourdi, „Bottom-Up Salvation? From Practical Cooperation Towards Joint Implementation Through the European Asylum Support Office", *European Papers* 1 (2017), p. 997–1031

Evangelia (Lilian) Tsourdi, „Monitoring and Steering through FRONTEX and EASO 2.0: The Rise of a New Model of AFSJ agencies?", eumigrationlawblog of 29/01/2018

Evangelia (Lilian) Tsourdi, „Holding the European Asylum Support Office Accountable for its role in Asylum Decision-Making: Mission Impossible?", *German Law Journal* 21 (2020), p. 506–531

Evangelia (Lilian) Tsourdi, „The New Pact and EU Agencies: An Ambivalent Approach Towards Administrative Integration", eumigrationlawblog of 06/11/2020

Evangelia (Lilian) Tsourdi, „Beyond the 'Migration Crisis': The Evolving Role of EU Agencies in the Administrative Governance of the Asylum and External Border Control Policies", in Johannes Pollak, Peter Slominski (ed.), *The Role of EU Agencies in the Eurozone and Migration Crisis. Impact and Future Challenges*, Palgrave Macmillan 2021, p. 175–203

Evangelia (Lilian) Tsourdi, Cathryn Costello, „'Systemic Violations' in EU Asylum Law: Cover or Catalyst?", *German Law Journal* 24 (2023), p. 982–994

Alexander Türk, *Judicial Review in EU Law*, Edward Elgar 2009

Alexander Türk, „Judicial review of integrated administration in the EU", in Herwig Hofmann, Alexander Türk (ed.), *Legal Challenges in EU Administrative Law: Towards an Integrated Administration*, Edward Elgar 2009, p. 218–256

Alexander H. Türk, „Liability and Accountability for Policies Announced to the Public and for Press Releases", *ECB Legal Conference 2017. Shaping a new legal order for Europe: a tale of crises and opportunities*, https://www.ecb.europa.eu/pub/pdf/other/ecblegalconferenceproceedings201712.en.pdf

Orcun Ulusoy, Hemme Battjes, „Situation of Readmitted Migrants and Refugees from Greece to Turkey under the EU-Turkey Statement", *VU Migration Law Series* (2017)

Unisys, *Study on the Feasibility of the Creation of a European System of Border Guards to Control the External Borders of the Union (ESBG), conducted for the European Commission*, 2014

Helene Urth, Mathilde Heegaard Bausager, Hanna-Maija Kuhn, Joanne Van Selm, *Study on the Feasibility and legal and practical implications of establishing a mechanism for the joint processing of asylum applications on the territory of the EU, conducted for the European Commission*, 2013

Ilse van Liempt, Maybritt Jill Alpes, Saima Hassan, Sevda Tunaboylu, Orcun Ulusoy, Annelies Zoomers, *Evidence-Based Assessment of Migration Deals. The case of the EU-Turkey Statement*, 2017

Maarten Vink, Claudia Engelmann, „Informal European Asylum Governance in an International Context", in Thomas Christiansen, Christine Neuhold (ed.), *International Handbook on Informal Governance*, Edward Elgar 2012, p. 534–553

Nikos Vogiatzis, *The European Ombudsman and Good Administration in the European Union*, Palgrave Macmillan 2018

Ellen Vos, „EU Agencies and Independence", in D Ritleng (ed.), *Independence and Legitimacy in the Institutional System of the European Union*, Oxford University Press 2016, p. 206–227

Jill Wakefield, *Judicial Protection through the Use of Article 288(2) EC*, Wolters Kluwer 2002

Angela Ward, „Damages under the EU Charter of Fundamental Rights", *ERA Forum* 12 (2012), p. 589–611

Ian Ward, *A Critical Introduction to European Law*, LexisNexis Buttersworths 1996

Martin Weitenberg, *Der Begriff der Kausalität in der haftungsrechtlichen Rechtsprechung der Unionsgerichte*, Nomos 2014

Matthias Wendel, „The Refugee Crisis and the Executive: On the Limits of Administrative Discretion in the Common European Asylum System", *German Law Journal* 17 (2016), p. 1005–1032

Wouter P. J. Wils, „Concurrent liability of the Community and a Member State", *European law review* 17 (1992), p. 191–206

Napoleon Xanthoulis, „Administrative factual conduct: Legal effects and judicial control in EU law", *Review of European Administrative Law* 12 (2019), p. 39–73

Jonathan Zeitlin, „EU experimentalist governance in times of crisis", *West European Politics* 39 (2016), p. 1073–1094

Catharina Ziebritzki, „A Hidden Success. Why the EU General Court's Frontex Judgment is Better Than it Seems", Verfassungsblog of 13/10/23

Catharina Ziebritzki, „Refugee Camps at the EU External Border – Is the Union responsible? The Integrated EU Hotspot Administration and the Potential of EU Public Liability Law", in Markus Kotzur, David Moya, Ülkü Sezgi Sözen, Andrea Romano (ed.), *The External Dimension of EU Migration and Asylum Policies. Human Rights, Development and Neighbourhood Policies in the Mediterranean Area*, Nomos 2020

Catharina Ziebritzki, „Warum die 'Instrumentalisierung' Asylsuchender kein Argument für die Aussetzung ihrer Grundrechte ist", *Kritische Justiz* 55 (2022), p. 152–166

Catharina Ziebritzki, *The EU's Responsibility in the Asylum Administration. Administrative Integration, Judicial Protection and the Case of the EU Hotspots*, Dissertation at Frankfurt University, Law Department January 2024

Catharina Ziebritzki, Robert Nestler, „Implementation of the EU-Turkey Statement: EU Hotspots and restriction of asylum seekers' freedom of movement", eumigrationlawblog of 22/06/2018

Catharina Ziebritzki, Robert Nestler, „'Hotspots' an der EU-Außengrenze. Eine rechtliche Bestandsaufnahme", *MPIL Research Paper Series (SSRN)* 17 (2017)